Dictionary of Holland Occupational Codes

Gary D. Gottfredson
Decision Research Associates

John L. Holland
Johns Hopkins University

Deborah Kimiko Ogawa
Decision Research Associates

Consulting Psychologists Press, Inc.
577 College Avenue, Palo Alto, CA 94306

ISBN: 0-89106-020

ACKNOWLEDGMENTS

We are grateful for the editorial counsel of Joseph Johnston, Jack Rayman, and Robert Reardon who read portions of earlier drafts, and for the technical assistance of Richard Joffe who helped us manage the data.

Table of Contents

List of Tables

Publisher's Foreword

In the early 1950's, R. B. Forer suggested that vocational interests were essentially expressions of personality, an idea that stimulated John Holland to develop the *Vocational Preference Inventory*, a deceptively simple personality test consisting entirely of occupational items. Using this device and other techniques in a variety of creative studies, Holland developed his theory that people and environments could be generally classified into six types, which he called Realistic, Investigative, Artistic, Social, Enterprising, and Conventional. In 1966 he published his lucid little book *The Psychology of Vocational Choice* (revised in 1973 as *Making Vocational Choices: A Theory of Careers*), which set forth his hexagonal structure of the world of work in detail.

No publication has so dominated and revolutionized the field of vocational psychology in the ensuing fifteen years, an observation clearly substantiated by tabulations of published research, bibliographic citations, and changes in the practice of interest measurement and career counseling. In 1970 Holland published his *Self-Directed Search*, now one of the most popular career counseling devices; in 1974 the prestigious *Strong Vocational Interest Blank* was revised to incorporate Holland's codes for all its occupational scales. In the past decade a number of imitations of Holland's SDS have also been published, and other inventories and career counseling workbooks have incorporated Holland's system.

In 1979 the U.S. Department of Labor published its *Guide to Occupational Exploration* with this acknowledgment:

> In recognition of the extensive research on the Holland model and its widespread use in vocational counseling today, the USES interest areas were arranged according to the Holland categories.

Similarly, the Canadian government published a dictionary of Holland codes with a similar acknowledgment:

> In order to accommodate the demand to access the CCDO using John L. Holland's approach to making vocational choices, all occupations . . . have been assigned Holland codes.

The *Dictionary of Holland Occupational Codes* can certainly be expected to stimulate further use of Holland's system because it makes job descriptions of all 12,099 occupational base titles in the *Dictionary of Occupational Titles* accessible through use of the Holland three-letter codes for the first time. Counselors can now provide their clients the opportunity to explore the entire spectrum of relevant occupations using their Holland codes. Researchers will also have a new tool for further studies of Holland's theory and other occupational studies.

To produce this volume, Gottfredson, Holland, and Ogawa used the job analysis data developed by the Department of Labor to create the current DOT, and Gottfredson devised a formula to translate these data into Holland codes. The job analyses included ratings of educational requirements, aptitudes, temperaments, interests, physical demands, and environmental conditions. The original results were validated on new job samples and carefully checked for anomalous codes.

We are pleased to be able to publish this new aid for workers in career guidance and are confident that it will enhance the usefulness of the *Self-Directed Search, Vocational Preference Inventory, Vocational Exploration and Insight Kit*, and of other counseling aids that provide Holland codes.

John D. Black
Publisher

Part I. Introduction

This volume is a translation of the *Dictionary of Occupational Titles* (DOT; U.S. Department of Labor, 1977) into the Holland (1973a) classification system. It makes the 12,099 occupational titles of the DOT more accessible to counselors, clients, and researchers using the Holland classification to find or to organize occupational information.

The classification uses six main groups—Realistic, Investigative, Artistic, Social, Enterprising, and Conventional—to characterize occupations. These six groups, sometimes abbreviated as R, I, A, S, E, and C, parallel the six types used to characterize persons with the *Self-Directed Search* (SDS; Holland, 1979). These main groups are used to form 88 three-letter subgroups that are useful in assessing the degree of congruence between a person's interests or preferences and any of thousands of occupations. Users of the SDS will see that the Classified Index (Part II) of this *Dictionary* forms a comprehensive *Occupations Finder*.

Counselors and clients can use this *Dictionary* to search for all the occupations suggested by a person's SDS assessment code. And, an Alphabetical Index (Part III) of the 12,099 occupations provides ready access to the Holland Code for any occupational title as well as the corresponding code in the *Guide for Occupational Exploration* (GOE; U.S. Department of Labor, 1979). Because this volume offers complete and rapid exploration of all occupations, clients will find taking the SDS a more helpful experience.

The codes listed in this volume are the result of the third major attempt to extend the Holland classification to all occupations. Earlier attempts (Holland, 1973a; Viernstein, 1972) were helpful and led to this reorganization, which we assume is superior to the earlier classifications. Although the present classification is the best and most recent, the codes listed are not carved in stone. They should be regarded as useful approximations. The results of future research will eventually lead to another revision as we strive to improve the classification system in response to new data.

Clients should explore several permutations of their three-letter codes. Most clients will find many occupations whose codes precisely match their SDS codes, but they should nevertheless be urged to expand their occupational exploration to include closely related codes.

The theoretical origin and statistical development of the translation is presented in Part IV. That section summarizes how the 44 ratings of each occupation were used to create the three-letter Holland code. The development of this *Dictionary* also produced some valuable by-products: a clearer knowledge of the distinguishing characteristics of each occupational class, the distribution of occupations among the categories, and more evidence of the validity of the classification. Counselors and scientists will find Part IV helpful in learning about the validity and interpretation of the codes both in practice and in research.

SOME INTERPRETATIONS AND CAUTIONS

Several cautions are important in making interpretations of any occupational information. Experienced counselors have long recognized the following points, but it is important to emphasize them for new users of the classification system.

1. The categories in the classification are not distinct—black or white, all or none. Even a casual review of the classification in Part II will reveal that the six main categories blend together at the edges. For example, CR occupations in the Conventional category resemble RC occupations in the Realistic category. In general, occupations at lower General Educational Development (GED) levels are less clearly identifiable as belonging to any major group than are occupations at higher levels. Successful performance in low-level occupations requires less education or training than successful performance in high-level occupations. Therefore, the distinctions among low-level occupations are somewhat blurred.

2. The average person has well-developed ideas about many occupations (O'Dowd and Beardslee, 1967). Although many

of these occupational perceptions have a moderate degree of validity, some perceptions form inaccurate stereotypes. The categories in the Holland classification appear to have undergone similar stereotyping: "Realistic jobs never require paperwork"; "Conventional jobs never involve tools"; "Investigative jobs never require artistic judgment." It is more accurate to think of the main categories in the Holland classification as bands or rings that blend into each other than to view the categories as six separate bins.

3. A person does not resemble one type and no other. An occupation does not fit into one main category and no other. For these reasons, the number of possible occupations or positions that are congruent with a particular person is large. When the levels of resemblance are also taken into account, this outcome is easily understood. Some people resemble two or three theoretical types to the same degree, and some occupations resemble two or more occupational groups to the same degree. Furthermore, the codes assigned to a few occupations shift from one study to the next. "Police officer" is a good example: S and R are the main categories suggested by divergent data at different times; one study suggests RSE and another suggests SRE. "Engineer" is another occupation for which I and R are the codes usually suggested by interest inventory data; but the positions of I and R change from study to study—even for the same engineering specialty.

4. A variety of types of people are found successfully working within any single occupation, but some types are found more frequently than others (see Holland & Holland, 1977; or Holland, 1979, p. 14). For example, most counselors have codes that include S, A, and E, but few have codes of C or R. In short, all occupations tolerate a range of types, but some types appear to cope more successfully with an occupation's demands than do others. See Holland's theory for a more complete explanation of person-environment fit (1973a).

SOME EXPECTED QUESTIONS

Does this classification supercede all earlier versions of the Holland classification? Yes. When in doubt, use this one.

Will the Occupations Finder (SDS) also be changed? Yes, but the codes in the current *Occupations Finder* (Holland, 1978a), and the codes assigned on the basis of occupational analysis information in this volume, are very similar. See Part IV of this volume.

Is this revision of codes ever going to end? I'm tired of revising my occupational information files. It is unlikely that revisions will cease, but a review of the successive revisions of the classification will show a decrease in major revisions. Information about occupations will always be imperfect due to errors in sampling, limitations in occupational analyses, and changes in job content over time. Therefore, codes will always be approximations or estimates, but the present estimates are a major improvement over the armchair codes on which counselors have usually had to rely.

Can I use this Dictionary *with other interest inventories such as the SCII?* This *Dictionary* is intended primarily for use with the SDS or *Vocational Preference Inventory* (VPI; Holland, 1978b), and it will be most compatible with these inventories. The *Dictionary* codes are expected to be compatible with the *Strong-Campbell Interest Inventory* (SCII; Campbell, 1977) and perhaps other inventories, but no empirical tests of compatibility have been made.

How about other inventories? In the past, codes based on the interests of males, using norms or raw scores, have been very similar. In contrast, codes based on the inventoried interests of women, using sex-based norms or so-called balanced scales, often produce codes that are at variance with the codes produced by raw scores. They also are at variance with the codes based on occupational analysis data presented here. In short, the *Dictionary* should be compatible with most other inventories for males, and for females with inventories reporting raw score profiles or profiles based on pooled norms. Users of inventories with sex-based norms or balanced scales should perform appropriate statistical studies before making use of the present *Dictionary* or the *Occupations Finder* with female clients.

Do occupational codes, and codes for fields of training, vary from region to region and from institution to institution? Yes, they do. If you have been collecting SDS or VPI data to create a local occupations finder, you should continue to do so. Your data will usually be most valid for your situation. This *Dictionary* is a supplement for what institutions cannot easily do for themselves.

What should I do when I find an occupation with a code that seems strange or in error? Locate and read the DOT definition. This review should clarify most apparent misclassifications—the occupational title itself does not always convey an accurate picture of the occupation. Also, review occupations with the identical code. For example, if you are in doubt about an RIE occupation, look at other RIE occupations to clarify for yourself the conceptual meaning of the category involved. Finally, review Table 15 of this volume for additional insights into the distinctions among the categories.

What should I do when I cannot find a code for a specific occupational title in the Alphabetical Index? All occupational titles in the DOT are included in this index. Any title, however, may have a number of synonyms. Try finding a synonymous title or transposing the words in the title. For example, "sales engineer" may be found under "engineer, sales." Finally, consult the DOT for alternate titles that are listed under defined titles.

What should I tell a client who wants to pursue an artistic career but who looks like a CES according to the SDS? Encourage the client to examine how he or she will use the CES interests, values, and competencies in an occupation dominated by Artistic types and tasks. Explore with the client the origin of the Artistic aspiration—what it means to him or her. Such exploration may reveal that the client can explain such a choice and that the explanation is backed by personal and other data, or that the client recognizes his or her aspiration as a fantasy that may easily be relinquished. Whatever happens, help the client explore both A as well as CES options.

Part II.   From Holland Codes to All Occupations

The Classified Index in this section lists occupations according to the Holland classification. It is a guide to career exploration for the person who has used the SDS or the VPI and who has therefore determined a range of occupations to explore. It is also a guide to career exploration for the person who already has a good idea of his or her general occupational preferences, has established a career and wants to examine similar occupations, or is reentering the work force with a clear notion of the general kind of work that would be satisfying.

THE OCCUPATIONAL CLASSIFICATION

The Classified Index groups together similar occupations.

R Occupations classified as Realistic (or R) tend to involve concrete and practical activity involving machines, tools, or materials.

I Occupations classified as Investigative (or I) tend to involve analytical or intellectual activity aimed at problem solving, trouble shooting, or the creation and use of knowledge.

A Occupations classified as Artistic (or A) generally involve creative work in the arts: music, writing, performance, sculpture, or other relatively unstructured and intellectual endeavors.

S Occupations classified as Social (or S) typically involve working with people in a helpful or facilitative way.

E Occupations classified as Enterprising (or E) tend to involve working with people in a supervisory or persuasive way, in order to achieve some organizational goal.

C Occupations classified as Conventional (or C) typically involve working with things, numbers, or machines in an orderly way to meet the regular and predictable needs of an organization.

If you are not familiar with the Holland classification, see *Making Vocational Choices: A Theory of Careers* (Holland, 1973a) or the *Professional Manual for the Self-Directed Search* (Holland, 1979).

Three-Letter Holland Codes

The Classified Index provides three-letter Holland codes. The first letter is the most important: It shows the major category into which the occupation falls and conveys the most information about the occupation. The second and third letters, in descending order of importance, provide supplementary information about the occupation by showing the categories that the occupation next most resembles. No individual person or occupation resembles a pure type and no other type. Therefore, describing both individuals and occupations in terms of their degree of resemblance to several types or groupings is useful but not precise.

In a few instances, a Holland code is also shown in parentheses after an occupational title. These are codes based on the SDS or on other interest inventory data. They are presented when there is a large discrepancy between the code derived using occupational analysis data and the code derived using interest inventory data. Users should consider both codes in exploring occupational possibilities. Fortunately, there are only 35 such discrepancies among 12,099 occupations.

Educational and Specific Vocational Preparation

Occupations differ in the level of general educational preparation and specific training required to perform at satisfactory levels. Anyone engaged in career planning will want to take into consideration the education and specific training required, for they are important determiners of access to employment.

General Educational Development (GED). The Classified Index shows the GED that is typically required to enter or to perform well in each occupation. A GED rating summarizes information about the level of reasoning, mathematical ability, or language performance demanded by an occupation. The rating includes the formal and informal education that develops reasoning, the ability to follow instructions, and the use of language and mathematics. These general ratings are only estimates, and they should not be regarded as precise requirements. Table 1 interprets the GED levels shown in the Classified Index.

Table 1
Interpretation of GED Levels

GED	Education	Demands
6	College required	Logic and abstract thinking Advanced mathematics or statistics Reading literature, scientific, or technical journals Writing books, manuals, critiques, songs, and the use of theory or persuasive speaking in educated speech
5	College	Logic or scientific thinking Application of algebra or statistics Language skills similar to level 6
4	High school or some college	Application of principles of bookkeeping, navigation, wiring, mechanics, and the like Some geometry, algebra, or shop math
3	High school	Common sense understanding Following written, diagrammed, or oral instructions Computation Reading manuals, rules, or instructions Use of grammar and correct speech
2	Elementary school	Common sense understanding Following detailed but uninvolved written or oral instructions Arithmetic Reading, writing, and understandable speech
1	Some elementary school	Common sense understanding Following one- or two-step instructions Simple arithmetic Recognize common words Print and speak simple sentences

Note: From Handbook for Analyzing Jobs, U.S. Department of Labor, 1972, 210-211.

Specific Vocational Preparation (SVP). The SVP ratings shown in the Classified Index indicate the training time required by an occupation. The ratings include training in school, at work, in the military, or through hobbies, but they exclude education that is not specifically vocational in nature. Table 2 shows the meanings of the SVP ratings.

Use the SVP ratings for an occupation to estimate the amount of time required to become proficient in that occupation.

Table 2
Interpretation of SVP Ratings

SVP Level	Training Time
9	Over 10 years
8	Over 4 years, up to and including 10 years
7	Over 2 years, up to and including 4 years
6	Over 1 year, up to and including 2 years
5	Over 6 months, up to and including 1 year
4	Over 3 months, up to and including 6 months
3	Over 30 days, up to and including 3 months
2	Anything beyond short demonstration, up to and including 30 days
1	Short demonstration only

Note: From Handbook for Analyzing Jobs, U.S. Department of Labor, 1972, 220.

Descriptions of Occupations

The Classified Index also shows the nine-digit *Dictionary of Occupational Titles* (DOT; U.S. Department of Labor, 1977) code for each occupation. This code will be useful for clients or counselors who wish to read more about the occupation. The DOT contains a narrative description of each occupation, and it is organized using these nine-digit numbers. The narratives tell what, in general, a worker in each occupation does, what kinds of tools or materials he or she works with, and what kind of special knowledge is required.

REALISTIC OCCUPATIONS

Code	Title	GED	SVP	DOT No.
RIA	LIGHTING-EQUIPMENT OPERATOR	4	6	962.381-014
RIA	TREATER	4	7	549.362-014
RIS	HEALTH PHYSICIST	6	8	079.021-010
RIS	APPRAISER	5	7	191.287-010
RIS	ASSAYER	5	7	022.281-010
RIS	ELECTRICAL-RESEARCH ENGINEER	5	8	003.061-026
RIS	ELECTRICAL-DESIGN ENGINEER	5	8	003.061-018
RIS	ELECTRONICS-DESIGN ENGINEER	5	8	003.061-034
RIS	ELECTRONICS-RESEARCH ENGINEER	5	8	003.061-038
RIS	FIELD ENGINEER	5	7	193.262-018
RIS	HELICOPTER PILOT	5	7	196.263-038
RIS	MECHANICAL ENGINEER	5	8	007.061-014
RIS	NUCLEAR MEDICAL TECHNOLOGIST	5	7	078.361-018
RIS	TOOL DESIGNER	5	8	007.061-026
RIS	TOOL-DESIGNER APPRENTICE	5	8	007.061-030
RIS	WEIGHT ANALYST	5	7	020.187-018
RIS	WELL-LOGGING CAPTAIN, MUD ANALYSIS	5	7	010.131-010
RIS	WRITER, TECHNICAL PUBLICATIONS	5	7	131.267-026
RIS	AIRCRAFT LAUNCH AND RECOVERY TECHNICIAN	4	5	912.682-010
RIS	BALANCER, SCALE	4	6	710.381-014
RIS	BATCH-AND-FURNACE OPERATOR	4	7	572.382-010
RIS	BIOLOGICAL PHOTOGRAPHER	4	6	143.362-010
RIS	BLOWER AND COMPRESSOR ASSEMBLER	4	6	801.361-010
RIS	CABINETMAKER	4	6	660.280-010
RIS	CABINETMAKER APPRENTICE	4	6	660.280-014
RIS	CARPENTER, ROUGH	4	7	860.381-042
RIS	CLOTH PRINTER	4	7	652.382-010
RIS	COLOR DEVELOPER	4	7	530.261-010
RIS	COMPOUNDER, FLAVORINGS	4	6	529.381-010
RIS	CONSERVATOR, ARTIFACTS	4	6	055.381-010
RIS	CUSTOM SKI MAKER	4	7	732.281-010
RIS	DECORATOR	4	6	740.381-010
RIS	DIE FINISHER	4	7	601.381-010
RIS	ELECTRICAL INSPECTOR	4	6	710.281-014
RIS	ELECTROMECHANICAL INSPECTOR	4	7	710.381-018
RIS	ELEVATOR REPAIRER	4	7	825.281-030
RIS	ELEVATOR-REPAIRER APPRENTICE	4	7	825.281-034
RIS	EMBALMER (SAC)	4	7	338.371-014
RIS	EMBALMER APPRENTICE	4	7	338.371-010
RIS	ENGINE TESTER	4	7	621.261-014
RIS	EXHAUST EQUIPMENT SET-UP MECHANIC	4	6	599.380-010
RIS	EXPERIMENTAL MECHANIC	4	8	600.260-014
RIS	FARMER, GENERAL	4	7	421.161-010
RIS	FIRE-FIGHTING-EQUIPMENT SPECIALIST	4	7	638.281-010
RIS	FIRER, KILN	4	5	573.662-010
RIS	FLAME-HARDENING-MACHINE SETTER	4	7	504.380-010

-1-

Code	Title	GED	SVP	DOT No.
RIS	FLOOR-COVERING LAYER	4	7	622.381-026
RIS	FOREIGN CLERK	4	5	214.467-010
RIS	FURNACE OPERATOR	4	5	512.362-014
RIS	GARDENER, SPECIAL EFFECTS AND INSTRUCTION MODELS	4	5	406.381-010
RIS	GLAZIER, STAINED GLASS	4	7	779.381-010
RIS	GUN EXAMINER	4	6	736.281-010
RIS	GUNSMITH, BALLISTICS LABORATORY	4	8	609.260-010
RIS	HONEY GRADER-AND-BLENDER	4	6	520.361-010
RIS	HOOD MAKER	4	5	804.481-010
RIS	INDUSTRIAL-GAS SERVICER	4	7	637.261-022
RIS	INSET CUTTER	4	6	739.381-038
RIS	INSPECTOR	4	6	612.261-010
RIS	KNIFE GRINDER	4	5	603.682-014
RIS	LANDSCAPE GARDENER	4	7	408.161-010
RIS	MACHINE TRY-OUT SETTER	4	7	600.360-010
RIS	MACHINIST, EXPERIMENTAL	4	8	600.280-038
RIS	MAINTENANCE MECHANIC	4	6	629.280-010
RIS	MALT-SPECIFICATIONS-CONTROL ASSISTANT	4	7	022.261-014
RIS	MEDICAL-APPARATUS MODEL MAKER	4	6	712.261-010
RIS	METAL FABRICATOR	4	7	619.360-014
RIS	METAL-FABRICATOR APPRENTICE	4	7	619.360-018
RIS	METALLURGICAL TECHNICIAN	4	6	011.261-010
RIS	MODEL MAKER	4	7	693.361-010
RIS	MODEL MAKER	4	7	700.281-018
RIS	MODEL MAKER, FLUORESCENT LIGHTING	4	7	723.361-010
RIS	MODEL MAKER, FIBERGLASS	4	8	777.381-010
RIS	MULTI-OPERATION-FORMING-MACHINE OPERATOR 1	4	6	616.360-026
RIS	MULTI-OPERATION-FORMING-MACHINE SETTER	4	7	616.260-014
RIS	OIL-WELL-SERVICE OPERATOR	4	6	939.462-010
RIS	OPERATING ENGINEER	4	6	859.683-010
RIS	OPERATING-ENGINEER APPRENTICE	4	6	859.683-014
RIS	ORNAMENTAL-IRON WORKER	4	7	809.381-022
RIS	ORNAMENTAL-IRON-WORKER APPRENTICE	4	7	809.381-026
RIS	PATTERN MARKER 1	4	7	761.381-022
RIS	PATTERNMAKER, PLASTICS	4	6	754.381-014
RIS	PHOTOENGRAVING PROOFER	4	8	971.381-038
RIS	PHOTOENGRAVING-PROOFER APPRENTICE	4	8	971.381-040
RIS	PIPE CUTTER	4	4	862.682-010
RIS	PLANT PROPAGATOR	4	6	405.361-010
RIS	PRIVATE-BRANCH-EXCHANGE INSTALLER	4	7	822.381-018
RIS	PROSPECTOR	4	7	024.284-010
RIS	PUMP ERECTOR	4	6	637.281-010
RIS	PUMPER	4	6	549.360-010
RIS	RADIOGRAPHER	4	5	199.361-010
RIS	RADIOISOTOPE-PRODUCTION OPERATOR	4	6	015.362-022
RIS	RELIEF-MAP MODELER	4	6	777.381-042
RIS	REPAIRER, WELDING, BRAZING, AND BURNING MACHINES	4	7	626.361-010
RIS	SALVAGE INSPECTOR	4	6	622.381-038
RIS	SAMPLE MAKER, APPLIANCES	4	8	600.280-054

Code	Title	GED	SVP	DOT No.
RIS	SAW MAKER	4	6	601.381-034
RIS	SECTION LEADER, SCREEN PRINTING	4	7	652.260-010
RIS	SEED ANALYST	4	7	040.361-014
RIS	SIDEROGRAPHER	4	6	979.381-030
RIS	STAMP CLASSIFIER	4	6	299.387-018
RIS	STEP-AND-REPEAT REDUCTION CAMERA OPERATOR	4	7	971.382-022
RIS	STOKER ERECTOR-AND-SERVICER	4	7	637.281-014
RIS	STONECUTTER, HAND	4	7	771.381-014
RIS	STREETCAR REPAIRER	4	6	807.381-026
RIS	SUBSTATION OPERATOR	4	7	952.362-026
RIS	SUBSTATION OPERATOR APPRENTICE	4	7	952.362-030
RIS	SUPERVISOR, KNITTING	4	7	685.130-010
RIS	SURFACE-PLATE FINISHER	4	7	775.281-010
RIS	TANK ERECTOR	4	7	860.381-070
RIS	TENONER OPERATOR	4	5	669.382-018
RIS	TEST TECHNICIAN	4	6	019.261-022
RIS	TRANSFORMER TESTER	4	7	724.281-010
RIS	TRANSMISSION TESTER	4	7	822.361-026
RIS	TUBE REBUILDER	4	6	725.381-010
RIS	WELDER APPRENTICE, ARC	4	5	810.384-010
RIS	WELDER, ARC	4	5	810.384-014
RIS	WOOD-TURNING-LATHE OPERATOR	4	5	664.382-014
RIS	YEAST-CULTURE DEVELOPER	4	5	022.381-010
RIS	BOAT-OAR MAKER	3	6	761.381-010
RIS	BULLET-SLUG-CASTING-MACHINE OPERATOR	3	5	502.382-010
RIS	COKE-CRUSHER OPERATOR	3	4	544.662-010
RIS	CUPOLA TENDER	3	4	512.662-010
RIS	DINKEY OPERATOR	3	4	919.663-014
RIS	HEAT TREATER 2	3	4	504.682-018
RIS	HOOP MAKER, MACHINE	3	4	619.682-030
RIS	HYDRO-SPRAYER OPERATOR	3	4	408.662-010
RIS	JOINTER OPERATOR	3	5	665.482-010
RIS	LAMBER	3	3	410.364-010
RIS	LOG-TRUCK DRIVER	3	4	904.683-010
RIS	MEASURER	3	3	869.367-014
RIS	MIXER OPERATOR	3	4	550.382-018
RIS	NEW-CAR GET-READY MECHANIC	3	6	806.361-026
RIS	POCKET CUTTER	3	4	667.482-014
RIS	PUNCH-PRESS OPERATOR 3	3	4	615.682-014
RIS	PUNCH-PRESS OPERATOR, AUTOMATIC	3	5	615.482-026
RIS	RESAW OPERATOR	3	6	667.682-058
RIS	ROTARY-SHEAR OPERATOR	3	4	615.482-030
RIS	SCREWDOWN OPERATOR	3	5	613.382-018
RIS	SHEAR OPERATOR 1	3	4	615.482-034
RIS	SLITTER-SCORER-CUT-OFF OPERATOR	3	5	649.682-038
RIS	STEVEDORE 1	3	5	911.663-014
RIS	STOPPING BUILDER	3	5	869.684-058
RIS	STOVE-CARRIAGE OPERATOR	3	4	590.662-022
RIS	SURVIVAL-EQUIPMENT REPAIRER	3	6	739.381-054
RIS	TEMPERER	3	4	504.682-026
RIS	UPSETTER	3	5	611.462-010

Code	Title	GED	SVP	DOT No.
RIE	GEOLOGIST, PETROLEUM	6	8	024.061-022
RIE	ORDNANCE ENGINEER	6	8	019.061-022
RIE	PHYSIATRIST	6	8	070.101-070
RIE	ADMEASURER	5	7	169.284-010
RIE	AERONAUTICAL TEST ENGINEER	5	8	002.061-018
RIE	AIRPLANE PILOT, COMMERCIAL	5	7	196.263-014
RIE	AUTO-DESIGN CHECKER	5	8	017.261-010
RIE	AUTOMOTIVE ENGINEER	5	8	007.061-010
RIE	BIOMEDICAL EQUIPMENT TECHNICIAN	5	7	719.261-010
RIE	CHEMICAL-TEST ENGINEER	5	8	008.061-026
RIE	COMMERCIAL ENGINEER	5	7	003.187-014
RIE	CONTROLLER, REMOTELY-PILOTED VEHICLE (RPV)	5	7	196.263-026
RIE	CUSTOMER-EQUIPMENT ENGINEER	5	8	003.187-018
RIE	DISTRIBUTION-FIELD ENGINEER	5	8	003.167-014
RIE	DRAFTER, DIRECTIONAL SURVEY	5	7	010.281-010
RIE	DRAFTER, GEOPHYSICAL	5	7	010.281-018
RIE	DRAINAGE-DESIGN COORDINATOR	5	8	005.167-014
RIE	ELECTRICAL ENGINEER	5	8	003.061-010
RIE	ELECTRONICS ENGINEER	5	8	003.061-030
RIE	ENGINEER-IN-CHARGE, TRANSMITTER	5	8	003.167-034
RIE	ESTIMATOR AND DRAFTER	5	7	019.261-014
RIE	EXECUTIVE PILOT	5	7	196.263-030
RIE	FACILITIES PLANNER	5	7	019.261-018
RIE	FACILITIES-FLIGHT-CHECK PILOT	5	8	196.263-034
RIE	FIELD-SERVICE ENGINEER	5	8	002.167-014
RIE	FLIGHT-OPERATIONS INSPECTOR	5	8	196.163-010
RIE	INDUCTION-COORDINATION POWER ENGINEER	5	8	003.167-038
RIE	INSPECTOR, AIR-CARRIER	5	7	168.264-010
RIE	INSPECTOR, INDUSTRIAL WASTE	5	6	168.267-054
RIE	MECHANICAL-DESIGN ENGINEER, FACILITIES	5	8	007.061-018
RIE	OCEANOGRAPHER, ASSISTANT	5	7	025.267-010
RIE	PETROLEUM ENGINEER	5	8	010.061-018
RIE	PILOT, SUBMERSIBLE	5	5	029.383-010
RIE	PLANT ENGINEER	5	8	007.167-014
RIE	PROTECTION ENGINEER	5	8	003.167-054
RIE	QUALITY-CONTROL TECHNICIAN	5	7	012.261-014
RIE	SALES ENGINEER, AERONAUTICAL PRODUCTS	5	8	002.151-010
RIE	STANDARDS ENGINEER	5	8	012.061-018
RIE	STRESS ANALYST	5	8	002.061-030
RIE	TEST PILOT	5	8	196.263-042
RIE	WINE MAKER	5	8	183.161-014
RIE	ACID-TANK LINER	4	7	861.381-010
RIE	AIR-CONDITIONING CHECK-OUT MECHANIC	4	7	621.281-010
RIE	AIRCRAFT BODY REPAIRER	4	7	807.261-010
RIE	AIRCRAFT LAY-OUT WORKER	4	7	693.381-010
RIE	AIRCRAFT MECHANIC, ELECTRICAL AND RADIO	4	7	825.381-010
RIE	AIRCRAFT-ARMAMENT MECHANIC	4	6	632.261-010
RIE	AIRFRAME-AND-POWER-PLANT-MECHANIC APPRENTICE	4	7	621.281-018

Code	Title	GED	SVP	DOT No.
RIE	AIRPLANE WOODWORKER	4	6	769.281-010
RIE	ALMOND-PASTE MIXER	4	8	529.361-010
RIE	ALTERATION TAILOR	4	7	785.261-010
RIE	ASSEMBLER-INSTALLER APPRENTICE, GENERAL	4	6	806.361-010
RIE	ASSEMBLER-INSTALLER, GENERAL	4	6	806.361-014
RIE	ASSEMBLER, PHOTOGRAPHIC EQUIPMENT	4	7	714.381-010
RIE	ASSEMBLER, WATCH TRAIN	4	6	715.381-014
RIE	ASSEMBLER, TUBING	4	6	806.381-034
RIE	ASSEMBLER, AIRCRAFT, STRUCTURES AND SURFACES	4	6	806.381-026
RIE	ASSEMBLER, ELECTRO-MECHANICAL	4	7	806.381-030
RIE	ASSEMBLER, INTERNAL COMBUSTION ENGINE	4	6	806.481-014
RIE	ASSEMBLY TECHNICIAN	4	6	633.261-010
RIE	AUTOMOBILE-BODY REPAIRER	4	7	807.381-010
RIE	AUTOMOTIVE TECHNICIAN, EXHAUST EMISSIONS	4	7	620.281-014
RIE	AUTOMOTIVE-MAINTENANCE-EQUIPMENT SERVICER	4	7	620.281-018
RIE	BAKERY-MACHINE MECHANIC	4	7	629.281-010
RIE	BALANCING-MACHINE SET-UP WORKER	4	7	809.382-010
RIE	BIOMEDICAL EQUIPMENT TECHNICIAN	4	6	019.261-010
RIE	BLACKSMITH	4	7	610.381-010
RIE	BLACKSMITH APPRENTICE	4	7	610.381-014
RIE	BLASTER	4	7	859.261-010
RIE	BLOCKER, METAL BASE	4	7	974.682-010
RIE	BOILERMAKER FITTER	4	7	805.361-014
RIE	BORING-MACHINE SET-UP OPERATOR, JIG	4	7	606.280-010
RIE	BORING-MILL SET-UP OPERATOR, HORIZONTAL	4	7	606.280-014
RIE	BOTTLE-HOUSE QUALITY-CONTROL TECHNICIAN	4	6	029.361-010
RIE	BOW MAKER, CUSTOM	4	7	732.381-010
RIE	BRASS-WIND-INSTRUMENT MAKER	4	7	730.381-018
RIE	BRAZING-MACHINE SETTER	4	7	813.360-010
RIE	BRICKLAYER APPRENTICE	4	8	861.381-022
RIE	CARBIDE OPERATOR	4	6	601.380-010
RIE	CARPENTER, MOLD	4	7	860.381-034
RIE	CARVER, HAND	4	8	761.281-010
RIE	CELLOPHANE-CASTING-MACHINE REPAIRER	4	6	629.281-014
RIE	CHASER	4	6	704.381-010
RIE	CHRONOMETER ASSEMBLER AND ADJUSTER	4	7	715.381-038
RIE	CHUCKING-MACHINE SET-UP OPERATOR	4	6	604.380-010
RIE	CHUCKING-MACHINE SET-UP OPERATOR, MULTIPLE SPINDLE, VERTICAL	4	6	604.380-014
RIE	CONFECTIONERY COOKER	4	7	526.382-014
RIE	CONSERVATION TECHNICIAN	4	6	102.261-010
RIE	CONTACT PRINTER, PHOTORESIST	4	6	719.381-010
RIE	CRUISER	4	7	459.387-010
RIE	CUTTING-MACHINE FIXER	4	6	585.380-010
RIE	CYLINDER-PRESS OPERATOR	4	7	651.362-010
RIE	CYLINDER-PRESS-OPERATOR APPRENTICE	4	7	651.362-014
RIE	DECORATOR	4	7	298.381-010

Code	Title	GED	SVP	DOT No.
RIE	DEEP SUBMERGENCE VEHICLE CREWMEMBER	4	5	623.281-014
RIE	DESIGNER AND PATTERNMAKER	4	7	788.281-010
RIE	DESULFURIZER OPERATOR	4	6	541.362-010
RIE	DETAILER	4	7	017.261-018
RIE	DETAILER, FURNITURE	4	7	017.261-022
RIE	DIAGRAMMER AND SEAMER	4	5	789.484-010
RIE	DIE DESIGNER	4	7	007.161-010
RIE	DIE MAKER	4	7	601.381-014
RIE	DIE MAKER	4	8	739.381-018
RIE	DIE MAKER	4	7	979.281-010
RIE	DIE MAKER, STAMPING	4	8	601.280-010
RIE	DIE MAKER, TRIM	4	7	601.280-014
RIE	DIE MAKER, WIRE DRAWING	4	7	601.280-018
RIE	DIE MAKER, BENCH, STAMPING	4	7	601.281-010
RIE	DIE SETTER	4	7	612.360-010
RIE	DIE SINKER	4	7	601.280-022
RIE	DIE-CASTING-MACHINE SETTER	4	7	514.360-010
RIE	DIE-DESIGNER APPRENTICE	4	7	007.161-014
RIE	DIE-MAKER APPRENTICE	4	7	601.381-022
RIE	DIE-MAKER APPRENTICE	4	8	739.381-022
RIE	DIE-TRY-OUT WORKER, STAMPING	4	7	601.281-014
RIE	DISTILLATION OPERATOR	4	6	552.462-010
RIE	DRAFTER, AUTOMOTIVE DESIGN LAY-OUT	4	7	017.281-026
RIE	DRAFTER, CASTINGS	4	7	007.261-014
RIE	DRAFTER, CARTOGRAPHIC	4	7	018.261-010
RIE	DRAFTER, DETAIL	4	7	017.261-030
RIE	DRAFTER, LANDSCAPE	4	7	001.261-014
RIE	DRAFTER, OIL AND GAS	4	7	017.281-030
RIE	DRAW-BENCH OPERATOR	4	5	614.682-010
RIE	DRILL-PRESS SET-UP OPERATOR, MULTIPLE SPINDLE	4	6	606.380-010
RIE	DRILL-PRESS SET-UP OPERATOR, RADIAL	4	6	606.380-014
RIE	DRILL-PRESS SET-UP OPERATOR, RADIAL, TOOL	4	6	606.380-018
RIE	DRIVEMATIC-MACHINE OPERATOR	4	6	619.360-010
RIE	DRY-CELL TESTER	4	6	727.381-018
RIE	DRY-WALL APPLICATOR	4	7	842.381-010
RIE	DUPLICATOR-PUNCH OPERATOR	4	5	615.482-014
RIE	EAR-MOLD LABORATORY TECHNICIAN	4	7	777.361-010
RIE	EDITOR, MAP	4	7	018.261-018
RIE	ELECTRIC-CABLE DIAGRAMER	4	6	728.281-010
RIE	ELECTRIC-METER REPAIRER	4	7	729.281-014
RIE	ELECTRIC-METER-REPAIRER APPRENTICE	4	7	729.281-018
RIE	ELECTRIC-METER TESTER	4	7	821.381-010
RIE	ELECTRIC-MOTOR REPAIRER	4	7	721.281-018
RIE	ELECTRIC-MOTOR-CONTROL ASSEMBLER	4	6	721.381-014
RIE	ELECTRICAL TECHNICIAN	4	7	003.161-010
RIE	ELECTRICAL-DISCHARGE-MACHINE SET-UP OPERATOR	4	7	609.380-010
RIE	ELECTRICAL-INSTRUMENT REPAIRER	4	6	729.281-026
RIE	ELECTRICIAN, AUTOMOTIVE	4	7	825.281-022
RIE	ELECTRICIAN, LOCOMOTIVE	4	7	825.281-026
RIE	ELECTROGALVANIZING-MACHINE OPERATOR	4	6	500.362-010
RIE	ELECTROMECHANICAL TECHNICIAN	4	7	710.281-018

Code	Title	GED	SVP	DOT No.
RIE	ELECTROMEDICAL-EQUIPMENT REPAIRER	4	6	729.281-030
RIE	ELECTRONIC-SALES-AND-SERVICE TECHNICIAN	4	7	828.251-010
RIE	ELECTRONICS INSPECTOR 1	4	6	726.381-010
RIE	ELECTROTYPER	4	8	974.381-010
RIE	ELECTROTYPER APPRENTICE	4	8	974.381-014
RIE	ELEVATOR CONSTRUCTOR	4	7	825.361-010
RIE	EMBOSSER	4	6	659.382-010
RIE	ENGINE REPAIRER, SERVICE	4	7	625.281-018
RIE	ENGINE REPAIRER, PRODUCTION	4	6	625.381-010
RIE	ENGINE-LATHE SET-UP OPERATOR, TOOL	4	7	604.280-010
RIE	ENGINE-LATHE SET-UP OPERATOR	4	6	604.380-018
RIE	ENGINEERING MODEL MAKER	4	8	600.260-010
RIE	ENGRAVER, HAND, HARD METALS	4	8	704.381-026
RIE	ENGRAVER, MACHINE	4	8	979.382-014
RIE	ENGRAVER, PICTURE	4	8	979.281-018
RIE	ETCHER APPRENTICE, PHOTOENGRAVING	4	8	971.381-010
RIE	ETCHER, PHOTOENGRAVING	4	8	971.381-014
RIE	EXPERIMENTAL-BOX TESTER	4	7	761.281-014
RIE	EXPERIMENTAL MECHANIC 2	4	7	621.281-022
RIE	EXPERIMENTAL MECHANIC 1	4	7	693.281-010
RIE	EXPERIMENTAL ASSEMBLER	4	6	739.381-026
RIE	FARMER, CASH GRAIN	4	7	401.161-010
RIE	FARMER, VINE-FRUIT CROPS	4	7	403.161-014
RIE	FERMENTATION OPERATOR	4	5	522.382-014
RIE	FIELD ENGINEER, SPECIALIST	4	7	010.261-010
RIE	FIELD-MAP EDITOR	4	6	018.262-010
RIE	FILM INSPECTOR	4	5	976.362-010
RIE	FILM LABORATORY TECHNICIAN 1	4	7	976.381-010
RIE	FINAL INSPECTOR, MOTORCYLES	4	7	806.281-018
RIE	FIRE-CONTROL MECHANIC	4	6	632.261-014
RIE	FIRER, LOCOMOTIVE	4	6	910.363-010
RIE	FIRESETTER	4	6	692.360-018
RIE	FITTER 1	4	7	801.261-014
RIE	FLIGHT-TEST SHOP MECHANIC	4	7	621.381-010
RIE	FLUID-POWER MECHANIC	4	7	600.281-010
RIE	FORM BUILDER	4	7	693.280-010
RIE	FORM BUILDER	4	7	860.381-046
RIE	FORMING-MACHINE ADJUSTER	4	5	629.281-026
RIE	FOUR-SLIDE-MACHINE OPERATOR 1	4	5	619.382-018
RIE	FUEL-INJECTION SERVICER	4	6	625.281-022
RIE	FURNITURE UPHOLSTERER	4	7	780.381-018
RIE	FURNITURE-UPHOLSTERER APPRENTICE	4	7	780.381-022
RIE	GAMBLING MONITOR	4	7	343.367-014
RIE	GAS-APPLIANCE SERVICER	4	7	637.261-018
RIE	GAS-MAIN FITTER	4	7	862.361-014
RIE	GAS-REGULATOR REPAIRER	4	7	710.381-026
RIE	GEAR INSPECTOR	4	6	602.362-010
RIE	GEAR-CUTTING-MACHINE SET-UP OPERATOR, TOOL	4	7	602.280-010
RIE	GEAR-CUTTING-MACHINE SET-UP OPERATOR	4	6	602.380-010
RIE	GOVERNOR ASSEMBLER, HYDRAULIC	4	7	721.381-018
RIE	GRAPHIC ARTS TECHNICIAN	4	5	979.382-018

Code	Title	GED	SVP	DOT No.
RIE	GRINDER MACHINE SETTER	4	6	603.380-010
RIE	GRINDER OPERATOR, EXTERNAL, TOOL	4	7	603.280-010
RIE	GRINDER OPERATOR, SURFACE, TOOL	4	7	603.280-014
RIE	GRINDER OPERATOR, TOOL	4	7	603.280-018
RIE	GRINDER SET-UP OPERATOR, GEAR, TOOL	4	7	602.360-010
RIE	GRINDER SET-UP OPERATOR, INTERNAL 1	4	7	603.280-022
RIE	GRINDER SET-UP OPERATOR, UNIVERSAL	4	7	603.280-030
RIE	GRINDER SET-UP OPERATOR, JIG	4	7	603.280-026
RIE	GRINDER SET-UP OPERATOR, THREAD TOOL	4	7	603.240-010
RIE	HARDENER	4	6	504.382-010
RIE	HARP-ACTION ASSEMBLER	4	6	730.381-030
RIE	HARPSICHORD MAKER	4	6	730.281-034
RIE	HEAT TREATER 1	4	7	504.382-014
RIE	HEAT-TREATER APPRENTICE	4	7	504.382-018
RIE	HIGH-ENERGY-FORMING WORKER	4	6	619.380-010
RIE	HONING-MACHINE SET-UP OPERATOR, TOOL	4	6	603.382-022
RIE	HORTICULTURAL-SPECIALTY GROWER, FIELD	4	7	405.161-014
RIE	HYDROELECTRIC-MACHINERY MECHANIC	4	7	631.261-010
RIE	IDENTIFICATION OFFICER	4	8	377.264-010
RIE	INFANTRY OPERATIONS SPECIALIST	4	6	378.367-022
RIE	INSIDE-METER TESTER	4	7	729.281-034
RIE	INSPECTOR	4	6	710.381-034
RIE	INSPECTOR OF DREDGING	4	6	850.387-010
RIE	INSPECTOR, GAGE AND INSTRUMENT	4	7	601.281-018
RIE	INSPECTOR, TOOL	4	8	601.281-022
RIE	INSPECTOR, METAL CAN	4	5	709.367-010
RIE	INSPECTOR, MECHANICAL AND ELECTRICAL	4	7	710.381-038
RIE	INSPECTOR, PHOTOGRAPHIC EQUIPMENT	4	6	714.381-014
RIE	INSPECTOR, AIRCRAFT LAUNCHING AND ARRESTING SYSTEMS	4	6	806.264-014
RIE	INSPECTOR, RAILROAD	4	7	168.287-018
RIE	INSPECTOR, CHIEF	4	7	956.267-010
RIE	INSPECTOR, REINFORCED PLASTICS	4	7	806.281-034
RIE	INSPECTOR, MISSILE	4	7	806.281-030
RIE	INSPECTOR, BENCH ASSEMBLY	4	7	806.281-026
RIE	INSPECTOR, PRECISION	4	7	716.381-010
RIE	INSTRUMENT MAKER	4	7	600.280-010
RIE	INSTRUMENT MECHANIC	4	3	710.381-042
RIE	INSTRUMENT REPAIRER	4	7	722.281-010
RIE	INSTRUMENT INSPECTOR	4	7	722.381-014
RIE	INSTRUMENT MECHANIC, WEAPONS SYSTEM	4	8	711.281-014
RIE	INSTRUMENT-MAKER APPRENTICE	4	7	600.280-018
RIE	INTERNAL CARVER	4	7	754.381-010
RIE	INTERNAL-COMBUSTION-ENGINE INSPECTOR	4	7	806.261-010
RIE	JIG-BORING MACHINE OPERATOR, NUMERICAL CONTROL	4	7	606.382-014
RIE	JOB PRINTER	4	8	973.381-018
RIE	JOB SETTER	4	7	600.380-014
RIE	JOB SETTER, HONING	4	6	603.280-034

Code	Title	GED	SVP	DOT No.
RIE	JOB-PRINTER APPRENTICE	4	8	973.381-022
RIE	KNITTER MECHANIC	4	7	685.360-010
RIE	LABORATORY TECHNICIAN	4	5	019.381-010
RIE	LABORATORY ASSISTANT	4	5	024.381-010
RIE	LAST-MODEL MAKER	4	6	761.381-018
RIE	LAST-PATTERN GRADER	4	7	693.382-010
RIE	LATHE OPERATOR, NUMERICAL CONTROL	4	6	604.362-010
RIE	LAY-OUT INSPECTOR	4	6	600.281-014
RIE	LAY-OUT WORKER	4	7	600.281-018
RIE	LAY-OUT WORKER	4	7	700.381-026
RIE	LAY-OUT WORKER 1	4	8	809.281-010
RIE	LEAD BURNER	4	7	819.281-010
RIE	LEAD-BURNER APPRENTICE	4	7	819.281-014
RIE	LINE INSTALLER, STREET RAILWAY	4	7	821.361-022
RIE	LINOTYPE OPERATOR	4	7	650.582-010
RIE	LOCATION-AND-MEASUREMENT TECHNICIAN	4	6	715.381-078
RIE	MACHINE BUILDER	4	7	600.281-022
RIE	MACHINE OPERATOR 1	4	6	616.360-018
RIE	MACHINE REPAIRER, MAINTENANCE	4	7	626.281-010
RIE	MACHINE SET-UP OPERATOR	4	6	600.380-018
RIE	MACHINE SETTER	4	7	600.380-022
RIE	MACHINE SETTER	4	6	616.360-022
RIE	MACHINE SETTER	4	7	669.280-010
RIE	MACHINIST	4	7	600.280-022
RIE	MACHINIST APPRENTICE	4	7	600.280-026
RIE	MACHINIST APPRENTICE, AUTOMOTIVE	4	7	600.280-030
RIE	MACHINIST APPRENTICE, OUTSIDE	4	7	623.281-022
RIE	MACHINIST APPRENTICE, WOOD	4	7	669.380-010
RIE	MACHINIST, AUTOMOTIVE	4	7	600.280-034
RIE	MACHINIST, OUTSIDE	4	7	623.281-030
RIE	MACHINIST, WOOD	4	7	669.380-014
RIE	MACHINIST, MOTION-PICTURE EQUIPMENT	4	8	714.281-018
RIE	MAIL-PROCESSING-EQUIPMENT MECHANIC	4	6	633.261-014
RIE	MAILING-MACHINE OPERATOR	4	5	208.462-010
RIE	MAINTENANCE MACHINIST	4	7	600.280-042
RIE	MAINTENANCE MECHANIC	4	7	620.281-046
RIE	MAINTENANCE MECHANIC, COMPRESSED-GAS PLANT	4	7	630.261-010
RIE	MAINTENANCE MECHANIC, TELEPHONE	4	7	822.281-018
RIE	MAINTENANCE REPAIRER, FACTORY OR MILL	4	7	899.281-014
RIE	MARBLE SETTER	4	7	861.381-030
RIE	METAL SPRAYER, MACHINED PARTS	4	6	505.380-010
RIE	METAL-SPRAYING-MACHINE OPERATOR, AUTOMATIC 1	4	7	505.382-010
RIE	METEOROLOGICAL-EQUIPMENT REPAIRER	4	7	823.281-018
RIE	METER REPAIRER	4	5	710.281-034
RIE	MICROFICHE DUPLICATOR	4	6	976.381-014
RIE	MILKING-SYSTEM INSTALLER	4	6	809.381-018
RIE	MILLING-MACHINE SET-UP OPERATOR 1	4	7	605.280-010
RIE	MILLING-MACHINE SET-UP OPERATOR 2	4	7	605.282-010
RIE	MINE-CAR REPAIRER	4	7	622.381-030
RIE	MINER	4	7	850.381-010
RIE	MINER 1	4	6	939.281-010

Code	Title	GED	SVP	DOT No.
RIE	MOCK-UP BUILDER	4	7	693.381-014
RIE	MOCK-UP BUILDER	4	7	693.381-018
RIE	MODEL MAKER	4	7	693.380-010
RIE	MODEL MAKER, SCALE	4	7	710.361-010
RIE	MODEL-AND-MOLD MAKER	4	6	777.381-014
RIE	MOLD MAKER, DIE-CASTING AND PLASTIC MOLDING	4	7	601.280-030
RIE	MOLDER	4	7	518.361-010
RIE	MOLDER APPRENTICE	4	7	518.361-014
RIE	MOLDER, SWEEP	4	7	518.361-018
RIE	MOTION-PICTURE PROJECTIONIST	4	6	960.362-010
RIE	NEEDLEMAKER	4	6	619.280-010
RIE	OBSERVER, ELECTRICAL PROSPECTING	4	6	010.261-014
RIE	OBSERVER, GRAVITY PROSPECTING	4	6	010.261-018
RIE	OBSERVER, SEISMIC PROSPECTING	4	7	010.161-018
RIE	OFFSET-PLATE MAKER	4	6	971.381-018
RIE	OFFSET-PRESS OPERATOR 1	4	7	651.482-010
RIE	OFFSET-PRESS-OPERATOR APPRENTICE	4	7	651.482-014
RIE	OIL-FIELD EQUIPMENT MECHANIC	4	6	629.381-014
RIE	OPERATING-TABLE ASSEMBLER	4	6	706.381-026
RIE	OPTICAL-INSTRUMENT ASSEMBLER	4	6	711.381-010
RIE	OUTBOARD-MOTOR MECHANIC	4	7	623.281-042
RIE	OUTSIDE PRODUCTION INSPECTOR	4	7	806.281-046
RIE	OVERHAULER	4	6	628.261-010
RIE	PANELBOARD OPERATOR	4	5	939.362-014
RIE	PARTS SALVAGER	4	7	638.281-026
RIE	PASTE-UP COPY-CAMERA OPERATOR	4	8	979.381-018
RIE	PASTE-UP COPY-CAMERA OPERATOR APPRENTICE	4	8	979.381-022
RIE	PATTERNMAKER APPRENTICE, METAL	4	8	600.280-046
RIE	PATTERNMAKER, METAL	4	8	600.280-050
RIE	PATTERNMAKER, ENVELOPE	4	7	649.361-010
RIE	PATTERNMAKER APPRENTICE, WOOD	4	8	661.281-018
RIE	PATTERNMAKER, WOOD	4	8	661.281-022
RIE	PATTERNMAKER, METAL, BENCH	4	8	693.281-018
RIE	PATTERNMAKER	4	7	703.381-010
RIE	PATTERNMAKER	4	7	709.381-034
RIE	PATTERNMAKER	4	7	751.381-010
RIE	PATTERNMAKER	4	8	772.381-014
RIE	PATTERNMAKER APPRENTICE, PLASTER	4	6	777.381-026
RIE	PATTERNMAKER, PLASTER	4	6	777.381-030
RIE	PHARMACIST ASSISTANT	4	6	074.381-010
RIE	PHOTOENGRAVER	4	8	971.381-022
RIE	PHOTOENGRAVER APPRENTICE	4	8	971.381-026
RIE	PHOTOENGRAVING FINISHER	4	8	971.381-030
RIE	PHOTOENGRAVING PRINTER	4	8	971.381-034
RIE	PHOTOGRAPHER, PHOTOENGRAVING	4	8	971.382-014
RIE	PHOTOGRAPHER, LITHOGRAPHIC (AIR)	4	7	972.382-014
RIE	PHOTOGRAPHER APPRENTICE, LITHOGRAPHIC	4	7	972.382-010
RIE	PHOTOGRAPHIC-PLATE MAKER	4	6	714.381-018
RIE	PHOTOGRAPHIC EQUIPMENT TECHNICIAN	4	8	714.281-022
RIE	PIPE FITTER	4	7	862.261-010
RIE	PIPE FITTER	4	8	862.381-018

Code	Title	GED	SVP	DOT No.
RIE	PIPE-FITTER APPRENTICE	4	8	862.381-026
RIE	PLANER SET-UP OPERATOR, TOOL	4	7	605.282-014
RIE	PLANER-TYPE-MILLING-MACHINE SET-UP OPERATOR	4	7	605.282-018
RIE	PLASTER MOLDER 1	4	7	777.381-034
RIE	PLASTER-PATTERN CASTER	4	7	777.381-038
RIE	PLASTERER, MOLDING	4	7	842.361-026
RIE	PLASTIC TOOL MAKER	4	7	601.381-026
RIE	PLASTIC-FIXTURE BUILDER	4	7	601.381-030
RIE	PLATE FINISHER	4	8	659.360-010
RIE	PLATEN-PRESS OPERATOR	4	7	651.362-018
RIE	PLATEN-PRESS-OPERATOR APPRENTICE	4	7	651.362-022
RIE	PLATER	4	7	500.380-010
RIE	PLATER APPRENTICE	4	7	500.380-014
RIE	PNEUMATIC-TOOL REPAIRER	4	7	630.281-010
RIE	POLYMERIZATION-KETTLE OPERATOR	4	7	558.382-050
RIE	POULTRY BREEDER	4	7	411.161-014
RIE	POWER-TRANSFORMER REPAIRER	4	7	821.361-034
RIE	PRECISION ASSEMBLER	4	7	828.381-014
RIE	PRECISION-LENS GRINDER	4	7	716.382-018
RIE	PRECISION-LENS-GRINDER APPRENTICE	4	7	716.382-022
RIE	PRESERVATION INSPECTOR, MARINE EQUIPMENT	4	6	929.367-010
RIE	PRESS MAINTAINER	4	8	627.281-010
RIE	PRINTER 2	4	8	651.380-010
RIE	PROCESS STRIPPER	4	7	972.281-014
RIE	PROFILING-MACHINE SET-UP OPERATOR, TOOL	4	7	605.280-018
RIE	PROFILING-MACHINE SET-UP OPERATOR 1	4	7	605.280-014
RIE	PROOF TECHNICIAN	4	6	199.171-010
RIE	PROPULSION-MOTOR-AND-GENERATOR REPAIRER	4	7	721.281-026
RIE	PROSTHETICS TECHNICIAN	4	6	712.381-038
RIE	PROTOTYPE-DEICER ASSEMBLER	4	6	759.261-010
RIE	PUMPER-GAGER	4	7	914.382-014
RIE	PUMPER-GAGER APPRENTICE	4	7	914.382-018
RIE	QUARRY SUPERVISOR, DIMENSION STONE	4	6	930.134-010
RIE	RADIOACTIVITY-INSTRUMENT MAINTENANCE TECHNICIAN	4	7	828.281-022
RIE	RECOVERY OPERATOR	4	5	552.362-018
RIE	RELAY TECHNICIAN	4	8	821.261-018
RIE	RELAY TESTER	4	7	729.281-038
RIE	REPRODUCTION TECHNICIAN	4	6	976.361-010
RIE	REPTILE FARMER	4	6	413.161-014
RIE	RESEARCH MECHANIC	4	7	002.280-010
RIE	RETICLE INSPECTOR	4	7	719.361-010
RIE	ROCKET-ENGINE MECHANIC	4	7	693.281-026
RIE	ROLL-FORMING-MACHINE SET-UP MECHANIC	4	6	613.360-010
RIE	ROLLER REPAIRER	4	7	979.381-026
RIE	ROLLER, PRIMARY MILL	4	7	613.362-014
RIE	ROTARY-HEAD-MILLING-MACHINE SET-UP OPERATOR	4	7	605.382-030
RIE	ROUTER SET-UP OPERATOR, NUMERICAL			

Code	Title	GED	SVP	DOT No.
	CONTROL	4	6	605.360-010
RIE	RUBBERIZING MECHANIC	4	7	630.281-030
RIE	SALVAGE INSPECTOR	4	6	806.287-010
RIE	SAMPLE STITCHER	4	6	785.361-018
RIE	SCIENTIFIC GLASS BLOWER	4	8	006.261-010
RIE	SCREEN MAKER, PHOTOGRAPHIC PROCESS	4	7	971.381-042
RIE	SCREEN MAKER, TEXTILE	4	7	971.381-046
RIE	SCREW-MACHINE SET-UP OPERATOR, MULTIPLE SPINDLE	4	8	604.280-014
RIE	SCREW-MACHINE SET-UP OPERATOR, SINGLE SPINDLE	4	7	604.280-018
RIE	SCREW-MACHINE SET-UP OPERATOR, SWISS-TYPE	4	7	604.260-010
RIE	SETTER, AUTOMATIC-SPINNING LATHE	4	6	604.360-010
RIE	SETTER, COLD-ROLLING MACHINE	4	7	617.682-022
RIE	SHAPER SET-UP OPERATOR, TOOL	4	6	605.382-038
RIE	SHEAR SETTER	4	6	615.380-010
RIE	SHIPFITTER	4	8	806.381-046
RIE	SHIPFITTER APPRENTICE	4	8	806.381-050
RIE	SHOEMAKER, CUSTOM	4	6	788.381-014
RIE	SHOP TAILOR	4	7	785.361-022
RIE	SHOP TAILOR APPRENTICE	4	7	785.361-026
RIE	SHOT-PEENING OPERATOR, TAPE CONTROL	4	6	617.280-010
RIE	SIGN ERECTOR 1	4	7	869.381-026
RIE	SIGNAL MAINTAINER	4	7	822.281-026
RIE	SKETCH MAKER, PHOTOENGRAVING	4	7	970.281-026
RIE	SMOKING-PIPE MAKER	4	7	761.381-030
RIE	SPECIAL EFFECTS SPECIALIST	4	6	962.281-018
RIE	SPECTROSCOPIST	4	7	011.281-014
RIE	SPINNER, HAND	4	7	619.362-018
RIE	SPINNER, HYDRAULIC	4	6	619.362-022
RIE	SPRING COILING MACHINE SETTER	4	7	616.260-018
RIE	SPRING MAKER	4	7	616.280-010
RIE	SPRING-MANUFACTURING SET-UP TECHNICIAN	4	7	619.280-018
RIE	STENCIL CUTTER	4	6	771.281-010
RIE	STENCIL CUTTER	4	7	970.381-038
RIE	STEREOTYPER	4	8	974.382-014
RIE	STEREOTYPER APPRENTICE	4	8	974.382-010
RIE	STONE-LATHE OPERATOR	4	7	674.662-010
RIE	STONECUTTER APPRENTICE, HAND	4	7	771.381-010
RIE	STORAGE BATTERY INSPECTOR AND TESTER	4	7	727.381-022
RIE	STREET-LIGHT REPAIRER	4	7	729.381-018
RIE	STRIPPER, PHOTOLITHOGRAPHIC	4	8	972.381-022
RIE	SUPERVISOR, PARACHUTE MANUFACTURING	4	7	789.132-026
RIE	SUPERVISOR, ASBESTOS-CEMENT SHEET	4	7	679.130-018
RIE	SUPPLY CONTROLLER	4	4	570.382-018
RIE	SWITCHBOARD OPERATOR	4	7	952.362-038
RIE	TAILOR APPRENTICE, ALTERATION	4	7	785.261-018
RIE	TAP-AND-DIE-MAKER TECHNICIAN	4	8	601.280-034
RIE	TAPE-RECORDER REPAIRER	4	7	720.281-014
RIE	TAXIMETER REPAIRER	4	6	710.281-038
RIE	TECHNICAL OPERATOR	4	6	930.167-010

Code	Title	GED	SVP	DOT No.
RIE	TECHNICAL TESTING ENGINEER	4	6	194.381-010
RIE	TECHNICIAN, PLANT AND MAINTENANCE	4	7	822.281-030
RIE	TELEVISION-CABLE INSTALLER	4	5	821.281-010
RIE	TEMPLATE MAKER, EXTRUSION DIE	4	7	601.280-038
RIE	TEMPLATE MAKER	4	7	601.381-038
RIE	TEMPLATE REPRODUCTION TECHNICIAN	4	7	971.381-058
RIE	TEST DRIVER 2	4	7	806.283-010
RIE	TEST-ENGINE EVALUATOR	4	7	010.261-026
RIE	TEST-ENGINE OPERATOR	4	6	029.261-018
RIE	TESTER	4	6	029.261-022
RIE	TESTER, MOTORS AND CONTROLS	4	6	721.281-030
RIE	TESTER, ROCKET ENGINE	4	8	806.261-022
RIE	THREAD INSPECTOR	4	6	862.381-038
RIE	THREADING-MACHINE SETTER	4	6	609.380-014
RIE	TOOL MAKER	4	7	601.280-042
RIE	TOOL MAKER, BENCH	4	7	601.281-026
RIE	TOOL-AND-DIE MAKER	4	7	601.280-046
RIE	TOOL-AND-DIE-MAKER APPRENTICE	4	7	601.280-050
RIE	TOOL-GRINDER OPERATOR	4	7	603.280-038
RIE	TOOL-MACHINE SET-UP OPERATOR	4	7	601.280-054
RIE	TOOL-MAKER APPRENTICE	4	7	601.280-058
RIE	TORSION SPRING COILING MACHINE SETTER	4	7	616.260-022
RIE	TRACER	4	7	779.381-022
RIE	TRANSFORMER ASSEMBLER	4	6	820.381-014
RIE	TRUCK-BODY BUILDER	4	7	807.281-010
RIE	TRUCK-BODY-BUILDER APPRENTICE	4	7	807.281-014
RIE	TURBINE OPERATOR	4	7	952.362-042
RIE	TURRET-LATHE SET-UP OPERATOR, TOOL	4	7	604.280-022
RIE	TURRET-LATHE SET-UP OPERATOR	4	6	604.380-026
RIE	TURRET-PUNCH-PRESS OPERATOR	4	5	615.482-038
RIE	WATCH ASSEMBLER	4	6	715.381-094
RIE	WEATHER OBSERVER	4	6	025.267-014
RIE	WEB-PRESS OPERATOR	4	7	651.362-030
RIE	WEB-PRESS-OPERATOR APPRENTICE	4	7	651.362-034
RIE	WELDER SETTER, RESISTANCE MACHINE	4	7	812.360-010
RIE	WELDER SETTER, ELECTRON-BEAM MACHINE	4	6	815.380-010
RIE	WELDER-FITTER	4	7	819.361-010
RIE	WELDER-FITTER APPRENTICE	4	7	819.361-014
RIE	WELDER, EXPERIMENTAL	4	8	819.281-022
RIE	WELDING-MACHINE OPERATOR, ARC	4	6	810.382-010
RIE	WELDING-MACHINE OPERATOR, ELECTRON BEAM	4	6	815.382-010
RIE	WELL-DRILL OPERATOR	4	7	859.362-010
RIE	WELL-LOGGING OPERATOR, MUD ANALYSIS	4	5	010.281-022
RIE	WIRE-MESH-FILTER FABRICATOR	4	6	709.381-046
RIE	WOOL SORTER	4	6	589.387-014
RIE	YARD INSPECTOR	4	7	869.281-018
RIE	ABRASIVE GRADER	3	4	570.682-010
RIE	AIRBORNE SENSOR SPECIALIST	3	6	378.382-010
RIE	ALINER, BARREL AND RECEIVER	3	3	736.684-010
RIE	ANGLE SHEAR OPERATOR	3	3	615.482-010
RIE	APPLIANCE REPAIRER	3	3	723.584-010

Code	Title	GED	SVP	DOT No.
RIE	ARCH-CUSHION-SKIVING-MACHINE OPERATOR	3	4	690.682-010
RIE	AUTOCLAVE OPERATOR 1	3	5	553.382-010
RIE	AVIATION SUPPORT EQUIPMENT REPAIRER	3	5	639.281-010
RIE	BELLOWS CHARGER 2	3	4	710.684-014
RIE	BELLY BUILDER	3	3	730.684-018
RIE	BELT-PRESS OPERATOR 1	3	5	553.362-010
RIE	BENZENE-WASHER OPERATOR	3	5	551.682-010
RIE	BEVELING-AND-EDGING-MACHINE OPERATOR	3	4	673.682-014
RIE	BLOOD TESTER, FOWL	3	2	411.364-010
RIE	BORING-MACHINE OPERATOR	3	5	606.682-010
RIE	BOX-FOLDING-MACHINE OPERATOR	3	4	649.682-010
RIE	BRAKE COUPLER, ROAD FREIGHT	3	4	910.367-010
RIE	BRAZER, FURNACE	3	4	813.482-010
RIE	BRAZER, INDUCTION	3	5	813.382-010
RIE	BRAZER, RESISTANCE	3	4	813.682-010
RIE	BRAZING-MACHINE OPERATOR	3	5	813.382-014
RIE	BRINE MAKER	3	3	550.685-018
RIE	BROACHING-MACHINE OPERATOR, PRODUCTION	3	4	605.682-014
RIE	BROACHING-MACHINE SET-UP OPERATOR	3	4	605.382-010
RIE	BUCKSHOT-SWAGE OPERATOR	3	4	612.682-010
RIE	BUFFING-MACHINE OPERATOR	3	4	603.382-010
RIE	BUFFING-MACHINE OPERATOR, SILVERWARE	3	4	603.682-010
RIE	BULK-STATION OPERATOR	3	5	570.362-010
RIE	BUS DRIVER, DAY-HAUL OR FARM CHARTER	3	3	913.363-010
RIE	CALENDER OPERATOR	3	4	554.362-010
RIE	CALENDER OPERATOR	3	4	590.682-010
RIE	CAPSULE-FILLING-MACHINE OPERATOR	3	4	559.682-010
RIE	CARBON-COATER-MACHINE OPERATOR	3	3	534.682-014
RIE	CARPET CUTTER	3	5	929.381-010
RIE	CASER, SHOE PARTS	3	3	788.687-026
RIE	CASTING-MACHINE OPERATOR, AUTOMATIC	3	4	502.482-014
RIE	CASTING-WHEEL OPERATOR	3	4	514.682-010
RIE	CATALYST-RECOVERY OPERATOR	3	3	551.685-022
RIE	CELL REPAIRER	3	5	826.384-010
RIE	CELL TESTER	3	4	558.584-010
RIE	CENTER-MACHINE OPERATOR	3	5	520.682-014
RIE	CHANNELING-MACHINE RUNNER	3	4	930.383-010
RIE	CHEMICAL COMPOUNDER	3	4	559.682-018
RIE	CHEMICAL OPERATOR 2	3	4	558.585-014
RIE	CLAY-STAIN MIXER	3	3	773.487-010
RIE	CLEAN-OUT DRILLER	3	5	930.363-010
RIE	CLOTH-SHRINKING TESTER	3	3	587.384-010
RIE	COAL-EQUIPMENT OPERATOR	3	4	921.683-022
RIE	COATER OPERATOR	3	6	509.382-010
RIE	COATING-MACHINE OPERATOR	3	5	584.382-010
RIE	COLOR MAKER	3	5	550.382-014
RIE	COLOR MATCHER	3	5	550.381-010
RIE	COLOR-PRINTER OPERATOR	3	3	976.382-014
RIE	COLORING CHECKER	3	4	735.587-010

Code	Title	GED	SVP	DOT No.
RIE	COMBINER OPERATOR	3	4	534.682-026
RIE	CONSOLE ASSEMBLER	3	4	730.684-030
RIE	CONSTRUCTION WORKER 1	3	4	869.664-014
RIE	CONTOUR-BAND-SAW OPERATOR, VERTICAL	3	4	607.382-010
RIE	CONVEYOR OPERATOR	3	4	921.683-026
RIE	CRUSHER OPERATOR	3	2	570.685-018
RIE	CUPROUS-CHLORIDE OPERATOR	3	4	558.382-034
RIE	CURB-MACHINE OPERATOR	3	4	853.683-010
RIE	CUT-AND-PRINT-MACHINE OPERATOR	3	4	659.682-010
RIE	CUT-OFF-SAW OPERATOR, METAL	3	4	607.682-010
RIE	CUTTING-MACHINE OPERATOR	3	4	640.682-018
RIE	DADO OPERATOR	3	5	669.382-010
RIE	DIE-CASTING-MACHINE OPERATOR 1	3	5	514.382-010
RIE	DOOR ASSEMBLER	3	3	806.684-050
RIE	DOOR-MACHINE OPERATOR	3	3	519.663-010
RIE	DRAW-BENCH OPERATOR	3	4	614.482-010
RIE	DRIER OPERATOR	3	4	543.682-014
RIE	DRILL-PRESS SET-UP OPERATOR, SINGLE SPINDLE	3	4	606.682-018
RIE	DRILLER, MACHINE	3	5	930.382-010
RIE	DRILLING-MACHINE OPERATOR	3	6	930.482-010
RIE	DRY-CHARGE-PROCESS ATTENDANT	3	4	590.685-026
RIE	DRY-PRESS OPERATOR	3	5	575.662-010
RIE	DUMP-TRUCK DRIVER	3	2	902.683-010
RIE	DYNAMIC-ETCHING PROCESSOR	3	6	704.381-014
RIE	ELECTRODE TURNER-AND-FINISHER	3	4	692.682-034
RIE	ELEVATING-GRADER OPERATOR	3	6	850.663-014
RIE	EXPANSION-JOINT BUILDER	3	4	759.664-014
RIE	EXTRUDER OPERATOR	3	5	614.482-014
RIE	EXTRUSION-PRESS ADJUSTER	3	5	614.380-010
RIE	FABRICATOR-ASSEMBLER, METAL PRODUCTS	3	5	809.381-010
RIE	FARM-MACHINE OPERATOR	3	3	409.683-010
RIE	FENCE-MAKING MACHINE OPERATOR	3	4	616.582-010
RIE	FILLING-MACHINE SET-UP MECHANIC	3	3	920.680-010
RIE	FINAL INSPECTOR	3	3	753.687-018
RIE	FITTER, VENTILATED RIB	3	5	736.381-014
RIE	FIXTURE REPAIRER-FABRICATOR	3	5	630.384-010
RIE	FLASH-DRIER OPERATOR	3	4	553.462-010
RIE	FLEXOGRAPHIC-PRESS OPERATOR	3	4	651.682-010
RIE	FORGING-PRESS OPERATOR 1	3	5	611.482-010
RIE	FORM-GRADER OPERATOR	3	4	850.683-022
RIE	FORMING-ROLL OPERATOR 1	3	4	617.482-014
RIE	FOUNDATION-DRILL OPERATOR	3	5	859.682-014
RIE	FOUR-SLIDE-MACHINE SETTER	3	6	616.380-010
RIE	FRAME STRAIGHTENER	3	5	807.484-010
RIE	FRUIT-BUYING GRADER	3	3	529.387-018
RIE	FUEL-SYSTEM-MAINTENANCE WORKER	3	7	638.381-010
RIE	FURNACE OPERATOR	3	4	513.462-010
RIE	GARBAGE COLLECTOR DRIVER	3	3	905.663-010
RIE	GEAR HOBBER SET-UP OPERATOR	3	5	602.382-010
RIE	GEAR REPAIRER	3	6	623.381-010
RIE	GEAR-GENERATOR SET-UP OPERATOR, SPIRAL BEVEL	3	5	602.382-014

Code	Title	GED	SVP	DOT No.
RIE	GEAR-GENERATOR SET-UP OPERATOR, STRAIGHT BEVEL	3	5	602.382-018
RIE	GEAR-LAPPING-MACHINE OPERATOR	3	5	602.482-010
RIE	GEAR-MILLING-MACHINE SET-UP OPERATOR	3	5	602.382-022
RIE	GEAR-SHAPER SET-UP OPERATOR	3	5	602.382-026
RIE	GEAR-SHAVER SET-UP OPERATOR	3	6	602.382-030
RIE	GRADER	3	4	669.587-010
RIE	GRANULATOR-MACHINE OPERATOR	3	5	559.382-026
RIE	GRINDER SET-UP OPERATOR, INTERNAL 2	3	4	603.482-018
RIE	GRINDER SET-UP OPERATOR, EXTERNAL	3	4	603.482-014
RIE	GROWTH-MEDIA MIXER, MUSHROOM	3	3	405.683-014
RIE	GUM-SCORING-MACHINE OPERATOR	3	5	520.682-022
RIE	HEAD SAWYER	3	7	667.662-010
RIE	HEADER	3	4	665.682-014
RIE	HEATER	3	6	542.362-010
RIE	HEATER	3	4	619.682-022
RIE	HEATER-PLANER OPERATOR	3	3	853.683-014
RIE	HIGH-DENSITY FINISHING OPERATOR	3	3	539.562-010
RIE	HONING-MACHINE OPERATOR, PRODUCTION	3	4	603.482-034
RIE	HOOKER INSPECTOR	3	3	689.685-078
RIE	HOSE MAKER	3	3	752.684-030
RIE	HOSTLER	3	4	909.663-010
RIE	HOSTLER	3	4	910.683-010
RIE	HYDROELECTRIC-MACHINERY-MECHANIC HELPER	3	3	631.364-010
RIE	IMPREGNATING-TANK OPERATOR	3	4	599.685-046
RIE	INDUSTRIAL-GAS FITTER	3	7	862.381-014
RIE	INSPECTOR	3	5	559.381-010
RIE	INSPECTOR	3	4	788.384-010
RIE	INSPECTOR, COLD WORKING	3	4	612.384-010
RIE	INSPECTOR, TYPEWRITER ASSEMBLY AND PARTS	3	6	706.381-022
RIE	IRON-PLASTIC BULLET MAKER	3	3	590.365-010
RIE	JOINT-CLEANING-AND-GROOVING-MACHINE OPERATOR	3	4	853.683-018
RIE	LABORER, CAR BARN	3	4	910.583-010
RIE	LEATHER GRADER	3	5	784.387-014
RIE	LINE TENDER, FLAKEBOARD	3	5	569.382-010
RIE	LOADING-MACHINE OPERATOR	3	5	932.683-014
RIE	LOCK-CORNER-MACHINE OPERATOR	3	4	665.382-014
RIE	LOG MARKER	3	3	454.687-018
RIE	LOZENGE MAKER	3	5	529.682-026
RIE	LYE TREATER	3	3	551.685-094
RIE	MACHINE MOLDER	3	4	518.682-010
RIE	MACHINE SET-UP OPERATOR, PAPER GOODS	3	5	649.380-010
RIE	MACHINE SETTER	3	5	690.380-010
RIE	MAJOR-ASSEMBLY INSPECTOR	3	6	801.381-018
RIE	METAL CONTROL WORKER	3	3	512.487-010
RIE	METAL SPRAYER, CORROSION PREVENTION	3	5	843.482-010
RIE	MILL ATTENDANT	3	3	555.565-010
RIE	MISSILE FACILITIES REPAIRER	3	4	828.281-018
RIE	MITER GRINDER OPERATOR	3	4	673.682-026

Code	Title	GED	SVP	DOT No.
RIE	MIXER	3	3	550.685-078
RIE	MIXER	3	3	550.685-074
RIE	MIXING-MACHINE OPERATOR	3	4	550.382-022
RIE	MIXING-MACHINE TENDER	3	4	550.685-090
RIE	MOLD SETTER	3	6	556.380-010
RIE	MORTISING-MACHINE OPERATOR	3	4	665.482-014
RIE	MOTOR OPERATOR	3	5	910.683-014
RIE	MOTORBOAT OPERATOR	3	5	911.663-010
RIE	MOTORCYCLE REPAIRER	3	6	620.281-054
RIE	MULTIPLE-DRUM SANDER	3	4	662.682-014
RIE	NEW-CAR INSPECTOR	3	4	919.363-010
RIE	OIL BOILER	3	5	543.362-010
RIE	OIL-RECOVERY-UNIT OPERATOR	3	3	549.382-014
RIE	OPENER-VERIFIER-PACKER, CUSTOMS	3	5	168.387-010
RIE	OPERATOR, CATALYST CONCENTRATION	3	5	550.382-026
RIE	ORDNANCE TRUCK INSTALLATION MECHANIC	3	3	806.684-098
RIE	OXYGEN-FURNACE OPERATOR	3	5	512.382-010
RIE	PACK-ROOM OPERATOR	3	4	559.684-010
RIE	PAINT-SPRAYER OPERATOR, AUTOMATIC	3	5	599.382-010
RIE	PAINTER, TUMBLING BARREL	3	3	599.685-070
RIE	PHARMACEUTICAL OPERATOR	3	5	559.382-042
RIE	PIGMENT FURNACE TENDER	3	3	553.685-086
RIE	PILE-DRIVER OPERATOR	3	5	859.682-018
RIE	PIPE TESTER	3	5	930.382-014
RIE	PIPE-WRAPPING-MACHINE OPERATOR	3	5	862.682-014
RIE	PLANER OPERATOR	3	4	665.682-022
RIE	PLANER, STONE	3	5	675.682-018
RIE	PLANT OPERATOR	3	4	570.682-014
RIE	PLASTICS BENCH MECHANIC	3	6	754.381-018
RIE	PLATE SETTER, FLEXOGRAPHIC PRESS	3	6	659.381-010
RIE	PLAYER-PIANO TECHNICIAN	3	4	730.381-050
RIE	PORCELAIN-ENAMEL REPAIRER	3	2	741.684-030
RIE	POT BUILDER	3	4	826.684-022
RIE	POTTERY-MACHINE OPERATOR	3	5	774.382-010
RIE	POULTRY INSEMINATOR	3	3	411.384-010
RIE	PREFITTER, DOORS	3	4	666.582-010
RIE	PRESS OPERATOR, HARDBOARD	3	5	569.682-014
RIE	PRESS SETTER	3	5	617.480-014
RIE	PRINTER, PLASTIC	3	5	651.382-026
RIE	PROCESSOR, SOLID PROPELLANT	3	4	590.464-010
RIE	PROFILE-SHAPER OPERATOR, AUTOMATIC	3	5	665.682-026
RIE	PROFILING-MACHINE SET-UP OPERATOR 2	3	5	605.382-026
RIE	PROOF-TECHNICIAN HELPER	3	4	736.387-014
RIE	PROPELLER LAY-OUT WORKER	3	6	600.381-010
RIE	PULP-AND-PAPER TESTER	3	5	539.364-010
RIE	PUNCH-PRESS SETTER	3	6	619.380-014
RIE	QUALITY TECHNICIAN, FIBERGLASS	3	4	579.384-014
RIE	QUALITY-CONTROL TESTER	3	4	559.367-010
RIE	RAFTER-CUTTING-MACHINE OPERATOR	3	4	669.382-014
RIE	REDEYE GUNNER	3	3	378.682-010
RIE	REPAIRER, HEAVY	3	6	620.381-022
RIE	ROAD-MIXER OPERATOR	3	5	859.683-026
RIE	ROCK-DRILL OPERATOR 2	3	5	850.662-014

Code	Title	GED	SVP	DOT No.
RIE	ROLL GRINDER	3	5	629.682-010
RIE	ROLL OPERATOR	3	5	554.682-018
RIE	ROLL-FORMING-MACHINE OPERATOR 1	3	5	617.482-018
RIE	ROLLER-MACHINE OPERATOR	3	4	611.482-014
RIE	ROLLER-PRINT TENDER	3	3	971.685-010
RIE	ROOF-CEMENT-AND-PAINT MAKER	3	5	550.382-030
RIE	ROTARY-SCREEN-PRINTING-MACHINE OPERATOR	3	4	652.582-014
RIE	ROUTER OPERATOR	3	6	605.382-034
RIE	ROUTER OPERATOR	3	4	665.682-030
RIE	ROUTER OPERATOR	3	3	676.462-010
RIE	RUBBER AND PLASTICS WORKER	3	4	891.684-014
RIE	SAFETY-PIN-ASSEMBLING-MACHINE OPERATOR	3	5	616.482-010
RIE	SAILOR, PLEASURE CRAFT	3	5	911.664-014
RIE	SANDBLASTER, STONE	3	6	673.382-010
RIE	SANDBLASTER, STONE APPRENTICE	3	6	673.382-014
RIE	SATURATION-EQUIPMENT OPERATOR	3	4	582.665-022
RIE	SATURATOR OPERATOR	3	5	558.362-018
RIE	SAW FILER	3	6	701.381-014
RIE	SCALPER OPERATOR	3	4	605.682-022
RIE	SCRAPER OPERATOR	3	5	850.683-038
RIE	SCREW-MACHINE SET-UP OPERATOR, PRODUCTION	3	5	604.380-022
RIE	SETTER, MOLDING-AND-COREMAKING MACHINES	3	4	518.380-010
RIE	SHAPER OPERATOR	3	5	665.682-034
RIE	SHELL-MACHINE OPERATOR	3	4	649.682-030
RIE	SHUTTLE-CAR OPERATOR	3	4	932.683-022
RIE	SILVERING APPLICATOR	3	5	574.582-010
RIE	SLAB-DEPILER OPERATOR	3	4	504.665-010
RIE	SODA-COLUMN OPERATOR	3	4	558.382-054
RIE	SOLDERER-ASSEMBLER	3	4	813.684-014
RIE	SPRAYER, HAND	3	4	408.684-014
RIE	STAMPER, MACHINE	3	4	652.682-022
RIE	STOCK CUTTER	3	4	667.482-018
RIE	STOCK GRADER	3	5	667.382-010
RIE	STOCK-PATCH SAWYER	3	4	667.682-082
RIE	STONE GRADER	3	6	670.384-010
RIE	STONE LAYOUT MARKER	3	3	670.587-010
RIE	STONECUTTER, MACHINE	3	6	677.682-022
RIE	STRAIGHT-PIN-MAKING-MACHINE OPERATOR	3	5	609.482-014
RIE	STRANDING-MACHINE OPERATOR	3	4	616.682-034
RIE	STROKE-BELT-SANDER OPERATOR	3	4	662.682-018
RIE	SWING-TYPE-LATHE OPERATOR	3	4	664.382-010
RIE	TABLET-MAKING-MACHINE OPERATOR	3	4	649.682-042
RIE	TARGET AIRCRAFT TECHNICIAN	3	6	378.281-010
RIE	TESTER, COMPRESSED GASES	3	3	549.364-010
RIE	THERMAL-CUTTING-MACHINE OPERATOR	3	5	816.482-010
RIE	THINNER	3	3	550.585-038
RIE	TIMBER-SIZER OPERATOR	3	4	665.482-018
RIE	TIN RECOVERY WORKER	3	4	512.382-018
RIE	TINTER	3	6	550.381-014

Code	Title	GED	SVP	DOT No.
RIE	TIRE BUILDER, AUTOMOBILE	3	3	750.384-010
RIE	TORCH-STRAIGHTENER-AND HEATER	3	4	709.684-086
RIE	TRACER-POWDER BLENDER	3	3	550.585-042
RIE	TRACK-MOVING-MACHINE OPERATOR	3	4	910.663-010
RIE	TRACK-SURFACING-MACHINE OPERATOR	3	3	910.683-018
RIE	TRACTOR-TRAILER-TRUCK DRIVER	3	4	904.383-010
RIE	TREATING INSPECTOR	3	3	569.367-010
RIE	TREATING-PLANT OPERATOR	3	4	563.662-010
RIE	TREE-SHEAR OPERATOR	3	4	454.683-010
RIE	TRIMMER SAWYER	3	4	667.482-022
RIE	TRUCK DRIVER, LIGHT	3	3	906.683-022
RIE	UNATTENDED-GROUND-SENSOR SPECIALIST	3	6	378.382-018
RIE	UTILITY-TRACTOR OPERATOR	3	4	850.683-046
RIE	VEHICLE-FUEL-SYSTEMS CONVERTER	3	6	620.281-070
RIE	VENEER-LATHE OPERATOR	3	4	664.662-010
RIE	VINEGAR MAKER	3	4	522.382-038
RIE	WASTEWATER-TREATMENT-PLANT ATTENDANT	3	4	955.585-010
RIE	WATER-TRUCK DRIVER 2	3	3	905.683-010
RIE	WAXING-MACHINE OPERATOR	3	5	534.482-010
RIE	WEIGHER-BULKER	3	5	550.582-014
RIE	WELDER APPRENTICE, GAS	3	4	811.684-010
RIE	WELDING-MACHINE OPERATOR, ELECTROSLAG	3	4	815.382-014
RIE	WELDING-MACHINE OPERATOR, THERMIT	3	3	815.682-014
RIE	WELL PULLER	3	5	930.382-030
RIE	WIRE DRAWER	3	4	614.382-010
RIE	WOOD-CARVING-MACHINE OPERATOR	3	4	665.382-018
RIE	YARD ENGINEER	3	5	910.363-018
RIE	YARD WORKER	3	3	929.583-010
RIE	BELT SANDER, STONE	2	2	673.666-010
RIE	BEVELER	2	2	673.685-022
RIE	CUT-OFF SAW TENDER, METAL	2	2	607.685-010
RIE	FURNACE-AND-WASH-EQUIPMENT OPERATOR	2	2	503.685-026
RIE	HEAT WELDER, PLASTICS	2	3	553.684-010
RIE	INFANTRY INDIRECT FIRE CREWMEMBER	2	5	378.684-022
RIE	LABORER, GENERAL	2	2	559.685-110
RIE	LABORER, POULTRY FARM	2	2	411.687-018
RIE	MILL HELPER	2	3	502.684-014
RIE	MIXER	2	2	737.687-090
RIE	POWDER BLENDER AND POURER	2	3	550.485-022
RIE	SINGER	2	3	585.685-106
RIE	SKI-TOP TRIMMER	2	2	690.685-370
RIE	SPLITTER TENDER	2	2	663.685-038
RIE	STABLE ATTENDANT	2	2	410.674-022
RIE	STRING LASTER	2	2	690.685-406
RIE	UTILITY BAG ASSEMBLER	2	2	783.684-030
RIC	OPTICAL ENGINEER	6	8	019.061-018
RIC	HEAT-TRANSFER TECHNICIAN	5	7	007.181-010
RIC	INSTRUMENTATION TECHNICIAN	5	7	003.261-010
RIC	OPTOMECHANICAL TECHNICIAN	5	8	007.161-030
RIC	RADIO STATION OPERATOR	5	6	193.262-026
RIC	ASSEMBLER AND TESTER, ELECTRONICS	4	6	710.281-010

Code	Title	GED	SVP	DOT No.
RSI	FARMER, DIVERSIFIED CROPS	4	7	407.161-010
RSI	FINAL TESTER	4	7	721.261-014
RSI	FIXER, BOARDING ROOM	4	7	580.380-010
RSI	FURNACE-COMBUSTION ANALYST	4	6	572.360-010
RSI	GLASS-BULB-MACHINE ADJUSTER	4	6	575.360-010
RSI	HARNESS BUILDER	4	6	683.380-010
RSI	HEAT-TREAT INSPECTOR	4	7	504.281-010
RSI	LINE MAINTAINER	4	7	821.261-014
RSI	LIVESTOCK RANCHER	4	7	410.161-018
RSI	MAKE-UP ARRANGER	4	8	973.381-026
RSI	ORTHOPTIST	4	6	079.371-014
RSI	PANTOGRAPH SETTER	4	6	979.380-010
RSI	PINSETTER ADJUSTER, AUTOMATIC	4	6	829.381-010
RSI	POLLUTION-CONTROL TECHNICIAN	4	6	029.261-014
RSI	PRIMER-CHARGING TOOL SETTER	4	6	694.360-010
RSI	RIGGER	4	7	823.281-022
RSI	SLITTER SERVICE AND SETTER	4	6	615.280-010
RSI	SPIDER ASSEMBLER	4	6	721.684-026
RSI	STOCK MAKER, CUSTOM	4	7	761.381-038
RSI	SUPERVISOR, ROLLER SHOP	4	7	979.131-014
RSI	SWITCHBOARD OPERATOR	4	7	952.362-034
RSI	TANK BUILDER AND ERECTOR	4	7	860.381-066
RSI	AMBULANCE DRIVER	3	4	913.683-010
RSI	ASSEMBLER, UNIT	3	4	809.681-010
RSI	BIOLOGICAL AIDE	3	6	049.384-010
RSI	BRAKE OPERATOR 1	3	6	617.360-010
RSI	CONTROL OPERATOR	3	5	511.482-010
RSI	GUIDE SETTER	3	6	613.361-010
RSI	INSPECTOR-REPAIRER, SANDSTONE	3	3	779.684-030
RSI	LOCOMOTIVE-CRANE OPERATOR	3	5	921.663-038
RSI	PICKLER, CONTINUOUS PICKLING LINE	3	6	503.362-010
RSI	PRINTER-SLOTTER OPERATOR	3	6	659.662-010
RSI	ROLLER MAKER	3	4	759.664-018
RSI	SLITTING-MACHINE OPERATOR 1	3	4	699.682-030
RSI	TANNER, ROTARY DRUM, CONTINUOUS PROCESS	3	5	582.482-014
RSI	TIRE-REGROOVING-MACHINE OPERATOR	3	4	690.662-010
RSE	CHECK PILOT	5	8	196.263-022
RSE	ORNAMENTAL-METALWORK DESIGNER	5	8	142.061-034
RSE	ORTHOTIST	5	8	078.261-018
RSE	PROSTHETIST	5	8	078.261-022
RSE	ACCORDION REPAIRER	4	7	730.281-014
RSE	AEROSPACE PHYSIOLOGICAL TECHNICIAN	4	6	199.682-010
RSE	AGING-DEPARTMENT SUPERVISOR	4	6	582.132-010
RSE	AIRPORT ELECTRICIAN	4	7	824.281-010
RSE	ASSEMBLER	4	7	715.381-010
RSE	AUDIO-VIDEO REPAIRER	4	6	729.281-010
RSE	AUTOMOBILE MECHANIC	4	7	620.261-010
RSE	AUTOMOBILE TESTER	4	7	620.261-014
RSE	AUTOMOBILE-REPAIR-SERVICE ESTIMATOR	4	7	620.261-018
RSE	AUTOMOBILE-MECHANIC APPRENTICE	4	7	620.261-012
RSE	AUTOMOTIVE-GENERATOR-AND-STARTER REPAIRER	4	6	721.281-010

Code	Title	GED	SVP	DOT No.
RSE	GLASS-CUT-OFF SUPERVISOR	4	7	677.131-010
RSE	GLASS-RIBBON-MACHINE OPERATOR	4	7	575.362-014
RSE	HARP MAKER	4	8	730.281-030
RSE	HEATING-PLANT SUPERINTENDENT	4	8	959.131-010
RSE	HOUSE MOVER	4	6	869.261-010
RSE	HOUSE-MOVER SUPERVISOR	4	7	869.131-022
RSE	HYDRAULIC-PRESSURE-AUTO-FRETTAGE-MACHINE-OPERATOR SUPERVISOR	4	7	619.130-010
RSE	IMMIGRATION INSPECTOR	4	5	168.167-022
RSE	INSPECTOR	4	7	710.384-014
RSE	INSPECTOR AND TESTER	4	6	624.361-010
RSE	INSPECTOR, FURNITURE AND BEDDING	4	6	168.267-046
RSE	INSTRUCTOR, DECORATING	4	7	740.221-010
RSE	KNITTING-MACHINE FIXER, HEAD	4	7	689.130-018
RSE	LINE INSTALLER-REPAIRER	4	7	822.381-014
RSE	LOOM FIXER	4	7	683.260-018
RSE	LOOM STARTER	4	7	683.360-014
RSE	MACHINE-CLOTHING REPLACER	4	7	629.361-010
RSE	MACHINIST APPRENTICE, MARINE ENGINE	4	7	623.281-018
RSE	MACHINIST SUPERVISOR, OUTSIDE	4	8	623.131-010
RSE	MACHINIST, MARINE ENGINE	4	7	623.281-026
RSE	MANNEQUIN-MOLD MAKER	4	7	739.381-046
RSE	MECHANIC, FLOWMETER TEST AND CERTIFICATION	4	7	621.381-018
RSE	MECHANICAL TECHNICIAN, LABORATORY	4	7	715.261-010
RSE	MODEL MAKER	4	7	731.280-010
RSE	MOLDER, BENCH	4	7	518.381-022
RSE	MONUMENT SETTER	4	7	861.361-014
RSE	NEON-SIGN SERVICER	4	7	824.281-018
RSE	OIL-WELL-SERVICES SUPERVISOR	4	8	939.132-014
RSE	ORIENTAL-RUG REPAIRER	4	6	782.381-014
RSE	ORNAMENTAL-METAL WORKER	4	8	619.260-008
RSE	ORNAMENTAL-METAL-WORKER APPRENTICE	4	8	619.260-010
RSE	ORTHOTICS ASSISTANT	4	7	078.361-022
RSE	PAPERHANGER	4	7	841.381-010
RSE	PATTERN-GRADER SUPERVISOR	4	7	693.132-010
RSE	PATTERNMAKER	4	7	784.361-010
RSE	PERMANENT-MOLD SUPERVISOR	4	7	514.130-010
RSE	PHOTOGRAPHER, SCIENTIFIC	4	7	143.062-026
RSE	PHOTOGRAPHER, AERIAL	4	7	143.062-014
RSE	PHOTOGRAPHIC-EQUIPMENT-MAINTENANCE TECHNICIAN	4	7	714.281-026
RSE	PIPE FITTER, DIESEL ENGINE 1	4	7	862.361-018
RSE	PIPE-FITTER SUPERVISOR	4	8	862.131-014
RSE	POULTRY FARMER	4	7	411.161-018
RSE	POWDER-LINE REPAIRER	4	6	629.261-018
RSE	PRINT CONTROLLER	4	6	976.360-010
RSE	PRIVATE-BRANCH-EXCHANGE REPAIRER	4	7	822.281-022
RSE	PROOFSHEET CORRECTOR	4	8	973.381-030
RSE	PROSTHETICS ASSISTANT	4	7	078.361-026
RSE	PUMP MECHANIC	4	6	629.281-034
RSE	QUILTER FIXER	4	6	689.260-014
RSE	RERECORDING MIXER	4	7	194.362-014
RSE	ROLL OPERATOR 1	4	7	619.362-014

Code	Title	GED	SVP	DOT No.
RSE	SCREEN-PRINTING-EQUIPMENT SETTER	4	7	979.360-010
RSE	SERVICE RESTORER, EMERGENCY	4	7	821.261-022
RSE	SET-UP MECHANIC, COIL-WINDING MACHINES	4	6	724.360-010
RSE	SET-UP MECHANIC	4	6	692.380-010
RSE	SOUND TECHNICIAN	4	6	829.281-022
RSE	SOUS CHEF	4	8	313.131-026
RSE	SPRING INSPECTOR 1	4	7	616.361-010
RSE	STATE-HIGHWAY POLICE OFFICER	4	6	375.263-018
RSE	STONEMASON	4	7	861.381-038
RSE	STONEMASON APPRENTICE	4	7	861.381-042
RSE	SUBSTATION INSPECTOR	4	7	952.261-010
RSE	SUPERVISOR	4	7	556.130-010
RSE	SUPERVISOR	4	7	679.130-010
RSE	SUPERVISOR	4	8	779.131-010
RSE	SUPERVISOR, VACUUM METALIZING	4	7	505.130-014
RSE	SUPERVISOR, LEAD REFINERY	4	8	519.130-018
RSE	SUPERVISOR, PULP HOUSE	4	7	529.130-030
RSE	SUPERVISOR, CIGAR-MAKING MACHINE	4	7	529.132-034
RSE	SUPERVISOR, NATURAL-GAS-FIELD PROCESSING	4	7	549.131-010
RSE	SUPERVISOR, FORMING DEPARTMENT 2	4	6	579.130-022
RSE	SUPERVISOR, AUTOMATIC MACHINES	4	7	609.130-022
RSE	SUPERVISOR, BLOOMING MILL	4	7	613.130-010
RSE	SUPERVISOR, PIPE FINISHING	4	7	619.130-038
RSE	SUPERVISOR, ELECTRONICS	4	7	726.130-010
RSE	SUPERVISOR, BURNING, FORMING, AND ASSEMBLY	4	7	727.130-010
RSE	SUPERVISOR, FIREWORKS ASSEMBLY	4	7	737.131-010
RSE	SUPERVISOR, BRIAR SHOP	4	7	761.130-010
RSE	SUPERVISOR, STITCHING DEPARTMENT	4	7	787.132-018
RSE	SUPERVISOR, RIDE ASSEMBLY	4	7	801.131-018
RSE	SUPERVISOR, BOILERMAKING	4	8	805.131-010
RSE	SUPERVISOR, RIGGER	4	8	806.131-030
RSE	SUPERVISOR, ENGINE ASSEMBLY	4	8	806.130-010
RSE	SUPERVISOR, PIPE-LINE MAINTENANCE	4	8	869.134-018
RSE	SUPERVISOR, SALVAGE	4	7	929.131-010
RSE	SUPERVISOR, PRODUCTION	4	8	939.131-014
RSE	SUPERVISOR, ALUMINUM BOAT ASSEMBLY	4	8	806.131-010
RSE	SUPERVISOR, CARDING	4	7	680.130-010
RSE	SUPERVISOR, PATTERN MARKING	4	7	781.131-010
RSE	SUPERVISOR, ORNAMENTAL IRONWORKING	4	7	809.131-014
RSE	SUPERVISOR, GRINDING AND SPRAYING	4	5	809.134-010
RSE	SUPERVISOR, QUALITY CONTROL	4	6	763.134-010
RSE	SUPERVISOR, SCREEN MAKING	4	8	971.131-014
RSE	SUPERVISOR, RADIO INTERFERENCE	4	8	823.131-022
RSE	SUPERVISOR, TOY PARTS FORMER	4	7	692.130-034
RSE	SUPERVISOR, MODEL MAKING	4	7	693.130-010
RSE	SUPERVISOR, ELECTROTYPING AND STEREOTYPING	4	8	974.131-010
RSE	SUPERVISOR, SAWMILL	4	7	669.130-026
RSE	SUPERVISOR, SCOURING PADS	4	7	759.135-010
RSE	SUPERVISOR, PASTE PLANT	4	7	549.132-026
RSE	SUPERVISOR, GAME FARM	4	5	412.131-010

Code	Title	GED	SVP	DOT No.
RSE	SUPERVISOR, CLOTH WINDING	4	6	689.130-022
RSE	SUPERVISOR, FARM-EQUIPMENT MAINTENANCE	4	7	624.131-010
RSE	SUPERVISOR, MAJOR APPLIANCE ASSEMBLY	4	7	827.131-014
RSE	SUPERVISOR, ELECTRICAL ASSEMBLIES	4	7	826.131-014
RSE	SUPERVISOR, AVIONICS SHOP	4	8	823.131-018
RSE	SUPERVISOR, ASBESTOS PIPE	4	7	679.130-014
RSE	SUPERVISOR, FISH BAIT PROCESSING	4	7	550.132-014
RSE	SUPERVISOR, REACTOR FUELING	4	6	929.132-010
RSE	SUPERVISOR, COMPONENT ASSEMBLER	4	8	762.134-010
RSE	SUPERVISOR, SANDING	4	7	662.132-010
RSE	SUPERVISOR, AUTOMOBILE ASSEMBLY	4	7	806.134-010
RSE	SUPERVISOR, FINISHING	4	8	775.130-010
RSE	SUPERVISOR, GLYCERIN	4	7	559.132-098
RSE	TELEGRAPH-PLANT MAINTAINER	4	7	822.381-022
RSE	TESTER, PLUMBING SYSTEMS	4	6	806.281-054
RSE	TILE SETTER	4	7	861.381-054
RSE	TILE SETTER APPRENTICE	4	7	861.381-058
RSE	TNT-LINE SUPERVISOR	4	7	559.131-018
RSE	TRAFFIC SERGEANT	4	7	375.137-026
RSE	TRANSMITTER OPERATOR	4	7	193.262-038
RSE	TROUBLE SHOOTER 2	4	8	821.261-026
RSE	TURBINE-BLADE ASSEMBLER	4	6	600.380-026
RSE	UPHOLSTERER, INSIDE	4	7	780.681-010
RSE	UTILITY SUPERVISOR, BOAT AND PLANT	4	7	899.131-022
RSE	VOLTAGE TESTER	4	7	821.381-014
RSE	WILDLIFE CONTROL AGENT	4	7	379.267-010
RSE	ANIMAL KEEPER	3	4	412.674-010
RSE	ANODE REBUILDER	3	5	630.684-010
RSE	ARCH-SUPPORT TECHNICIAN	3	5	712.381-010
RSE	ASSEMBLER	3	5	710.681-010
RSE	ASSEMBLER 1	3	5	736.381-010
RSE	ASSEMBLER, ROCKET ENGINES	3	4	806.684-034
RSE	ASSEMBLER, SUBASSEMBLY	3	5	806.484-010
RSE	ASSEMBLY-MACHINE-SET-UP MECHANIC	3	5	692.360-010
RSE	AUTOMATIC-WHEEL-LINE OPERATOR	3	6	609.682-010
RSE	AUTOMOBILE-RADIATOR MECHANIC	3	6	620.381-010
RSE	BAKER	3	6	313.381-010
RSE	BAKER	3	7	526.381-010
RSE	BAKER APPRENTICE	3	7	526.381-014
RSE	BAKER, PIZZA	3	5	313.381-014
RSE	BAKER, TEST	3	6	526.381-018
RSE	BALANCING-MACHINE OPERATOR	3	6	609.462-010
RSE	BARREL-ENDSHAKE ADJUSTER	3	6	715.381-030
RSE	BATTERY MAINTAINER, LARGE EMERGENCY STORAGE	3	6	820.381-010
RSE	BELL SPINNER	3	7	619.682-010
RSE	BINDING CUTTER, SYNTHETIC CLOTH	3	4	699.682-010
RSE	BLANKET-WINDER OPERATOR	3	4	641.682-010
RSE	BLAST-FURNACE KEEPER	3	6	502.664-010
RSE	BLEACHER, PULP	3	5	533.362-010
RSE	BOAT RIGGER	3	4	806.464-010
RSE	BOILERHOUSE INSPECTOR	3	6	805.667-010

Code	Title	GED	SVP	DOT No.
RSE	BOX-SEALING-MACHINE OPERATOR	3	4	641.662-010
RSE	BRICK-AND-TILE-MAKING-MACHINE OPERATOR	3	5	575.382-010
RSE	BRINE-WELL OPERATOR	3	4	559.685-026
RSE	BUTCHER, MEAT	3	6	316.681-010
RSE	CAKE TESTER	3	6	526.381-022
RSE	CALENDER OPERATOR, FOUR-ROLL	3	5	554.662-010
RSE	CANDY PULLER	3	5	520.685-046
RSE	CAR-DUMPER OPERATOR	3	4	921.662-010
RSE	CARBIDE-POWDER PROCESSOR	3	5	510.465-010
RSE	CARBON-AND-GRAPHITE-BRUSH-MACHINE OPERATOR	3	4	692.482-010
RSE	CARBURETOR MECHANIC	3	7	620.281-034
RSE	CARGO CHECKER	3	4	222.367-010
RSE	CATALYTIC-CONVERTER OPERATOR	3	7	558.362-010
RSE	CELL MAKER	3	5	844.681-010
RSE	CEMETERY WORKER	3	5	406.684-010
RSE	CENTRIFUGAL-CASTING-MACHINE OPERATOR 3	3	6	514.562-010
RSE	CHARCOAL BURNER, BEEHIVE KILN	3	4	563.682-010
RSE	CIGARETTE-AND-FILTER CHIEF INSPECTOR	3	5	529.367-010
RSE	CLAY-STRUCTURE BUILDER AND SERVICER	3	4	579.664-010
RSE	COATER	3	4	584.682-010
RSE	COATING-MACHINE OPERATOR	3	6	524.382-010
RSE	COCOA-BEAN ROASTER 1	3	7	523.362-010
RSE	COFFEE ROASTER	3	5	523.682-014
RSE	COIN-MACHINE-SERVICE REPAIRER	3	5	639.281-014
RSE	COMPRESSION-MOLDING-MACHINE OPERATOR	3	5	556.682-014
RSE	CONCHE OPERATOR	3	4	526.382-010
RSE	CONTINUOUS-MINING-MACHINE OPERATOR	3	5	930.683-010
RSE	CONTINUOUS-ABSORPTION-PROCESS OPERATOR	3	4	521.362-010
RSE	COOK	3	6	305.281-010
RSE	COOK, BARBECUE	3	5	313.381-022
RSE	COOK, KETTLE	3	6	526.381-026
RSE	COOK, SCHOOL CAFETERIA	3	6	313.381-030
RSE	COOK, SPECIALTY, FOREIGN FOOD	3	7	313.361-030
RSE	COOK, SPECIALTY	3	5	313.361-026
RSE	COOK, STATION	3	6	315.361-022
RSE	CORE WINDING OPERATOR	3	5	640.682-014
RSE	CORE-CUTTER AND REAMER	3	4	649.685-026
RSE	CORE-DRILL OPERATOR	3	6	930.682-010
RSE	CORRUGATOR OPERATOR	3	4	556.665-014
RSE	CORRUGATOR OPERATOR	3	5	641.562-010
RSE	CUPOLA OPERATOR, INSULATION	3	6	579.382-014
RSE	CUTTER	3	4	699.682-014
RSE	CYLINDER FILLER	3	3	559.565-010
RSE	DEPUTY SHERIFF, GRAND JURY	3	6	377.363-010
RSE	DEXTRINE MIXER	3	4	523.682-018
RSE	DIE-CUTTING-MACHINE OPERATOR, AUTOMATIC	3	4	686.462-010
RSE	DIFFUSER OPERATOR	3	4	523.562-010

Code	Title	GED	SVP	DOT No.
RSE	DOG GROOMER	3	4	418.674-010
RSE	DRESSMAKER	3	7	785.361-010
RSE	DRIER OPERATOR 1	3	6	559.562-010
RSE	DRIER TENDER	3	4	511.565-014
RSE	DROP-HAMMER OPERATOR	3	6	610.462-010
RSE	DRUM DRIER	3	4	523.682-026
RSE	DYNAMITE-PACKING-MACHINE OPERATOR	3	5	692.662-010
RSE	ENVIRONMENTAL-CONTROL-SYSTEM INSTALLER-SERVICER HELPER	3	6	637.664-010
RSE	EXPLOSIVES-TRUCK DRIVER	3	3	903.683-010
RSE	FABRICATOR, INDUSTRIAL FURNACE	3	6	826.381-010
RSE	FARMWORKER, FIELD CROP 1	3	5	404.663-010
RSE	FARMWORKER, LIVESTOCK	3	4	410.664-010
RSE	FENCE ERECTOR	3	5	869.684-022
RSE	FIGURE REFINISHER AND REPAIRER	3	5	739.381-034
RSE	FINISH-MACHINE TENDER	3	5	673.685-058
RSE	FINISHING-AREA OPERATOR	3	6	559.362-014
RSE	FIRE-EXTINGUISHER REPAIRER	3	3	709.384-010
RSE	FIRST HELPER	3	6	512.362-010
RSE	FLANGING-ROLL OPERATOR	3	6	619.362-010
RSE	FORMING-MACHINE OPERATOR	3	5	559.665-022
RSE	FUEL ATTENDANT	3	5	953.362-010
RSE	FUR NAILER	3	6	783.684-014
RSE	FURNACE OPERATOR	3	5	512.362-018
RSE	FURNACE OPERATOR	3	5	613.462-014
RSE	GARDE MANGER	3	7	313.361-034
RSE	GAS-METER CHECKER	3	5	953.367-014
RSE	GELATIN-DYNAMITE-PACKING OPERATOR	3	5	692.662-014
RSE	GILDER	3	6	749.381-010
RSE	GLASS-BULB-MACHINE FORMER, TUBULAR STOCK	3	5	575.382-018
RSE	GLAZE MAKER	3	4	570.485-014
RSE	GLAZIER	3	7	865.381-010
RSE	GLAZIER APPRENTICE	3	7	865.381-014
RSE	GLAZING OPERATOR, BLACK POWDER	3	4	550.686-022
RSE	GOLDBEATER	3	6	700.381-018
RSE	GRINDER OPERATOR	3	7	521.682-026
RSE	GUN-PERFORATOR LOADER	3	5	931.384-010
RSE	HARP REGULATOR	3	6	730.381-026
RSE	HAT MAKER	3	5	784.684-042
RSE	HIDE INSPECTOR	3	4	783.687-018
RSE	HOGSHEAD INSPECTOR	3	4	529.367-014
RSE	HORSESHOER	3	6	418.381-010
RSE	HOUSE WORKER, GENERAL	3	3	301.474-010
RSE	HOUSEHOLD-APPLIANCE INSTALLER	3	6	827.661-010
RSE	HYDRAULIC PRESS OPERATOR	3	4	616.662-010
RSE	ICING MIXER	3	3	520.685-114
RSE	IMPREGNATOR AND DRIER	3	5	599.462-010
RSE	INDUCTION-MACHINE SETTER	3	7	504.380-014
RSE	INSPECTION CLERK	3	4	739.587-010
RSE	INSPECTOR	3	5	549.367-010
RSE	IRISH-MOSS OPERATOR	3	5	529.382-030
RSE	JIG BUILDER	3	6	761.381-014
RSE	KILN OPERATOR, MALT HOUSE	3	4	523.682-030

Code	Title	GED	SVP	DOT No.
RSE	LAMP-SHADE SEWER	3	6	787.381-010
RSE	LAUNDRY-TUB MAKER	3	4	575.684-034
RSE	LEATHER WORKER	3	5	783.684-026
RSE	LINSEED-OIL REFINER	3	4	559.382-030
RSE	LOCKER-PLANT ATTENDANT	3	4	922.684-010
RSE	LUGGAGE REPAIRER	3	6	365.361-010
RSE	LUSTER APPLICATOR	3	6	740.381-014
RSE	MACHINE-TANK OPERATOR	3	5	667.662-014
RSE	MAGAZINE KEEPER	3	5	222.367-038
RSE	MANIPULATOR	3	5	613.682-010
RSE	MARINE RAILWAY OPERATOR	3	4	921.662-022
RSE	MEAT CUTTER	3	6	316.684-018
RSE	MEAT-CUTTER APPRENTICE	3	6	316.684-022
RSE	MECHANICAL OXIDIZER	3	5	590.662-014
RSE	MECHANICAL-SHOVEL OPERATOR	3	5	932.683-018
RSE	MESSENGER, BANK	3	4	230.367-014
RSE	MILLER, WET PROCESS	3	7	521.662-010
RSE	MOBILE-HOME-LOT UTILITY WORKER	3	6	899.484-010
RSE	MOLD STAMPER AND REPAIRER	3	6	709.381-026
RSE	MOLDER	3	6	575.381-010
RSE	MOLDING-MACHINE OPERATOR	3	4	575.682-014
RSE	MORTUARY BEAUTICIAN	3	6	339.361-010
RSE	MULTI-OPERATION-MACHINE OPERATOR	3	6	612.462-010
RSE	NEEDLE-LOOM SETTER	3	6	689.360-010
RSE	NEON-TUBE PUMPER	3	5	824.684-010
RSE	NEWSPAPER-DELIVERY DRIVER	3	4	292.363-010
RSE	NITRATOR OPERATOR	3	6	558.382-046
RSE	ORGAN-PIPE MAKER, METAL	3	7	709.381-030
RSE	PAINTER	3	7	840.381-010
RSE	PAINTER, RUG TOUCH-UP	3	6	364.381-010
RSE	PARAFFIN-PLANT OPERATOR	3	6	541.682-010
RSE	PARTITION-ASSEMBLY-MACHINE OPERATOR	3	5	649.582-010
RSE	PIE MAKER	3	6	313.361-038
RSE	PIG-MACHINE OPERATOR	3	5	514.362-010
RSE	PORTABLE SAWYER	3	3	899.684-030
RSE	POWDER-TRUCK DRIVER	3	3	903.683-014
RSE	PRESS OPERATOR	3	4	575.682-018
RSE	PRESS OPERATOR, HEAVY DUTY	3	7	617.260-010
RSE	PRIMER-INSERTING-MACHINE ADJUSTER	3	5	632.360-018
RSE	PRINTER	3	5	979.681-014
RSE	PRODUCTION REPAIRER	3	6	726.381-014
RSE	PROJECTION PRINTER	3	7	976.381-018
RSE	PUNCH-PRESS OPERATOR 1	3	5	615.482-022
RSE	PUTTY TINTER-MAKER	3	5	559.482-014
RSE	QUALITY-CONTROL INSPECTOR	3	4	529.367-018
RSE	RAILROAD-CAR-TRUCK BUILDER	3	3	806.684-114
RSE	REDRYING-MACHINE OPERATOR	3	5	522.662-014
RSE	REELING-MACHINE OPERATOR	3	5	613.682-014
RSE	REFRIGERATION UNIT REPAIRER	3	6	637.381-014
RSE	REFRIGERATOR TESTER	3	5	827.384-010
RSE	REPAIRER, ASSEMBLED WOOD PRODUCTS	3	5	769.684-038
RSE	REPAIRER, FINISHED METAL	3	5	809.684-034
RSE	RIVETER	3	4	800.684-010
RSE	ROASTER, GRAIN	3	4	523.585-034

Code	Title	GED	SVP	DOT No.
RSE	ROCKET-TEST-FIRE WORKER	3	5	806.384-022
RSE	ROLLING-MILL OPERATOR	3	6	613.462-018
RSE	ROTOR CASTING-MACHINE OPERATOR	3	5	502.482-018
RSE	ROVING SIZER	3	4	680.367-010
RSE	RUG INSPECTOR	3	4	369.687-030
RSE	SADDLE MAKER	3	8	783.381-026
RSE	SCREEN REPAIRER, CRUSHER	3	4	630.684-030
RSE	SEALER	3	5	710.684-038
RSE	SEPTIC-TANK INSTALLER	3	4	851.663-010
RSE	SETTER, TV TUBE COATING AND BAKING	3	4	574.382-010
RSE	SHOE REPAIRER	3	7	365.361-014
RSE	SHOOTER, SEISMOGRAPH	3	6	931.361-018
RSE	SHRINK-PIT OPERATOR	3	5	619.662-010
RSE	SIGN ERECTOR-AND-REPAIRER	3	6	869.361-018
RSE	SILK-SCREEN REPAIRER	3	3	979.684-038
RSE	SLITTING-MACHINE OPERATOR 2	3	5	615.662-010
RSE	SOLDERER	3	5	700.381-050
RSE	SPEED OPERATOR	3	6	613.362-022
RSE	SPIKEMAKING SUPERVISOR	3	7	612.130-010
RSE	STARTER	3	4	153.667-010
RSE	STEEL POURER	3	6	502.664-014
RSE	STEEL-DIE PRINTER	3	7	651.382-030
RSE	STEEPLE JACK	3	7	869.381-030
RSE	STOCK CHECKERER 1	3	5	761.381-034
RSE	STOCK CLERK, SELF-SERVICE STORE	3	4	299.367-014
RSE	STRAPPING-MACHINE OPERATOR	3	4	692.682-058
RSE	SUPPLIES PACKER	3	5	919.687-022
RSE	SWITCHBOARD OPERATOR ASSISTANT	3	7	952.367-014
RSE	TAG-PRESS OPERATOR	3	6	649.682-046
RSE	TANK TENDER	3	5	509.685-054
RSE	THERMOMETER MAKER	3	4	710.681-026
RSE	TOBACCO CURER	3	3	523.682-038
RSE	TONGUE-AND-GROOVE-MACHINE OPERATOR	3	5	669.662-018
RSE	TOOL REPAIRER	3	5	519.684-026
RSE	TOWER OPERATOR	3	5	910.362-010
RSE	TRACER-BULLET-CHARGING-MACHINE OPERATOR	3	4	694.382-014
RSE	TRAILER ASSEMBLER	3	5	806.381-058
RSE	TRANSFERRER	3	6	972.381-026
RSE	TREE TRIMMER	3	4	408.664-010
RSE	TRIPLE-AIR-VALVE TESTER	3	7	622.382-010
RSE	TRUCK DRIVER, HEAVY	3	4	905.663-014
RSE	TUBE-MACHINE OPERATOR	3	5	641.662-014
RSE	TUNER, PERCUSSION	3	6	730.381-058
RSE	TURNER	3	6	774.684-038
RSE	UPPER-LEATHER SORTER	3	4	788.387-010
RSE	UTILITY WORKER, ROLLER SHOP	3	3	628.684-034
RSE	VARIETY-SAW OPERATOR	3	5	667.682-086
RSE	VENEER-SLICING-MACHINE OPERATOR	3	3	663.682-018
RSE	WALLPAPER PRINTER 1	3	6	652.662-014
RSE	WARDROBE-SPECIALTY WORKER	3	7	969.381-010
RSE	WASTE-DISPOSAL ATTENDANT	3	5	955.383-010
RSE	WAX BLEACHER	3	3	551.685-158
RSE	WELDING-ROD COATER	3	6	505.382-014

Code	Title	GED	SVP	DOT No.
RSE	WIRER, CABLE	3	6	729.381-022
RSE	YARN EXAMINER	3	3	681.687-030
RSE	ASSEMBLER, LAY-UPS	2	2	677.685-014
RSE	BEAM RACKER	2	2	681.686-010
RSE	BREAKER	2	2	779.687-010
RSE	CAKE-PRESS-OPERATOR HELPER	2	2	556.686-010
RSE	CASTING-WHEEL-OPERATOR HELPER	2	2	514.667-010
RSE	CHAIN OFFBEARER	2	2	669.686-018
RSE	CHEMICAL-COMPOUNDER HELPER	2	2	550.687-010
RSE	CLEANER, INDUSTRIAL	2	2	381.687-018
RSE	CLOTH FRAMER	2	2	689.687-026
RSE	COLOR DIPPER	2	2	652.687-014
RSE	COMPOUNDER	2	3	550.685-050
RSE	DRIER OPERATOR 1	2	3	553.665-026
RSE	DYNAMITE RECLAIMER	2	2	551.687-018
RSE	FIELD HAULER	2	3	409.683-014
RSE	FLOOR SERVICE WORKER, SPRING	2	4	807.684-022
RSE	FLYER	2	3	962.687-018
RSE	FORGE HELPER	2	2	619.666-010
RSE	GLOBE MOUNTER	2	3	795.684-018
RSE	HEDDLE CLEANER, MACHINE	2	2	689.685-070
RSE	HELPER, ELECTRICAL	2	3	821.667-010
RSE	HULL AND DECK REMOVER	2	3	809.667-010
RSE	JOGGER	2	2	659.686-010
RSE	LABORER	2	2	590.687-010
RSE	LABORER, HOT-PLATE PLYWOOD PRESS	2	2	569.686-026
RSE	LABORER, SALVAGE	2	2	929.687-022
RSE	LABORER, SHIPYARD	2	2	809.687-022
RSE	LABORER, SOLDER MAKING	2	3	519.667-014
RSE	LABORER, TIN CAN	2	2	709.686-010
RSE	LEAD-BURNER HELPER	2	2	727.687-070
RSE	LIQUOR-BRIDGE-OPERATOR HELPER	2	3	521.687-078
RSE	LUMBER HANDLER	2	2	922.687-070
RSE	MACHINE HELPER	2	3	619.687-014
RSE	METAL-FABRICATING-SHOP HELPER	2	2	619.686-022
RSE	ORDNANCE-ARTIFICER HELPER	2	4	632.684-010
RSE	PNEUMATIC-HOIST OPERATOR	2	3	921.663-046
RSE	POLISHER	2	4	775.684-058
RSE	POWDER LOADER	2	2	931.667-010
RSE	RIGGER HELPER	2	3	921.687-026
RSE	SCAGLIOLA MECHANIC	2	5	556.484-010
RSE	SCRAPPER	2	2	794.687-050
RSE	SHEEP SHEARER	2	3	410.684-014
RSE	SKI REPAIRER, PRODUCTION	2	5	732.684-118
RSE	SLOT ROUTER	2	2	763.684-066
RSE	SPICE MIXER	2	2	520.585-026
RSE	STEAM-CONDITIONER OPERATOR	2	2	522.685-094
RSE	STEAM-TANK OPERATOR	2	4	573.683-010
RSE	STOCK CHECKER, APPAREL	2	2	299.667-014
RSE	STOVE REFINISHER	2	3	749.684-046
RSE	TANK-CAR INSPECTOR	2	4	622.684-022
RSE	TEST-DEPARTMENT HELPER	2	3	729.664-010
RSE	THERMAL CUTTER, HAND 2	2	2	816.684-010
RSE	UPHOLSTERY CLEANER	2	2	780.687-058

Code	Title	GED	SVP	DOT No.
RSE	UTILITY WORKER, FORGE	2	2	612.684-010
RSE	VACUUM-TANK TENDER	2	2	689.665-018
RSE	WALLPAPER INSPECTOR	2	4	652.687-042
RSE	WALLPAPER-PRINTER HELPER	2	2	652.687-050
RSE	WAX-PATTERN COATER	2	2	518.687-022
RSE	WOODEN-FRAME BUILDER	2	2	762.684-066
RSE	OFFAL ICER, POULTRY	1	1	525.687-054
RSE	OIL-BURNER-SERVICER-AND-INSTALLER HELPER	1	2	862.687-022
RSE	WHARF TENDER	1	2	542.667-010
RSC	MATHEMATICAL TECHNICIAN	5	7	020.162-010
RSC	ASSEMBLER, MINING MACHINERY	4	7	801.261-010
RSC	CABLE ASSEMBLER, MOCK-UP	4	7	806.381-042
RSC	CARPENTER INSPECTOR	4	7	860.261-010
RSC	COMPOSITOR	4	8	973.381-010
RSC	COMPOSITOR APPRENTICE	4	8	973.381-014
RSC	COOK, PSYCHIATRIC HOSPITAL	4	7	315.361-018
RSC	ELECTRIC-ORGAN INSPECTOR AND REPAIRER	4	6	730.281-018
RSC	ELECTRICIAN, RADIO	4	7	823.281-014
RSC	ELECTRICIAN SUPERVISOR	4	8	825.131-010
RSC	ELECTRONIC-PRODUCTION-LINE-MAINTENANCE MECHANIC	4	8	629.281-022
RSC	ENGRAVER, RUBBER	4	7	733.381-010
RSC	FLAME-ANNEALING-MACHINE SETTER	4	6	504.360-010
RSC	LINE INSPECTOR	4	7	822.267-010
RSC	LIQUEFACTION-AND-REGASIFICATION-PLANT OPERATOR	4	7	953.362-014
RSC	MASTER, YACHT	4	8	197.133-014
RSC	MECHANICAL INSPECTOR	4	7	549.261-010
RSC	MOLDER, PUNCH	4	7	502.381-014
RSC	PIPE-ORGAN TUNER AND REPAIRER	4	8	730.361-014
RSC	QUALITY-CONTROL INSPECTOR	4	6	701.261-010
RSC	RADIO INTERFERENCE INVESTIGATOR	4	7	823.261-014
RSC	RADIOTELEPHONE OPERATOR	4	7	193.262-034
RSC	RIGGER	4	6	921.260-010
RSC	RUBBER-STAMP MAKER	4	6	733.381-014
RSC	SILVERSMITH	4	7	700.281-022
RSC	SUPERVISOR, FRAMING MILL	4	8	669.130-018
RSC	SUPERVISOR, SHUTTLE VENEERING	4	7	669.130-038
RSC	SUPERVISOR, PHOTOENGRAVING	4	8	971.131-010
RSC	SUPERVISOR, DAIRY FARM	4	7	410.131-018
RSC	ACROBATIC RIGGER	3	6	962.684-010
RSC	ARMORED-CAR GUARD AND DRIVER	3	3	372.563-010
RSC	AUTOCLAVE OPERATOR	3	4	587.682-010
RSC	BENCH HAND	3	6	735.381-010
RSC	BICYCLE REPAIRER	3	4	639.681-010
RSC	BLENDER	3	4	550.665-010
RSC	BRAKE-LINING FINISHER, ASBESTOS	3	3	579.665-010
RSC	BRAZER, CONTROLLED ATMOSPHERIC FURNACE	3	4	813.685-010
RSC	BULLET-CASTING OPERATOR	3	4	502.682-010
RSC	BUTLER, SECOND	3	3	309.674-010

Code	Title	GED	SVP	DOT No.
RSC	CAGE MAKER	3	5	709.684-030
RSC	CAKE-PRESS OPERATOR	3	4	556.665-010
RSC	CHAIR UPHOLSTERER	3	5	780.684-034
RSC	CHIP TUNER	3	3	730.684-026
RSC	CHOCOLATE TEMPERER	3	5	523.682-010
RSC	CLASSIFIER OPERATOR	3	5	511.562-010
RSC	CLIP-LOADING-MACHINE ADJUSTER	3	4	694.362-010
RSC	COCOA-POWDER-MIXER OPERATOR	3	4	520.685-074
RSC	COLOR MATCHER	3	6	582.261-010
RSC	CONDUCTOR	3	4	910.667-014
RSC	CONTROL-PANEL OPERATOR	3	7	546.382-010
RSC	COOPER	3	6	764.684-022
RSC	CUT-OFF-SAW OPERATOR	3	4	667.682-022
RSC	CUTTER OPERATOR	3	4	699.682-018
RSC	DEPOSITING-MACHINE OPERATOR	3	4	524.682-010
RSC	DRAWING-IN-MACHINE TENDER	3	5	683.682-018
RSC	DUBBING-MACHINE OPERATOR	3	3	962.665-010
RSC	ENGRAVER, RUBBER	3	6	979.581-010
RSC	EXCAVATOR	3	3	850.684-010
RSC	FARM-EQUIPMENT MECHANIC 2	3	6	624.381-014
RSC	FEEDER-SWITCHBOARD OPERATOR	3	6	952.362-014
RSC	FELTING-MACHINE OPERATOR	3	4	586.662-010
RSC	FINAL INSPECTOR, PAPER	3	5	539.367-010
RSC	FINISHING-MACHINE OPERATOR	3	4	582.682-010
RSC	FLAT CLOTHIER	3	5	628.382-010
RSC	FORGING-ROLL OPERATOR	3	4	612.682-014
RSC	GLASS FINISHER	3	5	775.684-026
RSC	GLASS GRINDER	3	6	775.684-030
RSC	ION-EXCHANGE OPERATOR	3	5	558.685-038
RSC	IRONWORKER-MACHINE OPERATOR	3	4	615.482-018
RSC	IRRADIATED-FUEL HANDLER	3	5	921.663-034
RSC	KETTLE TENDER 1	3	4	519.685-022
RSC	KILN BURNER	3	5	573.682-010
RSC	KNIT-GOODS WASHER	3	4	582.685-094
RSC	LACQUER MAKER	3	5	559.682-030
RSC	LEAD-PRESS OPERATOR	3	4	691.382-014
RSC	LOCK OPERATOR	3	5	911.362-010
RSC	MAIL HANDLER	3	4	209.687-014
RSC	MAINTENANCE MECHANIC HELPER	3	5	620.664-014
RSC	MIXING-ROLL OPERATOR	3	4	590.662-018
RSC	MOBILE-LOUNGE DRIVER	3	3	913.663-014
RSC	NEEDLE-LOOM OPERATOR	3	5	689.662-010
RSC	NITROGLYCERIN NEUTRALIZER	3	5	558.685-050
RSC	OIL-PIPE-INSPECTOR HELPER	3	5	930.364-010
RSC	OPERATOR, PREFINISH	3	5	562.685-018
RSC	PLANISHING-PRESS OPERATOR	3	5	690.682-058
RSC	POWER-DRIVEN-BRUSH MAKER	3	5	692.682-050
RSC	PRESS OPERATOR	3	4	690.682-062
RSC	RADIAL-ARM-SAW OPERATOR	3	4	667.682-054
RSC	REFINING-MACHINE OPERATOR	3	3	529.685-198
RSC	RIGGER	3	5	921.664-014
RSC	ROOF ASSEMBLER 1	3	3	869.684-042
RSC	ROUTER OPERATOR, PORTABLE	3	4	804.684-018
RSC	RUG CUTTER	3	4	686.662-010

Code	Title	GED	SVP	DOT No.
RSC	SALAD MAKER	3	5	317.384-010
RSC	SEAMLESS-TUBE ROLLER	3	5	619.682-042
RSC	SIDER	3	3	860.684-014
RSC	SILVERER	3	3	574.684-014
RSC	SIZING-MACHINE-AND-DRIER OPERATOR	3	4	582.665-026
RSC	SOUNDER	3	2	911.667-018
RSC	SPIKE-MACHINE OPERATOR	3	7	612.662-010
RSC	SPINNER	3	6	520.682-030
RSC	STAVE-LOG-CUT-OFF SAW OPERATOR	3	4	667.682-078
RSC	STEAM-DRIER TENDER	3	5	581.685-058
RSC	STONE-MILL OPERATOR	3	3	555.682-022
RSC	STRIPE MATCHER	3	3	689.662-014
RSC	STRIPPING-SHOVEL OPERATOR	3	5	850.663-026
RSC	TANK-FARM ATTENDANT	3	4	559.665-038
RSC	TEMPLATE MAKER, TRACK	3	3	809.484-014
RSC	TOBACCO BLENDER	3	6	790.381-010
RSC	TOWER ERECTOR HELPER	3	5	821.684-014
RSC	TRUSS ASSEMBLER	3	3	762.684-062
RSC	VACUUM-CONDITIONER OPERATOR	3	3	522.685-102
RSC	VALVE REPAIRER	3	6	630.381-030
RSC	WAX BLENDER	3	3	550.585-046
RSC	WELDER, TACK	3	5	810.684-010
RSC	WET-MIX OPERATOR	3	4	558.382-058
RSC	BED SETTER	2	3	679.664-010
RSC	BENCH CARPENTER	2	3	760.684-010
RSC	BOTTOM-PRECIPITATOR OPERATOR	2	4	511.664-010
RSC	CARD TENDER	2	3	680.685-018
RSC	CLAMPER	2	2	669.685-030
RSC	COATER HELPER	2	3	584.665-010
RSC	COUNTING-MACHINE OPERATOR	2	3	649.685-030
RSC	CUTTER, WET MACHINE	2	2	539.686-010
RSC	DROSS SKIMMER	2	4	519.683-010
RSC	FORM-TAMPER OPERATOR	2	3	869.683-010
RSC	GATHERER	2	5	575.684-026
RSC	GLASS-CUTTER HELPER	2	3	775.687-018
RSC	INSPECTOR	2	3	739.687-110
RSC	POLISHING-WHEEL SETTER	2	3	776.684-014
RSC	PRIMER CHARGER	2	3	737.687-102
RSC	QUARRY PLUG-AND-FEATHER DRILLER	2	4	930.684-022
RSC	SANITARY LANDFILL OPERATOR	2	5	955.463-010
RSC	SCREEN PRINTER HELPER	2	2	979.687-022
RSC	SHIPWRIGHT HELPER	2	4	860.664-018
RSC	SLITTING-MACHINE-OPERATOR HELPER 1	2	2	699.587-010
RSC	STAND-IN	2	2	961.667-014
RSC	TOOL GRINDER 2	2	3	603.664-010
RSC	WEIGHER AND MIXER	2	4	550.685-122
RSC	WEIGHER, ALLOY	2	3	509.687-022
RSC	WINDER OPERATOR	2	2	590.665-018
RSC	TELEPHONE-DIRECTORY DELIVERER	1	1	230.667-014
REI	GENERAL SUPERVISOR	5	8	183.167-018
REI	LABORATORY ASSISTANT, LIAISON INSPECTION	5	7	169.167-026
REI	MATERIALS ENGINEER	5	8	019.061-014

Code	Title	GED	SVP	DOT No.
REI	MINING ENGINEER	5	8	010.061-014
REI	PRODUCTION PLANNER	5	7	012.167-050
REI	PROJECT MANAGER, ENVIRONMENTAL RESEARCH	5	8	029.167-014
REI	SAFETY ENGINEER, MINES	5	8	010.061-026
REI	SALES REPRESENTATIVE, AIRCRAFT	5	6	273.253-010
REI	TEST ENGINEER, MECHANICAL EQUIPMENT	5	8	007.161-034
REI	TRAFFIC TECHNICIAN	5	7	199.267-030
REI	AIRCRAFT MECHANIC, ARMAMENT	4	7	806.381-010
REI	AIRCRAFT MECHANIC, HEAT AND VENT	4	7	806.381-014
REI	AIRCRAFT MECHANIC, RIGGING AND CONTROLS	4	6	806.381-018
REI	ASSEMBLER, STEAM-AND-GAS TURBINE	4	8	600.261-010
REI	ASSEMBLER, GROUND SUPPORT EQUIPMENT	4	7	809.261-010
REI	ASSEMBLY MECHANIC, EXPERIMENTAL AIRCRAFT	4	7	806.381-038
REI	BARGE CAPTAIN	4	6	911.137-010
REI	BOATBUILDER APPRENTICE, WOOD	4	7	860.381-014
REI	BOATBUILDER, WOOD	4	7	860.381-018
REI	BOILER	4	7	553.382-014
REI	BRICKLAYER, FIREBRICK AND REFRACTORY TILE	4	8	861.381-026
REI	BUS INSPECTOR	4	7	620.281-030
REI	CAR REPAIRER, PULLMAN	4	7	622.381-018
REI	CARPENTER	4	7	860.381-022
REI	CARPENTER APPRENTICE	4	7	860.381-026
REI	CARPENTER, MAINTENANCE	4	7	860.281-010
REI	CARPENTER, SHIP	4	7	860.281-014
REI	CLAY MODELER	4	7	779.281-010
REI	COLD-MILL OPERATOR	4	7	613.462-010
REI	CONCRETE-STONE FINISHER	4	7	844.461-010
REI	CONTOUR WIRE SPECIALIST, DENTURE	4	7	712.381-014
REI	CORRECTIVE THERAPIST (SIR)	4	7	076.361-010
REI	CORROSION-CONTROL FITTER	4	7	820.361-010
REI	DAIRY-EQUIPMENT REPAIRER	4	7	629.281-018
REI	DAIRY-PROCESSING-EQUIPMENT OPERATOR	4	5	529.382-018
REI	DELINEATOR	4	7	970.281-014
REI	DENTAL-LABORATORY TECHNICIAN	4	8	712.381-018
REI	DENTAL-LABORATORY-TECHNICIAN APPRENTICE	4	8	712.381-022
REI	DIAMOND SELECTOR	4	8	770.281-010
REI	DIESEL MECHANIC	4	7	625.281-010
REI	DIESEL-ENGINE ERECTOR	4	7	625.361-010
REI	DIESEL-MECHANIC APPRENTICE	4	7	625.281-014
REI	DITCH RIDER	4	4	954.362-010
REI	DYER	4	7	364.361-010
REI	DYNAMOMETER TESTER, MOTOR	4	6	806.281-010
REI	ELECTRIC-MOTOR ASSEMBLER AND TESTER	4	7	721.281-014
REI	ELECTRIC-TOOL REPAIRER	4	6	729.281-022
REI	ELECTRICAL REPAIRER	4	7	829.281-014
REI	ELECTRICIAN	4	7	824.261-010
REI	ELECTRICIAN APPRENTICE	4	7	824.261-014
REI	ELECTRICIAN, AIRPLANE	4	7	825.281-018
REI	ENGRAVER, SEALS	4	6	704.381-034

Code	Title	GED	SVP	DOT No.
REI	EXPEDITION SUPERVISOR	4	6	461.134-010
REI	EXPERIMENTAL MECHANIC, ELECTRICAL	4	7	806.281-014
REI	EXPERIMENTAL-ROCKET-SLED MECHANIC	4	7	825.281-038
REI	FANCY-WIRE DRAWER	4	7	700.381-014
REI	FARMER, FIELD CROP	4	7	404.161-010
REI	FARMER, TREE-FRUIT-AND-NUT CROPS	4	7	403.161-010
REI	FARMER, VEGETABLE	4	7	402.161-010
REI	FILING-AND-POLISHING SUPERVISOR	4	7	603.137-010
REI	FILTER-PLANT SUPERVISOR	4	6	511.135-010
REI	FINE ARTS PACKER	4	7	102.367-010
REI	FIRE CHIEF'S AIDE	4	6	373.363-010
REI	FIREWORKS DISPLAY SPECIALIST	4	5	969.664-010
REI	FISH FARMER	4	6	446.161-010
REI	FORESTER AIDE	4	6	452.364-010
REI	FRETTED-INSTRUMENT REPAIRER	4	6	730.281-026
REI	FUMIGATOR	4	5	383.361-010
REI	FUR FARMER	4	6	410.161-014
REI	FURNACE INSTALLER-AND-REPAIRER, HOT AIR	4	7	869.281-010
REI	FURRIER	4	8	783.261-010
REI	GAME-BIRD FARMER	4	6	412.161-010
REI	GEMOLOGIST	4	7	199.281-010
REI	GLASS BENDER	4	8	772.381-010
REI	GLASS DECORATOR	4	6	775.381-014
REI	GLAZE SUPERVISOR	4	7	574.130-010
REI	GUIDE, ALPINE	4	7	353.164-010
REI	HEAVY FORGER	4	8	612.361-010
REI	HORTICULTURAL-SPECIALTY GROWER, INSIDE	4	7	405.161-018
REI	HOUSE REPAIRER	4	7	869.381-010
REI	INSPECTOR 3	4	6	737.367-010
REI	INSPECTOR, AGRICULTURAL COMMODITIES	4	7	168.287-010
REI	INSPECTOR, SET-UP AND LAY-OUT	4	8	601.261-010
REI	INSPECTOR, ASSEMBLIES AND INSTALLATIONS	4	7	806.281-022
REI	INSPECTOR, OPTICAL INSTRUMENT	4	7	711.281-010
REI	INSTRUMENT TECHNICIAN	4	8	710.281-030
REI	INSTRUMENT-TECHNICIAN APPRENTICE	4	8	710.281-008
REI	JEWEL-BEARING MAKER	4	7	770.381-030
REI	KNITTING-MACHINE FIXER	4	7	689.280-014
REI	LEAD OPERATOR	4	6	630.381-018
REI	LEAD-SECTION SUPERVISOR	4	8	619.132-010
REI	LIGHT TECHNICIAN	4	7	962.362-014
REI	LIQUOR BLENDER	4	6	522.382-018
REI	LITHOGRAPHIC PLATE MAKER	4	8	972.381-010
REI	LITHOGRAPHIC-PLATE-MAKER APPRENTICE	4	8	972.381-014
REI	LOGGING-EQUIPMENT MECHANIC	4	7	620.281-042
REI	LOOM CHANGER	4	7	683.360-010
REI	MACHINE FIXER	4	7	628.281-010
REI	MACHINERY ERECTOR	4	8	638.261-014
REI	MACHINING-AND-ASSEMBLY SUPERVISOR	4	5	619.131-010
REI	MACHINIST APPRENTICE, LINOTYPE	4	7	627.261-018
REI	MACHINIST, LINOTYPE	4	7	627.261-022
REI	MAGNETO REPAIRER	4	6	721.281-022

Code	Title	GED	SVP	DOT No.
REI	MAINTENANCE MECHANIC	4	7	638.281-014
REI	MAINTENANCE SUPERVISOR, FIRE-FIGHTING-EQUIPMENT	4	8	638.131-018
REI	MASTER, PASSENGER BARGE	4	7	197.163-014
REI	MATE, FISHING VESSEL	4	7	197.133-018
REI	MILL PLATFORM SUPERVISOR	4	7	521.132-010
REI	MODEL MAKER, WOOD	4	7	661.380-010
REI	MODEL MAKER	4	7	709.381-018
REI	MODEL-AND-MOLD MAKER, PLASTER	4	7	777.381-018
REI	MODEL-MAKER APPRENTICE	4	7	709.381-022
REI	MOLDER, PATTERN	4	7	693.381-022
REI	MUSEUM TECHNICIAN	4	7	102.381-010
REI	OPTICIAN	4	8	716.280-014
REI	OPTICIAN APPRENTICE	4	8	716.280-010
REI	ORDNANCE ARTIFICER	4	6	632.261-018
REI	OUTBOARD-MOTOR TESTER	4	6	623.261-014
REI	PACKAGING SUPERVISOR	4	6	920.132-010
REI	PAINTER, SIGN	4	7	970.381-026
REI	PARTS CATALOGER	4	6	229.267-010
REI	PATTERNMAKER, SAMPLE	4	7	693.281-022
REI	PILOT, SHIP	4	8	197.133-026
REI	PIPE COVERER AND INSULATOR	4	8	863.381-014
REI	PLUMBER	4	7	862.381-030
REI	PLUMBER APPRENTICE	4	7	862.381-034
REI	POLICE OFFICER, IDENTIFICATION AND RECORDS	4	7	375.384-010
REI	POWERHOUSE MECHANIC	4	8	631.261-014
REI	POWERHOUSE-MECHANIC APPRENTICE	4	8	631.261-018
REI	PROP MAKER	4	7	962.281-010
REI	RADIO MECHANIC	4	7	823.261-018
REI	RADIO REPAIRER	4	6	720.281-010
REI	RAIL-FLAW-DETECTOR OPERATOR	4	6	910.263-010
REI	REFRIGERATING ENGINEER	4	7	950.362-014
REI	REPAIRER	4	7	630.281-026
REI	REPEAT CHIEF	4	7	970.361-014
REI	REPEAT-PHOTOCOMPOSING-MACHINE OPERATOR	4	7	971.382-018
REI	ROAD SUPERVISOR OF ENGINES	4	7	910.137-034
REI	SALES-SERVICE REPRESENTATIVE, MILKING MACHINES	4	6	299.251-010
REI	SALVAGE ENGINEER	4	7	600.131-014
REI	SECTION LEADER AND MACHINE SETTER	4	7	689.260-018
REI	SERVICE MECHANIC, COMPRESSED-GAS EQUIPMENT	4	7	630.281-034
REI	SET-UP MECHANIC, AUTOMATIC LINE	4	6	692.380-014
REI	SHEET-METAL WORKER	4	7	804.281-010
REI	SHEET-METAL-WORKER APPRENTICE	4	7	804.281-014
REI	SHELLFISH GROWER	4	6	446.161-014
REI	SKETCH MAKER 2	4	7	972.381-018
REI	SNOW-REMOVING SUPERVISOR	4	6	955.137-010
REI	SPRINKLER-IRRIGATION-EQUIPMENT MECHANIC	4	6	624.361-014
REI	STATIONARY ENGINEER	4	7	950.382-026
REI	STATIONARY-ENGINEER APPRENTICE	4	7	950.382-030

Code	Title	GED	SVP	DOT No.
REI	STEAM SERVICE INSPECTOR	4	7	862.361-022
REI	STILL OPERATOR	4	6	522.382-026
REI	STREET-OPENINGS INSPECTOR	4	8	859.267-010
REI	STRIPPER	4	8	971.381-050
REI	STRIPPER APPRENTICE	4	8	971.381-054
REI	STUCCO MASON	4	7	842.381-014
REI	SUCTION-DREDGE-PIPE-LINE-PLACING SUPERVISOR	4	7	862.134-010
REI	SUPERVISOR, MINE	4	8	181.167-018
REI	SUPERVISOR, TREE-FRUIT-AND-NUT FARMING	4	7	403.131-010
REI	SUPERVISOR, HOT-DIP-TINNING	4	8	501.130-010
REI	SUPERVISOR, HOT-DIP PLATING	4	7	501.137-010
REI	SUPERVISOR, SOAKING PITS	4	8	509.132-010
REI	SUPERVISOR, STEFFEN HOUSE	4	8	529.132-086
REI	SUPERVISOR, BRINE	4	7	558.134-010
REI	SUPERVISOR, CELL-EFFICIENCY	4	7	558.134-018
REI	SUPERVISOR, CELL ROOM	4	7	558.134-014
REI	SUPERVISOR, HYDROCHLORIC AREA	4	7	558.134-022
REI	SUPERVISOR, CD-AREA	4	7	559.132-070
REI	SUPERVISOR, BEAM DEPARTMENT	4	7	589.134-010
REI	SUPERVISOR, MERCHANT-MILL ROLLING AND FINISHING	4	7	613.130-014
REI	SUPERVISOR, SPECIALTY MANUFACTURING	4	7	616.130-014
REI	SUPERVISOR, COLD ROLLING	4	6	619.130-018
REI	SUPERVISOR, FINISHING-AND-SHIPPING	4	6	619.132-026
REI	SUPERVISOR, BOTTLE-HOUSE CLEANERS	4	7	529.132-022
REI	SUPERVISOR, COREMAKER	4	7	640.132-010
REI	SUPERVISOR, PAPER PRODUCTS	4	8	649.130-010
REI	SUPERVISOR, METER SHOP	4	7	710.131-030
REI	SUPERVISOR, INSPECTION AND TESTING	4	7	721.131-014
REI	SUPERVISOR, COVERING AND LINING	4	8	780.134-010
REI	SUPERVISOR, GARMENT MANUFACTURING	4	6	786.132-010
REI	SUPERVISOR, METAL FABRICATING	4	8	809.130-014
REI	SUPERVISOR, SEWER MAINTENANCE	4	6	851.137-014
REI	SUPERVISOR, TUNNEL HEADING	4	7	859.137-018
REI	SUPERVISOR, MANUFACTURED BUILDINGS	4	7	869.131-030
REI	SUPERVISOR, METAL HANGING	4	7	809.134-014
REI	SUPERVISOR, NET MAKING	4	7	789.132-022
REI	SUPERVISOR, MOLD SHOP	4	8	777.131-010
REI	SUPERVISOR, SHEARING	4	7	615.132-010
REI	SUPERVISOR, FENCE MANUFACTURE	4	6	617.130-014
REI	SUPERVISOR, POWER-REACTOR	4	7	509.130-010
REI	SUPERVISOR, PLASTIC SHEETS	4	7	557.130-014
REI	SUPERVISOR, GRINDING	4	7	603.130-010
REI	SUPERVISORY WASTEWATER-TREATMENT-PLANT OPERATOR	4	7	955.130-010
REI	SWATCH CHECKER	4	7	683.260-022
REI	TECHNICIAN, SUBMARINE CABLE EQUIPMENT	4	7	822.281-034
REI	TELEVISION-AND-RADIO REPAIRER	4	7	720.281-018
REI	TERRAZZO WORKER	4	7	861.381-046
REI	TERRAZZO-WORKER APPRENTICE	4	7	861.381-050
REI	TIN ROLLER, HOT MILL	4	7	613.360-018

Code	Title	GED	SVP	DOT No.
REI	TOOLING COORDINATOR, PRODUCTION ENGINEERING	4	7	169.167-054
REI	TRACTOR MECHANIC	4	7	620.281-058
REI	TREATMENT-PLANT MECHANIC	4	6	630.281-038
REI	TREE SURGEON	4	6	408.181-010
REI	TUGBOAT CAPTAIN	4	8	197.133-030
REI	TUGBOAT MATE	4	7	197.133-034
REI	TURBINE OPERATOR, HEAD	4	7	952.137-022
REI	UNDERWATER HUNTER-TRAPPER	4	5	461.664-010
REI	WASHING-AND-SCREENING PLANT SUPERVISOR	4	7	570.132-018
REI	WASTEWATER-TREATMENT-PLANT OPERATOR	4	6	955.362-010
REI	WATCH REPAIRER	4	8	715.281-010
REI	WATCH REPAIRER APPRENTICE	4	8	715.281-014
REI	WELD INSPECTOR 1	4	7	819.281-018
REI	WOODS BOSS	4	7	459.137-010
REI	WORM GROWER	4	6	413.161-018
REI	X-RAY-EQUIPMENT TESTER	4	6	729.281-046
REI	ABSORPTION OPERATOR	3	5	551.382-010
REI	ACID EXTRACTOR	3	5	558.382-010
REI	AIRCRAFT MECHANIC, PLUMBING AND HYDRAULICS	3	7	862.381-010
REI	ALUM-PLANT OPERATOR	3	4	559.362-010
REI	AMALGAMATOR	3	3	511.685-010
REI	ANODE BUILDER	3	4	826.684-010
REI	ANODIZER	3	4	500.682-010
REI	AQUARIST	3	4	449.674-010
REI	AQUATIC PERFORMER	3	5	159.347-014
REI	ARBOR-PRESS OPERATOR 1	3	3	616.682-010
REI	ARC CUTTER	3	5	816.364-010
REI	ARMOR RECONNAISSANCE SPECIALIST	3	5	378.363-010
REI	ARTIFICIAL INSEMINATOR	3	3	418.384-010
REI	ARTILLERY OR NAVAL GUNFIRE OBSERVER	3	4	378.367-010
REI	ASSEMBLER, AIRCRAFT POWER PLANT	3	6	806.381-022
REI	ASSEMBLER, WIRE-MESH GATE	3	4	801.384-010
REI	ASSEMBLER, ALUMINUM BOATS	3	5	806.481-010
REI	ASSEMBLER, CAMPER	3	3	806.684-018
REI	AUTOMATIC PATTERN EDGER	3	3	673.682-010
REI	AUTOMATIC-DOOR MECHANIC	3	6	829.281-010
REI	AWNING HANGER	3	4	869.484-010
REI	AWNING MAKER-AND-INSTALLER	3	5	869.481-010
REI	BABBITTER	3	6	709.684-022
REI	BALL-TRUING-MACHINE OPERATOR	3	5	690.682-014
REI	BALLPOINT PEN CARTRIDGE TESTER	3	5	733.281-010
REI	BARREL-RIB MATTING-MACHINE OPERATOR	3	4	605.682-010
REI	BATTERY REPAIRER	3	6	727.381-014
REI	BATTERY TESTER	3	3	727.384-010
REI	BEADWORKER	3	6	789.381-010
REI	BED RUBBER	3	4	673.685-014
REI	BELLOWS TESTER	3	3	710.687-014
REI	BENCH HAND	3	6	706.381-014
REI	BEVELER	3	5	775.684-010
REI	BINDER TECHNICIAN	3	3	550.585-010
REI	BLENDING-PLANT OPERATOR	3	5	520.682-010

Code	Title	GED	SVP	DOT No.
REI	BLOCKER AND CUTTER, CONTACT LENS	3	5	716.681-010
REI	BLOCKER 2	3	4	971.684-010
REI	BLOW-UP OPERATOR	3	3	529.485-014
REI	BOAT OUTFITTER	3	4	806.484-014
REI	BODY-MAKER-MACHINE SETTER	3	6	616.360-010
REI	BONDING-MACHINE SETTER	3	5	589.360-010
REI	BORING-MACHINE OPERATOR	3	4	666.382-010
REI	BOW MAKER, PRODUCTION	3	5	732.684-038
REI	BOWLING-BALL GRADER AND MARKER	3	6	732.381-014
REI	BRICKLAYER	3	8	861.381-014
REI	BRILLIANDEER-LOPPER	3	6	770.261-010
REI	BROTH MIXER	3	4	520.585-014
REI	BUFFING-LINE SET-UP WORKER	3	5	603.360-010
REI	BUILDING-EQUIPMENT INSPECTOR	3	6	956.387-010
REI	BURNER OPERATOR	3	5	558.382-014
REI	BUS DRIVER	3	5	913.463-010
REI	BUTTERMAKER	3	6	529.362-010
REI	BUTTERMAKER, CONTINUOUS CHURN	3	3	529.382-010
REI	CABLE STRETCHER AND TESTER	3	4	806.685-010
REI	CALENDER OPERATOR, INSULATION BOARD	3	4	539.482-010
REI	CANAL-EQUIPMENT MECHANIC	3	6	899.281-010
REI	CARBON PRINTER	3	5	979.684-010
REI	CARPENTER 2	3	5	860.681-010
REI	CARPET LAYER	3	7	864.381-010
REI	CASING-IN-LINE SETTER	3	8	653.360-010
REI	CASKET ASSEMBLER	3	6	739.481-010
REI	CASKET ASSEMBLER, METAL	3	4	809.684-014
REI	CASTER	3	5	575.684-014
REI	CASTING-MACHINE OPERATOR	3	6	654.382-010
REI	CATALYST OPERATOR, GASOLINE	3	5	559.382-014
REI	CATHODE MAKER	3	4	554.585-010
REI	CAUSTIC OPERATOR	3	4	558.485-010
REI	CAUSTICISER	3	5	558.382-022
REI	CELL CHANGER	3	5	826.684-014
REI	CELL TENDER	3	5	558.382-026
REI	CENTRIFUGAL OPERATOR	3	3	521.682-010
REI	CHAMFERING-MACHINE OPERATOR 1	3	3	606.685-014
REI	CHAUFFEUR	3	3	913.663-010
REI	CHEESEMAKER HELPER	3	6	529.682-014
REI	CHEMICAL OPERATOR 3	3	7	559.382-018
REI	CHUCKING-MACHINE OPERATOR	3	5	665.382-010
REI	CIRCULAR SAWYER, STONE	3	4	677.462-010
REI	CLARIFYING-PLANT OPERATOR	3	4	955.382-010
REI	CLAY MAKER	3	5	570.482-010
REI	CLERK-OF-SCALES	3	3	153.467-010
REI	CLOTH EXAMINER, MACHINE	3	4	689.685-038
REI	CLOTH-FINISHING-RANGE TENDER	3	3	589.685-026
REI	CLOTH-FINISHING-RANGE OPERATOR, CHIEF	3	5	589.562-010
REI	COAGULATING-BATH MIXER	3	4	550.684-010
REI	COATER	3	5	554.382-010
REI	COATING-MACHINE OPERATOR	3	4	534.682-018
REI	COATING-MACHINE OPERATOR, HARDBOARD	3	5	534.682-022
REI	COLOR CHECKER, ROVING OR YARN	3	3	582.387-010

Code	Title	GED	SVP	DOT No.
REI	COLOR WEIGHER	3	4	590.487-010
REI	COLORER, HIDES AND SKINS	3	4	582.482-010
REI	COMPOSITION MIXER	3	4	550.665-014
REI	COMPOUNDER	3	4	550.685-046
REI	COMPRESSOR	3	4	556.382-010
REI	CONCRETE-FENCE BUILDER	3	6	869.681-010
REI	CONCRETE-MIXING-TRUCK DRIVER	3	3	900.683-010
REI	CONCRETE-PAVING-MACHINE OPERATOR	3	3	853.663-014
REI	CONCRETE-STONE FABRICATOR	3	7	575.461-010
REI	CONDUIT MECHANIC	3	7	869.361-010
REI	CONSTRUCTION-EQUIPMENT MECHANIC	3	7	620.261-022
REI	CONTACT-ACID-PLANT OPERATOR	3	5	558.585-018
REI	CONTOUR GRINDER	3	5	675.682-010
REI	CONVOLUTE-TUBE WINDER	3	4	640.682-010
REI	COOK	3	3	526.685-010
REI	COOK, SIRUP MAKER	3	4	526.682-018
REI	COOLING-PIPE INSPECTOR	3	5	862.687-010
REI	COPER, HAND	3	3	771.384-010
REI	CRUDE-OIL TREATER	3	5	541.382-014
REI	CURER, FOAM RUBBER	3	4	553.682-014
REI	CYLINDER-DIE-MACHINE OPERATOR	3	5	649.682-014
REI	CYLINDER-MACHINE OPERATOR	3	6	539.362-010
REI	DEBURRER, STRIP	3	6	603.482-010
REI	DECONTAMINATOR	3	6	199.384-010
REI	DECORATING-EQUIPMENT SETTER	3	5	652.380-010
REI	DEFENSIVE FIRE CONTROL SYSTEMS OPERATOR	3	7	378.382-014
REI	DENTAL-AMALGAM PROCESSOR	3	4	509.382-014
REI	DEVELOPER	3	4	976.681-010
REI	DIE BARBER	3	7	705.381-010
REI	DOUBLE-END-TRIMMER-AND-BORING-MACHINE OPERATOR	3	4	669.682-038
REI	DOUGH MIXER	3	5	520.582-010
REI	DOUGH-MIXER OPERATOR	3	5	520.462-010
REI	DOWEL-MACHINE OPERATOR	3	5	665.682-010
REI	DRAPER	3	7	962.381-010
REI	DRIER OPERATOR	3	3	553.685-042
REI	DRIER, BELT CONVEYOR	3	3	529.485-018
REI	DRILL OPERATOR, AUTOMATIC	3	4	676.682-010
REI	DRILL-PRESS OPERATOR, NUMERICAL CONTROL	3	6	606.362-010
REI	DRY-KILN OPERATOR	3	5	573.362-010
REI	DRY-PAN CHARGER	3	5	570.683-010
REI	DUST-COLLECTOR ATTENDANT	3	3	511.685-022
REI	DYE-RANGE OPERATOR, CLOTH	3	4	582.582-010
REI	DYER	3	3	554.384-010
REI	DYNAMITE-CARTRIDGE CRIMPER	3	4	692.685-078
REI	ELECTRIC-GOLF-CART REPAIRER	3	5	620.261-026
REI	ELECTRICIAN	3	4	824.681-010
REI	EMBOSSER OPERATOR	3	5	649.682-022
REI	EMBOSSING-PRESS OPERATOR, MOLDED GOODS	3	5	690.682-034
REI	EMBROIDERY-MACHINE OPERATOR	3	4	787.682-022
REI	ENGRAVER, PANTOGRAPH 1	3	6	704.382-010

Code	Title	GED	SVP	DOT No.
REI	ENGRAVER, TIRE MOLD	3	5	605.382-014
REI	ETCHER	3	6	704.684-010
REI	EXTERMINATOR, TERMITE	3	6	383.364-010
REI	EXTRUDER OPERATOR	3	5	557.382-010
REI	EXTRUSION-PRESS OPERATOR 1	3	5	614.482-018
REI	FABRIC-MACHINE OPERATOR 1	3	6	616.362-010
REI	FARMWORKER, GRAIN 1	3	4	401.683-010
REI	FARMWORKER, RICE	3	5	401.683-014
REI	FARMWORKER, FRUIT 1	3	5	403.683-010
REI	FILER, FINISH	3	5	705.481-010
REI	FILER, HAND, TOOL	3	6	705.484-010
REI	FILM-CASTING OPERATOR	3	4	559.682-022
REI	FINAL ASSEMBLER	3	6	706.381-018
REI	FINAL FINISHER, FORGING DIES	3	6	705.484-014
REI	FINAL INSPECTOR	3	5	779.387-010
REI	FINAL INSPECTOR	3	4	806.687-018
REI	FINISHING INSPECTOR	3	5	729.387-018
REI	FIRE INSPECTOR	3	5	373.367-010
REI	FLAVOR ROOM WORKER	3	4	529.685-130
REI	FOLDING-MACHINE OPERATOR	3	3	649.685-046
REI	FORM MAKER, PLASTER	3	4	777.684-010
REI	FORMING-MACHINE OPERATOR	3	7	575.382-014
REI	FOURDRINIER-MACHINE TENDER	3	6	539.362-014
REI	FRETTED-INSTRUMENT INSPECTOR	3	4	730.684-034
REI	FULLING-MACHINE OPERATOR	3	4	586.382-010
REI	FUR SORTER	3	7	783.384-010
REI	FURNACE OPERATOR	3	3	543.682-018
REI	FURNITURE ASSEMBLER-AND-INSTALLER	3	4	739.684-082
REI	GAS-ENGINE REPAIRER	3	6	625.281-026
REI	GAS-ENGINE OPERATOR	3	6	950.382-018
REI	GLASS CUTTER, HAND	3	4	716.681-014
REI	GLASS GRINDER, LABORATORY APPARATUS	3	5	775.382-010
REI	GLASS-ROLLING-MACHINE OPERATOR	3	6	575.382-022
REI	GLUE MAKER, BONE	3	5	559.382-022
REI	GREASE MAKER	3	5	549.682-010
REI	GRINDER SET-UP OPERATOR, SURFACE	3	4	603.482-022
REI	GRINDER-CHIPPER 1	3	4	705.684-030
REI	GRINDER, GEAR	3	5	602.382-034
REI	GRINDER, HARDBOARD	3	6	569.682-010
REI	GRINDING-WHEEL INSPECTOR	3	4	776.487-010
REI	HARDNESS INSPECTOR	3	4	504.387-010
REI	HARNESS PULLER	3	4	683.684-018
REI	HAT-BLOCK MAKER	3	6	661.381-010
REI	HAT-FORMING-MACHINE OPERATOR	3	3	586.685-030
REI	HEAD INSPECTOR	3	4	764.387-010
REI	HEAD SAWYER, AUTOMATIC	3	6	667.682-034
REI	HEAT-TREATING BLUER	3	4	504.682-022
REI	HIDE SPLITTER	3	4	690.580-010
REI	HONING-MACHINE SET-UP OPERATOR	3	5	603.382-018
REI	HORIZONTAL-EARTH-BORING-MACHINE OPERATOR	3	5	850.662-010
REI	HORTICULTURAL WORKER 1	3	3	405.684-014
REI	HOSE INSPECTOR AND PATCHER	3	4	759.364-010
REI	HUMIDIFIER OPERATOR	3	4	562.682-010

Code	Title	GED	SVP	DOT No.
REI	HYDRAULIC-PRESS SERVICER	3	6	626.381-018
REI	HYDROGENATION OPERATOR	3	4	529.382-026
REI	IDENTIFICATION TECHNICIAN	3	4	209.362-022
REI	IMPREGNATING-MACHINE OPERATOR	3	4	590.362-014
REI	IN-FLIGHT REFUELING SYSTEM REPAIRER	3	7	829.281-018
REI	INJECTION-MOLDING-MACHINE OPERATOR	3	5	556.382-014
REI	INSPECTOR	3	5	590.367-010
REI	INSPECTOR	3	6	619.381-010
REI	INSPECTOR	3	3	649.487-010
REI	INSPECTOR	3	5	774.364-010
REI	INSPECTOR, GRAIN MILL PRODUCTS	3	3	529.387-026
REI	INSPECTOR, FLOOR	3	6	609.361-010
REI	INSPECTOR, PAPER PRODUCTS	3	5	649.367-010
REI	INSPECTOR, MAGNETIC AND ZYGLO	3	5	709.364-010
REI	INSPECTOR, SURGICAL GARMENT	3	3	712.487-010
REI	INSPECTOR, EYEGLASS	3	5	713.384-014
REI	INSPECTOR, POISING	3	4	715.384-018
REI	INSPECTOR, GLASS OR MIRROR	3	4	779.687-022
REI	INSPECTOR, PROCUREMENT	3	5	806.384-010
REI	INSPECTOR, RETURNED MATERIALS	3	5	806.384-014
REI	INSPECTOR, EXHAUST EMISSIONS	3	5	806.364-010
REI	INSTALLER-INSPECTOR, FINAL	3	4	806.684-066
REI	INSTRUMENT-TECHNICIAN HELPER	3	4	710.684-030
REI	INSTRUMENT-REPAIRER HELPER	3	5	710.384-018
REI	IRRIGATION SYSTEM INSTALLER	3	5	851.383-010
REI	JIG FITTER	3	5	801.684-010
REI	JOB SETTER, SPLINE-ROLLING MACHINE	3	5	617.480-010
REI	KETTLE OPERATOR	3	5	558.382-042
REI	KETTLE OPERATOR	3	5	558.382-038
REI	KETTLE WORKER	3	4	553.685-070
REI	KEYSEATING-MACHINE SET-UP OPERATOR	3	4	605.382-018
REI	LABORATORY-EQUIPMENT INSTALLER	3	7	869.381-014
REI	LAPPING-MACHINE SET-UP OPERATOR	3	6	603.382-026
REI	LAST REMODELER-REPAIRER	3	4	739.684-106
REI	LAST TRIMMER	3	3	669.682-054
REI	LATEX-RIBBON-MACHINE OPERATOR	3	6	559.682-034
REI	LATHE OPERATOR, CONTACT LENS	3	5	716.382-010
REI	LAWN-SERVICE WORKER	3	4	408.684-010
REI	LAWN-SPRINKLER INSTALLER	3	5	869.684-030
REI	LAY-OUT TECHNICIAN	3	6	716.381-014
REI	LAY-OUT WORKER 2	3	5	809.381-014
REI	LENS POLISHER, HAND	3	5	716.681-018
REI	LENS-MOLD SETTER	3	5	713.381-010
REI	LIME-KILN OPERATOR	3	5	573.462-010
REI	LINEN-ROOM ATTENDANT	3	3	222.387-030
REI	LINK-AND-LINK-KNITTING-MACHINE OPERATOR	3	6	685.380-010
REI	LINTER-SAW SHARPENER	3	4	603.682-018
REI	LIQUID-SUGAR MELTER	3	4	520.382-014
REI	LITHOGRAPH-PRESS OPERATOR, TINWARE	3	7	651.382-014
REI	LITHOGRAPHIC-PROOFER APPRENTICE	3	5	651.582-014
REI	LIVESTOCK-YARD ATTENDANT	3	2	410.674-018
REI	LOAD CHECKER	3	6	952.367-010
REI	LOAD-OUT SUPERVISOR	3	4	921.133-014

Code	Title	GED	SVP	DOT No.
REI	LOCK TENDER 2	3	4	850.663-018
REI	LOG GRADER	3	6	455.367-010
REI	LOG SCALER	3	5	455.487-010
REI	LOG SORTER	3	3	455.684-010
REI	LOG-CUT-OFF SAWYER, AUTOMATIC	3	5	667.482-010
REI	MACHINE OPERATOR, CENTRIFUGAL- CONTROL SWITCHES	3	6	609.682-022
REI	MAINTENANCE MECHANIC, ENGINE	3	7	623.281-034
REI	MAKE-UP OPERATOR	3	5	559.382-034
REI	MARINE OILER	3	4	911.584-010
REI	MAT INSPECTOR	3	3	575.687-022
REI	MAT TESTER	3	3	579.387-010
REI	MATRIX-BATH ATTENDANT	3	5	500.384-014
REI	MEDICAL-INSTRUMENT-CABLE FABRICATOR	3	4	712.681-022
REI	MELTER OPERATOR	3	4	523.382-018
REI	METAL HANGER	3	4	809.684-030
REI	METAL-FINISH INSPECTOR	3	4	703.687-018
REI	MILK RECEIVER	3	3	222.585-010
REI	MILL OPERATOR	3	5	570.382-010
REI	MILL OPERATOR, ROLLS	3	4	613.482-010
REI	MILLER	3	7	555.682-010
REI	MILLER, DISTILLERY	3	4	521.362-014
REI	MILLER, HEAD, WET PROCESS	3	7	629.261-014
REI	MILLER, WOOD FLOUR	3	6	564.682-018
REI	MIXER, WET POUR	3	4	579.682-010
REI	MODEL BUILDER	3	7	709.381-014
REI	MOLASSES AND CARAMEL OPERATOR	3	4	526.382-022
REI	MOLASSES PREPARER	3	3	522.685-078
REI	MOLD LAMINATOR	3	4	806.684-086
REI	MOLD SETTER	3	3	502.684-018
REI	MOLDER, HAND	3	3	575.684-042
REI	MORGUE ATTENDANT	3	4	355.667-010
REI	MUD BOSS	3	4	519.585-014
REI	MVA-REACTOR OPERATOR	3	4	558.685-046
REI	NATURAL-GAS-TREATING-UNIT OPERATOR	3	6	549.382-010
REI	NEUTRALIZER	3	3	522.685-082
REI	NOODLE-PRESS OPERATOR	3	6	520.662-010
REI	NOVELTY MAKER 1	3	4	529.482-014
REI	NOVELTY MAKER 2	3	5	529.482-018
REI	NUMERICAL-CONTROL-MACHINE OPERATOR	3	5	609.662-010
REI	OPERATOR, AUTOMATED PROCESS	3	4	590.382-010
REI	ORDINARY SEAMAN	3	4	911.687-030
REI	OXYGEN-PLANT OPERATOR	3	4	552.362-014
REI	PACKAGE-DYEING-MACHINE OPERATOR	3	4	582.685-102
REI	PAINT-ROLLER-COVER-MACHINE SETTER	3	5	692.682-046
REI	PALEONTOLOGICAL HELPER	3	6	024.364-010
REI	PANTOGRAPH-MACHINE SET-UP OPERATOR	3	7	605.382-022
REI	PAPER-COATING-MACHINE OPERATOR	3	5	534.582-010
REI	PASTING-MACHINE OPERATOR	3	4	505.482-010
REI	PATTERN GRADER-CUTTER	3	6	781.381-022
REI	PELLET-PRESS OPERATOR	3	3	555.685-042
REI	PERCUSSION-INSTRUMENT REPAIRER	3	6	730.381-042
REI	PERISHABLE-FRUIT INSPECTOR	3	5	910.387-010
REI	PHOTOGRAPHER HELPER	3	4	976.667-010

Code	Title	GED	SVP	DOT No.
REI	PHOTOSTAT OPERATOR	3	5	976.382-022
REI	PLANER OPERATOR	3	5	675.682-014
REI	PLASTER MIXER, MACHINE	3	5	570.382-014
REI	PLASTIC DUPLICATOR	3	5	754.684-038
REI	PLATER, BARREL	3	5	500.362-014
REI	PLATER, PRODUCTION	3	4	500.365-010
REI	PLATFORM ATTENDANT	3	3	299.377-010
REI	PLUMBER	3	6	862.681-010
REI	PNEUMATIC-JACK OPERATOR	3	5	939.682-014
REI	POLISHING-MACHINE OPERATOR	3	4	603.682-026
REI	POLYSTYRENE-BEAD MOLDER	3	4	556.382-018
REI	POWER-SAW MECHANIC	3	6	625.281-030
REI	POWERED BRIDGE SPECIALIST	3	5	378.683-014
REI	PRECIPITATE WASHER	3	3	551.685-110
REI	PRECIPITATOR SUPERVISOR	3	5	511.132-010
REI	PRECISION-LENS POLISHER	3	7	716.682-018
REI	PRECISION-LENS CENTERER AND EDGER	3	6	716.462-010
REI	PRECISION-LENS GENERATOR	3	6	716.682-014
REI	PRESSURE CONTROLLER	3	7	953.362-018
REI	PRESSURE-TEST OPERATOR	3	4	737.387-018
REI	PRINT INSPECTOR	3	4	774.687-018
REI	PRINTING-ROLLER POLISHER	3	6	603.382-030
REI	PRODUCT TESTER, FIBERGLASS	3	5	589.384-010
REI	PROFILE-GRINDER TECHNICIAN	3	6	601.482-010
REI	PROOF-PRESS OPERATOR	3	5	651.582-010
REI	PROPERTY CUSTODIAN	3	5	222.387-042
REI	PROSPECTING DRILLER	3	6	930.382-018
REI	PULP GRINDER AND BLENDER	3	6	530.682-010
REI	PULP-REFINER OPERATOR	3	4	530.382-010
REI	PULPER, SYNTHETIC SOIL BLOCKS	3	4	530.582-010
REI	PUMP SERVICER	3	7	630.281-018
REI	PUMPER	3	5	914.682-010
REI	PUMPER, BREWERY	3	3	914.665-014
REI	PYRIDINE OPERATOR	3	6	552.382-010
REI	QUALITY-CONTROL TECHNICIAN	3	4	529.387-030
REI	QUALITY-CONTROL TECHNICIAN	3	3	637.684-014
REI	QUALITY-CONTROL INSPECTOR	3	4	194.387-010
REI	QUALITY-CONTROL INSPECTOR	3	4	750.367-010
REI	RAIL-TRACTOR OPERATOR	3	4	919.683-018
REI	RAILROAD-CAR LETTERER	3	7	845.681-010
REI	RECEIVER, FERMENTING CELLARS	3	4	522.662-010
REI	REFINED-SIRUP OPERATOR	3	4	520.485-022
REI	REPAIRER, GYROSCOPE	3	6	710.681-022
REI	REPAIRER, PENS AND PENCILS	3	3	733.384-010
REI	REPAIRER, TYPEWRITER	3	6	706.381-030
REI	REPAIRER, WELDING EQUIPMENT	3	6	626.381-022
REI	ROAD-OILING-TRUCK DRIVER	3	5	853.663-018
REI	ROCK SPLITTER	3	6	771.684-010
REI	ROLL TENDER	3	5	559.362-030
REI	ROLL-THREADER OPERATOR	3	5	619.462-010
REI	ROLLER 1	3	3	520.684-014
REI	ROOF FITTER	3	4	806.684-126
REI	ROOFING-MACHINE OPERATOR	3	4	554.682-022
REI	ROPE-MAKER, ROPEWALK	3	4	681.682-014

Code	Title	GED	SVP	DOT No.
REI	ROTARY DRILLER	3	6	930.382-026
REI	ROTARY-KILN OPERATOR	3	4	573.382-010
REI	ROTOGRAVURE-PRESS OPERATOR	3	7	651.362-026
REI	RUBBER LINER	3	4	759.684-050
REI	RUG SETTER, AXMINSTER	3	5	681.682-018
REI	RULING-MACHINE OPERATOR	3	5	659.682-022
REI	SAFE-AND-VAULT SERVICE MECHANIC	3	7	869.381-022
REI	SAMPLER	3	4	529.387-034
REI	SAND-MILL GRINDER	3	3	555.682-018
REI	SAW OPERATOR	3	4	607.682-018
REI	SAW SETTER	3	5	701.684-022
REI	SCOURING-TRAIN OPERATOR	3	4	589.662-010
REI	SCRAP HANDLER	3	3	509.685-050
REI	SCREEN-PRINTING-MACHINE OPERATOR	3	4	652.682-018
REI	SCREW-MACHINE OPERATOR, MULTIPLE SPINDLE	3	6	604.382-010
REI	SCREW-MACHINE OPERATOR, SINGLE SPINDLE	3	5	604.382-014
REI	SCREW-MACHINE OPERATOR, SWISS-TYPE	3	6	604.682-010
REI	SCUBA DIVER	3	4	379.384-010
REI	SECTION-PLOTTER OPERATOR	3	5	194.382-010
REI	SEED-YEAST OPERATOR	3	3	522.685-090
REI	SERVICE REPRESENTATIVE	3	3	959.574-010
REI	SEWER-PIPE CLEANER	3	3	899.664-014
REI	SHALE PLANER OPERATOR	3	4	930.663-010
REI	SHEAR-GRINDER OPERATOR	3	6	628.382-014
REI	SHELLFISH DREDGE OPERATOR	3	5	446.663-010
REI	SHIPPING AND RECEIVING CLERK	3	5	222.387-050
REI	SHIPPING CHECKER	3	4	222.687-030
REI	SHOT DROPPER	3	6	502.362-010
REI	SILO OPERATOR	3	4	529.682-030
REI	SILVER-SOLUTION MIXER	3	3	550.684-026
REI	SIRUP MAKER	3	4	520.485-026
REI	SIZE MAKER	3	5	550.682-010
REI	SIZING-MACHINE OPERATOR	3	4	649.582-014
REI	SKIFF OPERATOR	3	4	441.683-010
REI	SLURRY MIXER	3	4	539.362-018
REI	SLURRY-CONTROL TENDER	3	5	510.465-014
REI	SMOKE JUMPER	3	6	452.364-014
REI	SOAP MAKER	3	7	559.382-054
REI	SODA-ROOM OPERATOR	3	4	559.682-046
REI	SOLUTIONS OPERATOR	3	5	550.382-034
REI	SPECIALTIES OPERATOR	3	5	559.582-014
REI	SPIRAL-TUBE WINDER	3	4	640.682-022
REI	SPRAY-MACHINE OPERATOR	3	5	574.682-014
REI	SPRING FITTER	3	5	709.684-078
REI	SPRING FORMER, MACHINE	3	4	617.482-022
REI	STARCHMAKER	3	3	520.485-030
REI	STATIC BALANCER	3	3	724.384-014
REI	STEEL-SHOT-HEADER OPERATOR	3	4	611.682-010
REI	STOCK CLERK	3	4	222.387-058
REI	STOCK-PARTS INSPECTOR	3	4	763.684-070
REI	STONE DRILLER	3	4	676.682-014
REI	STONE POLISHER, MACHINE	3	6	673.382-018

Code	Title	GED	SVP	DOT No.
REI	STONE POLISHER, MACHINE APPRENTICE	3	6	673.382-022
REI	STONE ROUGHER	3	2	673.685-074
REI	STONE SETTER	3	7	700.381-054
REI	STONE-SETTER APPRENTICE	3	7	700.381-058
REI	STRAIGHTENER, HAND	3	5	709.484-014
REI	STRAIGHTENING-PRESS OPERATOR	3	5	617.482-026
REI	STRETCHER-LEVELER OPERATOR	3	5	619.582-010
REI	STRIP ROLLER	3	4	613.682-022
REI	STRUCTURAL-STEEL WORKER	3	7	801.361-014
REI	STRUCTURAL-STEEL-WORKER APPRENTICE	3	7	801.361-018
REI	SUBASSEMBLER	3	6	706.381-038
REI	SUPERVISOR, SPLIT LEATHER DEPARTMENT	3	6	589.130-030
REI	SWEEPER-BRUSH MAKER, MACHINE	3	4	692.682-066
REI	TAB-CARD-PRESS OPERATOR	3	5	651.382-034
REI	TANNING-SOLUTION MAKER	3	5	550.682-014
REI	TAPPER OPERATOR	3	4	606.682-022
REI	TESTER, MOTOR	3	4	806.384-026
REI	TESTER, REGULATOR	3	4	710.387-010
REI	THERMAL CUTTER, HAND 1	3	5	816.464-010
REI	THERMOSTAT REPAIRER	3	5	710.381-050
REI	THREAD-MILLING-MACHINE SET-UP OPERATOR	3	6	605.382-042
REI	THROWER	3	7	774.381-010
REI	TIN-WHIZ-MACHINE OPERATOR	3	4	582.685-154
REI	TIP INSERTER	3	4	669.682-066
REI	TIRE ADJUSTER	3	3	241.367-034
REI	TIRE BUFFER	3	3	690.685-422
REI	TIRE TECHNICIAN	3	5	750.382-010
REI	TOWER HELPER	3	3	558.385-014
REI	TOWER OPERATOR	3	4	559.362-034
REI	TRACK REPAIRER	3	4	910.682-010
REI	TRANSFER-TABLE OPERATOR	3	3	910.683-022
REI	TRANSFORMER REPAIRER	3	7	724.381-018
REI	TRIMMING ASSEMBLER	3	3	780.684-114
REI	TURBINE SUBASSEMBLER	3	6	706.381-042
REI	TYPE-CASTING MACHINE OPERATOR	3	6	654.582-010
REI	TYPE-ROLLING-MACHINE OPERATOR	3	4	619.382-022
REI	VACUUM CLEANER REPAIRER	3	6	723.381-014
REI	VARNISH MAKER	3	5	553.382-022
REI	VAULT WORKER	3	3	222.587-058
REI	WAD-COMPRESSOR OPERATOR-ADJUSTER	3	4	535.482-010
REI	WARE TESTER	3	5	579.384-018
REI	WASH HELPER	3	4	559.665-042
REI	WASHER, MACHINE	3	4	361.665-010
REI	WATER REGULATOR AND VALVE REPAIRER	3	5	862.684-030
REI	WATER-METER INSTALLER	3	4	954.564-010
REI	WATER-QUALITY TESTER	3	5	539.367-014
REI	WATER-TREATMENT-PLANT OPERATOR	3	5	954.382-014
REI	WEIGH-TANK OPERATOR	3	3	529.485-026
REI	WELDER, GAS	3	5	811.684-014
REI	WELDING-MACHINE OPERATOR, GAS	3	6	811.482-010
REI	WELDING-MACHINE OPERATOR, ULTRASONIC	3	4	814.682-010

Code	Title	GED	SVP	DOT No.
REI	WELDING-MACHINE OPERATOR, FRICTION	3	5	814.382-010
REI	WHARFINGER	3	5	184.387-010
REI	WHIPPED-TOPPING FINISHER	3	5	529.682-034
REI	WIND-TUNNEL MECHANIC	3	7	827.381-014
REI	WINDING INSPECTOR	3	4	729.384-022
REI	WIRE SAWYER	3	5	677.462-014
REI	WIRE-FRAME-LAMP-SHADE MAKER	3	5	709.684-098
REI	WOOD GRINDER OPERATOR	3	5	530.662-014
REI	WORT EXTRACTOR	3	3	526.485-010
REI	YARDAGE ESTIMATOR	3	6	221.484-010
REI	ZINC-PLATING-MACHINE OPERATOR	3	4	500.485-010
REI	ANTITANK ASSAULT GUNNER	2	3	378.464-010
REI	ASSEMBLER	2	3	762.684-010
REI	ASSEMBLER, FINGER BUFFS	2	2	739.685-010
REI	AUTOMATIC-MACHINE ATTENDANT	2	2	649.685-010
REI	AUTOMOBILE-MECHANIC HELPER	2	3	620.684-014
REI	BAG-MACHINE OPERATOR	2	3	649.685-014
REI	BAND-SAW OPERATOR	2	2	667.685-010
REI	BAND-SAW OPERATOR	2	2	525.685-010
REI	BATH-MIX OPERATOR	2	2	552.685-018
REI	BATTER-OUT	2	4	575.684-010
REI	BELT-BUILDER HELPER	2	3	759.684-018
REI	BENCH GRINDER	2	3	705.684-010
REI	BINDER SELECTOR	2	2	521.687-018
REI	BOIL-OFF-MACHINE OPERATOR, CLOTH	2	2	582.685-022
REI	BOOM-CONVEYOR OPERATOR	2	3	921.683-014
REI	BORING-MACHINE OPERATOR, PRODUCTION	2	3	606.685-010
REI	BOWL TURNER	2	2	664.684-010
REI	BRICK TESTER	2	4	579.384-010
REI	BRINE-TANK TENDER	2	2	529.685-030
REI	CALCINE-FURNACE TENDER	2	3	553.685-030
REI	CALENDER-LET-OFF HELPER	2	2	554.686-014
REI	CALENDER-MACHINE OPERATOR	2	3	583.585-010
REI	CALENDERING-MACHINE OPERATOR	2	3	580.485-010
REI	CARTON MARKER, MACHINE	2	2	652.685-018
REI	CARTON-FORMING-MACHINE TENDER	2	2	641.685-026
REI	CASE-LOADER OPERATOR	2	2	920.685-042
REI	CEMENT-BOAT-AND-BARGE LOADER	2	2	921.665-010
REI	CENTRIFUGE OPERATOR	2	3	521.685-050
REI	CENTRIFUGE OPERATOR	2	2	521.685-042
REI	CHANGE-HOUSE ATTENDANT	2	2	358.687-010
REI	CHAR PULLER	2	2	521.687-030
REI	CHEESE CUTTER	2	2	529.585-010
REI	CHRISTMAS-TREE GRADER	2	3	451.687-014
REI	CIRCULAR-SAWYER HELPER	2	3	677.486-010
REI	CLEAN-OUT-DRILLER HELPER	2	3	930.664-014
REI	CLEANER 2	2	1	919.687-014
REI	COATING-MACHINE-OPERATOR HELPER	2	2	590.686-010
REI	COCOA-BEAN CLEANER	2	2	521.685-066
REI	COILER	2	2	681.685-010
REI	CONTINUOUS-LINTER-DRIER OPERATOR	2	2	553.685-034
REI	COOK TENDER	2	2	553.665-022
REI	COOLER ROOM WORKER	2	2	525.687-022
REI	CORDUROY-BRUSHER OPERATOR	2	2	585.685-034

Code	Title	GED	SVP	DOT No.
REI	COVER STRIPPER	2	2	641.685-034
REI	CREPING-MACHINE-OPERATOR HELPER	2	2	534.687-014
REI	CROSSBAND LAYER	2	2	762.687-026
REI	CRUSHER TENDER	2	2	555.685-022
REI	CRUSHER TENDER	2	3	570.685-022
REI	CULLET CRUSHER-AND-WASHER	2	2	570.685-026
REI	CUT-OFF SAWYER, LOG	2	2	667.685-034
REI	CYLINDER-PRESS FEEDER	2	3	651.686-010
REI	CYLINDER-SANDER OPERATOR	2	2	662.685-014
REI	DECKHAND	2	4	911.687-022
REI	DECKHAND, FISHING VESSEL	2	3	449.667-010
REI	DEFINER	2	2	599.685-022
REI	DESIZING-MACHINE OPERATOR, HEAD-END	2	3	582.685-046
REI	DIE CLEANER	2	3	529.687-062
REI	DIP-LUBE OPERATOR	2	2	503.685-014
REI	DISTILLERY WORKER, GENERAL	2	2	529.687-066
REI	DOCK HAND	2	3	891.684-010
REI	DOCK HAND	2	4	919.683-010
REI	DRILLER HELPER	2	2	930.666-010
REI	DRILLER, HAND	2	2	809.684-018
REI	DRY CLEANER, HAND	2	3	362.684-010
REI	DUMPER	2	2	921.667-018
REI	DYE-REEL-OPERATOR HELPER	2	2	582.686-014
REI	EDGER-MACHINE OPERATOR	2	3	673.682-018
REI	ELECTRODE-CLEANING-MACHINE OPERATOR	2	2	559.685-062
REI	END STAPLER	2	3	669.685-054
REI	EQUIPMENT CLEANER	2	2	599.684-010
REI	EXCELSIOR-MACHINE TENDER	2	2	663.685-014
REI	EXTRUSION-PRESS OPERATOR 2	2	2	614.685-014
REI	FARM-MACHINE TENDER	2	2	409.685-010
REI	FEATHER MIXER	2	2	589.685-050
REI	FEATHER SEPARATOR	2	3	589.685-054
REI	FEED BLENDER	2	2	520.685-094
REI	FEED GRINDER	2	2	521.685-122
REI	FEED WEIGHER	2	2	920.685-058
REI	FELT CARBONIZER	2	3	586.687-010
REI	FERRYBOAT-OPERATOR HELPER	2	2	911.667-010
REI	FIELD ARTILLERY CREWMEMBER	2	3	378.684-018
REI	FILTER-PRESS TENDER, HEAD	2	3	521.665-018
REI	FILTER-SCREEN CLEANER	2	2	521.687-054
REI	FINISHER OPERATOR	2	2	521.685-142
REI	FISH SMOKER	2	3	522.685-066
REI	FISH-CAKE MAKER	2	4	529.685-122
REI	FISH-LIVER SORTER	2	2	521.687-062
REI	FISH-MACHINE FEEDER	2	2	521.686-034
REI	FISHER, POT	2	2	441.684-014
REI	FISHER, SPEAR	2	4	443.684-010
REI	FISHER, TERRAPIN	2	2	441.684-018
REI	FLAME CHANNELER	2	4	930.684-010
REI	FLOUR BLENDER	2	3	520.685-106
REI	FOAM-MACHINE OPERATOR	2	2	559.685-078
REI	FOOD-SERVICE DRIVER	2	3	906.683-010
REI	FORGING-PRESS OPERATOR 2	2	2	611.685-010
REI	FRAMER	2	3	666.684-010

Code	Title	GED	SVP	DOT No.
REI	FREIGHT-CAR CLEANER, DELTA SYSTEM	2	2	910.687-022
REI	FUEL-HOUSE ATTENDANT	2	2	951.686-010
REI	FURNACE CLEANER	2	2	891.687-014
REI	FURNACE HELPER	2	2	504.686-014
REI	GAS-APPLIANCE-SERVICER HELPER	2	4	637.684-010
REI	GREEN-CHAIN OFFBEARER	2	2	663.686-018
REI	GRINDER	2	2	555.685-026
REI	HAIR CLIPPER, POWER	2	2	789.684-022
REI	HANDLE MAKER	2	3	575.684-030
REI	HASHER OPERATOR	2	2	521.685-170
REI	HEAD TRIMMER	2	3	525.684-034
REI	HEAVY-FORGER HELPER	2	3	612.687-014
REI	HIDE HANDLER	2	2	525.687-038
REI	HIDE PULLER	2	2	525.685-022
REI	HOT-TOP LINER	2	3	709.684-046
REI	HYDRAULIC-BOOM OPERATOR	2	3	921.683-046
REI	INSPECTOR	2	3	739.687-106
REI	INSPECTOR, SHELLS	2	2	737.687-066
REI	IRRIGATOR, GRAVITY FLOW	2	2	409.687-014
REI	JET HANDLER	2	4	557.684-010
REI	KAPOK-AND-COTTON-MACHINE OPERATOR	2	2	689.685-082
REI	KELP CUTTER	2	2	447.687-022
REI	KETTLE TENDER	2	2	520.685-118
REI	KETTLE TENDER	2	2	526.665-014
REI	KILN-TRANSFER OPERATOR	2	3	569.683-010
REI	LABORER	2	2	529.687-130
REI	LABORER, CHEMICAL PROCESSING	2	3	559.687-050
REI	LABORER, CONCRETE PLANT	2	2	579.686-010
REI	LABORER, GENERAL	2	2	509.686-010
REI	LABORER, GENERAL	2	2	519.687-026
REI	LABORER, SHELLFISH PROCESSING	2	2	529.686-058
REI	LAUNDRY OPERATOR	2	3	369.684-014
REI	LAUNDRY WORKER 1	2	2	361.684-014
REI	LEAD CASTER	2	3	502.684-010
REI	LEAD-NITRATE PROCESSOR	2	3	558.585-030
REI	LEATHER SOFTENER	2	2	788.687-090
REI	LIGHT AIR DEFENSE ARTILLERY CREWMEMBER	2	3	378.684-030
REI	LINER REROLL TENDER	2	2	554.685-022
REI	LIQUOR-BRIDGE OPERATOR	2	3	521.565-010
REI	LOG MARKER	2	2	455.687-010
REI	MATERIAL HANDLER	2	3	929.687-030
REI	MATRIX INSPECTOR	2	3	654.687-010
REI	MILLED-RUBBER TENDER	2	2	553.685-078
REI	MILLER	2	3	570.685-046
REI	MILLER HELPER, DISTILLERY	2	3	521.687-082
REI	MIXER OPERATOR	2	3	520.685-150
REI	MIXING-MACHINE OPERATOR	2	2	680.685-066
REI	MOLDER-MACHINE TENDER	2	2	575.685-062
REI	MOTTLER-MACHINE FEEDER	2	2	550.686-034
REI	OILING-MACHINE OPERATOR	2	2	534.685-018
REI	PAINT MIXER, HAND	2	3	550.684-018
REI	PAINTER, SPRAY 2	2	2	741.687-018
REI	PATCH DRILLER	2	3	739.687-142

Code	Title	GED	SVP	DOT No.
REI	PELTER	2	2	410.687-018
REI	PICKER	2	2	669.687-022
REI	PIG-MACHINE-OPERATOR HELPER	2	3	514.667-014
REI	PLATER, HOT DIP	2	4	501.685-010
REI	POLE FRAMER	2	3	959.684-010
REI	POLISHER	2	2	599.685-078
REI	POLISHER	2	3	700.687-058
REI	POLISHING-MACHINE-OPERATOR HELPER	2	2	603.686-010
REI	POND TENDER	2	4	939.685-010
REI	POULTRY-PICKING MACHINE TENDER	2	2	525.685-026
REI	POWERHOUSE HELPER	2	3	550.685-098
REI	PRESSER, ALL-AROUND	2	3	363.682-014
REI	PRODUCTION HARDENER	2	3	504.685-026
REI	PUG-MILL-OPERATOR HELPER	2	2	570.685-074
REI	PUNCH-PRESS OPERATOR 2	2	3	615.685-030
REI	RACK-ROOM WORKER	2	2	920.665-014
REI	RAFTER	2	3	455.664-010
REI	RAW-CHEESE WORKER	2	2	529.686-078
REI	RESTRICTIVE-PREPARATION OPERATOR	2	3	559.685-154
REI	REWINDER OPERATOR	2	3	640.685-058
REI	RIVETING-MACHINE OPERATOR	2	2	616.685-058
REI	ROLLER-MACHINE OPERATOR	2	2	583.685-094
REI	RUBBER-MILL TENDER	2	3	550.685-102
REI	RUG CLEANER	2	2	689.687-066
REI	SAND-CUTTER OPERATOR	2	4	570.683-014
REI	SANDBLASTER	2	2	503.687-010
REI	SCRATCHER TENDER	2	3	555.685-050
REI	SCREENER OPERATOR	2	2	599.685-082
REI	SCREENER-AND-BLENDER OPERATOR	2	2	549.685-026
REI	SCUTCHER TENDER	2	2	589.685-090
REI	SECOND HELPER	2	3	512.684-010
REI	SECOND-FLOOR OPERATOR	2	3	557.685-022
REI	SEPARATOR TENDER	2	3	521.685-290
REI	SEWAGE-DISPOSAL WORKER	2	2	955.687-010
REI	SHAKER WASHER	2	2	521.687-114
REI	SHELLFISH-BED WORKER	2	3	446.684-014
REI	SHREDDER TENDER	2	2	555.665-010
REI	SILVER SPRAY WORKER	2	4	500.684-022
REI	SINK CUTTER	2	3	677.682-018
REI	SKIVING-MACHINE OPERATOR	2	4	664.682-018
REI	SNAG GRINDER	2	3	705.684-074
REI	SOAKER, HIDES	2	2	582.685-134
REI	SPICE CLEANER	2	2	521.685-322
REI	SPINNING-MACHINE TENDER	2	2	681.685-110
REI	SPLITTER OPERATOR	2	2	677.685-042
REI	SPONGE BUFFER	2	3	690.685-390
REI	SPOUT WORKER	2	2	514.667-018
REI	SPRAY-PAINTING-MACHINE OPERATOR	2	2	741.685-010
REI	SQUEEZER OPERATOR	2	3	669.685-082
REI	STAVE-LOG-RIPSAW OPERATOR	2	4	667.685-058
REI	STIFFENER	2	3	589.687-038
REI	STONE POLISHER, HAND	2	4	775.664-010
REI	STRAND-AND-BINDER CONTROLLER	2	2	680.685-106
REI	SWITCH TENDER	2	2	910.667-026

Code	Title	GED	SVP	DOT No.
REI	TAILINGS-DAM LABORER	2	2	511.687-026
REI	TANK CLEANER	2	2	891.687-022
REI	TANK CREWMEMBER	2	4	378.683-018
REI	THERMOSCREW OPERATOR	2	3	526.685-058
REI	THIRD HELPER	2	3	512.687-014
REI	TIMBER-FRAMER HELPER	2	3	869.687-042
REI	TIP STRETCHER	2	2	580.685-062
REI	TIRE REPAIRER	2	3	915.684-010
REI	TRACTOR-MECHANIC HELPER	2	4	620.684-030
REI	TRANSFER CONTROLLER	2	3	921.682-022
REI	TRIM-MACHINE OPERATOR	2	3	609.685-026
REI	TUBE DRAWER	2	3	614.685-022
REI	TUMBLER TENDER	2	2	581.685-062
REI	UPHOLSTERER HELPER	2	3	780.687-054
REI	UTILITY WORKER, WOOLEN MILL	2	2	689.686-050
REI	UTILITY WORKER, EXTRUSION	2	3	691.685-030
REI	VOTATOR-MACHINE OPERATOR	2	3	529.685-250
REI	WARP COILER	2	2	582.686-038
REI	WASH-HOUSE WORKER	2	2	529.685-254
REI	WASHING-MACHINE LOADER-AND-PULLER	2	2	361.686-010
REI	WASHING-MACHINE OPERATOR	2	2	599.685-118
REI	WATER-FILTER CLEANER	2	2	954.587-010
REI	WIRE-BORDER ASSEMBLER	2	3	780.685-018
REI	WIRE-COATING OPERATOR, METAL	2	2	501.485-010
REI	WOOD-WEB-WEAVING-MACHINE OPERATOR	2	3	692.685-262
REI	WOOL-FLEECE SORTER	2	3	410.687-026
REI	YEAST PUSHER	2	2	522.665-014
REI	BRINER	1	2	522.687-014
REI	BUTCHER, FISH	1	2	525.684-014
REI	CHRISTMAS-TREE FARM WORKER	1	2	451.687-010
REI	COMPOUND FILLER	1	2	550.686-014
REI	CRAB BUTCHER	1	2	525.684-022
REI	DRYING-OVEN ATTENDANT	1	1	581.686-022
REI	DUST-MILL OPERATOR	1	1	581.686-030
REI	FISH-EGG PACKER	1	2	529.687-086
REI	FRUIT-PRESS OPERATOR	1	2	521.685-146
REI	HAIR-SPINNING-MACHINE OPERATOR	1	1	689.686-030
REI	HOT-TOP-LINER HELPER	1	3	709.687-018
REI	ICE CUTTER	1	2	529.685-150
REI	LABORER	1	1	939.687-018
REI	LABORER, SIRUP MACHINE	1	1	521.687-074
REI	LABORER, WHARF	1	2	922.687-062
REI	NAPHTHALENE-OPERATOR HELPER	1	2	551.687-026
REI	POND WORKER	1	2	921.686-022
REI	ROTARY-CUTTER OPERATOR	1	2	551.585-022
REI	SHELLER 2	1	2	521.685-294
REI	SPREADER	1	1	581.687-022
REI	STONE-DRILLER HELPER	1	2	676.686-010
REA	CELLAR SUPERVISOR	4	8	529.131-010
REA	COOK, CHIEF	4	7	315.131-010
REA	DYE-HOUSE SUPERVISOR	4	7	582.131-010
REA	MACHINE-ADJUSTER LEADER	4	8	619.137-010
REA	MANAGER, MARINE SERVICE	4	8	187.167-130

Code	Title	GED	SVP	DOT No.
REA	PROCESS ARTIST	4	8	972.281-010
REA	PROCESS-ARTIST APPRENTICE	4	8	972.281-018
REA	SUPERVISOR, SOAKERS	4	6	529.132-082
REA	SUPERVISOR, FITTING	4	8	801.131-014
REA	SUPERVISOR, DIAMOND FINISHING	4	8	770.131-014
REA	WOOD GRINDER, HEAD	4	6	530.132-022
REA	WRECKING SUPERVISOR	4	7	869.137-014
REA	AERIALIST	3	6	159.247-014
REA	AMMONIA-STILL OPERATOR	3	5	559.382-010
REA	AUTOMATIC-WINDOW-SEAT-AND-TOP-LIFT REPAIRER	3	4	825.381-014
REA	BOAT PATCHER, PLASTIC	3	4	807.684-014
REA	CHAIN REPAIRER	3	5	683.684-010
REA	DENTAL CERAMIST ASSISTANT	3	6	712.664-010
REA	GRADE CHECKER	3	4	850.467-010
REA	HULLER OPERATOR	3	5	521.682-030
REA	MOTOR-GRADER OPERATOR	3	5	850.663-022
REA	PATTERN-LEASE INSPECTOR	3	4	683.384-010
REA	POLE-PEELING-MACHINE OPERATOR	3	3	663.682-014
REA	PRESS TENDER	3	4	520.685-186
REA	PRESSURE SEALER-AND-TESTER	3	4	806.684-110
REA	RENDERING-EQUIPMENT TENDER	3	3	529.685-202
REA	SUPERCALENDER OPERATOR	3	5	534.682-038
REA	SUPERVISOR, LIVESTOCK-YARD	3	6	410.134-010
REA	AIRPLANE-PILOT HELPER	2	3	409.667-010
REA	EXERCISER, HORSE	2	3	153.674-010
REA	LOCOMOTIVE OPERATOR HELPER	2	3	910.367-022
RES	AIRPLANE PILOT, PHOTOGRAMMETRY	5	7	196.263-018
RES	LOGGING-OPERATIONS INSPECTOR	5	7	168.267-070
RES	ACCIDENT-PREVENTION-SQUAD POLICE OFFICER	4	6	375.263-010
RES	ACCORDION MAKER	4	8	730.281-010
RES	ACOUSTICAL CARPENTER	4	7	860.381-010
RES	ACQUISITIONS LIBRARIAN (SAI)	4	6	100.267-010
RES	AIR-CONDITIONING INSTALLER-SERVICER, WINDOW UNIT	4	8	637.261-010
RES	AIRFRAME-AND-POWER-PLANT MECHANIC	4	7	621.281-014
RES	AIRPLANE INSPECTOR	4	8	621.261-010
RES	ALUMINA-PLANT SUPERVISOR	4	8	511.130-010
RES	ANIMAL BREEDER	4	6	410.161-010
RES	ANIMAL TRAINER	4	6	159.224-010
RES	ANODE-CREW SUPERVISOR	4	7	630.134-010
RES	ARTIFICIAL-GLASS-EYE MAKER	4	8	713.261-010
RES	ARTIFICIAL-PLASTIC-EYE MAKER	4	8	713.261-014
RES	ARTILLERY-MAINTENANCE SUPERVISOR	4	7	632.131-010
RES	ASSEMBLER AND WIRER, INDUSTRIAL EQUIPMENT	4	7	826.361-010
RES	AUDIO OPERATOR	4	7	194.262-010
RES	AUTOMATED EQUIPMENT ENGINEER-TECHNICIAN	4	7	638.261-010
RES	AUTOMATIC-EQUIPMENT TECHNICIAN	4	7	822.281-010
RES	AUTOMOBILE RACER	4	6	153.243-010
RES	AUTOMOTIVE-TIRE-TESTING SUPERVISOR	4	8	736.131-010

Code	Title	GED	SVP	DOT No.
RES	AUTOMOTIVE-TIRE TESTER	4	7	736.367-010
RES	BAKER, HEAD	4	7	313.131-010
RES	BAKERY SUPERVISOR	4	8	526.131-010
RES	BAKERY-MACHINE-MECHANIC SUPERVISOR	4	7	629.131-010
RES	BOAT REPAIRER	4	7	807.361-014
RES	BOATSWAIN	4	7	911.131-010
RES	BOILERHOUSE MECHANIC	4	7	805.361-010
RES	BOX TENDER	4	6	689.280-010
RES	BRAID-PATTERN SETTER	4	7	683.260-010
RES	BRUSH-FABRICATION SUPERVISOR	4	7	692.130-010
RES	CABIN-EQUIPMENT SUPERVISOR	4	7	869.131-010
RES	CABINETMAKER, SUPERVISOR	4	8	660.130-010
RES	CABLE SUPERVISOR	4	8	829.131-010
RES	CAPTAIN, FISHING VESSEL	4	7	197.133-010
RES	CAR REPAIRER	4	7	622.381-014
RES	CAR-REPAIRER APPRENTICE	4	7	622.381-022
RES	CARD CLOTHIER	4	7	628.381-010
RES	CARPENTER-LABOR SUPERVISOR	4	7	860.137-010
RES	CARPENTER, RAILCAR	4	7	860.381-038
RES	CARPENTER, BRIDGE	4	7	860.381-030
RES	CASH-REGISTER SERVICER	4	7	633.281-010
RES	CEMENT MASON	4	7	844.364-010
RES	CEMENT-MASON APPRENTICE	4	7	844.364-014
RES	CHAIN MAKER, HAND	4	6	700.381-010
RES	CHEESEMAKER	4	7	529.361-018
RES	CHEMICAL-PROCESSING SUPERVISOR	4	8	559.130-010
RES	CHIMNEY SUPERVISOR, BRICK	4	8	861.131-014
RES	CHOCOLATE-PRODUCTION-MACHINE OPERATOR	4	6	529.382-014
RES	CLEARING SUPERVISOR	4	7	869.133-010
RES	CLOTH-GRADER SUPERVISOR	4	7	689.134-010
RES	CLOTHING-PATTERN PREPARER	4	6	781.287-010
RES	COAL-YARD SUPERVISOR	4	8	921.137-010
RES	COCOA-BEAN ROASTER 2	4	7	523.380-010
RES	COMPOSING-ROOM MACHINIST	4	8	627.261-010
RES	COMPRESSOR-STATION ENGINEER, CHIEF	4	8	914.132-010
RES	CONCENTRATOR OPERATOR	4	7	511.462-010
RES	CONCRETING SUPERVISOR	4	7	869.131-014
RES	CONTROL-PANEL TESTER	4	7	827.381-010
RES	CONTROLLER REPAIRER-AND-TESTER	4	7	825.381-018
RES	COSTUMER	4	7	346.261-010
RES	CRANE-CREW SUPERVISOR	4	7	921.133-010
RES	CRUSHER SUPERVISOR	4	7	515.132-010
RES	CUSTOM TAILOR	4	8	785.261-014
RES	DEVELOPER PROVER, MECHANICAL	4	7	693.260-010
RES	DICTATING-TRANSCRIBING-MACHINE SERVICER	4	7	633.281-014
RES	DISPATCHER, RADIOACTIVE-WASTE-DISPOSAL	4	7	955.167-010
RES	DISTILLING-DEPARTMENT SUPERVISOR	4	7	522.131-010
RES	DIVER	4	7	899.261-010
RES	DOCK SUPERVISOR	4	7	891.131-010
RES	DREDGE OPERATOR SUPERVISOR	4	7	939.132-010
RES	DRIER OPERATOR	4	7	523.362-014

Code	Title	GED	SVP	DOT No.
RES	ELECTRIC-DISTRIBUTION CHECKER	4	8	824.281-014
RES	ELECTRIC-METER INSTALLER 1	4	7	821.361-014
RES	ELECTRIC-MOTOR FITTER	4	7	721.381-010
RES	ELECTRICAL AND RADIO MOCK-UP MECHANIC	4	7	825.381-022
RES	ELECTRICAL INSPECTOR	4	7	825.381-026
RES	ELECTRICAL-INSTALLATION SUPERVISOR	4	8	821.131-010
RES	ELECTRICIAN SUPERVISOR, SUBSTATION	4	8	820.131-010
RES	ELECTRICIAN APPRENTICE, POWERHOUSE	4	8	820.261-010
RES	ELECTRICIAN, POWERHOUSE	4	8	820.261-014
RES	ELECTRICIAN	4	7	825.281-014
RES	ELECTRICIAN SUPERVISOR	4	8	829.131-014
RES	ELECTRONICS ASSEMBLER, DEVELOPMENTAL	4	7	726.261-010
RES	ELECTRONICS TESTER 1	4	7	726.281-014
RES	ELECTRONICS MECHANIC	4	7	828.281-010
RES	ELECTRONICS-MECHANIC APPRENTICE	4	7	828.281-014
RES	ELEVATOR EXAMINER-AND-ADJUSTER	4	8	825.261-014
RES	ELEVATOR-CONSTRUCTOR SUPERVISOR	4	8	825.131-014
RES	EMBOSSING TOOLSETTER	4	6	616.260-010
RES	EMBROIDERY SUPERVISOR	4	7	689.130-010
RES	ENGINE-TESTING SUPERVISOR	4	8	625.131-010
RES	ENGINEER	4	8	197.130-010
RES	ENGRAVER, BLOCK	4	7	979.281-014
RES	ENGRAVING SUPERVISOR	4	8	704.131-010
RES	ENVIRONMENTAL-CONTROL-SYSTEM INSTALLER-SERVICER	4	8	637.261-014
RES	EQUIPMENT INSPECTOR	4	8	822.261-014
RES	EXPERIMENTAL MECHANIC, OUTBOARD MOTORS	4	7	623.261-010
RES	FARM-EQUIPMENT MECHANIC 1	4	7	624.281-010
RES	FARM-EQUIPMENT-MECHANIC APPRENTICE	4	7	624.281-014
RES	FIELD SERVICE TECHNICIAN, POULTRY	4	7	411.267-010
RES	FIELD SUPERVISOR, OIL-WELL SERVICES	4	7	930.131-010
RES	FIELD-ASSEMBLY SUPERVISOR	4	7	869.131-018
RES	FIELD-SERVICE REPRESENTATIVE	4	7	621.221-010
RES	FINGERPRINT CLASSIFIER	4	6	375.387-010
RES	FINISHING SUPERVISOR	4	7	692.130-014
RES	FINISHING-AREA SUPERVISOR	4	8	559.132-022
RES	FIRE CAPTAIN	4	7	373.134-010
RES	FIRE FIGHTER, CRASH, FIRE, AND RESCUE	4	5	373.663-010
RES	FIRE FIGHTER	4	6	373.364-010
RES	FISH AND GAME WARDEN	4	6	379.167-010
RES	FISHING-TOOL TECHNICIAN, OIL WELL	4	7	930.261-010
RES	FIXTURE MAKER	4	7	600.380-010
RES	FLIGHT ENGINEER	4	7	621.261-018
RES	FLOOR SUPERVISOR, ENDLESS-BELT-WEAVING DEPARTMENT	4	7	683.130-010
RES	FORGE-SHOP SUPERVISOR	4	8	612.131-010
RES	FORGE-SHOP-MACHINE REPAIRER	4	7	626.261-010
RES	FORMER, HAND	4	7	619.361-010
RES	FORMING-MACHINE UPKEEP MECHANIC	4	7	575.380-010
RES	FOUNDRY SUPERVISOR	4	7	519.131-010

Code	Title	GED	SVP	DOT No.
RES	FRETTED-INSTRUMENT MAKER, HAND	4	8	730.281-022
RES	FURNACE INSTALLER	4	7	862.361-010
RES	GAGER, CHIEF	4	7	914.134-010
RES	GASKET SUPERVISOR	4	6	569.130-010
RES	GEM CUTTER	4	6	770.281-014
RES	GLAZE SUPERVISOR	4	7	574.132-010
RES	GLUED WOOD TESTER	4	7	762.384-010
RES	GREASE MAKER, HEAD	4	8	549.132-010
RES	GREENSKEEPER 1	4	6	406.137-010
RES	GUNSMITH	4	8	632.281-010
RES	HEARING-AID REPAIRER	4	6	719.381-014
RES	HEAT-TREAT SUPERVISOR	4	7	504.131-010
RES	IN-FLIGHT REFUELING OPERATOR	4	6	912.662-010
RES	INSPECTION SUPERVISOR	4	8	609.131-010
RES	INSPECTION SUPERVISOR	4	7	736.131-018
RES	INSPECTION SUPERVISOR	4	8	737.134-010
RES	INSPECTION SUPERVISOR	4	8	709.137-010
RES	INSPECTOR, AIRCRAFT ACCESSORIES	4	6	709.261-010
RES	INSPECTOR, MOTORS AND GENERATORS	4	7	721.361-010
RES	INSTALLATION SUPERINTENDENT, PIN-SETTING MACHINE	4	8	829.131-018
RES	INSTRUCTOR	4	6	788.222-010
RES	INSTRUCTOR, WATCH ASSEMBLY	4	7	715.221-010
RES	INSTRUMENT-MAKER AND REPAIRER	4	7	600.280-014
RES	JOCKEY	4	6	153.244-010
RES	JOINER	4	7	860.381-050
RES	JOINER APPRENTICE	4	7	860.381-054
RES	KITCHEN STEWARD/STEWARDESS	4	6	318.137-010
RES	KITCHEN SUPERVISOR	4	7	310.137-014
RES	LABOR-CREW SUPERVISOR	4	8	899.131-010
RES	LABORATORY SUPERVISOR	4	8	706.131-010
RES	LIFT-SLAB OPERATOR	4	7	869.662-010
RES	LINE ERECTOR	4	7	821.361-018
RES	LINE REPAIRER	4	7	821.361-026
RES	LINE SUPERVISOR	4	8	821.131-014
RES	LINE-ERECTOR APPRENTICE	4	7	821.361-030
RES	LOCK MAINTENANCE SUPERVISOR	4	8	899.131-014
RES	LOCK TENDER, CHIEF OPERATOR	4	7	911.131-014
RES	LOCOMOTIVE INSPECTOR	4	7	622.281-010
RES	LOCOMOTIVE ENGINEER	4	7	910.363-014
RES	LOFT WORKER, HEAD	4	8	661.131-010
RES	LOFT WORKER	4	7	661.281-010
RES	LOFT WORKER APPRENTICE	4	7	661.281-014
RES	LOOM SETTER, WIRE WEAVING	4	7	616.360-014
RES	LOOM-FIXER SUPERVISOR	4	7	683.130-014
RES	MACHINE FIXER	4	6	689.260-010
RES	MACHINE-ASSEMBLER SUPERVISOR	4	8	638.131-014
RES	MACHINE-SHOP SUPERVISOR, TOOL	4	8	600.131-010
RES	MACHINE-SHOP SUPERVISOR, PRODUCTION	4	8	609.130-010
RES	MACHINIST APPRENTICE, COMPOSING ROOM	4	8	627.261-014
RES	MAINS-AND-SERVICE SUPERVISOR	4	7	862.137-010
RES	MAINTENANCE MECHANIC	4	6	629.281-030
RES	MAINTENANCE-MECHANIC SUPERVISOR	4	8	638.131-022

Code	Title	GED	SVP	DOT No.
RES	MAINTENANCE INSPECTOR	4	8	822.261-018
RES	MAINTENANCE REPAIRER, BUILDING	4	7	899.381-010
RES	MANAGER, HANDICRAFT-OR-HOBBY SHOP	4	7	187.161-014
RES	MANUFACTURER'S SERVICE REPRESENTATIVE	4	8	638.261-018
RES	MATERIAL INSPECTOR	4	5	764.387-014
RES	MATERIAL-HANDLING SUPERVISOR	4	7	921.133-018
RES	MECHANIC, ENDLESS TRACK VEHICLE	4	7	620.381-014
RES	MECHANIC, INDUSTRIAL TRUCK	4	7	620.281-050
RES	MECHANICAL-UNIT REPAIRER	4	7	620.381-018
RES	MECHANICAL-MAINTENANCE SUPERVISOR	4	8	638.131-026
RES	MECHANICAL-TEST TECHNICIAN	4	7	869.261-014
RES	METAL-CONTROL COORDINATOR	4	6	222.167-010
RES	MILL-LABOR SUPERVISOR	4	7	519.131-014
RES	MILLWRIGHT	4	7	638.281-018
RES	MILLWRIGHT APPRENTICE	4	7	638.281-022
RES	MODEL MAKER, FIREARMS	4	8	600.260-018
RES	MOLD MAKER 1	4	8	700.381-034
RES	MOLD-MAKER APPRENTICE	4	8	700.381-038
RES	MORTICIAN INVESTIGATOR	4	6	168.267-078
RES	MOTOR-ROOM CONTROLLER	4	8	820.662-010
RES	MOTORBOAT MECHANIC	4	7	623.281-038
RES	NITROGLYCERIN SUPERVISOR	4	7	559.132-038
RES	OFFICE-MACHINE SERVICER	4	7	633.281-018
RES	OFFICE-MACHINE-SERVICER APPRENTICE	4	7	633.281-022
RES	OIL-FIELD EQUIPMENT MECHANIC SUPERVISOR	4	8	629.131-014
RES	OPTICIAN	4	8	716.280-008
RES	ORGAN-PIPE VOICER	4	7	730.381-038
RES	PACKAGING TECHNICIAN	4	6	739.281-010
RES	PASTER SUPERVISOR	4	7	773.131-010
RES	PATTERN-CHAIN MAKER SUPERVISOR	4	7	683.132-010
RES	PATTERN-SHOP SUPERVISOR	4	8	693.131-010
RES	PATTERNMAKER	4	7	693.281-014
RES	PIPE FITTER, DIESEL ENGINE 2	4	7	862.381-022
RES	PIPE-FITTER SUPERVISOR	4	8	862.131-010
RES	PIPE-LINE-CONSTRUCTION INSPECTOR	4	8	869.367-018
RES	PIPE-ORGAN BUILDER	4	8	730.281-042
RES	PIPE-ORGAN INSTALLER	4	7	730.381-046
RES	PLASTERER	4	7	842.361-018
RES	PLASTERER APPRENTICE	4	7	842.361-022
RES	PLUMBER SUPERVISOR	4	8	862.131-018
RES	POT-LINING SUPERVISOR	4	7	519.134-010
RES	POT-ROOM SUPERVISOR	4	7	512.135-010
RES	POWDER-AND-PRIMER-CANNING LEADER	4	8	737.137-014
RES	POWER-PLANT OPERATOR	4	8	952.382-018
RES	POWER-REACTOR OPERATOR	4	7	952.362-022
RES	POWERHOUSE-MECHANIC SUPERVISOR	4	8	631.131-010
RES	PRESS SUPERVISOR	4	7	575.130-010
RES	PRESS-HAND SUPERVISOR	4	7	615.130-010
RES	PROCESS-AREA SUPERVISOR	4	7	559.132-042
RES	PRODUCTION SUPERVISOR	4	7	699.130-010
RES	PROTECTIVE-SIGNAL REPAIRER	4	7	822.361-022
RES	PUBLIC-ADDRESS SERVICER	4	7	823.261-010

Code	Title	GED	SVP	DOT No.
RES	PUMP-SERVICER SUPERVISOR	4	7	630.131-010
RES	QUALITY-CONTROL SUPERVISOR	4	7	559.131-014
RES	RAILROAD WHEELS AND AXLE INSPECTOR	4	6	622.381-034
RES	RAILROAD-CONSTRUCTION DIRECTOR	4	8	182.167-018
RES	RECLAMATION SUPERVISOR	4	7	512.132-014
RES	REFINERY OPERATOR	4	7	521.362-018
RES	REFINERY OPERATOR	4	8	549.260-010
RES	REFRIGERATION MECHANIC	4	8	637.261-026
RES	REFRIGERATION MECHANIC	4	7	827.361-014
RES	REFRIGERATING ENGINEER, HEAD	4	7	950.131-010
RES	REGULATOR INSPECTOR	4	7	820.361-018
RES	REMELT-FURNACE EXPEDITER	4	7	512.132-018
RES	REPAIRER	4	7	630.281-022
RES	RIGGER	4	7	806.261-014
RES	RIGGER APPRENTICE	4	7	806.261-018
RES	RIGGING SUPERVISOR	4	8	921.130-010
RES	ROOFING SUPERVISOR	4	7	866.131-010
RES	ROTARY-RIG ENGINE OPERATOR	4	7	950.382-022
RES	RUG DYER 1	4	8	364.361-014
RES	SAIL-LAY-OUT WORKER	4	8	781.381-030
RES	SALESPERSON, ELECTRIC MOTORS	4	6	271.354-010
RES	SAMPLE-BODY BUILDER	4	8	693.380-014
RES	SAMPLE-BODY-BUILDER APPRENTICE	4	8	693.380-018
RES	SAMPLER, FIRST	4	5	619.682-038
RES	SCALE ASSEMBLY SET-UP WORKER	4	7	710.360-010
RES	SCALE MECHANIC	4	7	633.281-026
RES	SCREW SUPERVISOR	4	7	609.130-014
RES	SENIOR TECHNICIAN, CONTROLS	4	7	828.261-018
RES	SERVICE SUPERVISOR 3	4	8	184.167-126
RES	SERVICE SUPERVISOR 2	4	8	821.131-018
RES	SHELL-SHOP SUPERVISOR	4	8	619.132-018
RES	SHIPWRIGHT	4	8	860.381-058
RES	SHIPWRIGHT APPRENTICE	4	8	860.381-062
RES	SHOP ESTIMATOR	4	6	807.267-010
RES	SHOP SUPERVISOR	4	7	619.131-014
RES	SHRINK-PIT SUPERVISOR	4	7	619.131-018
RES	SOAPING-DEPARTMENT SUPERVISOR	4	6	582.132-014
RES	SOFT-TILE SETTER	4	7	861.381-034
RES	SORTING SUPERVISOR	4	6	920.137-014
RES	SPOTTER	4	6	770.381-042
RES	SPRING REPAIRER, HAND	4	7	619.380-018
RES	STATION ENGINEER, CHIEF	4	8	914.132-014
RES	STATIONARY-ENGINEER SUPERVISOR	4	7	950.131-014
RES	STATISTICAL-MACHINE SERVICER	4	7	633.281-030
RES	STEAM-DISTRIBUTION SUPERVISOR	4	7	862.137-014
RES	STREET-LIGHT SERVICER	4	7	824.381-010
RES	SUBSTATION OPERATOR, CHIEF	4	8	952.131-010
RES	SUPERCHARGER-REPAIR SUPERVISOR	4	7	621.131-010
RES	SUPERINTENDENT, AMMUNITION STORAGE	4	8	189.167-038
RES	SUPERVISOR	4	7	500.131-010
RES	SUPERVISOR	4	7	559.132-054
RES	SUPERVISOR	4	6	559.132-058
RES	SUPERVISOR	4	7	589.132-010
RES	SUPERVISOR	4	7	609.130-018

Code	Title	GED	SVP	DOT No.
RES	SUPERVISOR	4	7	615.130-014
RES	SUPERVISOR	4	7	616.130-010
RES	SUPERVISOR	4	7	691.130-010
RES	SUPERVISOR	4	7	692.130-018
RES	SUPERVISOR	4	7	700.130-010
RES	SUPERVISOR	4	8	700.131-014
RES	SUPERVISOR	4	7	700.131-010
RES	SUPERVISOR	4	7	715.131-010
RES	SUPERVISOR	4	7	730.131-010
RES	SUPERVISOR	4	7	739.131-014
RES	SUPERVISOR	4	6	788.131-010
RES	SUPERVISOR	4	7	789.132-010
RES	SUPERVISOR	4	7	789.134-010
RES	SUPERVISOR	4	5	920.137-018
RES	SUPERVISOR	4	7	732.130-010
RES	SUPERVISOR 2	4	6	692.130-022
RES	SUPERVISOR	4	6	617.130-010
RES	SUPERVISOR	4	7	579.132-010
RES	SUPERVISOR, ASSEMBLY STOCK	4	6	222.137-042
RES	SUPERVISOR, MAINTENANCE	4	6	382.137-010
RES	SUPERVISOR, FIELD-CROP FARMING	4	7	404.131-010
RES	SUPERVISOR, PARK WORKERS	4	6	406.134-014
RES	SUPERVISOR, PICKING CREW	4	7	409.131-010
RES	SUPERVISOR, POULTRY FARM	4	7	411.131-010
RES	SUPERVISOR, STOCK RANCH	4	7	410.131-022
RES	SUPERVISOR, SHEET MANUFACTURING	4	7	500.132-010
RES	SUPERVISOR, MATRIX	4	6	500.134-010
RES	SUPERVISOR, CASTING-AND-PASTING	4	7	502.130-010
RES	SUPERVISOR, METALIZING	4	8	505.130-010
RES	SUPERVISOR, BLAST FURNACE	4	7	512.132-022
RES	SUPERVISOR, DIE CASTING	4	7	514.130-014
RES	SUPERVISOR, PIG-MACHINE	4	6	514.137-010
RES	SUPERVISOR, REVERBERATORY FURNACE	4	8	519.130-022
RES	SUPERVISOR, SINTERING PLANT	4	8	519.130-026
RES	SUPERVISOR, URANIUM PROCESSING	4	8	519.130-030
RES	SUPERVISOR, BLAST-FURNACE-AUXILIARIES	4	6	519.132-014
RES	SUPERVISOR, CELL OPERATION	4	7	519.132-018
RES	SUPERVISOR, SOLDER MAKING	4	6	519.132-022
RES	SUPERVISOR, SCRAP PREPARATION	4	6	519.137-014
RES	SUPERVISOR, MOLD YARD	4	7	519.137-010
RES	SUPERVISOR, LUMP ROOM	4	7	520.137-010
RES	SUPERVISOR, RICE MILLING	4	6	521.131-010
RES	SUPERVISOR, MELT HOUSE	4	7	522.130-010
RES	SUPERVISOR, CURED MEATS	4	6	525.132-010
RES	SUPERVISOR, TANK HOUSE	4	7	525.132-014
RES	SUPERVISOR, ABATTOIR	4	7	525.131-010
RES	SUPERVISOR, NUT PROCESSING	4	7	529.130-026
RES	SUPERVISOR, CHOCOLATE-AND-COCOA PROCESSING	4	8	529.130-014
RES	SUPERVISOR, FILTRATION	4	7	529.130-022
RES	SUPERVISOR, REFINING	4	7	529.130-034
RES	SUPERVISOR, SOFT SUGAR	4	7	529.130-038
RES	SUPERVISOR, WHITE SUGAR	4	7	529.130-042

Code	Title	GED	SVP	DOT No.
RES	SUPERVISOR, DAIRY PROCESSING	4	7	529.131-014
RES	SUPERVISOR, BREW HOUSE	4	8	529.132-026
RES	SUPERVISOR, CLEANING	4	7	699.137-010
RES	SUPERVISOR, COOK ROOM	4	7	529.132-038
RES	SUPERVISOR, DRIED YEAST	4	7	529.132-042
RES	SUPERVISOR, FEED HOUSE	4	8	529.132-050
RES	SUPERVISOR, LIQUID YEAST	4	7	529.132-066
RES	SUPERVISOR, MILL HOUSE	4	7	529.132-074
RES	SUPERVISOR, NUTRITIONAL YEAST	4	7	529.132-078
RES	SUPERVISOR, SUGAR REFINERY	4	8	529.132-094
RES	SUPERVISOR, TANK STORAGE	4	8	529.132-098
RES	SUPERVISOR, TEA AND SPICE	4	7	529.132-102
RES	SUPERVISOR, WASH HOUSE	4	7	529.132-106
RES	SUPERVISOR, CURING ROOM	4	7	529.137-038
RES	SUPERVISOR, WHIPPED TOPPING	4	7	529.137-066
RES	SUPERVISOR, SPECIALTY FOOD PRODUCTS	4	8	529.137-062
RES	SUPERVISOR, WOOD ROOM	4	7	530.132-018
RES	SUPERVISOR, COATING	4	7	534.130-010
RES	SUPERVISOR, HARDBOARD	4	7	539.130-010
RES	SUPERVISOR, WET ROOM	4	8	539.130-014
RES	SUPERVISOR, PAPER MACHINE	4	7	539.132-010
RES	SUPERVISOR, NATURAL-GAS PLANT	4	8	542.130-010
RES	SUPERVISOR, PASTE MIXING	4	6	550.137-014
RES	SUPERVISOR, PROCESSING	4	7	551.130-010
RES	SUPERVISOR, PLASTICS	4	7	556.130-014
RES	SUPERVISOR, FURNACE PROCESS	4	7	559.132-094
RES	SUPERVISOR, LIQUEFACTION	4	7	559.132-106
RES	SUPERVISOR, RECORD PRESS	4	7	559.130-018
RES	SUPERVISOR, LITHARGE	4	7	559.132-110
RES	SUPERVISOR, REFINING	4	7	559.132-126
RES	SUPERVISOR, VAT HOUSE	4	7	582.132-022
RES	SUPERVISOR, BLEACH	4	7	559.137-018
RES	SUPERVISOR, EVAPORATOR	4	7	559.137-026
RES	SUPERVISOR, FERTILIZER	4	6	559.132-090
RES	SUPERVISOR, ROCKET PROPELLANT PLANT	4	6	559.137-046
RES	SUPERVISOR, FORMING DEPARTMENT 1	4	7	575.130-018
RES	SUPERVISOR, PRECAST AND PRESTRESSED CONCRETE	4	7	575.131-014
RES	SUPERVISOR, CONCRETE-STONE FABRICATING	4	7	575.131-010
RES	SUPERVISOR, BOARD MILL	4	8	579.130-010
RES	SUPERVISOR, CONCRETE BLOCK PLANT	4	7	579.130-014
RES	SUPERVISOR, CONCRETE PIPE PLANT	4	7	579.130-018
RES	SUPERVISOR, PLEATING	4	8	583.137-010
RES	SUPERVISOR, FUR DRESSING	4	7	589.130-022
RES	SUPERVISOR, MILL	4	7	589.130-026
RES	SUPERVISOR, INSULATION	4	8	590.130-014
RES	SUPERVISOR, ROOFING PLANT	4	7	590.130-018
RES	SUPERVISOR, ROLL SHOP	4	7	604.130-010
RES	SUPERVISOR, MOLD MAKING	4	8	609.131-014
RES	SUPERVISOR, MOLD SHOP	4	8	609.131-018
RES	SUPERVISOR, STRUCTURAL ROLLING-AND-FINISHING	4	8	613.130-018
RES	SUPERVISOR, HOT-STRIP MILL	4	7	613.132-010

Code	Title	GED	SVP	DOT No.
RES	SUPERVISOR, DRAWING	4	7	614.132-010
RES	SUPERVISOR, EXTRUSION	4	7	614.132-014
RES	SUPERVISOR, SPRING PRODUCTION	4	8	616.130-018
RES	SUPERVISOR, STEEL DIVISION	4	7	616.130-022
RES	SUPERVISOR, ASSEMBLY DEPARTMENT	4	7	809.130-010
RES	SUPERVISOR, CONTINUOUS-WELD-PIPE MILL	4	8	619.130-022
RES	SUPERVISOR, HOT-WOUND SPRING PRODUCTION	4	8	619.130-026
RES	SUPERVISOR, LINE	4	8	619.130-030
RES	SUPERVISOR, PUNCH-AND-ASSEMBLY DEPARTMENT	4	7	619.130-042
RES	SUPERVISOR, MACHINE SETTER	4	8	619.130-034
RES	SUPERVISOR, WIRE-ROPE FABRICATION	4	7	691.130-014
RES	SUPERVISOR, PLATE HEATING, ROLLING, AND FINISHING	4	8	619.132-030
RES	SUPERVISOR, RAILROAD CAR REPAIR	4	8	622.131-010
RES	SUPERVISOR, WHEEL SHOP	4	8	622.131-018
RES	SUPERVISOR, ROUNDHOUSE	4	8	622.131-014
RES	SUPERVISOR, ENGINE-REPAIR	4	8	625.131-014
RES	SUPERVISOR, PRESS ROOM	4	8	651.130-010
RES	SUPERVISOR, PRINTING AND STAMPING	4	8	652.130-014
RES	SUPERVISOR, BINDERY	4	8	653.131-010
RES	SUPERVISOR, PRINTING-SHOP	4	8	659.130-010
RES	SUPERVISOR, ASSEMBLY ROOM	4	7	669.130-010
RES	SUPERVISOR, SHUTTLE FITTING	4	7	669.130-030
RES	SUPERVISOR, SHUTTLE PREPARATION	4	7	669.130-034
RES	SUPERVISOR, PREPARATION DEPARTMENT	4	7	681.130-010
RES	SUPERVISOR, WINDING AND TWISTING DEPARTMENT	4	7	681.130-014
RES	SUPERVISOR, SPINNING	4	8	682.130-010
RES	SUPERVISOR, ROVING DEPARTMENT	4	7	689.130-026
RES	SUPERVISOR, WEAVING	4	6	689.130-030
RES	SUPERVISOR, SLITTING-AND-SHIPPING	4	7	690.130-014
RES	SUPERVISOR, PAINT ROLLER COVERS	4	7	692.130-030
RES	SUPERVISOR, JEWELRY DEPARTMENT	4	7	700.131-018
RES	SUPERVISOR, METAL CANS	4	7	703.132-010
RES	SUPERVISOR, ENGRAVING	4	8	704.131-014
RES	SUPERVISOR, SPECIAL ASSEMBLIES	4	8	710.131-038
RES	SUPERVISOR, THERMOSTATIC CONTROLS	4	7	710.131-042
RES	SUPERVISOR, INSTRUMENT MAINTENANCE	4	8	710.131-014
RES	SUPERVISOR, INSTRUMENT MECHANICS	4	8	710.131-018
RES	SUPERVISOR, SHOP	4	8	710.131-034
RES	SUPERVISOR, TUMBLING AND ROLLING	4	7	715.131-030
RES	SUPERVISOR, FABRICATION DEPARTMENT	4	8	723.132-010
RES	SUPERVISOR, TOY ASSEMBLY	4	7	731.131-010
RES	SUPERVISOR, ASSEMBLY	4	7	733.137-010
RES	SUPERVISOR, BIT AND SHANK DEPARTMENT	4	7	739.130-010
RES	SUPERVISOR, ASSEMBLY ROOM	4	7	739.134-010
RES	SUPERVISOR, PIPE MANUFACTURE	4	7	739.137-018
RES	SUPERVISOR, COOPERAGE SHOP	4	7	764.134-010
RES	SUPERVISOR, FABRICATION	4	7	769.130-010
RES	SUPERVISOR, CLAY SHOP	4	7	774.130-010

Code	Title	GED	SVP	DOT No.
RES	SUPERVISOR, CONCRETE-STONE FINISHING	4	7	775.131-010
RES	SUPERVISOR, CUTTING-AND-SEWING DEPARTMENT	4	8	780.131-010
RES	SUPERVISOR, MATTRESS AND BOXSPRINGS	4	7	780.137-010
RES	SUPERVISOR, FURRIER SHOP	4	7	783.131-010
RES	SUPERVISOR, PACKING	4	7	788.137-010
RES	SUPERVISOR, WEBBING	4	7	789.137-014
RES	SUPERVISOR, REINFORCED-STEEL-PLACING	4	8	801.134-010
RES	SUPERVISOR, BOILER REPAIR	4	8	805.137-010
RES	SUPERVISOR, ERECTION SHOP	4	8	806.131-022
RES	SUPERVISOR, SHIPFITTERS	4	8	806.131-034
RES	SUPERVISOR, STRUCTURAL-STEEL ERECTION	4	8	809.131-018
RES	SUPERVISOR, LINE DEPARTMENT	4	7	825.137-010
RES	SUPERVISOR, ELECTRICAL REPAIR AND TELEPHONE LINE MAINTENANCE	4	8	829.131-022
RES	SUPERVISOR, LATHING	4	8	842.131-014
RES	SUPERVISOR, PILE DRIVING	4	8	859.137-014
RES	SUPERVISOR, BOATBUILDERS, WOOD	4	8	860.131-014
RES	SUPERVISOR, CARPENTERS	4	8	860.131-018
RES	SUPERVISOR, JOINERS	4	8	860.131-022
RES	SUPERVISOR, CANAL-EQUIPMENT MAINTENANCE	4	8	899.130-010
RES	SUPERVISOR, LABOR GANG	4	7	899.133-010
RES	SUPERVISOR, FIELD-PIPE-LINES	4	7	914.132-022
RES	SUPERVISOR, PACKING	4	6	920.130-010
RES	SUPERVISOR, CARTON AND CAN SUPPLY	4	7	920.132-014
RES	SUPERVISOR, CELLARS	4	7	914.132-018
RES	SUPERVISOR, OPEN-HEARTH STOCKYARD	4	8	922.137-022
RES	SUPERVISOR, FELLING-BUCKING	4	7	454.134-010
RES	SUPERVISOR, PUMPING STATION	4	7	954.130-010
RES	SUPERVISOR, POULTRY PROCESSING	4	7	525.134-014
RES	SUPERVISOR, FISH PROCESSING	4	7	525.134-010
RES	SUPERVISOR, LAST-MODEL DEPARTMENT	4	8	761.131-010
RES	SUPERVISOR, SPRING-UP	4	7	780.134-014
RES	SUPERVISOR, LIQUEFACTION-AND-REGASIFICATION	4	8	953.132-010
RES	SUPERVISOR, PLATING AND POINT ASSEMBLY	4	7	733.130-010
RES	SUPERVISOR, FABRICATION AND ASSEMBLY	4	7	809.131-010
RES	SUPERVISOR, SHELLFISH FARMING	4	6	446.133-010
RES	SUPERVISOR, FISH HATCHERY	4	7	446.134-010
RES	SUPERVISOR, CARBON-PAPER-COATING	4	7	534.137-010
RES	SUPERVISOR, TANK CLEANING	4	7	891.137-018
RES	SUPERVISOR, TYPESETTING	4	8	650.132-010
RES	SUPERVISOR, PIPE JOINTS	4	7	590.134-010
RES	SUPERVISOR, DRY-WALL APPLICATION	4	7	842.131-010
RES	SUPERVISOR, DIVERSIFIED CROPS	4	7	407.131-010
RES	SUPERVISOR, HORTICULTURAL-SPECIALTY FARMING	4	7	405.131-010
RES	SUPERVISOR, VINE-FRUIT FARMING	4	6	403.131-014

Code	Title	GED	SVP	DOT No.
RES	SUPERVISOR, VEGETABLE FARMING	4	7	402.131-010
RES	SUPERVISOR, CEMETERY WORKERS	4	6	406.134-010
RES	SUPERVISOR, INSULATION	4	8	863.134-014
RES	SUPERVISOR, MIRROR FABRICATION	4	7	679.137-014
RES	SUPERVISOR, TERRAZZO	4	8	861.131-026
RES	SUPERVISOR, MARBLE	4	8	861.131-022
RES	SUPERVISOR, RIGHT-OF-WAY MAINTENANCE	4	7	859.133-010
RES	SUPERVISOR, QUILTING	4	6	689.134-022
RES	SUPERVISOR, GEAR REPAIR	4	7	623.131-014
RES	SUPERVISOR, BRINEYARD	4	7	522.134-010
RES	SUPERVISOR, SANDBLASTER	4	7	503.137-010
RES	SUPERVISOR, ESTERS-AND-EMULSIFIERS	4	7	559.132-086
RES	SUPERVISOR, FERTILIZER PROCESSING	4	7	559.130-014
RES	SUPERVISOR, TILE-AND-MOTTLE	4	6	559.130-022
RES	SUPERVISOR, INSECTICIDE	4	7	559.132-102
RES	SUPERVISOR, GREEN END DEPARTMENT	4	7	663.132-010
RES	SUPERVISOR, GLAZING DEPARTMENT	4	7	582.130-010
RES	SUPERVISOR, ALUMINUM FABRICATION	4	8	619.130-014
RES	SUPERVISOR, TELEPHONE INFORMATION	4	7	237.137-010
RES	SUPERVISOR, EXTRUDING DEPARTMENT	4	8	557.130-010
RES	SUPERVISOR, CEREAL	4	7	529.132-030
RES	SURFACE SUPERVISOR	4	8	932.132-014
RES	TAILOR APPRENTICE, CUSTOM	4	8	785.261-022
RES	TAPPER SUPERVISOR	4	7	514.134-010
RES	TESTING-AND-REGULATING TECHNICIAN	4	7	822.261-026
RES	TOOL PUSHER	4	8	930.130-010
RES	TOOL-AND-DIE SUPERVISOR	4	8	601.130-010
RES	TOWER ERECTOR	4	7	821.361-038
RES	TRACK-LAYING SUPERVISOR	4	7	869.134-022
RES	TREATING-PLANT SUPERVISOR	4	7	561.131-010
RES	UTILITIES-AND-MAINTENANCE SUPERVISOR	4	8	899.131-018
RES	VIOLIN MAKER, HAND	4	8	730.281-046
RES	VIOLIN REPAIRER	4	7	730.281-050
RES	WATER-AND-SEWER-SYSTEMS SUPERVISOR	4	7	862.137-018
RES	WEAVE-ROOM SUPERVISOR	4	7	683.130-018
RES	WEAVING SUPERVISOR	4	8	683.130-022
RES	WELDER APPRENTICE, COMBINATION	4	6	819.384-008
RES	WELDER, COMBINATION	4	6	819.384-010
RES	WELDING SUPERVISOR	4	8	819.131-014
RES	WELDING TECHNICIAN	4	8	011.261-014
RES	WELDING-MACHINE OPERATOR, RESISTANCE	4	6	812.682-010
RES	WELL PULLER, HEAD	4	7	939.131-018
RES	WELL-POINT PUMPING SUPERVISOR	4	7	862.132-010
RES	WIREWORKER SUPERVISOR	4	8	821.131-026
RES	YARD SUPERVISOR	4	7	929.133-010
RES	ABLE SEAMAN	3	5	911.364-010
RES	ABRASIVE MIXER	3	4	570.485-010
RES	ABRASIVE-COATING-MACHINE OPERATOR	3	4	574.462-010
RES	ACID MAKER	3	5	559.662-010
RES	AGER OPERATOR	3	5	553.482-010
RES	AIR-COMPRESSOR OPERATOR	3	5	950.685-010

Code	Title	GED	SVP	DOT No.
RES	AIR-CONDITIONING MECHANIC	3	6	620.281-010
RES	AIR-CONDITIONING-UNIT TESTER	3	6	827.361-010
RES	AIR-CONDITIONING INSTALLER, DOMESTIC	3	4	827.464-010
RES	AIR-DRIER-MACHINE OPERATOR	3	5	534.682-010
RES	AIRFRAME-AND-POWER-PLANT-MECHANIC HELPER	3	4	621.684-010
RES	AIRPLANE COVERER	3	7	849.381-010
RES	AIRPORT ATTENDANT	3	5	912.364-010
RES	ALODIZE-MACHINE OPERATOR	3	5	509.462-010
RES	ALUMINUM-HYDROXIDE-PROCESS OPERATOR	3	4	559.685-014
RES	ALUMINUM-POOL INSTALLER	3	4	809.664-010
RES	ARCH-CUSHION-PRESS OPERATOR	3	4	556.362-010
RES	ASBESTOS-WIRE FINISHER	3	4	691.682-010
RES	ASPHALT-PAVING-MACHINE OPERATOR	3	5	853.663-010
RES	ASSEMBLER	3	5	710.381-010
RES	ASSEMBLER	3	4	869.684-010
RES	ASSEMBLER, PRODUCTION LINE	3	4	714.684-010
RES	ASSEMBLER, METAL BUILDING	3	6	801.381-010
RES	ASSEMBLER, METAL BONDING	3	5	806.684-030
RES	ASSEMBLER, DECK AND HULL	3	3	806.684-022
RES	ASSEMBLY INSPECTOR	3	5	706.361-014
RES	ASSEMBLY REPAIRER	3	5	624.381-010
RES	ASSISTANT-PRESS OPERATOR	3	6	651.585-010
RES	AUGER PRESS OPERATOR, MANUAL CONTROL	3	6	575.462-010
RES	AUTOMOBILE WRECKER	3	4	620.684-010
RES	AUTOMOBILE UPHOLSTERER	3	6	780.381-010
RES	AUTOMOBILE-UPHOLSTERER APPRENTICE	3	6	780.381-014
RES	AUTOMOBILE-SEAT-COVER-AND-CONVERTIBLE-TOP INSTALLER	3	6	780.384-010
RES	AUTOMOBILE-SERVICE-STATION ATTENDANT	3	3	915.467-010
RES	AUTOMOBILE-BODY CUSTOMIZER	3	6	807.361-010
RES	AUXILIARY-EQUIPMENT OPERATOR	3	5	952.362-010
RES	AWNING-FRAME MAKER	3	5	809.484-010
RES	BACK TENDER, PAPER MACHINE	3	6	534.662-010
RES	BAGGAGE CHECKER	3	3	357.477-010
RES	BARREL STRAIGHTENER 1	3	4	736.684-026
RES	BARREL-LATHE OPERATOR, INSIDE	3	4	664.682-010
RES	BASE-DRAW OPERATOR	3	3	504.685-010
RES	BATCH-STILL OPERATOR 1	3	4	552.685-014
RES	BATTER SCALER	3	4	526.682-010
RES	BATTERY INSPECTOR	3	4	829.684-010
RES	BATTERY RECHARGER	3	5	727.381-010
RES	BEATER ENGINEER	3	5	530.662-010
RES	BEEKEEPER	3	7	413.161-010
RES	BELL MAKER	3	7	730.381-014
RES	BEN-DAY ARTIST	3	6	970.681-010
RES	BENCH HAND	3	6	520.384-010
RES	BEVELER	3	5	771.484-010
RES	BITE-BLOCK MAKER	3	4	712.684-014
RES	BLACK-ASH-BURNER OPERATOR	3	4	553.682-010
RES	BLEACH-LIQUOR MAKER	3	5	550.662-010

Code	Title	GED	SVP	DOT No.
RES	BLENDER	3	6	540.462-010
RES	BLENDING-MACHINE OPERATOR	3	3	522.685-010
RES	BLOCKER AND POLISHER, GOLD WHEEL	3	5	715.381-034
RES	BLOCKER 1	3	7	979.682-010
RES	BLOCKER, HAND	3	3	716.684-010
RES	BOAT-RENTAL CLERK	3	2	295.467-014
RES	BOILERMAKER 2	3	7	805.381-010
RES	BOMB LOADER	3	3	737.684-014
RES	BONDING-MACHINE TENDER	3	4	589.665-010
RES	BONE-CHAR KILN OPERATOR	3	4	523.662-010
RES	BOOKBINDER	3	7	977.381-010
RES	BOOKBINDER, APPRENTICE	3	7	977.381-014
RES	BRAKE OPERATOR 2	3	4	619.685-026
RES	BRAKE REPAIRER	3	6	620.281-026
RES	BRIQUETTER OPERATOR	3	3	559.685-030
RES	BRUSH-MACHINE SETTER	3	5	692.360-014
RES	BUTCHER APPRENTICE	3	6	525.381-010
RES	BUTCHER, ALL-ROUND	3	6	525.381-014
RES	CABLE SWAGER	3	5	806.684-042
RES	CAGE MAKER, MACHINE	3	6	616.682-018
RES	CALCINER, GYPSUM	3	4	579.382-010
RES	CALIBRATION CHECKER 2	3	4	710.687-018
RES	CAMP TENDER	3	6	410.137-010
RES	CAR TRIMMER	3	3	806.684-046
RES	CAR-WASH SUPERVISOR	3	5	915.137-010
RES	CARBON SETTER	3	3	519.667-010
RES	CARGO AGENT	3	5	248.367-018
RES	CASE-FINISHING-MACHINE ADJUSTER	3	5	626.381-010
RES	CASKET LINER	3	4	780.684-030
RES	CASTING REPAIRER	3	6	619.281-010
RES	CASTING-ROOM OPERATOR	3	4	556.585-010
RES	CD-REACTOR OPERATOR, HEAD	3	7	558.362-014
RES	CENTRIFUGAL-CASTING-MACHINE OPERATOR 1	3	3	514.685-010
RES	CENTRIFUGAL-STATION OPERATOR, AUTOMATIC	3	5	521.585-010
RES	CENTRIFUGAL-DRIER OPERATOR	3	4	551.685-026
RES	CENTRIFUGE OPERATOR	3	4	529.682-010
RES	CHAR-FILTER-TANK TENDER, HEAD	3	4	521.665-010
RES	CHEESE GRADER	3	5	529.387-010
RES	CHEMICAL MIXER	3	4	550.585-018
RES	CHEMICAL MIXER	3	6	550.485-010
RES	CHILD-CARE ATTENDANT, SCHOOL	3	3	355.674-010
RES	CHIPPING-MACHINE OPERATOR	3	5	564.682-010
RES	CHLORINATOR OPERATOR	3	5	558.382-030
RES	CHOCOLATE MOLDER, MACHINE	3	4	529.685-054
RES	CIRCULATING PROCESS INSPECTOR	3	6	829.361-018
RES	CLAMPER	3	6	979.382-010
RES	CLAY ROASTER	3	4	573.685-014
RES	CLOTH GRADER	3	5	689.387-010
RES	COAL WASHER	3	5	541.382-010
RES	COAL-PIPE-LINE OPERATOR	3	4	914.362-010
RES	COATING-AND-EMBOSSING-UNIT OPERATOR	3	6	583.682-010
RES	COATING-MACHINE OPERATOR	3	7	501.362-010

Code	Title	GED	SVP	DOT No.
RES	COBBLER	3	5	788.381-010
RES	COCOA-PRESS OPERATOR	3	4	521.682-014
RES	COIL CONNECTOR	3	5	721.684-018
RES	COIN-MACHINE OPERATOR	3	3	217.585-010
RES	COKE BURNER	3	5	543.682-010
RES	COKE LOADER	3	5	921.563-010
RES	COLOR MAKER	3	5	550.382-010
RES	COMBAT SURVEILLANCE AND TARGET ACQUISITION NONCOMMISSIONED OFFICER	3	7	378.161-010
RES	COMMUTATOR ASSEMBLER	3	5	724.684-030
RES	COMPO CASTER	3	6	769.381-010
RES	COMPOSITION-ROLL MAKER AND CUTTER	3	4	559.482-010
RES	COMPOUNDER	3	7	540.382-010
RES	CONCRETE RUBBER	3	5	844.684-010
RES	CONTROLS OPERATOR, MOLDED GOODS	3	5	590.662-010
RES	CONVEYOR-MAINTENANCE MECHANIC	3	6	630.381-010
RES	COOK	3	6	315.361-010
RES	COOK	3	5	315.381-010
RES	COOK, DOG-AND-CAT FOOD	3	4	526.682-014
RES	COOK, MESS	3	6	315.371-010
RES	COOK, RAILROAD	3	6	315.381-018
RES	COOK, THIRD	3	6	315.381-022
RES	COOKER, PROCESS CHEESE	3	3	526.665-010
RES	CORNER-TRIMMER OPERATOR	3	5	667.682-018
RES	CORSET FITTER	3	7	782.361-010
RES	COTTAGE-CHEESE MAKER	3	4	522.382-010
RES	CRACKER-AND-COOKY-MACHINE OPERATOR	3	5	520.482-010
RES	CREMATOR	3	3	359.685-010
RES	CRIMPING-MACHINE OPERATOR	3	5	616.682-022
RES	CROOK OPERATOR	3	4	609.682-018
RES	CRUTCHER	3	4	550.685-054
RES	CUTTER, FABRICS AND MATERIALS	3	6	781.384-010
RES	CUTTER, MACHINE 1	3	5	781.684-014
RES	DEEP SUBMERGENCE VEHICLE OPERATOR	3	7	911.263-010
RES	DENSITY CONTROL PUNCHER	3	4	976.684-010
RES	DENTURE WAXER	3	6	712.681-010
RES	DENTURE-MODEL MAKER	3	5	712.681-014
RES	DEPOSITING-MACHINE OPERATOR	3	5	529.682-018
RES	DERRICK OPERATOR	3	4	921.663-022
RES	DEWATERER OPERATOR	3	5	511.565-010
RES	DIAL MAKER	3	6	715.381-046
RES	DIE MOUNTER	3	5	659.481-010
RES	DIE POLISHER	3	6	601.381-018
RES	DIGESTER OPERATOR	3	6	532.362-010
RES	DISSOLVER OPERATOR	3	4	558.682-014
RES	DISTILLER	3	4	552.682-014
RES	DISTRIBUTING CLERK	3	3	222.587-018
RES	DITCHER OPERATOR	3	4	850.683-014
RES	DIVER	3	4	349.247-010
RES	DIVIDING-MACHINE OPERATOR	3	3	520.685-086
RES	DOOR-CLOSER MECHANIC	3	7	630.381-014
RES	DOUGHNUT MAKER	3	5	526.684-010
RES	DRAGLINE OPERATOR	3	5	850.683-018

Code	Title	GED	SVP	DOT No.
RES	DRAPERY AND UPHOLSTERY MEASURER	3	6	299.364-010
RES	DRAPERY HANGER	3	5	869.484-014
RES	DRIER OPERATOR 2	3	4	553.582-010
RES	DRILLER-AND-REAMER, AUTOMATIC	3	4	606.382-010
RES	DRIVER-UTILITY WORKER	3	4	919.663-018
RES	DRY CLEANER	3	5	362.382-014
RES	DRY-CLEANER APPRENTICE	3	5	362.382-010
RES	DRY-PLACER-MACHINE OPERATOR	3	4	939.382-010
RES	DRY-STARCH OPERATOR	3	7	520.362-014
RES	DRY-STARCH OPERATOR, AUTOMATIC	3	7	529.362-014
RES	DRY-WALL SPRAYER	3	4	842.684-010
RES	EARTH-BORING-MACHINE OPERATOR	3	4	859.682-010
RES	EDGER, AUTOMATIC	3	5	667.682-026
RES	EDGING-MACHINE SETTER	3	5	673.680-010
RES	EFFERVESCENT-SALTS COMPOUNDER	3	4	559.685-058
RES	ELECTRIC-CELL TENDER	3	4	558.565-014
RES	ELECTRIC-MOTOR WINDER	3	6	721.484-010
RES	ELECTRIC-ORGAN ASSEMBLER AND CHECKER	3	6	730.381-022
RES	ELECTRICAL-EQUIPMENT TESTER	3	6	729.381-010
RES	ELECTRONICS UTILITY WORKER	3	6	726.361-010
RES	EMBOSSING-PRESS OPERATOR	3	7	659.682-014
RES	EMBOSSING-PRESS-OPERATOR APPRENTICE	3	7	659.682-018
RES	ENAMELER	3	5	509.684-010
RES	ENGRAVER	3	6	775.381-010
RES	ENGRAVER 1	3	5	979.381-010
RES	ENROBING-MACHINE OPERATOR	3	6	524.382-014
RES	ENVELOPE-FOLDING-MACHINE ADJUSTER	3	7	641.680-010
RES	EXTERMINATOR	3	5	389.684-010
RES	EXTRACTOR-PLANT OPERATOR	3	4	559.665-018
RES	EXTRUDER OPERATOR	3	5	520.682-018
RES	EXTRUSION BENDER	3	4	804.684-014
RES	FABRICATOR, SHOWER DOORS AND PANELS	3	5	739.381-030
RES	FALLER 1	3	6	454.384-010
RES	FARMWORKER, GENERAL 1	3	5	421.683-010
RES	FARMWORKER, DIVERSIFIED CROPS 1	3	4	407.663-010
RES	FARMWORKER, BULBS	3	5	405.683-010
RES	FEED-RESEARCH AIDE	3	4	049.364-010
RES	FERMENTATION OPERATOR	3	5	558.682-018
RES	FERRYBOAT OPERATOR	3	6	911.363-010
RES	FIELD-RING ASSEMBLER	3	6	721.484-014
RES	FILM DEVELOPER	3	6	976.382-018
RES	FILM LABORATORY TECHNICIAN 2	3	5	976.685-018
RES	FILM PRINTER	3	5	976.682-010
RES	FINAL INSPECTOR	3	5	730.367-010
RES	FINAL INSPECTOR, SHUTTLE	3	4	769.684-022
RES	FINISHER	3	6	613.382-014
RES	FINISHER, DENTURE	3	5	712.681-018
RES	FINISHING SUPERVISOR, PLASTIC SHEETS	3	6	554.137-010
RES	FIRER, HIGH PRESSURE	3	5	951.685-010
RES	FIRER, MARINE	3	5	951.685-018
RES	FIREWORKS MAKER	3	6	737.684-018
RES	FISH HATCHERY WORKER	3	5	446.684-010

Code	Title	GED	SVP	DOT No.
RES	FISHER, DIVING	3	4	443.664-010
RES	FITTER	3	7	801.381-014
RES	FLAKING-ROLL OPERATOR	3	3	520.685-102
RES	FLATWARE MAKER	3	7	700.682-010
RES	FLOOR LAYER	3	6	864.481-010
RES	FLOOR WINDER	3	4	681.685-050
RES	FLOOR-LAYER APPRENTICE	3	6	864.481-014
RES	FLUSHER	3	5	559.682-026
RES	FOLDING-MACHINE SETTER	3	8	653.360-014
RES	FOLDING-MACHINE OPERATOR	3	5	653.382-010
RES	FORMING-MACHINE TENDER	3	4	575.685-038
RES	FORMING-MACHINE UPKEEP-MECHANIC HELPER	3	3	575.687-014
RES	FORMING-PROCESS WORKER	3	5	590.362-010
RES	FOUNDATION MAKER	3	5	739.384-014
RES	FRAME REPAIRER	3	7	807.381-018
RES	FRAME-TABLE OPERATOR	3	5	669.662-014
RES	FREEZER OPERATOR	3	5	529.482-010
RES	FUN-HOUSE OPERATOR	3	3	342.665-010
RES	FUR BLENDER	3	6	783.681-010
RES	FUR CLEANER	3	5	362.684-014
RES	FUR CUTTER	3	7	783.381-010
RES	FUR DRESSER	3	7	589.361-010
RES	FUR FINISHER	3	6	783.381-014
RES	FUR-REPAIR INSPECTOR	3	8	783.387-010
RES	FURNACE OPERATOR	3	6	542.562-010
RES	FURNACE OPERATOR	3	4	558.482-010
RES	GAS-LEAK INSPECTOR	3	5	953.367-010
RES	GAS-LEAK INSPECTOR HELPER	3	4	953.667-010
RES	GAS-MASK INSPECTOR	3	4	712.687-022
RES	GAS-METER INSTALLER	3	6	953.364-010
RES	GAS-METER PROVER	3	7	710.281-022
RES	GAS-WELDING-EQUIPMENT MECHANIC	3	7	626.381-014
RES	GATHERING-MACHINE SETTER	3	8	653.360-018
RES	GELATIN MAKER, UTILITY	3	6	529.382-022
RES	GLASS-RIBBON-MACHINE-OPERATOR ASSISTANT	3	6	575.365-010
RES	GOLF-CLUB FACER	3	4	761.684-010
RES	GOLF-CLUB HEAD FORMER	3	6	732.381-018
RES	GOLF-CLUB REPAIRER	3	6	732.381-022
RES	GRADER, MEAT	3	5	525.387-010
RES	GRINDER SET-UP OPERATOR, CENTERLESS	3	5	603.382-014
RES	GRINDER SET-UP OPERATOR, THREAD	3	6	603.482-026
RES	GRIP	3	5	962.684-014
RES	GUN-REPAIR CLERK	3	3	222.387-022
RES	HAIR PREPARER	3	7	739.384-018
RES	HAIRSPRING TRUER	3	6	715.381-058
RES	HAIRSPRING VIBRATOR	3	6	715.381-062
RES	HAIRSPRING ASSEMBLER	3	5	715.381-054
RES	HAMMERSMITH	3	6	700.381-022
RES	HARNESS MAKER	3	7	783.381-018
RES	HATTER	3	6	369.384-010
RES	HEARSE UPHOLSTERER	3	5	780.381-026
RES	HEATER	3	6	613.362-010

Code	Title	GED	SVP	DOT No.
RES	HIGH RIGGER	3	6	962.664-010
RES	HONEYCOMB-BLANKET MAKER	3	5	806.684-062
RES	HOOK TENDER	3	7	921.131-010
RES	HORSE-RACE TIMER	3	3	153.367-014
RES	HOUSE BUILDER	3	7	869.281-014
RES	HUMIDIFIER ATTENDANT	3	6	950.485-010
RES	HYDRAULIC-PRESSURE-AUTO-FRETTAGE-MACHINE OPERATOR	3	5	694.682-014
RES	HYDRO-PNEUMATIC TESTER	3	4	862.687-018
RES	HYDROMETER CALIBRATOR	3	6	710.381-030
RES	IMPREGNATOR	3	4	590.682-014
RES	INCOMING-FREIGHT CLERK	3	5	248.362-010
RES	INDUSTRIAL-GAS-SERVICER HELPER	3	4	637.384-010
RES	INKER	3	4	659.667-010
RES	INSPECTOR	3	6	321.137-014
RES	INSPECTOR	3	4	579.664-014
RES	INSPECTOR	3	6	869.687-038
RES	INSPECTOR	3	4	709.687-022
RES	INSPECTOR AND SORTER	3	4	589.387-010
RES	INSPECTOR 1	3	6	619.364-010
RES	INSPECTOR 1	3	5	737.387-014
RES	INSPECTOR 4	3	5	559.387-010
RES	INSPECTOR, WIRE	3	5	691.367-010
RES	INSPECTOR, DIALS	3	4	715.687-066
RES	INSPECTOR, TOYS	3	4	731.687-022
RES	INSPECTOR, GOLF BALL	3	3	732.567-010
RES	INSPECTOR, SURFACE PROCESSING	3	5	806.387-010
RES	INSTALLER	3	4	869.684-026
RES	INSTALLER, MOVABLE BULKHEAD	3	4	806.684-074
RES	INSTRUCTOR, WEAVING	3	7	683.222-010
RES	INTELLIGENCE CLERK	3	6	249.387-014
RES	ION-EXCHANGE OPERATOR	3	3	558.685-034
RES	IRRIGATOR, HEAD	3	5	409.137-010
RES	JACQUARD-PLATE MAKER	3	5	685.381-010
RES	JANITOR	3	3	382.664-010
RES	KETTLE OPERATOR	3	4	522.682-010
RES	KETTLE TENDER, PLATINUM AND PALLADIUM	3	4	511.685-034
RES	KEYBOARD-ACTION ASSEMBLER	3	4	730.684-042
RES	LAPPER, HAND, TOOL	3	5	705.481-014
RES	LAUNDRY-MACHINE MECHANIC	3	6	629.261-010
RES	LAY-OUT WORKER	3	6	869.684-034
RES	LAY-OUT-MACHINE OPERATOR	3	4	781.684-034
RES	LEACHER	3	5	511.582-010
RES	LEAD BURNER, MACHINE	3	5	727.662-010
RES	LEAD OPERATOR, AUTOMATIC VULCANIZING	3	5	690.362-010
RES	LEATHER CUTTER	3	4	783.684-022
RES	LENS MOUNTER 2	3	6	713.681-010
RES	LETTERER	3	6	970.661-014
RES	LIME-KILN OPERATOR	3	4	559.685-118
RES	LINE MOVER	3	3	921.664-010
RES	LINE-UP EXAMINER	3	8	979.381-014
RES	LOAD-TEST MECHANIC	3	6	929.382-010

Code	Title	GED	SVP	DOT No.
RES	LOCK ASSEMBLER	3	6	706.684-070
RES	LOCKET MAKER	3	7	700.381-030
RES	LUBRICATION-EQUIPMENT SERVICER	3	6	630.381-022
RES	MACHINE ASSEMBLER	3	6	638.361-010
RES	MAINTENANCE-REPAIRER HELPER, FACTORY OR MILL	3	5	899.684-022
RES	MALT ROASTER	3	4	526.682-026
RES	MAPLE-SIRUP MAKER	3	5	523.382-014
RES	MARSHALL	3	4	153.384-010
RES	MASSEUR/MASSEUSE	3	4	334.374-010
RES	MAT-MACHINE OPERATOR	3	4	579.662-010
RES	MEAT DRESSER	3	6	525.664-010
RES	MECHANIC, AIRCRAFT ACCESSORIES	3	6	621.381-014
RES	MECHANIC, FIELD AND SERVICE	3	7	621.281-026
RES	MECHANICAL ASSEMBLER	3	4	806.684-082
RES	MENDER	3	4	782.684-042
RES	METAL-BONDING CRIB ATTENDANT	3	4	550.564-010
RES	METAL-BONDING PRESS OPERATOR	3	5	806.682-010
RES	MICROPHONE-BOOM OPERATOR	3	5	962.384-010
RES	MILLING-MACHINE OPERATOR, NUMERICAL CONTROL	3	7	605.380-010
RES	MIRROR-FINISHING-MACHINE OPERATOR	3	4	603.682-022
RES	MIXER OPERATOR, HOT METAL	3	5	509.362-010
RES	MIXER TENDER, BOARD	3	4	570.685-062
RES	MIXER-AND-BLENDER	3	4	520.685-154
RES	MIXING-MACHINE OPERATOR	3	4	550.485-014
RES	MOLD FINISHER	3	5	705.684-038
RES	MOLD MAKER 2	3	7	777.381-022
RES	MOLD MAKER	3	6	777.681-010
RES	MOLD STAMPER	3	6	709.684-054
RES	MOLDING SANDER	3	4	662.682-010
RES	MONOMER-PURIFICATION OPERATOR	3	5	552.362-010
RES	MOTOR AND CHASSIS INSPECTOR	3	6	806.281-042
RES	MOTORCYCLE ASSEMBLER	3	5	806.684-090
RES	MOTORCYCLE SUBASSEMBLER	3	5	806.684-094
RES	MOUTHPIECE MAKER	3	3	730.685-014
RES	MUD-PLANT OPERATOR	3	4	930.685-010
RES	MUFFLER INSTALLER	3	4	807.664-010
RES	MVA-REACTOR OPERATOR, HEAD	3	6	559.362-022
RES	NAIL-MAKING-MACHINE SETTER	3	6	616.460-010
RES	NET REPAIRER	3	6	449.664-010
RES	NICKEL-PLANT OPERATOR	3	6	519.362-010
RES	NICKING-MACHINE OPERATOR	3	5	609.682-026
RES	NITROCELLULOSE OPERATOR	3	4	553.684-014
RES	NUT FORMER	3	5	612.462-014
RES	ODD-SHOE EXAMINER	3	3	788.667-010
RES	OFFSET-DUPLICATING-MACHINE OPERATOR	3	5	207.682-018
RES	OFFSET-DUPLICATING-MACHINE OPERATOR	3	4	651.682-014
RES	OIL PUMPER	3	6	914.382-010
RES	OIL-BURNER-SERVICER-AND-INSTALLER	3	7	862.281-018
RES	OPAQUER	3	4	712.684-030
RES	OPTICAL-ELEMENT COATER	3	5	716.382-014
RES	OPTICAL-GLASS SILVERER	3	4	574.484-010
RES	ORTHODONTIC GOLD-BAND MAKER	3	6	712.381-026

Code	Title	GED	SVP	DOT No.
RES	OVEN OPERATOR, AUTOMATIC	3	4	526.682-030
RES	OVEN TENDER	3	4	526.685-030
RES	OVEN TENDER	3	3	553.685-082
RES	OVEN-EQUIPMENT REPAIRER	3	6	630.261-014
RES	PACKER, DENTURE	3	5	712.684-034
RES	PAINTER APPRENTICE, SHIPYARD	3	7	840.381-014
RES	PAINTER HELPER, SIGN	3	5	970.664-010
RES	PAINTER, AIRBRUSH	3	5	741.684-018
RES	PAINTER, SHIPYARD	3	7	840.381-018
RES	PAN HELPER	3	4	551.585-018
RES	PANEL-LAY-UP WORKER	3	4	761.684-018
RES	PANEL-MACHINE SETTER	3	6	640.360-010
RES	PANTOGRAPHER	3	4	979.382-022
RES	PARAFFIN-PLANT-SWEATER OPERATOR	3	4	543.682-022
RES	PARKING-METER SERVICER	3	4	710.384-026
RES	PASTEURIZER	3	2	523.585-026
RES	PEARL RESTORER	3	6	735.381-014
RES	PERCOLATOR OPERATOR	3	4	523.682-034
RES	PERFORATOR OPERATOR, OIL WELL	3	6	931.382-010
RES	PHOTOGRAPHIC-MACHINE OPERATOR	3	3	207.685-018
RES	PIE MAKER, MACHINE	3	4	526.685-038
RES	PIERCING-MACHINE OPERATOR	3	5	613.482-014
RES	PIPE INSTALLER	3	7	869.381-018
RES	PIPE-AND-TANK FABRICATOR	3	7	669.380-018
RES	PIPELINER	3	5	899.684-026
RES	PLANT OPERATOR, FURNACE PROCESS	3	5	559.362-026
RES	PLASTER MAKER	3	5	779.684-046
RES	PLASTER-DIE MAKER	3	5	774.684-026
RES	PLATE GRAINER	3	7	972.682-010
RES	PLATE MOLDER	3	4	556.582-010
RES	PLATE-GRAINER APPRENTICE	3	7	972.682-014
RES	PLATEN-PRESS OPERATOR	3	5	649.682-026
RES	PLATER	3	5	719.684-014
RES	PLODDER OPERATOR	3	4	556.682-018
RES	PLUGGING-MACHINE OPERATOR	3	4	669.682-062
RES	PNEUMATIC-TUBE REPAIRER	3	6	630.281-014
RES	PNEUMATIC-TOOL OPERATOR	3	7	809.381-030
RES	POLISHER	3	6	705.684-058
RES	POLISHER APPRENTICE	3	6	705.684-066
RES	PONY EDGER	3	6	667.682-050
RES	POT FIRER	3	5	553.582-014
RES	POT LINER	3	4	519.664-014
RES	POULTRY TENDER	3	5	411.364-014
RES	POWDER WORKER, TNT	3	4	737.684-030
RES	POWER OPERATOR	3	7	952.382-014
RES	POWER-SHOVEL OPERATOR	3	5	850.683-030
RES	PRECISION ASSEMBLER, BENCH	3	6	706.681-010
RES	PREDATORY-ANIMAL HUNTER	3	5	461.661-010
RES	PRESCRIPTION CLERK, LENS-AND-FRAMES	3	5	222.367-050
RES	PRINT-LINE OPERATOR	3	6	652.562-010
RES	PUG-MILL OPERATOR	3	4	510.685-022
RES	PULLEY-MORTISER OPERATOR	3	4	666.482-010
RES	PUMP INSTALLER	3	5	630.684-018
RES	PUMPER, HEAD	3	7	914.382-022

Code	Title	GED	SVP	DOT No.
RES	RAILROAD-CAR INSPECTOR	3	5	910.387-014
RES	RAW-SILK GRADER	3	4	689.687-062
RES	RECORDER	3	5	221.367-050
RES	RECORDING ENGINEER	3	7	194.362-010
RES	REED MAKER	3	6	709.381-038
RES	REFINER	3	4	712.684-038
RES	REFINING-MACHINE OPERATOR	3	6	521.682-034
RES	REGISTER REPAIRER	3	6	710.681-018
RES	REINFORCING-METAL WORKER	3	6	801.684-026
RES	REPAIRER 1	3	7	630.261-018
RES	REPAIRER 2	3	4	630.684-026
RES	REPAIRER, GENERAL	3	4	806.684-118
RES	REPAIRER, HANDTOOLS	3	5	701.381-010
RES	REPAIRER, MANUFACTURED BUILDINGS	3	4	869.384-010
RES	REPAIRER, SWITCHGEAR	3	5	729.684-038
RES	RETORT OPERATOR	3	5	526.682-034
RES	RETORT-OR-CONDENSER PRESS OPERATOR	3	4	575.382-026
RES	RETOUCHER, PHOTOENGRAVING	3	7	970.381-030
RES	RIGGER	3	4	869.683-014
RES	RIGGER HELPER	3	5	806.684-122
RES	RIGGING SLINGER	3	5	921.364-010
RES	RING MAKER	3	7	700.381-042
RES	RIVETER, PNEUMATIC	3	4	800.684-014
RES	RODEO PERFORMER	3	5	159.344-014
RES	ROLL BUILDER	3	5	801.564-010
RES	ROLL-TUBE SETTER	3	6	613.360-014
RES	ROLLER ENGRAVER, HAND	3	7	979.681-018
RES	ROLLER VARNISHER	3	6	979.682-022
RES	ROPE-MACHINE SETTER	3	6	681.380-010
RES	ROUGHER	3	7	613.362-018
RES	ROUTER OPERATOR, RADIAL	3	4	605.682-018
RES	ROVING INSPECTOR	3	5	710.367-010
RES	RUBBER TESTER	3	6	559.381-014
RES	RUG MEASURER	3	4	369.367-014
RES	RUG REPAIRER	3	6	782.381-018
RES	SAND MIXER, MACHINE	3	4	570.682-018
RES	SAWMILL WORKER	3	3	667.686-014
RES	SAWYER, OPTICAL GLASS	3	7	677.382-014
RES	SCANNER OPERATOR	3	6	972.282-010
RES	SCRAPER-LOADER OPERATOR	3	4	921.663-050
RES	SCRAPER, HAND	3	6	705.384-010
RES	SCREEN-AND-CYCLONE REPAIRER	3	4	630.664-014
RES	SECOND COOK AND BAKER	3	6	315.381-026
RES	SECTION LEADER AND MACHINE SETTER, POLISHING	3	5	689.260-022
RES	SERVICE MECHANIC	3	6	807.381-022
RES	SERVICE-UNIT OPERATOR, OIL WELL	3	7	930.361-010
RES	SET-UP MECHANIC, CROWN ASSEMBLY MACHINE	3	5	692.362-010
RES	SEWING-MACHINE REPAIRER	3	7	639.281-018
RES	SEWING-MACHINE ASSEMBLER	3	6	706.381-034
RES	SHACTOR	3	5	525.361-010
RES	SHAFT MECHANIC	3	5	899.684-034
RES	SHAKE SAWYER	3	4	667.682-070

Code	Title	GED	SVP	DOT No.
RES	SHEET-MILL SUPERVISOR	3	7	619.132-014
RES	SHIELD RUNNER	3	5	850.682-010
RES	SHOE-REPAIR SUPERVISOR	3	7	365.131-010
RES	SHOOTER	3	6	931.361-014
RES	SHREDDING-FLOOR-EQUIPMENT OPERATOR	3	5	559.382-050
RES	SILICA-FILTER OPERATOR	3	4	521.582-010
RES	SIRUP MIXER	3	5	529.462-010
RES	SIZER, MACHINE	3	7	716.360-010
RES	SKI MAKER, WOOD	3	5	761.381-026
RES	SKIN FITTER	3	7	806.381-054
RES	SLAB-CONDITIONER SUPERVISOR	3	6	609.132-010
RES	SLASHER TENDER	3	6	582.562-010
RES	SLIME-PLANT OPERATOR 1	3	6	510.685-030
RES	SLIPCOVER CUTTER	3	6	780.381-034
RES	SMOKE AND FLAME SPECIALIST	3	4	378.682-014
RES	SMOKE JUMPER SUPERVISOR	3	8	452.134-010
RES	SMOKER	3	4	525.682-010
RES	SOFT-SUGAR OPERATOR, HEAD	3	4	521.565-018
RES	SORTER-PRICER	3	5	222.387-054
RES	SORTING-GRAPPLE OPERATOR	3	6	921.683-066
RES	SOUND RANGING CREWMEMBER	3	5	378.362-010
RES	SOUVENIR AND NOVELTY MAKER	3	5	739.381-050
RES	SPAR-MACHINE OPERATOR	3	5	664.682-022
RES	SPEEDOMETER INSPECTOR	3	4	710.687-030
RES	SPINDLE CARVER	3	5	761.682-018
RES	SPONGE-PRESS OPERATOR	3	4	559.682-050
RES	SPOTTER	3	4	362.381-010
RES	SPRAY-DRIER OPERATOR	3	4	573.382-014
RES	SPRAY-GUN REPAIRER	3	7	630.381-026
RES	SPRING FORMER, HAND	3	7	709.381-042
RES	STEAK SAUCE MAKER	3	3	529.484-010
RES	STENCIL MAKER	3	6	979.381-038
RES	STERILE-PRODUCTS PROCESSOR	3	5	559.682-054
RES	STILL OPERATOR	3	4	522.685-098
RES	STILL-OPERATOR HELPER	3	3	552.685-030
RES	STOCK FITTER	3	6	788.685-018
RES	STOCK SHEETS CLEANER-INSPECTOR	3	4	779.687-034
RES	STONE REPAIRER	3	5	779.684-058
RES	STOREKEEPER	3	5	222.387-062
RES	STOVE TENDER	3	5	512.382-014
RES	STRAIGHT-LINE-PRESS SETTER	3	4	616.360-034
RES	STRAIGHTENING-ROLL OPERATOR	3	4	613.462-022
RES	STRETCH-MACHINE OPERATOR	3	5	559.682-058
RES	STRIPPING-SHOVEL OILER	3	6	850.684-018
RES	STROBOSCOPE OPERATOR	3	5	689.364-010
RES	STRONG-NITRIC OPERATOR	3	4	559.682-062
RES	SUGAR BOILER	3	6	522.382-034
RES	SUPERVISOR 1	3	5	575.130-014
RES	SUPERVISOR	3	6	690.130-010
RES	SUPERVISOR, LAUNDRY	3	6	361.137-010
RES	SUPERVISOR, PIT-AND-AUXILIARIES	3	6	514.137-014
RES	SUPERVISOR, MOLD CLEANING AND STORAGE	3	6	579.137-018
RES	SUPERVISOR, CONDITIONING YARD	3	8	619.134-010

Code	Title	GED	SVP	DOT No.
RES	SUPERVISOR, LOG SORTING	3	7	455.134-010
RES	SUPERVISOR, ALTERATION WORKROOM	3	6	785.131-010
RES	SUPERVISOR, CORNCOB PIPE MANUFACTURING	3	6	739.132-010
RES	SUPERVISOR, HARVESTING	3	5	939.137-022
RES	SUPERVISOR, EDGING	3	6	673.130-010
RES	SWAGING-MACHINE ADJUSTER	3	6	617.360-014
RES	TABLE OPERATOR	3	5	613.682-026
RES	TABLE TENDER	3	4	511.685-062
RES	TANK-HOUSE OPERATOR	3	6	519.362-014
RES	TAPER	3	5	842.664-010
RES	TEST DRIVER 1	3	6	806.281-050
RES	TESTER, CONVERTIBLE SOFA BEDSPRING	3	4	780.684-110
RES	TESTER, ELECTRONIC SCALE	3	6	710.381-046
RES	THREADING-MACHINE OPERATOR	3	5	604.682-014
RES	TIMBER FRAMER	3	6	869.381-034
RES	TIMING ADJUSTER	3	6	715.681-010
RES	TINNING-MACHINE SET-UP OPERATOR	3	5	653.682-022
RES	TIRE-FABRIC-IMPREGNATING-RANGE OPERATOR, CHIEF	3	5	589.662-014
RES	TONE CABINET ASSEMBLER	3	3	730.684-090
RES	TOOL DRESSER	3	5	601.682-010
RES	TOOL GRINDER 1	3	6	701.381-018
RES	TOOL-CRIB ATTENDANT	3	5	222.367-062
RES	TOP POLISHER	3	6	673.662-010
RES	TOWER-EXCAVATOR OPERATOR	3	5	850.683-042
RES	TRANSMISSION MECHANIC	3	7	620.281-062
RES	TRAPPER, ANIMAL	3	5	461.684-014
RES	TRAWL NET MAKER	3	6	789.381-018
RES	TREATING ENGINEER	3	6	561.362-010
RES	TRIM-MACHINE ADJUSTER	3	5	609.280-010
RES	TRIMMER OPERATOR	3	5	619.462-014
RES	TROUBLE SHOOTER 1	3	5	952.364-010
RES	TUBE BENDER, BRASS-WIND INSTRUMENTS	3	4	617.382-010
RES	TUBE BENDER, HAND 1	3	4	709.684-090
RES	TUNNEL-KILN OPERATOR	3	5	573.382-018
RES	TURBINE ATTENDANT	3	4	952.567-010
RES	USED-CAR RENOVATOR	3	4	620.684-034
RES	UTILITY WORKER, LINE ASSEMBLY	3	4	806.367-010
RES	UTILITY WORKER	3	5	869.684-074
RES	VACUUM-DRIER TENDER	3	4	553.685-106
RES	VALVE GRINDER	3	5	706.684-098
RES	VAN DRIVER	3	4	905.663-018
RES	VULCANIZED-FIBER-UNIT OPERATOR	3	5	539.565-010
RES	WARDROBE SUPERVISOR	3	7	346.361-010
RES	WEIGHER-AND-CRUSHER	3	4	515.567-010
RES	WELD INSPECTOR 2	3	4	819.687-010
RES	WELDER-ASSEMBLER	3	6	819.381-010
RES	WELDER, EXPLOSION	3	5	814.684-010
RES	WHEELWRIGHT	3	5	706.381-046
RES	WICKER WORKER	3	5	763.684-078
RES	WIRE WEAVER, CLOTH	3	7	616.382-014
RES	WIRE-ROPE-SLING MAKER	3	5	709.684-102
RES	WIRE-WRAPPING-MACHINE OPERATOR	3	4	692.662-022

Code	Title	GED	SVP	DOT No.
RES	WIRER	3	6	729.281-042
RES	WOOL-FLEECE GRADER	3	4	589.687-054
RES	YARD COUPLER	3	4	910.664-010
RES	YARDAGE-CONTROL OPERATOR, FORMING	3	5	575.662-014
RES	YARDING ENGINEER	3	6	921.663-066
RES	ACID DUMPER	2	2	727.687-010
RES	AIR-AND-WATER FILLER	2	2	764.687-010
RES	ALMOND-CUTTING-MACHINE TENDER	2	3	521.685-018
RES	AMPHIBIAN CREWMEMBER	2	3	378.683-010
RES	ANIMAL EVISCERATOR	2	3	525.687-010
RES	ASSEMBLER	2	2	733.685-010
RES	ASSEMBLER HELPER, INTERNAL COMBUSTION ENGINE	2	2	801.687-010
RES	ASSEMBLER, WET WASH	2	2	361.687-010
RES	ASSEMBLER, GARMENT FORM	2	2	739.687-022
RES	ASSEMBLER, BICYCLE 1	2	4	806.684-014
RES	ATTENDANT, CAMPGROUND	2	2	329.683-010
RES	AUTOMOBILE-ACCESSORIES INSTALLER	2	4	806.684-038
RES	AUTOMOBILE-BUMPER STRAIGHTENER	2	3	807.684-010
RES	AUTOMOBILE-BODY-REPAIRER HELPER	2	2	807.687-010
RES	AWNING-HANGER HELPER	2	3	869.687-010
RES	BACK WASHER	2	2	582.685-010
RES	BACKING-IN-MACHINE TENDER	2	2	590.685-010
RES	BAGGER	2	2	920.687-014
RES	BAKER HELPER	2	3	313.684-010
RES	BALE-TIE-MACHINE OPERATOR	2	4	616.682-014
RES	BALING-MACHINE TENDER	2	2	920.685-010
RES	BALL-FRINGE-MACHINE OPERATOR	2	3	689.685-010
RES	BALLOON DIPPER	2	2	599.687-010
RES	BANDING-MACHINE OPERATOR	2	3	619.685-018
RES	BARKER OPERATOR	2	3	663.682-010
RES	BARREL-ASSEMBLER HELPER	2	2	669.685-010
RES	BARREL-CHARRER HELPER	2	2	764.687-034
RES	BARREL-LATHE OPERATOR, OUTSIDE	2	4	664.682-014
RES	BARREL-RAISER HELPER	2	2	764.687-038
RES	BEATER-AND-PULPER FEEDER	2	2	530.686-010
RES	BINDER-AND-WRAPPER PACKER	2	2	922.687-014
RES	BINDERY WORKER	2	3	649.685-018
RES	BLACKSMITH HELPER	2	4	610.684-010
RES	BLANCHING-MACHINE OPERATOR	2	3	523.685-014
RES	BLANKET WASHER	2	2	511.687-010
RES	BLANKET-WINDER HELPER	2	2	641.686-010
RES	BLAST-FURNACE-KEEPER HELPER	2	3	502.687-010
RES	BLOCK-BREAKER OPERATOR	2	2	555.686-010
RES	BLOCK-MAKING-MACHINE OPERATOR	2	3	575.685-014
RES	BLOCK-SPLITTER OPERATOR	2	3	663.685-010
RES	BLOW-PIT HELPER	2	2	533.686-010
RES	BLOW-PIT OPERATOR	2	3	533.665-010
RES	BOARD-LINER OPERATOR	2	3	641.685-014
RES	BOAT-LOADER HELPER	2	2	911.687-010
RES	BOILER RELINER, PLASTIC BLOCK	2	4	849.484-010
RES	BOILER-ROOM HELPER	2	4	950.685-014
RES	BOILERMAKER HELPER 2	2	5	805.664-010
RES	BOILERMAKER HELPER 1	2	2	805.687-010

Code	Title	GED	SVP	DOT No.
RES	BOTTOM MAKER	2	3	509.687-010
RES	BOTTOM-HOLE-PRESSURE-RECORDING- OPERATOR HELPER	2	3	930.687-010
RES	BOTTOM-HOOP DRIVER	2	3	669.685-022
RES	BOTTOMER 1	2	3	932.667-010
RES	BOWLING-BALL MOLDER	2	3	556.685-018
RES	BOWLING-BALL-MOLD ASSEMBLER	2	2	556.687-010
RES	BOX-BLANK-MACHINE-OPERATOR HELPER	2	2	669.686-014
RES	BOX-SPRING MAKER 2	2	3	780.684-022
RES	BRAKE-LINING-FINISHER HELPER, ASBESTOS	2	2	579.687-010
RES	BRANDING-MACHINE TENDER	2	3	690.685-042
RES	BREAK-OFF WORKER	2	2	663.686-014
RES	BREAKING-MACHINE OPERATOR	2	2	521.685-034
RES	BRICKLAYER HELPER, FIREBRICK AND REFRACTORY TILE	2	3	861.687-010
RES	BRIQUETTE-MACHINE-OPERATOR HELPER	2	2	549.686-010
RES	BRUSH MAKER, MACHINE	2	2	739.685-014
RES	BURN-OUT TENDER, LACE	2	3	589.685-018
RES	BUSHER	2	2	502.687-014
RES	BUTTON GRADER	2	4	734.687-038
RES	CAGER	2	3	939.667-010
RES	CAGER OPERATOR	2	2	921.685-018
RES	CALENDER-OPERATOR HELPER	2	2	554.686-018
RES	CAMOUFLAGE SPECIALIST	2	4	378.684-010
RES	CANDLE MOLDER, MACHINE	2	4	692.685-038
RES	CAPACITOR-PACK-PRESS OPERATOR	2	4	726.684-010
RES	CAR ICER	2	2	910.687-018
RES	CARBON-PAPER INTERLEAFER	2	2	640.685-018
RES	CARPET-LAYER HELPER	2	3	864.687-010
RES	CARRIER PACKER	2	2	920.687-066
RES	CARTON-FORMING-MACHINE HELPER	2	2	641.686-014
RES	CASE-MAKING-MACHINE OPERATOR	2	4	653.685-018
RES	CASTER	2	3	502.482-010
RES	CASTER	2	4	575.684-018
RES	CASTER HELPER	2	3	700.687-022
RES	CASTING-HOUSE WORKER	2	2	514.687-014
RES	CASTING-MACHINE-OPERATOR HELPER	2	2	502.686-010
RES	CASTING-MACHINE-SERVICE OPERATOR	2	3	559.687-018
RES	CATCHER	2	3	613.686-010
RES	CELL CLEANER	2	2	559.687-022
RES	CELL PLASTERER	2	3	519.687-010
RES	CELL PREPARER	2	2	556.687-014
RES	CELL STRIPPER	2	2	556.686-014
RES	CEMENTER, HAND	2	2	788.687-030
RES	CENTRIFUGE OPERATOR	2	2	551.685-034
RES	CHAINSAW OPERATOR	2	2	454.687-010
RES	CHANNEL INSTALLER	2	2	764.687-046
RES	CHAR-DUST CLEANER AND SALVAGER	2	2	529.687-038
RES	CHAR-FILTER-OPERATOR HELPER	2	3	521.687-034
RES	CHASER	2	3	921.667-014
RES	CHASSIS INSPECTOR	2	3	806.687-014
RES	CHAUFFEUR	2	3	359.673-010
RES	CHAUFFEUR, FUNERAL CAR	2	4	359.673-014

Code	Title	GED	SVP	DOT No.
RES	CHERRY-PICKER OPERATOR	2	3	921.663-014
RES	CIRCUS LABORER	2	2	969.687-010
RES	CLAMP-JIG ASSEMBLER	2	2	762.687-022
RES	CLEANER	2	2	869.687-018
RES	CLEANER, LABORATORY EQUIPMENT	2	2	381.687-022
RES	CLIPPER	2	2	753.687-010
RES	CLOTH DOFFER	2	2	689.586-010
RES	CLOTH EXAMINER, HAND	2	3	781.687-014
RES	CLOTH SHADER	2	4	582.685-026
RES	CLOTH TEARER	2	2	781.687-018
RES	CLOTH-BOLT BANDER	2	2	920.587-010
RES	COAL TRIMMER	2	3	911.687-018
RES	COATING-MACHINE OPERATOR	2	2	692.685-054
RES	COATING-MIXER TENDER	2	2	530.685-010
RES	COCOA-BEAN-ROASTER HELPER	2	2	523.666-010
RES	COIL ASSEMBLER, MACHINE	2	4	616.685-018
RES	COIL BINDER	2	2	619.687-010
RES	COLD-PRESS LOADER	2	3	701.687-018
RES	COLUMN PRECASTER	2	2	869.667-010
RES	COMBAT RIFLE CREWMEMBER	2	3	378.684-014
RES	COMPOUND-COATING-MACHINE OFFBEARER	2	2	509.666-010
RES	COMPRESSOR OPERATOR	2	2	559.685-038
RES	CONDITIONER-TUMBLER OPERATOR	2	2	361.685-010
RES	CONDITIONER TENDER	2	3	587.685-022
RES	CONE TREATER	2	2	534.687-010
RES	CONSTRUCTION-EQUIPMENT-MECHANIC HELPER	2	3	620.664-010
RES	CONSTRUCTION WORKER 2	2	2	869.687-026
RES	CONTACT-ACID-PLANT-OPERATOR HELPER	2	2	559.687-026
RES	COOK HELPER, PASTRY	2	3	313.687-010
RES	COOK HELPER	2	2	317.687-010
RES	COOKER	2	3	526.685-022
RES	COOLER TENDER	2	4	520.585-018
RES	COOPER HELPER	2	2	764.687-050
RES	CORE-DRILL-OPERATOR HELPER	2	2	930.687-014
RES	CORN-PRESS OPERATOR	2	3	529.685-078
RES	CORNER FORMER	2	3	617.685-014
RES	CORRUGATOR-OPERATOR HELPER	2	2	641.686-018
RES	COUNTER-SUPPLY WORKER	2	2	319.687-010
RES	COVERING-MACHINE-OPERATOR HELPER	2	3	681.685-042
RES	CRATE LINER	2	2	920.687-078
RES	CRATE OPENER	GED	2	929.685-010
RES	CRIMP SETTER	2	3	680.685-026
RES	CRUSHER OPERATOR	2	3	521.685-090
RES	CRUSHER SETTER	2	3	933.664-010
RES	CRUTCHER HELPER	2	2	550.686-018
RES	CURING-BIN OPERATOR	2	3	522.685-038
RES	CUTTER-OPERATOR HELPER	2	2	930.687-018
RES	CUTTER, BANANA ROOM	2	2	929.687-010
RES	CUTTING-MACHINE-TENDER HELPER	2	2	690.686-030
RES	CYLINDER-DIE-MACHINE HELPER	2	2	649.686-018
RES	DAY WORKER	2	2	301.687-014
RES	DEHYDRATOR TENDER	2	3	523.685-054
RES	DEMOLITION SPECIALIST	2	4	737.687-034

Code	Title	GED	SVP	DOT No.
RES	DEODORIZER	2	3	522.685-046
RES	DERRICK WORKER, WELL SERVICE	2	3	930.683-018
RES	DEVULCANIZER CHARGER	2	2	558.666-010
RES	DEWAXER	2	2	710.687-022
RES	DIE TRIPPER	2	2	575.665-014
RES	DIGGER	2	3	739.687-070
RES	DISTILLATION-OPERATOR HELPER	2	2	552.687-010
RES	DISTRESSER	2	3	763.687-018
RES	DOLLY PUSHER	2	2	962.687-010
RES	DOOR CORE ASSEMBLER	2	2	762.687-030
RES	DRAW-BENCH-OPERATOR HELPER	2	2	614.686-010
RES	DRESSER	2	2	788.687-038
RES	DRIER OPERATOR	2	2	553.686-026
RES	DRIER TENDER	2	3	523.685-066
RES	DROPPER, FERMENTING CELLAR	2	2	522.685-054
RES	DRUM LOADER AND UNLOADER	2	2	522.685-058
RES	DRY CURER	2	2	525.687-026
RES	DRY-CLEANER HELPER	2	2	362.686-010
RES	DRY-KILN OPERATOR HELPER	2	3	573.687-014
RES	DUST PULLER	2	2	519.687-014
RES	DYE WEIGHER	2	3	550.684-014
RES	DYER	2	2	562.687-010
RES	DYER HELPER	2	3	364.687-010
RES	DYNAMITE-PACKING-MACHINE FEEDER	2	2	692.686-038
RES	EDGE SETTER	2	3	690.685-146
RES	EDGER-MACHINE HELPER	2	2	673.686-018
RES	ELASTIC-TAPE INSERTER	2	2	782.687-022
RES	ELECTROFORMER	2	4	500.684-010
RES	ELEVATOR OPERATOR, FREIGHT	2	2	921.683-038
RES	EMBOSSING-MACHINE TENDER	2	2	649.685-038
RES	ETCHER HELPER, HAND	2	2	971.687-010
RES	EXAMINER	2	4	979.687-010
RES	EXPANSION ENVELOPE MAKER, HAND	2	2	794.684-018
RES	EXTRACTOR OPERATOR	2	2	551.685-054
RES	EXTRACTOR OPERATOR	2	3	582.685-062
RES	EXTRACTOR-OPERATOR HELPER	2	2	552.686-010
RES	EXTRUDING-MACHINE OPERATOR	2	3	557.565-010
RES	EXTRUDING-PRESS OPERATOR	2	4	614.685-010
RES	FABRIC NORMALIZER	2	3	559.685-066
RES	FALLER 2	2	3	454.684-014
RES	FARMWORKER, DAIRY	2	4	410.684-010
RES	FELT HANGER	2	2	549.686-014
RES	FERRYBOAT OPERATOR, CABLE	2	3	911.664-010
RES	FIG CAPRIFIER	2	2	403.687-014
RES	FILM LOADER	2	2	962.687-014
RES	FILTER OPERATOR	2	3	521.685-126
RES	FILTER WASHER	2	2	559.687-042
RES	FINISHER	2	2	554.586-010
RES	FINISHER	2	4	749.684-026
RES	FIRER, KILN	2	3	523.685-078
RES	FIRER, LOW PRESSURE	2	5	951.685-014
RES	FISHER, NET	2	4	441.684-010
RES	FISHER, WEIR	2	4	441.684-022
RES	FITTER HELPER	2	3	801.687-014

Code	Title	GED	SVP	DOT No.
RES	FLAME-HARDENING-MACHINE OPERATOR	2	2	504.685-014
RES	FLATCAR WHACKER	2	3	807.667-010
RES	FLEECE TIER	2	2	410.687-010
RES	FLOOR ATTENDANT	2	2	579.687-018
RES	FLOOR WORKER, WELL SERVICE	2	3	930.684-014
RES	FOLDER	2	2	369.687-018
RES	FORCE-VARIATION EQUIPMENT TENDER	2	2	690.685-182
RES	FOREST WORKER	2	2	452.687-010
RES	FOREST-FIRE FIGHTER	2	2	452.687-014
RES	FOREST-PRODUCTS GATHERER	2	2	453.687-010
RES	FORMING-ROLL OPERATOR 2	2	3	619.685-046
RES	FOUNDRY WORKER, GENERAL	2	2	519.687-022
RES	FRAME-TABLE-OPERATOR HELPER	2	2	669.685-058
RES	FRAZER	2	3	664.685-022
RES	FREEZING-ROOM WORKER	2	2	523.587-018
RES	FRIT-MIXER-AND-BURNER	2	4	579.685-014
RES	FURNACE-INSTALLER-AND-REPAIRER HELPER, HOT AIR	2	2	869.687-030
RES	FURNITURE CLEANER	2	3	362.684-022
RES	FUSE MAKER	2	3	559.685-094
RES	GAS-PUMPING-STATION HELPER	2	4	953.684-010
RES	GILL-BOX TENDER	2	3	680.685-058
RES	GLAZE HANDLER	2	4	571.685-014
RES	GLUE-MILL OPERATOR	2	3	559.685-098
RES	GLUER	2	3	762.687-034
RES	GLUER AND SLICER, HAND	2	2	794.687-030
RES	GLUING-MACHINE OFFBEARER	2	2	569.686-022
RES	GOODS LAYER	2	2	781.687-038
RES	GRAIN DRIER	2	2	523.685-086
RES	GRAIN-WAFER-MACHINE OPERATOR	2	3	523.685-094
RES	GRAINING-PRESS OPERATOR	2	3	557.682-010
RES	GRAVES REGISTRATION SPECIALIST	2	3	355.687-014
RES	GRINDER-CHIPPER 2	2	3	809.684-026
RES	GRIP	2	5	962.687-022
RES	GROUND MIXER	2	2	550.685-066
RES	GUM PULLER	2	2	520.687-038
RES	HAIR-BOILER OPERATOR	2	2	582.685-086
RES	HANDLE ASSEMBLER	2	2	762.687-042
RES	HANDLE-MACHINE OPERATOR	2	3	649.685-050
RES	HARDWARE ASSEMBLER	2	2	762.684-046
RES	HARNESS-AND-BAG INSPECTOR	2	2	789.687-086
RES	HASSOCK MAKER	2	2	780.687-018
RES	HAT-STOCK-LAMINATING-MACHINE OPERATOR	2	4	584.685-026
RES	HATCH TENDER	2	2	911.667-014
RES	HEAD-MACHINE FEEDER	2	2	525.686-018
RES	HEADER	2	2	764.687-058
RES	HEAT READER	2	3	612.687-010
RES	HEATER HELPER	2	4	613.685-014
RES	HELPER, METAL BONDING	2	3	806.687-022
RES	HIDE TRIMMER	2	3	525.687-046
RES	HOGSHEAD COOPER 1	2	2	764.684-026
RES	HOGSHEAD COOPER 2	2	2	764.687-070
RES	HOGSHEAD COOPER 3	2	2	764.687-074

Code	Title	GED	SVP	DOT No.
RES	HOGSHEAD OPENER	2	2	920.687-102
RES	HONEYCOMB DECAPPER	2	3	521.687-070
RES	HOOP-MAKER HELPER, MACHINE	2	2	619.686-014
RES	HORTICULTURAL WORKER 2	2	2	405.687-014
RES	HOSE CUTTER, MACHINE	2	2	751.686-010
RES	HOSE WRAPPER	2	2	759.684-038
RES	HOSE-COUPLING JOINER	2	2	759.687-014
RES	HOSE-TUBING BACKER	2	2	559.686-018
RES	ICER, MACHINE	2	3	524.685-034
RES	INFANTRY WEAPONS CREWMEMBER	2	3	378.684-026
RES	INSPECTOR, FILTER TIP	2	3	529.667-010
RES	INSPECTOR, ALUMINUM BOAT	2	3	806.687-026
RES	INSTALLER	2	2	922.687-050
RES	INSTALLER, DOOR FURRING	2	2	806.687-034
RES	INSTALLER, METAL FLOORING	2	4	806.684-070
RES	JET-DYEING-MACHINE TENDER	2	3	582.685-090
RES	JEWEL-HOLE CORNERER	2	3	770.684-014
RES	KILN-BURNER HELPER	2	3	573.687-026
RES	KITCHEN HELPER	2	2	318.687-010
RES	KNOCK-UP ASSEMBLER	2	2	762.687-050
RES	LABORER	2	2	559.686-022
RES	LABORER, AIRPORT MAINTENANCE	2	2	899.687-014
RES	LABORER, AMMUNITION ASSEMBLY 1	2	3	737.687-070
RES	LABORER, AMMUNITION ASSEMBLY 2	2	2	737.687-074
RES	LABORER, AQUATIC LIFE	2	2	446.687-014
RES	LABORER, BOOT AND SHOE	2	2	788.687-066
RES	LABORER, CANVAS SHOP	2	2	789.687-090
RES	LABORER, CONSTRUCTION OR LEAK GANG	2	4	862.684-014
RES	LABORER, GENERAL	2	2	519.686-010
RES	LABORER, GENERAL	2	2	609.684-014
RES	LABORER, GENERAL	2	2	754.687-010
RES	LABORER, GOLD LEAF	2	2	700.687-038
RES	LABORER, LANDSCAPE	2	2	408.687-014
RES	LABORER, PETROLEUM REFINERY	2	3	549.687-018
RES	LABORER, PIE BAKERY	2	2	529.686-054
RES	LABORER, PIPE-LINES	2	2	914.687-010
RES	LABORER, POWERHOUSE	2	3	952.665-010
RES	LABORER, STARCH FACTORY	2	3	529.685-154
RES	LABORER, STORES	2	2	922.687-058
RES	LABORER, WOOD-PRESERVING PLANT	2	2	561.686-010
RES	LACE-PAPER-MACHINE OPERATOR	2	3	649.685-058
RES	LAMINATOR, PREFORMS	2	4	754.484-010
RES	LAMINATOR, HAND	2	3	763.684-050
RES	LATEXER	2	3	584.684-010
RES	LATHE SPOTTER	2	3	663.686-022
RES	LAUNDERER, HAND	2	2	361.684-010
RES	LEAD HANDLER	2	3	599.687-018
RES	LEASING-MACHINE TENDER	2	2	681.685-054
RES	LENS EXAMINER	2	4	716.687-022
RES	LENS-MOLDING-EQUIPMENT OPERATOR	2	3	575.685-054
RES	LINER REPLACER	2	3	801.664-010
RES	LINER-MACHINE OPERATOR	2	3	641.685-058
RES	LINER-MACHINE-OPERATOR HELPER	2	2	641.686-022
RES	LINES TENDER	2	2	911.687-026

Code	Title	GED	SVP	DOT No.
RES	LINING INSERTER	2	2	732.687-042
RES	LINKER	2	3	529.687-150
RES	LINSEED-OIL-PRESS TENDER	2	3	559.685-122
RES	LOADER	2	3	921.687-018
RES	LOADER-UNLOADER, SCREEN-PRINTING MACHINE	2	2	652.686-022
RES	LOADER, MAGAZINE GRINDER	2	2	530.686-014
RES	LOADING-SHOVEL OILER	2	3	932.667-014
RES	LOCKER-ROOM ATTENDANT	2	2	358.677-014
RES	LOGGER, ALL-ROUND	2	4	454.684-018
RES	LONG-GOODS HELPER, MACHINE	2	2	529.686-062
RES	LOOM CHANGEOVER OPERATOR	2	3	683.687-030
RES	LOOM-WINDER TENDER	2	2	681.685-062
RES	LOZENGE-DOUGH MIXER	2	4	520.685-122
RES	LUBRICATION SERVICER	2	4	915.687-018
RES	LUMBER STRAIGHTENER	2	2	669.687-018
RES	MACHINE HELPER	2	2	586.686-022
RES	MACHINE HELPER	2	2	819.666-010
RES	MAGNESIUM-MILL OPERATOR	2	2	607.686-010
RES	MATCHBOOK ASSEMBLER	2	3	649.685-074
RES	MECHANICAL ASSEMBLER, PANELING	2	3	807.684-030
RES	MELT-HOUSE DRAG OPERATOR	2	3	529.687-158
RES	MERCURY WASHER	2	3	551.685-098
RES	METAL FABRICATOR HELPER	2	4	619.685-066
RES	METAL-BED ASSEMBLER	2	3	706.684-082
RES	METAL-SPRAYING-MACHINE OPERATOR, AUTOMATIC 2	2	2	505.685-014
RES	MILL HAND, PLATE MILL	2	4	613.667-014
RES	MILLER	2	2	570.685-038
RES	MIXER	2	4	559.665-026
RES	MIXER OPERATOR	2	3	550.685-082
RES	MIXER, CHILI POWDER	2	3	520.685-158
RES	MIXER, WHIPPED TOPPING	2	3	520.385-010
RES	MIXING-MACHINE OPERATOR	2	2	520.665-014
RES	MOLD CLEANER	2	2	556.687-018
RES	MOLD CLOSER	2	3	518.684-018
RES	MOLD FILLER, PLASTIC DOLLS	2	3	731.687-026
RES	MOLD PARTER	2	2	556.587-010
RES	MOLD PRESSER	2	2	790.687-022
RES	MOLD-INSERT CHANGER	2	3	753.687-034
RES	MOLDER, FOAM RUBBER	2	3	556.685-046
RES	MOLDER, INFLATED BALL	2	2	732.687-054
RES	MOLDER, MEAT	2	2	520.685-174
RES	MOLDER, PIPE COVERING	2	3	556.665-018
RES	MOLDER, WAX BALL	2	2	732.687-058
RES	MOLDING-MACHINE TENDER	2	2	570.685-066
RES	MOTTLER OPERATOR	2	3	550.665-022
RES	MULTIPLE-DRUM-SANDER HELPER	2	2	662.686-014
RES	NITROGLYCERIN DISTRIBUTOR	2	2	559.664-010
RES	NOODLE MAKER	2	3	529.385-010
RES	NUT ROASTER	2	3	529.685-174
RES	OPENER TENDER	2	2	680.685-070
RES	ORNAMENTAL-METAL-WORKER HELPER	2	5	619.484-010
RES	OVEN OPERATOR	2	3	526.585-010

Code	Title	GED	SVP	DOT No.
RES	OVERLAY PLASTICIAN	2	4	806.684-106
RES	PACKAGER, HAND	2	2	920.587-018
RES	PACKER, AGRICULTURAL PRODUCE	2	2	920.687-134
RES	PACKER, INSULATION	2	2	579.685-038
RES	PACKING-FLOOR WORKER	2	2	920.686-026
RES	PAD MAKER	2	3	589.687-030
RES	PADDING GLUER	2	2	780.687-034
RES	PAINT MIXER, MACHINE	2	3	550.485-018
RES	PAINTER HELPER, SPRAY	2	2	741.687-014
RES	PAINTER, EMBOSSED OR IMPRESSED LETTERING	2	2	740.687-018
RES	PAPER-CUP-MACHINE OPERATOR	2	3	649.685-078
RES	PAPER-PROCESSING-MACHINE HELPER	2	2	534.686-010
RES	PARACHUTE FOLDER	2	3	789.684-034
RES	PASTING INSPECTOR	2	4	773.687-010
RES	PATCH FINISHER	2	2	582.684-010
RES	PEANUT-BUTTER MAKER	2	4	529.685-178
RES	PICKLE PUMPER	2	3	522.685-086
RES	PICKLING SOLUTION MAKER	2	3	522.485-010
RES	PIPE CHANGER	2	3	891.564-010
RES	PIPE-SMOKER-MACHINE OPERATOR	2	2	739.687-150
RES	PITCH FILLER	2	2	619.687-018
RES	PLASTIC-JOINT MAKER	2	3	590.687-014
RES	PLATE-TAKE-OUT WORKER	2	2	500.687-010
RES	PLOW-AND-BORING-MACHINE TENDER	2	2	665.685-018
RES	PLUGGER	2	2	613.687-010
RES	POPCORN-CANDY MAKER	2	3	526.685-042
RES	PORTER, MARINA	2	3	329.677-010
RES	PORTER, SAMPLE CASE	2	2	299.687-010
RES	POWDER-MILL OPERATOR	2	4	521.585-018
RES	POWER-CHISEL OPERATOR	2	2	701.687-030
RES	PRESS HELPER	2	2	651.586-010
RES	PRESS OPERATOR	2	2	551.685-114
RES	PRESS-MACHINE OPERATOR	2	2	590.665-014
RES	PRESSER	2	3	575.685-074
RES	PRETZEL COOKER	2	3	526.685-054
RES	PRINTER-SLOTTER HELPER	2	2	659.686-014
RES	PRINTING-ROLLER HANDLER	2	2	652.385-010
RES	PRIZER	2	2	920.687-142
RES	PULP-PRESS TENDER	2	3	532.685-026
RES	PULVERIZER	2	2	555.685-046
RES	PUMPER HELPER	2	2	914.687-018
RES	QUARRY WORKER	2	2	939.667-014
RES	REDUCING-SALON ATTENDANT	2	2	359.567-010
RES	REDUCTION-FURNACE-OPERATOR HELPER	2	2	559.686-038
RES	REELER	2	2	640.685-054
RES	REELER	2	3	549.685-022
RES	REELER	2	2	769.684-034
RES	REFRIGERATION-MECHANIC HELPER	2	2	637.687-014
RES	REPAIRER HELPER	2	3	630.664-010
RES	REVERSER	2	2	732.687-066
RES	RIBBON CUTTER	2	2	781.687-050
RES	RIVETER HELPER	2	3	800.687-010
RES	RODDING-ANODE WORKER	2	3	519.687-034

Code	Title	GED	SVP	DOT No.
RES	ROLL FINISHER	2	2	920.685-090
RES	ROLLER	2	3	806.687-046
RES	ROLLING-MACHINE OPERATOR	2	3	520.685-198
RES	ROUND-UP-RING HAND	2	3	579.587-010
RES	ROUNDING-MACHINE TENDER	2	2	663.685-026
RES	RUBBER	2	2	334.677-010
RES	RUBBER-CUTTING-MACHINE TENDER	2	2	690.685-342
RES	RUG-CLEANER HELPER	2	2	362.686-014
RES	RUG-DYER HELPER	2	3	364.687-014
RES	RUG-FRAME MOUNTER	2	3	687.464-010
RES	SALVAGER	2	3	729.687-030
RES	SALVAGER HELPER	2	4	709.687-034
RES	SAND FILLER	2	2	939.687-034
RES	SCARF GLUER	2	4	762.684-054
RES	SCORER HELPER	2	2	641.686-030
RES	SCRAP BALLER	2	3	509.685-046
RES	SCRAP SORTER	2	2	509.686-018
RES	SCREEN TENDER, CHIPS	2	3	533.685-026
RES	SCREEN-PRINTING-MACHINE-OPERATOR HELPER	2	2	652.686-038
RES	SENSITIZED-PAPER TESTER	2	3	714.667-010
RES	SERVICE-MECHANIC HELPER, COMPRESSED-GAS EQUIPMENT	2	4	630.664-018
RES	SEXTON	2	2	389.667-010
RES	SHAPER, BASEBALL GLOVE	2	2	732.684-106
RES	SHEAR-GRINDER-OPERATOR HELPER	2	2	628.687-014
RES	SHEEP HERDER	2	3	410.687-022
RES	SHINGLE PACKER	2	2	920.687-158
RES	SHIPPING PROCESSOR	2	2	920.687-162
RES	SHOE-REPAIRER HELPER	2	4	365.674-010
RES	SHORE HAND, DREDGE OR BARGE	2	4	939.667-018
RES	SHREDDED-FILLER HOPPER-FEEDER	2	2	529.687-182
RES	SHUTTLE SPOTTER	2	2	664.685-026
RES	SIGNALER	2	2	869.667-014
RES	SIZER	2	3	582.687-026
RES	SIZING-MACHINE TENDER	2	2	662.685-030
RES	SKEIN-YARN-DYER HELPER	2	2	582.686-022
RES	SKINNING-MACHINE FEEDER	2	2	525.686-022
RES	SLASHER-TENDER HELPER	2	2	582.686-026
RES	SLITTER-CREASER-SLOTTER OPERATOR	2	4	649.682-034
RES	SLITTER-CREASER-SLOTTER HELPER	2	2	649.686-030
RES	SLIVER-LAP-MACHINE TENDER	2	2	680.685-094
RES	SLOT-TAG INSERTER	2	2	222.567-018
RES	SLUNK-SKIN CURER	2	2	525.687-106
RES	SOAP GRINDER	2	2	555.685-062
RES	SOFTBALL CORE MOLDER	2	2	732.687-070
RES	SORTER	2	3	573.687-034
RES	SORTER OPERATOR	2	4	921.685-054
RES	SORTING-MACHINE OPERATOR	2	2	521.685-318
RES	SPAR-MACHINE-OPERATOR HELPER	2	3	664.685-030
RES	SPIKE-MACHINE HEATER	2	2	619.686-026
RES	SPIN-TABLE OPERATOR	2	3	732.687-074
RES	SPLASH-LINE OPERATOR	2	4	559.665-034
RES	SPOT PICKER, MOLDED GOODS	2	3	739.667-010

Code	Title	GED	SVP	DOT No.
RES	SPOUT TENDER	2	2	932.664-014
RES	SPRAY-MACHINE LOADER	2	2	574.686-010
RES	SPREADER	2	2	554.687-010
RES	SPREADER 1	2	2	781.687-058
RES	SPRING ASSEMBLER	2	4	706.684-090
RES	SPRING COVERER	2	2	780.687-038
RES	SPRING SALVAGE WORKER	2	4	610.684-014
RES	SPRING-REPAIRER HELPER, HAND	2	4	620.584-010
RES	SQUEAK, RATTLE, AND LEAK REPAIRER	2	4	620.364-010
RES	SQUEEGEE TENDER	2	3	750.685-010
RES	STACKING-MACHINE OPERATOR 2	2	2	739.685-038
RES	STAINER	2	2	739.687-174
RES	STAPLER, HAND	2	2	780.687-042
RES	STAVE JOINTER	2	3	665.685-030
RES	STEAM CLEANER	2	2	915.687-026
RES	STEAM-PRESS TENDER 1	2	4	553.665-046
RES	STEAMER-BLOCKER	2	2	784.684-070
RES	STEEL-PLATE CALKER	2	4	843.684-010
RES	STEEL-POST INSTALLER	2	3	821.687-010
RES	STEEL-POURER HELPER	2	5	502.664-018
RES	STERILIZER OPERATOR	2	3	523.685-114
RES	STERILIZER	2	2	920.687-182
RES	STEVEDORE 2	2	2	922.687-090
RES	STITCH-BONDING-MACHINE TENDER	2	3	689.685-126
RES	STITCHER OPERATOR	2	4	649.685-114
RES	STITCHING-MACHINE OPERATOR	2	2	669.685-086
RES	STONE GRADER	2	4	679.567-010
RES	STOPPER MAKER	2	3	519.684-022
RES	STOPPER-MAKER HELPER	2	2	519.687-038
RES	STRAIGHT-LINE EDGER	2	3	673.685-078
RES	STRANDING-MACHINE-OPERATOR HELPER	2	2	616.687-010
RES	STREETCAR-REPAIRER HELPER	2	3	807.687-014
RES	STRIPPER	2	2	749.687-030
RES	STUBBER	2	2	222.687-034
RES	SUGAR DRIER	2	3	523.665-010
RES	SUPPLY CLERK	2	3	339.687-010
RES	TABLE-TOP TILE SETTER	2	4	763.684-074
RES	TAPER OPERATOR	2	3	649.685-126
RES	TAPPER	2	2	514.664-014
RES	TARE WEIGHER	2	3	221.587-034
RES	TARGET TRIMMER	2	2	732.687-078
RES	TEMPERATURE REGULATOR, PYROMETER	2	2	512.667-010
RES	TESTER-OPERATOR HELPER	2	2	614.686-014
RES	THREADING-MACHINE FEEDER, AUTOMATIC 1	2	2	604.666-010
RES	TIE INSPECTOR	2	2	669.687-026
RES	TIE-UP WORKER	2	3	710.687-034
RES	TILE SORTER	2	3	573.687-038
RES	TIRE RECAPPER	2	4	750.685-014
RES	TOBACCO-CLOTH RECLAIMER	2	2	589.686-050
RES	TOP-DYEING-MACHINE LOADER	2	2	582.686-030
RES	TOW-TRUCK OPERATOR	2	3	919.663-026
RES	TOWEL INSPECTOR	2	3	652.686-042
RES	TOWER ATTENDANT	2	2	559.666-010

Code	Title	GED	SVP	DOT No.
RES	TRANSFER-TABLE OPERATOR HELPER	2	3	910.667-030
RES	TREE CUTTER	2	3	454.684-026
RES	TRUCK-DRIVER HELPER	2	2	905.687-010
RES	TUBING OILER	2	3	699.685-034
RES	TUBING-MACHINE OPERATOR	2	4	613.685-030
RES	TUBULAR-SPLITTING-MACHINE TENDER	2	2	686.685-070
RES	TUFTER, HAND	2	2	780.687-050
RES	TUMBLER OPERATOR	2	2	369.685-034
RES	UTILITY WORKER, MERCHANT MILL	2	5	801.664-014
RES	UTILITY WORKER, CLOTH PRINTING	2	2	652.586-010
RES	VACUUM CASTER	2	5	514.582-010
RES	VAN-DRIVER HELPER	2	3	905.687-014
RES	VAULT CUSTODIAN	2	3	369.587-010
RES	VENDOR	2	2	291.457-022
RES	VENEER-JOINTER OFFBEARER	2	2	665.686-022
RES	VENEER-STOCK LAYER	2	2	762.687-066
RES	VENETIAN-BLIND CLEANER AND REPAIRER	2	2	739.687-198
RES	VULCAN CREWMEMBER	2	3	378.663-010
RES	WASHER-AND-CRUSHER TENDER	2	3	939.685-014
RES	WEAVER, AXMINSTER	2	4	683.685-038
RES	WEIGHER AND GRADER	2	3	559.567-014
RES	WELDER HELPER	2	2	819.687-014
RES	WET INSPECTOR, OPTICAL GLASS	2	3	716.687-034
RES	WET-AND-DRY-SUGAR-BIN OPERATOR	2	3	529.665-018
RES	WHEEL ASSEMBLER	2	2	809.684-038
RES	WIRE CHARGER	2	2	614.586-010
RES	WIRE-WEAVER HELPER	2	3	616.687-014
RES	WIRE-WINDING-MACHINE OPERATOR	2	2	619.685-090
RES	WOOD HACKER	2	3	569.687-026
RES	WOODENWARE ASSEMBLER	2	2	762.687-070
RES	WOODWORKING-SHOP HAND	2	2	769.687-054
RES	WOOL SACKER	2	2	920.687-198
RES	WRAPPER OPERATOR	2	2	706.684-110
RES	WRAPPING-MACHINE OPERATOR	2	2	641.685-098
RES	YARD WORKER	2	2	301.687-018
RES	APRON CLEANER	1	2	680.687-010
RES	AUTOMATIC STACKER	1	2	619.686-010
RES	BACK FEEDER, PLYWOOD LAYUP LINE	1	2	569.686-010
RES	BARREL DRAINER	1	1	764.687-018
RES	BARREL FILLER	1	2	522.687-010
RES	BEVELING-AND-EDGING-MACHINE-OPERATOR HELPER	1	2	673.686-010
RES	BLENDER LABORER	1	1	520.687-010
RES	BLOWER FEEDER, DYED RAW STOCK	1	2	581.686-010
RES	BOAT-HOIST-OPERATOR HELPER	1	2	921.667-010
RES	BOBBIN CLEANER, HAND	1	2	689.687-014
RES	BOBBIN-WINDER TENDER	1	2	619.685-022
RES	BOLT LOADER	1	2	922.687-022
RES	BOX BENDER	1	1	641.687-010
RES	BULL-GANG WORKER	1	2	922.687-026
RES	BUZZSAW-OPERATOR HELPER	1	1	667.687-010
RES	CAKE PULLER	1	2	521.686-014
RES	CALCINE FURNACE LOADER	1	2	553.486-010
RES	CALENDER FEEDER	1	2	554.686-010

Code	Title	GED	SVP	DOT No.
RES	CALENDER-WIND-UP HELPER	1	2	554.686-022
RES	CAN DOFFER	1	2	680.686-010
RES	CAN FILLER	1	1	922.687-030
RES	CANVAS SHRINKER	1	2	587.687-010
RES	CAR PINCHER	1	1	922.687-034
RES	CARTON-COUNTER FEEDER	1	2	921.686-010
RES	CASER	1	3	930.664-010
RES	CD-MIXER HELPER	1	2	553.686-014
RES	CHIP WASHER	1	2	522.686-010
RES	CHOKE SETTER	1	2	921.687-014
RES	CHOPPER	1	1	564.687-010
RES	CIGARETTE-MAKING-MACHINE-HOPPER FEEDER	1	2	529.686-018
RES	CLEANER, WINDOW	1	2	389.687-014
RES	CLIPPER AND TURNER	1	2	780.687-014
RES	CLOTH FEEDER	1	2	589.686-014
RES	COFFEE WEIGHER	1	1	529.687-046
RES	COLOR STRAINER	1	2	550.687-014
RES	COMPANY LABORER	1	1	939.687-014
RES	CONVEYOR LOADER 1	1	2	525.687-018
RES	COTTON WASHER	1	1	559.687-030
RES	CUT-IN WORKER	1	1	521.686-030
RES	DECKHAND	1	2	553.686-022
RES	DRIER FEEDER	1	2	559.686-014
RES	DRIER-OPERATOR HELPER	1	2	553.686-030
RES	DRYING-UNIT-FELTING-MACHINE-OPERATOR HELPER	1	2	581.687-018
RES	DYE-HOUSE WORKER	1	2	582.686-010
RES	EDGE-BANDING-MACHINE OFFBEARER	1	2	762.686-010
RES	ELECTRIC-FORK OPERATOR	1	2	921.685-042
RES	EXTERMINATOR HELPER, TERMITE	1	2	383.687-010
RES	FARMWORKER, GRAIN 2	1	2	401.687-010
RES	FEATHER-CURLING-MACHINE OPERATOR	1	1	589.686-018
RES	FEATHER-DRYING-MACHINE OPERATOR	1	2	581.686-034
RES	FEED-IN WORKER	1	2	929.686-022
RES	FEED-MIXER HELPER	1	2	520.686-018
RES	FEEDER-CATCHER, TOBACCO	1	2	529.686-038
RES	FILLER ROOM ATTENDANT	1	2	522.687-022
RES	FILLER SPREADER	1	1	521.687-046
RES	FILLER-BLOCK INSERTER-REMOVER	1	1	652.687-018
RES	FISH CHOPPER, GANG KNIFE	1	2	521.687-058
RES	FISH DRIER	1	2	523.687-014
RES	FRAME HAND	1	2	689.687-046
RES	FURNACE HELPER	1	2	558.686-010
RES	GAMBRELER	1	2	525.687-030
RES	GAMBRELER HELPER	1	2	525.687-034
RES	GARBAGE COLLECTOR	1	1	909.687-010
RES	GATHERING-MACHINE FEEDER	1	2	653.686-018
RES	GRIZZLY WORKER	1	2	933.687-010
RES	HARDENER HELPER	1	2	504.686-018
RES	HOPPER FEEDER	1	2	619.686-018
RES	HOUSE-MOVER HELPER	1	2	869.687-034
RES	ICER	1	1	922.687-046
RES	INJECTION-MOLDING-MACHINE OFFBEARER	1	2	690.686-042

Code	Title	GED	SVP	DOT No.
RES	INNER-TUBE INSERTER	1	2	750.687-010
RES	LABORER	1	2	732.687-030
RES	LABORER, BRUSH CLEARING	1	2	459.687-010
RES	LABORER, GENERAL	1	1	579.667-010
RES	LABORER, PRESTRESSED CONCRETE	1	2	575.687-018
RES	LAST PUTTER-AWAY	1	2	922.687-066
RES	LITHOGRAPHED-PLATE INSPECTOR	1	2	651.687-010
RES	LUMBER SORTER	1	2	922.687-074
RES	MACHINE FEEDER, RAW STOCK	1	2	680.686-018
RES	MASH-FILTER-CLOTH CHANGER	1	2	529.667-014
RES	MATTRESS STRIPPER	1	4	780.687-026
RES	MEAT GRINDER	1	2	521.685-214
RES	MILK-POWDER GRINDER	1	2	521.685-222
RES	MIRROR-MACHINE FEEDER	1	2	579.686-022
RES	MIXING-MACHINE OPERATOR	1	2	520.685-166
RES	MIXING-MACHINE FEEDER	1	2	550.686-030
RES	NUT-PROCESS HELPER	1	2	529.486-010
RES	OFFBEARER, SEWER PIPE	1	2	579.686-026
RES	OILSEED-MEAT PRESSER	1	2	521.685-242
RES	PAPER STRIPPER	1	2	922.687-078
RES	PATCHER HELPER	1	2	861.687-014
RES	PIPE STRIPPER	1	2	575.687-026
RES	PLUG SHAPER, MACHINE	1	2	520.686-034
RES	PNEUMATIC JACKETER	1	2	691.667-010
RES	POLE-PEELING-MACHINE-OPERATOR HELPER	1	2	665.686-010
RES	PORCELAIN-ENAMEL LABORER	1	2	509.687-014
RES	POULTRY-DRESSING WORKER	1	2	525.687-082
RES	PRESS BUCKER	1	1	920.686-042
RES	PRESS PULLER	1	2	529.687-170
RES	PRINT-LINE FEEDER	1	1	652.686-026
RES	PROCESSOR HELPER	1	2	521.686-050
RES	PULP PILER	1	2	922.687-082
RES	RACK LOADER 1	1	2	529.686-074
RES	RENOVATOR-MACHINE OPERATOR	1	2	589.685-082
RES	REPAIRER, SHOE STICKS	1	2	619.685-074
RES	RETORT UNLOADER	1	2	569.686-034
RES	ROOF-CEMENT-AND-PAINT-MAKER HELPER	1	2	550.686-038
RES	RUBBER CUTTER	1	2	559.685-158
RES	SANDING-MACHINE OPERATOR	1	2	524.665-010
RES	SEED CUTTER	1	1	404.686-010
RES	SEEDLING PULLER	1	1	451.687-018
RES	SETTER HELPER	1	2	573.687-030
RES	SHACTOR HELPER	1	2	525.687-090
RES	SHAVER	1	2	362.687-018
RES	SHELL-SIEVE OPERATOR	1	2	694.585-010
RES	SIRUP-MIXER ASSISTANT	1	2	520.687-058
RES	SMOKE-ROOM OPERATOR	1	2	784.687-066
RES	SMOKED MEAT PREPARER	1	2	525.587-014
RES	SOAP CHIPPER	1	2	555.686-014
RES	SOLE SCRAPER	1	2	788.687-134
RES	SPLITTING-MACHINE-OPERATOR HELPER	1	2	677.666-010
RES	STEAMER	1	2	789.687-170
RES	STITCH-BONDING-MACHINE-TENDER			

Code	Title	GED	SVP	DOT No.
	HELPER	1	2	689.686-042
RES	STUNNER, ANIMAL	1	2	525.687-114
RES	SUCKER-MACHINE OPERATOR	1	3	529.685-234
RES	SUGAR-CHIPPER-MACHINE OPERATOR	1	2	521.685-354
RES	TAKER-OFF, HEMP FIBER	1	1	589.686-046
RES	TAPPER, HAND	1	1	737.687-134
RES	TIPPLE TENDER	1	2	521.685-366
RES	TUBER-MACHINE-OPERATOR HELPER	1	2	690.686-070
RES	VENEER-CLIPPER HELPER	1	2	663.686-030
RES	WASHER	1	1	733.687-078
RES	WHARF WORKER	1	2	921.667-026
REC	AUDITOR	5	8	160.162-014
REC	MARINE SURVEYOR	5	8	014.167-010
REC	AVIONICS TECHNICIAN	4	6	823.281-010
REC	CELL-FEED-DEPARTMENT SUPERVISOR	4	7	519.130-010
REC	CONSTRUCTION INSPECTOR	4	6	182.267-010
REC	ESTIMATOR, JEWELRY	4	6	221.387-022
REC	FELT-GOODS SUPERVISOR, NEEDLE PROCESS	4	8	689.130-014
REC	FINAL INSPECTOR	4	7	715.381-050
REC	FORMATION-TESTING OPERATOR	4	6	930.261-014
REC	HOT-CELL TECHNICIAN	4	7	015.362-018
REC	JEWEL SUPERVISOR	4	7	770.131-010
REC	JEWELER	4	7	700.281-010
REC	JEWELER APPRENTICE	4	7	700.281-014
REC	LOCKSMITH	4	6	709.281-010
REC	LOCKSMITH APPRENTICE	4	6	709.281-014
REC	MILLWRIGHT SUPERVISOR	4	8	638.131-030
REC	OIL-PIPE INSPECTOR	4	6	930.267-010
REC	PATTERNMAKER	4	7	781.381-026
REC	PIN-GAME-MACHINE INSPECTOR	4	5	729.381-014
REC	QUARRY SUPERVISOR, OPEN PIT	4	7	939.131-010
REC	RATE REVIEWER	4	6	214.387-014
REC	STEEL-PAN-FORM-PLACING SUPERVISOR	4	7	869.131-026
REC	SUPERVISOR, GREASE REFINING	4	7	553.132-010
REC	SUPERVISOR, PRODUCTION DEPARTMENT	4	8	621.131-018
REC	SUPERVISOR, LUBRICATION	4	7	699.131-010
REC	TANKAGE SUPERVISOR	4	7	869.131-034
REC	TUNE-UP MECHANIC	4	7	620.281-066
REC	AIR-CONDITIONING-COIL ASSEMBLER	3	3	706.684-010
REC	AIRCRAFT-EQUIPMENT-AND-ACCESSORIES ASSEMBLER	3	4	222.587-010
REC	AIRCRAFT-SHIPPING CHECKER	3	5	222.387-010
REC	ANKLE-PATCH MOLDER	3	4	692.682-010
REC	APPLIANCE ASSEMBLER, LINE	3	3	827.684-010
REC	BALLOON MAKER	3	3	752.684-010
REC	BANKING PIN ADJUSTER	3	5	715.381-018
REC	BARREL-BRIDGE ASSEMBLER	3	5	715.381-026
REC	BASIN OPERATOR	3	4	954.385-010
REC	BEAD MAKER	3	7	770.381-010
REC	BEAM-DYER OPERATOR	3	3	582.685-014
REC	BELLOWS MAKER	3	4	714.684-014
REC	BIAS-CUTTING-MACHINE OPERATOR	3	4	686.682-014

Code	Title	GED	SVP	DOT No.
REC	BLOCKER	3	3	363.684-010
REC	BONDED STRUCTURES REPAIRER	3	6	807.381-014
REC	BOOTMAKER, HAND	3	4	753.381-010
REC	BOX-BLANK-MACHINE OPERATOR	3	4	669.662-010
REC	BRAIDER OPERATOR	3	5	691.682-014
REC	BRIQUETTE-MACHINE OPERATOR	3	4	549.662-010
REC	BULLDOZER OPERATOR 1	3	5	850.683-010
REC	BULLET-ASSEMBLY-PRESS SETTER-OPERATOR	3	4	694.682-010
REC	CABLE MAINTAINER	3	5	952.464-010
REC	CALCINER OPERATOR	3	6	513.362-010
REC	CALIBRATOR 1	3	4	710.681-014
REC	CARBON CUTTER	3	4	677.685-018
REC	CARGO INSPECTOR	3	5	549.387-010
REC	CASKET INSPECTOR	3	5	739.387-010
REC	CASTER	3	6	502.381-010
REC	CHECKER, BAKERY PRODUCTS	3	3	222.487-010
REC	CHEMICAL-STRENGTH TESTER	3	2	582.587-010
REC	CHRONOMETER-BALANCE-AND-HAIRSPRING ASSEMBLER	3	6	715.381-042
REC	CHUCKING-AND-SAWING-MACHINE OPERATOR	3	4	669.682-026
REC	CIGARETTE TESTER	3	5	529.387-014
REC	CIGARETTE-MAKING-MACHINE OPERATOR	3	3	529.685-066
REC	CISTERN-ROOM OPERATOR	3	4	520.382-010
REC	COAGULATION OPERATOR	3	5	559.582-010
REC	COATING-MACHINE OPERATOR	3	4	590.685-014
REC	COIN COLLECTOR	3	3	292.483-010
REC	COLLET MAKER	3	5	609.682-014
REC	COMMUNITY-ANTENNA-TELEVISION LINE TECHNICIAN	3	6	821.261-010
REC	COMPOSITION-STONE APPLICATOR	3	7	861.361-010
REC	COMPOUND MIXER	3	4	509.485-010
REC	CONVERTER OPERATOR	3	4	526.382-018
REC	CONVEYOR OPERATOR, PNEUMATIC SYSTEM	3	4	921.382-010
REC	COOK	3	3	553.665-018
REC	CRABBER	3	2	582.685-038
REC	CRATER	3	3	920.484-010
REC	CRYOLITE-RECOVERY OPERATOR	3	5	511.482-014
REC	CUTTING-MACHINE OPERATOR	3	4	521.685-102
REC	CYLINDER INSPECTOR-AND-TESTER	3	4	953.387-010
REC	DECKER OPERATOR	3	4	533.682-010
REC	DEICER TESTER	3	4	729.387-014
REC	DENTAL CERAMIST	3	6	712.281-010
REC	DETHISTLER OPERATOR	3	3	521.685-106
REC	DIAL MAKER	3	4	710.684-018
REC	DIAMOND CLEAVER	3	6	770.381-014
REC	DIAMOND SIZER AND SORTER	3	4	770.687-014
REC	DIFFERENTIAL TESTER	3	4	806.382-010
REC	DISTILLER	3	5	552.682-010
REC	DRAPER	3	4	781.684-026
REC	DRAPERY AND UPHOLSTERY ESTIMATOR	3	5	299.387-010
REC	DREDGE OPERATOR	3	5	850.663-010
REC	DRIER OPERATOR	3	4	543.382-010

Code	Title	GED	SVP	DOT No.
REC	DRILL-PRESS OPERATOR, ACOUSTICAL TILE	3	5	649.682-018
REC	DRIP PUMPER	3	3	953.583-010
REC	DUMPER-BAILER OPERATOR	3	5	931.684-010
REC	DUST COLLECTOR, ORE CRUSHING	3	3	511.682-010
REC	ENGINE DISPATCHER	3	4	910.367-018
REC	ENGINE TURNER	3	6	704.381-018
REC	ENGINEER, EXHAUSTER	3	7	950.362-010
REC	EQUIPMENT CLEANER-AND-TESTER	3	4	630.584-010
REC	EVAPORATOR OPERATOR	3	5	521.382-010
REC	FANCY-WIRE DRAWER	3	4	614.682-014
REC	FARMWORKER, VEGETABLE 1	3	4	402.663-010
REC	FELT-CUTTING-MACHINE OPERATOR	3	4	686.682-018
REC	FERMENTER OPERATOR	3	4	559.685-070
REC	FILTER OPERATOR	3	5	521.682-018
REC	FILTER TENDER	3	4	522.665-010
REC	FILTRATION OPERATOR, POLYETHYLENE CATALYST	3	5	551.562-010
REC	FINAL INSPECTOR, MOVEMENT ASSEMBLY	3	4	715.684-094
REC	FINAL-DRESSING CUTTER	3	4	525.684-026
REC	FINGER-GRIP-MACHINE OPERATOR	3	3	673.685-054
REC	FINISH OPENER, JEWEL HOLE	3	5	673.682-022
REC	FOAM-GUN OPERATOR	3	3	741.684-014
REC	FOILING-MACHINE ADJUSTER	3	5	629.381-010
REC	FORMULA WEIGHER	3	4	559.685-082
REC	FOXING-CUTTING-MACHINE OPERATOR, AUTOMATIC	3	4	690.682-038
REC	FRAME WIRER	3	4	822.684-010
REC	FREEZING-MACHINE OPERATOR	3	3	559.685-090
REC	FURNACE-STOCK INSPECTOR	3	4	559.364-010
REC	GAGER	3	5	529.387-022
REC	GALLEY STRIPPER	3	5	973.681-010
REC	GAS TREATER	3	4	546.385-010
REC	GAS-METER MECHANIC 1	3	5	710.381-022
REC	GAS-PUMPING-STATION OPERATOR	3	5	953.382-010
REC	GAS-REGULATOR-REPAIRER HELPER	3	5	710.384-010
REC	GEAR-SORTING-AND-INSPECTING MACHINE OPERATOR	3	4	602.362-014
REC	GERMINATION WORKER	3	5	522.585-014
REC	GLASS-LINED TANK REPAIRER	3	3	779.684-026
REC	GREEN INSPECTOR	3	4	726.367-010
REC	GRINDER-MILL OPERATOR	3	4	519.485-010
REC	HANDLER	3	5	774.684-022
REC	HARDNESS TESTER	3	3	519.585-010
REC	HAT BLOCKER	3	4	363.684-014
REC	HEAD-SAW OPERATOR, INSULATION BOARD	3	6	677.682-010
REC	HOUSE-PIPING INSPECTOR	3	5	953.367-018
REC	HYPOID-GEAR TESTER	3	4	806.382-014
REC	INKER AND OPAQUER	3	7	970.681-018
REC	INSPECTOR	3	6	779.387-014
REC	INSPECTOR, FIBROUS WALLBOARD	3	4	539.487-010
REC	INSPECTOR, INSULATION	3	5	691.387-010
REC	INSPECTOR, AUTOMATIC TYPEWRITER	3	4	706.387-010
REC	INSPECTOR, MULTIFOCAL LENS	3	3	716.687-018

Code	Title	GED	SVP	DOT No.
REC	INSPECTOR, HAIRSPRING 1	3	6	715.381-066
REC	INSPECTOR, WATCH PARTS	3	6	715.384-022
REC	INSPECTOR, WATCH ASSEMBLY	3	6	715.381-070
REC	INSPECTOR, TIMING	3	5	715.685-034
REC	INSPECTOR, WOODWIND INSTRUMENTS	3	4	730.684-038
REC	INSPECTOR, FABRICATION	3	6	806.361-022
REC	INSPECTOR, PACKAGING MATERIALS	3	4	920.387-010
REC	INSTRUMENT CHECKER	3	3	710.687-026
REC	INSULATION-WORKER APPRENTICE	3	6	863.364-010
REC	JACQUARD-LOOM WEAVER	3	5	683.662-010
REC	JOB SETTER	3	5	616.380-014
REC	KETTLE OPERATOR	3	4	519.685-018
REC	KETTLE TENDER 2	3	4	511.685-030
REC	KILN OPERATOR	3	6	563.382-010
REC	KNIFE OPERATOR	3	5	579.382-018
REC	KNIFE SETTER	3	4	638.684-014
REC	LAMINATING-MACHINE OPERATOR	3	5	584.682-014
REC	LATHE HAND	3	6	700.682-014
REC	LATHE WINDER	3	4	619.482-010
REC	LEATHER CLEANER	3	3	362.684-026
REC	LENS-BLANK GAGER	3	3	716.687-026
REC	LIQUEFACTION-PLANT OPERATOR	3	4	559.362-018
REC	LOADING-UNIT TOOL-SETTER	3	5	632.380-014
REC	LOCKSTITCH-SEWING-MACHINE OPERATOR, COMPLETE GARMENT	3	4	786.682-174
REC	LUGGAGE MAKER	3	7	783.381-022
REC	MANNEQUIN SANDER AND FINISHER	3	3	739.684-122
REC	MANOMETER TECHNICIAN	3	3	519.387-010
REC	MANUGRAPHER	3	4	970.681-022
REC	MAP-AND-CHART MOUNTER	3	5	979.684-022
REC	MASHER	3	4	522.482-010
REC	MATERIAL CLERK	3	5	222.387-034
REC	MATRIX PLATER	3	4	500.384-010
REC	MICA SPLITTER	3	4	779.681-010
REC	MILK-RECEIVER, TANK TRUCK	3	3	222.485-010
REC	MINER, PLACER	3	4	939.684-014
REC	MOLDER, MACHINE	3	4	556.685-050
REC	MOLDING-MACHINE OPERATOR	3	6	520.682-026
REC	MUSICAL-STRING MAKER	3	4	730.684-050
REC	OUTFITTER, CABIN	3	5	806.684-102
REC	OVERLOCK-MACHINE OPERATOR, COMPLETE GARMENT	3	4	786.682-198
REC	PAINTER, MIRROR	3	4	741.684-022
REC	PALLET-STONE INSERTER	3	6	715.381-082
REC	PALLET-STONE POSITIONER	3	6	715.381-086
REC	PAPIER MACHE MOLDER	3	4	794.684-026
REC	PATTERN CHART-WRITER	3	5	789.381-014
REC	PERFECT-BINDER SETTER	3	8	653.380-010
REC	PHARMACY HELPER	3	3	074.387-010
REC	PHONOGRAPH-NEEDLE-TIP MAKER	3	5	770.382-014
REC	PIANO TECHNICIAN	3	7	730.281-038
REC	PINSETTER MECHANIC, AUTOMATIC	3	4	638.261-022
REC	PLASTER MOLDER 2	3	4	518.484-010
REC	PLASTICS FABRICATOR	3	5	754.684-042

Code	Title	GED	SVP	DOT No.
REC	PLEATING-MACHINE OPERATOR	3	4	583.685-082
REC	POACHER OPERATOR	3	4	551.685-106
REC	POTLINE MONITOR	3	4	512.467-010
REC	PROFILER, HAND	3	4	715.685-054
REC	PUMP OPERATOR, BYPRODUCTS	3	5	541.362-014
REC	PUMP-STATION OPERATOR, WATERWORKS	3	5	954.382-010
REC	PURIFICATION OPERATOR	3	2	551.685-122
REC	QUALITY-CONTROL TECHNICIAN	3	5	529.367-022
REC	RECORDIST	3	6	962.382-010
REC	RECOVERY OPERATOR	3	5	519.582-010
REC	REFINERY OPERATOR HELPER	3	6	542.362-014
REC	REFRIGERATOR GLAZIER	3	4	865.684-022
REC	RETURNED-TELEPHONE-EQUIPMENT APPRAISER	3	5	222.387-046
REC	RIVETER, HYDRAULIC	3	5	800.662-010
REC	RIVETER, PORTABLE PINCH	3	4	800.682-010
REC	ROOFER	3	7	866.381-010
REC	ROOFER APPRENTICE	3	7	866.381-014
REC	ROTARY DERRICK OPERATOR	3	5	930.382-022
REC	ROUTER	3	5	979.682-026
REC	SAFETY INSPECTOR, TRUCK	3	4	919.687-018
REC	SALT WASHER	3	4	551.685-126
REC	SAMPLE MAKER 1	3	7	700.381-046
REC	SCREEN OPERATOR	3	4	511.685-050
REC	SCREEN TENDER	3	4	533.685-022
REC	SCREWHEAD POLISHER	3	5	715.381-090
REC	SET-UP WORKER	3	5	715.660-010
REC	SEWING-MACHINE OPERATOR	3	4	783.682-014
REC	SHINGLE TRIMMER	3	4	667.685-050
REC	SHIPPING-AND-RECEIVING WEIGHER	3	2	222.367-058
REC	SHRIMP-PEELING-MACHINE OPERATOR	3	5	521.682-038
REC	SHUTTLE INSPECTOR	3	4	769.684-046
REC	SIGHT MOUNTER	3	5	736.481-010
REC	SILK FINISHER	3	4	363.681-010
REC	SILK-SCREEN CUTTER	3	5	979.681-022
REC	SINTER FEEDER	3	4	513.685-010
REC	SKETCH MAKER 1	3	4	979.381-034
REC	SLIDING-JOINT MAKER	3	3	730.684-078
REC	SLIME-PLANT OPERATOR 2	3	4	511.685-054
REC	SMALL-ENGINE MECHANIC	3	6	625.281-034
REC	SPECIAL TESTER	3	3	529.487-010
REC	SPINNER	3	5	700.684-074
REC	STAVE-SAW OPERATOR	3	4	667.685-062
REC	STILL OPERATOR	3	5	543.682-026
REC	STITCHING-MACHINE SETTER	3	5	653.680-010
REC	SWIMMING-POOL SERVICER	3	4	891.684-018
REC	TANK ASSEMBLER	3	4	764.684-030
REC	TANK TENDER	3	3	529.585-014
REC	TANK-TRUCK DRIVER	3	3	903.683-018
REC	TAPPER, BALANCE-WHEEL SCREW HOLE	3	3	715.682-022
REC	THERMOMETER TESTER	3	5	710.384-030
REC	TOOTH POLISHER	3	5	715.682-026
REC	TOY-ELECTRIC-TRAIN REPAIRER	3	3	731.684-022
REC	TRUCK-CRANE OPERATOR	3	5	921.663-062

Code	Title	GED	SVP	DOT No.
REC	TRUCKLOAD CHECKER	3	3	222.367-066
REC	UTILITY OPERATOR 1	3	5	559.682-066
REC	UTILITY OPERATOR	3	4	786.682-262
REC	V-BELT CURER	3	4	553.682-026
REC	VENTILATOR	3	5	739.384-022
REC	WATERSHED TENDER	3	5	954.382-018
REC	WEED INSPECTOR	3	5	408.381-014
REC	WHARF ATTENDANT	3	3	342.667-010
REC	WHEEL INSPECTOR	3	8	806.387-014
REC	WINERY WORKER	3	3	521.685-370
REC	WINK-CUTTER OPERATOR	3	4	557.382-014
REC	WIRE DRAWER	3	4	614.382-014
REC	ZINC-CHLORIDE OPERATOR	3	4	511.385-010
REC	ABRASIVE-MIXER HELPER	2	2	570.686-014
REC	ADJUSTER	2	3	709.684-010
REC	AIR-CONDITIONING INSTALLER-SERVICER HELPER, WINDOW UNIT	2	3	637.687-010
REC	AIR-TABLE OPERATOR	2	2	549.685-010
REC	ALMOND HULLER	2	2	521.685-010
REC	ALODIZE-MACHINE HELPER	2	3	509.685-010
REC	ARMATURE-WINDER HELPER, REPAIR	2	3	721.684-010
REC	ARROWSMITH	2	2	732.684-010
REC	ASSEMBLER	2	2	734.687-014
REC	ASSEMBLER-ARRANGER	2	2	739.687-010
REC	ASSEMBLER, SURGICAL GARMENT	2	3	712.684-010
REC	ASSEMBLER, LIQUID CENTER	2	2	732.684-018
REC	ASSEMBLER, MECHANICAL PENCILS AND BALLPOINT PENS	2	2	733.687-014
REC	ASSEMBLER, CARDS AND ANNOUNCEMENTS	2	2	794.687-010
REC	ASSEMBLER, AUTOMOBILE	2	2	806.684-010
REC	ASSEMBLER, INSULATION AND FLOORING	2	3	806.684-026
REC	ASSEMBLER, PING-PONG TABLE	2	2	732.684-022
REC	AUTOCLAVE OPERATOR	2	2	587.585-010
REC	BACK TENDER, CLOTH PRINTING	2	2	652.685-010
REC	BAG CUTTER	2	2	789.687-010
REC	BAG-MACHINE-OPERATOR HELPER	2	2	649.686-010
REC	BAGGAGE HANDLER	2	2	910.687-010
REC	BAGGER	2	3	553.685-014
REC	BAKER HELPER	2	2	526.686-010
REC	BALER	2	2	690.685-022
REC	BAND CUTTER	2	3	690.685-026
REC	BAND-MACHINE OPERATOR	2	4	690.685-030
REC	BANDING-MACHINE OPERATOR	2	2	619.685-014
REC	BARLEY STEEPER	2	2	522.585-010
REC	BARREL RAISER	2	4	764.684-018
REC	BARREL-DEDENTING-MACHINE OPERATOR	2	4	617.682-010
REC	BASE-FILLER OPERATOR	2	2	732.685-010
REC	BATCH MAKER	2	2	515.685-010
REC	BATCH MIXER	2	2	570.687-010
REC	BATTERY-PARTS ASSEMBLER	2	3	727.687-038
REC	BEAD PREPARER	2	3	692.685-022
REC	BEAD-MACHINE OPERATOR	2	2	583.686-010
REC	BEAMER	2	3	681.585-010
REC	BEAMING INSPECTOR	2	3	585.687-010

Code	Title	GED	SVP	DOT No.
REC	BEDDER	2	3	573.687-010
REC	BELTING-AND-WEBBING INSPECTOR	2	2	683.487-010
REC	BENCH WORKER	2	3	713.684-018
REC	BENDER, HAND	2	2	769.684-018
REC	BENDER, MACHINE	2	3	641.685-010
REC	BENDING-MACHINE OPERATOR 2	2	3	617.685-010
REC	BILLPOSTER	2	2	299.667-010
REC	BINDERY WORKER	2	4	653.685-010
REC	BLANKET-CUTTING-MACHINE OPERATOR	2	3	689.585-010
REC	BLEACH-BOILER FILLER	2	2	533.685-010
REC	BLEACH-RANGE OPERATOR	2	2	582.685-018
REC	BLENDER-CONVEYOR OPERATOR	2	2	529.685-022
REC	BLENDER-MACHINE OPERATOR	2	2	520.685-018
REC	BLOCK-PRESS OPERATOR	2	2	556.685-014
REC	BLOCKER	2	2	673.685-026
REC	BLOCKER	2	2	689.685-014
REC	BLOCKER	2	4	715.684-034
REC	BLOCKER, HAND 1	2	3	580.684-010
REC	BOAT LOADER 1	2	3	911.364-014
REC	BOBBIN DISKER	2	2	734.687-022
REC	BOILING-TUB OPERATOR	2	2	551.685-014
REC	BOLTER	2	3	521.685-030
REC	BONE CRUSHER	2	2	555.685-014
REC	BONER, MEAT	2	4	525.684-010
REC	BOOK REPAIRER	2	3	977.684-010
REC	BOOK-SEWING-MACHINE OPERATOR 1	2	4	653.685-014
REC	BOTTLE PACKER	2	2	920.685-026
REC	BOTTOM PRESSER	2	2	690.685-034
REC	BOTTOM WHEELER	2	3	788.684-030
REC	BOX-LINING-MACHINE FEEDER	2	2	641.685-018
REC	BOX-SPRING MAKER 1	2	3	780.684-018
REC	BRAIDING-MACHINE TENDER	2	3	692.665-010
REC	BRAILLE-DUPLICATING-MACHINE OPERATOR	2	2	207.685-010
REC	BREAKER TENDER	2	3	544.685-010
REC	BREWERY CELLAR WORKER	2	2	522.685-014
REC	BRIM CURLER	2	2	583.685-014
REC	BRIM RAISER	2	2	784.687-010
REC	BRINE MAKER 1	2	3	522.685-018
REC	BRINE MAKER	2	3	551.687-014
REC	BROOM BUNDLER	2	2	692.685-030
REC	BROWN-STOCK WASHER	2	2	533.685-014
REC	BROWNING PROCESSOR	2	3	505.685-010
REC	BRUSH OPERATOR	2	2	587.685-010
REC	BRUSHER, MACHINE	2	2	587.685-014
REC	BUCKER	2	3	454.684-010
REC	BUCKET CHUCKER	2	3	664.685-014
REC	BUCKLE-FRAME SHAPER	2	3	692.685-034
REC	BUFFER, MACHINE	2	3	585.685-018
REC	BUFFING-AND-POLISHING-WHEEL REPAIRER	2	3	739.684-030
REC	BUFFING-WHEEL FORMER, AUTOMATIC	2	2	689.685-034
REC	BULK-SEALER OPERATOR	2	2	554.685-010
REC	BULL-CHAIN OPERATOR	2	2	921.685-014

Code	Title	GED	SVP	DOT No.
REC	BULLET-ASSEMBLY-PRESS OPERATOR	2	3	694.685-014
REC	BUNDLE TIER AND LABELER	2	2	920.585-010
REC	BURNER TENDER	2	2	571.685-010
REC	BURRING-MACHINE OPERATOR	2	2	615.685-010
REC	BUTTON-AND-BUCKLE MAKER	2	3	734.687-046
REC	BUTTON-CUTTING-MACHINE OPERATOR	2	3	734.384-010
REC	BUTTON-FACING-MACHINE OPERATOR	2	2	690.685-066
REC	CABLE PULLER	2	4	829.684-018
REC	CAKE FORMER	2	2	520.685-038
REC	CAKE STRIPPER	2	2	520.685-042
REC	CAN-CONVEYOR FEEDER	2	2	529.685-046
REC	CANDLE MOLDER, HAND	2	3	739.687-054
REC	CANNERY WORKER	2	2	529.686-014
REC	CANVAS REPAIRER	2	4	782.684-010
REC	CAR DROPPER	2	3	932.683-010
REC	CAR SCRUBBER	2	3	845.684-010
REC	CAR-DUMPER-OPERATOR HELPER	2	2	921.687-010
REC	CAR-WASH ATTENDANT, AUTOMATIC	2	2	915.667-010
REC	CARBONIZER	2	3	581.585-010
REC	CARCASS SPLITTER	2	3	525.684-018
REC	CARPET CUTTER 1	2	4	781.684-010
REC	CARROTING-MACHINE OPERATOR	2	2	586.685-010
REC	CARTON-FORMING-MACHINE OPERATOR	2	2	641.685-022
REC	CASE PACKER AND SEALER	2	3	920.685-038
REC	CASING CLEANER	2	2	525.686-010
REC	CASKET COVERER	2	3	780.684-026
REC	CASTER	2	4	754.684-022
REC	CASTING-MACHINE OPERATOR	2	2	520.685-062
REC	CAUSTIC OPERATOR	2	3	554.684-010
REC	CELL-TENDER HELPER	2	4	558.685-022
REC	CEMENT FITTINGS MAKER	2	4	779.684-010
REC	CEMENTER AND FOLDER, MACHINE	2	3	690.685-070
REC	CENTRIFUGAL SPINNER	2	2	575.664-010
REC	CHAMFERING-MACHINE OPERATOR 2	2	2	606.685-018
REC	CHAR-CONVEYOR TENDER	2	2	529.685-050
REC	CHICK SEXER	2	4	411.687-014
REC	CHILLER TENDER	2	3	523.585-014
REC	CHIMNEY SWEEP	2	3	891.687-010
REC	CHIPPER	2	2	564.685-014
REC	CIRCLE EDGER	2	2	673.685-038
REC	CLAM SORTER	2	2	446.687-010
REC	CLARIFIER	2	2	521.685-054
REC	CLARIFIER-OPERATOR HELPER	2	3	511.667-010
REC	CLASSIFIER	2	2	361.687-014
REC	CLAY MIXER	2	2	570.685-014
REC	CLEAN-RICE GRADER AND REEL TENDER	2	3	521.685-062
REC	CLEANER	2	3	503.684-010
REC	CLEANER	2	2	739.687-058
REC	CLEANER 3	2	2	911.687-014
REC	CLEANER-TOUCH-UP WORKER	2	3	706.587-010
REC	CLEARANCE CUTTER	2	2	615.685-014
REC	CLINCHING-MACHINE OPERATOR	2	2	616.685-014
REC	CLIP-BOLTER AND WRAPPER	2	3	709.684-038
REC	CLOTH FOLDER, HAND	2	2	589.687-014

Code	Title	GED	SVP	DOT No.
REC	CLOTH INSPECTOR	2	4	685.687-010
REC	CLOTH-DOUBLING-AND-WINDING-MACHINE OPERATOR	2	3	689.685-050
REC	CLOTH-FINISHING-RANGE OPERATOR	2	2	589.665-014
REC	CLOTH-SHRINKING-MACHINE OPERATOR	2	3	587.685-018
REC	CLOTH-STOCK SORTER	2	2	789.687-034
REC	CLOTH-WASHER OPERATOR	2	2	582.685-030
REC	COAT-HANGER-SHAPER-MACHINE OPERATOR	2	3	669.685-034
REC	COATING-MACHINE OPERATOR	2	2	584.685-018
REC	COIL-REWIND-MACHINE OPERATOR	2	2	619.685-030
REC	COILER	2	2	712.687-014
REC	COMB-MACHINE OPERATOR	2	3	640.685-022
REC	COMPOUNDER, CORK	2	2	560.587-010
REC	COMPRESSED-GAS-PLANT WORKER	2	2	549.587-010
REC	CONCRETE-PIPE-MAKING-MACHINE OPERATOR	2	2	575.665-010
REC	CONCRETE-VAULT MAKER	2	2	579.684-010
REC	CONTINUOUS-TOWEL ROLLER	2	2	361.685-014
REC	CONVEYOR LOADER 2	2	2	525.686-014
REC	COOK, VACUUM KETTLE	2	2	526.685-018
REC	COOKER, CASING	2	3	520.685-082
REC	COOKER, MEAL	2	3	523.685-034
REC	COOLING-MACHINE OPERATOR	2	2	523.685-042
REC	COPY-LATHE TENDER	2	3	664.685-018
REC	CORE CHECKER	2	3	518.687-010
REC	CORE FEEDER, PLYWOOD LAYUP LINE	2	3	569.685-018
REC	CORE LAYER, PLYWOOD LAYUP LINE	2	2	569.686-014
REC	CORE SETTER	2	2	518.684-010
REC	CORE SHAPER	2	2	692.685-058
REC	CORE-COMPOSER FEEDER	2	3	669.685-038
REC	COREMAKER, PIPE	2	3	518.684-014
REC	COREMAKER, MACHINE 3	2	2	518.685-022
REC	CORK GRINDER	2	2	662.685-010
REC	CORN COOKER	2	2	522.685-034
REC	CORN GRINDER	2	3	521.685-082
REC	CORNER CUTTER	2	2	640.685-030
REC	CORRUGATED-FASTENER DRIVER	2	2	669.685-042
REC	COSMETICS PRESSER	2	3	556.685-026
REC	COTTON BALER	2	3	920.465-010
REC	COUNTER, HAND	2	3	794.687-018
REC	COVERER, LOOSELEAF BINDER	2	4	795.687-010
REC	CRACKING-AND-FANNING-MACHINE OPERATOR	2	3	521.385-010
REC	CRAYON-SORTING-MACHINE FEEDER	2	2	929.686-018
REC	CRIMPING-MACHINE OPERATOR	2	3	680.685-030
REC	CROWN-ASSEMBLY-MACHINE OPERATOR	2	2	692.685-062
REC	CRYSTALLIZER OPERATOR	2	3	523.585-018
REC	CRYSTALLIZER OPERATOR	2	3	523.685-050
REC	CURTAIN-STRETCHER ASSEMBLER	2	2	762.684-030
REC	CUSHION BUILDER	2	2	780.684-050
REC	CUT-OFF-SAW OPERATOR, PIPE BLANKS	2	3	677.685-026
REC	CUTCH CLEANER	2	2	700.687-030
REC	CUTTER HELPER	2	2	781.687-022
REC	CUTTER, FROZEN MEAT	2	2	521.685-098

Code	Title	GED	SVP	DOT No.
REC	CUTTING-MACHINE OFFBEARER	2	2	689.686-018
REC	CYLINDER BATCHER	2	3	582.665-010
REC	DAIRY HELPER	2	2	529.686-026
REC	DEBUBBLIZER	2	3	553.585-010
REC	DEBURRER, MACHINE	2	3	715.685-018
REC	DECATING-MACHINE OPERATOR	2	2	582.685-042
REC	DEFECTIVE-CIGARETTE SLITTER	2	2	529.685-090
REC	DEHAIRING-MACHINE TENDER	2	3	525.685-018
REC	DEHYDRATING-PRESS OPERATOR	2	2	551.685-046
REC	DELIVERER, CAR RENTAL	2	3	919.663-010
REC	DESIGN PRINTER, BALLOON	2	2	651.685-014
REC	DESK-PEN-SET ASSEMBLER	2	2	733.687-034
REC	DESTATICIZER FEEDER	2	2	715.686-010
REC	DEVULCANIZER TENDER	2	3	558.585-026
REC	DICER OPERATOR	2	2	690.685-130
REC	DIGESTER-OPERATOR HELPER	2	2	532.686-010
REC	DIPPER	2	2	556.685-030
REC	DIPPER	2	2	599.685-026
REC	DIPPING-MACHINE OPERATOR	2	3	556.685-034
REC	DISPLAY-SCREEN FABRICATOR	2	2	725.685-010
REC	DOFFER	2	2	689.686-022
REC	DOOR ASSEMBLER	2	3	762.684-034
REC	DOPE-DRY-HOUSE OPERATOR	2	2	559.685-046
REC	DOUGH-BRAKE-MACHINE OPERATOR	2	3	520.685-090
REC	DOWEL-INSERTING-MACHINE OPERATOR	2	4	669.682-042
REC	DRAPERY-HEAD FORMER	2	2	781.684-030
REC	DRAW-FRAME TENDER	2	3	680.685-034
REC	DRAWER-IN HELPER, HAND	2	2	683.687-010
REC	DRAWER-IN, STITCH-BONDING MACHINE	2	2	689.684-014
REC	DRAWING-FRAME TENDER	2	3	680.685-038
REC	DRIER ATTENDANT	2	3	523.685-058
REC	DRIER OPERATOR	2	3	581.685-018
REC	DRIER-AND-PULVERIZER TENDER	2	2	559.685-050
REC	DRIER, LONG GOODS	2	2	523.585-022
REC	DRIER, SHORT GOODS	2	3	523.587-010
REC	DRIVER HELPER, SALES ROUTE	2	2	292.667-010
REC	DRY-HOUSE TENDER	2	2	559.585-010
REC	DRYING-MACHINE OPERATOR, PACKAGE YARNS	2	2	581.685-026
REC	DUAL-HOSE CEMENTER	2	2	690.685-134
REC	DUCT MAKER	2	2	809.687-010
REC	DUMP OPERATOR	2	3	921.685-038
REC	DUST SAMPLER	2	3	939.585-010
REC	DUSTING-AND-BRUSHING-MACHINE OPERATOR	2	2	559.685-054
REC	DYE-REEL OPERATOR	2	3	582.665-014
REC	DYE-TANK TENDER	2	3	582.685-054
REC	DYE-TUB OPERATOR	2	3	582.585-014
REC	DYE-WEIGHER HELPER	2	2	550.687-018
REC	DYER HELPER	2	2	589.685-042
REC	EAR-MUFF ASSEMBLER	2	2	784.687-022
REC	EDGE BURNISHER, UPPERS	2	3	690.685-138
REC	EDGER, HAND	2	2	775.684-014
REC	ELECTRICIAN HELPER, AUTOMOTIVE	2	2	825.684-010

Code	Title	GED	SVP	DOT No.
REC	ELECTRIFIER OPERATOR	2	3	585.685-042
REC	ELECTROLESS PLATER	2	3	505.684-010
REC	EMBOSSER	2	2	690.685-158
REC	ENROBING-MACHINE CORDER	2	4	524.684-018
REC	EXAMINER	2	2	739.687-082
REC	EXTRACTOR OPERATOR	2	2	581.685-042
REC	EXTRUDER-OPERATOR HELPER	2	2	557.564-010
REC	FABRIC STRETCHER	2	3	709.667-010
REC	FABRIC-LAY-OUT WORKER	2	2	589.687-022
REC	FABRIC-MACHINE OPERATOR 2	2	3	616.685-022
REC	FARMWORKER, FRUIT 2	2	2	403.687-010
REC	FARMWORKER, GENERAL 2	2	2	421.687-010
REC	FEATHER WASHER	2	2	582.685-066
REC	FELT-STRIP FINISHER	2	3	586.685-018
REC	FILLER	2	2	780.684-066
REC	FILLER SHREDDER, MACHINE	2	3	529.685-110
REC	FILM SPOOLER	2	2	692.685-082
REC	FILTER CLEANER	2	2	559.687-038
REC	FILTER HELPER	2	2	551.685-074
REC	FILTER-PRESS OPERATOR	2	3	551.685-082
REC	FILTER-TANK OPERATOR	2	2	551.585-010
REC	FILTERING-MACHINE TENDER	2	3	521.685-138
REC	FINAL ASSEMBLER	2	2	789.687-046
REC	FINISHER	2	4	774.684-018
REC	FINISHER, BRUSH	2	3	739.684-062
REC	FINISHER, FIBERGLASS BOAT PARTS	2	3	809.684-022
REC	FIREWORKS ASSEMBLER	2	2	737.587-014
REC	FISH CLEANER MACHINE TENDER	2	2	529.685-118
REC	FISH PACKER	2	2	920.687-086
REC	FISH-BIN TENDER	2	2	529.687-082
REC	FISH-NET STRINGER	2	3	782.684-026
REC	FISHER, LINE	2	3	442.684-010
REC	FISHING-LINE-WINDING-MACHINE OPERATOR	2	2	689.685-066
REC	FLAKER OPERATOR	2	3	559.685-074
REC	FLATWORK FINISHER	2	2	363.686-010
REC	FLOCKER	2	2	789.687-054
REC	FLOORWORKER, LASTING	2	2	788.687-046
REC	FLOWER-POT-PRESS OPERATOR	2	2	575.685-034
REC	FLUMER 1	2	3	922.665-010
REC	FOLDER, HAND	2	3	794.687-022
REC	FOLDING-MACHINE OPERATOR	2	2	208.685-014
REC	FOLDING-MACHINE OPERATOR	2	2	369.686-010
REC	FOLDING-MACHINE OPERATOR	2	2	583.685-042
REC	FOLDING-MACHINE OPERATOR	2	2	589.685-058
REC	FOLDING-MACHINE OPERATOR	2	2	689.585-014
REC	FOLDING-MACHINE FEEDER	2	2	641.685-050
REC	FOLDING-MACHINE TENDER	2	2	788.685-014
REC	FOOD MIXER	2	2	520.687-034
REC	FOOT WORKER	2	2	934.687-010
REC	FOREPART LASTER	2	2	690.685-186
REC	FOUNDRY LABORER, COREROOM	2	2	518.687-014
REC	FOXING PAINTER	2	2	584.685-022
REC	FRAME STRIPPER	2	2	559.685-086

Code	Title	GED	SVP	DOT No.
REC	FRAME TRIMMER 2	2	2	769.687-022
REC	FRESH-WORK INSPECTOR	2	3	529.687-090
REC	FRINGING-MACHINE OPERATOR	2	2	685.686-010
REC	FURNACE HELPER	2	2	553.687-014
REC	GARAGE SERVICER, INDUSTRIAL	2	3	915.687-014
REC	GARLAND-MACHINE OPERATOR	2	2	692.685-090
REC	GARMENT STEAMER	2	2	582.685-078
REC	GAS CHARGER	2	2	827.485-010
REC	GAS-AND-OIL SERVICER	2	2	915.587-010
REC	GAS-MASK ASSEMBLER	2	4	712.684-022
REC	GAS-METER-INSTALLER HELPER	2	2	953.687-010
REC	GLASS SANDER, BELT	2	2	775.684-042
REC	GLASS TINTER	2	5	840.684-010
REC	GLASS-UNLOADING-EQUIPMENT TENDER	2	2	677.665-010
REC	GLOVE CLEANER, HAND	2	2	362.687-010
REC	GLOVE PAIRER	2	2	784.687-034
REC	GLUE-SPREADING-MACHINE OPERATOR	2	2	584.665-014
REC	GLUING-MACHINE OPERATOR	2	3	569.685-046
REC	GOAT HERDER	2	3	410.687-014
REC	GOLD BURNISHER	2	2	775.687-022
REC	GRADER, GREEN MEAT	2	3	529.687-106
REC	GRAIN-DRIER OPERATOR	2	3	523.685-090
REC	GRAINER, MACHINE	2	2	652.686-014
REC	GRANULATING-MACHINE OPERATOR	2	2	521.685-158
REC	GRANULATOR OPERATOR	2	3	523.685-098
REC	GRAPHITE PAN-DRIER TENDER	2	4	549.685-014
REC	GREASE-REFINER OPERATOR	2	3	551.685-086
REC	GREASER OPERATOR	2	3	582.685-082
REC	GREEN-COFFEE BLENDER	2	2	520.685-110
REC	GREY-CLOTH TENDER, PRINTING	2	2	652.686-018
REC	GRINDER OPERATOR	2	3	555.685-034
REC	GRINDING-MACHINE OPERATOR, AUTOMATIC	2	2	690.685-194
REC	GUNNER	2	2	523.382-010
REC	HAMMER-MILL OPERATOR	2	3	515.687-010
REC	HAMMER-MILL OPERATOR	2	3	570.685-030
REC	HARDENER	2	4	784.684-034
REC	HARDENING-MACHINE OPERATOR	2	3	586.685-026
REC	HAT-BLOCKING-MACHINE OPERATOR 1	2	4	580.685-026
REC	HEAT-TREATER HELPER	2	2	504.685-018
REC	HEATING-ELEMENT WINDER	2	3	723.685-010
REC	HELPER, MANUFACTURING	2	2	809.687-014
REC	HIDE INSPECTOR	2	3	525.687-042
REC	HOG TENDER	2	2	564.685-018
REC	HOGSHEAD MAT ASSEMBLER	2	2	764.687-082
REC	HONEY PROCESSOR	2	3	522.685-070
REC	HOOKER-LASTER	2	3	753.684-018
REC	HOP WEIGHER	2	3	520.687-042
REC	HOPPER ATTENDANT	2	2	521.685-182
REC	HORIZONTAL-EARTH-BORING-MACHINE-OPERATOR HELPER	2	2	850.684-014
REC	HORSERADISH MAKER	2	2	529.685-142
REC	HOT-ROOM ATTENDANT	2	2	335.677-014
REC	HOTHOUSE WORKER	2	2	549.687-014

Code	Title	GED	SVP	DOT No.
REC	HOUSECLEANER	2	2	323.687-018
REC	HYDRAULIC-PRESS OPERATOR	2	2	583.685-054
REC	ICE CREAM FREEZER ASSISTANT	2	2	529.685-146
REC	ICE MAKER	2	3	523.685-102
REC	INJECTION-MOLDING-MACHINE TENDER	2	2	556.685-038
REC	INK PRINTER	2	2	652.685-038
REC	INSERTING-MACHINE OPERATOR	2	2	208.685-018
REC	INSPECTOR	2	4	780.687-022
REC	INSPECTOR	2	3	784.387-010
REC	INSPECTOR AND TESTER	2	3	809.687-018
REC	INSPECTOR 2	2	2	727.687-062
REC	INSPECTOR, CANNED FOOD RECONDITIONING	2	4	529.687-118
REC	INSPECTOR, EYEGLASS FRAMES	2	3	713.687-022
REC	INSPECTOR, CLIP-ON SUNGLASSES	2	3	713.667-010
REC	INSPECTOR, OIL FILTERS	2	2	739.687-114
REC	INSULATION-BLANKET MAKER	2	3	806.684-078
REC	INSULATION-POWER-UNIT TENDER	2	4	863.685-010
REC	IRISH-MOSS BLEACHER	2	2	447.687-014
REC	IRRIGATOR, VALVE PIPE	2	3	409.684-010
REC	IRRIGATOR, SPRINKLING SYSTEM	2	2	409.685-014
REC	JAMMER OPERATOR	2	3	921.683-054
REC	JEWEL-CORNER-BRUSHING-MACHINE OPERATOR	2	3	770.685-026
REC	JIG BUILDER	2	3	761.684-014
REC	JIGGER	2	3	582.665-018
REC	KILN DRAWER	2	2	573.667-010
REC	KILN PLACER	2	2	573.686-026
REC	KILN-FURNITURE CASTER	2	4	579.684-018
REC	KILN-OPERATOR HELPER	2	2	573.685-022
REC	KNIFE-MACHINE OPERATOR	2	4	584.685-030
REC	KNITTING-MACHINE OPERATOR HELPER	2	2	685.686-014
REC	KNOCK-OUT HAND	2	3	754.684-034
REC	KNOTTING-MACHINE OPERATOR	2	2	649.685-054
REC	LABEL DRIER	2	2	532.687-010
REC	LABORER, CHEESEMAKING	2	2	529.686-050
REC	LABORER, CONCRETE-MIXING PLANT	2	2	579.665-014
REC	LABORER, ELECTROPLATING	2	2	500.686-010
REC	LABORER, GRINDING AND POLISHING	2	2	705.687-014
REC	LABORER, TANBARK	2	3	454.687-014
REC	LACE-ROLLER OPERATOR	2	2	920.685-070
REC	LACER	2	3	732.687-034
REC	LACQUER-DIPPING-MACHINE OPERATOR	2	2	509.685-034
REC	LAGGING-MACHINE OPERATOR	2	2	691.685-014
REC	LAMINATION SPINNER	2	2	729.687-018
REC	LANE-MARKER INSTALLER	2	3	859.684-010
REC	LAST PULLER	2	2	788.687-086
REC	LAST REPAIRER	2	3	739.684-110
REC	LAST SCOURER	2	4	662.685-018
REC	LASTER	2	3	753.684-022
REC	LATEX SPOOLER	2	4	559.685-114
REC	LATHE SANDER	2	2	761.682-010
REC	LAUNDRY WORKER 2	2	2	361.685-018
REC	LAUNDRY-MACHINE TENDER	2	3	589.685-066

Code	Title	GED	SVP	DOT No.
REC	LEAF COVERER	2	3	519.684-014
REC	LEASE-OUT WORKER	2	3	683.684-022
REC	LEGEND MAKER	2	3	979.684-018
REC	LEVEL-VIAL INSPECTOR-AND-TESTER	2	3	701.687-026
REC	LEVER TENDER	2	4	612.685-010
REC	LIME SLAKER	2	4	570.685-034
REC	LIME-SLUDGE MIXER	2	3	550.585-026
REC	LINE-OUT WORKER 2	2	2	920.687-114
REC	LINGO CLEANER	2	2	683.687-026
REC	LINKING-MACHINE OPERATOR	2	2	529.685-162
REC	LIQUID-SUGAR FORTIFIER	2	4	520.585-022
REC	LIQUOR-GRINDING-MILL OPERATOR	2	3	521.685-202
REC	LOADING-MACHINE-OPERATOR HELPER	2	3	939.686-010
REC	LOCK INSTALLER	2	3	706.684-078
REC	LOG COOKER	2	2	562.665-010
REC	LUBRICATING-MACHINE TENDER	2	2	509.685-038
REC	MACHINE CLEANER	2	2	699.687-014
REC	MACHINE FEEDER	2	2	819.686-010
REC	MACHINE-CASTINGS PLASTERER	2	2	519.687-030
REC	MAILER	2	3	222.587-030
REC	MAINTENANCE-MECHANIC HELPER	2	4	638.684-018
REC	MANGLER	2	2	583.685-070
REC	MARKER	2	2	369.687-026
REC	MARKER, HAND	2	2	788.584-014
REC	MARKING-MACHINE OPERATOR	2	2	652.685-050
REC	MASH GRINDER	2	2	520.685-130
REC	MASKER	2	3	749.687-018
REC	MASKING-MACHINE FEEDER	2	2	920.586-010
REC	MAT PUNCHER	2	2	690.685-286
REC	MAT SEWER	2	2	529.687-154
REC	MATTING-PRESS TENDER	2	2	556.685-042
REC	MATTRESS-FILLING-MACHINE TENDER	2	2	780.685-010
REC	MELLOWING-MACHINE OPERATOR	2	2	585.685-066
REC	MERCURY PURIFIER	2	4	551.585-014
REC	MESS ATTENDANT	2	3	350.677-010
REC	METAL SPRAYER, PRODUCTION	2	3	505.684-014
REC	METAL-WASHING-MACHINE OPERATOR	2	2	503.685-034
REC	MEXICAN FOOD MAKER, HAND	2	2	520.687-046
REC	MICA-LAMINATING-MACHINE FEEDER	2	2	579.686-018
REC	MILL-AND-COAL-TRANSPORT OPERATOR	2	3	544.665-010
REC	MILLER	2	2	570.685-042
REC	MILLER, HEAD, ASSISTANT, WET PROCESS	2	5	629.684-014
REC	MILLWRIGHT HELPER	2	3	638.484-010
REC	MIX-CRUSHER OPERATOR	2	2	544.585-010
REC	MIXER	2	2	570.685-050
REC	MIXER	2	3	680.685-062
REC	MIXER OPERATOR HELPER, HOT METAL	2	2	509.566-010
REC	MIXER OPERATOR	2	2	520.685-142
REC	MOLDER, LEAD INGOT	2	2	502.685-010
REC	MOLDER, SHOE PARTS	2	2	788.687-094
REC	MOLDER, TOILET PRODUCTS	2	3	556.687-022
REC	MOP MAKER	2	2	739.685-026
REC	MOP-HANDLE ASSEMBLER	2	2	739.687-122

Code	Title	GED	SVP	DOT No.
REC	MOTORBOAT-MECHANIC HELPER	2	3	623.684-010
REC	MUD-MILL TENDER	2	3	519.685-026
REC	MUD-MIXER OPERATOR	2	2	570.685-070
REC	MULTI-OPERATION-FORMING-MACHINE OPERATOR 2	2	2	616.685-042
REC	MUNITIONS HANDLER	2	2	929.687-034
REC	NAILING-MACHINE OPERATOR	2	4	669.682-058
REC	NARROW-FABRIC CALENDERER	2	2	583.685-074
REC	NEUTRALIZER	2	3	558.585-034
REC	NOODLE-CATALYST MAKER	2	2	559.685-126
REC	NOVELTY WORKER	2	2	524.686-014
REC	NUT STEAMER	2	2	521.687-090
REC	ODD-PIECE CHECKER	2	2	221.587-018
REC	OFFAL SEPARATOR	2	2	525.684-038
REC	OFFSET-PRESS OPERATOR 2	2	3	651.685-018
REC	OIL DIPPER	2	3	769.684-026
REC	ORDER FILLER, LINSEED OIL	2	2	920.686-022
REC	OVEN OPERATOR	2	3	590.665-010
REC	PACKAGER, MACHINE	2	2	920.685-078
REC	PACKING-MACHINE CAN FEEDER	2	2	920.686-030
REC	PAD-EXTRACTOR TENDER	2	3	589.485-010
REC	PADDING-MACHINE OPERATOR	2	2	582.685-106
REC	PAGER	2	2	654.687-014
REC	PAINT-ROLLER COVERMAKER	2	2	739.684-142
REC	PANEL-MACHINE OPERATOR	2	2	640.685-038
REC	PARACHUTE MARKER	2	2	789.587-018
REC	PARAFFIN-MACHINE OPERATOR	2	2	534.685-026
REC	PASTER	2	3	773.684-014
REC	PATCH-MACHINE OPERATOR	2	2	641.685-066
REC	PATCHER	2	3	769.684-030
REC	PATCHER	2	4	861.684-014
REC	PATTERN GATER	2	4	801.684-014
REC	PATTERN MARKER 2	2	2	761.684-022
REC	PEARL-GLUE OPERATOR	2	3	550.685-094
REC	PERSONAL ATTENDANT	2	3	309.674-014
REC	PHOTOCOPYING-MACHINE OPERATOR	2	2	207.685-014
REC	PHOTOGRAPH FINISHER	2	2	976.487-010
REC	PHOTOSTAT-OPERATOR HELPER	2	2	979.687-014
REC	PICKING-MACHINE OPERATOR	2	2	680.685-082
REC	PICKLER	2	3	522.684-010
REC	PICKLER	2	2	522.687-034
REC	PICKLER HELPER, CONTINUOUS PICKLING LINE	2	3	503.686-010
REC	PILLING-MACHINE OPERATOR	2	4	556.685-058
REC	PIN MAKER	2	2	575.686-018
REC	PINSETTER-MECHANIC HELPER	2	2	829.667-014
REC	PLASTER-MACHINE TENDER	2	4	842.665-010
REC	PLATE GAGER	2	3	979.687-018
REC	PLATE WORKER	2	2	535.685-010
REC	PLATEN BUILDER-UP	2	4	651.384-010
REC	PLATING-MACHINE OPERATOR	2	2	649.686-026
REC	PLUG-OVERWRAP-MACHINE TENDER	2	3	529.685-186
REC	PLYWOOD-SCARFER TENDER	2	4	665.685-022
REC	POLISHING-PAD MOUNTER	2	2	739.687-154

Code	Title	GED	SVP	DOT No.
REC	POLYMERIZATION-OVEN OPERATOR	2	3	556.585-014
REC	POLYSTYRENE-MOLDING-MACHINE TENDER	2	2	556.685-062
REC	PORTER	2	2	357.677-010
REC	POULTRY DEBEAKER	2	3	411.687-026
REC	POWDER-CUTTING OPERATOR	2	2	559.685-134
REC	POWDERER	2	2	784.687-058
REC	POWER-PRESS TENDER	2	3	617.685-026
REC	PRECAST MOLDER	2	3	579.685-042
REC	PRESERVATIVE FILLER, MACHINE	2	3	529.685-190
REC	PRESS OPERATOR	2	2	363.685-010
REC	PRESS OPERATOR	2	2	551.685-118
REC	PRESS OPERATOR	2	3	559.685-138
REC	PRESS OPERATOR, PIERCE AND SHAVE	2	2	715.685-050
REC	PRESS TENDER	2	2	556.685-066
REC	PRESSER, AUTOMATIC	2	3	363.685-014
REC	PRESSER, BUFFING WHEEL	2	2	583.685-090
REC	PRESSER, FORM	2	2	363.685-018
REC	PRESSER, HAND	2	2	363.684-018
REC	PRESSURE-TANK OPERATOR	2	3	523.385-010
REC	PRINT WASHER	2	3	976.684-022
REC	PRINT-SHOP HELPER	2	3	979.684-026
REC	PRINTER, FLOOR COVERING	2	3	652.685-066
REC	PRINTER, FLOOR COVERING, ASSISTANT	2	2	652.687-038
REC	PROGRESSIVE ASSEMBLER AND FITTER	2	3	801.684-022
REC	PROJECT-CREW WORKER	2	3	891.687-018
REC	PULP-DRIER FIRER	2	3	523.585-030
REC	PUMP TENDER, CEMENT BASED MATERIALS	2	4	849.665-010
REC	PUNCHBOARD-FILLING-MACHINE OPERATOR	2	2	649.685-094
REC	QUILT STUFFER	2	2	789.687-130
REC	RAG-CUTTING-MACHINE FEEDER	2	2	530.666-010
REC	RAW-STOCK-DRIER TENDER	2	2	581.685-046
REC	RAWHIDE-BONE ROLLER	2	2	789.684-042
REC	REAMING-MACHINE TENDER	2	2	606.685-034
REC	RECLAMATION KETTLE TENDER, METAL	2	3	512.685-022
REC	RECORD-CHANGER TESTER	2	2	720.687-014
REC	REFRACTORY MIXER	2	3	570.685-078
REC	REFRACTORY-GRINDER OPERATOR	2	2	677.682-014
REC	RIVER	2	2	454.684-022
REC	RIVETER	2	2	616.685-054
REC	ROAD-ROLLER OPERATOR	2	3	859.683-030
REC	ROCK-DUST SPRAYER	2	2	939.687-026
REC	ROD-AND-TUBE STRAIGHTENER	2	2	559.587-010
REC	ROLLER OPERATOR	2	2	580.685-046
REC	ROLLER-LEVELER OPERATOR	2	2	613.685-022
REC	ROLLING-DOWN-MACHINE OPERATOR	2	2	589.685-086
REC	ROLLING-MACHINE OPERATOR	2	2	585.685-078
REC	ROLLING-MACHINE OPERATOR	2	2	640.685-070
REC	ROLLING-MILL-OPERATOR HELPER	2	3	613.685-026
REC	ROOF-TRUSS-MACHINE TENDER	2	2	669.685-070
REC	ROPE MAKER, MACHINE	2	3	681.685-082
REC	ROTARY-FURNACE TENDER	2	3	553.685-094
REC	ROUGH-RICE TENDER	2	3	521.685-274
REC	ROVING-WEIGHT GAGER	2	4	680.687-018
REC	RUG-DRY-ROOM ATTENDANT	2	2	369.685-026

Code	Title	GED	SVP	DOT No.
REC	RUG-DRYING-MACHINE OPERATOR	2	3	581.685-050
REC	SAGGER PREPARER	2	3	570.685-086
REC	SALVAGER	2	2	713.687-038
REC	SAMPLER	2	2	549.587-018
REC	SAMPLER-TESTER	2	3	579.585-010
REC	SAND PLANT ATTENDANT	2	2	934.685-014
REC	SANDBLAST OPERATOR	2	3	503.685-038
REC	SANDWICH-MACHINE OPERATOR	2	2	529.685-210
REC	SAUSAGE MIXER	2	3	520.685-206
REC	SAWYER	2	2	677.686-010
REC	SCREEN HANDLER	2	2	539.685-026
REC	SCREEN PRINTER	2	3	979.684-034
REC	SCREEN TENDER	2	3	534.665-010
REC	SCREEN-TENDER HELPER	2	2	533.687-010
REC	SCROLL-MACHINE OPERATOR	2	2	616.685-062
REC	SCRUBBING-MACHINE OPERATOR	2	3	582.685-122
REC	SCULLION	2	2	318.687-014
REC	SEALER	2	2	461.684-010
REC	SEALING-AND-CANCELING-MACHINE OPERATOR	2	2	208.685-026
REC	SEALING-MACHINE OPERATOR	2	2	641.685-074
REC	SEED-CLEANER OPERATOR	2	2	599.665-010
REC	SEPARATOR OPERATOR	2	4	521.382-014
REC	SEPARATOR OPERATOR, SHELLFISH MEATS	2	2	521.685-286
REC	SEWING-MACHINE OPERATOR, ZIPPER	2	2	787.685-034
REC	SHAKE BACKBOARD NOTCHER	2	2	663.685-030
REC	SHAKER REPAIRER	2	2	769.664-010
REC	SHAKER TENDER	2	3	541.665-010
REC	SHALE PLANER OPERATOR HELPER	2	2	930.667-010
REC	SHAVER	2	2	525.687-094
REC	SHEAR OPERATOR 2	2	3	615.685-034
REC	SHEEPSKIN PICKLER	2	2	582.685-126
REC	SHELL ASSEMBLER	2	5	737.684-038
REC	SHELLACKER	2	3	737.687-130
REC	SHELLFISH-PROCESSING-MACHINE TENDER	2	2	529.685-214
REC	SHIPFITTER HELPER	2	2	806.687-050
REC	SHIRRING-MACHINE OPERATOR, AUTOMATIC	2	3	787.685-038
REC	SHIRT PRESSER	2	2	363.685-026
REC	SHOE TURNER	2	2	788.687-130
REC	SHOT BAGGER	2	2	920.687-170
REC	SHOT-COAT TENDER	2	2	575.665-018
REC	SHRINKING-MACHINE OPERATOR	2	3	586.685-034
REC	SHUTTLE HAND	2	2	689.686-038
REC	SIEVE MAKER	2	2	529.684-018
REC	SIEVE-GRADER TENDER	2	2	521.665-026
REC	SILVER STRIPPER, MACHINE	2	2	579.685-054
REC	SINGER	2	2	525.687-098
REC	SINGER	2	2	784.687-062
REC	SIZER, HAND	2	3	784.684-054
REC	SIZER, MACHINE	2	2	784.684-058
REC	SKEIN WINDER	2	3	681.685-098
REC	SKEIN-YARN DYER	2	3	582.685-130
REC	SKEINER	2	2	681.685-102

Code	Title	GED	SVP	DOT No.
REC	SKIN-LAP BONDER	2	3	806.684-130
REC	SLICING-MACHINE TENDER	2	3	663.685-034
REC	SLIDE-MACHINE TENDER	2	2	641.685-078
REC	SLIME-PLANT-OPERATOR HELPER	2	3	511.685-058
REC	SLUG-PRESS OPERATOR	2	2	556.685-074
REC	SNUFF-BOX FINISHER	2	2	920.687-174
REC	SOFT CRAB SHEDDER	2	4	446.684-018
REC	SOLDERER, BARREL RIBS	2	3	736.684-038
REC	SPARK-PLUG ASSEMBLER	2	2	729.684-046
REC	SPEED-BELT-SANDER TENDER	2	2	662.685-034
REC	SPEEDER TENDER	2	2	681.685-106
REC	SPICE MILLER	2	3	521.685-326
REC	SPINNING-LATHE OPERATOR, AUTOMATIC	2	2	619.685-082
REC	SPIRAL RUNNER	2	4	934.685-022
REC	SPIRAL-TUBE-WINDER HELPER	2	2	640.687-014
REC	SPLICING-MACHINE OPERATOR	2	4	689.682-018
REC	SPLITTING-MACHINE OPERATOR	2	2	690.685-386
REC	SPONGE HOOKER	2	2	447.684-010
REC	SPOOLER OPERATOR, AUTOMATIC	2	2	681.686-018
REC	SPOOLER, SEQUINS	2	2	920.686-046
REC	SPOOLING-MACHINE OPERATOR	2	3	691.685-026
REC	SPRAY-GUN-REPAIRER HELPER	2	3	630.684-034
REC	SPRAYER, MACHINE	2	2	599.685-094
REC	SPREADER, MACHINE	2	3	781.685-010
REC	SPRING ASSEMBLER	2	2	780.684-098
REC	STACKER	2	2	222.587-046
REC	STACKER-AND-SORTER OPERATOR	2	3	921.682-018
REC	STACKER, MACHINE	2	2	569.685-066
REC	STAINER	2	2	589.687-034
REC	STAINING-MACHINE OPERATOR	2	3	582.685-142
REC	STAMPER	2	2	734.685-010
REC	STAPLING-MACHINE OPERATOR	2	2	692.685-202
REC	STAVE-PLANER TENDER	2	2	665.686-014
REC	STEAM-OVEN OPERATOR	2	3	526.382-026
REC	STEAMER TENDER	2	2	582.685-146
REC	STICKER, ANIMAL	2	3	525.684-050
REC	STOCK CHECKERER 2	2	2	665.685-034
REC	STOCK SHAPER	2	3	761.684-046
REC	STONE CLEANER	2	2	529.687-190
REC	STONE SPLITTER	2	2	677.685-050
REC	STOVE-BOTTOM WORKER	2	2	590.667-010
REC	STRAND-FORMING-MACHINE OPERATOR	2	3	681.685-118
REC	STREET-LIGHT CLEANER	2	2	952.667-010
REC	STREET-SWEEPER OPERATOR	2	3	919.683-022
REC	STRETCHER	2	2	580.685-054
REC	STRIP POLISHER	2	2	673.685-082
REC	STRIP-TANK TENDER	2	3	503.685-046
REC	STRIPPER-CUTTER, MACHINE	2	2	521.685-342
REC	STUFFER	2	2	520.685-210
REC	STUFFING-MACHINE OPERATOR	2	2	732.685-034
REC	SUBSTATION-OPERATOR HELPER	2	5	952.687-010
REC	SUCTION-PLATE-CARRIER CLEANER	2	2	529.687-194
REC	SUGAR CONTROLLER	2	3	529.565-010
REC	SULFATE DRIER-MACHINE OPERATOR	2	4	551.685-142

Code	Title	GED	SVP	DOT No.
REC	SUNGLASS-CLIP ATTACHER	2	2	713.687-042
REC	SWEDGER	2	2	735.687-038
REC	SWEET-GOODS-MACHINE OPERATOR	2	3	520.685-214
REC	SWEET-POTATO DISINTEGRATOR	2	2	521.685-358
REC	SYNTHETIC-FILAMENT EXTRUDER	2	3	557.565-014
REC	TABLE-COVER FOLDER	2	2	920.687-186
REC	TABLET-MACHINE OPERATOR	2	2	529.685-238
REC	TAG-MACHINE OPERATOR	2	2	649.685-118
REC	TANK CLEANER	2	3	559.684-022
REC	TANK CLEANER	2	2	559.687-062
REC	TANK PUMPER, PANELBOARD	2	3	529.685-242
REC	TANK-HOUSE-OPERATOR HELPER	2	3	519.565-014
REC	TAPER, MACHINE	2	2	692.685-214
REC	TARRING-MACHINE OPERATOR	2	3	584.685-046
REC	TAXI SERVICER	2	2	915.687-030
REC	TERRAZZO-TILE MAKER	2	3	575.684-046
REC	TESTING-MACHINE OPERATOR	2	2	703.685-014
REC	TETRYL-SCREEN OPERATOR	2	2	551.685-146
REC	THERMAL MOLDER	2	3	553.585-022
REC	THREADER	2	2	689.687-078
REC	TICKET TAKER, FERRYBOAT	2	2	911.677-010
REC	TIE PRESSER	2	2	789.687-178
REC	TILE-POWER-SHEAR OPERATOR	2	2	692.685-222
REC	TIP BANDER	2	2	733.685-030
REC	TIPPLE OPERATOR	2	3	921.662-026
REC	TIPPLE TENDER	2	2	669.685-090
REC	TIRE BUILDER	2	3	750.684-022
REC	TIRE MOUNTER	2	2	739.684-158
REC	TIRE VULCANIZER	2	3	750.684-038
REC	TRANSFER OPERATOR	2	3	921.685-066
REC	TRAVELER CHANGER	2	2	682.687-010
REC	TRAY-CASTING-MACHINE OPERATOR	2	2	520.685-218
REC	TREE-SURGEON HELPER 2	2	2	408.687-018
REC	TRIMMER	2	2	869.684-066
REC	TRIPE COOKER	2	2	526.685-062
REC	TROMMEL TENDER	2	2	511.685-066
REC	TRUER, PINION AND WHEEL	2	3	715.684-194
REC	TUBBER	2	2	599.685-098
REC	TUBE ASSEMBLER, CATHODE RAY	2	3	725.684-022
REC	TUBE CLEANER	2	2	891.687-030
REC	TUBE COATER	2	2	599.685-102
REC	TUBE SORTER	2	3	559.687-066
REC	TUBE-BUILDING-MACHINE OPERATOR	2	3	559.685-174
REC	TUBE-MACHINE-OPERATOR HELPER	2	2	641.686-038
REC	TUMBLER OPERATOR	2	2	550.685-118
REC	TUMBLER OPERATOR	2	2	553.585-026
REC	TUMBLER OPERATOR	2	2	599.685-110
REC	TURNER	2	3	669.685-094
REC	TURNING-SANDER OPERATOR	2	3	662.685-038
REC	TWISTING-MACHINE OPERATOR	2	2	619.485-014
REC	UNLEAVENED-DOUGH MIXER	2	2	520.685-226
REC	UTILITY WORKER	2	2	529.686-086
REC	VACUUM-PAN OPERATOR 1	2	2	551.685-150
REC	VACUUM-PAN OPERATOR 2	2	3	551.685-154

Code	Title	GED	SVP	DOT No.
REC	VARNISH-MAKER HELPER	2	2	553.686-042
REC	VENETIAN-BLIND ASSEMBLER	2	3	739.684-166
REC	VULCANIZER	2	2	690.685-462
REC	WAFER-MACHINE OPERATOR	2	3	526.685-066
REC	WAIST PLEATER	2	4	583.684-014
REC	WARP-DYEING-VAT TENDER	2	4	582.685-158
REC	WARP-TENSION TESTER	2	2	683.687-034
REC	WASH-MILL OPERATOR	2	3	559.485-010
REC	WASHER	2	2	529.687-210
REC	WASHER	2	3	582.685-162
REC	WASHER	2	2	599.687-030
REC	WASHER	2	2	715.687-126
REC	WASHER, HAND	2	2	361.687-030
REC	WASHER, MACHINE	2	2	599.685-114
REC	WASHROOM OPERATOR	2	2	529.665-014
REC	WASTE CHOPPER	2	2	689.686-054
REC	WELD INSPECTOR	2	2	724.685-014
REC	WELT WHEELER	2	2	690.685-482
REC	WELT-BUTTER, HAND	2	2	788.687-162
REC	WET-MACHINE TENDER	2	3	539.685-030
REC	WICK-AND-BASE ASSEMBLER	2	2	739.687-202
REC	WINDER HELPER	2	3	539.685-034
REC	WINDING-LATHE OPERATOR	2	3	619.685-086
REC	WIRE DRAWER	2	2	735.687-042
REC	WIRE-DRAWING-MACHINE TENDER	2	3	614.685-026
REC	WIRE-FRAME DIPPER	2	2	734.684-026
REC	WIRE-WINDING-MACHINE TENDER	2	2	690.685-490
REC	WIREWORKER	2	4	709.684-106
REC	WOOD CALKER	2	3	843.384-010
REC	WOOD-HEEL BACK-LINER	2	2	662.685-042
REC	WOODWORKING-MACHINE FEEDER	2	2	669.686-030
REC	WOODWORKING-MACHINE OFFBEARER	2	2	669.686-034
REC	WORK-TICKET DISTRIBUTOR	2	2	221.667-010
REC	WORM PICKER	2	1	413.687-010
REC	WORM-FARM LABORER	2	1	413.687-014
REC	WRAPPER-HANDS SPRAYER	2	2	522.687-042
REC	WREATH MACHINE TENDER	2	2	739.685-058
REC	WRINGER OPERATOR	2	2	522.685-106
REC	WRINGER OPERATOR	2	2	551.685-162
REC	YARDAGE-CONTROL CLERK	2	2	221.587-050
REC	YARN-MERCERIZER OPERATOR 2	2	3	584.685-058
REC	YEAST-FERMENTATION ATTENDANT	2	3	522.685-110
REC	ZIPPER CUTTER	2	2	616.685-090
REC	ALMOND BLANCHER, HAND	1	1	521.687-010
REC	ASBESTOS-SHINGLE SHEARING-MACHINE OPERATOR	1	2	679.686-010
REC	ASSEMBLER	1	2	731.687-010
REC	ASSEMBLER, BICYCLE 2	1	2	806.687-010
REC	AUTOMATIC-NAILING-MACHINE FEEDER	1	2	669.686-010
REC	BACK-STRIP-MACHINE OPERATOR	1	2	690.685-018
REC	BAG LOADER	1	1	737.687-014
REC	BAGGER	1	2	582.687-010
REC	BAKERY WORKER	1	2	929.686-010
REC	BALE SEWER	1	2	920.687-022

Code	Title	GED	SVP	DOT No.
REC	BAND SALVAGER	1	1	929.686-014
REC	BAND TUMBLER	1	2	551.685-010
REC	BASE REMOVER	1	2	692.686-014
REC	BASTING PULLER	1	2	782.687-010
REC	BATTERY STACKER	1	2	727.687-030
REC	BATTERY-CONTAINER-FINISHING HAND	1	2	727.687-034
REC	BEADER	1	2	739.687-034
REC	BELT PICKER	1	1	939.687-010
REC	BEVELING-MACHINE OPERATOR	1	2	690.686-010
REC	BIAS-MACHINE-OPERATOR HELPER	1	2	690.686-014
REC	BIN CLEANER	1	2	529.687-014
REC	BLEACH PACKER	1	1	558.687-010
REC	BLENDER	1	2	520.585-010
REC	BLINTZE ROLLER	1	2	520.687-014
REC	BLOCK INSPECTOR	1	2	739.687-038
REC	BOAT BUFFER, PLASTIC	1	3	849.684-010
REC	BOBBIN WINDER, MACHINE	1	2	681.685-022
REC	BOBBIN-CLEANING-MACHINE OPERATOR	1	2	689.686-014
REC	BORDER MEASURER AND CUTTER	1	1	780.687-010
REC	BOTTOM BLEACHER	1	2	788.687-014
REC	BOX-TRUCK WASHER	1	1	529.687-018
REC	BRAKE-LINING CURER	1	2	573.686-010
REC	BREAKER-UP-MACHINE OPERATOR	1	2	589.685-014
REC	BRIMER	1	2	700.687-018
REC	BROOMCORN SEEDER	1	2	692.686-018
REC	BRUSHER	1	2	788.687-018
REC	BUFFER, AUTOMATIC	1	2	690.685-050
REC	BULLET-LUBRICATING-MACHINE OPERATOR	1	2	694.685-018
REC	BUNDLE BREAKER	1	2	689.687-018
REC	CAKE WRAPPER	1	2	589.687-010
REC	CANDY SPREADER	1	2	520.687-022
REC	CARROTING-MACHINE OFFBEARER	1	1	586.686-010
REC	CASING-IN-LINE FEEDER	1	2	653.686-010
REC	CASING-RUNNING-MACHINE TENDER	1	2	525.685-014
REC	CEMENT SPRAYER HELPER, NOZZLE	1	2	844.687-010
REC	CHALK CUTTER	1	2	733.687-022
REC	CHANNEL OPENER, OUTSOLES	1	2	690.685-082
REC	CHARGER-OPERATOR HELPER	1	2	504.686-010
REC	CHASER, TAR	1	2	549.687-010
REC	CHERRY CUTTER	1	1	524.687-010
REC	CHIP-BIN CONVEYOR TENDER	1	2	921.685-022
REC	CLAMPER	1	2	733.687-026
REC	CLEANER	1	2	704.687-010
REC	CLEANER AND PREPARER	1	2	721.687-010
REC	CLEANER, COMMERCIAL OR INSTITUTIONAL	1	2	381.687-014
REC	CLEANER, WALL	1	2	381.687-026
REC	CLEAT FEEDER	1	2	669.687-010
REC	CLIPPER	1	2	789.687-030
REC	CLOTH SANDER	1	2	581.685-010
REC	CLOTH-SHRINKING-MACHINE-OPERATOR HELPER	1	2	587.686-010
REC	CLOTHESPIN-MACHINE OPERATOR	1	2	667.686-010
REC	COFFEE-ROASTER HELPER	1	2	523.687-010

Code	Title	GED	SVP	DOT No.
REC	COKE DRAWER, HAND	1	2	543.687-010
REC	COMPENSATOR	1	2	640.685-026
REC	COMPOUND WORKER	1	2	559.686-010
REC	CONVEYOR TENDER	1	2	921.685-026
REC	COOKER CLEANER	1	2	529.687-054
REC	COOKER LOADER	1	2	921.685-030
REC	CORK-PRESSING-MACHINE OPERATOR	1	2	569.686-018
REC	CORN POPPER	1	2	526.685-026
REC	COTTON PULLER	1	1	521.686-022
REC	COTTON TIER	1	2	920.687-074
REC	CUSTOM-FEED-MILL-OPERATOR HELPER	1	2	521.686-026
REC	CUTTER	1	2	692.686-030
REC	CUTTER, HAND 3	1	2	781.687-030
REC	DEBRANDER	1	2	753.687-014
REC	DEOILING-MACHINE AND PASTEURIZING-MACHINE OPERATOR	1	2	529.685-094
REC	DETACKER	1	2	589.685-030
REC	DIPPER	1	2	733.687-038
REC	DIPPER AND DRIER	1	2	749.687-010
REC	DISTRIBUTOR-CLEANER	1	1	529.687-070
REC	DRIER ATTENDANT	1	1	581.686-018
REC	DRIER OPERATOR	1	2	523.685-062
REC	DRIER TENDER 1	1	2	523.685-074
REC	DRIER-OPERATOR HELPER	1	2	553.685-058
REC	DRIP-BOX TENDER	1	1	521.687-038
REC	DRUM ATTENDANT	1	2	582.685-050
REC	DRY-PRESS-OPERATOR HELPER	1	2	575.686-010
REC	DRYING-ROOM ATTENDANT	1	2	553.585-018
REC	DRYING-ROOM ATTENDANT	1	1	581.687-014
REC	DULSER	1	2	447.687-010
REC	DUMPER	1	1	922.686-010
REC	DUST-BRUSH ASSEMBLER	1	2	739.687-074
REC	DYE-STAND LOADER	1	2	589.587-010
REC	DYER	1	2	582.687-014
REC	EGG BREAKER	1	2	521.687-042
REC	EGG-BREAKING-MACHINE OPERATOR	1	2	521.685-114
REC	EXTRACTOR OPERATOR	1	2	581.685-038
REC	EXTRACTOR-MACHINE OPERATOR	1	2	521.665-014
REC	FACTORY HELPER	1	2	529.686-034
REC	FARMWORKER, FIELD CROP 2	1	2	404.687-010
REC	FEATHER RENOVATOR	1	2	362.685-010
REC	FEATHER-CUTTING-MACHINE FEEDER	1	1	585.686-010
REC	FELTING-MACHINE-OPERATOR HELPER	1	2	586.686-014
REC	FILLER-SHREDDER HELPER	1	2	529.687-078
REC	FILTER CHANGER	1	2	521.687-050
REC	FIRST-BREAKER FEEDER	1	2	680.686-014
REC	FISH BAILER	1	2	914.685-010
REC	FISH CLEANER	1	2	525.684-030
REC	FLAME DEGREASER	1	2	503.685-022
REC	FLOOR WORKER	1	1	739.687-098
REC	FLOTATION-TENDER HELPER	1	1	511.687-018
REC	FLOUR-BLENDER HELPER	1	2	520.686-022
REC	FLUMER	1	1	521.686-038
REC	FLUMER 2	1	1	521.686-042

Code	Title	GED	SVP	DOT No.
REC	FOILING-MACHINE OPERATOR	1	2	692.685-086
REC	FOLDER	1	2	789.687-058
REC	FOLDING-MACHINE FEEDER	1	2	653.686-014
REC	FOLDING-MACHINE FEEDER	1	2	920.686-018
REC	FRAME FEEDER	1	2	553.686-034
REC	FUR-FLOOR WORKER	1	2	589.686-022
REC	FUSING-MACHINE TENDER	1	2	583.685-046
REC	GARMENT TURNER	1	2	789.687-074
REC	GENERAL HELPER	1	2	522.686-014
REC	GENERAL HELPER	1	2	529.686-046
REC	GENERAL HELPER	1	2	529.687-094
REC	GLOVE FORMER	1	3	363.687-010
REC	GLOVE TURNER AND FORMER, AUTOMATIC	1	2	583.686-018
REC	GLOVE TURNER	1	2	784.687-038
REC	GLUTEN-SETTLING TENDER	1	2	521.685-150
REC	GREASER	1	2	736.687-010
REC	GREENS TIER	1	1	920.687-094
REC	HACKER	1	2	573.686-022
REC	HAM-ROLLING-MACHINE OPERATOR	1	2	529.685-138
REC	HAMMER ADJUSTER	1	1	715.687-046
REC	HARNESS CLEANER	1	2	699.687-010
REC	HARVEST WORKER, FIELD CROP	1	1	404.687-014
REC	HAT-BLOCKING-MACHINE OPERATOR 2	1	2	580.685-030
REC	HAY SORTER	1	1	732.686-010
REC	HOGSHEAD HOOPER	1	2	764.687-078
REC	HONEY EXTRACTOR	1	2	521.685-174
REC	HOOK PULLER	1	1	683.687-022
REC	HOOP COILER	1	2	617.686-010
REC	HOPPER FEEDER	1	2	551.686-018
REC	HOT-WORT SETTLER	1	2	521.685-186
REC	IRISH-MOSS GATHERER	1	2	447.687-018
REC	IRONER, SOCK	1	1	363.687-014
REC	KEG VARNISHER	1	2	749.687-014
REC	KILN LOADER	1	2	523.687-018
REC	LABORER, COOK HOUSE	1	2	551.687-022
REC	LABORER, GENERAL	1	2	909.687-014
REC	LABORER, TREE TAPPING	1	2	453.687-014
REC	LABORER, VAT HOUSE	1	2	559.686-030
REC	LACER AND TIER	1	2	724.687-010
REC	LACER 1	1	2	788.687-070
REC	LACING-STRING CUTTER	1	1	788.687-074
REC	LATRINE CLEANER	1	2	939.687-022
REC	LAUNDRY LABORER	1	2	361.687-018
REC	LAUNDRY-BAG-PUNCH OPERATOR	1	2	649.685-062
REC	LEAD FORMER	1	2	575.685-050
REC	LEAF CONDITIONER	1	2	522.687-026
REC	LEAF-CONDITIONER HELPER	1	2	522.687-030
REC	LEATHER COATER	1	1	584.687-010
REC	LEVELER 1	1	2	764.687-094
REC	LINING SCRUBBER	1	2	362.687-014
REC	LOOSE-END FINDER, BOBBIN	1	2	681.687-014
REC	LOWERATOR OPERATOR	1	2	922.686-014
REC	MACHINE FEEDER	1	2	699.686-010
REC	MANGLE-PRESS CATCHER	1	2	583.686-022

Code	Title	GED	SVP	DOT No.
REC	MASH-FILTER OPERATOR	1	2	521.565-014
REC	MEAL-GRINDER TENDER	1	2	521.685-210
REC	MILL FEEDER	1	2	520.685-134
REC	MILL-OPERATOR HELPER	1	2	599.686-010
REC	MILLER	1	2	521.585-014
REC	MIXER OPERATOR	1	2	570.685-058
REC	MOLD CLEANER	1	2	732.687-046
REC	MOLD STRIPPER	1	2	732.687-050
REC	MOLDER HELPER	1	2	575.686-014
REC	MOLDING-MACHINE-OPERATOR HELPER	1	2	520.686-030
REC	MOSQUITO SPRAYER	1	3	379.687-014
REC	MOTOR POLARIZER	1	2	715.687-090
REC	MOUNTER 2	1	3	692.685-126
REC	MUD-MIXER HELPER	1	2	549.687-022
REC	NECK SKEWER	1	2	525.687-050
REC	NEEDLE-PUNCH-MACHINE-OPERATOR HELPER	1	2	689.686-034
REC	NUT-AND-BOLT ASSEMBLER	1	2	929.587-010
REC	ODD BUNDLE WORKER	1	2	529.687-166
REC	OPENER	1	2	559.686-034
REC	OPENER 2	1	2	589.686-030
REC	ORDER RUNNER	1	2	525.687-058
REC	OYSTER FLOATER	1	1	449.687-010
REC	PACKER-FUSER	1	1	737.687-094
REC	PAD-MACHINE FEEDER	1	2	920.686-034
REC	PAINTER, PANEL EDGE	1	2	740.687-022
REC	PALLBEARER	1	1	359.687-010
REC	PAPER-BAG-PRESS OPERATOR	1	2	641.686-026
REC	PARTITION ASSEMBLER	1	1	762.687-054
REC	PEANUT BLANCHER	1	2	521.685-246
REC	PEELED-POTATO INSPECTOR	1	2	521.687-094
REC	PERFECT-BINDER FEEDER-OFFBEARER	1	2	653.686-022
REC	PICK REMOVER	1	2	689.687-058
REC	PICKER	1	2	521.687-098
REC	PICKING-TABLE WORKER	1	1	521.687-102
REC	PILLOW CLEANER	1	1	789.687-122
REC	PLUG SHAPER, HAND	1	3	520.687-050
REC	POINTING-MACHINE OPERATOR	1	2	690.685-310
REC	POULTRY DRESSER	1	2	525.687-070
REC	POULTRY EVISCERATOR	1	2	525.687-074
REC	POULTRY HANGER	1	1	525.687-078
REC	POULTRY KILLER	1	2	525.684-042
REC	POURER	1	2	739.687-158
REC	PREPARATION-ROOM WORKER	1	2	570.686-018
REC	PRESS FEEDER	1	2	583.686-030
REC	PRESS HAND	1	2	583.687-010
REC	PRESS MACHINE FEEDER	1	2	529.686-066
REC	PRESS OPERATOR, MEAT	1	2	520.685-182
REC	PRESSER, HANDKERCHIEF	1	2	363.685-022
REC	PRINT-LINE TAILER	1	1	652.686-030
REC	PRODUCTION HELPER	1	1	691.687-010
REC	PULPER TENDER	1	2	521.685-262
REC	PUTTY MIXER AND APPLIER	1	1	769.687-038
REC	RACK LOADER	1	1	590.687-018

Code	Title	GED	SVP	DOT No.
REC	RACKER	1	2	715.687-106
REC	RACKER, SILK-SCREEN PRINTING	1	2	659.687-014
REC	RAKER	1	2	789.687-138
REC	RAW-STOCK-MACHINE LOADER	1	2	582.686-018
REC	ROLL CUTTER	1	2	690.685-322
REC	ROLL TURNER	1	2	689.685-110
REC	ROLLER CLEANER	1	2	680.687-014
REC	ROUGE MIXER	1	2	570.685-082
REC	RUG CUTTER	1	1	590.687-022
REC	RUG-INSPECTOR HELPER	1	2	589.686-038
REC	RUG-SAMPLE BEVELER	1	2	781.684-050
REC	SAMPLE WASHER	1	2	939.687-030
REC	SANDER, HAND	1	2	761.687-010
REC	SCREEN CLEANER	1	2	569.687-018
REC	SEAM STEAMER	1	1	789.687-166
REC	SEEDLING SORTER	1	2	451.687-022
REC	SHACKLER	1	2	525.687-086
REC	SHAKER	1	1	521.687-110
REC	SHAKER	1	2	589.685-094
REC	SHAKER, WEARING APPAREL	1	2	361.687-026
REC	SHANK-PIECE TACKER	1	2	788.687-118
REC	SHAPING-MACHINE OPERATOR	1	2	690.685-354
REC	SHEET TURNER	1	2	762.687-062
REC	SHOE COVERER	1	2	788.687-126
REC	SHROUDER	1	2	525.587-010
REC	SINGER	1	2	585.687-030
REC	SKEIN-YARN DRIER	1	2	581.685-054
REC	SKIN LIFTER, BACON	1	1	521.687-126
REC	SKULL GRINDER	1	2	521.687-130
REC	SLAT TWISTER	1	2	616.685-066
REC	SLAT-BASKET MAKER HELPER, MACHINE	1	2	669.686-026
REC	SLEEVER	1	2	641.686-034
REC	SLICING-MACHINE TENDER	1	1	663.686-026
REC	SLOTTER-OPERATOR HELPER	1	2	640.686-014
REC	SNOW SHOVELER	1	1	955.687-014
REC	SODA-ROOM OPERATOR	1	2	551.687-034
REC	SORTER, AGRICULTURAL PRODUCE	1	2	529.687-186
REC	SPLICER	1	2	692.687-010
REC	SPLITTER, HAND	1	2	734.687-086
REC	SPOOL MAKER	1	2	641.685-082
REC	SPREADER OPERATOR, AUTOMATIC	1	2	529.685-222
REC	STEAM-TUNNEL FEEDER	1	1	562.686-010
REC	STEAMER	1	1	525.687-110
REC	STEM-DRYER MAINTAINER	1	2	529.685-230
REC	STENCILER	1	2	920.687-178
REC	STITCHING-MACHINE FEEDER-OFFBEARER	1	2	653.686-026
REC	STRAW-HAT-WASHER OPERATOR	1	1	784.687-078
REC	STRIPPER	1	2	556.686-018
REC	SUGAR PRESSER	1	2	521.685-350
REC	SUMATRA OPENER	1	2	529.687-198
REC	SUPPOSITORY-MOLDING-MACHINE OPERATOR	1	2	556.686-022
REC	SWEATBAND FLANGER	1	2	690.686-058
REC	SWEATBAND-CUTTING-MACHINE OPERATOR	1	2	690.686-062

Code	Title	GED	SVP	DOT No.
REC	TAPE COATER	1	2	692.685-210
REC	TENNIS-BALL-COVER CEMENTER	1	2	795.687-030
REC	THREAD-PULLING-MACHINE ATTENDANT	1	1	689.686-046
REC	TIGHTENING-MACHINE OPERATOR	1	2	640.685-082
REC	TIMBER PACKER	1	2	922.687-094
REC	TIN STACKER	1	1	922.687-098
REC	TOGGLE-PRESS FOLDER-AND-FEEDER	1	2	690.686-066
REC	TOPPER	1	2	685.687-026
REC	TRAY DRIER	1	2	581.686-038
REC	TREE PLANTER	1	1	452.687-018
REC	TRIMMER, HAND	1	2	585.684-010
REC	TRIMMER, MEAT	1	2	525.684-054
REC	TROLLEY CLEANER	1	2	529.687-206
REC	TUBE COVERER	1	2	589.687-046
REC	TUBE HANDLER	1	2	582.686-034
REC	TURNER	1	2	522.687-038
REC	TURNER	1	2	789.687-182
REC	TWISTING-MACHINE OPERATOR	1	2	691.686-010
REC	UMBRELLA FINISHER	1	2	739.687-190
REC	VENEER-DRIER FEEDER	1	1	563.686-014
REC	WASHER, AGRICULTURAL PRODUCE	1	2	529.685-258
REC	WASHER, CARCASS	1	1	525.687-122
REC	WASHROOM CLEANER	1	2	529.687-214
REC	WAX-BALL KNOCK-OUT WORKER	1	2	732.687-082
REC	WEEDER-THINNER	1	1	409.687-018
REC	WET-COTTON FEEDER	1	2	581.686-042
REC	WOOD HANDLER	1	2	921.687-034
REC	WOOD-POLE TREATER	1	1	561.687-010
REC	WORM PACKER	1	1	920.687-202
REC	WRAPPING MACHINE HELPER	1	2	529.687-222
REC	WRINGER-MACHINE OPERATOR	1	2	589.685-098
REC	YARN-MERCERIZER-OPERATOR HELPER	1	2	584.686-010
RCI	ACCELERATOR OPERATOR	5	7	015.362-010
RCI	CALIBRATION LABORATORY TECHNICIAN	5	7	019.281-010
RCI	UTILIZATION ENGINEER	5	8	007.061-034
RCI	ASSEMBLER	4	7	722.381-010
RCI	CLEARING-HOUSE CLERK	4	5	216.382-026
RCI	CONSTRUCTION CHECKER	4	6	821.367-010
RCI	DRAFTER, ARCHITECTURAL	4	7	001.261-010
RCI	ELECTROCARDIOGRAPH TECHNICIAN	4	6	078.362-018
RCI	ESTIMATOR, PAPERBOARD BOXES	4	6	221.362-018
RCI	GRAVEL INSPECTOR	4	5	859.281-010
RCI	INSPECTOR, FIREARMS	4	6	632.381-014
RCI	MONOTYPE-KEYBOARD OPERATOR	4	6	650.582-014
RCI	PHOTOTYPESETTER OPERATOR	4	5	650.582-022
RCI	STEREO-PLOTTER OPERATOR	4	7	018.281-010
RCI	SURGICAL-ELASTIC KNITTER, HAND FRAME	4	5	685.382-010
RCI	ASSEMBLER, PRODUCT	3	3	706.684-018
RCI	BALANCE-BRIDGE ASSEMBLER	3	3	715.684-022
RCI	CARPET SEWER	3	3	787.682-014
RCI	CASE HARDENER	3	4	504.682-014
RCI	COREMAKER	3	5	518.381-014

Code	Title	GED	SVP	DOT No.
RCI	COREMAKER APPRENTICE	3	5	518.381-018
RCI	EXTRUDING-MACHINE OPERATOR	3	4	691.382-010
RCI	INSULATING-MACHINE OPERATOR	3	4	691.682-018
RCI	INVENTORY CLERK	3	4	222.387-026
RCI	RUBBER-GOODS CUTTER-FINISHER	3	4	690.680-010
RCI	RUBBER-PRINTING-MACHINE OPERATOR	3	4	652.462-010
RCI	SEWING-MACHINE TESTER	3	5	709.382-010
RCI	SPLITTING-MACHINE OPERATOR	3	3	677.685-046
RCI	SWITCH INSPECTOR	3	5	952.381-010
RCI	TILE DECORATOR	3	4	773.381-010
RCI	TIRE REPAIRER	3	3	750.681-010
RCI	NIGHT-PATROL INSPECTOR	2	2	824.683-010
RCS	ACCOUNTANT (CRS)	5	8	160.167-010
RCS	ACCOUNTANT, BUDGET (CRS)	5	8	160.167-014
RCS	SURVEYOR, OIL-WELL DIRECTIONAL	5	7	010.261-022
RCS	AIRCRAFT-PHOTOGRAPHIC-EQUIPMENT MECHANIC	4	8	714.281-010
RCS	ATOMIC-FUEL ASSEMBLER	4	4	709.381-010
RCS	BIOLOGY SPECIMEN TECHNICIAN	4	7	041.381-010
RCS	CABLE SPLICER	4	7	829.361-010
RCS	CABLE-SPLICER APPRENTICE	4	7	829.361-014
RCS	CAMERA OPERATOR, TITLE	4	7	976.382-010
RCS	DIESEL-PLANT OPERATOR	4	6	952.382-010
RCS	DRAFTER, ASSISTANT	4	7	017.281-018
RCS	ELECTROENCEPHALOGRAPHIC TECHNOLOGIST	4	6	078.362-022
RCS	ENGRAVING-PRESS OPERATOR	4	7	651.382-010
RCS	FLASH-DRIER OPERATOR	4	7	529.582-014
RCS	HULL INSPECTOR	4	8	806.264-010
RCS	HYDROELECTRIC-STATION OPERATOR	4	7	952.362-018
RCS	INSTRUMENT MECHANIC	4	7	710.281-026
RCS	INSTRUMENT REPAIRER	4	8	710.261-010
RCS	LABORATORY ASSISTANT, METALLURGICAL	4	7	011.261-010
RCS	LABORATORY TECHNICIAN, ARTIFICIAL BREEDING	4	5	040.361-010
RCS	LOADING-MACHINE TOOL-SETTER	4	6	694.260-010
RCS	MARGIN CLERK 2	4	5	216.382-046
RCS	MASH-TUB-COOKER OPERATOR	4	5	522.382-022
RCS	MECHANIC, AIRCRAFT RIGGING AND CONTROLS	4	7	806.281-038
RCS	MUSIC LIBRARIAN, INTERNATIONAL BROADCAST	4	6	100.367-026
RCS	ORTHOPEDIC-BOOT-AND-SHOE DESIGNER AND MAKER	4	7	788.261-010
RCS	PROTECTIVE-SIGNAL INSTALLER	4	7	822.361-018
RCS	RADIATION MONITOR	4	6	199.167-010
RCS	REACTOR OPERATOR, TEST-AND-RESEARCH	4	7	015.362-026
RCS	SAFETY INSPECTOR	4	6	168.264-014
RCS	SOUND MIXER	4	7	194.262-018
RCS	STATION INSTALLER-AND-REPAIRER	4	7	822.261-022
RCS	SUPERVISOR	4	7	706.131-014
RCS	SUPERVISOR, ENDLESS TRACK VEHICLE	4	7	620.131-010
RCS	SUPERVISOR, PIPE-LINES	4	7	862.131-022

Code	Title	GED	SVP	DOT No.
RCS	TANK SETTER	4	7	801.361-022
RCS	TROUBLE LOCATOR, TEST DESK	4	6	822.361-030
RCS	WASTE-TREATMENT OPERATOR	4	6	955.382-014
RCS	WATCH MANUFACTURING SUPERVISOR	4	7	609.130-026
RCS	WIND-INSTRUMENT REPAIRER	4	7	730.281-054
RCS	YIELD-LOSS INSPECTOR	4	5	529.367-030
RCS	ACCORDION TUNER	3	6	730.381-010
RCS	AGATE SETTER	3	4	710.684-010
RCS	AIR-COMPRESSOR MECHANIC	3	6	622.684-010
RCS	AIR-VALVE REPAIRER	3	6	622.381-010
RCS	ALINER, TYPEWRITER	3	4	706.381-010
RCS	AMMONIUM-NITRATE CRYSTALLIZER	3	4	553.685-010
RCS	ANIMAL-RIDE ATTENDANT	3	2	349.674-010
RCS	ANNEALER	3	4	504.682-010
RCS	ARMATURE BANDER	3	5	724.684-010
RCS	ARTIFICIAL-BREEDING TECHNICIAN	3	6	418.384-014
RCS	ARTIFICIAL-CANDY MAKER	3	5	739.684-010
RCS	ASSEMBLER	3	5	706.361-010
RCS	ASSEMBLER, PIANO	3	4	730.384-010
RCS	AUTOCLAVE OPERATOR 2	3	6	709.682-010
RCS	AUXILIARY-EQUIPMENT TENDER	3	6	869.665-010
RCS	BAND-SAW OPERATOR	3	4	686.682-010
RCS	BARBED-WIRE-MACHINE OPERATOR	3	5	616.382-010
RCS	BARREL ASSEMBLER	3	4	669.682-014
RCS	BARREL ASSEMBLER	3	6	715.381-022
RCS	BATTER MIXER	3	4	520.685-010
RCS	BEAD-FORMING-MACHINE OPERATOR	3	4	692.682-014
RCS	BELLOWS CHARGER 1	3	3	710.664-010
RCS	BENCH-SHEAR OPERATOR	3	5	703.684-010
RCS	BENDING-MACHINE OPERATOR 1	3	5	617.482-010
RCS	BILLET ASSEMBLER	3	4	614.684-010
RCS	BINDING FOLDER, MACHINE	3	4	788.684-018
RCS	BLENDER	3	4	520.387-010
RCS	BLUEPRINTING-MACHINE OPERATOR	3	5	979.682-014
RCS	BOTTOM-SAW OPERATOR	3	4	667.682-014
RCS	BOX MAKER, WOOD	3	3	760.684-014
RCS	BRACELET AND BROOCH MAKER	3	7	735.681-010
RCS	BRIDGE OPERATOR, SLIP	3	4	919.682-010
RCS	BRIDGE-OR-GANTRY-CRANE OPERATOR	3	5	921.663-010
RCS	BUILDER, BEAM	3	3	860.684-010
RCS	BUMPER OPERATOR	3	5	617.682-014
RCS	CALENDER-ROLL PRESS OPERATOR	3	4	692.462-010
RCS	CANDY-MAKER HELPER	3	4	520.685-050
RCS	CAPACITOR ASSEMBLER	3	4	729.684-014
RCS	CAR INSPECTOR	3	4	910.667-010
RCS	CARBON-PAPER-COATING-MACHINE SETTER	3	5	534.380-010
RCS	CARPET WEAVER	3	4	683.682-010
RCS	CARPET WEAVER, JACQUARD LOOM	3	4	683.682-014
RCS	CARVER	3	4	316.661-010
RCS	CASE PREPARER-AND-LINER	3	4	509.384-010
RCS	CASTING OPERATOR	3	5	514.662-010
RCS	CASTING-AND-CURING OPERATOR	3	5	559.682-014
RCS	CASTING-MACHINE OPERATOR	3	4	502.682-014
RCS	CELL INSTALLER	3	6	826.684-018

Code	Title	GED	SVP	DOT No.
RCS	CENTRIFUGAL-CASTING-MACHINE OPERATOR	3	5	502.682-018
RCS	CENTRIFUGAL-CASTING-MACHINE TENDER	3	3	556.385-010
RCS	CHAIN BUILDER, LOOM CONTROL	3	5	683.381-010
RCS	CHARGE-MACHINE OPERATOR	3	5	921.662-014
RCS	CHARGER OPERATOR	3	4	504.565-010
RCS	CHARGING-MACHINE OPERATOR	3	5	512.683-010
RCS	CHIP-MIXING-MACHINE OPERATOR	3	3	560.465-010
RCS	CHUCKING-AND-BORING-MACHINE OPERATOR	3	4	669.682-022
RCS	CIRCULAR SAW OPERATOR	3	5	869.682-010
RCS	CLICKING-MACHINE OPERATOR	3	5	789.382-010
RCS	CLOTH-MERCERIZER OPERATOR	3	3	584.685-014
RCS	CLUTCH REBUILDER	3	4	620.684-022
RCS	COATER	3	4	503.685-010
RCS	COATING-MACHINE OPERATOR	3	5	584.562-010
RCS	COLOR-PASTE MIXER	3	3	550.685-038
RCS	COMBINING-MACHINE OPERATOR	3	4	554.685-018
RCS	CONSTRUCTION-AND-MAINTENANCE INSPECTOR	3	5	914.362-014
RCS	CORE-DRILL OPERATOR	3	5	869.682-014
RCS	COREMAKING-MACHINE OPERATOR	3	4	692.682-030
RCS	CORK INSULATOR, REFRIGERATION PLANT	3	7	863.381-010
RCS	CORNER-BRACE-BLOCK-MACHINE OPERATOR	3	4	669.682-030
RCS	COTTON-BALL-MACHINE TENDER	3	4	580.685-022
RCS	COUPLING-MACHINE OPERATOR	3	4	619.682-014
RCS	CRACKING-UNIT OPERATOR	3	5	558.682-010
RCS	CREPING-MACHINE OPERATOR	3	3	534.682-030
RCS	CRUSHER TENDER	3	3	515.685-014
RCS	CRUSHER-AND-BLENDER OPERATOR	3	4	544.582-010
RCS	CUTTER APPRENTICE, HAND	3	5	781.584-010
RCS	CUTTER OPERATOR	3	3	555.585-010
RCS	CUTTER OPERATOR	3	6	930.683-014
RCS	CUTTER, BARREL DRUM	3	4	690.682-026
RCS	CUTTER, HAND 1	3	5	781.584-014
RCS	CUTTING-AND-PRINTING-MACHINE OPERATOR	3	3	652.685-022
RCS	CYLINDER GRINDER	3	7	500.381-010
RCS	DEICER ASSEMBLER, ELECTRIC	3	5	739.684-050
RCS	DIPPER	3	5	774.684-014
RCS	DIVER PUMPER	3	4	899.682-010
RCS	DRAWING-KILN OPERATOR	3	3	575.362-010
RCS	DRESSER TENDER	3	4	681.682-010
RCS	DRIER OPERATOR	3	4	523.682-022
RCS	DRIER OPERATOR 3	3	5	553.685-050
RCS	DRIER OPERATOR	3	4	553.385-010
RCS	DRIER-AND-GRINDER TENDER	3	4	579.685-010
RCS	DRILL-PRESS OPERATOR	3	3	606.682-014
RCS	DRIVER	3	3	919.663-014
RCS	DRY-END OPERATOR	3	3	559.665-014
RCS	DRY-WALL APPLICATOR	3	6	842.681-010
RCS	ELECTRIC-SIGN ASSEMBLER	3	3	729.684-022
RCS	ELECTRICAL-LINE SPLICER	3	5	728.684-014
RCS	ELECTRONIC-SENSING-EQUIPMENT			

Code	Title	GED	SVP	DOT No.
RCS	INSPECTOR, BARREL ASSEMBLY	3	6	715.684-114
RCS	JACK SETTER	3	5	939.684-010
RCS	JACQUARD-LOOM WEAVER	3	5	683.682-022
RCS	JEWEL BLOCKER AND SAWYER	3	6	770.381-026
RCS	JIGSAW OPERATOR	3	4	667.682-042
RCS	JOINER HELPER	3	4	860.664-014
RCS	KICK PRESS SETTER	3	5	617.380-010
RCS	KILN OPERATOR	3	4	513.565-010
RCS	KNIFE SETTER	3	4	663.380-010
RCS	LAMINATING-MACHINE OPERATOR	3	3	692.685-106
RCS	LATHER	3	6	842.361-010
RCS	LATHER APPRENTICE	3	6	842.361-014
RCS	LEAD RECOVERER, CONTINUOUS-NAPHTHA-TREATING PLANT	3	4	541.685-014
RCS	LEATHER TOOLER	3	5	763.684-054
RCS	LEVERS-LACE MACHINE OPERATOR	3	6	683.682-026
RCS	LOADING-MACHINE ADJUSTER	3	4	632.360-014
RCS	LOG-CHIPPER OPERATOR	3	4	564.662-010
RCS	LOGGING-TRACTOR OPERATOR	3	4	929.683-010
RCS	MACHINE SETTER	3	6	692.260-010
RCS	MARK-UP DESIGNER	3	3	775.684-050
RCS	MATTRESS MAKER	3	4	780.684-074
RCS	MEASURER	3	4	869.487-010
RCS	MERCHANDISE DISTRIBUTOR	3	3	219.367-018
RCS	METAL-REED TUNER	3	7	730.381-034
RCS	MICA INSPECTOR	3	4	779.687-026
RCS	MOLDER OPERATOR	3	5	665.682-018
RCS	MONITOR CAR OPERATOR	3	6	939.682-010
RCS	MOSAIC WORKER	3	5	779.381-014
RCS	NAIL-ASSEMBLY-MACHINE OPERATOR	3	4	616.682-030
RCS	NEEDLE-FELT-MAKING-MACHINE OPERATOR	3	5	689.362-010
RCS	NEEDLE-LOOM TENDER	3	3	689.685-090
RCS	OIL-WELL-SERVICE-OPERATOR HELPER	3	5	939.684-018
RCS	OPERATOR, CAVITY PUMP	3	4	729.682-010
RCS	ORDERING-MACHINE OPERATOR	3	4	522.682-014
RCS	ORTHOPEDIC ASSISTANT	3	4	712.661-010
RCS	OUTSOLE CUTTER, AUTOMATIC	3	4	690.462-010
RCS	OVERHAULER HELPER	3	3	628.664-010
RCS	PAD HAND	3	5	780.381-030
RCS	PAINT-SPRAY TENDER	3	4	574.685-014
RCS	PAINTER, STAGE SETTINGS	3	7	840.681-010
RCS	PANTRY GOODS MAKER	3	3	317.684-014
RCS	PARTS CLERK	3	5	222.367-042
RCS	PATTERN WHEEL MAKER	3	5	685.684-010
RCS	PATTERNMAKER	3	6	779.584-010
RCS	PEN-AND-PENCIL REPAIRER	3	4	733.684-014
RCS	PHOTOCOMPOSING-MACHINE OPERATOR	3	6	650.582-018
RCS	PIANO TUNER	3	5	730.361-010
RCS	PLATE FORMER	3	4	500.684-018
RCS	PLATE STACKER, MACHINE	3	4	692.382-014
RCS	PLUMBING ASSEMBLER-INSTALLER	3	4	862.684-026
RCS	PLUSH WEAVER	3	4	683.682-030
RCS	PNEUMATIC TESTER AND MECHANIC	3	6	621.381-022
RCS	POLISHER	3	5	715.682-018

Code	Title	GED	SVP	DOT No.
RCS	POT TENDER	3	3	512.685-018
RCS	PRECIPITATOR 2	3	4	511.685-042
RCS	PREFORM PLATE MAKER	3	5	751.684-026
RCS	PRESS OPERATOR, CARBON BLOCKS	3	4	514.682-014
RCS	PRIMER-POWDER BLENDER, WET	3	4	550.582-010
RCS	PRIMER-WATERPROOFING-MACHINE ADJUSTER	3	5	632.380-018
RCS	PRINTING-MACHINE OPERATOR, TAPE RULES	3	5	652.662-010
RCS	PROCESS INSPECTOR	3	6	736.381-018
RCS	PRODUCTION-SUPPLY-EQUIPMENT TENDER	3	4	921.685-050
RCS	PROFILE TRIMMER	3	4	607.682-014
RCS	PROFILE-SAW OPERATOR	3	3	700.682-018
RCS	PROOF INSPECTOR	3	3	736.384-010
RCS	PULVERIZING-AND-SIFTING OPERATOR	3	4	550.485-026
RCS	PUMP-PRESS OPERATOR	3	4	539.685-022
RCS	PUNCHER	3	4	689.582-010
RCS	QUILTING-MACHINE OPERATOR	3	4	689.685-106
RCS	REAMER, HAND	3	5	709.684-058
RCS	RECORDING STUDIO SET-UP WORKER	3	4	962.664-014
RCS	RECOVERY OPERATOR	3	4	558.682-022
RCS	REED REPAIRER	3	5	628.484-010
RCS	RIPSAW OPERATOR	3	4	667.682-066
RCS	RIVET HEATER	3	4	504.485-010
RCS	ROCK-DRILL OPERATOR 1	3	5	850.683-034
RCS	ROLLER-MILL OPERATOR	3	5	555.682-014
RCS	ROTARY-KILN OPERATOR	3	4	513.682-010
RCS	ROUGHER OPERATOR	3	5	613.662-014
RCS	ROUSTABOUT	3	5	869.684-046
RCS	RUBBER-GOODS TESTER	3	6	759.381-014
RCS	RUBBER-GOODS REPAIRER	3	4	759.684-054
RCS	RUG CLEANER, MACHINE	3	4	361.682-010
RCS	RUG CLEANER, HAND	3	5	369.384-014
RCS	SADDLE-STITCHING-MACHINE OPERATOR	3	6	653.662-010
RCS	SAFETY-GLASS INSTALLER	3	6	865.484-010
RCS	SALVAGE WORKER	3	4	619.387-010
RCS	SALVAGER	3	5	709.684-070
RCS	SAMPLE SHOE INSPECTOR AND REWORKER	3	5	788.684-098
RCS	SAMPLE TESTER	3	5	553.364-010
RCS	SAMPLE-TAKER OPERATOR	3	5	931.361-010
RCS	SAWYER	3	5	690.482-010
RCS	SELF-SEALING-FUEL-TANK BUILDER	3	4	752.684-046
RCS	SHEETER OPERATOR	3	4	690.382-010
RCS	SHINGLE SAWYER	3	4	667.485-010
RCS	SIDE-STITCHING-MACHINE OPERATOR	3	6	653.562-010
RCS	SINTER-MACHINE OPERATOR	3	5	510.685-026
RCS	SOLE-CONFORMING-MACHINE OPERATOR	3	4	690.682-070
RCS	SPAGHETTI-MACHINE OPERATOR	3	4	690.682-074
RCS	SPICE FUMIGATOR	3	2	529.685-218
RCS	SPINDLE PLUMBER	3	5	628.684-030
RCS	SPOTTER	3	3	361.684-018
RCS	SPRING TESTER 1	3	4	612.685-014
RCS	SPRINGER	3	4	780.684-106
RCS	STACKING-MACHINE OPERATOR 1	3	4	692.682-054

Code	Title	GED	SVP	DOT No.
RCS	STILL-PUMP OPERATOR	3	5	549.362-010
RCS	STITCHER, SPECIAL MACHINE	3	4	690.682-078
RCS	STOCK-PARTS FABRICATOR	3	3	769.684-050
RCS	STRIPER	3	5	651.682-018
RCS	SURVEYOR HELPER	3	4	869.567-010
RCS	SWITCH REPAIRER	3	5	622.684-018
RCS	TANK-CAR INSPECTOR	3	4	910.384-010
RCS	TANNING-DRUM OPERATOR	3	4	582.482-018
RCS	TAPE TRANSFERRER	3	5	194.382-014
RCS	TELEVISION INSTALLER	3	6	823.361-010
RCS	TETRYL-DISSOLVER OPERATOR	3	3	550.685-114
RCS	THIRD-RAIL INSTALLER	3	5	825.381-038
RCS	TOOL FILER	3	5	701.684-030
RCS	TOP-PRECIPITATOR OPERATOR	3	4	511.465-010
RCS	TRACTOR-CRANE OPERATOR	3	4	921.663-058
RCS	TRANSFORMER-STOCK CLERK	3	3	222.587-054
RCS	TRIMMER	3	4	705.682-014
RCS	TRIMMING-MACHINE OPERATOR	3	4	690.682-090
RCS	TROMBONE-SLIDE ASSEMBLER	3	7	730.381-054
RCS	TROPHY ASSEMBLER	3	5	735.684-018
RCS	TWISTING-MACHINE OPERATOR	3	5	692.682-070
RCS	ULTRASONIC TESTER	3	3	709.687-054
RCS	UPHOLSTERER	3	5	869.684-070
RCS	UPHOLSTERY REPAIRER	3	6	780.684-122
RCS	UTILITY OPERATOR 2	3	3	709.684-094
RCS	V-BELT BUILDER	3	4	759.684-066
RCS	VACUUM-PAN OPERATOR	3	3	559.585-022
RCS	VARNISHING-UNIT TOOL SETTER	3	3	632.380-026
RCS	VENEER JOINTER	3	4	665.682-038
RCS	VENEER STAPLER	3	4	869.684-078
RCS	VIBRATOR-EQUIPMENT TESTER	3	6	825.361-014
RCS	WAFER-MACHINE OPERATOR	3	4	692.662-018
RCS	WARE FINISHER	3	6	772.381-018
RCS	WARP-KNITTING-MACHINE OPERATOR	3	4	685.665-018
RCS	WEAVER, BENCH LOOM	3	5	616.681-010
RCS	WEAVER, NARROW FABRICS	3	5	683.682-046
RCS	WEAVER, NEEDLE LOOM	3	4	683.665-010
RCS	WEAVER, TIRE CORD	3	4	683.682-050
RCS	WET-END OPERATOR 1	3	4	559.685-186
RCS	WET-PLANT OPERATOR	3	4	519.665-018
RCS	WIRE COILER	3	5	724.361-010
RCS	WOOL-AND-PELT GRADER	3	4	589.387-018
RCS	YEAST DISTILLER	3	4	522.362-010
RCS	ALMOND-PASTE MOLDER	2	5	520.684-010
RCS	ANIMAL CARETAKER	2	4	410.674-010
RCS	ASSEMBLER	2	2	781.667-010
RCS	ASSEMBLER-AND-GLUER, LAMINATED PLASTICS	2	3	754.684-014
RCS	AUTOMATIC-PAD-MAKING-MACHINE OPERATOR HELPER	2	2	689.686-010
RCS	BACK TENDER	2	2	589.686-010
RCS	BALL SORTER	2	2	609.685-010
RCS	BAND MAKER	2	2	619.685-010
RCS	BAND-REAMER-MACHINE OPERATOR	2	3	603.685-010

Code	Title	GED	SVP	DOT No.
RCS	BANDER, HAND	2	2	920.687-030
RCS	BAR AND FILLER ASSEMBLER	2	2	706.684-034
RCS	BARK-PRESS OPERATOR	2	2	563.685-010
RCS	BARREL FINISHER	2	4	736.684-018
RCS	BARREL LINER	2	2	764.687-026
RCS	BASE-PLY HAND	2	3	759.684-014
RCS	BEAMER HELPER	2	2	681.686-014
RCS	BELT BUILDER	2	2	752.684-014
RCS	BEVELER	2	3	673.685-018
RCS	BLASTER HELPER	2	3	859.687-010
RCS	BLENDING-MACHINE OPERATOR	2	3	680.685-010
RCS	BLOCKER, AUTOMATIC	2	2	673.685-030
RCS	BOLTER	2	3	667.685-022
RCS	BONE-PROCESS OPERATOR	2	4	559.665-010
RCS	BOTTOM FILLER	2	2	788.684-026
RCS	BOTTOMING-MACHINE OPERATOR	2	3	649.685-022
RCS	BOX REPAIRER 2	2	2	762.687-018
RCS	BRUSH MATERIAL PREPARER	2	5	739.684-022
RCS	BUCKET TURNER	2	4	669.682-018
RCS	BUFFER	2	2	759.684-022
RCS	BUFFER 1	2	4	705.684-014
RCS	BUFFING-AND-SUEDING-MACHINE OPERATOR	2	2	753.684-010
RCS	BURNING-PLANT OPERATOR	2	2	509.685-018
RCS	CABLE-SPLICER HELPER	2	3	829.667-010
RCS	CALENDER OPERATOR, ARTIFICIAL LEATHER	2	3	584.685-010
RCS	CALENDER-WIND-UP TENDER	2	2	554.665-010
RCS	CANOE INSPECTOR, FINAL	2	4	769.687-018
RCS	CARD DECORATOR	2	2	649.686-014
RCS	CARNALLITE-PLANT OPERATOR	2	4	519.484-010
RCS	CARPET CUTTER 2	2	3	585.687-014
RCS	CASER	2	4	795.684-010
RCS	CASTING-OPERATOR HELPER	2	3	514.687-018
RCS	CHECKER	2	2	369.687-014
RCS	CHECKER-IN	2	2	221.587-014
RCS	CIGARETTE INSPECTOR	2	3	529.567-010
RCS	CIRCLE BEVELER	2	3	673.685-034
RCS	CLOTH REELER	2	2	689.685-042
RCS	CLOTH SPREADER, SCREEN PRINTING	2	3	652.687-010
RCS	CLOTH TRIMMER, MACHINE	2	3	585.685-026
RCS	CLOTH-PRINTER HELPER	2	2	652.686-010
RCS	CLUTCH INSPECTOR	2	3	706.687-014
RCS	COFFEE MAKER	2	2	317.684-010
RCS	COIN WRAPPER	2	2	217.686-010
RCS	COLLATOR OPERATOR	2	2	208.685-010
RCS	COMBER TENDER	2	3	680.665-010
RCS	COMPOUND FINISHER	2	3	550.685-042
RCS	CONCRETE-PIPE MAKER	2	3	779.684-014
RCS	CONDENSER SETTER	2	2	512.687-010
RCS	CONDENSER-TUBE TENDER	2	2	511.685-018
RCS	CORE-OVEN TENDER	2	2	518.685-010
RCS	CORK MOLDER	2	3	569.685-030
RCS	COTTON DISPATCHER	2	2	780.684-038

Code	Title	GED	SVP	DOT No.
RCS	CROSSCUTTER, ROLLED GLASS	2	2	575.684-022
RCS	CUFF CUTTER	2	3	686.685-018
RCS	CUPOLA CHARGER	2	2	512.686-010
RCS	DECORATOR, STREET AND BUILDING	2	4	899.687-010
RCS	DEICER-KIT ASSEMBLER	2	3	759.684-030
RCS	DIAL REFINISHER	2	5	715.584-010
RCS	DIAMOND-POWDER TECHNICIAN	2	3	673.685-046
RCS	DIPPER	2	2	735.687-010
RCS	DRAWER LINER	2	2	763.684-030
RCS	DRAWING-IN-MACHINE-TENDER HELPER	2	4	683.685-022
RCS	DRIER TENDER	2	3	523.685-070
RCS	DRY-HOUSE ATTENDANT	2	3	553.585-014
RCS	DUST COLLECTOR-TREATER	2	3	511.687-014
RCS	ELECTRICAL-APPLIANCE PREPARER	2	3	827.584-010
RCS	ETCHER, PRINTED CIRCUITS	2	2	590.685-030
RCS	FARMWORKER, POULTRY	2	3	411.584-010
RCS	FEATHER SAWYER	2	2	732.685-014
RCS	FILLING-MACHINE OPERATOR	2	2	733.685-014
RCS	FINISHER	2	2	775.687-010
RCS	FIRE-HOSE CURER	2	2	553.685-062
RCS	FIRER, RETORT	2	3	553.685-066
RCS	FLAMER	2	2	788.684-050
RCS	FLASHER ADJUSTER	2	2	723.684-022
RCS	FORMER HELPER, HAND	2	3	619.684-010
RCS	FOXING CUTTER, HOT KNIFE	2	2	751.684-022
RCS	FURNACE TENDER	2	3	512.685-010
RCS	FURNACE WORKER	2	2	543.666-010
RCS	GARMENT SORTER	2	2	222.687-014
RCS	GLASS CUT-OFF TENDER	2	2	677.685-030
RCS	GLASS CUTTER, OVAL OR CIRCULAR	2	3	779.684-022
RCS	GLASS INSTALLER	2	3	865.684-014
RCS	GOLD RECLAIMER	2	3	709.685-010
RCS	GOLF-BALL-COVER TREATER	2	2	559.685-102
RCS	GOLF-CLUB WEIGHER	2	2	732.587-014
RCS	GOLF-RANGE ATTENDANT	2	2	341.683-010
RCS	GRANULATOR TENDER	2	4	519.665-010
RCS	GREASER	2	4	624.684-010
RCS	GRINDER	2	2	555.685-030
RCS	HAND STAMPER	2	3	709.684-042
RCS	HEATER TENDER	2	2	553.665-038
RCS	HOT-PRESS OPERATOR	2	3	575.685-042
RCS	HOT-WIRE GLASS-TUBE CUTTER	2	2	772.684-014
RCS	HYDRAULIC OPERATOR	2	3	611.685-014
RCS	HYDRAULIC-PRESS OPERATOR	2	2	920.685-062
RCS	IMPREGNATOR	2	2	509.685-030
RCS	IMPREGNATOR-AND-DRIER HELPER	2	3	599.685-050
RCS	INDUCTION-MACHINE OPERATOR	2	2	504.685-022
RCS	INJECTION-MOLDING-MACHINE OFFBEARER	2	2	690.686-038
RCS	INSPECTOR-GRADER, AGRICULTURAL ESTABLISHMENT	2	3	409.687-010
RCS	INSPECTOR, FIREWORKS	2	3	737.687-062
RCS	INSTALLER, FUEL-BAY LINING	2	3	752.687-010
RCS	JACKHAMMER OPERATOR	2	2	930.684-018
RCS	KILN OPERATOR	2	3	509.565-010

Code	Title	GED	SVP	DOT No.
RCS	KILN-OPERATOR HELPER	2	3	513.587-010
RCS	KNURLING-MACHINE OPERATOR	2	3	604.685-018
RCS	LABORATORY HELPER	2	3	821.564-010
RCS	LABORER, GENERAL	2	2	589.686-026
RCS	LADLE LINER	2	3	519.684-010
RCS	LADLE POURER	2	4	514.684-014
RCS	LAMINATING-MACHINE TENDER	2	2	554.665-014
RCS	LEAD BURNER	2	3	727.684-022
RCS	LOAD TESTER	2	3	616.685-034
RCS	LOCK ASSEMBLER	2	3	706.684-074
RCS	LOG INSPECTOR	2	3	667.687-014
RCS	LOG ROLLER	2	2	677.687-010
RCS	MACHINE OPERATOR, GENERAL	2	3	649.685-070
RCS	MACHINIST HELPER, OUTSIDE	2	3	623.687-010
RCS	MAGAZINE REPAIRER	2	3	653.685-022
RCS	MAKE-UP OPERATOR HELPER	2	3	550.587-010
RCS	MEAT CLERK	2	2	222.684-010
RCS	METAL-CLEANER, IMMERSION	2	2	503.685-030
RCS	MIXER	2	3	510.685-018
RCS	MOLD MAKER	2	4	518.664-010
RCS	MOLD POLISHER	2	3	579.685-030
RCS	MOLD PREPARER	2	2	809.687-026
RCS	MOLD-MAKER HELPER	2	3	518.687-018
RCS	NIBBLER OPERATOR	2	3	615.685-026
RCS	OBSERVER HELPER, SEISMIC PROSPECTING	2	4	939.364-010
RCS	OIL-SPOT WASHER	2	2	689.687-050
RCS	OILER	2	3	699.687-018
RCS	OVEN DAUBER	2	2	543.687-014
RCS	OXIDIZED-FINISH PLATER	2	2	599.685-062
RCS	PACKER	2	2	920.687-130
RCS	PACKER	2	3	929.684-010
RCS	PAINT-BRUSH MAKER	2	4	733.684-010
RCS	PAINTER HELPER, AUTOMOTIVE	2	4	845.684-014
RCS	PASTE MIXER	2	3	550.585-034
RCS	PELLET-PRESS OPERATOR	2	3	694.685-034
RCS	PIANO STRINGER	2	4	730.684-054
RCS	PIPE BUFFER	2	2	705.684-054
RCS	PIPE FINISHER	2	3	779.684-042
RCS	PLASTIC-TOP ASSEMBLER	2	2	763.684-062
RCS	PLASTICS-SEASONER OPERATOR	2	2	553.665-042
RCS	PORTER, USED-CAR LOT	2	2	915.687-022
RCS	POTATO-CHIP FRIER	2	3	526.685-046
RCS	POURER, METAL	2	2	514.684-022
RCS	PREASSEMBLER AND INSPECTOR	2	4	730.684-058
RCS	PRIMER BOXER	2	2	737.587-018
RCS	PRIMING-MIXTURE CARRIER	2	2	922.587-010
RCS	PRINT DEVELOPER, AUTOMATIC	2	4	976.685-026
RCS	PRODUCTION ASSEMBLER	2	3	737.684-034
RCS	PRODUCTION-MACHINE TENDER	2	2	619.365-010
RCS	PROPELLANT-CHARGE-ZONE ASSEMBLER	2	3	737.687-110
RCS	PULPER	2	2	530.685-014
RCS	PUMP-SERVICER HELPER	2	5	630.684-022
RCS	PUTTY GLAZER	2	3	749.684-042

Code	Title	GED	SVP	DOT No.
RCS	RAG-CUTTING-MACHINE TENDER	2	2	530.665-014
RCS	RASPER	2	2	788.684-094
RCS	REEL ASSEMBLER	2	3	762.484-010
RCS	ROLL-UP-GUIDER OPERATOR	2	4	590.685-050
RCS	ROPE-SILICA-MACHINE OPERATOR	2	3	582.685-114
RCS	ROUGH OPENER, JEWEL HOLE	2	2	770.684-018
RCS	ROUND-CORNER-CUTTER OPERATOR	2	2	640.685-074
RCS	ROVING WINDER, FIBERGLASS	2	3	681.485-010
RCS	RUBBER	2	3	742.684-010
RCS	RUG INSPECTOR	2	4	585.685-090
RCS	RUG-INSPECTOR HELPER	2	3	789.687-158
RCS	SAMPLE-COLOR MAKER	2	2	550.584-014
RCS	SAMPLER	2	3	599.684-014
RCS	SANDER	2	2	761.684-030
RCS	SANDER-AND-BUFFER	2	3	730.684-066
RCS	SCRAPER	2	2	700.687-066
RCS	SECOND CUTTER	2	3	779.684-054
RCS	SETTER	2	4	573.684-014
RCS	SHELL MOLDER	2	2	518.685-026
RCS	SHOE CLEANER	2	2	788.687-122
RCS	SHOELACE-TIPPING-MACHINE OPERATOR	2	2	686.685-062
RCS	SHOTGUN-SHELL-ASSEMBLY-MACHINE OPERATOR	2	3	694.385-010
RCS	SIDING STAPLER	2	2	762.684-058
RCS	SILICA-SPRAY MIXER	2	3	570.685-090
RCS	SKIMMER, REVERBERATORY	2	3	511.687-022
RCS	SLOTTER OPERATOR	2	3	640.685-078
RCS	SNUFF-CONTAINER INSPECTOR	2	3	920.667-014
RCS	SPRAY-UNIT FEEDER	2	2	599.686-014
RCS	STAINER	2	3	742.684-014
RCS	STAPLE-PROCESSING-MACHINE OPERATOR	2	3	680.585-014
RCS	STOCK PREPARER	2	3	751.387-010
RCS	STRAW-HAT BRUSHER	2	2	784.687-074
RCS	STRIPPER	2	2	673.666-014
RCS	STRIPPER AND TAPER	2	3	899.684-038
RCS	SUGAR GRINDER	2	3	521.685-346
RCS	SWEEPING-COMPOUND BLENDER	2	3	550.685-110
RCS	TANKER	2	3	561.665-010
RCS	TAPE-FOLDING-MACHINE OPERATOR	2	3	689.685-134
RCS	TEAMSTER	2	3	919.664-010
RCS	TESTER OPERATOR	2	3	614.684-014
RCS	THAW-SHED HEATER TENDER	2	4	543.685-022
RCS	THRESHER, BROOMCORN	2	2	429.685-014
RCS	TIRE GROOVER	2	3	750.684-026
RCS	TIRE MOLDER	2	3	553.685-102
RCS	TIRE SORTER	2	3	750.687-022
RCS	TIRE TRIMMER, HAND	2	2	750.684-034
RCS	TONE REGULATOR	2	4	730.684-094
RCS	TOP-PRECIPITATOR-OPERATOR HELPER	2	2	511.586-010
RCS	TRIMMER, HAND	2	2	781.687-070
RCS	TUBE BALANCER	2	3	750.684-046
RCS	TUBE REPAIRER	2	3	750.684-050
RCS	TURNING-MACHINE-OPERATOR HELPER	2	2	667.686-022
RCS	UPHOLSTERER, OUTSIDE	2	4	780.684-118

Code	Title	GED	SVP	DOT No.
RCS	VARNISH INSPECTOR	2	3	559.584-014
RCS	VENEER GRADER	2	3	569.587-010
RCS	VENEER-STOCK GRADER	2	2	769.687-050
RCS	WARPER	2	4	681.685-146
RCS	WASHER-ENGINEER HELPER	2	2	533.686-014
RCS	WASTE-MACHINE OFFBEARER	2	2	680.686-022
RCS	WATER TENDER	2	4	599.685-122
RCS	WEBBING TACKER	2	3	780.684-130
RCS	WEIGHER OPERATOR	2	3	559.687-070
RCS	WELDER, GUN	2	2	810.664-010
RCS	WELDER, PRODUCTION LINE	2	2	819.684-010
RCS	WHEEL LACER AND TRUER	2	4	706.684-106
RCS	WINDER	2	3	715.687-130
RCS	WINDOW REPAIRER	2	4	899.684-042
RCS	WIRE SETTER	2	2	579.665-018
RCS	WRINKLE CHASER	2	2	788.684-130
RCS	YARD WORKER	2	4	921.683-086
RCS	YARD WORKER, USED BUILDING MATERIALS	2	3	922.667-010
RCS	ADHESIVE PRIMER	1	2	732.687-010
RCS	CANDLE CUTTER	1	2	739.687-050
RCS	CURING-PRESS OPERATOR	1	2	553.686-018
RCS	GROOVER	1	2	692.686-042
RCS	GUIDER	1	2	590.686-014
RCS	HARVEST WORKER, FRUIT	1	2	403.687-018
RCS	HEAD-GAGE-UNIT OPERATOR	1	2	619.685-054
RCS	LABORER, GENERAL	1	2	559.686-026
RCS	PACKAGE CRIMPER	1	2	589.686-034
RCS	PLUG SORTER	1	2	769.687-034
RCS	RIGGER, THIRD	1	2	921.687-030
RCS	SMOOTHER	1	2	784.684-066
RCS	TINNING-EQUIPMENT TENDER	1	2	501.685-014
RCS	TREE-TRIMMER HELPER	1	2	408.667-010
RCS	WAXER, FLOOR	1	2	381.687-034
RCE	SUPERINTENDENT, GENERATING PLANT	5	8	184.167-166
RCE	AIRBRUSH ARTIST	4	7	970.281-010
RCE	CAMERA REPAIRER	4	8	714.281-014
RCE	CORRESPONDENCE CLERK	4	6	209.262-010
RCE	DESIGNER AND TEMPLATE MAKER, COVERINGS	4	6	781.381-014
RCE	ELECTRICIAN, OFFICE	4	7	822.261-010
RCE	ELECTRONIC INTELLIGENCE OPERATIONS SPECIALIST	4	7	193.382-010
RCE	ESTIMATOR	4	7	160.267-018
RCE	GLAZIER SUPERVISOR	4	7	865.131-010
RCE	INSPECTOR, METAL FABRICATING	4	7	619.261-010
RCE	INSPECTOR, WATCH TRAIN	4	7	715.381-074
RCE	OPTICIAN APPRENTICE, DISPENSING	4	7	713.361-010
RCE	OPTICIAN, DISPENSING 1	4	7	713.361-014
RCE	ORTHODONTIC TECHNICIAN	4	6	712.381-030
RCE	PANELBOARD OPERATOR	4	7	950.562-010
RCE	PHOSPHORIC-ACID OPERATOR	4	7	558.582-010
RCE	RADIO OFFICER	4	7	193.262-022

Code	Title	GED	SVP	DOT No.
RCE	RADIO-INTELLIGENCE OPERATOR	4	6	193.362-014
RCE	ROLLING ATTENDANT	4	6	613.662-010
RCE	SAMPLE MAKER 2	4	6	735.381-018
RCE	SOUND CONTROLLER	4	7	194.262-014
RCE	STONEMASON SUPERVISOR	4	8	861.131-018
RCE	TELECINE OPERATOR	4	7	194.362-018
RCE	ABRASIVE-WHEEL MOLDER	3	4	575.685-010
RCE	ACID-POLYMERIZATION OPERATOR	3	3	558.685-010
RCE	ADDRESSING-MACHINE OPERATOR	3	4	208.582-010
RCE	ADJUSTER, ELECTRICAL CONTACTS	3	6	724.381-010
RCE	ADZING-AND-BORING-MACHINE OPERATOR	3	5	669.682-010
RCE	ARMATURE WINDER, REPAIR	3	4	724.684-018
RCE	ASSEMBLER FOR PULLER-OVER, HAND	3	3	788.684-010
RCE	ASSEMBLER, TYPE-BAR-AND-SEGMENT	3	3	706.684-026
RCE	ASSEMBLER, IGNITER	3	6	737.381-010
RCE	ASSEMBLER, COMPONENT	3	3	762.684-014
RCE	ASSEMBLER, SUBASSEMBLY	3	3	869.684-018
RCE	ASSEMBLY CLEANER	3	3	519.664-010
RCE	ASSORTER	3	4	703.687-010
RCE	AUTOMATIC-PAD-MAKING-MACHINE OPERATOR	3	4	689.382-010
RCE	BALANCE TRUER	3	4	715.684-018
RCE	BAND-SCROLL-SAW OPERATOR	3	5	667.682-010
RCE	BASEBALL INSPECTOR AND REPAIRER	3	3	732.684-030
RCE	BATTING-MACHINE OPERATOR, INSULATION	3	5	677.382-010
RCE	BED LASTER	3	5	690.682-018
RCE	BED OPERATOR	3	4	613.585-010
RCE	BIAS-MACHINE OPERATOR	3	4	690.682-022
RCE	BINDER	3	4	787.682-010
RCE	BLOW-MOLDING-MACHINE OPERATOR	3	3	556.682-010
RCE	BOARD-MACHINE SET-UP OPERATOR	3	6	579.380-010
RCE	BOAT-CANVAS MAKER-INSTALLER	3	6	789.261-010
RCE	BORING-AND-FILLING-MACHINE OPERATOR	3	5	692.682-018
RCE	BRAKE-DRUM-LATHE OPERATOR	3	5	620.682-010
RCE	BRIGHT CUTTER	3	3	700.684-018
RCE	BROOM STITCHER	3	4	692.682-022
RCE	BULLET-GROOVING-SIZING-AND-LUBRICATING-MACHINE OPERATOR	3	4	619.382-010
RCE	CALENDER-LET-OFF OPERATOR	3	4	554.682-010
RCE	CAP-JEWEL PLATE ASSEMBLER	3	3	715.684-050
RCE	CAR-RETARDER OPERATOR	3	5	910.382-010
RCE	CARD CUTTER, JACQUARD	3	5	683.582-010
RCE	CASE FITTER	3	3	763.684-026
RCE	CHECKERING-MACHINE ADJUSTER	3	7	669.360-010
RCE	CHIMNEY REPAIRER	3	5	899.364-010
RCE	CHURN TENDER	3	3	550.685-034
RCE	CLARIFIER OPERATOR	3	4	511.662-010
RCE	CLERK, ROUTE	3	4	235.562-010
RCE	COATING OPERATOR	3	4	550.585-022
RCE	COATING-AND-BAKING OPERATOR	3	3	554.685-014
RCE	COIL SHAPER	3	5	724.684-022
RCE	COIL WINDER, REPAIR	3	5	724.381-014
RCE	COILER OPERATOR	3	6	613.382-010

Code	Title	GED	SVP	DOT No.
RCE	COLORER	3	4	773.684-010
RCE	COLORER	3	4	970.681-014
RCE	COMPARATOR OPERATOR	3	4	699.384-010
RCE	CONTROL CLERK, DATA PROCESSING 2	3	4	221.687-010
RCE	CONTROL CLERK	3	6	221.387-018
RCE	COPRA PROCESSOR	3	3	555.685-018
RCE	COVER INSPECTOR	3	3	789.687-038
RCE	COVERING-MACHINE OPERATOR	3	5	653.682-014
RCE	CROCHET-MACHINE OPERATOR	3	4	685.682-010
RCE	CROCHETER, HAND	3	5	782.684-014
RCE	CROZE-MACHINE OPERATOR	3	4	669.682-034
RCE	CUPBOARD BUILDER	3	4	703.684-014
RCE	CUSTOMER SERVICE REPRESENTATIVE	3	6	959.361-010
RCE	DE-IONIZER OPERATOR	3	4	558.685-026
RCE	DEICER INSPECTOR, ELECTRIC	3	4	729.387-010
RCE	DERRICK-BOAT OPERATOR	3	5	921.683-034
RCE	DIAMOND MOUNTER	3	4	739.384-010
RCE	DIAMOND-DIE POLISHER	3	5	770.381-022
RCE	DICE MAKER	3	6	731.381-010
RCE	DIE PRESSER	3	3	575.685-026
RCE	DOUGHNUT-MACHINE OPERATOR	3	4	526.682-022
RCE	DRAPERY OPERATOR	3	4	787.682-018
RCE	DRAWER-IN, HAND	3	4	683.684-014
RCE	DRIER TENDER	3	4	563.585-010
RCE	DUPLICATING-MACHINE OPERATOR 1	3	4	207.682-010
RCE	DUST MIXER	3	4	510.685-010
RCE	DUST-COLLECTOR OPERATOR	3	3	511.482-018
RCE	ELECTRIC POWERLINE EXAMINER	3	6	959.367-010
RCE	ELECTRICAL REPAIRER	3	6	825.281-010
RCE	ELECTRICAL-DISCHARGE-MACHINE OPERATOR, PRODUCTION	3	4	609.482-010
RCE	ELECTRICIAN HELPER	3	3	829.684-022
RCE	ELEVATOR-CONSTRUCTOR HELPER	3	3	825.664-010
RCE	ELEVATOR-REPAIRER HELPER	3	3	825.684-014
RCE	EMBLEM DRAWER-IN	3	3	689.380-010
RCE	ENGRAVER APPRENTICE, DECORATIVE	3	7	704.381-022
RCE	ENGRAVER 2	3	6	979.684-014
RCE	ENGRAVER, HAND, SOFT METALS	3	7	704.381-030
RCE	ENGRAVER, MACHINE 2	3	3	704.582-010
RCE	ENGRAVER, PANTOGRAPH 2	3	3	704.682-014
RCE	EXTRACTOR OPERATOR	3	5	552.682-018
RCE	EYEGLASS-LENS CUTTER	3	3	716.682-010
RCE	FABRIC WORKER	3	5	782.684-022
RCE	FACER	3	4	770.582-010
RCE	FARE-REGISTER REPAIRER	3	6	729.384-014
RCE	FIELD RECORDER	3	4	229.367-010
RCE	FILM LABORATORY TECHNICIAN	3	3	976.684-014
RCE	FINISHING-MACHINE OPERATOR	3	4	674.682-010
RCE	FIRE-EQUIPMENT INSPECTOR	3	4	739.484-014
RCE	FISHING-LURE ASSEMBLER	3	3	732.684-058
RCE	FLAKE MILLER, WHEAT AND OATS	3	5	521.682-022
RCE	FLUX MIXER	3	4	550.584-010
RCE	FOOD-SERVICE WORKER, HOSPITAL	3	2	355.677-010
RCE	FREEZER TUNNEL OPERATOR	3	3	523.685-082

Code	Title	GED	SVP	DOT No.
RCE	FUEL-OIL CLERK	3	7	222.387-018
RCE	FUR-MACHINE OPERATOR	3	7	786.682-122
RCE	FUR-MACHINE OPERATOR	3	6	783.682-010
RCE	FURNACE CHARGER	3	4	512.483-010
RCE	GAGER	3	6	914.384-010
RCE	GANG SAWYER	3	5	667.682-030
RCE	GANG SAWYER, STONE	3	5	670.362-010
RCE	GARMENT FITTER	3	6	785.361-014
RCE	GARNETTER	3	3	680.685-054
RCE	GLASS CALIBRATOR	3	3	775.584-010
RCE	GLASS INSTALLER	3	4	865.684-010
RCE	GLASS-BLOWING-LATHE OPERATOR	3	6	772.482-010
RCE	GLAZIER, METAL FURNITURE	3	5	865.684-018
RCE	GLUE MIXER	3	3	550.685-062
RCE	GLUING-MACHINE OPERATOR, AUTOMATIC	3	4	641.682-014
RCE	GREEN-TIRE INSPECTOR	3	4	750.684-018
RCE	GRINDER OPERATOR, PRODUCTION	3	3	603.685-062
RCE	GRINDER 1	3	5	603.482-030
RCE	GRINDING-MILL OPERATOR	3	6	515.382-010
RCE	HAIRSPRING ADJUSTER	3	4	715.684-102
RCE	HARVESTER OPERATOR	3	4	930.683-022
RCE	HEAD-BANDER-AND-LINER OPERATOR	3	3	653.682-018
RCE	HEADING-SAW OPERATOR	3	4	667.682-038
RCE	HEMMER	3	4	787.682-026
RCE	HOOP-FLARING-AND-COILING-MACHINE OPERATOR	3	4	619.682-034
RCE	HYDRATE-CONTROL TENDER	3	4	511.585-010
RCE	INGREDIENT SCALER	3	2	529.684-014
RCE	INLETTER	3	4	669.682-050
RCE	INSPECTING-MACHINE ADJUSTER	3	4	632.380-010
RCE	INSPECTOR AND ADJUSTER, GOLF CLUB HEAD	3	4	732.384-014
RCE	INSPECTOR, OPEN DIE	3	4	701.684-014
RCE	INSPECTOR, ALINING	3	4	706.687-022
RCE	INSPECTOR, HAIRSPRING TRUING	3	4	715.684-118
RCE	INSPECTOR, MECHANISM	3	4	715.384-014
RCE	INSPECTOR, SLIDE FASTENERS	3	4	734.687-062
RCE	INSPECTOR, ASSEMBLY	3	4	736.387-010
RCE	INSTRUMENT-PANEL ASSEMBLER	3	4	706.684-066
RCE	INTERNAL-COMBUSTION-ENGINE SUBASSEMBLER	3	5	706.481-010
RCE	ION-EXCHANGE OPERATOR	3	4	558.685-030
RCE	JEWEL GAGER	3	4	770.687-018
RCE	JEWEL-BEARING BROACHER	3	5	770.682-010
RCE	JEWEL-BEARING DRILLER	3	4	770.682-014
RCE	JEWEL-BEARING FACER	3	4	770.682-018
RCE	JEWEL-BEARING GRINDER	3	4	770.685-018
RCE	JEWEL-BEARING POLISHER	3	4	770.685-022
RCE	JEWEL-BEARING TURNER	3	4	770.682-022
RCE	JEWEL-HOLE DRILLER	3	5	770.682-026
RCE	KICK-PRESS OPERATOR 1	3	4	616.682-026
RCE	KITCHEN CLERK	3	4	222.587-022
RCE	KNITTING-MACHINE OPERATOR, FULL-FASHIONED HOSIERY, AUTOMATIC	3	5	684.682-010

Code	Title	GED	SVP	DOT No.
RCE	LABORATORY CLERK	3	3	222.587-026
RCE	LABORATORY TESTER	3	4	689.384-014
RCE	LACQUERER	3	3	749.684-034
RCE	LASER-BEAM-MACHINE OPERATOR	3	4	815.682-010
RCE	LATHE OPERATOR	3	6	770.382-010
RCE	LEATHER FINISHER	3	4	363.682-010
RCE	LEATHER STAMPER	3	5	781.381-018
RCE	LETTERER	3	6	979.681-010
RCE	LOADING INSPECTOR	3	4	910.667-018
RCE	LOG LOADER	3	4	921.683-058
RCE	LONG-WALL-MINING-MACHINE TENDER	3	5	930.665-010
RCE	LOOPER	3	4	689.682-010
RCE	LUMBER SCALER	3	3	221.487-010
RCE	MACHINE TESTER	3	4	629.382-010
RCE	MANNEQUIN MOUNTER	3	5	739.684-118
RCE	MARKER	3	4	652.582-010
RCE	MARKER 1	3	4	781.384-014
RCE	MASKING-MACHINE OPERATOR	3	4	554.682-014
RCE	MATURITY CHECKER	3	2	529.485-022
RCE	MESH CUTTER	3	3	700.684-050
RCE	METER INSPECTOR	3	4	710.384-022
RCE	MINCEMEAT MAKER	3	3	520.485-018
RCE	MOLD MAKER	3	5	777.684-014
RCE	MOLDED-PARTS INSPECTOR	3	3	727.687-074
RCE	MOLYBDENUM-STEAMER OPERATOR	3	4	511.485-010
RCE	MOTOR-POWER CONNECTOR	3	5	962.684-018
RCE	MOTORCYCLE TESTER	3	5	620.384-010
RCE	MOTORCYCLE SUBASSEMBLY REPAIRER	3	5	620.684-026
RCE	MUCKING-MACHINE OPERATOR	3	3	850.683-026
RCE	MUSIC ENGRAVER	3	6	972.681-010
RCE	MUSIC GRAPHER	3	6	970.581-010
RCE	NEEDLE-CONTROL CHENILLER	3	3	687.685-010
RCE	NITRATING-ACID MIXER	3	5	550.585-030
RCE	OLIVING-MACHINE OPERATOR	3	5	770.381-034
RCE	OPEN-DEVELOPER OPERATOR	3	4	582.685-098
RCE	OPTICAL-GLASS ETCHER	3	4	716.681-022
RCE	ORDER FILLER	3	3	222.487-014
RCE	ORNAMENTAL-MACHINE OPERATOR	3	4	690.682-054
RCE	PAIL BAILER	3	3	703.685-010
RCE	PAINTER APPRENTICE, AUTOMOTIVE	3	6	845.381-010
RCE	PAINTER, SPRAY 1	3	5	741.684-026
RCE	PAINTER, TRANSPORTATION EQUIPMENT	3	6	845.381-014
RCE	PALLETIZER OPERATOR 1	3	4	921.682-014
RCE	PANELBOARD OPERATOR	3	4	582.362-010
RCE	PARACHUTE RIGGER	3	5	912.684-010
RCE	PARCEL-POST CLERK	3	4	222.387-038
RCE	PATTERNMAKER, ACOUSTICAL TILE	3	4	649.685-086
RCE	PIANO REGULATOR-INSPECTOR	3	5	730.681-010
RCE	PICTURE FRAMER	3	5	739.684-146
RCE	PIPE-CLEANING-AND-PRIMING-MACHINE OPERATOR	3	6	862.662-010
RCE	PIPE-FITTER HELPER	3	5	862.684-018
RCE	PISTON MAKER	3	5	730.681-014
RCE	PLASTIC MOLDER	3	3	779.684-050

Code	Title	GED	SVP	DOT No.
RCE	PLATEN GRINDER	3	3	690.385-010
RCE	PLAYGROUND-EQUIPMENT ERECTOR	3	3	801.684-018
RCE	PLEAT PATTERNMAKER	3	5	781.484-010
RCE	POCKET SETTER, LOCKSTITCH	3	4	786.682-210
RCE	POLE INSPECTOR	3	5	869.387-010
RCE	POLISHER, SAND	3	6	705.684-070
RCE	POLYMERIZATION HELPER	3	4	558.585-038
RCE	POWER-BARKER OPERATOR	3	3	669.485-010
RCE	POWERHOUSE-MECHANIC HELPER	3	5	631.684-010
RCE	PRECIPITATOR 1	3	4	511.685-038
RCE	PREFORM-MACHINE OPERATOR	3	4	556.380-014
RCE	PREPARER, MAKING DEPARTMENT	3	6	700.684-058
RCE	PREPLEATER	3	3	686.685-046
RCE	PROCESS CHECKER	3	3	737.364-010
RCE	PROOF-COIN COLLECTOR	3	4	709.687-030
RCE	QUALITY-CONTROL INSPECTOR	3	3	579.367-010
RCE	RAM-PRESS OPERATOR	3	5	575.682-022
RCE	RECLAMATION WORKER	3	4	621.684-014
RCE	RECORD TESTER	3	4	194.387-014
RCE	RECORDS CUSTODIAN	3	5	206.387-026
RCE	REFINERY OPERATOR, ASSISTANT	3	6	521.462-010
RCE	REPAIR OPERATOR	3	3	786.682-214
RCE	REPAIRER	3	5	709.684-062
RCE	RETORT-LOAD EXPEDITER	3	5	221.167-022
RCE	REVIVAL CLERK	3	4	219.362-050
RCE	RICE CLEANING MACHINE TENDER	3	3	521.665-022
RCE	RING-ROLLING-MACHINE OPERATOR	3	4	690.682-066
RCE	RIP-AND-GROOVE-MACHINE OPERATOR	3	4	667.682-062
RCE	RIPENING-ROOM ATTENDANT	3	4	559.682-038
RCE	RIVETING-MACHINE OPERATOR 1	3	5	699.482-010
RCE	ROLLER	3	4	613.682-018
RCE	ROLLER COVERER	3	4	628.682-010
RCE	ROOF BOLTER	3	4	930.683-026
RCE	RUBBER-GOODS INSPECTOR-TESTER	3	4	759.584-010
RCE	RUBBER-MILL OPERATOR	3	5	559.682-042
RCE	RUG INSPECTOR 2	3	4	789.587-022
RCE	SALVAGE REPAIRER 2	3	5	729.384-018
RCE	SALVAGE-MACHINE OPERATOR	3	4	694.382-010
RCE	SALVAGER 2	3	3	737.687-118
RCE	SAMPLE TESTER-GRINDER	3	4	519.585-018
RCE	SAND TESTER	3	6	777.381-046
RCE	SAPPHIRE-STYLUS GRINDER	3	5	770.381-038
RCE	SCALE-RECLAMATION TENDER	3	4	515.585-010
RCE	SCOOPING-MACHINE TENDER	3	4	665.685-026
RCE	SEAM HAMMERER	3	3	730.684-070
RCE	SELECTOR	3	3	739.687-166
RCE	SETTER, INDUCTION-HEATING EQUIPMENT	3	5	813.360-014
RCE	SETTLEMENT CLERK	3	4	214.382-030
RCE	SEWING-MACHINE OPERATOR	3	4	780.682-010
RCE	SEWING-MACHINE OPERATOR	3	4	787.682-058
RCE	SEWING-MACHINE OPERATOR	3	5	787.682-046
RCE	SHAPER, HAND	3	4	761.684-038
RCE	SHELL-GRADER	3	4	734.687-070
RCE	SHIP RUNNER	3	4	222.567-014

Code	Title	GED	SVP	DOT No.
RCE	SHOTGUN-SHELL-ASSEMBLY-MACHINE			
	ADJUSTER	3	4	616.360-030
RCE	SIGN ERECTOR 2	3	3	869.684-054
RCE	SIRUP MAKER	3	5	529.482-022
RCE	SKEIN WINDER	3	5	721.484-022
RCE	SLAB GRINDER	3	5	673.682-030
RCE	SOCKET PULLER	3	4	730.682-010
RCE	SODA DIALYZER	3	4	551.685-134
RCE	SOLE SEWER, HAND	3	6	788.684-110
RCE	STAGER	3	4	971.684-014
RCE	STARCH-TREATING ASSISTANT	3	4	520.665-018
RCE	STATION ENGINEER, MAIN LINE	3	7	914.362-018
RCE	STEEL-WOOL-MACHINE OPERATOR	3	5	605.482-010
RCE	STILL OPERATOR	3	5	522.382-030
RCE	STILL TENDER	3	3	552.685-026
RCE	STITCHER	3	4	689.682-022
RCE	STITCHER, STANDARD MACHINE	3	4	690.682-082
RCE	STOPBOARD ASSEMBLER	3	4	730.684-082
RCE	STRAP-FOLDING-MACHINE OPERATOR	3	2	554.485-014
RCE	STRICKLER ATTENDANT	3	4	652.665-014
RCE	SURGICAL-FORCEPS FABRICATOR	3	4	712.681-026
RCE	SYNTHETIC-STAPLE EXTRUDER	3	4	557.665-010
RCE	TAMPING-MACHINE OPERATOR	3	5	869.683-018
RCE	TARGETEER	3	3	736.684-042
RCE	TENONER OPERATOR	3	4	677.682-026
RCE	TEST-SKEIN WINDER	3	3	575.685-082
RCE	TESTER	3	6	730.684-086
RCE	TESTING-MACHINE OPERATOR	3	4	586.685-038
RCE	THREADER	3	5	685.680-010
RCE	TILE-CONDUIT LAYER	3	6	861.381-062
RCE	TIRE CLASSIFIER	3	3	750.387-010
RCE	TIRE INSPECTOR	3	4	750.684-030
RCE	TOOTH CUTTER, ESCAPE WHEEL	3	4	605.682-026
RCE	TOWER-LOADER OPERATOR	3	5	921.683-074
RCE	TRACTOR OPERATOR	3	3	929.683-014
RCE	TRANSFER OPERATOR	3	4	651.382-038
RCE	TRANSFER-MACHINE OPERATOR	3	3	609.685-022
RCE	TRANSMISSION TESTER	3	4	806.684-134
RCE	TREE PRUNER	3	4	408.684-018
RCE	TRIP FOLLOWER	3	3	209.367-050
RCE	TUBER-MACHINE OPERATOR	3	4	690.662-014
RCE	TUFTING-MACHINE OPERATOR	3	3	687.685-018
RCE	TUNGSTEN REFINER	3	5	511.382-010
RCE	TURNER, MACHINE	3	4	770.685-034
RCE	TYPESETTING-MACHINE TENDER	3	4	650.685-010
RCE	VACUUM DRIER OPERATOR	3	2	523.685-122
RCE	VALVE MAKER 2	3	6	730.681-018
RCE	VENTILATION EQUIPMENT TENDER	3	4	950.585-010
RCE	WAD-BLANKING-PRESS ADJUSTER	3	4	690.360-010
RCE	WARE DRESSER	3	4	774.684-042
RCE	WARP-TYING-MACHINE TENDER	3	4	683.685-034
RCE	WASH OPERATOR	3	5	559.662-014
RCE	WASH-OIL-PUMP OPERATOR	3	5	549.382-018
RCE	WATCH-CRYSTAL MOLDER	3	4	772.684-022

Code	Title	GED	SVP	DOT No.
RCE	WATER-SOFTENER SERVICER-AND-INSTALLER	3	3	862.684-034
RCE	WATER-TREATMENT-PLANT OPERATOR	3	4	551.485-010
RCE	WAY INSPECTOR	3	5	910.367-030
RCE	WEATHERSTRIP-MACHINE OPERATOR	3	4	690.382-014
RCE	WEAVER	3	5	683.682-038
RCE	WEAVER	3	5	683.682-034
RCE	WEAVER APPRENTICE	3	5	683.682-042
RCE	WEFT STRAIGHTENER	3	4	580.682-010
RCE	WELT-TRIMMING-MACHINE OPERATOR	3	3	686.685-074
RCE	WHEEL CUTTER	3	5	605.682-030
RCE	WINCH DRIVER	3	4	921.683-082
RCE	WIRE REPAIRER	3	3	628.684-038
RCE	WOODWORK-SALVAGE INSPECTOR	3	4	769.387-010
RCE	YEAST WASHER	3	2	529.685-278
RCE	ACETYLENE-PLANT OPERATOR	2	3	549.585-010
RCE	AGER OPERATOR	2	2	582.585-010
RCE	AIR-BAG CURER	2	2	556.685-010
RCE	AIR-HOLE DRILLER	2	2	692.685-018
RCE	AMPOULE FILLER	2	2	559.685-018
RCE	AMPOULE SEALER	2	2	559.687-014
RCE	AMPOULE-WASHING-MACHINE OPERATOR	2	2	559.685-022
RCE	ANVIL-SEATING-PRESS OPERATOR	2	3	694.685-010
RCE	APPLE-PACKING HEADER	2	2	920.687-010
RCE	APPLIQUER, ZIGZAG	2	3	786.682-010
RCE	ARMHOLE BASTER, JUMPBASTING	2	3	786.682-014
RCE	ARMHOLE-SEW-AND-TRIM OPERATOR, LOCKSTITCH	2	3	786.682-022
RCE	ARMORING-MACHINE OPERATOR	2	2	691.685-010
RCE	ARTIFICIAL-LOG-MACHINE OPERATOR	2	4	569.685-010
RCE	ASPHALT-DISTRIBUTOR TENDER	2	2	853.665-010
RCE	ASPHALT-HEATER TENDER	2	3	853.685-010
RCE	ASSEMBLER	2	2	701.687-010
RCE	ASSEMBLER	2	2	737.687-010
RCE	ASSEMBLER	2	4	754.684-010
RCE	ASSEMBLER FOR PULLER-OVER, MACHINE	2	3	690.685-010
RCE	ASSEMBLER 2	2	2	723.684-018
RCE	ASSEMBLER, PRODUCTION	2	2	706.687-010
RCE	ASSEMBLER, GOLD FRAME	2	2	713.384-010
RCE	ASSEMBLER, MOLDED FRAMES	2	2	713.684-014
RCE	ASSEMBLER, CLIP-ON SUNGLASSES	2	3	713.684-010
RCE	ASSEMBLER, METAL FURNITURE	2	2	709.684-014
RCE	ASSEMBLER, FILTERS	2	3	739.687-018
RCE	ASSEMBLER, FAUCETS	2	2	764.687-014
RCE	ASSEMBLER, PRODUCTION LINE	2	3	809.684-010
RCE	ASSEMBLER, SKYLIGHTS	2	3	869.684-014
RCE	ASSEMBLY ADJUSTER	2	3	720.684-010
RCE	ASSEMBLY OPERATOR	2	3	762.684-018
RCE	ASSEMBLY-INSPECTOR HELPER	2	3	801.663-010
RCE	ASSEMBLY-MACHINE OPERATOR	2	2	692.686-010
RCE	ATOMIZER ASSEMBLER	2	2	706.684-030
RCE	AUTOMATIC LUMP MAKING MACHINE TENDER	2	2	529.685-014
RCE	AUTOMOBILE-SEAT-COVER INSTALLER	2	2	915.687-010

Code	Title	GED	SVP	DOT No.
RCE	AUXILIARY-EQUIPMENT TENDER	2	3	570.685-010
RCE	BACK MAKER, LOCKSTITCH	2	3	786.682-026
RCE	BAG SEWER	2	2	787.686-010
RCE	BALL-WARPER TENDER	2	3	681.685-010
RCE	BALLING-MACHINE OPERATOR	2	2	681.685-014
RCE	BAND-SAWING-MACHINE OPERATOR	2	3	690.485-010
RCE	BAND-TOP MAKER	2	3	780.684-014
RCE	BANDER	2	2	733.687-018
RCE	BANDER-AND-CELLOPHANER, MACHINE	2	2	920.685-014
RCE	BANDER-AND-CELLOPHANER HELPER, MACHINE	2	2	920.686-010
RCE	BARREL BRANDER	2	2	764.684-010
RCE	BARREL CHARRER	2	4	764.684-014
RCE	BARREL FILLER	2	3	914.485-010
RCE	BARREL FINISHER	2	3	715.682-010
RCE	BARREL LOADER AND CLEANER	2	2	736.587-010
RCE	BARREL MARKER	2	2	764.687-030
RCE	BARREL REPAIRER	2	5	736.684-022
RCE	BARREL-CAP SETTER	2	3	715.687-014
RCE	BARTENDER HELPER	2	2	312.687-010
RCE	BASKET ASSEMBLER 1	2	2	669.685-014
RCE	BASKET ASSEMBLER 2	2	2	769.684-010
RCE	BASKET GRADER	2	2	769.687-010
RCE	BASKET PATCHER	2	2	769.684-014
RCE	BASTING-MACHINE OPERATOR	2	3	786.682-030
RCE	BATCH FREEZER	2	2	523.685-010
RCE	BATCH MIXER	2	3	550.685-010
RCE	BATTER MIXER	2	2	520.685-014
RCE	BATTERY CHARGER, CONVEYOR LINE	2	2	727.687-026
RCE	BATTING-MACHINE OPERATOR	2	2	680.585-010
RCE	BB SHOT PACKER	2	2	920.685-018
RCE	BEADING SAWYER	2	2	667.685-018
RCE	BEAM-WARPER TENDER, AUTOMATIC	2	4	681.685-018
RCE	BEARINGNIZER	2	2	603.685-018
RCE	BEATER-ENGINEER HELPER	2	2	530.665-010
RCE	BELL-NECK HAMMERER	2	2	730.684-014
RCE	BELT REPAIRER	2	4	630.684-014
RCE	BELT-PRESS OPERATOR 2	2	3	553.665-010
RCE	BENCH HAND	2	3	706.684-046
RCE	BENCH WORKER	2	3	616.485-010
RCE	BENCH WORKER, HOLLOW HANDLE	2	2	700.687-010
RCE	BENDER, MACHINE	2	3	569.685-014
RCE	BEVELER	2	3	715.684-030
RCE	BINDER LAYER	2	2	529.685-018
RCE	BINDER, CHAINSTITCH	2	3	786.682-034
RCE	BINDER, COVERSTITCH	2	3	786.682-038
RCE	BINDER, LOCKSTITCH	2	3	786.682-042
RCE	BISQUE CLEANER	2	4	774.684-010
RCE	BIT SHARPENER	2	3	603.685-026
RCE	BLADE GROOVER	2	2	705.582-010
RCE	BLASTING-CAP ASSEMBLER	2	2	737.687-018
RCE	BLEACHER OPERATOR	2	3	558.685-018
RCE	BLEACHER, LARD	2	2	521.685-026
RCE	BLENDER	2	2	550.685-014

Code	Title	GED	SVP	DOT No.
RCE	BLENDER, SNUFF	2	2	520.685-022
RCE	BLENDING-LINE ATTENDANT	2	3	520.685-026
RCE	BLENDING-TANK TENDER	2	2	520.685-030
RCE	BLIND-SLAT-STAPLING-MACHINE OPERATOR	2	2	669.685-018
RCE	BLOCK FEEDER	2	2	663.686-010
RCE	BLOCK SEALER	2	2	599.685-010
RCE	BLOCKER	2	2	920.685-022
RCE	BLOCKER, HAND 2	2	2	580.684-014
RCE	BLOCKING-MACHINE TENDER	2	3	716.685-010
RCE	BLOWER INSULATOR	2	5	863.664-010
RCE	BOAT LOADER 2	2	3	921.685-010
RCE	BOBBIN PRESSER	2	2	689.685-018
RCE	BOBBIN STRIPPER	2	2	689.685-022
RCE	BOBBIN WINDER, MACHINE	2	2	681.585-014
RCE	BOBBIN WINDER, SEWING MACHINE	2	3	681.685-026
RCE	BOILER-OUT	2	2	700.687-014
RCE	BONE-DRIER OPERATOR	2	2	553.685-022
RCE	BONER	2	2	789.687-018
RCE	BOOK TRIMMER	2	3	640.685-010
RCE	BOOK-SEWING-MACHINE OPERATOR 2	2	4	653.682-010
RCE	BOOSTER ASSEMBLER	2	2	737.687-022
RCE	BOTTLED-BEVERAGE INSPECTOR	2	3	529.685-026
RCE	BOTTOM-TURNING-LATHE TENDER	2	3	665.685-010
RCE	BOW MAKER	2	2	788.684-034
RCE	BOWLING-BALL FINISHER	2	2	690.685-038
RCE	BOWLING-BALL ENGRAVER	2	3	732.584-010
RCE	BOX MAKER	2	2	762.684-026
RCE	BOX MAKER, PAPERBOARD	2	2	794.684-014
RCE	BOX-SEALING INSPECTOR	2	2	641.687-014
RCE	BRAIDER SETTER	2	2	759.664-010
RCE	BRAIDING-MACHINE OPERATOR	2	3	683.685-010
RCE	BRAKE HOLDER	2	3	932.664-010
RCE	BRAN MIXER	2	2	599.685-014
RCE	BREAKER-MACHINE OPERATOR	2	4	564.685-010
RCE	BREAKER-MACHINE TENDER	2	2	583.685-010
RCE	BRIAR CUTTER	2	2	664.685-010
RCE	BRIM PRESSER 1	2	2	583.685-018
RCE	BRIM-POUNCING-MACHINE OPERATOR	2	3	585.685-010
RCE	BRIM-STRETCHING-MACHINE OPERATOR	2	3	580.685-010
RCE	BRIQUETTING-MACHINE OPERATOR	2	3	519.685-010
RCE	BRUSH-HEAD MAKER	2	2	739.685-018
RCE	BUCKET OPERATOR	2	3	575.683-010
RCE	BUCKLE SORTER	2	3	734.687-030
RCE	BUDDER	2	2	405.684-010
RCE	BUFFER	2	3	585.685-014
RCE	BUFFER	2	3	690.685-046
RCE	BUFFER	2	3	739.684-026
RCE	BUFFER	2	2	752.684-022
RCE	BUFFER, INFLATED-PAD	2	3	690.685-054
RCE	BUFFING-MACHINE TENDER	2	2	603.665-010
RCE	BUFFING-WHEEL INSPECTOR	2	2	789.687-026
RCE	BUFFING-WHEEL FORMER, HAND	2	3	789.684-014
RCE	BULK FILLER	2	3	529.687-022

Code	Title	GED	SVP	DOT No.
RCE	BUNCH MAKER, HAND	2	4	790.684-010
RCE	BUNDLER, SEASONAL GREENERY	2	2	920.687-046
RCE	BUTCHER, CHICKEN AND FISH	2	3	316.684-010
RCE	BUTTER LIQUEFIER	2	3	523.585-010
RCE	BUTTON-ATTACHING-MACHINE OPERATOR	2	2	699.685-010
RCE	BUTTON-DECORATING-MACHINE OPERATOR	2	2	690.685-062
RCE	BUTTON-SEWING-MACHINE OPERATOR	2	2	786.685-010
RCE	BUTTONHOLE MAKER	2	3	788.684-038
RCE	BUTTONHOLE-MACHINE OPERATOR	2	2	786.685-014
RCE	BUZZSAW OPERATOR	2	3	667.685-026
RCE	CADMIUM-LIQUOR MAKER	2	2	553.685-026
RCE	CAFETERIA ATTENDANT	2	2	311.677-010
RCE	CALENDER OPERATOR	2	3	583.685-026
RCE	CALIBRATOR	2	4	701.684-010
RCE	CAN PATCHER	2	2	920.687-054
RCE	CANDLE WRAPPING-MACHINE OPERATOR	2	2	920.685-030
RCE	CANDY CUTTER, HAND	2	2	790.687-010
RCE	CANVAS BASTER, JUMPBASTING	2	3	786.682-050
RCE	CAPPING-MACHINE OPERATOR	2	3	692.685-042
RCE	CAR-REPAIRER HELPER	2	4	622.684-014
RCE	CARD CHANGER, JACQUARD LOOM	2	4	683.685-014
RCE	CARD LACER, JACQUARD	2	2	683.685-018
RCE	CARD STRIPPER	2	3	680.685-014
RCE	CARDER	2	2	920.685-034
RCE	CARROTER	2	2	784.687-014
RCE	CASING GRADER	2	2	529.687-026
RCE	CASING SEWER	2	2	529.687-030
RCE	CASING-FLUID TENDER	2	3	520.685-054
RCE	CASING-MACHINE OPERATOR	2	3	522.685-030
RCE	CASTER	2	4	514.684-010
RCE	CASTING-MACHINE OPERATOR	2	3	520.685-058
RCE	CATALYTIC-CONVERTER-OPERATOR HELPER	2	5	558.585-010
RCE	CATCHER, FILTER TIP	2	2	529.666-010
RCE	CD-MIXER	2	3	550.685-022
RCE	CD-STORAGE-AND-MATERIALS MAKE-UP HELPER	2	4	559.685-034
RCE	CELL COVERER	2	2	727.687-042
RCE	CEMENT LOADER	2	2	921.565-010
RCE	CEMENT MIXER	2	3	550.685-026
RCE	CEMENTER	2	5	711.684-014
RCE	CEMENTER, MACHINE JOINER	2	2	690.685-074
RCE	CENTRIFUGAL-CASTING-MACHINE OPERATOR 2	2	3	514.685-014
RCE	CENTRIFUGE OPERATOR	2	2	551.685-030
RCE	CENTRIFUGE-SEPARATOR OPERATOR	2	2	551.685-038
RCE	CERAMIC COATER, MACHINE	2	2	509.685-022
RCE	CHALK-EXTRUDING-MACHINE OPERATOR	2	3	575.685-018
RCE	CHALK-MOLDING-MACHINE OPERATOR	2	3	575.685-022
RCE	CHANNELER, INSOLE	2	3	690.685-086
RCE	CHARGER 2	2	2	700.687-026
RCE	CHECKER 1	2	2	222.687-010
RCE	CHICK GRADER	2	2	411.687-010
RCE	CHIN-STRAP CUTTER	2	2	686.685-010
RCE	CHINCHILLA-MACHINE OPERATOR	2	2	585.685-022

Code	Title	GED	SVP	DOT No.
RCE	CHIP-APPLYING-MACHINE TENDER	2	3	641.685-030
RCE	CHOCOLATE TEMPERER	2	3	523.685-022
RCE	CHOPPED-STRAND OPERATOR	2	2	680.685-022
RCE	CHOPPING-MACHINE OPERATOR	2	4	520.685-066
RCE	CHURN OPERATOR, MARGARINE	2	2	520.685-070
RCE	CIGAR BRANDER	2	2	920.685-046
RCE	CIGAR MAKER	2	5	790.684-014
RCE	CIGAR-HEAD PIERCER	2	2	529.685-058
RCE	CIGARETTE-MAKING-MACHINE CATCHER	2	2	529.666-014
RCE	CIGARETTE-PACKAGE EXAMINER	2	4	920.667-010
RCE	CIGARETTE-PACKING-MACHINE OPERATOR	2	3	920.685-050
RCE	CLEANER, SIGNS	2	2	739.687-062
RCE	CLIPPER	2	2	739.685-022
RCE	CLIPPER, AUTOMATIC	2	4	663.585-010
RCE	CLOCK ASSEMBLER	2	3	715.684-058
RCE	CLOTH DRIER	2	2	580.685-014
RCE	CLOTH EXAMINER, HAND	2	2	689.687-022
RCE	CLOTH MEASURER, MACHINE	2	3	589.685-022
RCE	CLOTH WINDER	2	2	689.685-046
RCE	CLOTH-EDGE SINGER	2	2	585.687-018
RCE	CLOTHES-ROOM WORKER	2	2	355.687-010
RCE	COAT JOINER, LOCKSTITCH	2	3	786.682-058
RCE	COATING OPERATOR	2	3	524.685-018
RCE	COCOA-BUTTER-FILTER OPERATOR	2	2	521.685-070
RCE	COCOA-ROOM OPERATOR	2	3	521.685-074
RCE	COIL WINDER	2	4	724.684-026
RCE	COILER	2	4	613.685-010
RCE	COLLAR BASTER, JUMPBASTING	2	3	786.682-062
RCE	COLLAR FELLER, HANDSTITCHING MACHINE	2	2	786.682-066
RCE	COLLAR SETTER, LOCKSTITCH	2	3	786.682-070
RCE	COLLAR SETTER, OVERLOCK	2	3	786.682-074
RCE	COLLAR-TURNER OPERATOR	2	2	580.685-018
RCE	COLLATING-MACHINE OPERATOR	2	4	653.585-010
RCE	COLLET DRILLER	2	2	715.684-062
RCE	COLLETER	2	3	715.684-066
RCE	COMPACT ASSEMBLER	2	2	739.687-066
RCE	COMPOUNDER HELPER	2	2	540.686-010
RCE	CONCAVING-MACHINE OPERATOR	2	2	585.685-030
RCE	CONCRETE-BUILDING ASSEMBLER	2	4	869.664-010
RCE	CONCRETE-FLOAT MAKER	2	2	869.687-022
RCE	CONE OPERATOR	2	3	934.685-010
RCE	CONTACT-LENS MOLDER	2	3	690.685-090
RCE	CONTACT-LENS-FLASHING PUNCHER	2	2	713.687-014
RCE	CONTAINER WASHER, MACHINE	2	2	529.685-074
RCE	CONTINUOUS PILLOWCASE CUTTER	2	3	686.685-014
RCE	CONTINUOUS-CRUSHER OPERATOR	2	2	586.685-014
RCE	COOK HELPER	2	3	529.687-050
RCE	COOK-BOX FILLER	2	2	523.685-030
RCE	COOK, FRY, DEEP FAT	2	2	526.685-014
RCE	COOKER TENDER	2	3	532.685-014
RCE	COOLING-PAN TENDER	2	2	523.685-046
RCE	CORDUROY-CUTTER OPERATOR	2	3	585.565-010
RCE	CORE-COMPOSER-MACHINE TENDER	2	3	569.685-022

Code	Title	GED	SVP	DOT No.
RCE	CORE-LAYING-MACHINE OPERATOR	2	4	569.685-026
RCE	COREMAKER, MACHINE 1	2	3	518.685-014
RCE	COREMAKER, MACHINE 2	2	2	518.685-018
RCE	CORN-GRINDER OPERATOR, AUTOMATIC	2	2	521.685-086
RCE	COTTON SAMPLER	2	2	922.687-042
RCE	COTTON-BALL BAGGER	2	2	920.686-014
RCE	COTTON-ROLL PACKER	2	2	920.685-054
RCE	COUNTER CUTTER	2	3	690.685-094
RCE	COUNTER ROLLER	2	2	690.685-106
RCE	COUNTERSINKER	2	3	715.682-014
RCE	COVERING-MACHINE OPERATOR	2	3	681.685-038
RCE	CROWN ATTACHER	2	2	715.684-070
RCE	CRUSHER-AND-BINDER OPERATOR	2	2	689.685-054
RCE	CRYSTAL CUTTER	2	3	715.684-078
RCE	CUP SETTER, LOCKSTITCH	2	3	786.682-082
RCE	CUP-TRIMMING-MACHINE OPERATOR	2	2	615.685-018
RCE	CUPOLA CHARGER, INSULATION	2	3	572.686-010
RCE	CUPOLA TAPPER	2	2	514.664-010
RCE	CURING-PRESS MAINTAINER	2	2	629.684-010
RCE	CUSHION BUILDER	2	3	780.684-046
RCE	CUSHION MAKER 1	2	4	780.684-054
RCE	CUT-LACE-MACHINE OPERATOR	2	3	585.685-038
RCE	CUT-OFF-MACHINE OPERATOR	2	3	640.685-034
RCE	CUT-OUT-AND-MARKING-MACHINE OPERATOR	2	3	690.685-110
RCE	CUT-OUT-MACHINE OPERATOR	2	2	690.685-114
RCE	CUTTER	2	2	686.685-022
RCE	CUTTER	2	2	690.685-118
RCE	CUTTER, ALUMINUM SHEET	2	2	804.684-010
RCE	CUTTER, HAND	2	2	751.684-014
RCE	CUTTER, ROTARY SHEAR	2	3	781.684-018
RCE	CUTTER, V-GROOVE	2	3	715.685-014
RCE	CUTTER, WOODWIND REEDS	2	2	730.686-010
RCE	CUTTING-MACHINE OPERATOR	2	2	686.585-010
RCE	CUTTING-MACHINE TENDER, DECORATIVE	2	2	775.685-010
RCE	DAMPENER OPERATOR	2	2	534.685-010
RCE	DE-ALCOHOLIZER	2	3	522.685-042
RCE	DEBLOCKER	2	3	716.687-010
RCE	DECAL APPLIER	2	2	749.684-010
RCE	DEICER REPAIRER	2	4	759.684-026
RCE	DEICER-ELEMENT WINDER, MACHINE	2	4	692.685-066
RCE	DENTAL FLOSS PACKER	2	2	920.687-082
RCE	DEVELOPER, AUTOMATIC	2	2	976.685-014
RCE	DIAMOND BLENDER	2	4	590.685-018
RCE	DIE-CASTING-MACHINE OPERATOR 2	2	2	514.685-018
RCE	DIESEL-MECHANIC HELPER	2	4	625.684-010
RCE	DIGESTION OPERATOR	2	3	519.565-010
RCE	DIPPER	2	3	590.685-022
RCE	DOMER	2	2	641.685-038
RCE	DORR OPERATOR	2	3	522.685-050
RCE	DOUBLING-MACHINE OPERATOR	2	2	681.685-046
RCE	DOVETAIL-MACHINE OPERATOR	2	2	669.685-046
RCE	DRAPERY-ROD ASSEMBLER	2	3	706.484-010
RCE	DRAW-MACHINE OPERATOR	2	3	680.665-014

Code	Title	GED	SVP	DOT No.
RCE	DRAWER UPFITTER	2	4	706.684-050
RCE	DRIER	2	2	581.686-014
RCE	DRIER TENDER	2	3	543.685-014
RCE	DRIER-TAKE-OFF TENDER	2	2	921.685-034
RCE	DRIFTER	2	3	503.685-018
RCE	DRILL-PRESS OPERATOR, PRODUCTION	2	2	606.685-026
RCE	DRILL-PUNCH OPERATOR	2	2	649.685-034
RCE	DRILLER	2	3	716.685-014
RCE	DRILLER	2	3	700.684-026
RCE	DROP-WIRE BUILDER	2	2	689.687-034
RCE	DRUM STRAIGHTENER 1	2	2	619.685-034
RCE	DRY-CANS OPERATOR	2	2	581.685-022
RCE	DRY-HOUSE ATTENDANT	2	3	563.685-018
RCE	DRY-PAN OPERATOR	2	4	570.665-010
RCE	DRYING-MACHINE TENDER	2	2	581.685-030
RCE	DRYING-ROOM ATTENDANT	2	2	523.587-014
RCE	DRYING-UNIT-FELTING-MACHINE OPERATOR	2	4	581.685-034
RCE	DUPLICATING-MACHINE OPERATOR 2	2	4	207.682-014
RCE	DUSTER	2	2	587.685-026
RCE	EDGE BANDER, MACHINE	2	2	762.685-010
RCE	EDGE GRINDER	2	3	690.685-142
RCE	EDGE ROLLER	2	3	780.684-058
RCE	EDGE STAINER 2	2	3	749.684-022
RCE	EDGE TRIMMER	2	4	690.685-150
RCE	EDGE-GLUE-MACHINE TENDER	2	2	569.685-034
RCE	EDGER, TOUCH-UP	2	3	775.684-018
RCE	ELASTIC ATTACHER, CHAINSTITCH	2	3	786.682-086
RCE	ELASTIC ATTACHER, COVERSTITCH	2	3	786.682-090
RCE	ELASTIC ATTACHER, OVERLOCK	2	3	786.682-094
RCE	ELASTIC ATTACHER, ZIGZAG	2	3	786.682-098
RCE	ELECTRICIAN HELPER	2	3	829.684-026
RCE	ELECTRONIC-COMPONENT PROCESSOR	2	3	590.684-014
RCE	ELECTRONICS WORKER	2	2	726.687-010
RCE	EMBOSSER	2	3	583.685-030
RCE	EMBOSSING-MACHINE-OPERATOR HELPER	2	2	583.685-038
RCE	EMBOSSING-MACHINE OPERATOR	2	4	617.685-018
RCE	EMBOSSING-MACHINE OPERATOR	2	2	619.685-038
RCE	ENCAPSULATOR	2	2	726.684-030
RCE	END FINDER, ROVING DEPARTMENT	2	2	689.687-038
RCE	END FINDER, TWISTING DEPARTMENT	2	2	689.687-042
RCE	END FRAZER	2	3	665.685-014
RCE	ENGRAVER TENDER	2	3	673.685-050
RCE	ENROBING-MACHINE OPERATOR	2	2	524.685-026
RCE	ENVELOPE-MACHINE OPERATOR	2	4	649.685-042
RCE	ETCHER, ELECTROLYTIC	2	2	500.685-010
RCE	ETCHER, MACHINE	2	4	619.685-042
RCE	EXAMINER	2	3	789.687-042
RCE	EXPANDING MACHINE OPERATOR	2	3	617.685-022
RCE	EXPLOSIVE OPERATOR 2	2	2	737.687-046
RCE	EXTENSION EDGER	2	2	641.685-046
RCE	EXTRACTOR LOADER AND UNLOADER	2	2	551.686-014
RCE	EXTRACTOR OPERATOR	2	3	551.685-058
RCE	EXTRUDER OPERATOR	2	2	569.685-038

Code	Title	GED	SVP	DOT No.
RCE	EYEGLASS-FRAME TRUER	2	3	713.684-026
RCE	FACING BASTER, JUMPBASTING	2	3	786.682-102
RCE	FASTENER-SEWING-MACHINE OPERATOR	2	2	787.685-010
RCE	FASTENER, MACHINE	2	2	690.685-162
RCE	FEATHER SHAPER	2	2	734.684-010
RCE	FEATHER STITCHER	2	3	732.684-050
RCE	FEATHEREDGER AND REDUCER, MACHINE	2	2	690.685-166
RCE	FEED MIXER	2	2	520.685-098
RCE	FELLED-SEAM OPERATOR, CHAINSTITCH	2	3	786.682-106
RCE	FELT CUTTER	2	2	686.685-026
RCE	FERTILIZER MIXER	2	2	550.665-018
RCE	FETTLER	2	3	779.684-018
RCE	FIBERGLASS-CONTAINER-WINDING OPERATOR	2	4	579.584-010
RCE	FILER AND SANDER	2	3	705.684-018
RCE	FILLER MIXER	2	2	520.687-030
RCE	FILLING MACHINE TENDER	2	3	524.685-030
RCE	FILTER OPERATOR	2	2	551.685-078
RCE	FILTER WASHER AND PRESSER	2	2	599.685-038
RCE	FILTER-PRESS TENDER	2	3	599.685-042
RCE	FILTER-TANK-TENDER HELPER, HEAD	2	2	521.685-134
RCE	FINISHER-CARD TENDER	2	2	680.685-042
RCE	FINISHER, HAND	2	2	731.587-010
RCE	FINISHER, HAND	2	3	754.684-030
RCE	FINISHER, MACHINE	2	2	690.685-170
RCE	FINISHING TRIMMER	2	2	788.687-042
RCE	FITTER 2	2	5	706.684-054
RCE	FIXING-MACHINE OPERATOR	2	3	732.685-018
RCE	FLAGGER	2	2	372.667-022
RCE	FLATLOCK-SEWING-MACHINE OPERATOR	2	3	786.682-110
RCE	FLAVOR EXTRACTOR	2	3	529.685-126
RCE	FLOOR WORKER	2	2	920.687-090
RCE	FLOUR MIXER	2	2	520.485-010
RCE	FOAM CHARGER	2	3	827.585-010
RCE	FOAM DISPENSER	2	3	554.684-014
RCE	FOCUSER	2	3	725.687-018
RCE	FOLDER-SEAMER, AUTOMATIC	2	3	787.685-014
RCE	FOLDER, HAND	2	2	788.687-050
RCE	FOLDER, MACHINE	2	3	690.685-174
RCE	FOOT STRAIGHTENER	2	2	715.687-030
RCE	FORMING-PROCESS-LINE WORKER	2	2	727.687-058
RCE	FOUNDATION MAKER	2	2	784.684-030
RCE	FOUNTAIN PEN TURNER	2	3	690.685-190
RCE	FOUR-CORNER-STAYER-MACHINE OPERATOR	2	2	641.685-054
RCE	FOUR-SLIDE-MACHINE OPERATOR 2	2	3	619.685-050
RCE	FRAME BANDER	2	3	628.684-014
RCE	FRAME CHANGER	2	2	689.686-026
RCE	FRICTION-PAINT-MACHINE TENDER	2	2	534.685-014
RCE	FRONT MAKER, LOCKSTITCH	2	4	786.682-114
RCE	FRONT-EDGE-TAPE SEWER, LOCKSTITCH	2	4	786.682-118
RCE	FRONT-END LOADER OPERATOR	2	3	921.683-042
RCE	FROZEN PIE MAKER	2	2	529.684-010
RCE	FRUIT DISTRIBUTOR	2	2	921.685-046
RCE	FRUIT-BAR MAKER	2	2	529.685-134

Code	Title	GED	SVP	DOT No.
RCE	FUMIGATOR AND STERILIZER	2	2	582.685-074
RCE	FUR-BLOWER OPERATOR	2	4	680.685-046
RCE	FURNACE HELPER	2	2	512.666-010
RCE	FUSING-FURNACE LOADER	2	2	573.686-014
RCE	GAME-FARM HELPER	2	3	412.684-010
RCE	GARNETT-MACHINE OPERATOR	2	3	680.685-050
RCE	GAS-LEAK TESTER	2	2	827.584-014
RCE	GEAR-CUTTING-MACHINE OPERATOR, PRODUCTION	2	3	602.685-010
RCE	GETTERING-FILAMENT-MACHINE OPERATOR	2	3	509.685-026
RCE	GLASS CHECKER	2	2	716.687-014
RCE	GLASS POLISHER	2	3	775.684-038
RCE	GLASS-CLEANING-MACHINE TENDER	2	3	579.685-018
RCE	GLASS-FURNACE TENDER	2	2	572.685-010
RCE	GLASS-VIAL-BENDING-CONVEYOR FEEDER	2	2	573.686-018
RCE	GLASS-WOOL-BLANKET-MACHINE FEEDER	2	3	579.685-022
RCE	GLOVE PRINTER	2	3	652.685-034
RCE	GLUE-MACHINE OPERATOR	2	2	692.685-094
RCE	GLUE-SIZE-MACHINE OPERATOR	2	2	562.685-010
RCE	GLUER-AND-WEDGER	2	2	762.687-038
RCE	GLUING-MACHINE OPERATOR, ELECTRONIC	2	4	569.685-050
RCE	GOLF-SHOE-SPIKE ASSEMBLER	2	2	788.687-054
RCE	GRADER TENDER	2	3	521.685-154
RCE	GRATED-CHEESE MAKER	2	3	521.685-162
RCE	GREASE-AND-TALLOW PUMPER	2	2	559.585-014
RCE	GREENSKEEPER 2	2	3	406.683-010
RCE	GREY-GOODS MARKER	2	2	229.587-010
RCE	GRINDER 1	2	3	705.684-026
RCE	GRINDING-MACHINE OPERATOR, PORTABLE	2	3	910.684-010
RCE	GRIP WRAPPER	2	3	732.684-082
RCE	GROOVER AND TURNER	2	2	690.685-198
RCE	GROOVING-LATHE TENDER	2	2	690.685-202
RCE	GROUND LAYER	2	3	574.684-010
RCE	GROUNDSKEEPER, INDUSTRIAL-COMMERCIAL	2	3	406.684-014
RCE	GROUT-MACHINE TENDER	2	2	519.685-014
RCE	HACKLER, DOLL WIGS	2	2	731.687-018
RCE	HAIRSPRING CUTTER 2	2	2	715.687-042
RCE	HANDBAG FRAMER	2	2	739.684-090
RCE	HANDER-IN	2	2	683.687-018
RCE	HANDKERCHIEF FOLDER	2	2	920.687-098
RCE	HANDLE-AND-VENT-MACHINE OPERATOR	2	2	686.685-034
RCE	HARDWARE ASSEMBLER	2	2	762.687-046
RCE	HAT-LINING BLOCKER	2	2	583.685-050
RCE	HEADING-MACHINE OPERATOR	2	2	669.685-062
RCE	HEAT CURER	2	2	581.586-010
RCE	HEAVY-MEDIA OPERATOR	2	3	541.685-010
RCE	HEDDLE-MACHINE OPERATOR	2	3	616.685-026
RCE	HEEL ATTACHER, WOOD	2	4	788.684-058
RCE	HEEL BUILDER, MACHINE	2	3	690.685-206
RCE	HEEL PRICKER	2	3	690.685-218
RCE	HEEL SPRAYER, MACHINE	2	3	590.685-038
RCE	HEEL-SEAT FITTER, HAND	2	4	788.684-062
RCE	HEEL-SEAT LASTER, MACHINE	2	3	690.685-230

Code	Title	GED	SVP	DOT No.
RCE	HEEL-WASHER-STRINGING-MACHINE OPERATOR	2	2	619.685-058
RCE	HELMET COVERER	2	3	689.685-074
RCE	HEMMING-AND-TACKING-MACHINE OPERATOR	2	2	787.685-022
RCE	HEMSTITCHING-MACHINE OPERATOR	2	2	786.682-142
RCE	HOOKING-MACHINE OPERATOR	2	3	580.685-034
RCE	HOSE CUTTER, HAND	2	3	751.687-010
RCE	HOT-CAR OPERATOR	2	3	519.663-014
RCE	HOT-PLATE-PLYWOOD-PRESS OPERATOR	2	3	569.685-054
RCE	HYDRAULIC BLOCKER	2	4	580.685-038
RCE	HYDRAULIC-BILLET MAKER	2	3	575.685-046
RCE	HYDRAULIC-PRESS OPERATOR	2	3	569.685-058
RCE	HYDROELECTRIC-PLANT MAINTAINER	2	3	952.687-010
RCE	ICE MAKER, SKATING RINK	2	2	969.687-014
RCE	ICER, HAND	2	3	524.684-022
RCE	IMPREGNATOR OPERATOR	2	4	559.685-106
RCE	IMPREGNATOR	2	2	562.685-014
RCE	INDUSTRIAL-TRUCK OPERATOR	2	3	921.683-050
RCE	INKER, MACHINE	2	2	690.685-234
RCE	INSEAM TRIMMER	2	2	690.685-238
RCE	INSECTICIDE MIXER	2	2	550.685-070
RCE	INSOLE REINFORCER	2	3	690.685-246
RCE	INSPECTOR, WREATH	2	3	739.687-118
RCE	INSPECTOR, TYPE	2	3	706.687-026
RCE	INSPECTOR, SOLDERING	2	3	715.687-070
RCE	INSPECTOR, PICTURE FRAMES	2	3	769.687-030
RCE	INSPECTOR, TIMERS	2	3	715.687-074
RCE	INSTALLER, SOFT TOP	2	2	807.684-026
RCE	INTERLACER	2	3	788.684-070
RCE	IRONER	2	2	590.685-042
RCE	JEWEL GRINDER 2	2	3	770.684-010
RCE	JEWEL GRINDER 1	2	3	770.685-014
RCE	JEWEL STAKER	2	3	715.684-134
RCE	JEWEL-CUPPING-MACHINE OPERATOR	2	3	770.685-030
RCE	JIGGER-CROWN-POUNCING-MACHINE OPERATOR	2	3	585.685-058
RCE	JIGSAWYER	2	4	700.684-046
RCE	JOINER	2	2	673.687-010
RCE	JOINT CUTTER, MACHINE	2	2	690.685-250
RCE	JUNCTION MAKER	2	5	862.684-010
RCE	KERFER-MACHINE OPERATOR	2	3	667.685-042
RCE	KEY CUTTER	2	2	709.684-050
RCE	KEYING-MACHINE OPERATOR	2	2	652.685-042
RCE	KILN CLEANER	2	2	573.687-018
RCE	KILN-DOOR BUILDER	2	3	573.684-010
RCE	KNIFE SETTER, GRINDER MACHINE	2	3	564.684-010
RCE	KNITTER, FULL-FASHIONED GARMENT	2	4	685.665-010
RCE	KNITTER, WIRE MESH	2	2	616.685-030
RCE	KNITTING-MACHINE OPERATOR	2	3	685.665-014
RCE	LABEL REMOVER	2	2	920.687-106
RCE	LABEL-CUTTING-AND-FOLDING-MACHINE OPERATOR, AUTOMATIC	2	2	689.685-086
RCE	LABELING-MACHINE OPERATOR	2	2	920.685-066

Code	Title	GED	SVP	DOT No.
RCE	LABORATORY MILLER	2	3	521.685-194
RCE	LABORATORY-SAMPLE CARRIER	2	2	922.687-054
RCE	LABORER, GENERAL	2	2	559.567-010
RCE	LABORER, HOISTING	2	3	921.667-022
RCE	LABORER, RAGS	2	2	539.587-010
RCE	LACE WINDER	2	2	685.687-018
RCE	LACER	2	2	789.687-094
RCE	LACQUERER	2	3	599.685-054
RCE	LAG SCREWER	2	2	763.684-046
RCE	LAMINATOR	2	3	584.685-034
RCE	LAMINATOR 1	2	2	690.685-258
RCE	LAMP-SHADE ASSEMBLER	2	2	739.684-094
RCE	LAPEL PADDER, BLINDSTITCH	2	3	786.682-150
RCE	LAPPING-MACHINE OPERATOR, PRODUCTION	2	3	603.685-070
RCE	LARRY OPERATOR	2	3	519.683-014
RCE	LAST IRONER	2	3	739.684-098
RCE	LAST SAWYER	2	2	690.685-262
RCE	LASTER, HAND	2	2	788.684-074
RCE	LASTING-MACHINE OPERATOR, HAND METHOD	2	4	788.684-078
RCE	LATEXER 1	2	3	584.685-038
RCE	LATHE OPERATOR, PRODUCTION	2	3	604.685-026
RCE	LAUNDRY WORKER, DOMESTIC	2	2	302.685-010
RCE	LAUNDRY WORKER 3	2	3	369.387-010
RCE	LEAD-OXIDE-MILL TENDER	2	3	558.685-042
RCE	LEADER TIER	2	2	732.687-038
RCE	LEHR TENDER	2	3	573.685-026
RCE	LENS MATCHER	2	2	713.687-030
RCE	LIGHT-BULB ASSEMBLER	2	2	692.685-118
RCE	LIGHTOUT EXAMINER	2	3	529.687-146
RCE	LIME MIXER TENDER	2	3	514.685-022
RCE	LINEN GRADER	2	2	361.687-022
RCE	LINER ASSEMBLER	2	3	613.667-010
RCE	LINING BASTER, JUMPBASTING	2	4	786.682-154
RCE	LINING FELLER, BLINDSTITCH	2	3	786.682-158
RCE	LINING SETTER, LOCKSTITCH	2	3	786.682-166
RCE	LINING-MACHINE OPERATOR	2	2	575.565-010
RCE	LINTER TENDER	2	3	521.685-198
RCE	LIP CUTTER AND SCORER	2	2	690.685-270
RCE	LIQUOR INSPECTOR	2	2	522.667-010
RCE	LOG-HAUL CHAIN FEEDER	2	2	921.686-018
RCE	LONG-CHAIN BEAMER	2	3	681.685-058
RCE	LUMITE INJECTOR	2	2	690.685-278
RCE	LUMP-MACHINE OPERATOR	2	2	520.685-126
RCE	MACHINE OPERATOR 2	2	3	619.685-062
RCE	MACHINE SNELLER	2	2	732.685-026
RCE	MAILER APPRENTICE	2	3	222.587-032
RCE	MAINSPRING WINDER AND OILER	2	2	715.685-038
RCE	MAINSPRING FORMER, ARBOR END	2	2	715.687-078
RCE	MAINSPRING FORMER, BRACE END	2	2	715.687-082
RCE	MANIPULATOR OPERATOR	2	5	612.683-010
RCE	MARBLE-MACHINE TENDER	2	3	575.685-058
RCE	MARKER 2	2	2	920.687-126

Code	Title	GED	SVP	DOT No.
RCE	MARKER, MACHINE	2	3	690.685-282
RCE	MARKING STITCHER	2	2	781.687-046
RCE	MAT PACKER	2	2	579.686-014
RCE	MAT REPAIRER	2	2	759.684-042
RCE	MAT-MAKING MACHINE TENDER	2	2	692.685-122
RCE	MATRIX WORKER	2	2	500.684-014
RCE	MATRIX-DRIER TENDER	2	3	532.585-010
RCE	MATTRESS-SPRING ENCASER	2	2	780.687-030
RCE	MEAT BLENDER	2	2	529.685-166
RCE	MEAT-GRADING-MACHINE OPERATOR	2	2	521.685-218
RCE	MELTER	2	2	700.687-042
RCE	METAL FINISHER	2	4	705.684-034
RCE	METAL-SPONGE-MAKING-MACHINE OPERATOR	2	3	616.685-038
RCE	MICA-PLATE LAYER	2	2	579.685-026
RCE	MICA-PLATE LAYER, HAND	2	2	579.684-022
RCE	MICA-WASHER GLUER	2	2	729.687-022
RCE	MILKER, MACHINE	2	2	410.685-010
RCE	MILL ATTENDANT	2	2	555.685-038
RCE	MILL OPERATOR	2	3	599.685-058
RCE	MILL-ROLL REWINDER	2	4	690.585-010
RCE	MILLING-MACHINE OPERATOR, PRODUCTION	2	3	605.685-030
RCE	MINGLER OPERATOR	2	3	520.665-010
RCE	MIRROR SPECIALIST	2	3	779.684-038
RCE	MIXER	2	3	520.685-138
RCE	MIXER HELPER	2	2	530.384-010
RCE	MIXER, DIAMOND POWDER	2	4	570.484-010
RCE	MIXER, DRY-FOOD PRODUCTS	2	3	520.685-162
RCE	MIXER, FOAM RUBBER	2	2	550.685-086
RCE	MIXING-MACHINE TENDER	2	3	560.585-010
RCE	MIXING-TANK OPERATOR	2	2	520.685-170
RCE	MOISTURE-CONDITIONER OPERATOR	2	4	532.685-022
RCE	MOLD DRESSER	2	4	519.684-018
RCE	MOLD FILLER AND DRAINER	2	2	753.687-030
RCE	MOLD MAKER, TERRA COTTA	2	3	575.684-038
RCE	MOLD-FILLING OPERATOR	2	4	556.684-018
RCE	MOLDED-RUBBER-GOODS CUTTER	2	2	690.685-290
RCE	MOLDER	2	4	580.685-042
RCE	MOLDER, FIBERGLASS LUGGAGE	2	2	575.685-066
RCE	MOLDER, WAX	2	4	549.685-018
RCE	MOLDING CUTTER	2	2	663.685-018
RCE	MONORAIL CRANE OPERATOR	2	3	921.663-042
RCE	MOTOR TEST HELPER	2	2	806.687-038
RCE	MOTOR-VEHICLE-LIGHT ASSEMBLER	2	3	729.684-034
RCE	MOTTLE-LAY-UP OPERATOR	2	4	690.585-014
RCE	MOUNTER, AUTOMATIC	2	2	976.685-022
RCE	MOUNTER, HAND	2	3	725.684-014
RCE	MOUNTER, SMOKING PIPE	2	2	739.684-130
RCE	MULTIFOCAL-LENS ASSEMBLER	2	3	713.684-034
RCE	MULTINEEDLE-CHAINSTITCH-MACHINE OPERATOR	2	3	786.682-178
RCE	NAIL-MAKING-MACHINE TENDER	2	2	617.665-010
RCE	NAIL-POLISH-BRUSH-MACHINE FEEDER,			

Code	Title	GED	SVP	DOT No.
	AUTOMATIC	2	2	692.686-054
RCE	NAILER, HAND	2	3	762.684-050
RCE	NAILING-MACHINE OPERATOR, AUTOMATIC	2	2	669.685-066
RCE	NAPPER TENDER	2	3	585.685-070
RCE	NAPPER TENDER	2	2	585.665-010
RCE	NECKTIE OPERATOR, POCKETS AND PIECES	2	3	786.682-182
RCE	NECKTIE-CENTRALIZING-MACHINE OPERATOR 2	2	3	786.682-190
RCE	NECKTIE-CENTRALIZING-MACHINE OPERATOR 1	2	3	786.682-186
RCE	NEEDLE POLISHER	2	3	705.684-046
RCE	NETTING INSPECTOR	2	3	782.487-010
RCE	NICKER	2	2	690.685-298
RCE	NOTCH GRINDER	2	3	673.685-070
RCE	NOZZLE TENDER	2	3	512.685-014
RCE	NOZZLE-AND-SLEEVE WORKER	2	3	514.684-018
RCE	NUMBERER AND WIRER	2	2	689.587-010
RCE	NUT-SORTER OPERATOR	2	3	521.685-238
RCE	OBSERVER HELPER, GRAVITY PROSPECTING	2	3	939.663-010
RCE	OILER	2	2	715.684-146
RCE	OPENER 1	2	2	784.687-054
RCE	ORIENTAL-RUG STRETCHER	2	2	580.687-010
RCE	ORNAMENT SETTER	2	3	789.685-010
RCE	OVEN TENDER	2	2	534.565-010
RCE	OVEN TENDER	2	3	543.685-018
RCE	OVEN TENDER	2	2	573.585-010
RCE	OVEN-HEATER HELPER	2	3	542.665-010
RCE	OXIDIZER	2	2	700.684-054
RCE	PACKAGE SEALER, MACHINE	2	2	920.685-074
RCE	PACKAGER, HEAD	2	4	667.682-046
RCE	PACKING-LINE WORKER	2	2	753.687-038
RCE	PACKING-MACHINE-PILOT CAN ROUTER	2	2	920.685-086
RCE	PAD CUTTER	2	3	690.685-302
RCE	PAINT-LINE OPERATOR	2	3	599.685-066
RCE	PAINT-ROLLER WINDER	2	3	739.685-030
RCE	PAINTER HELPER, SHIPYARD	2	3	840.687-010
RCE	PAINTER, BRUSH	2	2	740.684-022
RCE	PAIRING-MACHINE OPERATOR	2	3	691.685-022
RCE	PALLET ASSEMBLER	2	3	715.684-154
RCE	PALLET RECTIFIER	2	4	715.684-158
RCE	PANEL EDGE SEALER	2	2	769.685-010
RCE	PANTS OUTSEAMER, CHAINSTITCH	2	3	786.682-202
RCE	PAPER CONDITIONER	2	3	659.685-010
RCE	PAPER-CONE-MACHINE TENDER	2	2	641.685-062
RCE	PAPER-REEL OPERATOR	2	3	640.685-046
RCE	PAPERBACK-MACHINE OPERATOR	2	3	616.685-046
RCE	PAPERHANGER	2	2	574.585-010
RCE	PARACHUTE INSPECTOR	2	2	789.687-114
RCE	PARACHUTE-LINE TIER	2	2	789.687-118
RCE	PARTITION-MAKING-MACHINE OPERATOR	2	2	649.685-082
RCE	PASTER, HAND OR MACHINE	2	2	783.687-026
RCE	PATCH WASHER	2	2	582.685-110

Code	Title	GED	SVP	DOT No.
RCE	PATCH WORKER	2	3	790.684-018
RCE	PATCHER	2	2	723.687-010
RCE	PATCHER, BOWLING BALL	2	3	759.684-046
RCE	PATROLLER	2	2	685.687-022
RCE	PATTERN DUPLICATOR	2	2	683.685-026
RCE	PEARLER	2	2	715.684-162
RCE	PELOTA MAKER	2	4	732.684-090
RCE	PERFORATING-MACHINE OPERATOR	2	4	649.685-090
RCE	PERFORATING-MACHINE OPERATOR	2	2	686.685-038
RCE	PHONOGRAPH-CARTRIDGE ASSEMBLER	2	5	720.684-014
RCE	PICK-PULLING-MACHINE OPERATOR	2	2	689.685-094
RCE	PICKER-MACHINE OPERATOR	2	3	680.685-078
RCE	PIERCING-MILL OPERATOR	2	3	613.685-018
RCE	PIGMENT PUMPER	2	4	914.665-010
RCE	PILLOWCASE TURNER	2	3	583.685-078
RCE	PIN INSERTER, REGULATOR	2	3	715.684-166
RCE	PIN-OR-CLIP FASTENER	2	2	735.687-022
RCE	PIPE-FITTER HELPER	2	3	862.684-022
RCE	PLASTERER	2	2	749.687-026
RCE	PLASTIC MIXER	2	4	559.684-014
RCE	PLASTICS REPAIRER	2	3	754.684-046
RCE	PLATEN-PRESS FEEDER	2	3	651.685-022
RCE	PLUG WIRER	2	3	726.687-014
RCE	PLUMBING-HARDWARE ASSEMBLER	2	2	706.684-086
RCE	POLISHER	2	2	761.684-026
RCE	POLISHER AND BUFFER 2	2	2	705.684-062
RCE	POLISHER, DIAL	2	3	715.684-170
RCE	POLISHER, EYEGLASS FRAMES	2	2	713.684-038
RCE	POTATO-PANCAKE FRIER	2	2	526.685-050
RCE	POTATO-PEELING-MACHINE OPERATOR	2	2	521.685-250
RCE	POULTICE-MACHINE OPERATOR	2	4	692.685-134
RCE	POUNCING-LATHE OPERATOR	2	2	585.685-074
RCE	POUNDER	2	3	690.685-314
RCE	PREPARER	2	2	700.687-062
RCE	PRESS FEEDER	2	3	652.685-058
RCE	PRESS FEEDER, BROOMCORN	2	2	429.686-010
RCE	PRESS OPERATOR	2	3	559.665-030
RCE	PRESS OPERATOR	2	3	575.685-070
RCE	PRESS OPERATOR	2	4	583.685-086
RCE	PRESS TENDER, PYROTECHNICS	2	2	694.685-038
RCE	PRESSER	2	2	559.685-142
RCE	PRESSER	2	2	690.685-318
RCE	PRESSER, MACHINE	2	2	363.682-018
RCE	PRIMER ASSEMBLER	2	3	737.687-098
RCE	PRIMER-INSERTING-MACHINE OPERATOR	2	2	694.685-042
RCE	PRIMER-POWDER BLENDER, DRY	2	3	550.565-010
RCE	PRIMER-WATERPROOFING-MACHINE OPERATOR	2	2	694.685-046
RCE	PRINTER	2	3	652.685-062
RCE	PROCESS-MACHINE OPERATOR	2	3	640.685-050
RCE	PROCESSOR	2	3	557.685-018
RCE	PRODUCTION-MACHINE TENDER	2	3	609.685-018
RCE	PROFILE-STITCHING-MACHINE OPERATOR	2	2	786.685-026
RCE	PROPELLANT-CHARGE LOADER	2	2	737.487-010

Code	Title	GED	SVP	DOT No.
RCE	PULLER OVER, MACHINE	2	4	788.684-090
RCE	PULVERIZER	2	2	770.687-030
RCE	PUMP INSTALLER-AND-TESTER	2	4	806.384-018
RCE	PUNCH-PRESS OPERATOR	2	2	692.665-014
RCE	PUNCHBOARD ASSEMBLER 1	2	2	794.687-042
RCE	PUNCHER	2	2	663.685-022
RCE	PUSH-CONNECTOR ASSEMBLER	2	2	706.687-030
RCE	PUSHER OPERATOR	2	3	519.663-018
RCE	QUILLER OPERATOR	2	4	681.685-070
RCE	RACKER	2	2	749.587-010
RCE	RAG INSPECTOR	2	2	530.687-010
RCE	RAKER, BUFFING WHEEL	2	3	589.684-010
RCE	REAMER, CENTER HOLE	2	2	715.687-110
RCE	RECORD-CHANGER ASSEMBLER	2	2	720.687-010
RCE	RECORD-PRESS TENDER	2	3	556.685-070
RCE	RED-LEAD BURNER	2	2	558.685-054
RCE	REELING-MACHINE OPERATOR	2	3	681.685-078
RCE	REJECT OPENER	2	3	790.687-026
RCE	RELISH BLENDER	2	3	520.685-194
RCE	REMELTER	2	2	502.685-014
RCE	REPACK-ROOM WORKER	2	2	920.687-146
RCE	RESERVE OPERATOR	2	3	529.685-206
RCE	RESIN COATER	2	2	562.687-014
RCE	RETURNED-GOODS SORTER	2	2	922.687-086
RCE	RIBBON-LAP-MACHINE TENDER	2	2	680.685-086
RCE	RIGGER	2	2	789.684-046
RCE	RIM-FIRE-PRIMING OPERATOR	2	3	694.685-050
RCE	RING STAMPER	2	5	700.684-066
RCE	RING-MAKING-MACHINE OPERATOR	2	2	649.685-098
RCE	RIPPER	2	2	617.685-030
RCE	RIPPER	2	2	782.687-038
RCE	RIVETER, HAND	2	2	709.684-066
RCE	ROD-MILL TENDER	2	2	519.685-030
RCE	ROD-PULLER AND COILER	2	2	619.685-078
RCE	ROLL BUILDER	2	3	759.484-010
RCE	ROLL RECLAIMER	2	2	640.685-062
RCE	ROLL-FORMING-MACHINE OPERATOR 2	2	2	617.685-034
RCE	ROLL-OR-TAPE-EDGE-MACHINE OPERATOR	2	3	787.682-038
RCE	ROLL-OVER-PRESS OPERATOR	2	2	690.685-326
RCE	ROLL-SLICING-MACHINE TENDER	2	2	640.685-066
RCE	ROLL-TENSION TESTER	2	3	559.584-010
RCE	ROLLER OPERATOR	2	2	652.685-078
RCE	ROLLER-SKATE ASSEMBLER	2	2	732.684-098
RCE	ROLLER, GOLD LEAF	2	3	709.685-018
RCE	ROLLER, HAND	2	5	790.684-022
RCE	ROPE-LAYING-MACHINE OPERATOR	2	3	681.685-086
RCE	ROTARY CUTTER	2	3	585.685-082
RCE	ROTARY-CUTTER FEEDER	2	2	640.686-010
RCE	ROTARY-DRIER FEEDER	2	2	553.686-038
RCE	ROTARY-DRILLER HELPER	2	4	930.684-026
RCE	ROUGH-AND-TRUEING-MACHINE OPERATOR	2	3	690.685-330
RCE	ROUGH-ROUNDER, MACHINE	2	3	690.685-334
RCE	ROUNDER	2	3	690.685-338
RCE	ROUTE AIDE	2	2	239.687-010

Code	Title	GED	SVP	DOT No.
RCE	ROUTING CLERK	2	2	222.687-022
RCE	ROUTING-EQUIPMENT TENDER	2	3	521.685-278
RCE	RUBBER MOLDER	2	4	556.684-026
RCE	RUG CLIPPER	2	3	781.684-046
RCE	RUG-CUTTER HELPER	2	2	686.686-014
RCE	SADDLE-AND-SIDE WIRE STITCHER	2	2	692.685-146
RCE	SAGGER MAKER	2	3	774.684-030
RCE	SALVAGE INSPECTOR	2	3	529.687-174
RCE	SALVAGE WINDER AND INSPECTOR	2	3	649.685-102
RCE	SAMPLE MAKER, HAND	2	3	794.684-030
RCE	SAMPLE SELECTOR	2	4	789.387-014
RCE	SAMPLE-BOOK MAKER	2	2	659.685-014
RCE	SAMPLER, WOOL	2	3	222.587-042
RCE	SAND-SLINGER OPERATOR	2	3	518.683-010
RCE	SANDBLAST-OR-SHOTBLAST-EQUIPMENT TENDER	2	2	503.685-042
RCE	SANDER, MACHINE	2	3	761.682-014
RCE	SANDWICH MAKER	2	2	317.684-018
RCE	SAUSAGE MAKER	2	2	520.685-202
RCE	SAUSAGE-MEAT TRIMMER	2	2	521.687-106
RCE	SAVE-ALL OPERATOR	2	2	533.685-018
RCE	SAWYER	2	2	677.685-038
RCE	SCALE OPERATOR	2	2	555.687-010
RCE	SCALER-PACKER	2	3	929.687-046
RCE	SCALLOP CUTTER, MACHINE	2	2	686.685-058
RCE	SCORER	2	2	641.685-070
RCE	SCREEN MAKER	2	3	739.684-150
RCE	SCREEN OPERATOR	2	3	551.685-130
RCE	SCREEN TACKER	2	2	762.687-058
RCE	SCREEN-ROOM OPERATOR	2	3	521.685-282
RCE	SCREENER-PERFUMER	2	3	559.685-162
RCE	SCREW REMOVER	2	2	788.684-102
RCE	SCREW-MACHINE OPERATOR, PRODUCTION	2	4	604.685-034
RCE	SCROLL ASSEMBLER	2	3	710.584-010
RCE	SEALING-MACHINE OPERATOR	2	3	692.685-162
RCE	SEAT JOINER, CHAINSTITCH	2	3	786.682-218
RCE	SECONDS HANDLER	2	2	782.687-050
RCE	SECTIONAL-BELT-MOLD ASSEMBLER	2	3	752.685-010
RCE	SELF-SEALING-FUEL-TANK REPAIRER	2	4	759.384-010
RCE	SELVAGE-MACHINE OPERATOR	2	2	681.685-094
RCE	SEMICONDUCTOR PROCESSOR	2	3	590.684-022
RCE	SEPARATOR OPERATOR	2	2	559.685-166
RCE	SEPARATOR OPERATOR	2	2	692.685-166
RCE	SEWING-MACHINE-REPAIRER HELPER	2	4	639.684-010
RCE	SEWING-MACHINE OPERATOR	2	3	787.682-054
RCE	SHAKER TENDER	2	3	934.685-018
RCE	SHAKER-PLATE OPERATOR	2	2	737.685-014
RCE	SHAVING-MACHINE OPERATOR	2	3	585.685-094
RCE	SHEARER AND TRIMMER, WIRE SCREEN AND FABRIC	2	3	709.684-074
RCE	SHEARING-MACHINE FEEDER	2	3	585.685-098
RCE	SHEARING-MACHINE OPERATOR	2	2	585.685-102
RCE	SHELL-MOLD-BONDING-MACHINE OPERATOR	2	2	518.685-030
RCE	SHELLFISH SHUCKER	2	3	521.687-122

Code	Title	GED	SVP	DOT No.
RCE	SHIRT-FOLDING-MACHINE OPERATOR	2	2	369.685-030
RCE	SHOE PACKER	2	2	920.687-166
RCE	SHOT POLISHER AND INSPECTOR	2	3	509.485-014
RCE	SHOT-GRINDER OPERATOR	2	2	603.685-074
RCE	SHOT-TUBE-MACHINE TENDER	2	2	649.685-106
RCE	SHOULDER JOINER, LOCKSTITCH	2	3	786.682-222
RCE	SHREDDER OPERATOR	2	3	555.685-058
RCE	SHREDDER TENDER, PEAT	2	2	599.685-086
RCE	SHUTTLER	2	2	689.687-070
RCE	SIDE LASTER, CEMENT	2	3	690.685-358
RCE	SIDE LASTER, STAPLE	2	3	690.685-362
RCE	SIGNAL MAINTAINER HELPER	2	3	822.684-018
RCE	SILK SPREADER	2	3	680.685-090
RCE	SILK-SCREEN PRINTER	2	2	726.687-018
RCE	SILO TENDER	2	3	579.685-050
RCE	SILVER WRAPPER	2	1	318.687-018
RCE	SILVERWARE ASSEMBLER	2	2	700.684-070
RCE	SINGE WINDER	2	3	681.585-018
RCE	SINKER WINDER	2	2	732.685-030
RCE	SINTERING-PRESS OPERATOR	2	2	617.685-038
RCE	SIPHON OPERATOR	2	2	599.687-026
RCE	SIZING-MACHINE TENDER	2	3	584.665-018
RCE	SKI BASE TRIMMER	2	2	732.684-110
RCE	SKIN FORMER	2	3	752.684-050
RCE	SKIN GRADER	2	2	525.687-102
RCE	SKIN-PEELING-MACHINE OPERATOR	2	2	525.685-030
RCE	SKINNER	2	2	525.684-046
RCE	SKIP OPERATOR	2	4	921.683-062
RCE	SKIVER	2	4	690.685-374
RCE	SKIVER, BLOCKERS	2	2	585.685-110
RCE	SLASHER	2	3	690.665-010
RCE	SLASHER OPERATOR	2	2	667.685-054
RCE	SLAT-BASKET MAKER, MACHINE	2	2	669.685-074
RCE	SLEEVE SETTER, LOCKSTITCH	2	4	786.682-230
RCE	SLEEVE SETTER, OVERLOCK	2	3	786.682-234
RCE	SLICE-PLUG-CUTTER OPERATOR	2	2	521.685-298
RCE	SLICING-MACHINE OPERATOR	2	2	521.685-302
RCE	SLICING-MACHINE OPERATOR	2	2	521.685-306
RCE	SLICING-MACHINE OPERATOR	2	2	692.685-174
RCE	SLIDER ASSEMBLER	2	2	734.687-078
RCE	SLINGER, SEQUINS	2	2	692.685-178
RCE	SLIP-SEAT COVERER	2	3	780.684-094
RCE	SLUBBER TENDER	2	3	680.685-098
RCE	SMOKING-PIPE DRILLER AND THREADER	2	2	669.685-078
RCE	SMOKING-TOBACCO-CUTTER OPERATOR	2	2	521.685-310
RCE	SNAILER	2	2	603.685-078
RCE	SNUFF GRINDER AND SCREENER	2	4	521.685-314
RCE	SNUFF-PACKING-MACHINE OPERATOR	2	2	920.685-094
RCE	SOCK BOARDER	2	2	589.686-042
RCE	SOLDERER, TORCH 1	2	2	813.684-026
RCE	SORTER	2	3	734.687-082
RCE	SORTER	2	3	735.687-030
RCE	SORTER	2	2	753.587-010
RCE	SORTER, MACHINE	2	2	692.685-182

Code	Title	GED	SVP	DOT No.
RCE	SPIKE-MACHINE FEEDER	2	2	612.666-010
RCE	SPINNER	2	3	557.685-026
RCE	SPINNER, MULE	2	4	682.685-014
RCE	SPIRAL SPRING WINDER	2	3	616.685-070
RCE	SPIRAL WEAVER	2	3	616.685-074
RCE	SPLICER OPERATOR	2	4	569.685-062
RCE	SPLICING-MACHINE OPERATOR, AUTOMATIC	2	2	689.685-122
RCE	SPLITTER, MACHINE	2	2	585.685-114
RCE	SPLITTING-MACHINE TENDER	2	3	663.685-042
RCE	SPOOL WINDER	2	2	619.485-010
RCE	SPORT-SHOE-SPIKE ASSEMBLER	2	3	690.685-394
RCE	SPOTTER	2	2	772.687-014
RCE	SPRAY-MACHINE OPERATOR	2	2	582.685-138
RCE	SPRING COILER	2	3	616.485-014
RCE	SPUN-PASTE-MACHINE OPERATOR	2	2	692.685-190
RCE	STACKER TENDER	2	3	921.685-062
RCE	STAIN APPLICATOR	2	2	561.585-010
RCE	STAMP MOUNTER	2	2	733.684-018
RCE	STAMP-PAD MAKER	2	2	733.687-070
RCE	STAMPER	2	2	556.685-078
RCE	STAMPER	2	2	652.685-082
RCE	STAMPING-MACHINE OPERATOR	2	4	690.685-398
RCE	STAMPING-MACHINE OPERATOR	2	2	692.685-194
RCE	STAMPING-MILL TENDER	2	3	515.685-018
RCE	STANDPIPE TENDER	2	2	519.665-014
RCE	STAPLE CUTTER	2	2	680.685-102
RCE	STAPLER, MACHINE	2	3	692.685-198
RCE	STAVE-BOLT EQUALIZER	2	4	667.682-074
RCE	STAVE-MACHINE TENDER	2	2	663.685-046
RCE	STEAM-BOX OPERATOR	2	2	562.665-014
RCE	STEAM-CLEANING-MACHINE OPERATOR	2	4	891.685-010
RCE	STEAM-PRESS TENDER 2	2	3	553.665-050
RCE	STEAMER	2	2	529.685-226
RCE	STEEL-BOX-TOE INSERTER	2	2	788.687-138
RCE	STEEL-TIE ADJUSTER, AUTOMATIC	2	2	649.685-110
RCE	STEEPING-PRESS TENDER	2	3	551.685-138
RCE	STEM MOUNTER	2	2	725.684-018
RCE	STEM-PROCESSING-MACHINE OPERATOR	2	2	739.685-042
RCE	STEMHOLE BORER	2	2	666.685-010
RCE	STENCIL-MACHINE OPERATOR	2	3	652.685-086
RCE	STICKER	2	2	563.686-010
RCE	STONE TRIMMER	2	3	670.685-010
RCE	STONER AND POLISHER, BEVEL FACE	2	3	603.685-082
RCE	STONER, HAND	2	3	715.584-018
RCE	STOP ATTACHER	2	2	692.685-206
RCE	STRADDLE-TRUCK OPERATOR	2	3	921.683-070
RCE	STRAINER TENDER	2	4	551.365-010
RCE	STRAP BUCKLER, MACHINE	2	3	689.665-010
RCE	STRAW-HAT-PLUNGER OPERATOR	2	2	583.685-114
RCE	STREET-LIGHT-REPAIRER HELPER	2	3	729.684-050
RCE	STRETCH-BOX TENDER	2	2	680.685-110
RCE	STRETCHER	2	3	700.684-078
RCE	STRETCHER-DRIER OPERATOR	2	2	363.687-022

Code	Title	GED	SVP	DOT No.
RCE	STRETCHER-LEVELER-OPERATOR HELPER	2	2	619.686-030
RCE	STRETCHING-MACHINE OPERATOR	2	3	580.685-058
RCE	STRIKE-OFF-MACHINE OPERATOR	2	3	652.685-090
RCE	STRINGER-MACHINE TENDER	2	2	692.485-010
RCE	STRIP-CUTTING-MACHINE OPERATOR	2	2	686.685-066
RCE	STRIP-METAL-PUNCH-AND-STRAIGHTENER OPERATOR	2	3	615.685-038
RCE	STRIPPING CUTTER AND WINDER	2	3	585.685-118
RCE	STUDDER, HAIRSPRING	2	3	715.684-186
RCE	STUFFER	2	2	731.685-014
RCE	STUFFING-MACHINE OPERATOR	2	3	780.685-014
RCE	STULL INSTALLER	2	2	869.684-062
RCE	SURFBOARD MAKER	2	3	732.684-126
RCE	SUTURE POLISHER	2	2	712.687-030
RCE	SWAGER OPERATOR	2	2	616.685-078
RCE	SWAGING-MACHINE OPERATOR	2	2	617.585-010
RCE	SWEATBAND SEPARATOR	2	2	585.685-122
RCE	SWEEP-PRESS OPERATOR	2	2	616.685-082
RCE	TABLE WORKER	2	2	788.687-142
RCE	TACKING-MACHINE OPERATOR	2	2	786.685-034
RCE	TANK-SETTER HELPER	2	2	801.687-018
RCE	TANKROOM TENDER	2	3	559.585-018
RCE	TAPER, MACHINE	2	3	690.685-414
RCE	TAPPER	2	2	529.685-246
RCE	TAPPER 2	2	3	715.685-062
RCE	TAPPER, BIT	2	2	739.685-046
RCE	TAPPER, SHANK	2	2	739.685-050
RCE	TASSEL-MAKING-MACHINE OPERATOR	2	2	689.685-142
RCE	TELEPHONE-DIRECTORY-DISTRIBUTOR DRIVER	2	3	906.683-018
RCE	TENNIS-BALL COVERER, HAND	2	2	795.687-026
RCE	TENSIONING-MACHINE OPERATOR	2	3	616.665-010
RCE	TENTER-FRAME OPERATOR	2	2	580.585-010
RCE	TEST PREPARER	2	4	509.584-010
RCE	THRASHER FEEDER	2	2	533.685-030
RCE	THREAD CUTTER	2	2	789.684-050
RCE	THREAD MARKER	2	2	782.687-058
RCE	THREAD WINDER, AUTOMATIC	2	2	681.685-122
RCE	THREADING-MACHINE OPERATOR	2	4	604.685-038
RCE	THRESHING-MACHINE OPERATOR	2	2	521.685-362
RCE	TICKET PRINTER AND TAGGER	2	2	652.685-094
RCE	TICKET SCHEDULER	2	3	221.587-038
RCE	TICKET-CHOPPER ASSEMBLER	2	5	739.684-154
RCE	TIE BINDER	2	2	920.687-190
RCE	TIER-AND-DETONATOR	2	2	931.664-010
RCE	TINSEL-MACHINE OPERATOR	2	2	692.685-226
RCE	TIPPER	2	3	795.684-022
RCE	TIPPING-MACHINE OPERATOR	2	2	733.685-034
RCE	TOBACCO-DRIER OPERATOR	2	2	523.685-118
RCE	TOE FORMER, STITCHDOWNS	2	3	690.685-426
RCE	TOE LASTER, AUTOMATIC	2	3	690.685-430
RCE	TOE-CLOSING-MACHINE TENDER	2	2	787.685-046
RCE	TONGUE PRESSER	2	2	788.685-022
RCE	TOOL-MAINTENANCE WORKER	2	3	701.384-010

Code	Title	GED	SVP	DOT No.
RCE	TOP FORMER	2	2	788.685-026
RCE	TOPSTITCHER, LOCKSTITCH	2	3	786.682-238
RCE	TOPSTITCHER, ZIGZAG	2	3	786.682-242
RCE	TORQUE TESTER	2	3	715.685-066
RCE	TRACK OILER	2	2	910.687-026
RCE	TRACKMOBILE OPERATOR	2	3	919.683-026
RCE	TRANSFER-CAR OPERATOR	2	2	921.683-078
RCE	TRANSFER-CAR OPERATOR, DRIER	2	2	921.583-010
RCE	TRANSFER-MACHINE OPERATOR	2	2	659.685-022
RCE	TRAY FILLER	2	2	920.686-050
RCE	TRAY-DRIER OPERATOR	2	3	553.665-054
RCE	TREATER HELPER	2	4	549.685-030
RCE	TREATING-ENGINEER HELPER	2	2	561.685-010
RCE	TREE DRILLER	2	3	788.684-118
RCE	TRIM ATTACHER	2	2	692.685-230
RCE	TRIM-STENCIL MAKER	2	3	781.684-058
RCE	TRIMMER HELPER	2	2	667.686-018
RCE	TRIMMER, HAND	2	2	788.687-150
RCE	TRIMMER, MACHINE	2	2	585.685-126
RCE	TRIMMER, MACHINE 1	2	3	690.685-434
RCE	TRIMMER, MACHINE	2	2	781.682-010
RCE	TRIMMING SEWER, AUTOMATIC	2	3	787.685-050
RCE	TRIMMING-MACHINE OPERATOR	2	2	583.685-122
RCE	TRUER	2	4	616.484-010
RCE	TUBE BENDER, HAND 2	2	2	709.687-050
RCE	TUBE MOLDER, FIBERGLASS	2	2	690.685-438
RCE	TUBE SPLICER	2	3	690.685-442
RCE	TUBE WINDER, HAND	2	2	692.685-234
RCE	TUBE-AND-MANIFOLD BUILDER	2	3	759.684-062
RCE	TUBE-CLEANING OPERATOR	2	2	514.685-026
RCE	TUBING-MACHINE TENDER	2	3	715.685-070
RCE	TUFTER	2	4	687.684-014
RCE	TUFTING-MACHINE OPERATOR	2	3	687.685-014
RCE	TUMBLER	2	2	599.685-106
RCE	TUMBLER-MACHINE OPERATOR	2	2	559.685-178
RCE	TUNNEL-ELASTIC OPERATOR, CHAINSTITCH	2	3	786.682-246
RCE	TUNNEL-ELASTIC OPERATOR, LOCKSTITCH	2	3	786.682-250
RCE	TUNNEL-ELASTIC OPERATOR, ZIGZAG	2	3	786.682-254
RCE	TURKEY-ROLL MAKER	2	2	525.684-058
RCE	TURNING-MACHINE OPERATOR	2	2	689.685-146
RCE	TURNING-MACHINE OPERATOR	2	2	667.685-066
RCE	TURRET-PUNCH-PRESS OPERATOR, TAPE-CONTROL	2	3	615.685-042
RCE	TWISTER TENDER	2	3	681.685-130
RCE	TWISTER TENDER, PAPER	2	4	681.685-134
RCE	TYING-MACHINE OPERATOR, LUMBER	2	2	929.685-018
RCE	TYPE-SOLDERING-MACHINE TENDER	2	3	706.685-010
RCE	UMBRELLA REPAIRER	2	4	369.684-018
RCE	UMBRELLA TIPPER, HAND	2	2	739.684-162
RCE	UPHOLSTERY TRIMMER	2	3	780.684-126
RCE	UPTWISTER TENDER	2	3	681.685-138
RCE	V-BELT COVERER	2	2	690.685-450
RCE	V-BELT FINISHER	2	3	690.685-454

Code	Title	GED	SVP	DOT No.
RCE	V-BELT SKIVER	2	3	690.685-458
RCE	VACUUM-APPLICATOR OPERATOR	2	2	692.685-238
RCE	VACUUM-DRIER OPERATOR	2	4	581.685-066
RCE	VACUUM-METALIZER OPERATOR	2	3	505.685-018
RCE	VALVING-MACHINE OPERATOR	2	2	641.685-094
RCE	VAMP CREASER	2	2	788.687-154
RCE	VARNISHING-MACHINE OPERATOR	2	2	534.685-030
RCE	VENDING-MACHINE ASSEMBLER	2	2	706.684-102
RCE	VENEER CLIPPER	2	4	663.585-014
RCE	VENEER DRIER	2	2	563.685-022
RCE	VENEER REDRIER	2	2	563.685-026
RCE	VULCANIZING-PRESS OPERATOR	2	3	690.685-466
RCE	WAD IMPREGNATOR	2	2	590.685-054
RCE	WAD-PRINTING-MACHINE OPERATOR	2	2	652.685-102
RCE	WAFER-LINE WORKER	2	2	727.687-082
RCE	WAISTLINE JOINER, LOCKSTITCH	2	3	786.682-270
RCE	WAISTLINE JOINER, OVERLOCK	2	4	786.682-274
RCE	WARE CLEANER	2	2	774.687-022
RCE	WARP SPOOLER	2	3	681.685-142
RCE	WASH-OIL-PUMP OPERATOR HELPER	2	3	549.685-034
RCE	WASH-TANK TENDER	2	3	559.685-182
RCE	WATCH-CRYSTAL EDGE GRINDER	2	4	775.684-062
RCE	WATCHER, PANTOGRAPH	2	4	689.685-154
RCE	WAX-PATTERN ASSEMBLER	2	2	518.684-022
RCE	WAX-PATTERN REPAIRER	2	2	518.684-026
RCE	WAX-POT TENDER	2	2	553.685-110
RCE	WEAVING INSPECTOR	2	3	683.684-034
RCE	WEDGER, MACHINE	2	2	701.687-034
RCE	WELDING-MACHINE TENDER	2	3	819.685-010
RCE	WELT BEATER	2	3	690.685-470
RCE	WELT BUTTER, MACHINE	2	2	690.685-474
RCE	WET-END OPERATOR 2	2	3	559.685-190
RCE	WHEEL-AND-CASTER REPAIRER	2	2	630.684-038
RCE	WHEEL-MILL OPERATOR	2	2	555.685-066
RCE	WHEEL-TRUING MACHINE TENDER	2	2	706.685-014
RCE	WHITING-MACHINE OPERATOR	2	4	562.485-010
RCE	WICKER, MOLDED CANDLES	2	3	692.685-242
RCE	WIDTH STRIPPER	2	3	690.685-486
RCE	WINDER	2	2	692.685-246
RCE	WINDER OPERATOR, AUTOMATIC	2	2	681.685-150
RCE	WINDING-MACHINE OPERATOR	2	2	619.665-010
RCE	WINDING-RACK OPERATOR	2	3	581.685-074
RCE	WINE PASTEURIZER	2	3	523.685-126
RCE	WING-MAILER-MACHINE OPERATOR	2	2	208.685-034
RCE	WIPER	2	2	723.687-022
RCE	WIPER	2	2	742.687-010
RCE	WIRE COINER	2	3	616.685-086
RCE	WIRE THREADER	2	2	604.686-010
RCE	WIRE-BASKET MAKER	2	2	709.687-062
RCE	WIRE-FRAME MAKER	2	3	734.481-010
RCE	WOVEN-WOOD SHADE ASSEMBLER	2	3	739.684-178
RCE	WRAP TURNER	2	2	788.685-030
RCE	WRAPPER	2	3	920.685-102
RCE	WRAPPER COUNTER	2	2	929.687-050

Code	Title	GED	SVP	DOT No.
RCE	WRAPPER LAYER	2	3	529.685-266
RCE	WREATH AND GARLAND MAKER	2	2	739.684-182
RCE	YARN CLEANER	2	2	681.687-026
RCE	YARN SORTER	2	2	689.687-086
RCE	YARN WINDER	2	3	681.685-154
RCE	YARN-POLISHING-MACHINE OPERATOR	2	2	583.685-126
RCE	ZIPPER SETTER, CHAINSTITCH	2	3	786.682-282
RCE	ZIPPER SETTER, LOCKSTITCH	2	3	786.682-286
RCE	ZIPPER-MACHINE OPERATOR	2	2	692.685-270
RCE	ABRASIVE-GRADER HELPER	1	2	570.686-010
RCE	ADVERTISING-MATERIAL DISTRIBUTOR	1	2	230.687-010
RCE	AIR PURIFIER SERVICER	1	2	389.687-010
RCE	ANTICHECKING-IRON WORKER	1	2	563.687-010
RCE	ANTISQUEAK FILLER	1	2	788.687-010
RCE	ARTIFICIAL-PEARL MAKER	1	2	770.687-010
RCE	ASSEMBLER, DRY CELL AND BATTERY	1	2	727.687-022
RCE	ASSEMBLER, FISHING FLOATS	1	2	732.687-014
RCE	BAG LINER	1	2	789.687-014
RCE	BAGGER	1	1	920.687-018
RCE	BAGGING SALVAGER	1	1	689.687-010
RCE	BALL-MACHINE OPERATOR	1	2	520.686-010
RCE	BAND ATTACHER	1	2	715.687-010
RCE	BAND-SAW OPERATOR	1	2	667.685-014
RCE	BANDER	1	2	762.687-010
RCE	BANDER, HAND	1	1	920.687-026
RCE	BANDOLEER PACKER	1	1	920.687-034
RCE	BANDOLEER STRAIGHTENER-STAMPER	1	2	737.587-010
RCE	BASE FILLER	1	1	732.687-018
RCE	BASKET FILLER	1	1	529.687-010
RCE	BATCH TRUCKER	1	2	550.686-010
RCE	BATTERY LOADER	1	2	683.686-010
RCE	BEAD PICKER	1	1	551.686-010
RCE	BENCH HAND	1	2	715.684-026
RCE	BIN FILLER	1	2	922.687-010
RCE	BINDER CUTTER, HAND	1	2	521.687-014
RCE	BLADE BALANCER	1	2	701.687-014
RCE	BLOW-OFF WORKER	1	2	763.687-010
RCE	BONE PICKER	1	1	521.687-022
RCE	BONE PICKER	1	1	551.687-010
RCE	BOOKER	1	1	599.687-014
RCE	BRASSIERE-SLIDE-MAKING-MACHINE TENDER, AUTOMATIC	1	2	692.685-026
RCE	BREADING MACHINE TENDER	1	2	524.685-010
RCE	BRINE-TANK-SEPARATOR OPERATOR	1	2	521.685-038
RCE	BUCKLER AND LACER	1	2	788.687-022
RCE	BUFFING TURNER-AND-COUNTER	1	2	789.687-022
RCE	BULB FILLER	1	1	692.686-022
RCE	BULKER, CUT TOBACCO	1	2	529.685-034
RCE	BUNCH TRIMMER, MOLD	1	1	521.687-026
RCE	BUNG DRIVER	1	1	764.687-042
RCE	BURLAP SPREADER	1	1	581.687-010
RCE	BURNISHER	1	3	690.685-058
RCE	BURR GRINDER	1	1	673.686-014
RCE	BUTTON RECLAIMER	1	2	734.687-042

Code	Title	GED	SVP	DOT No.
RCE	CAMOUFLAGE ASSEMBLER	1	2	869.687-014
RCE	CARBON ROD INSERTER	1	2	692.686-026
RCE	CARDBOARD INSERTER	1	1	920.687-062
RCE	CARDING-MACHINE OPERATOR	1	2	681.685-030
RCE	CARTRIDGE LOADER	1	1	779.687-014
RCE	CASING SPLITTER	1	1	525.687-014
RCE	CASING TIER	1	1	529.687-034
RCE	CASTING-PLUG ASSEMBLER	1	2	732.687-022
RCE	CELL TUBER, HAND	1	2	727.687-046
RCE	CEMENTER, MACHINE APPLICATOR	1	2	690.686-018
RCE	CHECKER	1	2	919.687-010
RCE	CHILLING-HOOD OPERATOR	1	2	523.685-018
RCE	CHUTE LOADER	1	1	932.687-010
RCE	CIGAR INSPECTOR	1	2	529.687-042
RCE	CIRCLE-CUTTING-SAW OPERATOR	1	2	669.685-026
RCE	CLAMP REMOVER	1	2	569.687-010
RCE	CLEANER AND POLISHER	1	2	709.687-010
RCE	CLEANER, FURNITURE	1	2	709.687-014
RCE	CLIP-LOADING-MACHINE FEEDER	1	2	694.686-010
RCE	CLIPPER, MACHINE	1	2	684.686-010
RCE	CLOTH-BALE HEADER	1	2	782.687-018
RCE	CLOTHESPIN-DRIER OPERATOR	1	2	563.685-014
RCE	COATING-MACHINE FEEDER	1	2	690.686-022
RCE	COB SAWYER	1	2	667.685-030
RCE	COFFEE GRINDER	1	2	521.685-078
RCE	CONFECTIONERY-DROPS-MACHINE OPERATOR	1	2	520.685-078
RCE	CONVEYOR FEEDER-OFFBEARER	1	2	921.686-014
RCE	CORE LOADER	1	1	737.687-030
RCE	COVERED-BUCKLE ASSEMBLER	1	3	734.687-050
RCE	CREELER	1	2	689.687-030
RCE	CRIMPER	1	2	690.686-026
RCE	CRUSHING-MACHINE OPERATOR	1	2	521.685-094
RCE	CRYSTAL ATTACHER	1	2	715.687-018
RCE	CUFF FOLDER	1	2	685.687-014
RCE	CUTLET MAKER, PORK	1	2	529.686-022
RCE	CUTTER	1	2	529.685-082
RCE	DEADENER	1	1	845.687-010
RCE	DESIGN ASSEMBLER	1	2	692.686-034
RCE	DESSERT-CUP-MACHINE FEEDER	1	2	520.686-014
RCE	DIPPER	1	2	589.687-018
RCE	DIPPER, CLOCK AND WATCH HANDS	1	2	715.687-026
RCE	DOWEL INSPECTOR	1	2	669.687-014
RCE	DRAWER WAXER	1	1	763.687-022
RCE	DRIED FRUIT WASHER	1	2	521.685-110
RCE	DROP-WIRE HANGER	1	2	683.687-014
RCE	DRUMMER	1	2	589.685-034
RCE	DUMPING-MACHINE OPERATOR	1	2	529.685-102
RCE	DUST-MOP MAKER	1	2	739.687-078
RCE	EDGING-MACHINE FEEDER	1	2	673.686-022
RCE	EGG WASHER, MACHINE	1	1	529.686-030
RCE	ELECTRODE CLEANER	1	1	729.687-014
RCE	END-TOUCHING-MACHINE OPERATOR	1	1	662.686-010
RCE	FARMWORKER, MACHINE	1	1	409.686-010

Code	Title	GED	SVP	DOT No.
RCE	FELT-TIPPING-MACHINE TENDER	1	1	686.686-010
RCE	FILLER	1	2	739.687-090
RCE	FILLER FEEDER	1	2	529.686-042
RCE	FINAL ASSEMBLER	1	2	713.687-018
RCE	FINISHING-MACHINE OPERATOR	1	1	649.686-022
RCE	FLARE BREAKER	1	2	788.685-010
RCE	FLOWER PICKER	1	1	405.687-010
RCE	FOLDING-MACHINE OPERATOR	1	2	690.686-034
RCE	FRAME STRIPPER	1	1	559.687-046
RCE	FRINGER	1	2	789.687-062
RCE	FRUIT CUTTER	1	1	521.687-066
RCE	FUNNEL COATER, HAND	1	2	740.687-014
RCE	FUSE-CUP EXPANDER	1	2	694.685-022
RCE	GARMENT FOLDER	1	2	789.687-066
RCE	GARNISHER	1	1	524.687-014
RCE	GETTERER	1	2	725.687-022
RCE	GLASS-BULB SILVERER	1	2	779.687-018
RCE	GLUCOSE-AND-SIRUP WEIGHER	1	2	520.686-026
RCE	GLUER	1	2	795.687-014
RCE	GRINDER, HAND	1	2	734.687-054
RCE	HARVEST WORKER, VEGETABLE	1	1	402.687-014
RCE	HEEL COMPRESSOR	1	2	690.685-210
RCE	HEEL DIPPER	1	2	788.687-058
RCE	HELPER, METAL HANGING	1	2	806.667-010
RCE	IGNITER CAPPER	1	1	737.687-050
RCE	INSOLE-AND-HEEL-STIFFENER	1	2	788.687-062
RCE	IRONER	1	2	302.687-010
RCE	JIGGER	1	2	705.687-010
RCE	KETTLE TENDER	1	2	869.685-010
RCE	KILN WORKER	1	2	573.687-022
RCE	KISS SETTER, HAND	1	4	529.687-122
RCE	KNIFE CHANGER	1	2	638.684-010
RCE	LABORER, HIGH-DENSITY PRESS	1	2	929.687-018
RCE	LACQUER-PIN-PRESS OPERATOR	1	1	737.687-078
RCE	LACQUERER	1	2	715.684-138
RCE	LAMINATED-PLASTIC-TABLETOP-MOLDING WRAPPER	1	2	692.686-046
RCE	LAMP-SHADE JOINER	1	2	692.685-110
RCE	LAST CLEANER	1	1	788.687-082
RCE	LEAF TIER	1	1	529.687-138
RCE	LEAF-SIZE PICKER	1	2	529.687-142
RCE	LENS INSERTER	1	2	713.687-026
RCE	LIGHT-FIXTURE SERVICER	1	2	389.687-018
RCE	LINER INSERTER	1	2	929.687-026
RCE	LINING CEMENTER	1	1	795.687-022
RCE	LOG LOADER HELPER	1	2	921.687-022
RCE	LOG WASHER	1	2	569.687-014
RCE	LYE-PEEL OPERATOR	1	2	521.685-206
RCE	MACHINE FEEDER	1	1	715.686-014
RCE	MACHINE-PACK ASSEMBLER	1	2	920.687-122
RCE	MANUAL-PLATE FILLER	1	2	737.687-082
RCE	MASKER	1	2	715.687-086
RCE	MERCURY-CRACKING TESTER	1	2	737.687-086
RCE	MIXER	1	2	789.687-098

Code	Title	GED	SVP	DOT No.
RCE	MIXER HELPER	1	2	550.686-026
RCE	MOLD-MAKER HELPER	1	2	700.687-050
RCE	MONITOR-AND-STORAGE-BIN TENDER	1	2	521.685-230
RCE	MOPHEAD TRIMMER-AND-WRAPPER	1	2	789.687-106
RCE	MOUNTER 1	1	2	692.686-050
RCE	MOUNTER, CLOCK AND WATCH HANDS	1	2	715.687-094
RCE	NECKER	1	2	692.686-058
RCE	NET WASHER	1	2	599.687-022
RCE	NUT CHOPPER	1	2	521.686-046
RCE	OUTSOLE FLEXER	1	2	583.686-026
RCE	PAD-MACHINE OFF-BEARER	1	1	569.686-030
RCE	PAINTER, BOTTOM	1	2	788.687-098
RCE	PAINTER, CLOCK AND WATCH HANDS	1	2	715.687-098
RCE	PAINTER, DEPILATORY	1	1	525.687-062
RCE	PAIRER	1	1	789.687-110
RCE	PAN GREASER, MACHINE	1	2	526.685-034
RCE	PAPER INSERTER	1	2	920.687-138
RCE	PAPER-CONE-DRYING-MACHINE OPERATOR	1	1	532.686-014
RCE	PARTS REMOVER	1	2	715.687-102
RCE	PASTER, SCREEN PRINTING	1	2	652.687-026
RCE	PATCH SANDER	1	2	775.684-054
RCE	PATCH WORKER	1	2	381.687-030
RCE	PATCHING-MACHINE OPERATOR	1	2	361.685-022
RCE	PINNER	1	2	782.687-026
RCE	PITCH WORKER	1	2	551.666-010
RCE	PLASTIC-DESIGN APPLIER	1	1	690.686-046
RCE	PLATE STACKER, HAND	1	2	729.687-026
RCE	PLEATER	1	2	589.685-074
RCE	PLUG-CUTTING-MACHINE OPERATOR	1	2	529.685-182
RCE	PLUGGER	1	1	764.687-098
RCE	POMPOM MAKER	1	1	789.687-126
RCE	POTATO-CHIP SORTER	1	1	526.687-010
RCE	POULTRY BONER	1	2	525.687-066
RCE	POURER	1	2	556.687-026
RCE	POWER-SCREWDRIVER OPERATOR	1	2	699.685-026
RCE	PRETZEL TWISTER	1	2	520.587-010
RCE	PUFF IRONER	1	1	363.687-018
RCE	PULLER-THROUGH	1	1	782.687-030
RCE	PULLEY MAINTAINER	1	3	630.687-010
RCE	RACKER	1	1	524.687-018
RCE	RACKER	1	2	735.687-026
RCE	RAG SORTER AND CUTTER	1	2	789.687-134
RCE	RAISED PRINTER	1	2	652.686-034
RCE	RAW-JUICE WEIGHER	1	2	529.685-194
RCE	REDUCING-MACHINE OPERATOR	1	2	614.685-018
RCE	REMNANTS CUTTER	1	1	789.687-150
RCE	RIDDLER OPERATOR	1	2	521.685-270
RCE	RIVETING-MACHINE OPERATOR 2	1	2	699.685-030
RCE	ROLL COVERER, BURLAP	1	2	929.687-042
RCE	ROLLING-MACHINE TENDER	1	2	689.685-114
RCE	ROPE CLEANER	1	2	699.687-022
RCE	ROSIN-BARREL FILLER	1	1	920.687-150
RCE	ROUGE SIFTER AND MILLER	1	2	579.685-046
RCE	RUBBER-ROLLER GRINDER	1	1	690.686-050

Code	Title	GED	SVP	DOT No.
RCE	SAWYER, CORK SLABS	1	2	667.685-046
RCE	SCRAP SORTER	1	2	788.687-106
RCE	SCREW-EYE ASSEMBLER	1	1	737.687-122
RCE	SEED-POTATO ARRANGER	1	2	404.685-010
RCE	SEQUINS STRINGER	1	2	754.687-014
RCE	SET-KEY DRIVER	1	2	715.687-118
RCE	SHANK TAPER	1	2	788.687-114
RCE	SHELLER 1	1	1	521.687-118
RCE	SLABBER	1	2	559.686-042
RCE	SLICE-PLUG-CUTTER-OPERATOR HELPER	1	2	521.686-054
RCE	SMOKING-PIPE LINER	1	2	739.687-170
RCE	SORTER 1	1	2	569.687-022
RCE	SPANNER	1	2	689.687-074
RCE	SPIRAL BINDER	1	2	653.685-030
RCE	SPIRAL-MACHINE OPERATOR	1	2	692.685-186
RCE	SPLITTING-MACHINE FEEDER	1	2	690.686-054
RCE	SPOOLING-MACHINE OPERATOR	1	2	681.685-114
RCE	STAMP-PAD FINISHER	1	1	733.687-066
RCE	STARCHER	1	2	739.687-178
RCE	STEAK TENDERIZER, MACHINE	1	2	529.686-082
RCE	STEEL-BARREL REAMER	1	2	703.687-022
RCE	STEM SIZER	1	2	692.686-062
RCE	STEM-ROLLER-OR-CRUSHER OPERATOR	1	2	521.685-330
RCE	STEMMER, HAND	1	2	521.687-134
RCE	STEMMER, MACHINE	1	2	521.685-334
RCE	STICKER	1	2	784.687-070
RCE	STREET CLEANER	1	1	955.687-018
RCE	STRINGER	1	1	509.687-018
RCE	STRIP PRESSER	1	2	583.685-118
RCE	STRIP-CUTTING-MACHINE OPERATOR	1	2	521.685-338
RCE	STUFFER	1	1	780.687-046
RCE	SWEEPER-CLEANER, INDUSTRIAL	1	2	389.683-010
RCE	SWITCHBOX ASSEMBLER 1	1	2	722.687-010
RCE	TABLE HAND	1	2	521.687-138
RCE	TABLE WORKER	1	2	739.687-182
RCE	TABLE WORKER	1	1	783.687-030
RCE	TACK PULLER, MACHINE	1	2	690.685-410
RCE	TACK PULLER	1	2	788.687-146
RCE	TAMALE-MACHINE FEEDER	1	2	520.686-038
RCE	TEST WORKER	1	2	519.687-042
RCE	THIRD DRY-CELL-ASSEMBLING-MACHINE TENDER	1	1	692.686-066
RCE	THREAD SEPARATOR	1	2	789.687-174
RCE	TIER	1	2	525.687-118
RCE	TIN-CONTAINER STRIAGHTENER	1	1	709.687-046
RCE	TRAVERSE-ROD ASSEMBLER	1	2	739.687-186
RCE	TREATER	1	2	582.687-030
RCE	TRIMMING-MACHINE OPERATOR	1	2	732.685-038
RCE	TROLLEY OPERATOR	1	2	524.565-010
RCE	TUBE CLEANER	1	2	589.687-042
RCE	TWISTER, HAND	1	2	790.687-030
RCE	TYING-MACHINE OPERATOR	1	2	929.685-014
RCE	UMBRELLA TIPPER, MACHINE	1	2	739.685-054
RCE	UNSCRAMBLER	1	2	921.685-070

Code	Title	GED	SVP	DOT No.
RCE	VAMP-STRAP IRONER	1	2	788.687-158
RCE	VARNISHER	1	2	569.685-070
RCE	WARE SERVER	1	2	652.686-046
RCE	WASTE-MACHINE TENDER	1	2	680.685-114
RCE	WASTE-PAPER-HAMMERMILL OPERATOR	1	1	530.686-018
RCE	WAXER	1	2	779.687-038
RCE	WHITE-SHOE RAGGER	1	2	788.687-166
RCE	WIRE BENDER	1	3	709.687-058
RCE	WIRE CUTTER	1	1	731.687-038
RCE	WIRE-TURNING-MACHINE OPERATOR	1	2	692.685-258
RCE	WIREWORKER	1	2	728.687-010
RCE	WRAPPER-LAYER-AND-EXAMINER, SOFT WORK	1	2	529.685-270
RCE	YARD LABORER	1	1	922.687-102

INVESTIGATIVE OCCUPATIONS

Code	Title	GED	SVP	DOT No.
IRA	VETERINARIAN, POULTRY	5	8	073.101-014
IRS	AERONAUTICAL ENGINEER	6	8	002.061-014
IRS	AGRONOMIST	6	8	040.061-010
IRS	ANESTHESIOLOGIST	6	8	070.101-010
IRS	ANIMAL BREEDER	6	8	041.061-014
IRS	ANIMAL SCIENTIST	6	8	040.061-014
IRS	BIOCHEMIST	6	8	041.061-026
IRS	BOTANIST	6	8	041.061-038
IRS	CARDIOLOGIST	6	8	070.101-014
IRS	CERAMIC ENGINEER	6	8	006.061-014
IRS	CHEMIST, WATER PURIFICATION	6	7	022.281-014
IRS	CRYSTALLOGRAPHER	6	8	024.061-010
IRS	CURATOR	6	9	102.017-010
IRS	DAIRY TECHNOLOGIST	6	8	040.061-022
IRS	DENTIST	6	8	072.101-010
IRS	ENTOMOLOGIST	6	8	041.061-046
IRS	FIBER TECHNOLOGIST	6	8	040.061-026
IRS	FLIGHT SURGEON	6	8	070.101-030
IRS	FOREST ECOLOGIST	6	8	040.061-030
IRS	GENERAL PRACTITIONER	6	8	070.101-022
IRS	GENETICIST	6	8	041.061-050
IRS	GEOPHYSICIST	6	8	024.061-030
IRS	GYNECOLOGIST	6	8	070.101-034
IRS	HISTOPATHOLOGIST	6	8	041.061-054
IRS	HORTICULTURIST	6	8	040.061-038
IRS	INTERN	6	8	070.101-038
IRS	INTERNIST	6	9	070.101-042
IRS	MEDICAL OFFICER	6	8	070.101-046
IRS	MEDICAL PHYSICIST	6	8	079.021-014
IRS	MICROBIOLOGIST	6	8	041.061-058
IRS	MYCOLOGIST	6	8	041.061-062
IRS	NEMATOLOGIST	6	8	041.061-066
IRS	NEUROLOGIST	6	8	070.101-050
IRS	OBSTETRICIAN	6	8	070.101-054
IRS	ORTHODONTIST	6	8	072.101-022
IRS	OSTEOPATHIC PHYSICIAN	6	8	071.101-010

Code	Title	GED	SVP	DOT No.
IRS	OTOLARYNGOLOGIST	6	8	070.101-062
IRS	PARASITOLOGIST	6	8	041.061-070
IRS	PEDIATRICIAN	6	8	070.101-066
IRS	PLANT BREEDER	6	8	041.061-082
IRS	PLANT PATHOLOGIST	6	8	041.061-086
IRS	POLICE SURGEON	6	8	070.101-082
IRS	POULTRY SCIENTIST	6	8	040.061-042
IRS	PROCTOLOGIST	6	8	070.101-086
IRS	PROSTHODONTIST	6	8	072.101-034
IRS	PSYCHOLOGIST, DEVELOPMENTAL	6	7	045.061-010
IRS	PSYCHOLOGIST, ENGINEERING	6	8	045.061-014
IRS	PSYCHOLOGIST, EXPERIMENTAL	6	8	045.061-018
IRS	RADIOLOGIST	6	8	070.101-090
IRS	RANGE MANAGER	6	8	040.061-046
IRS	SOIL SCIENTIST	6	8	040.061-058
IRS	STRATIGRAPHER	6	8	024.061-054
IRS	UROLOGIST	6	8	070.101-098
IRS	WOOD TECHNOLOGIST	6	8	040.061-062
IRS	AIR ANALYST	5	5	012.261-010
IRS	CHEMICAL DESIGN ENGINEER, PROCESSES	5	8	008.061-014
IRS	CHEMICAL RESEARCH ENGINEER	5	8	008.061-022
IRS	CHEMICAL-LABORATORY TECHNICIAN	5	7	022.261-010
IRS	CHIROPRACTOR	5	7	079.101-010
IRS	HYDRAULIC ENGINEER	5	7	005.061-018
IRS	INSPECTOR, ELEVATORS	5	8	168.167-038
IRS	MATERIAL SCHEDULER	5	7	012.187-010
IRS	METEOROLOGIST	5	7	025.062-010
IRS	NURSE PRACTITIONER	5	8	075.264-010
IRS	OPTOMETRIST	5	7	079.101-018
IRS	PHYSICIAN ASSISTANT	5	7	079.364-018
IRS	RAILROAD ENGINEER	5	8	005.061-026
IRS	RESTORER, LACE AND TEXTILES	5	7	102.361-010
IRS	STRUCTURAL ENGINEER	5	8	005.061-034
IRS	TAXIDERMIST	5	7	199.261-010
IRS	VETERINARIAN	5	8	073.101-010
IRS	CLOTH TESTER	4	5	029.381-010
IRS	HYDROGRAPHER	4	6	025.264-010
IRS	LABORATORY ASSISTANT	4	5	029.381-014
IRS	RESPIRATORY THERAPIST	4	6	079.361-010
IRS	SCIENTIFIC HELPER	4	6	199.364-014
IRE	AERODYNAMIST	6	8	002.061-010
IRE	AERONAUTICAL-RESEARCH ENGINEER	6	8	002.061-026
IRE	ANATOMIST	6	8	041.061-010
IRE	ANTHROPOLOGIST	6	7	055.067-010
IRE	ANTHROPOLOGIST, PHYSICAL	6	7	055.067-014
IRE	APICULTURIST	6	8	041.061-018
IRE	AQUATIC BIOLOGIST	6	8	041.061-022
IRE	ARCHEOLOGIST	6	7	055.067-018
IRE	ARCHITECT, MARINE	6	9	001.061-014
IRE	BIOLOGIST	6	8	041.061-030
IRE	BIOMEDICAL ENGINEER	6	8	019.061-010
IRE	BIOPHYSICIST	6	8	041.061-034
IRE	CENTRAL-OFFICE EQUIPMENT ENGINEER	6	8	003.187-010

Code	Title	GED	SVP	DOT No.
IRE	CHEMICAL ENGINEER	6	8	008.061-018
IRE	CHEMIST	6	8	022.061-010
IRE	CHEMIST, FOOD	6	7	022.061-014
IRE	CHIEF ENGINEER, RESEARCH	6	8	010.161-010
IRE	CHIEF PETROLEUM ENGINEER	6	9	010.161-014
IRE	COMPUTER-APPLICATIONS ENGINEER	6	8	020.062-010
IRE	COST-ANALYSIS ENGINEER	6	7	002.167-010
IRE	CYTOLOGIST	6	8	041.061-042
IRE	DAIRY SCIENTIST	6	8	040.061-018
IRE	ELECTRICAL ENGINEER, POWER SYSTEM	6	8	003.167-018
IRE	ELECTRICAL-PROSPECTING ENGINEER	6	8	003.061-022
IRE	ELECTRO-OPTICAL ENGINEER	6	8	023.061-010
IRE	ENGINEERING ANALYST	6	7	020.067-010
IRE	ENVIRONMENTAL ANALYST	6	8	029.081-010
IRE	ETHNOLOGIST	6	7	055.067-022
IRE	FAMILY PRACTITIONER	6	8	070.101-026
IRE	GEODESIST	6	8	024.061-014
IRE	GEOGRAPHER	6	7	029.067-010
IRE	GEOLOGIST	6	8	024.061-018
IRE	GEOPHYSICAL-LABORATORY CHIEF	6	9	024.167-010
IRE	HYDROLOGIST	6	8	024.061-034
IRE	MARINE ENGINEER	6	8	014.061-014
IRE	MATERIALS SCIENTIST	6	7	029.081-014
IRE	METALLURGIST, EXTRACTIVE	6	8	011.061-018
IRE	METALLURGIST, PHYSICAL	6	8	011.061-022
IRE	NUCLEAR ENGINEER	6	8	015.061-014
IRE	OPERATIONS-RESEARCH ANALYST	6	7	020.067-018
IRE	ORAL PATHOLOGIST	6	8	072.061-010
IRE	ORAL SURGEON	6	8	072.101-018
IRE	PATHOLOGIST	6	8	070.061-010
IRE	PEDODONTIST	6	8	072.101-026
IRE	PERIODONTIST	6	8	072.101-030
IRE	PHARMACOLOGIST	6	8	041.061-074
IRE	PHYSICIST	6	8	023.061-014
IRE	PHYSICIST, THEORETICAL	6	8	023.067-010
IRE	PHYSIOLOGIST	6	8	041.061-078
IRE	PLANNING ENGINEER, CENTRAL OFFICE FACILITIES	6	8	003.061-050
IRE	PROGRAMER, ENGINEERING AND SCIENTIFIC	6	8	020.167-022
IRE	PUBLIC-HEALTH DENTIST	6	8	072.101-038
IRE	QUALITY-CONTROL ENGINEER	6	8	012.167-054
IRE	SOIL CONSERVATIONIST	6	8	040.061-054
IRE	STATISTICIAN, MATHEMATICAL	6	8	020.067-022
IRE	SYSTEMS ENGINEER, ELECTRONIC DATA PROCESSING	6	8	003.167-062
IRE	VETERINARY PATHOLOGIST	6	8	073.061-030
IRE	ZOOLOGIST	6	8	041.061-090
IRE	ACCOUNTANT, PROPERTY (CER)	5	8	160.167-022
IRE	ACUPUNCTURIST	5	6	079.271-010
IRE	AGRICULTURAL ENGINEER	5	8	013.061-010
IRE	AGRICULTURAL-ENGINEERING TECHNICIAN	5	7	013.161-010
IRE	AGRICULTURAL-RESEARCH ENGINEER	5	8	013.061-014
IRE	AIRPLANE PILOT	5	6	196.263-010

Code	Title	GED	SVP	DOT No.
IRE	BALLISTICS EXPERT, FORENSIC	5	7	199.267-010
IRE	CABLE ENGINEER, OUTSIDE PLANT	5	8	003.167-010
IRE	CERAMIC DESIGN ENGINEER	5	8	006.061-010
IRE	CERAMIC RESEARCH ENGINEER	5	8	006.061-018
IRE	CERAMICS TEST ENGINEER	5	8	006.061-022
IRE	CHEMICAL-ENGINEERING TECHNICIAN	5	8	008.261-010
IRE	CHEMISTRY TECHNOLOGIST	5	7	078.261-010
IRE	CHIEF ENGINEER, WATERWORKS	5	9	005.167-010
IRE	COLORIST	5	7	022.161-014
IRE	CREDIT ANALYST, CHIEF	5	8	160.267-010
IRE	DESIGN DRAFTER, ELECTROMECHANISMS	5	7	017.261-014
IRE	DESIGN ENGINEER, MINING-AND-OILFIELD EQUIPMENT	5	8	010.061-010
IRE	DESIGN ENGINEER, NUCLEAR EQUIPMENT	5	8	015.061-010
IRE	DESIGN ENGINEER, MARINE EQUIPMENT	5	8	014.061-010
IRE	DESIGN-ENGINEER, AGRICULTURAL EQUIPMENT	5	8	013.061-018
IRE	DIE-DRAWING CHECKER	5	7	007.167-010
IRE	DRAFTER APPRENTICE	5	7	017.281-014
IRE	DRAFTER, AUTOMOTIVE DESIGN	5	7	017.281-022
IRE	DRAFTER, CIVIL	5	7	005.281-010
IRE	DRAFTER, COMMERCIAL	5	6	017.261-026
IRE	DRAFTER, ELECTRONIC	5	7	003.281-014
IRE	DRAFTER, MARINE	5	7	014.281-010
IRE	DRAFTER, MECHANICAL	5	7	007.281-010
IRE	DRAFTER, PATENT	5	7	007.261-018
IRE	DRAFTER, TOPOGRAPHICAL	5	7	018.261-014
IRE	ELECTROLYSIS-AND-CORROSION-CONTROL ENGINEER	5	8	003.167-022
IRE	ELECTRONICS TECHNICIAN	5	7	003.161-014
IRE	EXAMINER, QUESTIONED DOCUMENTS	5	6	199.267-022
IRE	FOREST ENGINEER	5	7	005.167-018
IRE	FOUNDRY METALLURGIST	5	8	011.061-010
IRE	ILLUMINATING ENGINEER	5	8	003.061-046
IRE	INDUSTRIAL ENGINEERING TECHNICIAN	5	7	012.267-010
IRE	INDUSTRIAL HYGIENIST	5	8	079.161-010
IRE	INSPECTOR, QUALITY ASSURANCE	5	7	168.287-014
IRE	IRRIGATION ENGINEER	5	8	005.061-022
IRE	LABORATORY ASSISTANT	5	6	029.361-018
IRE	LASER TECHNICIAN	5	7	019.181-010
IRE	MANUFACTURING ENGINEER	5	8	012.167-042
IRE	MECHANICAL RESEARCH ENGINEER	5	8	007.161-022
IRE	MECHANICAL-ENGINEERING TECHNICIAN	5	7	007.161-026
IRE	MEDICAL TECHNOLOGIST	5	7	078.361-014
IRE	MEDICAL-LABORATORY TECHNICIAN	5	5	078.381-014
IRE	METALLOGRAPHER	5	8	011.061-014
IRE	MICROBIOLOGY TECHNOLOGIST	5	6	078.261-014
IRE	OUTSIDE-PLANT ENGINEER	5	8	003.167-042
IRE	PHOTO-OPTICS TECHNICIAN	5	6	029.280-010
IRE	POWER-DISTRIBUTION ENGINEER	5	8	003.167-046
IRE	POWER-TRANSMISSION ENGINEER	5	8	003.167-050
IRE	RESEARCH ENGINEER, MINING-AND-OIL-WELL EQUIPMENT	5	8	010.061-022
IRE	RESEARCH ENGINEER, NUCLEAR			

Code	Title	GED	SVP	DOT No.
	EQUIPMENT	5	8	015.061-018
IRE	RESEARCH ENGINEER, MARINE EQUIPMENT	5	8	014.061-018
IRE	SALES ENGINEER, CERAMIC PRODUCTS (ERI)	5	8	006.151-010
IRE	SALES ENGINEER, NUCLEAR EQUIPMENT (ERI)	5	8	015.151-010
IRE	SALES ENGINEER, MARINE EQUIPMENT (ERI)	5	8	014.151-010
IRE	SANITARY ENGINEER	5	8	005.061-030
IRE	SEMICONDUCTOR-DEVELOPMENT TECHNICIAN	5	7	003.161-018
IRE	SILVICULTURIST	5	7	040.061-050
IRE	STATISTICIAN, APPLIED	5	7	020.167-026
IRE	SUPERVISING AIRPLANE PILOT	5	8	196.163-014
IRE	SUPERVISOR, ELECTRONICS SYSTEMS MAINTENANCE	5	8	828.161-010
IRE	SUPERVISOR, METALLURGICAL-AND-QUALITY-CONTROL-TESTING	5	8	011.161-010
IRE	SURVEYOR, MINE	5	7	018.167-050
IRE	TECHNICAL ILLUSTRATOR	5	7	017.281-034
IRE	TEST ENGINEER, MINING-AND-OILFIELD EQUIPMENT	5	8	010.061-030
IRE	TEST ENGINEER, NUCLEAR EQUIPMENT	5	8	015.061-022
IRE	TEST ENGINEER, MARINE EQUIPMENT	5	8	014.061-022
IRE	TEST ENGINEER, AGRICULTURAL EQUIPMENT	5	8	013.061-022
IRE	TEST TECHNICIAN	5	7	019.161-014
IRE	TIME-STUDY ENGINEER	5	8	012.167-070
IRE	TOOL PLANNER	5	8	012.167-074
IRE	TOOL PROGRAMER, NUMERICAL CONTROL	5	8	007.167-018
IRE	TOOL-DRAWING CHECKER	5	7	007.167-022
IRE	TRANSMISSION-AND-PROTECTION ENGINEER	5	8	003.167-066
IRE	VETERINARIAN, LABORATORY ANIMAL CARE	5	8	073.061-010
IRE	VETERINARY ANATOMIST	5	8	073.061-014
IRE	VETERINARY BACTERIOLOGIST	5	8	073.061-018
IRE	VETERINARY EPIDEMIOLOGIST	5	8	073.061-022
IRE	VETERINARY PARASITOLOGIST	5	8	073.061-026
IRE	VETERINARY PHARMACOLOGIST	5	8	073.061-034
IRE	VETERINARY PHYSIOLOGIST	5	8	073.061-038
IRE	VETERINARY VIROLOGIST	5	8	073.061-042
IRE	VETERINARY LIVESTOCK INSPECTOR	5	7	073.161-010
IRE	VETERINARY MEAT-INSPECTOR	5	8	073.264-010
IRE	WELDING ENGINEER	5	8	011.061-026
IRE	AUTO-DESIGN DETAILER	4	6	017.281-010
IRE	DOCUMENT RESTORER	4	6	979.361-010
IRE	EMBROIDERY PATTERNMAKER	4	6	782.361-014
IRE	LABORATORY TESTER	4	6	022.281-018
IRE	MEDICAL-LABORATORY ASSISTANT	4	4	078.381-010
IRE	PILOT-CONTROL OPERATOR	4	7	559.382-046
IRE	ROCKET-ENGINE-COMPONENT MECHANIC	4	7	621.281-030
IRE	CHEMICAL PREPARER 1	3	4	550.685-030
IRE	INSPECTOR, PLATING	3	3	500.287-010
IRE	LINE-SERVICE ATTENDANT	3	2	912.687-010
IRE	MILK DRIVER	3	3	905.483-010
IRE	PAINTER, TOUCH-UP	3	4	749.684-038

Code	Title	GED	SVP	DOT No.
IRE	PLASTICS-SPREADING-MACHINE OPERATOR	3	4	554.382-014
IRE	SAMPLE CHECKER	3	3	229.687-010
IRE	SUPERVISOR, FINISHING DEPARTMENT	3	4	679.137-010
IRE	TAXI DRIVER	3	3	913.463-018
IRC	CRIMINALIST	5	7	029.281-010
IRC	DRAFTER, AERONAUTICAL	5	7	002.261-010
IRC	DRAFTER, ELECTRICAL	5	7	003.281-010
IRC	DRAFTER, GEOLOGICAL	5	6	010.281-014
IRC	DRAFTER, HEATING AND VENTILATING	5	7	017.261-034
IRC	DRAFTER, PLUMBING	5	7	017.261-038
IRC	DRAFTER, STRUCTURAL	5	7	005.281-014
IRC	DRAFTER, TOOL DESIGN	5	7	007.261-022
IRC	ENGINEERING ASSISTANT, MECHANICAL			
	EQUIPMENT	5	7	007.161-018
IRC	FLIGHT-TEST-DATA TRANSCRIBER	5	5	002.281-010
IRC	PHOTOGRAMMETRIST	4	7	018.261-026
IAS	APPRAISER, ART	5	8	191.287-014
ISR	DERMATOLOGIST	6	8	070.101-018
ISR	DIETITIAN, RESEARCH	6	8	077.061-010
ISR	FOOD TECHNOLOGIST	6	7	041.081-010
ISR	MINERALOGIST	6	8	024.061-038
ISR	OPHTHALMOLOGIST	6	8	070.101-058
ISR	PALEONTOLOGIST	6	8	024.061-042
ISR	PETROLOGIST	6	8	024.061-046
ISR	PHYSICIAN, HEAD	6	8	070.101-074
ISR	SAFETY ENGINEER	6	8	012.061-014
ISR	SANITARIAN	6	8	079.117-018
ISR	AIRPORT ENGINEER	5	8	005.061-010
ISR	AUDIOLOGIST	5	7	076.101-010
ISR	CIVIL ENGINEER	5	8	005.061-014
ISR	FOOD TESTER	5	5	029.361-014
ISR	LABORATORY TECHNICIAN, VETERINARY	5	6	073.361-010
ISR	NURSE, PRIVATE DUTY	5	7	075.374-018
ISR	TRANSPORTATION ENGINEER	5	8	005.061-038
ISA	INSPECTOR, HEATING AND			
	REFRIGERATION	5	7	168.167-046
ISA	VIDEO OPERATOR	5	7	194.282-010
ISE	ASTRONOMER	6	8	021.067-010
ISE	ENDODONTIST	6	8	072.101-014
ISE	PRODUCT-SAFETY ENGINEER	6	8	012.061-010
ISE	PSYCHIATRIST	6	8	070.107-014
ISE	SURGEON 1	6	8	070.101-094
ISE	ACTUARY	5	8	020.167-010
ISE	AERIAL-PHOTOGRAPH INTERPRETER	5	7	029.167-010
ISE	CORONER	5	7	168.161-010
ISE	CUSTOMS IMPORT SPECIALIST	5	8	168.267-018
ISE	DRAFTER, CHIEF, DESIGN	5	8	017.161-010
ISE	FURNITURE REPRODUCER	5	7	149.281-010
ISE	NURSE ANESTHETIST	5	7	075.371-010

Code	Title	GED	SVP	DOT No.
ISE	NURSE, STAFF, OCCUPATIONAL HEALTH NURSING	5	7	075.374-022
ISE	NURSE, SUPERVISOR, COMMUNITY-HEALTH NURSING	5	7	075.127-026
ISE	PERFUMER	5	7	022.161-018
ISE	PHOTOGRAPHIC ENGINEER	5	8	019.081-014
ISE	RESEARCH WORKER, ENCYCLOPEDIA	5	6	109.267-014
ISC	PUBLIC-HEALTH MICROBIOLOGIST	6	7	041.261-010
ISC	SCIENTIFIC LINGUIST	6	8	059.067-014
ISC	TRANSLATOR	6	7	137.267-018
ISC	BURSAR	5	7	160.167-042
IER	ABSORPTION-AND-ADSORPTION ENGINEER	6	8	008.061-010
IER	CHIEF ENGINEER	6	9	010.167-010
IER	ENGINEER, SOILS	6	7	024.161-010
IER	GEOGRAPHER, PHYSICAL	6	7	029.067-014
IER	GEOPHYSICAL PROSPECTOR	6	8	024.061-026
IER	MATHEMATICIAN	6	8	020.067-014
IER	POLLUTION-CONTROL ENGINEER	6	8	019.081-018
IER	PSYCHOLOGIST, EDUCATIONAL	6	8	045.067-010
IER	RESEARCH WORKER, SOCIAL WELFARE	6	7	054.067-010
IER	SEISMOLOGIST	6	8	024.061-050
IER	TECHNICAL DIRECTOR, CHEMICAL PLANT	6	8	008.167-010
IER	CHIEF PILOT	5	9	196.167-010
IER	CONSULTANT	5	8	189.167-010
IER	DISTRICT SUPERVISOR, MUD-ANALYSIS WELL LOGGING	5	8	010.167-014
IER	ENGINEER OF SYSTEM DEVELOPMENT	5	8	003.167-026
IER	ENGINEER-IN-CHARGE, STUDIO OPERATIONS	5	8	003.167-030
IER	FACTORY LAY-OUT ENGINEER	5	8	012.167-018
IER	FIRE-INVESTIGATION LIEUTENANT	5	7	373.267-018
IER	GEODETIC COMPUTER	5	6	018.167-014
IER	INDUSTRIAL THERAPIST	5	7	076.167-010
IER	INFORMATION SCIENTIST	5	7	109.067-010
IER	MANAGER, LAND SURVEYING	5	8	018.167-022
IER	MANAGER, PRODUCTION, SEED CORN	5	7	180.161-010
IER	MECHANICAL-DESIGN ENGINEER, PRODUCTS	5	8	007.061-022
IER	NAVIGATOR	5	6	196.167-014
IER	PHARMACIST	5	7	074.161-010
IER	PROJECT ENGINEER	5	8	019.167-014
IER	SALES ENGINEER, AGRICULTURAL EQUIPMENT	5	8	013.151-010
IER	SCOUT	5	6	010.267-010
IER	SPECIFICATION WRITER	5	7	019.267-010
IER	SUPERINTENDENT, SYSTEM OPERATION	5	8	184.167-210
IER	SUPERINTENDENT, TRANSMISSION	5	8	184.167-222
IER	SUPERVISOR, MICROWAVE	5	8	003.167-058
IER	SURVEYOR ASSISTANT, INSTRUMENTS	5	7	018.167-034
IER	SURVEYOR, GEOPHYSICAL PROSPECTING	5	6	018.167-042
IER	SURVEYOR, MARINE	5	7	018.167-046
IER	SYSTEMS ANALYST, ELECTRONIC DATA			

Code	Title	GED	SVP	DOT No.
	PROCESSING	5	7	012.167-066
IER	TEACHER, INDUSTRIAL ARTS	5	7	091.221-010
IER	FIELD ARTILLERY OPERATIONS SPECIALIST	4	5	378.367-014
IEA	ARCHITECT	6	8	001.061-010
IEA	CHEMICAL-LABORATORY CHIEF	6	8	022.161-010
IEA	DIRECTOR, QUALITY CONTROL	6	8	012.167-014
IEA	MANAGER, ELECTRONIC DATA PROCESSING	6	8	169.167-030
IEA	RELIABILITY ENGINEER	6	8	019.081-022
IEA	SUPERINTENDENT, WATER-AND-SEWER SYSTEMS	6	9	184.161-014
IEA	CHIEF OF PARTY	5	7	018.167-010
IEA	LAND SURVEYOR	5	7	018.167-018
IEA	MEDICAL TECHNOLOGIST, CHIEF	5	7	078.161-010
IEA	SCHOOL-PLANT CONSULTANT	5	6	001.167-010
IEA	STILL OPERATOR, BATCH OR CONTINUOUS	4	6	552.362-022
IES	ALLERGIST-IMMUNOLOGIST	6	9	070.107-010
IES	MASTER, SHIP	6	8	197.167-010
IES	METROLOGIST	6	8	012.067-010
IES	SAFETY MANAGER	6	8	012.167-058
IES	SOCIOLOGIST	6	7	054.067-014
IES	APPRAISER	5	7	188.167-010
IES	ELECTRICAL TEST ENGINEER	5	8	003.061-014
IES	ELECTRONICS-TEST ENGINEER	5	8	003.061-042
IES	JOB ANALYST	5	6	166.267-018
IES	NURSE, SUPERVISOR, OCCUPATIONAL HEALTH NURSING	5	7	075.137-010
IES	OCCUPATIONAL ANALYST	5	7	166.067-010
IES	PSYCHOMETRIST	5	7	045.067-018
IES	PUBLIC HEALTH SERVICE OFFICER	5	8	187.117-050
IEC	HIGHWAY-ADMINISTRATIVE ENGINEER	6	9	005.167-022
IEC	PHOTOGRAMMETRIC ENGINEER	6	8	018.167-026
IEC	FIRE-PROTECTION ENGINEER	5	7	012.167-026
IEC	PROGRAMER, INFORMATION SYSTEM	5	7	020.187-010
IEC	TISSUE TECHNOLOGIST	5	6	078.361-030
ICR	CHIEF DRAFTER	5	7	007.261-010
ICR	CYTOTECHNOLOGIST	5	6	078.281-010
ICR	MANAGEMENT ANALYST	5	7	161.167-010
ICR	PROGRAMER, PROCESS CONTROL	5	7	020.187-014

ARTISTIC OCCUPATIONS

Code	Title	GED	SVP	DOT No.
ARI	MODEL MAKER 1	5	7	777.261-010
ARI	MODELER	4	5	777.081-010
ARE	DISPLAYER, MERCHANDISE	4	6	298.081-010
ARE	LAY-OUT FORMER	4	7	970.381-018
ARE	MINIATURE-SET CONSTRUCTOR	4	7	962.381-018
ARE	PAINTER, HAND	4	7	970.381-022
ARE	PASTRY CHEF	4	8	315.131-014

Code	Title	GED	SVP	DOT No.
ARE	CAKE DECORATOR	3	6	524.381-010
ARE	ENGROSSER	3	8	970.661-010
AIR	LANDSCAPE ARCHITECT	5	8	001.061-018
AIE	ILLUSTRATOR, MEDICAL AND SCIENTIFIC	5	7	141.061-026
AIE	SET DESIGNER	5	8	142.061-046
ASR	CLOTHES DESIGNER	5	7	142.061-018
ASR	PAINTINGS RESTORER	5	8	102.261-014
ASE	CLERGY MEMBER	6	8	120.007-010
ASE	COMPOSER	6	9	152.067-014
ASE	EDITOR, TECHNICAL AND SCIENTIFIC PUBLICATIONS	6	9	132.017-018
ASE	HUMORIST	6	8	131.067-026
ASE	LIBRETTIST	6	7	131.067-030
ASE	LYRICIST	6	7	131.067-034
ASE	PLAYWRIGHT	6	8	131.067-038
ASE	PSYCHOLOGIST, SOCIAL	6	8	045.067-014
ASE	STORY EDITOR	6	8	132.037-026
ASE	CROSSWORD-PUZZLE MAKER	5	6	139.087-010
ASE	DIRECTOR, INSTRUCTIONAL MATERIAL	5	8	099.167-018
ASE	QUICK SKETCH ARTIST	5	6	149.041-010
ASE	STAINED GLASS ARTIST	5	8	142.061-054
ASE	TEACHER, ART	5	7	149.021-010
ASE	INSTRUCTOR, MODELING	4	4	099.227-026
ASE	PASTRY CHEF	4	8	313.131-022
ASE	PURIFICATION OPERATOR	4	7	551.362-010
AER	CONTINUITY WRITER	5	7	131.087-010
AER	CRYPTANALYST	5	8	199.267-014
AER	MUSICIAN, INSTRUMENTAL	5	8	152.041-010
AER	SAFETY-CLOTHING-AND-EQUIPMENT DEVELOPER	5	8	142.061-038
AER	SCULPTOR	5	8	144.061-018
AER	TRAFFIC-SAFETY ADMINISTRATOR	5	8	188.167-102
AER	BANK-NOTE DESIGNER	4	8	142.061-010
AER	CLOTH DESIGNER	4	7	142.061-014
AER	DANCER	4	7	151.047-010
AER	MAKE-UP ARTIST	4	7	333.071-010
AER	MEMORIAL DESIGNER	4	7	142.061-030
AER	SALESPERSON, FLOWERS	4	4	260.357-026
AER	VENTRILOQUIST	4	7	159.044-010
AER	ACROBAT	3	5	159.247-010
AER	DOUBLE	3	3	961.364-010
AER	EQUESTRIAN	3	6	159.344-010
AER	WIRE WALKER	3	6	159.347-022
AER	AMUSEMENT PARK ENTERTAINER	2	2	159.647-010
AEI	ARRANGER	6	8	152.067-010
AEI	INTELLIGENCE RESEARCH SPECIALIST	6	8	059.167-010
AEI	ORCHESTRATOR	6	8	152.067-022
AEI	PATENT AGENT	6	7	119.167-014

Code	Title	GED	SVP	DOT No.
AEI	SCREEN WRITER	6	7	131.087-018
AEI	COMMERCIAL DESIGNER	5	7	141.081-014
AEI	DIRECTOR, STATE-ASSESSED PROPERTIES	5	7	188.167-042
AEI	FASHION ARTIST	5	7	141.061-014
AEI	ILLUSTRATOR	5	7	141.061-022
AEI	ILLUSTRATOR, SET	5	8	141.061-030
AEI	MIME	5	7	159.047-022
AEI	PACKAGE DESIGNER	5	7	142.081-018
AEI	PAINTER	5	8	144.061-010
AEI	PUPPETEER	5	8	159.041-014
AES	AUDIOVISUAL PRODUCTION SPECIALIST	6	7	149.061-010
AES	BAR EXAMINER	6	8	110.167-010
AES	CRITIC	6	8	131.067-018
AES	EDITOR, BOOK	6	8	132.067-014
AES	EDITOR, CITY	6	8	132.037-014
AES	EDITOR, NEWSPAPER	6	9	132.017-014
AES	EDITOR, PUBLICATIONS	6	8	132.037-022
AES	POET	6	7	131.067-042
AES	WRITER, PROSE, FICTION AND NONFICTION	6	8	131.067-046
AES	ACCOUNT EXECUTIVE	5	8	164.167-010
AES	ACTOR	5	7	150.047-010
AES	ARCHIVIST	5	8	101.167-010
AES	ART DIRECTOR	5	8	141.031-010
AES	ART DIRECTOR	5	8	142.031-010
AES	BUREAU CHIEF	5	8	132.067-010
AES	CARTOONIST	5	7	141.061-010
AES	CARTOONIST, MOTION PICTURES	5	7	141.081-010
AES	CHORAL DIRECTOR	5	8	152.047-010
AES	CHOREOGRAPHER	5	8	151.027-010
AES	COLOR EXPERT	5	7	141.051-010
AES	COMEDIAN	5	5	159.047-014
AES	COMMISSIONER, CONSERVATION OF RESOURCES	5	8	188.117-026
AES	CONDUCTOR, ORCHESTRA	5	9	152.047-014
AES	COPY WRITER	5	7	131.067-014
AES	CREATIVE DIRECTOR	5	8	141.067-010
AES	DIRECTOR OF PHOTOGRAPHY	5	8	143.062-010
AES	DIRECTOR, CLASSIFICATION AND TREATMENT	5	7	188.167-026
AES	DIRECTOR, MUSIC	5	9	152.047-018
AES	DIRECTOR, PROGRAM	5	8	184.167-030
AES	DIRECTOR, STAGE	5	8	150.067-010
AES	DIRECTOR, SECURITIES AND REAL ESTATE	5	7	188.167-038
AES	DISPLAY DESIGNER	5	7	142.051-010
AES	DRAMATIC COACH	5	7	150.027-010
AES	EDITOR, DEPARTMENT	5	8	132.037-018
AES	EDITOR, FILM	5	8	962.264-010
AES	EDITOR, GREETING CARD	5	6	132.067-022
AES	EDITORIAL WRITER	5	8	131.067-022
AES	FOREIGN-SERVICE OFFICER	5	8	188.117-106
AES	FURNITURE DESIGNER	5	7	142.061-022

Code	Title	GED	SVP	DOT No.
AES	GRAPHIC DESIGNER	5	7	141.061-018
AES	INDUSTRIAL DESIGNER	5	7	142.061-026
AES	INSPECTOR, PLUMBING	5	7	168.167-050
AES	INSTRUCTOR, DANCING	5	7	151.027-014
AES	INTELLIGENCE SPECIALIST	5	7	059.267-010
AES	INTERIOR DESIGNER	5	7	142.051-014
AES	MANAGER, CREDIT CARD OPERATIONS	5	8	186.167-022
AES	MANAGER, DISPLAY	5	7	142.031-014
AES	MANAGER, PERSONNEL	5	8	166.117-018
AES	NARRATOR	5	5	150.147-010
AES	PRINTMAKER	5	8	144.061-014
AES	READER	5	6	131.087-014
AES	REHABILITATION CENTER MANAGER	5	7	195.167-038
AES	SALES REPRESENTATIVE, GRAPHIC ART	5	7	254.251-010
AES	SALES-SERVICE PROMOTER	5	7	165.167-010
AES	SET DECORATOR	5	8	142.061-042
AES	SET DESIGNER	5	8	142.061-050
AES	SILHOUETTE ARTIST	5	6	149.051-010
AES	SUPERVISOR, HISTORIC SITES	5	7	102.117-010
AES	SUPERVISOR, SCENIC ARTS	5	8	149.031-010
AES	TEACHER, MUSIC	5	8	152.021-010
AES	YOUNG-ADULT LIBRARIAN	5	7	100.167-034
AES	ARTIST AND REPERTOIRE MANAGER	4	7	159.167-010
AES	CONTESTANT COORDINATOR	4	5	166.167-010
AES	COPYIST	4	6	142.281-010
AES	DECORATOR	4	6	524.381-014
AES	IMPERSONATOR	4	6	159.047-018
AES	MILLINER	4	6	784.261-010
AES	PHOTOGRAPHER, APPRENTICE	4	7	143.062-018
AES	PHOTOGRAPHER, STILL	4	7	143.062-030
AES	PHOTOGRAPHER, MOTION PICTURE	4	7	143.062-022
AES	SIGHT-EFFECTS SPECIALIST	4	8	962.267-010
AES	SINGER	4	8	152.047-022
AES	WEDDING CONSULTANT	4	6	299.357-018
AES	AUCTIONEER	3	6	294.257-010
AES	INSTRUCTOR, PAINTING	3	4	297.451-010
AES	MODEL, ARTISTS'	3	3	961.667-010
AES	MODEL, PHOTOGRAPHERS'	3	4	961.367-010
AES	PLAYROOM ATTENDANT	3	3	359.677-026
AES	SALES REPRESENTATIVE, DANCING INSTRUCTIONS	3	4	259.357-014
AEC	EDITOR, NEWS	5	8	132.067-026
AEC	MAGICIAN	4	6	159.041-010
AEC	PHOTOJOURNALIST	4	7	143.062-034
AEC	PSYCHIC READER	3	3	159.647-018
AEC	TATTOO ARTIST	3	5	339.571-010
ACS	FUR DESIGNER	4	7	142.081-014
ACS	GRAPHOLOGIST	3	4	159.247-018

Code	Title	GED	SVP	DOT No.

SOCIAL OCCUPATIONS

Code	Title	GED	SVP	DOT No.
SRI	RADIOLOGIC TECHNOLOGIST	5	6	078.362-026
SRI	STOCK-CONTROL CLERK	4	5	219.367-034
SRI	SUPERVISOR, CORDUROY CUTTING	4	6	585.130-010
SRE	APPRENTICESHIP CONSULTANT	5	8	188.117-010
SRE	ATHLETIC TRAINER	5	8	153.224-010
SRE	COMMUNITY DIETITIAN	5	8	077.127-010
SRE	DIETETIC TECHNICIAN	5	8	077.121-010
SRE	INSTRUCTOR, FLYING 1	5	7	196.223-010
SRE	INSTRUCTOR, PILOT	5	8	196.223-014
SRE	OCCUPATIONAL THERAPIST	5	7	076.121-010
SRE	ANIMAL KEEPER, HEAD	4	7	412.137-010
SRE	CARTOON DESIGNER	4	7	781.381-010
SRE	CHIROPRACTOR ASSISTANT	4	6	079.364-010
SRE	COATING-MIXER SUPERVISOR	4	7	530.132-010
SRE	COMMUNICATIONS ELECTRICIAN SUPERVISOR	4	8	823.131-010
SRE	COOK, LARDER	4	7	315.381-014
SRE	COOKING, CASING, AND DRYING SUPERVISOR	4	7	529.135-010
SRE	COSMETICS SUPERVISOR	4	7	550.131-010
SRE	DETECTIVE, NARCOTICS AND VICE	4	7	375.267-014
SRE	FURNITURE FINISHER	4	7	763.381-010
SRE	FURNITURE-FINISHER APPRENTICE	4	7	763.381-014
SRE	INSTRUCTOR, ROCKET-MOTOR CASE ASSEMBLY	4	5	806.227-010
SRE	INVESTIGATOR, NARCOTICS	4	7	375.267-018
SRE	MUSIC LIBRARIAN	4	6	100.367-022
SRE	OPTICIAN, DISPENSING 2	4	6	299.474-010
SRE	PLANT SUPERVISOR	4	7	529.132-014
SRE	RACEHORSE TRAINER	4	6	153.224-014
SRE	RECRUITER	4	5	166.267-026
SRE	SULKY DRIVER	4	6	153.244-014
SRE	SUPERVISOR	4	6	550.132-010
SRE	SUPERVISOR, SHIPPING	4	7	550.137-018
SRE	SUPERVISOR, CHAR HOUSE	4	7	523.132-010
SRE	SUPERVISOR, CLAY PREPARATION	4	8	570.130-010
SRE	SUPERVISOR, COOLER SERVICE	4	7	637.131-010
SRE	SUPERVISOR, CUTTING DEPARTMENT	4	7	669.130-014
SRE	SUPERVISOR, ASSEMBLY	4	8	806.131-014
SRE	SUPERVISOR, POND	4	7	939.130-010
SRE	SUPERVISOR, FILM PROCESSING	4	7	976.131-014
SRE	SUPERVISOR, MOLD CONSTRUCTION	4	7	860.131-026
SRE	SUPERVISOR, ROLLER PRINTING	4	7	652.130-018
SRE	SUPERVISOR, DECORATING	4	7	749.131-010
SRE	SUPERVISOR, PAPER COATING	4	8	534.132-014
SRE	SUPERVISOR, SILK-SCREEN CUTTING AND PRINTING	4	8	979.131-018
SRE	SUPERVISOR, TUFTING	4	6	687.132-010
SRE	SUPERVISOR, MIXING	4	7	680.130-014
SRE	SUPERVISOR, LACE TEARING	4	7	689.134-014
SRE	WEAVER, HAND LOOM	4	6	683.684-030

Code	Title	GED	SVP	DOT No.
SRE	ANIMAL TREATMENT INVESTIGATOR	3	5	379.263-010
SRE	BORDER GUARD	3	5	375.363-010
SRE	CHECKER, DUMP GROUNDS	3	3	219.367-010
SRE	GLOVE-PARTS INSPECTOR	3	4	781.687-034
SRE	INSPECTOR, SHIPPING	3	4	801.667-010
SRE	KENNEL MANAGER, DOG TRACK	3	6	349.367-010
SRE	MANNEQUIN WIG MAKER	3	6	739.381-042
SRE	ORDERLY	3	4	355.674-018
SRE	QUALITY-CONTROL CHECKER	3	5	789.387-010
SRE	SAMPLE CLERK, PAPER	3	3	209.587-046
SRE	SKI MOLDER	3	3	732.684-114
SRE	SUPERVISOR, WOOD-CREW	3	6	669.137-010
SRE	TILE SHADER	3	5	574.367-010
SRE	WIG MAKER	3	7	739.381-058
SRC	RADIOLOGIC TECHNOLOGIST, CHIEF	5	7	078.162-010
SRC	AUDIOMETRIST	4	6	078.362-010
SRC	CANARY BREEDER	4	5	411.161-010
SRC	COOK, PASTRY, PSYCHIATRIC HOSPITAL	4	7	315.361-014
SRC	HOOF AND SHOE INSPECTOR	4	6	153.287-010
SRC	PHOTOGRAPH RETOUCHER	4	6	970.281-018
SRC	PHOTOGRAPHER, FINISH	4	6	143.382-014
SRC	PROFESSIONAL ATHLETE	4	8	153.341-010
SRC	REPAIRER, ART OBJECTS	4	7	779.381-018
SRC	SUPERVISOR, FILM PROCESSING	4	6	976.132-010
SRC	SUPERVISOR, PHOSPHORIC ACID	4	8	558.132-014
SRC	BRANNER-MACHINE TENDER	3	4	509.685-014
SRC	MAIL CARRIER	3	4	230.367-010
SRC	STRIPER, HAND	3	6	740.484-010
SRC	BAG PRINTER	2	4	651.685-010
SRC	CANDLEMAKER	2	4	739.664-010
SIR	PHYSICIAN, OCCUPATIONAL	6	8	070.101-078
SIR	COACH, PROFESSIONAL ATHLETES	5	8	153.227-010
SIR	DOCTOR, NATUROPATHIC	5	7	079.101-014
SIR	NURSE-MIDWIFE	5	7	075.264-014
SIR	NURSE, OFFICE	5	7	075.374-014
SIR	ORIENTATION THERAPIST FOR THE BLIND	5	7	076.221-010
SIA	EDITOR, DICTIONARY	6	8	132.067-018
SIA	SHOE-LAY-OUT PLANNER	5	8	012.187-014
SIE	DIRECTOR, CORRECTIONAL AGENCY	6	8	188.117-054
SIE	MEDICAL-RECORD ADMINISTRATOR	6	8	079.167-014
SIE	PSYCHOLOGIST, CLINICAL	6	8	045.107-022
SIE	SPEECH PATHOLOGIST	6	7	076.107-010
SIE	AUDITOR, INTERNAL	5	8	160.167-034
SIE	CLAIM EXAMINER	5	7	168.267-014
SIE	CONSULTANT, EDUCATIONAL, STATE BOARD OF NURSING	5	8	075.117-010
SIE	DIETETIC INTERN	5	6	077.167-010
SIE	DIETITIAN, TEACHING	5	8	077.127-022
SIE	DIETITIAN, CLINICAL	5	7	077.127-014
SIE	DISTRICT SUPERVISOR	5	6	184.117-018

Code	Title	GED	SVP	DOT No.
SIE	INVESTIGATOR	5	6	168.267-062
SIE	NURSE, GENERAL DUTY	5	7	075.374-010
SIE	NURSE, HEAD	5	7	075.127-018
SIE	NURSE, SCHOOL	5	7	075.124-010
SIE	NURSE, STAFF, COMMUNITY HEALTH	5	7	075.124-014
SIE	PHYSICAL THERAPIST	5	7	076.121-014
SIE	VETERINARY VIRUS-SERUM INSPECTOR	5	7	073.261-010
SIE	COMPARISON SHOPPER	4	3	296.367-014
SIE	SUPERVISOR, MIXING	4	5	680.135-010
SIC	EDITOR, INDEX	5	7	132.367-010
SAE	GRADUATE ASSISTANT	6	8	090.227-014
SAE	TITLE ATTORNEY	6	8	110.117-042
SAE	FOOD AND DRUG INSPECTOR	5	6	168.267-042
SER	DIRECTOR, INSTITUTION	6	8	187.117-018
SER	ADMINISTRATOR, HOSPITAL	5	8	187.117-010
SER	AUDITOR, TAX	5	8	160.167-038
SER	CHIEF LIBRARIAN, BRANCH OR DEPARTMENT	5	7	100.127-010
SER	CHIEF, FISHERY DIVISION	5	8	188.117-018
SER	CHILDREN'S LIBRARIAN	5	7	100.167-018
SER	COMMISSIONER, PUBLIC WORKS	5	8	188.117-030
SER	COORDINATOR OF REHABILITATION SERVICES	5	8	076.117-010
SER	COUNSELOR	5	7	045.107-010
SER	COUNSELOR, NURSES' ASSOCIATION	5	8	045.107-014
SER	CUSTOMS PATROL OFFICER	5	8	168.167-010
SER	DIRECTOR, ATHLETIC	5	9	090.117-022
SER	DIRECTOR, AGRICULTURAL SERVICES	5	8	188.117-038
SER	DIRECTOR, ARTS-AND-HUMANITIES COUNCIL	5	8	188.117-042
SER	DIRECTOR, COMMISSION FOR THE BLIND	5	8	094.117-010
SER	DIRECTOR, CONSUMER AFFAIRS	5	8	188.117-050
SER	DIRECTOR, EDUCATIONAL, COMMUNITY-HEALTH NURSING	5	8	075.117-018
SER	DIRECTOR, FIELD REPRESENTATIVES	5	8	188.117-062
SER	DIRECTOR, INDUSTRIAL RELATIONS	5	8	166.117-010
SER	DIRECTOR, LICENSING AND REGISTRATION	5	8	188.117-074
SER	DIRECTOR, UNEMPLOYMENT INSURANCE	5	8	188.117-094
SER	DISTRICT CUSTOMS DIRECTOR	5	8	188.117-098
SER	EXECUTIVE CHEF	5	8	187.161-010
SER	EXECUTIVE DIRECTOR, SHELTERED WORKSHOP	5	8	187.117-026
SER	FACTORER	5	8	186.117-026
SER	GENERAL MANAGER, ROAD PRODUCTION	5	8	187.117-034
SER	HEALTH OFFICER, FIELD	5	6	168.167-018
SER	HOUSING-MANAGEMENT OFFICER	5	8	188.117-110
SER	INSTRUCTOR, CORRESPONDENCE SCHOOL	5	7	099.227-014
SER	LEASE BUYER	5	7	191.117-030
SER	LIBRARIAN, SPECIAL COLLECTIONS	5	8	100.267-014
SER	MANAGER, CHRISTMAS-TREE FARM	5	7	180.117-010

CLASSIFIED INDEX

Code	Title	GED	SVP	DOT No.
SER	MANAGER, DEPARTMENT STORE	5	8	185.117-010
SER	MANAGER, PROMOTION	5	8	163.117-018
SER	MANAGER, RECREATION ESTABLISHMENT	5	7	187.117-042
SER	POLICE CHIEF	5	9	375.117-010
SER	PRESIDENT	5	9	189.117-026
SER	PRINCIPAL	5	8	099.117-018
SER	RENTAL MANAGER, PUBLIC EVENTS FACILITIES	5	8	186.117-062
SER	RESEARCH ASSISTANT	5	7	109.267-010
SER	STEWARD, RACETRACK	5	8	153.117-022
SER	SUPERINTENDENT, SCHOOLS	5	9	099.117-022
SER	VOCATIONAL-REHABILITATION COUNSELOR	5	8	045.107-042
SER	WILDLIFE AGENT, REGIONAL	5	7	379.137-018
SER	AIR-TRAFFIC COORDINATOR	4	8	193.162-010
SER	AIR-TRAFFIC-CONTROL SPECIALIST, TOWER	4	8	193.162-018
SER	ANIMAL-RIDE MANAGER	4	6	349.224-010
SER	ASSEMBLY SUPERVISOR	4	7	739.137-010
SER	ATTENDANCE OFFICER	4	7	168.367-010
SER	BANK BOSS	4	7	932.132-010
SER	BURNING SUPERVISOR	4	7	573.132-010
SER	COOK, HEAD, SCHOOL CAFETERIA	4	6	313.131-018
SER	CORRECTION OFFICER, HEAD	4	6	372.137-010
SER	COSMETOLOGIST APPRENTICE	4	6	332.271-014
SER	DETECTIVE	4	7	375.267-010
SER	DREDGE CAPTAIN	4	8	197.161-010
SER	ELECTRONIC-COMPUTER-SUBASSEMBLY SUPERVISOR	4	7	726.131-010
SER	EMERGENCY MEDICAL SERVICES COORDINATOR	4	8	079.117-010
SER	FOLLOW-UP CLERK	4	6	221.367-018
SER	FREIGHT-LOADING SUPERVISOR	4	6	910.137-026
SER	GENERAL CLAIMS AGENT	4	8	186.117-030
SER	GUIDE, CHIEF AIRPORT	4	5	353.137-010
SER	HAIR STYLIST	4	6	332.271-018
SER	HIGHWAY-MAINTENANCE SUPERVISOR	4	8	899.134-010
SER	HOMEMAKER	4	5	309.354-010
SER	INSPECTOR, HEALTH CARE FACILITIES	4	6	168.167-042
SER	INSTRUCTOR	4	6	689.222-010
SER	INSTRUCTOR, DRIVING	4	4	099.223-010
SER	INVESTIGATOR, VICE	4	7	375.267-022
SER	JOCKEY AGENT	4	5	191.117-026
SER	LICENSE INSPECTOR	4	7	168.267-066
SER	MANAGER, CASINO	4	7	187.167-070
SER	MANAGER, DUDE RANCH	4	7	187.167-094
SER	MANAGER, FAST FOOD SERVICES	4	7	185.137-010
SER	MANAGER, HOTEL RECREATIONAL FACILITIES	4	7	187.167-122
SER	MANAGER, INTERNAL SECURITY	4	7	376.137-010
SER	MILLER SUPERVISOR	4	7	521.130-010
SER	PADDOCK JUDGE	4	7	153.167-010
SER	PAWNBROKER	4	6	191.157-010
SER	PHARMACEUTICAL-COMPOUNDING SUPERVISOR	4	7	559.131-010

Code	Title	GED	SVP	DOT No.
SER	POLICE OFFICER 1	4	6	375.263-014
SER	ROUTE SUPERVISOR	4	6	239.137-018
SER	SAFETY INSPECTOR	4	8	821.367-014
SER	SANITARY-LANDFILL SUPERVISOR	4	7	955.133-010
SER	SECTION SUPERVISOR	4	7	939.137-018
SER	SENIOR-COMMISSARY AGENT	4	7	922.137-010
SER	STEWARD/STEWARDESS, THIRD	4	7	350.137-026
SER	STRUCTURAL-MILL SUPERVISOR	4	6	619.132-022
SER	SUPERINTENDENT, LABOR UTILIZATION	4	8	189.167-042
SER	SUPERVISOR	4	7	188.137-010
SER	SUPERVISOR, MAILS	4	6	243.137-010
SER	SUPERVISOR, MAIL CARRIERS	4	6	230.137-018
SER	SUPERVISOR, DELIVERY DEPARTMENT	4	6	230.137-014
SER	SUPERVISOR, KOSHER DIETARY SERVICE	4	7	319.137-026
SER	SUPERVISOR, HAND SILVERING	4	7	574.134-010
SER	SUPERVISOR, TUMBLERS	4	7	599.132-010
SER	SUPERVISOR, ELECTRONIC COILS	4	8	724.130-010
SER	SUPERVISOR, COIN-MACHINE	4	7	706.130-010
SER	SUPERVISOR, METER-AND-REGULATOR SHOP	4	8	710.137-014
SER	SUPERVISOR, SMALL APPLIANCE ASSEMBLY	4	7	723.131-010
SER	SUPERVISOR, SAMPLE	4	7	754.137-010
SER	SUPERVISOR, ORDNANCE TRUCK INSTALLATION	4	7	806.137-014
SER	SUPERVISOR, BLUEPRINTING-AND-PHOTOCOPY	4	8	979.130-010
SER	SUPERVISOR, PUBLICATIONS PRODUCTION	4	8	979.131-010
SER	SUPERVISOR, HOSPITALITY HOUSE	4	6	359.137-010
SER	SUPERVISOR, AUTOMOBILE BODY REPAIR	4	7	807.137-010
SER	SUPERVISOR, SCREEN PRINTING	4	8	652.137-014
SER	SUPERVISOR, FINISHING	4	7	742.134-010
SER	SUPERVISOR, CALENDERING	4	8	534.132-010
SER	SUPERVISOR, COMMISSARY PRODUCTION	4	7	319.137-022
SER	SUPERVISOR, ARTIFICIAL BREEDING RANCH	4	7	410.131-014
SER	SUPERVISOR, ASSEMBLY	4	7	710.137-010
SER	SUPERVISOR, READY-MIXED FOOD PREPARATION	4	5	529.137-054
SER	SUPERVISOR, DENTAL LABORATORY	4	7	712.131-010
SER	SUPERVISOR, AUDIT CLERKS	4	6	210.132-010
SER	SUPERVISOR, ELECTRICAL ASSEMBLY	4	6	729.130-010
SER	TASTER	4	7	529.281-010
SER	TEACHER, ADULT EDUCATION	4	7	099.227-030
SER	TELLER, HEAD	4	8	211.132-010
SER	TESTING AND ANALYSIS DEPARTMENT SUPERVISOR	4	7	523.131-010
SER	TRANSFER-AND-PUMPHOUSE OPERATOR, CHIEF	4	7	559.132-138
SER	TRANSPORTATION INSPECTOR	4	7	168.167-082
SER	WAITER/WAITRESS, CAPTAIN	4	6	311.137-018
SER	WARD-SERVICE SUPERVISOR	4	6	245.137-010
SER	BIRTH ATTENDANT	3	4	354.377-010
SER	CLOTH-PRINTING INSPECTOR	3	4	652.567-010

Code	Title	GED	SVP	DOT No.
SER	COMPANION	3	3	309.677-010
SER	CORRECTION OFFICER	3	4	372.667-018
SER	DEPUTY SHERIFF, CIVIL DIVISION	3	3	377.667-018
SER	DOG CATCHER	3	3	379.673-010
SER	EDITOR, SCHOOL PHOTOGRAPH	3	5	976.687-010
SER	HOME ATTENDANT	3	3	354.377-014
SER	NURSE AIDE	3	4	355.674-014
SER	NURSE, PRACTICAL	3	4	354.374-010
SER	NURSERY SCHOOL ATTENDANT	3	4	359.677-018
SER	PAINTER	3	5	740.381-018
SER	POLICE OFFICER 2	3	5	375.367-010
SER	POLICE SERGEANT, PRECINCT 1	3	6	375.133-010
SER	PROTECTIVE OFFICER	3	4	372.363-010
SER	SHERIFF, DEPUTY	3	5	377.263-010
SER	SUPERVISOR, HOUSECLEANER	3	6	323.137-010
SER	SUPERVISOR, SLATE SPLITTING	3	5	771.137-010
SER	SUPERVISOR, PARKING LOT	3	4	915.133-010
SER	VENEER MATCHER	3	4	769.687-046
SER	ATTENDANT, LODGING FACILITIES	2	3	329.467-010
SER	COWPUNCHER	2	4	410.674-014
SER	MERCHANT PATROLLER	2	3	372.667-038
SEI	COMMUNITY-SERVICES-AND-HEALTH-EDUCATION OFFICER	6	8	079.167-010
SEI	DIRECTOR, REVENUE	6	8	188.117-090
SEI	EXECUTIVE DIRECTOR, NURSES' ASSOCIATION	6	8	075.117-034
SEI	FACULTY MEMBER, COLLEGE OR UNIVERSITY	6	8	090.227-010
SEI	HEARING OFFICER	6	9	119.107-010
SEI	INSURANCE ATTORNEY	6	8	110.117-014
SEI	PRESIDENT, FINANCIAL INSTITUTION	6	9	186.117-054
SEI	PRODUCER	6	8	159.117-010
SEI	PSYCHOLOGIST, COUNSELING	6	8	045.107-026
SEI	PSYCHOLOGIST, INDUSTRIAL-ORGANIZATIONAL	6	8	045.107-030
SEI	PSYCHOLOGIST, SCHOOL	6	8	045.107-034
SEI	RESEARCH-CONTRACTS SUPERVISOR	6	8	162.117-030
SEI	ANALYST, FOOD AND BEVERAGE	5	8	310.267-010
SEI	DIANETIC COUNSELOR	5	6	199.207-010
SEI	DIETITIAN, CONSULTANT	5	8	077.127-018
SEI	DIRECTOR OF GUIDANCE IN PUBLIC SCHOOLS	5	8	045.117-010
SEI	DIRECTOR, LABOR STANDARDS	5	8	188.117-066
SEI	DIRECTOR, LAW ENFORCEMENT	5	7	188.117-070
SEI	INSTRUCTOR, GROUND SERVICES	5	7	099.227-018
SEI	LOAN OFFICER	5	7	186.267-018
SEI	NURSE, SUPERVISOR	5	7	075.127-022
SEI	PARK NATURALIST	5	7	049.127-010
SEI	PROGRAM AIDE, GROUP WORK	5	6	195.227-010
SEI	RECREATION LEADER	5	7	195.227-014
SEI	SERVICE REPRESENTATIVE	5	7	191.167-022
SEI	EVALUATOR	4	4	249.367-034
SEI	FIRE ASSISTANT	4	6	169.167-022

Code	Title	GED	SVP	DOT No.
SEI	SUPERVISOR, QUALITY CONTROL	4	7	976.131-022
SEI	UTILITIES SERVICE INVESTIGATOR	4	6	821.364-010
SEI	ARMORED-CAR GUARD	3	3	372.567-010
SEA	APPEALS REVIEWER, VETERAN	6	9	119.117-010
SEA	CUE SELECTOR	6	9	152.067-018
SEA	DIRECTOR, SPECIAL EDUCATION	6	9	094.117-014
SEA	EDITOR, MANAGING, NEWSPAPER	6	8	132.017-010
SEA	ACADEMIC DEAN	5	9	090.117-010
SEA	ARBITRATOR	5	8	169.107-010
SEA	ART CONSERVATOR	5	8	102.167-010
SEA	CASEWORKER, CHILD WELFARE	5	7	195.107-014
SEA	CASEWORKER, FAMILY	5	7	195.107-018
SEA	CHIEF CONTROLLER	5	7	193.167-010
SEA	CHRISTIAN SCIENCE PRACTITIONER	5	6	129.107-014
SEA	CHRISTMAS-TREE CONTRACTOR	5	7	162.117-010
SEA	DEAN OF STUDENTS 1	5	8	090.117-018
SEA	DEAN OF STUDENTS 2	5	8	091.107-010
SEA	DIRECTOR, AERONAUTICS COMMISSION	5	8	188.117-034
SEA	DIRECTOR, COMMUNITY ORGANIZATION	5	8	187.117-014
SEA	DIRECTOR, COMPLIANCE	5	7	188.117-046
SEA	DIRECTOR, PUBLIC SERVICE	5	8	184.117-010
SEA	DIRECTOR, RESEARCH	5	8	052.167-010
SEA	DIRECTOR, RELIGIOUS EDUCATION	5	8	129.107-022
SEA	DIRECTOR, RECORDS MANAGEMENT	5	8	161.117-014
SEA	DIRECTOR, TELEVISION	5	8	159.067-014
SEA	DISTRICT EXTENSION SERVICE AGENT	5	8	096.167-010
SEA	DYER, SUPERVISOR	5	7	582.131-014
SEA	EDUCATION SUPERVISOR, CORRECTIONAL INSTITUTION	5	8	099.117-014
SEA	FIELD CONTRACTOR	5	7	162.117-022
SEA	FIRE CHIEF	5	8	373.117-010
SEA	HOME ECONOMIST	5	7	096.121-014
SEA	INSERVICE COORDINATOR, AUXILIARY PERSONNEL	5	7	079.127-010
SEA	INSTRUCTOR, EXTENSION WORK	5	8	090.227-018
SEA	INSTRUCTOR, MILITARY SCIENCE	5	9	099.227-022
SEA	MANAGER, EMPLOYEE WELFARE	5	7	166.117-014
SEA	PROGRAM DIRECTOR, GROUP WORK	5	8	187.117-046
SEA	PUBLIC HEALTH EDUCATOR	5	8	079.117-014
SEA	SOCIAL GROUP WORKER	5	8	195.107-022
SEA	SOCIAL WORKER, DELINQUENCY PREVENTION	5	7	195.107-026
SEA	SOCIAL WORKER, PSYCHIATRIC	5	7	195.107-034
SEA	SUPERVISOR, LIQUOR STORES AND AGENCIES	5	8	185.167-062
SEA	TEACHER, DRAMA	5	7	150.027-014
SEA	BOOKING MANAGER	4	6	191.117-014
SEA	COSMETOLOGIST	4	6	332.271-010
SEA	OCCUPATIONAL THERAPY AIDE	4	5	355.377-010
SEA	QUALITY-CONTROL TECHNICIAN	4	6	976.267-010
SEA	SUPERVISOR	4	5	734.131-010
SEA	SUPERVISOR, PUBLIC MESSAGE SERVICE	4	7	239.137-026
SEA	SUPERVISOR, FERMENTING CELLARS	4	7	529.132-058

Code	Title	GED	SVP	DOT No.
SEA	SUPERVISOR, PRODUCTION	4	6	979.137-018
SEA	SUPERVISOR, SAMPLE PREPARATION	4	7	979.137-022
SEA	SUPERVISOR, PRODUCT INSPECTION	4	6	689.134-018
SEA	SUPERVISOR, PRODUCTION	4	7	589.135-010
SEA	SUPERVISOR, CIGAR TOBACCO PROCESSING	4	6	529.137-034
SEA	CHECKROOM CHIEF	3	5	358.137-010
SEC	CLAIM AGENT	6	7	191.167-014
SEC	LIBRARY DIRECTOR	6	8	100.117-010
SEC	POLITICAL SCIENTIST	6	8	051.067-010
SEC	ASSIGNMENT EDITOR	5	8	132.137-010
SEC	CASE AIDE	5	6	195.367-010
SEC	CASEWORK SUPERVISOR	5	7	195.137-010
SEC	CASEWORKER	5	7	195.107-010
SEC	CLAIMS ADJUDICATOR	5	7	169.267-010
SEC	CLERICAL-METHODS ANALYST	5	7	161.267-010
SEC	COMMUNITY-RELATIONS-AND-SERVICES ADVISOR, PUBLIC HOUSING	5	7	195.167-014
SEC	CONTINUITY DIRECTOR	5	8	132.037-010
SEC	CONTRACT CLERK	5	7	119.267-018
SEC	COORDINATOR, VOLUNTEER SERVICES	5	7	187.167-022
SEC	COUNTY HOME-DEMONSTRATION AGENT	5	7	096.121-010
SEC	COUNTY-AGRICULTURAL AGENT	5	7	096.127-010
SEC	DIRECTOR, COMMUNITY-HEALTH NURSING	5	8	075.117-014
SEC	DIRECTOR, CASTING	5	7	159.267-010
SEC	DIRECTOR, EMPLOYMENT RESEARCH AND PLANNING	5	8	050.117-010
SEC	DIRECTOR, MOTION PICTURE	5	8	159.067-010
SEC	DIRECTOR, NURSING SERVICE	5	8	075.117-022
SEC	DIRECTOR, OPERATIONS, BROADCAST	5	8	184.167-022
SEC	DIRECTOR, SCHOOL OF NURSING	5	8	075.117-030
SEC	DIRECTOR, TRANSLATION	5	8	137.137-010
SEC	DIRECTOR, UTILITY ACCOUNTS	5	8	160.267-014
SEC	DIRECTOR, VOLUNTEER SERVICES	5	7	187.167-038
SEC	DISK JOCKEY	5	5	159.147-014
SEC	EDUCATIONAL THERAPIST	5	7	094.227-010
SEC	EMPLOYMENT INTERVIEWER	5	5	166.267-010
SEC	EXTENSION SERVICE SPECIALIST	5	8	096.127-014
SEC	FEDERAL AID COORDINATOR	5	7	188.167-054
SEC	FINANCIAL-AIDS OFFICER	5	8	090.117-030
SEC	FOREIGN-STUDENT ADVISER	5	7	090.107-010
SEC	FUND RAISER 1	5	6	293.157-010
SEC	IMPORT-EXPORT AGENT	5	7	184.117-022
SEC	INSTITUTION LIBRARIAN	5	7	100.167-022
SEC	INSTRUCTOR, PHYSICAL EDUCATION	5	7	099.224-010
SEC	LIBRARIAN	5	7	100.127-014
SEC	LIBRARIAN, SPECIAL LIBRARY	5	7	100.167-026
SEC	MANAGER, CITY	5	8	188.117-114
SEC	MANAGER, PRODUCTION	5	7	184.167-074
SEC	MANAGER, SCHEDULE PLANNING	5	8	184.167-058
SEC	MANAGER, SOUND EFFECTS	5	7	962.167-010
SEC	NURSE, CONSULTANT	5	7	075.127-014
SEC	PARALEGAL ASSISTANT	5	7	119.267-026

Code	Title	GED	SVP	DOT No.
SEC	PAROLE OFFICER	5	7	195.167-030
SEC	PRISONER-CLASSIFICATION INTERVIEWER	5	7	166.267-022
SEC	PROBATION OFFICER	5	7	195.167-034
SEC	RESIDENCE COUNSELOR	5	7	045.107-038
SEC	RETIREMENT OFFICER	5	7	166.267-030
SEC	SOCIAL WORKER, SCHOOL	5	7	195.107-038
SEC	SUPERVISOR, EDUCATION	5	8	099.117-026
SEC	TEACHER, BLIND	5	7	094.227-014
SEC	TEACHER, DEAF	5	7	094.224-010
SEC	TEACHER, ELEMENTARY SCHOOL	5	7	092.227-010
SEC	TEACHER, HANDICAPPED STUDENTS	5	7	094.227-018
SEC	TEACHER, KINDERGARTEN	5	7	092.227-014
SEC	TEACHER, MENTALLY RETARDED	5	7	094.227-022
SEC	TEACHER, SECONDARY SCHOOL	5	7	091.227-010
SEC	TITLE CLERK	5	6	162.267-010
SEC	TRAINING REPRESENTATIVE	5	7	166.227-010
SEC	TUTOR	5	7	099.227-034
SEC	WELFARE DIRECTOR	5	8	188.117-126
SEC	AGENT-LICENSING CLERK	4	5	209.367-010
SEC	AIRPLANE-DISPATCH CLERK	4	5	248.367-010
SEC	ASTROLOGER	4	4	159.207-010
SEC	AUTOMOBILE-CLUB-SAFETY-PROGRAM COORDINATOR	4	6	249.167-010
SEC	CENTRAL-OFFICE-OPERATOR SUPERVISOR	4	6	235.132-010
SEC	CHILDREN'S TUTOR	4	5	099.227-010
SEC	CHRISTIAN SCIENCE NURSE	4	7	129.107-010
SEC	CLERK, TELEGRAPH SERVICE	4	5	219.362-022
SEC	COPYRIGHT EXPERT	4	7	249.267-010
SEC	COUNSELOR, CAMP	4	6	159.124-010
SEC	CUSTOMER-COMPLAINT CLERK	4	5	241.367-014
SEC	CUSTOMER-SERVICE REPRESENTATIVE SUPERVISOR	4	6	239.137-014
SEC	CUSTOMER-SERVICE-REPRESENTATIVE INSTRUCTOR	4	6	239.227-010
SEC	DISPATCHER	4	6	193.262-014
SEC	DISPATCHER	4	6	932.167-010
SEC	DISPATCHER, TRAFFIC OR SYSTEM	4	7	919.162-010
SEC	DOCUMENTATION SUPERVISOR	4	7	214.137-010
SEC	ELIGIBILITY-AND-OCCUPANCY INTERVIEWER	4	5	168.267-038
SEC	FINANCIAL-AID COUNSELOR	4	5	169.267-018
SEC	FIRE INSPECTOR	4	7	373.267-010
SEC	FLIGHT ATTENDANT, RAMP	4	6	352.367-014
SEC	HYPNOTHERAPIST	4	7	079.157-010
SEC	INFORMATION CLERK, AUTOMOBILE CLUB	4	5	237.267-010
SEC	INSTRUCTOR, APPAREL MANUFACTURE	4	6	789.222-010
SEC	INVESTIGATOR, FRAUD	4	7	376.267-014
SEC	LABOR EXPEDITER	4	5	249.167-018
SEC	MANAGEMENT AIDE	4	5	195.367-014
SEC	MANAGER, AQUATIC FACILITY	4	7	187.167-054
SEC	MANAGER, STATEMENT CLERKS	4	7	214.137-014
SEC	MANAGER, TOURING PRODUCTION	4	7	191.117-038
SEC	MEDICAL-SERVICE TECHNICIAN	4	7	079.367-018
SEC	NEWS ASSISTANT	4	3	209.367-038

Code	Title	GED	SVP	DOT No.
SEC	NURSE, LICENSED PRACTICAL	4	6	079.374-014
SEC	PHOTOGRAPHIC SUPERVISOR	4	7	976.137-010
SEC	POLICE LIEUTENANT, COMMUNITY RELATIONS	4	8	375.137-018
SEC	PRIVATE-BRANCH-EXCHANGE SERVICE ADVISER	4	6	235.222-010
SEC	RECORDIST, CHIEF	4	7	962.134-010
SEC	RECREATIONAL THERAPIST	4	6	076.124-014
SEC	RESIDENCE SUPERVISOR	4	6	187.167-186
SEC	SCOUT, PROFESSIONAL SPORTS	4	8	153.117-018
SEC	SHELVING SUPERVISOR	4	6	109.137-010
SEC	SHIPPING-AND-RECEIVING SUPERVISOR	4	6	222.137-030
SEC	SKIP TRACER	4	4	241.367-026
SEC	SUPERVISOR 1	4	6	692.132-010
SEC	SUPERVISOR, TELLERS	4	8	211.137-022
SEC	SUPERVISOR, ACCOUNTS RECEIVABLE	4	8	214.137-022
SEC	SUPERVISOR, CONTACT AND SERVICE CLERKS	4	7	249.137-014
SEC	SUPERVISOR, SURVEY WORKERS	4	6	205.137-014
SEC	SUPERVISOR, EXTERMINATION	4	6	389.134-010
SEC	SUPERVISOR, CANDY	4	7	529.130-010
SEC	SUPERVISOR, OPTICAL INSTRUMENT ASSEMBLY	4	7	711.137-010
SEC	SUPERVISOR, RUBBER STAMPS AND DIES	4	7	733.131-010
SEC	SUPERVISOR, DOPING	4	7	843.134-010
SEC	SUPERVISOR, CIRCUS	4	6	969.137-010
SEC	SUPERVISOR, RIDES	4	7	342.137-010
SEC	SUPERVISOR, PAPER TESTING	4	8	539.134-010
SEC	SUPERVISOR, INSPECTING	4	7	979.137-014
SEC	SUPERVISOR, ANIMAL CRUELTY INVESTIGATION	4	7	379.137-010
SEC	SUPERVISOR, FINISHING DEPARTMENT	4	6	976.137-014
SEC	SUPERVISOR, WATER SOFTENER SERVICE	4	8	862.134-014
SEC	SUPERVISOR, CREDIT AND LOAN COLLECTIONS	4	5	241.137-010
SEC	SUPERVISOR, CODING CLERKS	4	7	209.137-022
SEC	SUPERVISOR, FERRY TERMINAL	4	5	911.137-026
SEC	TEACHER, PRESCHOOL	4	7	092.227-018
SEC	TELEPHONE OPERATOR, CHIEF	4	6	235.137-010
SEC	TRAVEL COUNSELOR, AUTOMOBILE CLUB	4	5	238.167-014
SEC	AMBULANCE ATTENDANT	3	3	355.374-010
SEC	CHAPERON	3	2	359.667-010
SEC	CHILD MONITOR	3	3	301.677-010
SEC	COLORIST, PHOTOGRAPHY	3	6	970.381-010
SEC	COMMUNITY SERVICE OFFICER, PATROL	3	3	372.367-010
SEC	DETECTIVE 1	3	4	376.367-014
SEC	ESCORT	3	2	359.367-010
SEC	FIRST-AID ATTENDANT	3	3	354.677-010
SEC	FOSTER PARENT	3	3	309.677-014
SEC	GUARD, SECURITY	3	3	372.667-034
SEC	HORSE TRAINER	3	7	419.224-010
SEC	INSTRUCTOR, PHYSICAL	3	6	153.227-014
SEC	JUGGLER	3	6	159.341-010
SEC	MATERIAL EXPEDITER	3	4	221.367-042

Code	Title	GED	SVP	DOT No.
SEC	PASSENGER SERVICE REPRESENTATIVE	3	3	359.677-022
SEC	PATROL CONDUCTOR	3	3	372.677-010
SEC	PSYCHIATRIC AIDE	3	4	355.377-014
SEC	REGISTRAR	3	5	205.367-038
SEC	SUPERVISOR, MARKING ROOM	3	6	209.137-026
SEC	UNDERCOVER OPERATOR	3	4	376.367-026
SEC	WIG DRESSER	3	6	332.361-010
SEC	SCHOOL BUS MONITOR	2	2	372.667-042
SCR	PHILOLOGIST	5	8	059.067-010
SCR	CHIEF PROJECTIONIST	4	8	960.132-010
SCR	EXTENSION CLERK	4	5	219.362-030
SCR	MEDICAL ASSISTANT	4	6	079.367-010
SCR	PHYSICAL THERAPIST ASSISTANT	4	6	076.224-010
SCR	SUPERVISOR, SULFURIC-ACID PLANT	4	8	558.132-018
SCR	ARTIST, MANNEQUIN COLORING	3	4	741.684-010
SCR	BOW REHAIRER	3	6	730.684-022
SCR	INSPECTOR	3	3	732.364-010
SCR	LIBRARY CLERK, TALKING BOOKS	3	3	209.387-026
SCR	NITROGLYCERIN-SEPARATOR OPERATOR	3	4	551.685-102
SCR	OFFICE COPY SELECTOR	3	3	249.687-010
SCI	ECONOMIST (IAS)	5	7	050.067-010
SCI	EDITORIAL ASSISTANT	5	7	132.267-014
SCI	NURSE, INSTRUCTOR	5	7	075.121-010
SCI	PACKAGING ENGINEER	5	7	019.187-010
SCI	MEDICAL-RECORD CLERK	4	4	245.362-010
SCI	OPTOMETRIC ASSISTANT	4	6	079.364-014
SCA	SIGN WRITER, HAND	4	5	970.281-022
SCE	APPEALS REFEREE	6	8	119.267-014
SCE	CONSULTANT, EDUCATION	6	8	099.167-014
SCE	AGENT-CONTRACT CLERK	5	5	241.267-010
SCE	ANNOUNCER	5	6	159.147-010
SCE	APPRAISER, REAL ESTATE	5	7	191.267-010
SCE	CONTACT REPRESENTATIVE	5	6	169.167-018
SCE	COPYIST	5	7	152.267-010
SCE	COST-AND-SALES-RECORD SUPERVISOR	5	7	216.137-010
SCE	DIRECTOR, OCCUPATIONAL HEALTH NURSING	5	8	075.117-026
SCE	DIRECTOR, STATE-HISTORICAL SOCIETY	5	8	052.067-014
SCE	INSTRUCTOR, PSYCHIATRIC AIDE	5	7	075.127-010
SCE	MARKET-RESEARCH ANALYST 1 (IAS)	5	7	050.067-014
SCE	SUPERINTENDENT, RADIO COMMUNICATIONS	5	8	193.167-018
SCE	AIR-TRAFFIC-CONTROL SPECIALIST, STATION	4	7	193.162-014
SCE	BONDING AGENT	4	6	186.267-010
SCE	CAREER-GUIDANCE TECHNICIAN	4	6	249.367-014
SCE	COMMUNICATION-CENTER COORDINATOR	4	5	235.132-014
SCE	COMPUTER OPERATOR (ISC)	4	6	213.362-010
SCE	ELIGIBILITY WORKER	4	6	195.267-010
SCE	FIELD CASHIER	4	7	219.137-010

Code	Title	GED	SVP	DOT No.
SCE	INTERPRETER, DEAF	4	5	137.267-014
SCE	INVESTIGATOR, CASH SHORTAGE	4	6	376.267-010
SCE	MOHEL	4	6	129.271-010
SCE	MORTGAGE-CLOSING CLERK	4	5	219.362-038
SCE	OCCUPATIONAL THERAPY ASSISTANT	4	6	076.364-010
SCE	PODIATRIC ASSISTANT	4	6	079.374-018
SCE	REVIEWING OFFICER, DRIVER'S LICENSE	4	7	168.167-074
SCE	SUPERVISOR, WATERPROOFING	4	7	843.137-010
SCE	SUPERVISOR, AGENCY APPOINTMENTS	4	7	209.137-018
SCE	SUPERVISOR, CORRESPONDENCE SECTION	4	6	249.137-018
SCE	SUPERVISOR, CUTTING AND SPLICING	4	6	976.134-010
SCE	SUPERVISOR, MICROFILM DUPLICATING UNIT	4	7	976.131-018
SCE	SUPERVISOR, TRUST ACCOUNTS	4	7	219.132-014
SCE	SUPERVISOR, DATA-CONTROL CLERK	4	6	219.137-014
SCE	SUPERVISOR, SECURITIES VAULT	4	7	216.132-014
SCE	TEACHER AIDE 1	4	6	099.327-010
SCE	BLIND AIDE	3	3	359.573-010
SCE	DECORATOR, LIGHTING FIXTURES	3	3	749.684-018
SCE	SCOUT	3	4	408.381-010
SCE	STUNT PERFORMER	3	6	159.341-014
SCE	TAXICAB COORDINATOR	3	5	215.367-018
SCE	BLOOD-DONOR-UNIT ASSISTANT	2	2	245.367-014
SCE	JOCKEY-ROOM CUSTODIAN	2	3	346.667-010
SCE	PRINT-LINE INSPECTOR	2	2	652.687-034

ENTERPRISING OCCUPATIONS

Code	Title	GED	SVP	DOT No.
ERI	CHEMICAL-EQUIPMENT SALES ENGINEER	5	8	008.151-010
ERI	MAINTAINABILITY ENGINEER	5	8	019.081-010
ERI	MANAGER, BULK PLANT	5	8	181.117-010
ERI	REVENUE AGENT	5	7	160.167-050
ERI	SALES ENGINEER, MECHANICAL EQUIPMENT	5	8	007.151-010
ERI	SPECIAL AGENT	5	7	375.167-042
ERI	SUPERINTENDENT, DRILLING AND PRODUCTION	5	8	181.167-014
ERI	SUPERINTENDENT, MAINTENANCE OF WAY	5	8	182.167-030
ERI	SUPERINTENDENT, LOGGING	5	8	183.167-038
ERI	SUPERINTENDENT OF GENERATION	5	8	184.167-138
ERI	SUPERINTENDENT, METERS	5	8	184.167-194
ERI	SUPERINTENDENT, MAINTENANCE	5	8	189.167-046
ERI	DRAWING-KILN SUPERVISOR	4	5	575.137-010
ERI	FIELD ENGINEER	4	7	828.261-014
ERI	FUEL-SYSTEM-MAINTENANCE SUPERVISOR	4	7	638.131-010
ERI	MANAGER, BRANCH OPERATION EVALUATION	4	6	187.167-062
ERI	MANAGER, LAUNDROMAT	4	6	369.167-010
ERI	ROAD SUPERVISOR	4	6	913.133-010
ERI	SCHEDULE MAKER	4	5	913.167-018
ERI	SUPERINTENDENT, GREENS	4	7	406.137-014
ERI	SUPERVISOR, MACHINE-RECORDS UNIT	4	7	213.132-014
ERI	SUPERVISOR, CARBON ELECTRODES	4	6	549.137-010
ERI	SUPERVISOR, VENEER	4	6	569.135-010

Code	Title	GED	SVP	DOT No.
ERI	SUPERVISOR, PARTICLE BOARD	4	6	569.132-010
ERI	TRAFFIC-MAINTENANCE SUPERVISOR	4	7	869.137-010
ERI	DRIER OPERATOR 4 (REI)	3	4	553.685-054
ERI	KILN DRAWER (REI)	2	2	929.687-014
ERI	LOADER, MALT HOUSE (REI)	2	3	921.682-010
ERA	PARK SUPERINTENDENT	5	7	188.167-062
ERA	SUPERINTENDENT, MEASUREMENT	5	8	184.167-190
ERA	CONVERTER SUPERVISOR	4	6	513.132-010
ERA	SANITARIAN	4	7	529.137-014
ERA	SUPERINTENDENT, MAINTENANCE	4	7	184.167-170
ERA	SUPERVISOR, THRESHING DEPARTMENT	4	5	521.132-014
ERA	SUPERVISOR, OVENS	4	8	542.132-014
ERA	SUPERVISOR, COAL HANDLING	4	7	549.132-018
ERA	SUPERVISOR, COKE HANDLING	4	8	549.132-022
ERA	SUPERVISOR, RECLAMATION	4	7	850.133-010
ERA	SUPERVISOR, MARINA SALES AND SERVICE	4	5	299.137-026
ERA	CARBON-FURNACE OPERATOR (REA)	3	5	543.562-010
ERA	RAILWAY-EQUIPMENT OPERATOR	3	4	859.683-018
ERA	DUST BOX WORKER (RSE)	2	2	574.667-010
ERS	MANAGER, HARBOR DEPARTMENT	6	9	184.117-042
ERS	BROKER'S FLOOR REPRESENTATIVE	5	8	162.157-014
ERS	CHIEF BANK EXAMINER	5	8	160.167-046
ERS	COMMISSIONER OF CONCILIATION	5	8	188.217-010
ERS	CREDIT OFFICER, DEALER ACCOUNTS	5	7	161.267-014
ERS	DIRECTOR, RESEARCH AND DEVELOPMENT	5	8	189.117-014
ERS	LIAISON WORKER, TOOL FABRICATION	5	7	012.167-038
ERS	MANAGER, GAME BREEDING FARM	5	7	180.167-034
ERS	MANAGER, VEHICLE LEASING AND RENTAL	5	8	187.167-162
ERS	PILOT, HIGHWAY PATROL	5	6	375.163-014
ERS	RELOCATION COMMISSIONER	5	8	188.167-070
ERS	SALES ENGINEER, MINING-AND-OIL-WELL EQUIPMENT AND SERVICES	5	8	010.151-010
ERS	SALES REPRESENTATIVE, FOUNDRY AND MACHINE SHOP PRODUCTS	5	7	274.257-010
ERS	SUPERINTENDENT, OIL-WELL SERVICES	5	8	010.167-018
ERS	SUPERINTENDENT, CONSTRUCTION	5	8	182.167-026
ERS	SUPERINTENDENT, CAR CONSTRUCTION	5	8	183.167-034
ERS	SUPERINTENDENT, COMPRESSOR STATIONS	5	8	184.167-146
ERS	SUPERINTENDENT, DISTRIBUTION 2	5	8	184.167-154
ERS	SUPERINTENDENT, TERMINAL	5	8	184.167-214
ERS	ADMITTING OFFICER	4	7	205.137-010
ERS	AIRPORT-MAINTENANCE CHIEF	4	7	899.137-010
ERS	APPLIANCE-SERVICE SUPERVISOR	4	7	187.167-010
ERS	APPRAISER, AUTOMOBILE DAMAGE	4	7	241.267-014
ERS	BAGGAGE-AND-MAIL AGENT	4	6	910.137-010
ERS	BANK BOSS	4	7	851.137-010
ERS	BLENDING SUPERVISOR	4	6	520.132-010
ERS	BRICKLAYER SUPERVISOR	4	8	861.131-010
ERS	CABLE SUPERVISOR	4	8	184.161-010
ERS	CHEST-PAINTING AND SEALING SUPERVISOR	4	8	749.137-010

Code	Title	GED	SVP	DOT No.
ERS	CHIEF LOAD DISPATCHER	4	7	952.137-010
ERS	CLOTH FINISHER	4	7	589.130-010
ERS	COMMANDER, IDENTIFICATION AND RECORDS	4	8	375.137-010
ERS	CONDUCTOR, PULLMAN	4	6	198.167-014
ERS	CONTAINER COORDINATOR	4	6	248.367-022
ERS	COOK, MEXICAN FOOD	4	7	526.134-010
ERS	CUSTOMER-FACILITIES SUPERVISOR	4	7	822.131-014
ERS	DERRICK-BOAT CAPTAIN	4	7	911.137-014
ERS	DINING-SERVICE INSPECTOR	4	7	168.267-030
ERS	DISASTER OR DAMAGE CONTROL SPECIALIST	4	6	378.267-014
ERS	DISPATCHER	4	7	239.167-014
ERS	DISPATCHER, BUS AND TROLLEY	4	7	913.167-014
ERS	DISPATCHER, CHIEF 2	4	7	914.167-010
ERS	ESTIMATOR, PRINTING	4	6	221.367-014
ERS	EXAMINER	4	6	169.267-014
ERS	EXPLOSIVE-OPERATOR SUPERVISOR	4	8	694.132-010
ERS	FABRIC-COATING SUPERVISOR	4	8	589.130-014
ERS	FENCE-ERECTOR SUPERVISOR	4	7	869.134-010
ERS	FIRE MARSHAL	4	7	373.167-018
ERS	FIREARMS-ASSEMBLY SUPERVISOR	4	7	736.131-014
ERS	FLASH RANGING CREWMEMBER	4	5	378.367-018
ERS	FLIGHT-INFORMATION EXPEDITER	4	5	912.367-010
ERS	FOREST NURSERY SUPERVISOR	4	6	451.137-010
ERS	GAS DISPATCHER	4	8	953.167-010
ERS	GAS-PUMPING-STATION SUPERVISOR	4	7	953.137-010
ERS	GENERAL-HANDLING SUPERVISOR	4	6	929.137-010
ERS	GUIDE, HUNTING AND FISHING	4	7	353.161-010
ERS	HARVEST CONTRACTOR	4	7	409.117-010
ERS	HEAD OPERATOR, SULFIDE	4	8	559.132-026
ERS	HEATING-AND-BLENDING SUPERVISOR	4	8	559.132-030
ERS	HYDROELECTRIC-STATION OPERATOR, CHIEF	4	7	952.137-014
ERS	INCINERATOR-PLANT-GENERAL SUPERVISOR	4	6	184.167-046
ERS	INSPECTOR, GOVERNMENT PROPERTY	4	6	168.267-050
ERS	INSPECTOR, CHIEF	4	7	514.131-010
ERS	INSPECTOR, CHIEF	4	7	737.137-010
ERS	INSTRUCTOR, FLYING 2	4	6	097.227-010
ERS	INTELLIGENCE SPECIALIST	4	7	059.267-014
ERS	LINE SUPERVISOR	4	7	822.131-018
ERS	LOAD DISPATCHER	4	8	952.167-014
ERS	MAINTENANCE SUPERVISOR	4	7	891.137-010
ERS	MANAGER, AUTOMOBILE SERVICE STATION	4	7	185.167-014
ERS	MANAGER, INDUSTRIAL CAFETERIA	4	6	319.137-018
ERS	MANAGER, POULTRY HATCHERY	4	7	180.167-046
ERS	MANAGER, SALES	4	7	187.167-138
ERS	MANAGER, SERVICE DEPARTMENT	4	7	187.167-142
ERS	MANAGER, TRAFFIC 1	4	8	184.167-098
ERS	MATERIAL-CREW SUPERVISOR	4	7	921.137-014
ERS	MELTER SUPERVISOR	4	7	512.132-010
ERS	ORDER-DEPARTMENT SUPERVISOR	4	7	169.167-038
ERS	PIT SUPERVISOR	4	7	939.137-014

Code	Title	GED	SVP	DOT No.
ERS	POLEYARD SUPERVISOR	4	7	929.137-014
ERS	POLICE CAPTAIN, PRECINCT	4	7	375.167-034
ERS	PRESSURE SUPERVISOR	4	7	953.137-014
ERS	PRIMER SUPERVISOR	4	7	737.132-010
ERS	PRODUCTION MANAGER, REPRODUCTION	4	7	652.137-010
ERS	PROPERTY COORDINATOR	4	7	962.167-018
ERS	PROTECTIVE-SIGNAL SUPERINTENDENT	4	7	822.131-022
ERS	REDUCTION-PLANT SUPERVISOR	4	7	512.130-010
ERS	RETREAD SUPERVISOR	4	5	750.132-010
ERS	SALES CORRESPONDENT	4	6	221.367-062
ERS	SALES REPRESENTATIVE, RADIO AND TELEVISION TIME	4	6	259.357-018
ERS	SALES REPRESENTATIVE, INDUSTRIAL MACHINERY	4	5	274.357-038
ERS	SALES REPRESENTATIVE, ULTRASONIC EQUIPMENT	4	5	271.352-014
ERS	SALESPERSON, CORSETS	4	5	261.354-010
ERS	SALESPERSON, SEWING MACHINES	4	6	270.352-010
ERS	SALVAGE SUPERVISOR	4	7	559.137-010
ERS	SAMPLER, HEAD	4	7	519.130-014
ERS	SERVICE OBSERVER	4	4	239.367-026
ERS	SERVICE SUPERVISOR 1	4	7	953.137-018
ERS	SEWING SUPERVISOR	4	6	787.132-010
ERS	SIGNAL SUPERVISOR	4	7	822.131-026
ERS	STAMP ANALYST	4	6	299.387-014
ERS	STEEL-POST-INSTALLER SUPERVISOR	4	7	821.131-022
ERS	STEWARD/STEWARDESS	4	7	310.137-018
ERS	STEWARD/STEWARDESS, BANQUET	4	7	310.137-022
ERS	STOCKING-AND-BOX-SHOP SUPERVISOR	4	7	769.137-010
ERS	SUPERCARGO	4	7	248.167-010
ERS	SUPERINTENDENT, INDUSTRIES, CORRECTIONAL FACILITY	4	8	188.167-094
ERS	SUPERINTENDENT, BUILDING	4	7	187.167-190
ERS	SUPERINTENDENT, LAUNDRY	4	7	187.167-194
ERS	SUPERINTENDENT, TRACK	4	6	899.137-014
ERS	SUPERINTENDENT, STEVEDORING	4	7	911.137-022
ERS	SUPERVISOR	4	7	549.132-014
ERS	SUPERVISOR 2	4	7	559.137-014
ERS	SUPERVISOR	4	8	737.137-018
ERS	SUPERVISOR	4	7	750.130-010
ERS	SUPERVISOR 1	4	7	759.137-010
ERS	SUPERVISOR	4	5	783.132-010
ERS	SUPERVISOR	4	7	784.132-010
ERS	SUPERVISOR, DRY CLEANING	4	7	369.137-010
ERS	SUPERVISOR, AREA	4	7	401.137-010
ERS	SUPERVISOR, TREE-TRIMMING	4	6	408.137-014
ERS	SUPERVISOR, BLAST FURNACE	4	6	519.132-010
ERS	SUPERVISOR, COMPRESSED YEAST	4	7	520.132-014
ERS	SUPERVISOR, POWDERED SUGAR	4	7	521.130-014
ERS	SUPERVISOR, CUTTING AND BONING	4	7	525.131-014
ERS	SUPERVISOR, BEET END	4	7	529.132-018
ERS	SUPERVISOR, YARD	4	8	529.137-070
ERS	SUPERVISOR, MALTED MILK	4	7	529.132-070
ERS	SUPERVISOR, PULP PLANT	4	7	539.132-014

Code	Title	GED	SVP	DOT No.
ERS	SUPERVISOR, WET END	4	7	539.131-010
ERS	SUPERVISOR, BYPRODUCTS	4	7	542.132-010
ERS	SUPERVISOR, TOWER	4	7	549.130-010
ERS	SUPERVISOR, TREATING AND PUMPING	4	8	549.132-034
ERS	SUPERVISOR, PURIFICATION	4	7	549.132-030
ERS	SUPERVISOR, SPECIALTY PLANT	4	7	549.137-018
ERS	SUPERVISOR, COLOR-PASTE MIXING	4	7	550.135-010
ERS	SUPERVISOR, CHEMICAL	4	7	558.132-010
ERS	SUPERVISOR, ALUM PLANT	4	7	559.132-062
ERS	SUPERVISOR, BONE PLANT	4	8	559.132-066
ERS	SUPERVISOR, PHOSPHORUS PROCESSING	4	8	559.132-118
ERS	SUPERVISOR, PIGMENT MAKING	4	7	559.132-122
ERS	SUPERVISOR, VARNISH	4	8	559.132-134
ERS	SUPERVISOR, COOK HOUSE	4	7	559.132-074
ERS	SUPERVISOR, DRY PASTE	4	7	559.132-082
ERS	SUPERVISOR, PUTTY AND CALKING	4	7	559.137-042
ERS	SUPERVISOR, PAINTING DEPARTMENT	4	7	692.137-010
ERS	SUPERVISOR, MIRROR MANUFACTURING DEPARTMENT	4	7	579.131-010
ERS	SUPERVISOR, RECEIVING AND PROCESSING	4	7	579.137-026
ERS	SUPERVISOR, TAN ROOM	4	7	582.132-018
ERS	SUPERVISOR, PRESSING DEPARTMENT	4	7	583.132-010
ERS	SUPERVISOR, FINISHING ROOM	4	7	589.130-018
ERS	SUPERVISOR, SPLIT AND DRUM ROOM	4	7	589.132-014
ERS	SUPERVISOR, GARAGE	4	7	620.131-014
ERS	SUPERVISOR, MOTORCYCLE REPAIR SHOP	4	8	620.131-018
ERS	SUPERVISOR, AIRCRAFT MAINTENANCE	4	8	621.131-014
ERS	SUPERVISOR, DECORATING	4	6	652.130-010
ERS	SUPERVISOR, MACHINING	4	7	669.130-022
ERS	SUPERVISOR, ASSEMBLY-AND-PACKING	4	7	701.137-010
ERS	SUPERVISOR, GAS METER REPAIR	4	8	710.131-010
ERS	SUPERVISOR, METER REPAIR SHOP	4	8	710.131-026
ERS	SUPERVISOR, DIALS	4	7	715.131-014
ERS	SUPERVISOR, HAIRSPRING FABRICATION	4	7	715.131-018
ERS	SUPERVISOR, MAINSPRING FABRICATION	4	7	715.131-026
ERS	SUPERVISOR, INSPECTION	4	7	715.131-022
ERS	SUPERVISOR, COIL WINDING	4	7	724.131-010
ERS	SUPERVISOR, FINISHING DEPARTMENT	4	7	733.137-014
ERS	SUPERVISOR, INSPECTION	4	7	733.137-018
ERS	SUPERVISOR, BELT-AND-LINK ASSEMBLY	4	8	737.137-022
ERS	SUPERVISOR, LAMP SHADES	4	7	739.137-014
ERS	SUPERVISOR, FINISHING	4	8	749.134-010
ERS	SUPERVISOR, CHIMNEY CONSTRUCTION	4	8	801.131-010
ERS	SUPERVISOR, INSPECTION AND TESTING	4	8	806.131-026
ERS	SUPERVISOR, PAINTING	4	8	840.131-010
ERS	SUPERVISOR, LABOR GANG	4	6	850.137-014
ERS	SUPERVISOR, MIXING PLACE	4	7	853.137-010
ERS	SUPERVISOR, ASPHALT PAVING	4	8	853.133-010
ERS	SUPERVISOR, GRADING	4	7	859.137-010
ERS	SUPERVISOR, CAB	4	7	913.133-014
ERS	SUPERVISOR, PUMPING	4	7	914.131-010
ERS	SUPERVISOR, LOADING AND UNLOADING	4	6	922.137-018
ERS	SUPERVISOR, EGG PROCESSING	4	7	529.137-042

Code	Title	GED	SVP	DOT No.
ERS	SUPERVISOR, ICE HOUSE	4	7	523.137-010
ERS	SUPERVISOR, LOGGING	4	7	459.133-010
ERS	SUPERVISOR, ACOUSTICAL TILE CARPENTERS	4	8	860.131-010
ERS	SUPERVISOR, REPULPING	4	8	539.132-018
ERS	SUPERVISOR, BROOMMAKING	4	6	692.130-026
ERS	SUPERVISOR, PLASTERING	4	7	842.131-018
ERS	SUPERVISOR, SHED WORKERS	4	7	404.131-014
ERS	SUPERVISOR, ASSEMBLY	4	7	769.137-014
ERS	SUPERVISOR, DRYING	4	6	563.135-010
ERS	SUPERVISOR, DIMENSION WAREHOUSE	4	7	769.134-010
ERS	SURGICAL TECHNICIAN	4	6	079.374-022
ERS	TIRE-SERVICE SUPERVISOR	4	6	915.134-010
ERS	TRACER-BULLET-SECTION SUPERVISOR	4	8	694.131-010
ERS	TRANSFORMER ASSEMBLY SUPERVISOR	4	7	820.137-010
ERS	TRUCK SUPERVISOR	4	8	909.137-018
ERS	UNCLAIMED PROPERTY OFFICER	4	7	188.167-106
ERS	WAREHOUSE SUPERVISOR	4	7	929.137-018
ERS	WHARFINGER, CHIEF	4	8	184.167-274
ERS	WOOD-CREW SUPERVISOR	4	7	564.132-010
ERS	YARD MANAGER	4	6	910.137-046
ERS	YARD SUPERVISOR, COTTON GIN	4	6	929.137-034
ERS	YARD SUPERVISOR, BUILDING MATERIALS OR LUMBER	4	7	929.137-030
ERS	YARD SUPERVISOR	4	7	929.137-026
ERS	BARTENDER	3	3	312.474-010
ERS	CAR CHASER	3	6	910.167-010
ERS	CAR-CLEANING SUPERVISOR	3	6	910.137-014
ERS	COACH DRIVER	3	3	349.677-014
ERS	COIN-MACHINE-COLLECTOR SUPERVISOR	3	5	292.137-010
ERS	ELEVATOR STARTER	3	6	388.367-010
ERS	EXPRESS CLERK	3	4	222.367-022
ERS	FIBERGLASS LAMINATOR	3	4	806.684-054
ERS	FIELD ARTILLERY SENIOR SERGEANT	3	8	378.132-010
ERS	FLIGHT OPERATIONS SPECIALIST	3	6	248.387-010
ERS	GATE AGENT	3	4	238.367-010
ERS	HORSE-RACE STARTER	3	4	153.267-010
ERS	IDENTIFIER, HORSE	3	3	153.387-010
ERS	INFANTRY UNIT LEADER	3	7	378.137-010
ERS	INSPECTOR-REPAIRER	3	4	734.684-018
ERS	LITHO-MAKE-READY ASSISTANT	3	6	972.664-010
ERS	MAINTENANCE DATA ANALYST	3	5	221.367-038
ERS	MANAGER, APARTMENT HOUSE	3	6	186.167-018
ERS	PERSONAL PROPERTY ASSESSOR	3	4	191.367-010
ERS	PIGMENT PROCESSOR	3	3	559.685-130
ERS	PRINT INSPECTOR	3	5	976.687-022
ERS	RADIO-MESSAGE ROUTER	3	5	235.387-010
ERS	RECONNAISSANCE CREWMEMBER	3	4	378.367-030
ERS	SALES CLERK, FOOD	3	3	290.477-018
ERS	SALES REPRESENTATIVE	3	5	250.357-022
ERS	SCALP-TREATMENT OPERATOR	3	5	339.371-014
ERS	SKI PATROLLER	3	6	379.664-010
ERS	STEWARD/STEWARDESS, WINE	3	4	350.677-026
ERS	STREETCAR OPERATOR	3	3	913.463-014

Code	Title	GED	SVP	DOT No.
ERS	SUPERVISOR	3	5	570.137-010
ERS	SUPERVISOR, CHRISTMAS-TREE FARM	3	5	451.137-014
ERS	SUPERVISOR, FEED MILL	3	7	529.132-054
ERS	SUPERVISOR, RAG ROOM	3	5	539.137-010
ERS	SUPERVISOR, MOLD-MAKING PLASTICS SHEETS	3	6	579.137-022
ERS	SUPERVISOR, SKI PRODUCTION	3	6	692.132-018
ERS	SUPERVISOR, CIGAR MAKING, HAND	3	6	790.134-010
ERS	TANK AND AMPHIBIAN TRACTOR OPERATIONS CHIEF	3	7	620.137-010
ERS	WATCH-AND-CLOCK-REPAIR CLERK	3	5	299.367-018
ERS	YARD SUPERVISOR	3	6	922.137-030
ERS	BELLHOP	2	2	324.677-010
ERS	CANTEEN OPERATOR	2	3	311.674-010
ERS	CARETAKER	2	2	301.687-010
ERS	COMBAT SURVEILLANCE AND TARGET ACQUISITION CREWMEMBER	2	2	378.687-010
ERS	DELIVERER, MERCHANDISE	2	2	299.477-010
ERS	DEPUTY SHERIFF, BUILDING GUARD	2	3	377.667-014
ERS	DOORKEEPER	2	2	324.677-014
ERS	FUR GLAZER	2	2	369.684-010
ERS	LUNCH-TRUCK DRIVER	2	2	292.463-010
ERS	PHOTOFINISHING LABORATORY WORKER	2	3	976.687-018
ERS	PORTER, BAGGAGE	2	2	324.477-010
ERS	STRIPER, MACHINE	2	2	749.686-010
ERS	TAILER	2	3	930.666-014
ERS	VAULT ATTENDANT	2	2	249.677-010
ERS	PAINT POURER	1	1	652.687-022
ERC	CEPHALOMETRIC ANALYST	4	6	078.384-010
ERC	DENTAL HYGIENIST (SAI)	4	6	078.361-010
ERC	LEAD-BURNER SUPERVISOR	4	7	819.131-010
ERC	MILL SUPERVISOR	4	7	515.130-010
ERC	SUPERVISOR, INSTRUMENT REPAIR	4	7	710.131-022
ERC	ASSEMBLER, MECHANICAL ORDNANCE	3	3	737.684-010
ERC	AUTOMOBILE-RENTAL CLERK	3	4	295.477-010
ERC	BABY-STROLLER AND WHEELCHAIR RENTAL CLERK	3	2	295.367-014
ERC	CAUSTICISER	3	4	558.382-018
ERC	CIRCULATION CLERK	3	3	209.362-010
ERC	CONTROLLER, COAL OR ORE	3	6	939.167-010
ERC	SHEET WRITER	3	2	211.467-026
ERC	SMOKING-PIPE REPAIRER	3	5	739.484-018
ERC	BAR ATTENDANT	2	2	312.477-010
ERC	BICYCLE-RENTAL CLERK	2	2	295.467-010
ERC	BOLTER HELPER	2	2	521.686-010
ERC	BONE-CHAR OPERATOR	2	2	553.686-010
ERC	CABANA ATTENDANT	2	3	349.677-010
ERC	CUPROUS-CHLORIDE HELPER	2	2	558.585-022
ERC	EXPELLER OPERATOR	2	4	529.685-106
ERC	EXTRA	2	2	159.647-014
ERC	FILTER-PRESS TENDER	2	2	521.685-130
ERC	INSTANTIZER OPERATOR	2	3	523.685-106
ERC	SERVICE ATTENDANT, SLEEPING CAR	2	2	351.677-010

Code	Title	GED	SVP	DOT No.
ERC	SKI TOPPER	2	2	692.685-170
ERC	TANK PROCESSOR	2	2	891.687-026
ERC	TAPROOM ATTENDANT	2	2	312.677-010
ERC	TRAFFIC CHECKER	2	2	205.367-058
ERC	BULKER	1	2	522.687-018
ERC	BUNDLES HANGER	1	1	529.686-010
ERC	FARMWORKER, VEGETABLE 2	1	2	402.687-010
ERC	MOLD SHEET CLEANER	1	2	700.687-046
EIR	BUSINESS-ENTERPRISE OFFICER	5	6	188.117-014
EIR	FOREIGN-EXCHANGE TRADER	5	8	186.167-014
EIR	INDUSTRIAL ENGINEER	5	7	012.167-030
EIR	MAINTENANCE SUPERVISOR	5	8	184.167-050
EIR	PORT ENGINEER	5	8	014.167-014
EIR	PROGRAM MANAGER	5	8	189.167-030
EIR	SALES REPRESENTATIVE, WEIGHING AND FORCE-MEASUREMENT INSTRUMENTS	5	6	276.257-014
EIR	SECRETARY, BOARD-OF-EDUCATION	5	7	169.267-022
EIR	SUPERVISOR, WATERWORKS	5	7	184.167-246
EIR	SUPERVISOR, SEWER SYSTEM	5	8	184.167-238
EIR	SURVEYOR, GEODETIC	5	7	018.167-038
EIR	CONTRACTOR	4	7	182.167-010
EIR	INSTRUCTOR, BUS, TROLLEY, AND TAXI	4	6	919.223-010
EIR	SUPERINTENDENT, PRODUCTION	4	7	180.167-058
EIR	COSTUMER ASSISTANT	3	4	346.374-010
EIR	MOTORCYCLE RACER	3	5	153.243-014
EIA	AUDITOR, COUNTY OR CITY	5	6	160.167-030
EIA	COMMUNICATIONS CONSULTANT	5	6	253.157-010
EIA	SUPERVISOR, VENDOR QUALITY	5	7	012.167-062
EIS	EDUCATIONAL SPECIALIST	6	8	099.167-022
EIS	MANAGER, EDUCATION AND TRAINING	6	7	166.167-026
EIS	BATTALION CHIEF	5	8	373.167-010
EIS	BUYER, GRAIN	5	8	162.167-010
EIS	CONTROLLER	5	8	186.117-014
EIS	DIRECTOR, FOOD SERVICES	5	7	187.167-026
EIS	EXECUTIVE HOUSEKEEPER	5	6	187.167-046
EIS	LABORATORY SUPERVISOR	5	7	022.137-010
EIS	MANAGER, DENTAL LABORATORY	5	7	187.167-090
EIS	MANUAL-ARTS THERAPIST (SRE)	4	7	076.124-010
EIC	INDUSTRIAL-HEALTH ENGINEER	5	7	012.167-034
EIC	PRODUCTION ENGINEER	5	7	012.167-046
EAR	FIRE WARDEN	5	7	452.167-010
EAR	LOCATION MANAGER	4	6	191.167-018
EAR	SUPERINTENDENT, CONCRETE-MIXING PLANT	4	6	182.167-022
EAR	SUPERVISOR, PREPARATION PLANT	4	7	549.137-014
EAR	SUPERVISOR, SEWING ROOM	4	5	787.132-014
EAI	DEPARTMENT HEAD, COLLEGE OR UNIVERSITY	6	8	090.167-010

Code	Title	GED	SVP	DOT No.
EAI	DIRECTOR OF VITAL STATISTICS	5	8	188.167-022
EAI	MANAGER, RECORDS ANALYSIS	5	8	161.167-018
EAI	SALES REPRESENTATIVE, ELEVATORS, ESCALATORS, AND DUMBWAITERS	5	5	274.157-010
EAI	SUPERVISOR, WOOL-SHEARING	4	7	410.134-014
EAI	SUPERVISOR, INSECT AND DISEASE INSPECTION	4	6	408.137-010
EAS	COLUMNIST/COMMENTATOR	6	7	131.067-010
EAS	AUDIOVISUAL LIBRARIAN	5	7	100.167-010
EAS	BROKER-AND-MARKET OPERATOR, GRAIN	5	7	162.157-010
EAS	DIRECTOR, COUNCIL ON AGING	5	8	188.117-058
EAS	FASHION COORDINATOR	5	7	185.157-010
EAS	FIELD REPRESENTATIVE	5	6	163.267-010
EAS	FIELD SUPERVISOR, SEED PRODUCTION	5	6	180.167-014
EAS	MANAGER, FORMS ANALYSIS	5	8	161.167-014
EAS	MANAGER, HOUSING PROJECT	5	7	186.167-030
EAS	MANAGER, REPORTS ANALYSIS	5	8	161.167-022
EAS	MUSIC SUPERVISOR	5	8	099.167-026
EAS	PUBLIC-RELATIONS REPRESENTATIVE	5	7	165.067-010
EAS	REPORTER	5	7	131.267-018
EAS	SUPERINTENDENT, TESTS	5	9	184.167-218
EAS	ARTIFICIAL-BREEDING DISTRIBUTOR	4	7	180.167-010
EAS	COMMISSION AGENT, LIVESTOCK	4	6	162.157-026
EAS	CRATING-AND-MOVING ESTIMATOR	4	5	252.357-010
EAS	MILL SUPERVISOR	4	7	559.132-034
EAS	RING CONDUCTOR	4	6	159.367-010
EAS	SALES REPRESENTATIVE, UPHOLSTERY AND FURNITURE REPAIR	4	5	259.357-026
EAS	SALES REPRESENTATIVE, WATER-SOFTENING EQUIPMENT	4	5	279.357-034
EAS	SALESPERSON, SHOES	4	3	261.357-062
EAS	SALESPERSON, MEN'S AND BOYS' CLOTHING	4	5	261.357-050
EAS	SALESPERSON, MILLINERY	4	3	261.357-058
EAS	SALESPERSON, WOMEN'S APPAREL AND ACCESSORIES	4	3	261.357-066
EAS	SALESPERSON, YARD GOODS	4	3	261.357-070
EAS	SUPERVISOR	4	7	579.137-010
EAS	SUPERVISOR, FRUIT GRADING	4	6	529.137-046
EAS	IMPERSONATOR, CHARACTER	3	2	299.647-010
EAS	MODEL	3	3	297.667-014
EAC	CLOWN	4	6	159.047-010
EAC	MINE INSPECTOR	4	6	168.267-074
ESR	ASSESSOR-COLLECTOR, IRRIGATION TAX	5	8	188.167-014
ESR	BUSINESS MANAGER, COLLEGE OR UNIVERSITY	5	8	186.117-010
ESR	CLAIM ADJUSTER	5	6	241.217-010
ESR	CLEAN-RICE BROKER	5	7	162.167-018
ESR	CONFIGURATION MANAGEMENT ANALYST	5	8	012.167-010
ESR	COUNTERINTELLIGENCE AGENT	5	7	378.267-010
ESR	CREDIT ANALYST	5	8	191.267-014

Code	Title	GED	SVP	DOT No.
ESR	CUSTOMS-HOUSE BROKER	5	8	186.117-018
ESR	DEPUTY INSURANCE COMMISSIONER	5	8	186.117-022
ESR	DIRECTOR, EMPLOYMENT SERVICES	5	8	188.117-078
ESR	DIRECTOR, MEDICAL FACILITIES SECTION	5	8	188.117-082
ESR	DIRECTOR, PHOTOGRAMMETRY FLIGHT OPERATIONS	5	8	184.167-026
ESR	DIRECTOR, SUMMER SESSIONS	5	9	090.167-026
ESR	DIRECTOR, SPORTS	5	8	184.167-034
ESR	DIRECTOR, TRANSPORTATION	5	8	184.117-014
ESR	EXECUTIVE SECRETARY, STATE BOARD OF NURSING	5	8	169.117-010
ESR	FIELD-CONTACT TECHNICIAN	5	7	162.117-026
ESR	FREIGHT-TRAFFIC CONSULTANT	5	8	184.267-010
ESR	GENERAL MANAGER, FARM	5	8	180.167-018
ESR	GENERAL SUPERINTENDENT, MILLING	5	8	183.167-014
ESR	HARBOR MASTER	5	8	375.167-026
ESR	HEAD COACH	5	9	153.117-010
ESR	INSPECTOR, MOTOR VEHICLES	5	7	168.267-058
ESR	MANAGER, AGRICULTURAL-LABOR CAMP	5	7	187.167-050
ESR	MANAGER, AIRPORT	5	8	184.117-026
ESR	MANAGER, ATHLETE	5	7	153.117-014
ESR	MANAGER, AUTOMOTIVE SERVICES	5	8	184.117-034
ESR	MANAGER, BROKERAGE OFFICE	5	8	186.117-034
ESR	MANAGER, CARGO-AND-RAMP-SERVICES	5	8	184.167-058
ESR	MANAGER, COMPENSATION	5	8	166.167-022
ESR	MANAGER, CUSTOMER TECHNICAL SERVICES	5	8	189.117-018
ESR	MANAGER, FINANCIAL INSTITUTION	5	8	186.117-038
ESR	MANAGER, FLIGHT CONTROL	5	8	184.167-066
ESR	MANAGER, FOOD PROCESSING PLANT	5	8	183.167-026
ESR	MANAGER, HOTEL OR MOTEL	5	8	187.117-038
ESR	MANAGER, INDUSTRIAL ORGANIZATION	5	8	189.117-022
ESR	MANAGER, IRRIGATION DISTRICT	5	9	184.117-046
ESR	MANAGER, LABOR RELATIONS	5	8	166.167-034
ESR	MANAGER, LEASING	5	8	186.117-046
ESR	MANAGER, OPERATIONS	5	8	184.117-050
ESR	MANAGER, PROPERTY	5	8	186.167-046
ESR	MANAGER, REGIONAL	5	8	184.117-054
ESR	MANAGER, STATION	5	8	184.117-062
ESR	MANAGER, TRAFFIC	5	8	184.167-094
ESR	MANAGER, UTILITY SALES AND SERVICE	5	8	163.167-022
ESR	MANAGER, WAREHOUSE	5	8	184.167-114
ESR	MINE SUPERINTENDENT	5	8	181.117-014
ESR	NEWSCASTER	5	7	131.267-010
ESR	NEWSWRITER	5	7	131.267-014
ESR	PERMIT AGENT, GEOPHYSICAL PROSPECTING	5	6	191.117-042
ESR	POLICE COMMISSIONER I	5	8	188.117-118
ESR	PORT PURSER	5	8	166.167-038
ESR	PRESIDENT, EDUCATIONAL INSTITUTION	5	9	090.117-034
ESR	PRODUCTION SUPERINTENDENT	5	8	183.117-014
ESR	PROPERTY-DISPOSAL OFFICER	5	7	163.167-026
ESR	REAL-ESTATE AGENT	5	8	186.117-058

Code	Title	GED	SVP	DOT No.
ESR	REGULATORY ADMINISTRATOR	5	8	168.167-070
ESR	RIGHT-OF-WAY AGENT	5	7	191.117-046
ESR	ROADS SUPERVISOR	5	8	188.167-078
ESR	SAFETY INSPECTOR	5	8	168.167-078
ESR	SALES REPRESENTATIVE, COMPUTERS AND EDP SYSTEMS	5	6	275.257-010
ESR	SECRETARY OF STATE	5	8	188.167-082
ESR	SECTIONAL CENTER MANAGER, POSTAL SERVICE	5	8	188.167-086
ESR	SHERIFF, DEPUTY, CHIEF	5	9	377.117-010
ESR	SUPERINTENDENT, COMMISSARY	5	8	184.117-078
ESR	SUPERINTENDENT, COMMUNICATIONS	5	8	184.117-082
ESR	SUPERINTENDENT, DIVISION	5	8	184.167-158
ESR	SUPERINTENDENT, MARINE	5	8	184.167-182
ESR	SUPERINTENDENT, PIPE-LINES	5	8	184.167-198
ESR	SUPERINTENDENT, POWER	5	8	184.167-202
ESR	SUPERINTENDENT, TRANSPORTATION	5	8	184.167-226
ESR	SUPERINTENDENT, PLANT PROTECTION	5	8	189.167-050
ESR	TRAFFIC AGENT	5	7	252.257-010
ESR	TRANSPORTATION-MAINTENANCE SUPERVISOR	5	8	184.167-266
ESR	TREASURER	5	8	161.117-018
ESR	TREASURER, FINANCIAL INSTITUTION	5	9	186.117-070
ESR	TRUST OFFICER	5	8	186.117-074
ESR	URBAN PLANNER (IRE)	5	8	199.167-014
ESR	VICE PRESIDENT, FINANCIAL INSTITUTION	5	8	186.117-078
ESR	VICE PRESIDENT	5	8	189.117-034
ESR	ACID SUPERVISOR	4	7	559.132-010
ESR	ADMISSIONS EVALUATOR	4	6	205.367-010
ESR	ADVANCE AGENT	4	7	191.167-010
ESR	AIRPLANE-FLIGHT ATTENDANT	4	3	352.367-010
ESR	ANNOUNCER	4	6	159.347-010
ESR	BARN BOSS	4	7	410.131-010
ESR	BOAT DISPATCHER	4	7	184.167-010
ESR	BOOKING SUPERVISOR	4	6	248.137-010
ESR	BOOKMOBILE LIBRARIAN	4	7	100.167-014
ESR	BOXING-AND-PRESSING SUPERVISOR	4	6	789.137-010
ESR	BUS DISPATCHER, INTERSTATE	4	5	913.167-010
ESR	BUYER, ASSISTANT	4	6	162.157-022
ESR	CALENDER SUPERVISOR	4	7	559.132-014
ESR	CATALYST OPERATOR, CHIEF	4	7	559.132-018
ESR	CHEF	4	7	313.131-014
ESR	CHIEF CLERK, PRINT SHOP	4	6	207.137-010
ESR	CIRCUS AGENT	4	7	191.117-022
ESR	CLAIMS CLERK	4	5	241.387-010
ESR	COMMANDING OFFICER, HOMICIDE SQUAD	4	7	375.167-010
ESR	COMMANDING OFFICER, INVESTIGATION DIVISION	4	7	375.167-014
ESR	COMMISSARY MANAGER	4	6	185.167-010
ESR	COMMISSION AGENT, AGRICULTURAL PRODUCE	4	6	260.357-010
ESR	CONCRETE-BATCHING AND MIXING-PLANT SUPERVISOR	4	7	570.132-010

Code	Title	GED	SVP	DOT No.
ESR	CONDUCTOR, YARD	4	6	910.137-022
ESR	CONTROL CLERK, HEAD	4	6	221.137-010
ESR	CREDIT ANALYST	4	7	241.267-022
ESR	CREW SCHEDULER, CHIEF	4	7	215.137-010
ESR	DEALER-COMPLIANCE REPRESENTATIVE	4	6	168.267-026
ESR	DEPUTY SHERIFF, CHIEF	4	8	377.167-010
ESR	DEPUTY SHERIFF, COMMANDER, CIVIL DIVISION	4	7	377.137-010
ESR	DIRECTOR, FUNERAL	4	7	187.167-030
ESR	DISPATCHER	4	6	849.137-010
ESR	DISPATCHER, READY-MIX PLANT	4	6	849.137-014
ESR	DISPATCHER, OIL	4	7	914.167-014
ESR	DISPATCHER, SERVICE OR WORK	4	7	952.167-010
ESR	DISPATCHER, CHIEF, SERVICE OR WORK	4	7	959.137-010
ESR	DISPATCHER, SERVICE, CHIEF	4	7	959.137-014
ESR	DREDGE MATE	4	7	197.137-010
ESR	DRIVER SUPERVISOR	4	7	909.137-010
ESR	ELECTRIC MOTOR REPAIRING SUPERVISOR	4	7	721.131-010
ESR	ELECTRICAL-APPLIANCE-SERVICER SUPERVISOR	4	7	827.131-010
ESR	ELECTRICIAN, CHIEF	4	7	824.137-010
ESR	EXAMINATION PROCTOR	4	5	199.267-018
ESR	EXHIBIT-DISPLAY REPRESENTATIVE	4	5	297.367-010
ESR	FILM-VAULT SUPERVISOR	4	7	222.137-010
ESR	FIRE MARSHAL	4	7	373.267-014
ESR	FOOD-SERVICE SUPERVISOR	4	6	319.137-010
ESR	GENERAL SUPERVISOR	4	8	183.167-022
ESR	GRIP BOSS	4	8	962.137-010
ESR	HOST/HOSTESS, RESTAURANT	4	6	310.137-010
ESR	HOUSEKEEPER, HOME	4	6	301.137-010
ESR	INSTRUCTOR, SPORTS	4	8	153.227-018
ESR	INVESTIGATOR, UTILITY-BILL COMPLAINTS	4	6	241.267-034
ESR	JAILER, CHIEF	4	7	372.167-018
ESR	LABORATORY CHIEF	4	8	976.131-010
ESR	LAND-LEASING EXAMINER	4	7	237.367-026
ESR	LANDSCAPE CONTRACTOR	4	8	182.167-014
ESR	LINEN-ROOM SUPERVISOR	4	6	222.137-014
ESR	LOAN CLOSER	4	6	249.367-050
ESR	MAGAZINE SUPERVISOR	4	6	222.137-018
ESR	MAILROOM SUPERVISOR	4	6	209.137-010
ESR	MAILROOM SUPERVISOR	4	7	222.137-022
ESR	MANAGEMENT TRAINEE	4	6	189.167-018
ESR	MANAGER, BUS TRANSPORTATION	4	8	184.167-054
ESR	MANAGER, CAMP	4	6	187.167-066
ESR	MANAGER, CARDROOM	4	7	343.137-010
ESR	MANAGER, CEMETERY	4	7	187.167-074
ESR	MANAGER, CUSTOMER SERVICES	4	8	187.167-082
ESR	MANAGER, DAIRY FARM	4	8	180.167-026
ESR	MANAGER, DEPARTMENT	4	6	299.137-010
ESR	MANAGER, FIELD PARTY, GEOPHYSICAL PROSPECTING	4	6	181.167-010
ESR	MANAGER, FOOD SERVICE	4	7	187.167-106
ESR	MANAGER, FRONT OFFICE	4	6	187.167-110

Code	Title	GED	SVP	DOT No.
ESR	MANAGER, HEALTH CLUB	4	7	339.137-010
ESR	MANAGER, LAND LEASES-AND-RENTALS	4	7	186.167-038
ESR	MANAGER, LIQUOR ESTABLISHMENT	4	6	187.167-126
ESR	MANAGER, LODGING FACILITIES	4	7	320.137-014
ESR	MANAGER, MACHINERY-OR-EQUIPMENT, RENTAL AND LEASING	4	6	185.167-026
ESR	MANAGER, MERCHANDISE	4	7	185.167-034
ESR	MANAGER, OFFICE	4	7	169.167-034
ESR	MANAGER, OFFICE	4	8	188.167-058
ESR	MANAGER, RETAIL STORE	4	7	185.167-046
ESR	MANAGER, RESERVATIONS	4	5	238.137-010
ESR	MANAGER, SKATING RINK	4	6	187.167-146
ESR	MANAGER, SOLID-WASTE-DISPOSAL	4	7	184.167-078
ESR	MANAGER, THEATER	4	7	187.167-154
ESR	MANAGER, TOBACCO WAREHOUSE	4	8	185.167-054
ESR	MANAGER, TRUCK TERMINAL	4	8	184.167-110
ESR	MANAGER, TRAVEL AGENCY	4	7	187.167-158
ESR	MASTER, RIVERBOAT	4	7	197.163-018
ESR	MATERIAL COORDINATOR	4	6	221.167-014
ESR	MILLING SUPERVISOR	4	7	570.132-014
ESR	OFFICE-MACHINE-SERVICE SUPERVISOR	4	7	633.131-010
ESR	PACKING-HOUSE SUPERVISOR	4	6	920.137-010
ESR	PARK RANGER	4	7	169.167-042
ESR	PAYROLL CLERK, CHIEF	4	8	215.137-014
ESR	PERSONAL SHOPPER	4	5	296.357-010
ESR	PIT STEWARD	4	6	153.167-014
ESR	POLICE INSPECTOR 1	4	7	375.267-026
ESR	POLICE INSPECTOR 2	4	5	375.267-030
ESR	POLICE LIEUTENANT, PATROL	4	8	375.167-038
ESR	POLICE-ACADEMY INSTRUCTOR	4	7	375.227-010
ESR	PORCELAIN-ENAMELING SUPERVISOR	4	7	590.131-010
ESR	POSTMASTER	4	7	188.167-066
ESR	POTATO-CHIP-PROCESSING SUPERVISOR	4	6	526.137-010
ESR	PREPARATION SUPERVISOR	4	7	529.137-010
ESR	PRIZE COORDINATOR	4	5	162.167-026
ESR	PRODUCTION COORDINATOR	4	6	221.167-018
ESR	PRODUCTION SUPERVISOR, ANHYDROUS AMMONIA	4	8	559.132-046
ESR	PROGRAM ASSISTANT	4	5	962.167-014
ESR	PUBLIC HEALTH REGISTRAR	4	7	169.167-046
ESR	PURCHASING-AND-CLAIMS SUPERVISOR	4	6	248.137-014
ESR	ROW BOSS, HOEING	4	7	409.137-014
ESR	SACK-DEPARTMENT SUPERVISOR	4	6	229.137-010
ESR	SALES AGENT, INSURANCE	4	6	250.257-010
ESR	SALES AGENT, PEST CONTROL SERVICE	4	6	251.357-018
ESR	SALES REPRESENTATIVE, PUBLIC UTILITIES	4	6	253.357-010
ESR	SALES REPRESENTATIVE, SIGNS AND DISPLAYS	4	6	254.257-010
ESR	SALES REPRESENTATIVE, ADVERTISING	4	6	254.357-014
ESR	SALES REPRESENTATIVE, EDUCATION COURSES	4	5	259.257-010
ESR	SALES REPRESENTATIVE, ANIMAL-FEED PRODUCTS	4	6	272.357-010

Code	Title	GED	SVP	DOT No.
ESR	SALES REPRESENTATIVE, CANVAS PRODUCTS	4	6	261.357-014
ESR	SALES REPRESENTATIVE, MEN'S AND BOYS' APPAREL	4	6	261.357-022
ESR	SALES REPRESENTATIVE, PETROLEUM PRODUCTS	4	6	269.357-014
ESR	SALES REPRESENTATIVE, INDUSTRIAL RUBBER GOODS	4	6	274.357-042
ESR	SALES REPRESENTATIVE, ABRASIVES	4	6	274.357-010
ESR	SALES REPRESENTATIVE, METALS	4	6	274.357-054
ESR	SALES REPRESENTATIVE, WIRE ROPE	4	6	274.357-078
ESR	SALES REPRESENTATIVE, BUILDING EQUIPMENT AND SUPPLIES	4	6	274.357-018
ESR	SALES REPRESENTATIVE, CONSTRUCTION MACHINERY	4	6	274.357-022
ESR	SALES REPRESENTATIVE, MATERIAL-HANDLING EQUIPMENT	4	5	274.357-050
ESR	SALES REPRESENTATIVE, OILFIELD SUPPLIES AND EQUIPMENT	4	6	274.357-058
ESR	SALES REPRESENTATIVE, TEXTILE MACHINERY	4	6	274.357-070
ESR	SALES REPRESENTATIVE, WELDING EQUIPMENT	4	6	274.357-074
ESR	SALES REPRESENTATIVE, DAIRY SUPPLIES	4	6	274.357-030
ESR	SALES REPRESENTATIVE, FARM AND GARDEN EQUIPMENT AND SUPPLIES	4	5	272.357-014
ESR	SALES REPRESENTATIVE, POULTRY EQUIPMENT AND SUPPLIES	4	6	272.357-018
ESR	SALES REPRESENTATIVE, COMMUNICATION EQUIPMENT	4	6	271.257-010
ESR	SALES REPRESENTATIVE, ELECTRONICS PARTS	4	6	271.357-010
ESR	SALES REPRESENTATIVE, AIRCRAFT EQUIPMENT AND PARTS	4	6	273.357-010
ESR	SALES REPRESENTATIVE, MOTOR VEHICLES AND SUPPLIES	4	5	273.357-022
ESR	SALES REPRESENTATIVE, RAILROAD EQUIPMENT AND SUPPLIES	4	6	273.357-026
ESR	SALES REPRESENTATIVE, BOTTLES AND BOTTLING EQUIPMENT	4	5	274.357-014
ESR	SALES REPRESENTATIVE, CHURCH FURNITURE AND RELIGIOUS SUPPLIES	4	5	275.357-014
ESR	SALES REPRESENTATIVE, OFFICE MACHINES	4	5	275.357-034
ESR	SALES REPRESENTATIVE, SCHOOL EQUIPMENT AND SUPPLIES	4	5	275.357-042
ESR	SALES REPRESENTATIVE, DENTAL AND MEDICAL EQUIPMENT AND SUPPLIES	4	6	276.257-010
ESR	SALES REPRESENTATIVE, VETERINARIAN SUPPLIES	4	6	276.357-018
ESR	SALES REPRESENTATIVE, PRECISION INSTRUMENTS	4	6	276.357-014
ESR	SALES REPRESENTATIVE, ARCHITECTURAL			

Code	Title	GED	SVP	DOT No.
	AND ENGINEERING SUPPLIES	4	6	276.357-010
ESR	SALES REPRESENTATIVE, MUSICAL INSTRUMENTS AND ACCESSORIES	4	6	277.357-014
ESR	SALES REPRESENTATIVE, CONTAINERS	4	5	274.357-026
ESR	SALES REPRESENTATIVE, MORTICIAN SUPPLIES	4	6	275.357-030
ESR	SALES REPRESENTATIVE, FRANCHISE	4	5	251.357-022
ESR	SALES REPRESENTATIVE, AUDIOVISUAL PROGRAM PRODUCTIONS	4	5	259.157-010
ESR	SALES REPRESENTATIVE, AUTOMOTIVE-LEASING	4	5	273.357-014
ESR	SALES SUPERVISOR, MALT LIQUORS	4	5	299.137-014
ESR	SALESPERSON, ORTHOPEDIC SHOES	4	6	276.257-018
ESR	SALESPERSON, HEARING AIDS	4	5	276.354-010
ESR	SALESPERSON, PIANOS AND ORGANS	4	6	277.354-010
ESR	SALESPERSON, SHEET MUSIC	4	5	277.357-054
ESR	SAMPLE-ROOM SUPERVISOR	4	7	299.137-018
ESR	SECRETARY OF POLICE	4	7	375.137-022
ESR	SECURITY OFFICER	4	7	189.167-034
ESR	SENIOR RESERVATIONS AGENT	4	6	238.137-014
ESR	SERVICE MANAGER	4	6	185.167-058
ESR	SERVICE OBSERVER, CHIEF	4	7	239.137-022
ESR	SERVICE SUPERVISOR, LEASED MACHINERY AND EQUIPMENT	4	7	183.167-030
ESR	SHIFT SUPERINTENDENT, CAUSTIC CRESYLATE	4	8	552.132-010
ESR	STATION AGENT 1	4	6	910.137-038
ESR	STEWARD/STEWARDESS, RAILROAD DINING CAR	4	7	310.137-026
ESR	STEWARD/STEWARDESS, CHIEF, CARGO VESSEL	4	7	350.137-014
ESR	STEWARD/STEWARDESS, CHIEF, PASSENGER SHIP	4	7	350.137-018
ESR	STEWARD/STEWARDESS, SECOND	4	7	350.137-022
ESR	STOCK SUPERVISOR	4	6	222.137-034
ESR	STOCK-CONTROL SUPERVISOR	4	6	222.137-038
ESR	STREET-LIGHT-SERVICER SUPERVISOR	4	7	824.137-014
ESR	SUPERINTENDENT, COLD STORAGE	4	8	184.167-142
ESR	SUPERINTENDENT, MARINE OIL TERMINAL	4	8	184.167-186
ESR	SUPERINTENDENT, LOCAL	4	7	952.137-018
ESR	SUPERVISOR OF SALES	4	7	185.157-014
ESR	SUPERVISOR	4	7	529.137-026
ESR	SUPERVISOR	4	7	739.131-010
ESR	SUPERVISOR	4	6	789.132-014
ESR	SUPERVISOR	4	7	789.132-018
ESR	SUPERVISOR 2	4	6	692.132-014
ESR	SUPERVISOR, INSPECTION	4	6	183.161-010
ESR	SUPERVISOR, CONTINGENTS	4	6	205.367-050
ESR	SUPERVISOR, TELEPHONE CLERKS	4	5	239.132-010
ESR	SUPERVISOR, ROUTE SALES-DELIVERY DRIVERS	4	5	292.137-014
ESR	SUPERVISOR, ICE STORAGE, SALE, AND DELIVERY	4	6	299.137-022
ESR	SUPERVISOR, ADVERTISING-MATERIAL			

Code	Title	GED	SVP	DOT No.
	DISTRIBUTORS	4	6	230.137-010
ESR	SUPERVISOR, CARDROOM	4	6	343.137-014
ESR	SUPERVISOR, JANITORIAL SERVICES	4	6	381.137-010
ESR	SUPERVISOR, POULTRY HATCHERY	4	6	411.137-010
ESR	SUPERVISOR, SPRAY, LAWN AND TREE SERVICE	4	7	408.131-010
ESR	SUPERVISOR, POWDERED METAL	4	7	509.130-010
ESR	SUPERVISOR, PICKING	4	7	521.137-010
ESR	SUPERVISOR, MALT HOUSE	4	7	522.132-010
ESR	SUPERVISOR, CURED-MEAT PACKING	4	7	529.135-014
ESR	SUPERVISOR, COFFEE	4	7	529.130-018
ESR	SUPERVISOR, GRAIN AND YEAST PLANTS	4	7	529.132-062
ESR	SUPERVISOR, SUGAR HOUSE	4	8	529.132-090
ESR	SUPERVISOR, BEATER ROOM	4	7	530.132-014
ESR	SUPERVISOR, PAINT	4	7	559.132-114
ESR	SUPERVISOR, GELATIN PLANT	4	8	559.137-030
ESR	SUPERVISOR, GLUE SPECIALTY	4	7	559.137-034
ESR	SUPERVISOR, SILVERING DEPARTMENT	4	7	574.132-014
ESR	SUPERVISOR, WET POUR	4	7	575.137-014
ESR	SUPERVISOR, LIME	4	8	579.132-014
ESR	SUPERVISOR, ASBESTOS TEXTILE	4	7	579.137-014
ESR	SUPERVISOR, CANDLE MAKING	4	7	590.132-010
ESR	SUPERVISOR, FACEPIECE LINE	4	7	712.137-010
ESR	SUPERVISOR, FINAL ASSEMBLY AND PACKING	4	7	712.137-014
ESR	SUPERVISOR, MOTION-PICTURE EQUIPMENT	4	8	714.131-010
ESR	SUPERVISOR, ELECTRONICS PROCESSING	4	7	590.130-010
ESR	SUPERVISOR, DRY-CELL ASSEMBLY	4	7	727.137-010
ESR	SUPERVISOR, UPHOLSTERY DEPARTMENT	4	7	780.131-014
ESR	SUPERVISOR, CAP-AND-HAT PRODUCTION	4	7	784.130-010
ESR	SUPERVISOR, SEWING DEPARTMENT	4	6	689.137-010
ESR	SUPERVISOR, ASSEMBLY	4	7	801.137-010
ESR	SUPERVISOR, INSPECTION	4	7	801.137-014
ESR	SUPERVISOR, CORE DRILLING	4	7	850.137-010
ESR	SUPERVISOR, TICKET SALES	4	6	238.137-022
ESR	SUPERVISOR, INSPECTION	4	7	559.137-038
ESR	SUPERVISOR, PROP-MAKING	4	8	962.137-022
ESR	SUPERVISOR, COMPOSING-ROOM	4	7	973.137-010
ESR	SUPERVISOR, FINISHING ROOM	4	7	979.137-010
ESR	SUPERVISOR, BOAT OUTFITTING	4	8	806.131-018
ESR	SUPERVISOR, FIBERGLASS BOAT ASSEMBLY	4	8	806.134-014
ESR	SUPERVISOR, SHIPPING TRACK	4	7	806.137-018
ESR	SUPERVISOR, PRODUCTION CONTROL	4	8	221.137-018
ESR	SUPERVISOR, DOG LICENSE OFFICER	4	7	379.137-014
ESR	SUPERVISOR, OFFSET-PLATE PREPARATION	4	8	972.130-010
ESR	SUPERVISOR, METAL FURNITURE ASSEMBLY	4	7	709.134-010
ESR	SUPERVISOR, ROSE-GRADING	4	7	405.137-010
ESR	SUPERVISOR, IDENTIFICATION AND COMMUNICATIONS	4	8	377.134-010
ESR	SUPERVISOR, SIRUP SHED	4	6	529.137-058

Code	Title	GED	SVP	DOT No.
ESR	PASSENGER REPRESENTATIVE	3	4	910.367-026
ESR	PROTECTIVE-SIGNAL OPERATOR	3	5	379.362-014
ESR	RATER, TRAVEL ACCOMMODATIONS	3	6	168.367-014
ESR	REPOSSESSOR	3	3	241.367-022
ESR	SALES ATTENDANT	3	2	299.677-010
ESR	SALES CLERK	3	3	290.477-014
ESR	SALES REPRESENTATIVE, SHIPPING SERVICES	3	5	252.357-014
ESR	SALESPERSON, PHONOGRAPH RECORDS AND TAPE RECORDINGS	3	3	277.357-046
ESR	SALESPERSON, ART OBJECTS	3	4	277.457-010
ESR	SELF-SERVICE-LAUNDRY-AND-DRY-CLEANING ATTENDANT	3	2	369.677-010
ESR	SUBSCRIPTION CREW LEADER	3	5	291.157-010
ESR	SUPERINTENDENT, SERVICE	3	7	329.137-010
ESR	SUPERVISOR, SAFETY DEPOSIT	3	6	186.137-010
ESR	SUPERVISOR, DETASSELING CREW	3	6	401.137-014
ESR	SUPERVISOR, HIDE HOUSE	3	7	922.137-014
ESR	SUPERVISOR, WALL MIRROR DEPARTMENT	3	5	739.137-022
ESR	SUPERVISOR, BEEHIVE KILN	3	6	563.137-010
ESR	SURVIVAL SPECIALIST	3	5	378.227-018
ESR	THRILL PERFORMER	3	5	159.347-018
ESR	TOOL-AND-EQUIPMENT-RENTAL CLERK	3	4	295.357-014
ESR	TRAILER-RENTAL CLERK	3	4	295.467-022
ESR	TRANSPORTATION AGENT	3	5	912.367-014
ESR	UTILITY WORKER, FILM PROCESSING	3	3	976.685-030
ESR	WAITER/WAITRESS, BAR (RSE)	3	3	311.477-018
ESR	WAITER/WAITRESS, ROOM SERVICE (RSE)	3	3	311.477-034
ESR	WAITER/WAITRESS, TAKE OUT (RSE)	3	3	311.477-038
ESR	WAREHOUSE TRAFFIC SUPERVISOR	3	5	922.137-026
ESR	BAILIFF	2	3	377.667-010
ESR	BOUNCER	2	3	376.667-010
ESR	CAR HOP	2	2	311.477-010
ESR	ESCORT	2	2	353.667-010
ESR	FLAGGER	2	2	372.667-026
ESR	FUNERAL ATTENDANT	2	3	359.677-014
ESR	JOCKEY VALET	2	3	346.677-010
ESR	SOAP INSPECTOR (RES)	2	2	559.687-058
ESI	CERTIFICATION AND SELECTION SPECIALIST	6	8	099.167-010
ESI	MAGISTRATE	6	9	111.107-014
ESI	MUSIC THERAPIST	6	7	076.127-014
ESI	SECURITIES TRADER 2	6	8	186.167-058
ESI	TAX ATTORNEY	6	8	110.117-038
ESI	BUDGET OFFICER	5	8	161.117-010
ESI	CREDIT COUNSELOR	5	7	160.207-010
ESI	DIETITIAN, CHIEF	5	8	077.117-010
ESI	DISPATCHER	5	8	912.167-010
ESI	DISTRICT CUSTOMS DIRECTOR, DEPUTY	5	7	188.167-046
ESI	ESTATE PLANNER	5	7	186.167-010
ESI	GROUP WORKER	5	7	195.164-010
ESI	MANAGER, FLIGHT OPERATIONS	5	8	184.117-038
ESI	MANAGER, LAND DEVELOPMENT	5	8	186.117-042

Code	Title	GED	SVP	DOT No.
ESI	MANAGER, TRAFFIC 2	5	8	184.167-106
ESI	NEGOTIATOR, LETTER OF CREDIT	5	7	186.117-050
ESI	PRODUCER	5	7	187.167-178
ESI	PROJECT DIRECTOR	5	8	189.117-030
ESI	REVENUE OFFICER	5	7	188.167-074
ESI	SALES AGENT, SECURITIES	5	7	251.157-010
ESI	SALES-ENGINEER, ELECTRONICS PRODUCTS AND SYSTEMS	5	8	003.151-014
ESI	SALES-ENGINEER, ELECTRICAL PRODUCTS	5	8	003.151-010
ESI	SERVICE REPRESENTATIVE, ELEVATORS, ESCALATORS, AND DUMBWAITERS	5	5	259.257-018
ESI	SUPERINTENDENT, SANITATION	5	7	188.167-098
ESI	SUPERVISOR, ESTIMATOR AND DRAFTER	5	8	019.161-010
ESI	SUPERVISOR, SPECIAL SERVICES	5	6	169.267-026
ESI	SUPERVISOR, BRIDGES AND BUILDINGS	5	7	182.167-034
ESI	SUPERVISOR, COMPUTER OPERATIONS	5	7	213.132-010
ESI	VENDING-STAND SUPERVISOR	5	7	185.167-066
ESI	ART THERAPIST	4	7	076.127-010
ESI	BLENDING SUPERVISOR	4	5	520.136-010
ESI	CHEESE BLENDER	4	6	520.487-010
ESI	DIRECTOR, MERIT SYSTEM	4	5	188.117-086
ESI	EMERGENCY MEDICAL TECHNICIAN	4	5	079.374-010
ESI	FERRYBOAT CAPTAIN	4	7	197.163-010
ESI	HANDICAPPER, HARNESS RACING	4	4	219.267-010
ESI	INSTRUCTOR, VOCATIONAL TRAINING	4	7	097.227-014
ESI	INVESTIGATOR, PRIVATE	4	5	376.267-018
ESI	LIBRARY TECHNICAL ASSISTANT	4	5	100.367-018
ESI	OPERATIONS MANAGER	4	6	184.167-118
ESI	SAFETY COORDINATOR	4	7	909.127-010
ESI	LIFEGUARD	3	4	379.667-014
ESA	ADMINISTRATOR, SOCIAL WELFARE	6	8	195.117-010
ESA	DIRECTOR OF PLACEMENT	6	8	166.167-014
ESA	DIRECTOR, EXTENSION WORK	6	9	090.117-026
ESA	DISTRICT ATTORNEY	6	8	110.117-010
ESA	JUDGE	6	9	111.107-010
ESA	LAWYER	6	8	110.107-010
ESA	LAWYER, ADMIRALTY	6	8	110.117-018
ESA	LAWYER, CORPORATION	6	8	110.117-022
ESA	LAWYER, CRIMINAL	6	8	110.107-014
ESA	LAWYER, PATENT	6	8	110.117-026
ESA	LAWYER, PROBATE	6	8	110.117-030
ESA	LAWYER, REAL ESTATE	6	8	110.117-034
ESA	MANAGER, ADVERTISING	6	8	164.117-010
ESA	PRODUCER	6	8	187.167-174
ESA	ALUMNI SECRETARY	5	8	090.117-014
ESA	ARTIST'S MANAGER	5	7	191.117-010
ESA	ASSOCIATION EXECUTIVE	5	8	189.117-010
ESA	BREWING DIRECTOR	5	8	183.167-010
ESA	BUSINESS REPRESENTATIVE, LABOR UNION	5	8	187.167-018
ESA	BUSINESS-OPPORTUNITY-AND-PROPERTY-INVESTMENT BROKER	5	7	189.157-010
ESA	CAPTAIN, FIRE-PREVENTION BUREAU	5	8	373.167-014

Code	Title	GED	SVP	DOT No.
ESA	CHIEF WARDEN	5	6	188.167-018
ESA	CIVIL PREPAREDNESS OFFICER	5	6	188.117-022
ESA	COMMUNITY ORGANIZATION WORKER	5	7	195.167-010
ESA	CONCILIATOR	5	8	169.207-010
ESA	CONTRACT ADMINISTRATOR	5	8	162.117-014
ESA	CONTRACT SPECIALIST	5	8	162.117-018
ESA	DEMONSTRATOR, ELECTRIC-GAS APPLIANCES	5	6	297.357-010
ESA	DIRECTOR OF COUNSELING	5	8	045.107-018
ESA	DIRECTOR OF ADMISSIONS	5	8	090.167-014
ESA	DIRECTOR OF RELIGIOUS ACTIVITIES	5	8	129.107-018
ESA	DIRECTOR, CAMP	5	7	195.167-018
ESA	DIRECTOR, FUNDRAISING	5	8	165.117-010
ESA	DIRECTOR, FIELD	5	7	195.167-022
ESA	DIRECTOR, NEWS	5	8	184.167-014
ESA	DIRECTOR, RECREATION CENTER	5	7	195.167-026
ESA	DIRECTOR, SAFETY COUNCIL	5	8	188.167-034
ESA	DIRECTOR, TECHNICAL	5	8	962.162-010
ESA	DIRECTOR, VOCATIONAL TRAINING	5	8	097.167-010
ESA	DISTRICT ADVISER	5	8	187.117-022
ESA	DIVISION MANAGER, CHAMBER OF COMMERCE	5	7	187.167-042
ESA	ECONOMIC DEVELOPMENT COORDINATOR	5	8	188.117-102
ESA	ELECTION ASSISTANT	5	7	188.167-050
ESA	EQUAL-OPPORTUNITY REPRESENTATIVE	5	8	168.167-014
ESA	EXECUTIVE VICE PRESIDENT, CHAMBER OF COMMERCE	5	8	187.117-030
ESA	FIELD REPRESENTATIVE	5	8	189.267-010
ESA	FOUR-H CLUB AGENT	5	7	096.127-022
ESA	HOME-SERVICE DIRECTOR	5	8	096.161-010
ESA	INTERPRETER	5	6	137.267-010
ESA	LEGAL INVESTIGATOR	5	7	119.267-022
ESA	LITERARY AGENT	5	7	191.117-034
ESA	LOAN COUNSELOR	5	7	186.267-014
ESA	LOBBYIST	5	7	165.017-010
ESA	MANAGER, ADVERTISING	5	8	163.167-010
ESA	MANAGER, ADVERTISING AGENCY	5	8	164.117-014
ESA	MANAGER, AREA DEVELOPMENT	5	8	184.117-030
ESA	MANAGER, BRANCH	5	8	183.117-010
ESA	MANAGER, CONVENTION	5	7	187.167-078
ESA	MANAGER, CUSTOMER SERVICE	5	8	168.167-058
ESA	MANAGER, EXPORT	5	8	163.117-014
ESA	MANAGER, FISH HATCHERY	5	7	180.167-030
ESA	MANAGER, GAME PRESERVE	5	8	180.167-038
ESA	MANAGER, PROFESSIONAL EQUIPMENT SALES-AND-SERVICE	5	7	185.167-042
ESA	MANAGER, SALES	5	8	163.167-018
ESA	MANAGER, STATION	5	8	184.167-082
ESA	MANAGER, TRAFFIC	5	8	184.117-066
ESA	MANAGER, WORLD TRADE AND MARITIME DIVISION	5	7	187.167-170
ESA	MEDIA SPECIALIST, SCHOOL LIBRARY	5	7	100.167-030
ESA	MEMBERSHIP DIRECTOR	5	7	189.167-026
ESA	OPERATIONS MANAGER	5	8	184.117-070

Code	Title	GED	SVP	DOT No.
ESA	PHARMACEUTICAL DETAILER	5	7	262.157-010
ESA	PORT-TRAFFIC MANAGER	5	8	184.167-122
ESA	PRODUCER, ASSISTANT	5	7	187.167-182
ESA	PROPERTY-UTILIZATION OFFICER	5	8	188.117-122
ESA	RECREATION SUPERVISOR	5	8	187.137-010
ESA	REPRESENTATIVE, PERSONAL SERVICE	5	6	236.252-010
ESA	REVENUE-SETTLEMENTS ADMINISTRATOR	5	8	184.117-074
ESA	RIGHT-OF-WAY SUPERVISOR	5	8	191.117-050
ESA	RISK AND INSURANCE MANAGER	5	8	186.117-066
ESA	SALES AGENT, PSYCHOLOGICAL TESTS AND INDUSTRIAL RELATIONS	5	7	251.257-014
ESA	SALES AGENT, FINANCIAL SERVICES	5	6	251.257-010
ESA	SALES REPRESENTATIVE, TELEPHONE SERVICES	5	6	253.257-010
ESA	SALES REPRESENTATIVE, TRAVELERS' CHECKS	5	7	251.257-018
ESA	SALES REPRESENTATIVE, ELECTROPLATING	5	7	259.257-014
ESA	SALESPERSON, SURGICAL APPLIANCES	5	6	276.257-022
ESA	SOCIAL WORKER, MEDICAL	5	7	195.107-030
ESA	SPECIALIST-IN-CHARGE, EXTENSION SERVICE	5	8	096.167-014
ESA	SUPERINTENDENT	5	7	180.167-054
ESA	SUPERINTENDENT, RECREATION	5	8	187.117-054
ESA	SUPERINTENDENT, MAINTENANCE	5	8	184.167-174
ESA	SUPERINTENDENT, SALES	5	7	250.157-010
ESA	SUPERVISING FILM EDITOR	5	8	962.137-014
ESA	SUPERVISOR, TERMINAL OPERATIONS	5	8	184.167-242
ESA	TESTING-AND-REGULATING CHIEF	5	8	184.167-258
ESA	VETERANS CONTACT REPRESENTATIVE	5	7	187.167-198
ESA	WATER CONTROL SUPERVISOR	5	8	184.167-270
ESA	WHOLESALER 2	5	7	185.157-018
ESA	WHOLESALER 1	5	8	185.167-070
ESA	BLOOD-DONOR RECRUITER	4	3	293.357-010
ESA	BUILDING CONSULTANT	4	5	250.357-010
ESA	BUYER	4	6	162.157-018
ESA	BUYER, TOBACCO, HEAD	4	7	162.167-014
ESA	CD-STORAGE-AND-MATERIALS-MAKE-UP OPERATOR, HEAD	4	7	559.167-010
ESA	CHEF, PASSENGER VESSEL	4	7	315.137-010
ESA	CIRCULATION-SALES REPRESENTATIVE	4	6	299.167-010
ESA	CIRCUS-TRAIN SUPERVISOR	4	6	910.137-018
ESA	CIVIL PREPAREDNESS TRAINING OFFICER	4	6	169.127-010
ESA	COLLECTION CLERK	4	4	241.357-010
ESA	CONDUCTOR, PASSENGER CAR	4	8	198.167-010
ESA	DIRECTOR, PRESCHOOL	4	7	092.137-010
ESA	DISPATCHER, SECURITY GUARD	4	6	372.167-010
ESA	GARBAGE-COLLECTION SUPERVISOR	4	6	909.137-014
ESA	GUIDE, ESTABLISHMENT	4	5	353.367-014
ESA	LAUNCH COMMANDER, HARBOR POLICE	4	6	375.167-030
ESA	LEASING AGENT, RESIDENCE	4	5	250.357-014
ESA	LINEN CONTROLLER	4	6	299.357-010
ESA	MANAGER, ARMORED TRANSPORT SERVICE	4	6	372.167-022
ESA	MANAGER, DANCE STUDIO	4	6	187.167-086

Code	Title	GED	SVP	DOT No.
ESA	MANAGER, DEPARTMENT	4	7	189.167-022
ESA	MANAGER, MEAT SALES AND STORAGE	4	6	185.167-030
ESA	MANAGER, NURSERY	4	7	180.167-042
ESA	MANAGER, PARTS	4	7	185.167-038
ESA	MANAGER, TELEGRAPH OFFICE	4	8	184.167-086
ESA	MANAGER, TEXTILE CONVERSION	4	6	185.167-050
ESA	MANUFACTURERS' REPRESENTATIVE	4	6	279.157-010
ESA	OUTSIDE PROPERTY AGENT	4	7	162.157-030
ESA	PATROL JUDGE	4	8	153.267-014
ESA	PURCHASING AGENT	4	7	162.157-038
ESA	REPORTS ANALYST	4	7	161.267-026
ESA	SALES AGENT, REAL ESTATE	4	5	250.357-018
ESA	SALES AGENT, BUSINESS SERVICES	4	5	251.357-010
ESA	SALES AGENT, FINANCIAL-REPORT SERVICE	4	5	251.357-014
ESA	SALES REPRESENTATIVE, PRINTING	4	5	254.357-018
ESA	SALES REPRESENTATIVE, SIGNS	4	6	254.357-022
ESA	SALES REPRESENTATIVE, TELEVISION CABLE SERVICE	4	3	259.357-022
ESA	SALES REPRESENTATIVE, WEATHER-FORECASTING SERVICE	4	4	259.357-030
ESA	SALES REPRESENTATIVE, LIVESTOCK	4	5	260.257-010
ESA	SALES REPRESENTATIVE, FOOD PRODUCTS	4	5	260.357-014
ESA	SALES REPRESENTATIVE, TOBACCO PRODUCTS AND SMOKING SUPPLIES	4	5	260.357-022
ESA	SALES REPRESENTATIVE, APPAREL TRIMMINGS	4	5	261.357-010
ESA	SALES REPRESENTATIVE, FOOTWEAR	4	6	261.357-018
ESA	SALES REPRESENTATIVE, UNIFORMS	4	6	261.357-034
ESA	SALES REPRESENTATIVE, WOMEN'S AND GIRLS' APPAREL	4	5	261.357-038
ESA	SALES REPRESENTATIVE, LEATHER GOODS	4	5	279.357-022
ESA	SALES REPRESENTATIVE, WRITING AND MARKING PENS	4	3	277.357-030
ESA	SALES REPRESENTATIVE, PAPER AND PAPER PRODUCTS	4	5	279.357-026
ESA	SALES REPRESENTATIVE, PRESSURE-SENSITIVE TAPE	4	4	275.357-038
ESA	SALES REPRESENTATIVE, CHEMICALS AND DRUGS	4	5	262.357-010
ESA	SALES REPRESENTATIVE, TOILET PREPARATIONS	4	5	262.357-014
ESA	SALES REPRESENTATIVE, FUELS	4	4	269.357-010
ESA	SALES REPRESENTATIVE, HOME FURNISHINGS	4	5	270.357-010
ESA	SALES REPRESENTATIVE, HOTEL AND RESTAURANT EQUIPMENT AND SUPPLIES	4	6	275.357-026
ESA	SALES REPRESENTATIVE, HARDWARE SUPPLIES	4	5	274.357-034
ESA	SALES REPRESENTATIVE, RADIOGRAPHIC-INSPECTION EQUIPMENT AND SERVICES	4	6	271.352-010
ESA	SALES REPRESENTATIVE, SAFETY APPAREL AND EQUIPMENT	4	4	261.357-026
ESA	SALES REPRESENTATIVE, TEXTILE			

Code	Title	GED	SVP	DOT No.
	DESIGNS	4	5	274.357-066
ESA	SALES REPRESENTATIVE, HOUSEHOLD APPLIANCES	4	5	270.357-014
ESA	SALES REPRESENTATIVE, BOATS AND MARINE SUPPLIES	4	5	273.357-018
ESA	SALES REPRESENTATIVE, PRINTING SUPPLIES	4	5	274.357-062
ESA	SALES REPRESENTATIVE, BARBER AND BEAUTY EQUIPMENT AND SUPPLIES	4	5	275.357-010
ESA	SALES REPRESENTATIVE, CORDAGE	4	5	275.357-022
ESA	SALES REPRESENTATIVE, SHOE LEATHER AND FINDINGS	4	5	275.357-046
ESA	SALES REPRESENTATIVE, VENDING AND COIN MACHINES	4	5	275.357-050
ESA	SALES REPRESENTATIVE, COMMERCIAL EQUIPMENT AND SUPPLIES	4	4	275.357-018
ESA	SALES REPRESENTATIVE, JEWELRY	4	6	279.357-018
ESA	SALES REPRESENTATIVE, RECREATION AND SPORTING GOODS	4	5	277.357-026
ESA	SALES REPRESENTATIVE, HOBBIES AND CRAFTS	4	5	277.357-010
ESA	SALES REPRESENTATIVE, GENERAL MERCHANDISE	4	5	279.357-014
ESA	SALES REPRESENTATIVE, NOVELTIES	4	4	277.357-018
ESA	SALES REPRESENTATIVE, PUBLICATIONS	4	5	277.357-022
ESA	SALES REPRESENTATIVE, TEXTILES	4	6	261.357-030
ESA	SALES REPRESENTATIVE, MALT LIQUORS	4	4	260.357-018
ESA	SALES REPRESENTATIVE, HERBICIDE SERVICE	4	5	251.357-026
ESA	SALES-PROMOTION REPRESENTATIVE	4	3	269.357-018
ESA	SALESPERSON, BURIAL NEEDS	4	5	279.357-042
ESA	SALESPERSON, FURS	4	5	261.357-042
ESA	SALESPERSON, MEN'S FURNISHINGS	4	4	261.357-054
ESA	SALESPERSON, INFANTS' AND CHILDREN'S WEAR	4	3	261.357-046
ESA	SALESPERSON, FLOOR COVERINGS	4	4	270.357-026
ESA	SALESPERSON, CHINA AND SILVERWARE	4	4	270.357-018
ESA	SALESPERSON, CURTAINS AND DRAPERIES	4	4	270.357-022
ESA	SALESPERSON, FURNITURE	4	4	270.357-030
ESA	SALESPERSON, GENERAL HARDWARE	4	4	279.357-050
ESA	SALESPERSON, HORTICULTURAL AND NURSERY PRODUCTS	4	4	272.357-022
ESA	SALESPERSON, STEREO EQUIPMENT	4	4	270.357-038
ESA	SALESPERSON, HOUSEHOLD APPLIANCES	4	4	270.357-034
ESA	SALESPERSON, AUTOMOBILES	4	5	273.353-010
ESA	SALESPERSON, TRAILERS AND MOTOR HOMES	4	5	273.357-034
ESA	SALESPERSON, AUTOMOBILE ACCESSORIES	4	4	273.357-030
ESA	SALESPERSON, JEWELRY	4	5	279.357-058
ESA	SALESPERSON, PHOTOGRAPHIC SUPPLIES AND EQUIPMENT	4	5	277.357-050
ESA	SALESPERSON, SPORTING GOODS	4	5	277.357-058
ESA	SALESPERSON, MUSICAL INSTRUMENTS AND ACCESSORIES	4	6	277.357-038

Code	Title	GED	SVP	DOT No.
ESA	SALESPERSON, FLORIST SUPPLIES	4	4	275.357-054
ESA	SALESPERSON, PETS AND PET SUPPLIES	4	4	277.357-042
ESA	SALESPERSON, STAMPS OR COINS	4	5	277.357-062
ESA	SALESPERSON, FLYING SQUAD	4	6	279.357-046
ESA	SALESPERSON, GENERAL MERCHANDISE	4	4	279.357-054
ESA	SALESPERSON-DEMONSTRATOR, PARTY PLAN	4	4	279.357-038
ESA	SONG PLUGGER	4	5	165.157-010
ESA	SOUS CHEF	4	7	315.137-014
ESA	SPECIAL AGENT	4	5	372.267-014
ESA	SUPERVISOR	4	7	684.137-010
ESA	SUPERVISOR, RUG CLEANING	4	7	369.137-014
ESA	SUPERVISOR, MAPLE PRODUCTS	4	6	529.137-050
ESA	SUPERVISOR, TAR DISTILLATION	4	7	542.130-014
ESA	SUPERVISOR, TANK CLEANING	4	6	559.137-050
ESA	SUPERVISOR, CHANNEL PROCESS	4	7	559.137-022
ESA	SUPERVISOR, PACKING ROOM	4	7	589.137-010
ESA	SUPERVISOR, RECLAMATION	4	6	621.137-010
ESA	SUPERVISOR, PAINT DEPARTMENT	4	7	749.131-014
ESA	SUPERVISOR, PAINTING, SHIPYARD	4	8	840.131-014
ESA	SUPERVISOR, RIPRAP PLACING	4	6	850.137-018
ESA	SUPERVISOR, MAINTENANCE	4	7	899.137-018
ESA	SUPERVISOR, DOCK	4	7	914.137-018
ESA	SUPERVISOR, PROPERTIES	4	8	962.137-026
ESA	SUPERVISOR, COSTUMING	4	7	962.137-018
ESA	SUPERVISOR, AIRPLANE-FLIGHT ATTENDANT	4	7	352.137-010
ESA	SUPERVISOR, TRAVEL-INFORMATION CENTER	4	6	237.137-014
ESA	SUPERVISOR, CUSTOMER SERVICES	4	6	248.137-018
ESA	TICKET BROKER	4	6	259.357-034
ESA	WAITER/WAITRESS, BANQUET, HEAD	4	6	311.137-014
ESA	WAITER/WAITRESS, HEAD	4	6	311.137-022
ESA	ALARM INVESTIGATOR	3	3	376.367-010
ESA	BARKER	3	2	342.657-010
ESA	CATERER HELPER	3	3	319.677-010
ESA	CIGARETTE VENDOR	3	2	291.457-010
ESA	DETECTIVE 2	3	4	376.667-014
ESA	FIRE LOOKOUT	3	5	452.367-010
ESA	FUND RAISER 2	3	2	293.357-014
ESA	HOUSE OFFICER	3	4	376.367-018
ESA	PHOTO CHECKER AND ASSEMBLER (CRA)	3	4	976.687-014
ESA	PHOTOGRAPHER	3	3	143.457-010
ESA	SALES EXHIBITOR	3	3	279.357-010
ESA	SALES REPRESENTATIVE, DOOR-TO-DOOR	3	2	291.357-010
ESA	SALESPERSON, COSMETICS AND TOILETRIES	3	4	262.357-018
ESA	SALESPERSON, WIGS	3	4	261.351-010
ESA	SHOW-HORSE DRIVER	3	5	159.344-018
ESA	TOBACCO-WAREHOUSE AGENT	3	3	259.357-038
ESA	TRACK SUPERVISOR	3	4	921.132-010
ESA	WEIGHT GUESSER	3	2	342.357-010
ESA	WINE STEWARD/STEWARDESS	3	6	310.357-010

Code	Title	GED	SVP	DOT No.
ESC	DIRECTOR OF INSTITUTIONAL RESEARCH	6	8	090.167-018
ESC	ADJUDICATOR	5	7	119.167-010
ESC	ADMINISTRATIVE ASSISTANT	5	7	169.167-010
ESC	ADMINISTRATIVE SECRETARY	5	8	169.167-014
ESC	BIOGRAPHER (ASE)	5	7	052.067-010
ESC	BUSINESS MANAGER	5	7	191.117-018
ESC	DIRECTOR OF STUDENT AFFAIRS	5	8	090.167-022
ESC	DIRECTOR, EDUCATIONAL PROGRAM	5	8	099.117-010
ESC	DIRECTOR, NURSES' REGISTRY	5	6	187.167-034
ESC	DIRECTOR, OPERATIONS	5	8	184.167-018
ESC	DIRECTOR, SERVICE	5	7	189.167-014
ESC	DISPATCHER, CHIEF 1	5	8	184.167-038
ESC	FIELD SUPERVISOR, BROADCAST	5	7	193.167-014
ESC	GENEALOGIST	5	7	052.067-018
ESC	HISTORIAN	5	7	052.067-022
ESC	HISTORIAN, DRAMATIC ARTS	5	7	052.067-026
ESC	LOGISTICS ENGINEER	5	8	019.167-010
ESC	MANAGER, CIRCULATION	5	8	163.167-014
ESC	MANAGER, CONTRACTS	5	7	163.117-010
ESC	MANAGER, COMMUNICATIONS STATION	5	8	184.167-062
ESC	MANAGER, CREDIT AND COLLECTION	5	8	168.167-054
ESC	MANAGER, CREDIT UNION	5	7	186.167-026
ESC	MANAGER, DISTRIBUTION WAREHOUSE	5	6	185.167-018
ESC	MANAGER, EMPLOYMENT	5	8	166.167-030
ESC	MANAGER, FLIGHT-RESERVATIONS	5	8	184.167-070
ESC	MANAGER, INSURANCE OFFICE	5	8	186.167-034
ESC	MANAGER, TRAFFIC 1	5	8	184.167-102
ESC	MANAGER, TRAFFIC	5	7	184.167-090
ESC	OPERATIONS OFFICER	5	7	186.167-050
ESC	REGISTRAR, COLLEGE OR UNIVERSITY	5	8	090.167-030
ESC	RESERVE OFFICER	5	9	186.167-054
ESC	SECURITIES TRADER 1	5	7	162.157-042
ESC	SPECIAL AGENT	5	8	166.167-046
ESC	SPECIAL AGENT, GROUP INSURANCE	5	7	169.167-050
ESC	STATIONS-RELATIONS-CONTACT REPRESENTATIVE	5	8	184.167-134
ESC	SUPERINTENDENT, STATIONS	5	6	184.167-206
ESC	SUPERVISOR OF WAY	5	7	184.167-234
ESC	AIRPLANE-CHARTER CLERK	4	3	295.367-010
ESC	ALARM OPERATOR	4	6	379.162-010
ESC	BOOKMAKER	4	6	187.167-014
ESC	BUTLER	4	6	309.137-010
ESC	CAR CLERK, PULLMAN	4	6	215.167-010
ESC	CAR DISTRIBUTOR	4	5	910.367-014
ESC	CHIEF DISPATCHER	4	7	939.137-010
ESC	CLAIM EXAMINER	4	7	241.267-018
ESC	COMMANDING OFFICER, MOTOR EQUIPMENT	4	8	375.167-018
ESC	COMMERCIAL-INSTRUCTOR SUPERVISOR	4	8	239.137-010
ESC	COMMUNICATIONS COORDINATOR	4	7	239.167-010
ESC	DEMONSTRATOR, KNITTING	4	5	297.354-014
ESC	DENTAL ASSISTANT (SAI)	4	6	079.371-010
ESC	DEPOSIT CLERK	4	6	241.267-026
ESC	DESK OFFICER	4	7	375.137-014
ESC	DETECTIVE CHIEF	4	7	375.167-022

Code	Title	GED	SVP	DOT No.
ESC	DIRECTOR, FINANCIAL RESPONSIBILITY DIVISION	4	6	188.167-030
ESC	DIRECTOR, RADIO	4	6	159.167-014
ESC	DIRECTOR, SOCIAL	4	6	352.167-010
ESC	DISPATCHER, TUGBOAT	4	6	911.167-010
ESC	FEED AND FARM MANAGEMENT ADVISER	4	7	096.127-018
ESC	FILM-RENTAL CLERK	4	5	295.367-018
ESC	FORMS ANALYST	4	7	161.267-018
ESC	FRUIT COORDINATOR	4	5	529.167-010
ESC	GENERAL AGENT, OPERATIONS	4	8	184.167-042
ESC	GUIDE, TRAVEL	4	6	353.167-010
ESC	HOSPITAL-INSURANCE REPRESENTATIVE	4	6	166.267-014
ESC	INSTRUCTOR, BRIDGE	4	8	159.227-010
ESC	INSTRUMENT-SHOP SUPERVISOR	4	7	722.131-010
ESC	INVESTIGATOR	4	5	241.267-030
ESC	LOADING-RACK SUPERVISOR	4	7	914.137-014
ESC	LOAN INTERVIEWER	4	6	241.367-018
ESC	MAIL-DISTRIBUTION-SCHEME EXAMINER	4	5	239.367-018
ESC	MANAGER, BARBER OR BEAUTY SHOP	4	7	187.167-058
ESC	MANAGER, BENEFITS	4	7	166.167-018
ESC	MANAGER, EMPLOYMENT AGENCY	4	7	187.167-098
ESC	MANAGER, FISH-AND-GAME CLUB	4	6	187.167-102
ESC	MANAGER, FLIGHT KITCHEN	4	7	319.137-014
ESC	MANAGER, MARKET	4	7	186.167-042
ESC	MANAGER, STAGE	4	7	159.167-018
ESC	MANAGER, WINTER SPORTS	4	6	187.167-166
ESC	MEMBERSHIP SOLICITOR	4	4	293.357-022
ESC	METER READER, CHIEF	4	6	209.137-014
ESC	OFFICE SUPERVISOR, ANIMAL HOSPITAL	4	6	249.137-010
ESC	ORDER DISPATCHER, CHIEF	4	6	959.137-018
ESC	PETROLEUM-INSPECTOR SUPERVISOR	4	7	222.137-026
ESC	PURSER	4	7	197.167-014
ESC	RACING SECRETARY AND HANDICAPPER	4	8	153.167-018
ESC	RATE SUPERVISOR	4	6	214.137-018
ESC	RECORDS-MANAGEMENT ANALYST	4	7	161.267-022
ESC	RECREATION-FACILITY ATTENDANT	4	3	341.367-010
ESC	ROUTING CLERK	4	3	209.567-018
ESC	SALES REPRESENTATIVE, HOTEL SERVICES	4	6	259.157-014
ESC	SALES REPRESENTATIVE, PLASTIC PRODUCTS	4	4	279.357-030
ESC	SALES REPRESENTATIVE, LUBRICATING EQUIPMENT	4	5	274.357-046
ESC	SALES REPRESENTATIVE, VIDEOTAPE	4	3	271.357-014
ESC	SALESPERSON, BOOKS	4	4	277.357-034
ESC	SALESPERSON, PARTS	4	6	279.357-062
ESC	SALESPERSON, TOY TRAINS AND ACCESSORIES	4	3	277.357-066
ESC	SPECIAL AGENT-IN-CHARGE	4	7	376.167-010
ESC	STATION MANAGER	4	7	184.167-130
ESC	STOCK-TRANSFER CLERK, HEAD	4	6	216.137-014
ESC	SUPERINTENDENT, GRAIN ELEVATOR	4	6	529.137-022
ESC	SUPERVISOR	4	7	529.137-030
ESC	SUPERVISOR OF COMMUNICATIONS	4	8	184.167-230

CLASSIFIED INDEX

Code	Title	GED	SVP	DOT No.
ESC	SUPERVISOR, FORCE ADJUSTMENT	4	7	215.137-018
ESC	SUPERVISOR, CLASSIFIED ADVERTISING	4	6	247.137-014
ESC	SUPERVISOR, CUSTOMER RECORDS DIVISION	4	7	249.137-022
ESC	SUPERVISOR, COMPOUNDING-AND-FINISHING	4	8	550.137-010
ESC	SUPERVISOR, COATING	4	7	554.137-014
ESC	SUPERVISOR, TOILET-AND-LAUNDRY SOAP	4	7	559.132-130
ESC	SUPERVISOR, CUTTING DEPARTMENT	4	6	781.134-010
ESC	SUPERVISOR, CAR INSTALLATIONS	4	7	806.137-010
ESC	SUPERVISOR, AIRCRAFT CLEANING	4	7	891.137-014
ESC	SUPERVISOR, FILES	4	6	206.137-010
ESC	SUPERVISOR, CASHIERS	4	7	211.137-010
ESC	SUPERVISOR, BLOOD-DONOR RECRUITERS	4	6	293.137-010
ESC	SUPERVISOR, TAPING	4	6	842.134-010
ESC	SUPERVISOR, CUSTOMER-COMPLAINT SERVICE	4	5	241.137-014
ESC	SUPERVISOR, SURGICAL GARMENT ASSEMBLY	4	7	712.132-010
ESC	SUPERVISOR, ORDER TAKERS	4	5	249.137-026
ESC	TERMINAL SUPERINTENDENT	4	8	184.167-254
ESC	TESTER, FOOD PRODUCTS	4	6	199.251-010
ESC	TRAVEL CLERK	4	7	238.167-010
ESC	TYPING SECTION CHIEF	4	6	203.137-014
ESC	VAULT CASHIER	4	5	222.137-050
ESC	YARD MANAGER	4	7	184.167-278
ESC	ANIMAL-HOSPITAL CLERK	3	4	245.367-010
ESC	APPAREL-RENTAL CLERK	3	3	295.357-010
ESC	CARDROOM ATTENDANT 1	3	4	343.467-010
ESC	CLAIMS CLERK 2	3	4	205.367-018
ESC	CLASSIFIER (CRE)	3	3	753.467-010
ESC	CLOCKER	3	2	153.367-010
ESC	COLLECTOR	3	4	241.367-010
ESC	COMMUNICATION-CENTER OPERATOR	3	5	235.662-014
ESC	CUSTOMER-SERVICE CLERK	3	4	299.367-010
ESC	DEMONSTRATOR	3	3	297.354-010
ESC	DESK CLERK, BOWLING FLOOR	3	3	340.367-010
ESC	DISPATCHER, MOTOR VEHICLE	3	5	249.167-014
ESC	DRIVER'S LICENSE EXAMINER	3	4	168.267-034
ESC	DUDE WRANGLER	3	3	353.364-010
ESC	EMPLOYMENT-AND-CLAIMS AIDE	3	5	169.367-010
ESC	GOLF-COURSE RANGER	3	4	379.667-010
ESC	GOODWILL AMBASSADOR	3	2	293.357-018
ESC	GROUP-SALES REPRESENTATIVE	3	3	259.357-010
ESC	GUIDE	3	3	353.367-010
ESC	GUIDE, PLANT	3	3	353.367-018
ESC	GUIDE, REAL ESTATE	3	2	297.667-010
ESC	GUIDE, SIGHTSEEING	3	4	353.363-010
ESC	HOST/HOSTESS, HEAD	3	2	349.667-014
ESC	LEASING AGENT, OUTDOOR ADVERTISING	3	4	254.357-010
ESC	LOST-AND-FOUND CLERK	3	3	222.367-034
ESC	OPERATIONS AND INTELLIGENCE ASSISTANT	3	5	378.367-026
ESC	PAY-STATION ATTENDANT	3	5	237.367-034

-205-

Code	Title	GED	SVP	DOT No.
ESC	PHYSICAL THERAPY AIDE	3	4	355.354-010
ESC	PROCESS SERVER	3	3	249.367-062
ESC	RECEIVER-DISPATCHER	3	4	239.367-022
ESC	RECEIVING-BARN CUSTODIAN	3	3	349.367-014
ESC	RECRUIT INSTRUCTOR	3	4	378.227-014
ESC	SCORER	3	4	153.387-014
ESC	SENIOR ENLISTED ADVISOR	3	5	166.167-042
ESC	SHOPPING INVESTIGATOR	3	3	376.267-022
ESC	STEWARD/STEWARDESS	3	3	350.677-022
ESC	SUPERVISOR, FILLING-AND-PACKING	3	5	920.137-022
ESC	TEACHER AIDE 2	3	3	249.367-074
ESC	TELEPHONE SOLICITOR	3	3	299.357-014
ESC	TRAVEL CLERK	3	4	238.367-030
ESC	USHER, HEAD	3	4	344.137-010
ESC	WAITER/WAITRESS, INFORMAL	3	3	311.477-030
ESC	BODYGUARD	2	3	372.667-014
ESC	DRESSER	2	3	346.674-010
ESC	GRADER	2	3	529.687-098
ESC	GUARD, SCHOOL-CROSSING	2	2	371.567-010
ESC	LEI SELLER	2	2	291.454-010
ESC	MANICURIST	2	3	331.674-010
ESC	NEWSPAPER CARRIER	2	2	292.457-010
ESC	PATROLLER	2	3	376.667-018
ESC	PEDDLER	2	3	291.457-018
ESC	WAITER/WAITRESS, CLUB	2	2	352.677-018
ECR	SUPERVISOR, MAPPING	4	7	018.167-030
ECR	TEST-DESK SUPERVISOR	4	7	822.131-030
ECR	DISPATCHER, RELAY	3	5	221.362-014
ECR	JOB TRACER	3	4	221.387-034
ECR	SAMPLER	3	4	579.484-010
ECR	TRAPPER, BIRD	3	4	461.684-018
ECR	COAL SAMPLER	2	2	922.687-038
ECR	COUNTER ATTENDANT, CAFETERIA	2	3	311.677-014
ECR	GRAIN RECEIVER	2	2	921.365-010
ECR	LABORER, POULTRY HATCHERY	2	2	411.687-022
ECR	LARD REFINER	2	3	529.685-158
ECR	MALT-HOUSE OPERATOR	2	3	522.685-074
ECR	OFFICE HELPER	2	2	239.567-010
ECR	SIFTER	2	2	551.687-030
ECR	SORTING-MACHINE OPERATOR	2	2	649.665-010
ECI	SUPERINTENDENT, DISTRIBUTION 1	5	9	184.167-150
ECI	SUPERINTENDENT, ELECTRIC POWER	5	8	184.167-162
ECI	TOWN CLERK	4	5	243.367-018
ECS	ACCOUNTANT, TAX	5	8	160.162-010
ECS	OCCUPATIONAL-SAFETY-AND-HEALTH INSPECTOR	5	6	168.167-062
ECS	PURCHASE-PRICE ANALYST	5	7	162.167-030
ECS	BUILDING-INSULATION SUPERVISOR	4	7	863.134-010
ECS	CENTRAL-OFFICE-REPAIRER SUPERVISOR	4	7	822.131-010
ECS	CONDUCTOR, ROAD FREIGHT	4	8	198.167-018
ECS	DISPATCHER, SERVICE	4	4	959.167-010

Code	Title	GED	SVP	DOT No.
ECS	DISTRIBUTION SUPERVISOR	4	6	914.137-010
ECS	ESCROW OFFICER	4	8	119.367-010
ECS	INFORMATION CLERK	4	4	237.367-022
ECS	MANAGER, GOLF CLUB	4	6	187.167-114
ECS	MANAGER, PROCUREMENT SERVICES	4	7	162.167-022
ECS	PRODUCTION SUPERVISOR, DEFLUORINATED PHOSPHATE	4	7	559.132-050
ECS	RIGGER SUPERVISOR	4	7	823.131-014
ECS	SERVICE-LIAISON REPRESENTATIVE	4	6	221.367-074
ECS	SUPERINTENDENT, MAINTENANCE OF EQUIPMENT	4	8	184.167-178
ECS	SUPERVISOR, DRY-STARCH	4	7	529.132-046
ECS	SUPERVISOR, DEHYDROGENATION	4	8	559.132-078
ECS	TRAIN DISPATCHER	4	7	184.167-262
ECS	ALTERATIONS WORKROOM CLERK	3	3	221.367-010
ECS	AUTOMOBILE LOCATOR	3	3	296.367-010
ECS	BOOKING CLERK	3	5	248.367-014
ECS	BOOKMOBILE DRIVER	3	3	249.363-010
ECS	CARD PLAYER	3	4	343.367-010
ECS	CASHIER, COURTESY BOOTH	3	4	211.467-010
ECS	CHARTER	3	3	249.367-018
ECS	DEMONSTRATOR, SEWING TECHNIQUES	3	3	297.454-010
ECS	FACILITY EXAMINER	3	6	959.367-014
ECS	FOOD ORDER EXPEDITER	3	3	319.467-010
ECS	HOSPITAL-ADMITTING CLERK	3	6	205.362-018
ECS	HOTEL CLERK	3	4	238.362-010
ECS	MANAGER, BRANCH STORE	3	3	369.467-010
ECS	ORDER-CONTROL CLERK, BLOOD BANK	3	3	245.367-026
ECS	OUTBOARD-MOTOR INSPECTOR	3	4	806.687-042
ECS	PASSENGER SERVICE REPRESENTATIVE 1	3	3	352.677-010
ECS	POST-OFFICE CLERK	3	4	243.367-014
ECS	REPRODUCTION ORDER PROCESSOR	3	5	221.367-058
ECS	SAFE-DEPOSIT-BOX RENTAL CLERK	3	3	295.367-022
ECS	SCHEDULER, MAINTENANCE	3	4	221.367-066
ECS	SERVICE CLERK	3	4	221.367-070
ECS	SERVICE-ESTABLISHMENT ATTENDANT	3	3	369.477-014
ECS	STEEP TENDER	3	4	522.465-010
ECS	SUGAR-REPROCESS OPERATOR, HEAD	3	6	529.137-018
ECS	TRAVEL AGENT	3	4	252.157-010
ECS	WARD CLERK	3	3	245.362-014
ECS	FIELD INSPECTOR, DISEASE AND INSECT CONTROL	2	2	408.687-010
ECS	HOST/HOSTESS, DANCE HALL	2	2	349.667-010
ECS	LOUNGE-CAR ATTENDANT	2	2	291.457-014
ECS	PRESS-BOX CUSTODIAN	2	2	344.677-010
ECS	ROCK BREAKER	2	2	770.687-034
ECS	ROOM-SERVICE CLERK	2	2	324.577-010
ECS	SAMPLER	2	3	549.587-014

Code	Title	GED	SVP	DOT No.

CONVENTIONAL OCCUPATIONS

Code	Title	GED	SVP	DOT No.
CRI	PROGRAMER, BUSINESS	5	7	020.162-014
CRI	FIXED-CAPITAL CLERK	4	5	210.382-042
CRI	RECEIPT-AND-REPORT CLERK	4	5	216.382-054
CRI	LIQUID-FERTILIZER SERVICER	3	3	906.683-014
CRS	AERONAUTICAL-DESIGN ENGINEER (IRE)	5	8	002.061-022
CRS	BOOKKEEPING-MACHINE OPERATOR 1	4	5	210.382-022
CRS	COLLATERAL-AND-SAFEKEEPING CLERK	4	5	216.382-030
CRS	CONTROL CLERK, DATA PROCESSING 1	4	4	221.382-014
CRS	COST CLERK	4	5	216.382-034
CRS	GENERAL-LEDGER BOOKKEEPER	4	5	210.382-046
CRS	INTERLINE CLERK	4	5	214.382-022
CRS	MEDIA CLERK	4	5	247.382-010
CRS	MORTGAGE-ACCOUNTING CLERK	4	3	216.362-026
CRS	NIGHT AUDITOR	4	5	210.382-054
CRS	PROGRAMER, DETAIL	4	5	219.367-026
CRS	PROGRESS CLERK	4	5	221.362-022
CRS	RADIOTELEGRAPH OPERATOR	4	7	193.262-030
CRS	SOUND CUTTER	4	6	962.382-014
CRS	STOCK-TRANSFER CLERK	4	5	216.382-070
CRS	TONNAGE-COMPILATION CLERK	4	5	248.387-014
CRS	TRANSIT CLERK	4	5	217.382-014
CRS	ACCOUNTING CLERK, DATA PROCESSING	3	5	216.382-010
CRS	AIRCRAFT-LOG CLERK	3	4	221.362-010
CRS	ANNEALER	3	3	573.685-010
CRS	ANTENNA INSTALLER	3	4	823.684-010
CRS	ARMATURE TESTER 1	3	4	724.384-010
CRS	ASSEMBLER, CARBON BRUSHES	3	4	721.684-014
CRS	ASSEMBLER, MUSICAL INSTRUMENTS	3	3	730.684-010
CRS	ASSEMBLY INSPECTOR	3	5	763.684-010
CRS	ASSEMBLY-LINE INSPECTOR	3	4	709.684-018
CRS	AUDIT-MACHINE OPERATOR	3	4	216.482-018
CRS	BALL-MILL OPERATOR	3	3	558.685-014
CRS	BANDING-MACHINE OPERATOR	3	4	679.682-010
CRS	BATTERY ASSEMBLER	3	4	727.684-010
CRS	BILLING-MACHINE OPERATOR	3	4	214.482-010
CRS	BOAT-HOIST OPERATOR	3	3	921.683-010
CRS	BODY WIRER	3	4	829.684-014
CRS	BONE-COOKING OPERATOR	3	3	551.685-018
CRS	BOOKING PRIZER	3	3	216.462-010
CRS	BOX PRINTER	3	4	652.682-010
CRS	BRAILLE OPERATOR	3	4	203.582-010
CRS	CANDLE-EXTRUSION-MACHINE OPERATOR	3	4	692.682-026
CRS	CANER 1	3	3	763.684-018
CRS	CANNON-PINION ADJUSTER	3	3	715.684-046
CRS	CANOPY STRINGER	3	4	789.684-018
CRS	CARBONATION EQUIPMENT TENDER	3	3	522.685-026
CRS	CARPENTER 1	3	4	860.664-010
CRS	CARPET INSPECTOR, FINISHED	3	4	689.564-010
CRS	CHAIN MAKER, MACHINE	3	3	700.684-022
CRS	CHAR-FILTER OPERATOR	3	5	521.365-010
CRS	CHART CHANGER	3	4	221.584-010

Code	Title	GED	SVP	DOT No.
CRS	CHECKER 2	3	4	209.687-010
CRS	CLASSIFIER TENDER	3	4	511.685-014
CRS	COATER OPERATOR	3	3	554.585-014
CRS	COILED-COIL INSPECTOR	3	3	725.684-010
CRS	COLORING-MACHINE OPERATOR	3	3	582.685-034
CRS	CONTROL INSPECTOR	3	4	539.667-010
CRS	CONVEYOR-SYSTEM DISPATCHER	3	3	921.662-018
CRS	CREASER	3	4	783.685-014
CRS	CREW SCHEDULER	3	5	215.362-010
CRS	CRIPPLE WORKER	3	3	788.684-042
CRS	CROWN-WHEEL ASSEMBLER	3	3	715.684-074
CRS	CUPOLA HOIST OPERATOR	3	4	921.683-030
CRS	CUPOLA PATCHER	3	4	861.684-010
CRS	CURING-OVEN TENDER	3	4	553.685-038
CRS	CUT-FILE CLERK	3	4	222.367-014
CRS	CUTTING-MACHINE TENDER	3	3	690.685-122
CRS	DIALER	3	3	715.684-086
CRS	DIAMOND DRILLER	3	5	770.381-018
CRS	DIE CUTTER	3	4	699.682-022
CRS	DIVER HELPER	3	3	899.664-010
CRS	DRAWBRIDGE OPERATOR	3	4	371.362-010
CRS	EARRING MAKER	3	3	700.684-030
CRS	ELECTRONIC-SCALE SUBASSEMBLER	3	3	726.684-014
CRS	ELECTRONICS INSPECTOR 2	3	3	726.684-022
CRS	ELECTRONICS TESTER 2	3	3	726.684-026
CRS	ELECTRONICS ASSEMBLER	3	3	726.684-018
CRS	ELEMENT WINDER	3	3	724.685-010
CRS	EMBOSSING-MACHINE OPERATOR 2	3	4	208.682-010
CRS	EMBOSSING-MACHINE OPERATOR 1	3	4	208.582-014
CRS	EMBOSSOGRAPH OPERATOR	3	4	652.682-014
CRS	FABRIC-AND-ACCESSORIES ESTIMATOR	3	3	221.482-010
CRS	FAT-PURIFICATION WORKER	3	3	551.685-070
CRS	FIBERGLASS-DOWEL-DRAWING-MACHINE OPERATOR	3	4	575.682-010
CRS	FILE CUTTER	3	4	605.685-014
CRS	FILER	3	3	700.684-034
CRS	FILLER	3	5	710.684-022
CRS	FILM-OR-TAPE LIBRARIAN	3	5	222.367-026
CRS	FILTER TENDER, JELLY	3	3	529.685-114
CRS	FINGER COBBLER	3	4	788.684-046
CRS	FLOWER-MACHINE OPERATOR	3	4	687.682-010
CRS	FUNCTIONAL TESTER, TYPEWRITERS	3	4	706.382-010
CRS	FUR CLEANER, HAND	3	5	362.684-018
CRS	FUR PLUCKER	3	6	585.681-014
CRS	FURNITURE ASSEMBLER	3	4	763.684-038
CRS	FUSE ASSEMBLER	3	3	737.684-022
CRS	GLASS-CUTTING-MACHINE OPERATOR, AUTOMATIC	3	3	677.562-010
CRS	GLOVE SEWER	3	4	784.682-010
CRS	HEEL-SEAT FITTER, MACHINE	3	4	690.682-046
CRS	HIGHWAY-MAINTENANCE WORKER	3	3	899.684-014
CRS	HOBBING-PRESS OPERATOR	3	4	617.682-018
CRS	ICICLE-MACHINE OPERATOR	3	4	920.482-010
CRS	INLAYER	3	4	977.684-014

Code	Title	GED	SVP	DOT No.
CRS	INSPECTOR	3	4	700.687-034
CRS	INSPECTOR	3	4	776.667-010
CRS	INSPECTOR-REPAIRER	3	3	783.684-018
CRS	INSPECTOR, WHEEL AND PINION	3	4	715.684-126
CRS	INSPECTOR, RUBBER-STAMP DIE	3	4	733.687-054
CRS	INSULATOR TESTER	3	4	729.387-026
CRS	IRON-LAUNDER OPERATOR	3	4	511.565-018
CRS	JACKET PREPARER	3	3	221.387-030
CRS	JEWEL INSPECTOR	3	4	770.687-022
CRS	JOB PUTTER-UP AND TICKET PREPARER	3	3	788.587-010
CRS	LEATHER ETCHER	3	3	583.685-066
CRS	LINE WALKER	3	4	869.564-010
CRS	LINER	3	5	740.681-010
CRS	LOADER 1	3	5	914.667-010
CRS	LUMBER ESTIMATOR	3	5	221.482-014
CRS	MAGNETIC-TAPE-TYPEWRITER OPERATOR	3	4	203.582-034
CRS	MARGIN CLERK 1	3	5	216.382-042
CRS	MATTRESS FINISHER	3	3	780.684-070
CRS	MENDER, KNIT GOODS	3	3	782.684-046
CRS	METAL-FINISH INSPECTOR	3	5	703.687-014
CRS	METER-REPAIRER HELPER	3	4	710.684-034
CRS	MOLD OPERATOR	3	4	729.684-030
CRS	MONEY COUNTER	3	3	211.467-014
CRS	MORTGAGE-PROCESSING CLERK	3	5	203.382-022
CRS	MOTHER REPAIRER	3	4	705.684-042
CRS	MOTOR-AND-GENERATOR-BRUSH MAKER	3	4	724.684-038
CRS	MUSIC COPYIST	3	5	209.582-010
CRS	NAPHTHA-WASHING-SYSTEM OPERATOR	3	5	559.382-038
CRS	NEEDLE STRAIGHTENER	3	4	628.684-018
CRS	OUTSIDE CUTTER, HAND	3	4	788.684-082
CRS	OVEREDGE SEWER	3	4	787.682-034
CRS	PANTRY WORKER	3	3	520.487-018
CRS	PARACHUTE MENDER	3	3	789.684-038
CRS	PARTS-ORDER-AND-STOCK CLERK	3	5	249.367-058
CRS	PAYROLL CLERK	3	4	215.482-010
CRS	POLICY-VALUE CALCULATOR	3	5	216.382-050
CRS	PRESS-PIPE INSPECTOR	3	2	575.687-030
CRS	PRESSER	3	4	977.684-018
CRS	PRINTER OPERATOR, BLACK-AND-WHITE	3	5	976.682-014
CRS	PROPERTY CLERK	3	5	222.367-054
CRS	PROTECTIVE-SIGNAL-INSTALLER HELPER	3	5	822.664-010
CRS	PUMP TESTER	3	4	557.564-014
CRS	PUT-IN-BEAT ADJUSTER	3	3	715.684-174
CRS	REAGENT TENDER	3	4	511.685-046
CRS	RECEIVING CHECKER	3	3	222.687-018
CRS	RECONCILEMENT CLERK	3	5	210.382-058
CRS	REDUCTION-FURNACE OPERATOR	3	4	553.682-022
CRS	REINFORCING-STEEL-MACHINE OPERATOR	3	4	859.683-022
CRS	RETURNED-ITEM CLERK	3	4	216.382-058
CRS	ROOFER APPLICATOR	3	6	866.684-010
CRS	RUG DYER 2	3	5	364.684-010
CRS	SAFETY-LAMP KEEPER	3	4	729.684-042
CRS	SAIL CUTTER	3	4	781.384-018
CRS	SCREEN PRINTER	3	3	979.684-030

CLASSIFIED INDEX

Code	Title	GED	SVP	DOT No.
CRS	SCREWMAKER, AUTOMATIC	3	5	609.682-030
CRS	SEAMLESS-HOSIERY KNITTER	3	3	684.685-010
CRS	SERGING-MACHINE OPERATOR, AUTOMATIC	3	3	787.685-030
CRS	SEWER AND INSPECTOR	3	3	684.682-014
CRS	SEWING-MACHINE OPERATOR	3	4	787.682-066
CRS	SEWING-MACHINE OPERATOR	3	3	787.682-074
CRS	SHIRRING-MACHINE OPERATOR	3	4	787.682-078
CRS	SHUTTLE FIXER	3	3	628.684-026
CRS	SIZER	3	3	684.687-018
CRS	SLIP-COVER SEWER	3	4	780.682-014
CRS	SMASH HAND	3	3	683.684-026
CRS	SPORTS-EQUIPMENT REPAIRER	3	4	732.684-122
CRS	STATISTICAL CLERK	3	4	216.382-062
CRS	STATISTICAL CLERK, ADVERTISING	3	4	216.382-066
CRS	STERILIZER	3	3	599.585-010
CRS	STONE-SPREADER OPERATOR	3	5	853.663-022
CRS	STRAP-MACHINE OPERATOR	3	4	534.682-034
CRS	STREET-LIGHT-SERVICER HELPER	3	4	824.664-010
CRS	SUBASSEMBLER	3	4	706.684-094
CRS	TERMINAL-MAKEUP OPERATOR	3	5	208.382-010
CRS	TESTER, ELECTRICAL CONTINUITY	3	3	729.684-058
CRS	TESTER, SOUND	3	4	706.382-014
CRS	THICKENER OPERATOR	3	4	511.485-014
CRS	THREAD-CUTTER TENDER	3	2	689.665-014
CRS	TICKET-DISPENSER CHANGER	3	3	349.680-010
CRS	TIP PRINTER	3	3	651.682-022
CRS	TITLE SEARCHER	3	5	209.367-046
CRS	TRAFFIC CLERK	3	4	214.587-014
CRS	TRAFFIC CLERK	3	4	209.382-022
CRS	TRIMMER, MACHINE 2	3	4	690.682-086
CRS	TRUST-SECURITIES CLERK	3	4	219.362-062
CRS	TUFT-MACHINE OPERATOR	3	4	687.682-014
CRS	UPHOLSTERY SEWER	3	4	780.682-018
CRS	WASTE SALVAGER	3	3	781.684-062
CRS	WEATHER CLERK	3	3	248.362-014
CRS	WEAVER, HAND	3	5	782.381-022
CRS	WINDING INSPECTOR AND TESTER	3	4	724.364-010
CRS	WIRER, SUBASSEMBLIES	3	4	729.684-062
CRS	WOODEN-SHADE HARDWARE INSTALLER	3	3	739.684-174
CRS	ACETYLENE-CYLINDER-PACKING MIXER	2	2	549.665-010
CRS	ADDING-MACHINE OPERATOR	2	3	216.482-014
CRS	AERIAL-TRAM OPERATOR	2	2	932.685-010
CRS	AIRLINE SECURITY REPRESENTATIVE	2	2	372.667-010
CRS	AMPOULE EXAMINER	2	3	559.687-010
CRS	ARBORER	2	2	700.684-010
CRS	ASSEMBLER	2	3	369.687-010
CRS	ASSEMBLER, SMALL PARTS	2	2	706.684-022
CRS	ASSEMBLER, MARKING DEVICES	2	2	733.687-010
CRS	ASSEMBLER, MOVEMENT	2	3	715.684-014
CRS	BALCONY WORKER	2	2	575.687-010
CRS	BAND BUILDER	2	3	750.684-010
CRS	BEAD BUILDER	2	3	750.684-014
CRS	BEVEL POLISHER	2	3	603.685-022
CRS	BILLPOSTER	2	2	841.684-010

Code	Title	GED	SVP	DOT No.
CRS	BINDER AND BOX BUILDER	2	2	628.684-010
CRS	BINDING PRINTER	2	2	652.685-014
CRS	BIT BENDER	2	3	752.684-018
CRS	BIT-SHARPENER OPERATOR	2	2	603.685-030
CRS	BLEMISH REMOVER	2	4	788.684-022
CRS	BLENDER HELPER	2	2	550.586-010
CRS	BOBBIN SORTER	2	2	922.687-018
CRS	BOTTOM POLISHER	2	2	603.685-034
CRS	BOW MAKER	2	3	784.684-010
CRS	BOW-STRING MAKER	2	3	732.684-042
CRS	BOX INSPECTOR	2	2	762.687-014
CRS	BOXING INSPECTOR	2	3	789.587-010
CRS	BRIM IRONER, HAND	2	2	784.684-014
CRS	BRIM STITCHER 1	2	2	784.685-014
CRS	BRUSH POLISHER	2	3	603.685-038
CRS	BULLET-LUBRICANT MIXER	2	2	543.685-010
CRS	CAN RECONDITIONER	2	3	920.687-058
CRS	CANDY DIPPER, HAND	2	4	524.684-010
CRS	CANDY MOLDER, HAND	2	3	520.687-018
CRS	CANER 2	2	3	763.684-022
CRS	CAPONIZER	2	2	411.684-010
CRS	CARTON INSPECTOR	2	3	920.687-070
CRS	CARTON-PACKAGING-MACHINE OPERATOR	2	2	920.665-010
CRS	CELL INSPECTOR	2	4	556.684-010
CRS	CHAIN-TESTING-MACHINE OPERATOR	2	4	616.685-010
CRS	CHICLE-GRINDER FEEDER	2	2	521.686-018
CRS	CHURNER	2	2	520.565-010
CRS	COILER	2	3	725.687-014
CRS	COIN-MACHINE ASSEMBLER	2	3	731.684-010
CRS	COLOR-CARD MAKER	2	2	794.687-014
CRS	COMPRESSION-MOLDING-MACHINE TENDER	2	2	556.685-022
CRS	CRAYON GRADER	2	3	579.684-014
CRS	CURB ATTENDANT	2	2	369.477-010
CRS	CURTAIN-ROLLER ASSEMBLER	2	3	739.684-042
CRS	CUT-AND-COVER LINE WORKER	2	2	753.684-014
CRS	CUT-OFF-MACHINE OPERATOR	2	2	615.685-022
CRS	CUTTER-INSPECTOR	2	2	751.684-010
CRS	CUTTER, HAND 2	2	2	781.687-026
CRS	CUTTER, HOT KNIFE	2	3	751.684-018
CRS	DECAY-CONTROL OPERATOR	2	2	529.685-086
CRS	DECORATOR	2	2	739.684-046
CRS	DECORATOR	2	4	749.684-014
CRS	DEICER FINISHER	2	4	739.684-054
CRS	DELI CUTTER-SLICER	2	2	316.684-014
CRS	DETONATOR ASSEMBLER	2	2	737.687-038
CRS	DIELECTRIC-PRESS OPERATOR	2	2	692.685-074
CRS	DINING ROOM ATTENDANT	2	2	311.677-018
CRS	DIPPER AND BAKER	2	2	599.685-030
CRS	DISASSEMBLER	2	3	715.684-090
CRS	DOWEL POINTER	2	2	667.685-038
CRS	DOWELING-MACHINE OPERATOR	2	3	669.685-050
CRS	DRIER	2	3	581.685-014
CRS	DRIER OPERATOR, DRUM	2	2	529.685-098
CRS	DRILLER, MACHINE	2	2	676.685-014

Code	Title	GED	SVP	DOT No.
CRS	DRYING-RACK CHANGER	2	2	581.686-026
CRS	EDGE BANDER, HAND	2	2	762.684-038
CRS	EDGE STRIPPER	2	4	795.684-014
CRS	ENROBING-MACHINE FEEDER	2	2	524.686-010
CRS	FAN-BLADE ALINER	2	2	706.687-018
CRS	FELT-WASHING-MACHINE TENDER	2	3	582.685-070
CRS	FELTMAKER AND WEIGHER	2	3	586.685-022
CRS	FIBERGLASS-BONDING-MACHINE TENDER	2	2	574.665-010
CRS	FIRE-EQUIPMENT-INSPECTOR HELPER	2	3	739.687-094
CRS	FISH-STRINGER ASSEMBLER	2	2	732.684-054
CRS	FLY TIER	2	4	732.684-074
CRS	FORMULA WEIGHER	2	3	550.663-014
CRS	FORMULA-ROOM WORKER	2	3	520.487-014
CRS	FORWARDER	2	3	794.687-026
CRS	FRAME TRIMMER 1	2	2	749.684-030
CRS	FRUIT-GRADER OPERATOR	2	2	529.665-010
CRS	FUR BLOWER	2	2	369.685-010
CRS	GASSER	2	2	585.685-050
CRS	GLASS DRILLER	2	2	775.687-014
CRS	GLASS GRINDER	2	2	775.684-034
CRS	GLASS-WORKER, PRESSED OR BLOWN	2	2	772.687-010
CRS	GOLD-NIB GRINDER	2	2	705.682-010
CRS	GOLF-CLUB WEIGHTER	2	2	732.687-026
CRS	GRINDER OPERATOR, AUTOMATIC	2	2	603.685-058
CRS	GROOVER	2	2	673.685-062
CRS	GROUNDSKEEPER, PARKS AND GROUNDS	2	2	406.687-010
CRS	GUIDE WINDER	2	3	732.684-086
CRS	HAND FILER, BALANCE WHEEL	2	3	715.684-106
CRS	HANDS ASSEMBLER	2	3	715.684-110
CRS	HARDWARE ASSEMBLER	2	3	763.684-042
CRS	HAT-FORMING-MACHINE FEEDER	2	2	586.686-018
CRS	HOT BOX OPERATOR	2	2	709.685-014
CRS	INKER	2	2	788.684-066
CRS	INSOLE BEVELER	2	2	690.685-242
CRS	INSPECTOR	2	3	733.687-042
CRS	INSPECTOR	2	3	769.687-026
CRS	INSPECTOR	2	2	529.687-114
CRS	INSPECTOR, BALANCE WHEEL MOTION	2	3	715.687-054
CRS	INSPECTOR, BALL POINTS	2	3	733.687-046
CRS	INSPECTOR, BARREL	2	3	736.687-014
CRS	INSPECTOR, BULLET SLUGS	2	3	737.687-058
CRS	JEWEL INSERTER	2	3	715.684-130
CRS	JEWEL STRIPPER	2	2	605.685-022
CRS	LAP CUTTER-TRUER OPERATOR	2	2	604.685-022
CRS	LEAD PONY RIDER	2	2	153.674-014
CRS	LEAK HUNTER	2	2	764.687-090
CRS	LENS-BLOCK GAGER	2	2	716.687-030
CRS	LEVEL-VIAL SETTER	2	3	701.684-018
CRS	LEVEL-VIAL SEALER	2	2	779.684-034
CRS	LIME-SLUDGE KILN OPERATOR	2	2	553.685-074
CRS	LUMP INSPECTOR	2	2	790.687-018
CRS	MACHINE OPERATOR, CERAMICS	2	3	679.685-010
CRS	MACHINE-MADE-SHOE UNIT WORKER	2	2	753.584-010
CRS	MECHANISM ASSEMBLER	2	3	715.684-142

Code	Title	GED	SVP	DOT No.
CRS	MIDDLE-CARD TENDER	2	2	680.665-018
CRS	MIXER OPERATOR, CARBON PASTE	2	4	540.585-010
CRS	MOLD WORKER	2	3	514.567-010
CRS	MOLDER, SHOULDER PAD	2	2	789.684-026
CRS	MONOGRAM-AND-LETTER PASTER	2	2	789.687-102
CRS	NAME-PLATE STAMPER	2	2	652.685-054
CRS	NAPHTHALENE OPERATOR	2	3	551.665-010
CRS	NEEDLE-PUNCH-MACHINE OPERATOR	2	3	689.682-014
CRS	NIB FINISHER	2	4	705.684-050
CRS	NYLON-HOT-WIRE CUTTER	2	3	781.684-038
CRS	OIL-SEAL ASSEMBLER	2	3	739.684-138
CRS	OLIVE BRINE TESTER	2	3	522.584-010
CRS	ORDER CALLER	2	2	209.667-014
CRS	ORNAMENT MAKER, HAND	2	3	739.687-130
CRS	OUTSOLE SCHEDULER	2	2	221.587-022
CRS	OVERCOILER	2	3	715.684-150
CRS	PADDED-PRODUCTS FINISHER	2	3	752.684-034
CRS	PAPER CUTTER	2	2	640.565-010
CRS	PAPER-PATTERN INSPECTOR	2	2	649.687-018
CRS	PARKING-LOT ATTENDANT	2	2	915.473-010
CRS	PASSEMENTERIE WORKER	2	4	782.684-050
CRS	PIANO CASE AND BENCH ASSEMBLER	2	2	763.684-058
CRS	PILOT-CONTROL-OPERATOR HELPER	2	5	559.664-014
CRS	PINION POLISHER	2	3	715.685-042
CRS	PINNER	2	3	782.684-054
CRS	PLANISHER	2	2	700.687-054
CRS	POLE INSPECTOR	2	3	561.587-010
CRS	POULTRY VACCINATOR	2	2	411.684-014
CRS	PRIMER EXPEDITOR AND DRIER	2	3	553.385-014
CRS	PRIMER INSPECTOR	2	3	737.687-106
CRS	PRIMING-POWDER-PREMIX BLENDER	2	3	550.684-022
CRS	PRODUCTION HELPER	2	2	529.686-070
CRS	QUILL-BUNCHER-AND-SORTER	2	3	734.687-066
CRS	QUILLING-MACHINE OPERATOR, AUTOMATIC	2	3	681.685-074
CRS	REAGENT TENDER HELPER	2	2	511.686-010
CRS	REED-PRESS FEEDER	2	2	669.686-022
CRS	REPAIRER	2	4	753.684-026
CRS	ROLLER-SKATE REPAIRER	2	4	732.684-102
CRS	ROLLER-STITCHER	2	2	753.684-030
CRS	ROTOR ASSEMBLER	2	2	715.687-114
CRS	ROUNDER, HAND	2	2	784.684-050
CRS	RUBBER-TUBING SPLICER	2	2	752.684-042
CRS	RUG INSPECTOR 1	2	3	689.667-010
CRS	RUG-BACKING STENCILER	2	3	781.687-054
CRS	SAMPLE MAKER, VENEER	2	3	769.684-042
CRS	SANDING-MACHINE TENDER	2	2	662.685-026
CRS	SAW-EDGE FUSER, CIRCULAR	2	3	701.684-026
CRS	SEALER 1	2	3	727.684-030
CRS	SEALER, DRY CELL	2	3	692.685-158
CRS	SHADE-CLOTH FINISHER	2	2	585.687-026
CRS	SHANK THREADER	2	2	739.685-034
CRS	SLITTER	2	2	781.684-054
CRS	SOLDERER-DIPPER	2	2	813.684-018

Code	Title	GED	SVP	DOT No.
CRS	SOLDERER, PRODUCTION LINE	2	2	813.684-022
CRS	SOLDERER, ULTRASONIC, HAND	2	3	813.684-030
CRS	SORTER, UPHOLSTERY PARTS	2	3	780.587-010
CRS	SORTING-MACHINE OPERATOR	2	3	208.685-030
CRS	SPOILAGE WORKER	2	4	709.587-014
CRS	SPRING CLIPPER	2	3	780.684-102
CRS	SPRING LAYER	2	2	715.687-122
CRS	SPRING TESTER 2	2	2	709.687-042
CRS	STARCHMAKER	2	3	526.687-014
CRS	STEAM-PRESS TENDER	2	3	583.685-106
CRS	STENCIL INSPECTOR	2	2	733.687-074
CRS	STICKER-ON	2	2	774.684-034
CRS	STOCKLAYER	2	2	753.687-042
CRS	STONER	2	4	735.684-014
CRS	STRIKE-OUT-MACHINE OPERATOR	2	2	587.685-030
CRS	SURGICAL-DRESSING MAKER	2	2	689.685-130
CRS	SWATCH CLERK	2	2	222.587-050
CRS	TEMPERATURE INSPECTOR	2	3	529.687-202
CRS	TESTER	2	3	899.487-010
CRS	THERMAL-SURFACING-MACHINE OPERATOR	2	2	679.685-018
CRS	THERMOSTAT-ASSEMBLY-MACHINE TENDER, AUTOMATIC	2	4	692.685-218
CRS	TIP FINISHER	2	2	690.685-418
CRS	TIRE BALANCER	2	2	750.687-014
CRS	TIRE-BLADDER MAKER	2	2	750.684-042
CRS	TOY ASSEMBLER	2	3	731.684-018
CRS	TUBE BUILDER, AIRPLANE	2	4	750.384-014
CRS	TURRET-LATHE OPERATOR, TUMBLE TAILSTOCK	2	3	604.685-042
CRS	VARNISHING-UNIT OPERATOR	2	2	737.687-138
CRS	WARM-IN WORKER	2	3	772.684-018
CRS	WARP-YARN SORTER	2	2	681.687-022
CRS	WASHER ENGINEER	2	3	533.685-034
CRS	WEAVE-DEFECT-CHARTING CLERK	2	2	221.587-042
CRS	WELT CUTTER	2	4	690.685-478
CRS	WRONG-ADDRESS CLERK	2	3	209.587-050
CRS	X-RAY INSPECTOR	2	2	529.685-274
CRS	INSPECTOR, LIVE AMMUNITION	1	2	736.687-018
CRS	PASTING-MACHINE OFFBEARER	1	2	509.686-014
CRS	PULVERIZER	1	2	521.685-266
CRS	RETURNED-CASE INSPECTOR	1	2	929.687-038
CRE	AIRLINE-RADIO OPERATOR	4	7	193.262-010
CRE	AUDIT CLERK	4	5	210.382-010
CRE	BOOKKEEPER 1	4	6	210.382-014
CRE	BOOKKEEPING-MACHINE OPERATOR 2	4	5	210.382-026
CRE	CENTRAL-OFFICE REPAIRER	4	7	822.281-014
CRE	FOREIGN-EXCHANGE-POSITION CLERK	4	5	210.367-014
CRE	MATERIAL LISTER	4	5	229.387-010
CRE	PHOTORADIO OPERATOR	4	6	193.362-010
CRE	SERVICES CLERK	4	5	214.387-018
CRE	ABRASIVE GRINDER	3	3	673.685-010
CRE	ASSEMBLER 1	3	3	723.684-014
CRE	ASSEMBLER, ELECTRICAL ACCESSORIES 2	3	3	729.384-010

Code	Title	GED	SVP	DOT No.
CRE	ASSEMBLER, BILLIARD-TABLE	3	3	732.384-010
CRE	ASSEMBLER, LEATHER GOODS 1	3	3	783.684-010
CRE	ASSIGNMENT CLERK	3	4	219.387-010
CRE	AUTOMOBILE TESTER	3	4	379.364-010
CRE	BALANCE ASSEMBLER	3	3	715.384-010
CRE	BATTERY-CHARGER TESTER	3	3	729.684-010
CRE	BOOK-JACKET-COVER-MACHINE OPERATOR	3	3	640.685-014
CRE	BOTTLE GAGER	3	3	529.587-010
CRE	BURLER	3	3	689.684-010
CRE	CALCINER-OPERATOR HELPER	3	4	513.667-010
CRE	CANTILEVER-CRANE OPERATOR	3	5	921.683-018
CRE	CARBON-FURNACE-OPERATOR HELPER	3	3	543.664-010
CRE	CHIP TESTER	3	3	539.387-010
CRE	CHRONOGRAPH OPERATOR	3	3	739.484-010
CRE	CLOTH TESTER, QUALITY	3	4	689.384-010
CRE	COKE INSPECTOR	3	4	542.567-010
CRE	COMMODITY-LOAN CLERK	3	4	210.382-034
CRE	COOK, SHORT ORDER 2	3	3	313.671-010
CRE	COUNTER MOLDER	3	3	690.685-102
CRE	CRYSTALLIZER OPERATOR	3	4	559.685-042
CRE	CURRENCY SORTER	3	4	217.485-010
CRE	CUTTING INSPECTOR	3	3	781.684-022
CRE	DECORATING-MACHINE OPERATOR	3	3	652.685-026
CRE	DEICER INSPECTOR, PNEUMATIC	3	4	759.687-010
CRE	DEMURRAGE CLERK	3	5	214.362-010
CRE	DIRECT-MAIL CLERK	3	4	209.587-018
CRE	DISTRIBUTION-ACCOUNTING CLERK	3	5	210.362-010
CRE	DRILLER AND BROACHER	3	5	715.685-022
CRE	DROP TESTER	3	3	737.387-010
CRE	DUSTLESS OPERATOR	3	3	550.685-058
CRE	ELECTRICAL-CONTROL ASSEMBLER	3	4	729.684-026
CRE	ELECTROLOGIST (SAC)	3	5	339.371-010
CRE	ELECTROTYPE SERVICER	3	3	659.462-010
CRE	ENGRAVER, MACHINE 1	3	3	704.682-010
CRE	ETCHED-CIRCUIT PROCESSOR	3	4	590.684-018
CRE	EVAPORATIVE-COOLER INSTALLER	3	6	637.381-010
CRE	FIBER-MACHINE TENDER	3	3	575.685-030
CRE	FIRE-EXTINGUISHER-SPRINKLER INSPECTOR	3	4	379.687-010
CRE	FLOTATION TENDER	3	4	511.685-026
CRE	FOOD CHECKER	3	3	211.482-014
CRE	FOOD-AND-BEVERAGE CHECKER	3	3	211.482-018
CRE	FUR IRONER	3	3	369.685-018
CRE	GAGER	3	4	715.687-034
CRE	GOLD CUTTER	3	4	700.684-038
CRE	HAT TRIMMER	3	5	782.381-010
CRE	HAT-AND-CAP SEWER	3	3	784.682-014
CRE	HEDDLES TIER, JACQUARD LOOM	3	5	683.680-014
CRE	HEMMER, AUTOMATIC	3	3	787.685-018
CRE	INJECTOR ASSEMBLER	3	5	706.684-062
CRE	INSPECTOR 1	3	4	729.387-022
CRE	INSPECTOR, FABRIC	3	3	789.587-014
CRE	INSULATION CUTTER AND FORMER	3	3	721.484-018
CRE	KNITTER, HAND	3	5	782.684-034

Code	Title	GED	SVP	DOT No.
CRE	LAMINATION ASSEMBLER	3	3	729.484-010
CRE	LAUNDRY PRICING CLERK	3	3	216.482-030
CRE	MACHINE TESTER	3	4	706.387-014
CRE	MANUAL WINDER	3	3	730.684-046
CRE	MELTER CLERK	3	4	221.387-042
CRE	MENDER	3	4	787.682-030
CRE	MILL RECORDER, COMPUTERIZED MILL	3	5	221.367-046
CRE	MORTGAGE CLERK	3	5	249.382-010
CRE	PERISHABLE-FREIGHT INSPECTOR	3	3	910.667-022
CRE	PHOTOCOMPOSITION-KEYBOARD OPERATOR	3	4	203.582-046
CRE	PLATE ASSEMBLER, SMALL BATTERY	3	3	727.684-026
CRE	PLEATER	3	3	787.685-026
CRE	PREPARER, SAMPLES AND REPAIRS	3	4	700.684-062
CRE	PROOF-MACHINE OPERATOR	3	4	217.382-010
CRE	PROTECTIVE-SIGNAL-REPAIRER HELPER	3	6	822.684-014
CRE	QUALITY-CONTROL TECHNICIAN	3	4	579.367-014
CRE	QUALITY-CONTROL TESTER	3	4	684.384-010
CRE	QUARTERMASTER	3	6	911.363-014
CRE	RABBLE-FURNACE TENDER	3	3	553.685-090
CRE	RACKER, OCTAVE BOARD	3	3	730.684-062
CRE	RACKET STRINGER	3	5	732.684-094
CRE	RAW SAMPLER	3	4	519.484-014
CRE	RECTIFICATION PRINTER	3	4	976.682-018
CRE	RETORT-CONDENSER ATTENDANT	3	3	552.685-022
CRE	REVISING CLERK	3	4	214.382-026
CRE	ROUNDING-AND-BACKING-MACHINE OPERATOR	3	4	653.685-026
CRE	RUG HOOKER	3	5	687.684-010
CRE	SATURATOR TENDER	3	3	582.685-118
CRE	SEWING-MACHINE OPERATOR	3	4	787.682-042
CRE	SEWING-MACHINE OPERATOR	3	4	787.682-070
CRE	SEWING-MACHINE OPERATOR	3	4	787.682-050
CRE	SIDER	3	4	863.684-014
CRE	SILK-SCREEN-FRAME ASSEMBLER	3	3	709.484-010
CRE	SPACE-AND-STORAGE CLERK	3	3	219.387-026
CRE	SPECIAL-CERTIFICATE DICTATOR	3	6	209.382-014
CRE	SPRAY-MACHINE TENDER	3	4	599.685-090
CRE	SWITCHBOARD OPERATOR, POLICE DISTRICT	3	4	235.562-014
CRE	TABULATING-MACHINE OPERATOR	3	5	213.682-010
CRE	THREAD LASTER	3	3	788.684-114
CRE	TRANSFERRER	3	3	715.684-190
CRE	TUCKING-MACHINE OPERATOR	3	4	787.682-082
CRE	TYPESETTER-PERFORATOR OPERATOR	3	4	203.582-062
CRE	VARITYPE OPERATOR	3	5	203.382-026
CRE	VENETIAN-BLIND INSTALLER	3	4	869.484-018
CRE	WATER-SERVICE DISPATCHER	3	4	954.367-010
CRE	WATERWAY TRAFFIC CHECKER	3	3	248.367-030
CRE	WIRER, STREET LIGHT	3	3	821.684-018
CRE	ZIPPER SETTER	3	4	787.682-086
CRE	ABRASIVE SAWYER	2	2	677.685-010
CRE	ACETONE-RECOVERY WORKER	2	3	552.685-010
CRE	ACID ADJUSTER	2	2	727.484-010
CRE	ACID FILLER	2	2	727.687-014

CLASSIFIED INDEX

Code	Title	GED	SVP	DOT No.
CRE	ACID PURIFIER	2	3	559.685-010
CRE	ADHESIVE-BANDAGE-MACHINE OPERATOR	2	3	692.685-014
CRE	ADJUSTER, ALARM MECHANISM	2	2	715.684-010
CRE	AIRPLANE-GAS-TANK-LINER ASSEMBLER	2	2	759.684-010
CRE	ALMOND-BLANCHER OPERATOR	2	2	521.685-014
CRE	ALUMINUM-CONTAINER TESTER	2	3	727.687-018
CRE	ANNEALER	2	2	504.687-010
CRE	ARMATURE CONNECTOR 2	2	3	724.684-014
CRE	ARMHOLE FELLER, HANDSTITCHING MACHINE	2	2	786.682-018
CRE	ARTIFICIAL-FLOWER MAKER	2	3	739.684-014
CRE	ASBESTOS-SHINGLE INSPECTOR	2	3	679.687-010
CRE	ASSEMBLER	2	3	700.684-014
CRE	ASSEMBLER	2	3	723.684-010
CRE	ASSEMBLER	2	3	732.684-014
CRE	ASSEMBLER 2	2	3	736.684-014
CRE	ASSEMBLER, REGULATORS	2	3	719.684-010
CRE	ASSEMBLER, ELECTRICAL WIRE GROUP	2	3	728.384-010
CRE	ASSEMBLER, ELECTRICAL ACCESSORIES 1	2	2	729.687-010
CRE	ASSEMBLER, CORNCOB PIPES	2	2	739.687-014
CRE	ASSEMBLER, OIL FILTERS	2	2	739.687-026
CRE	ASSEMBLER, SANDAL PARTS	2	2	788.684-014
CRE	ASSEMBLY LOADER	2	3	711.684-010
CRE	ASSEMBLY-PRESS OPERATOR	2	2	690.685-014
CRE	AUTO ROLLER	2	2	529.685-010
CRE	AUTOMAT-CAR ATTENDANT	2	2	319.464-010
CRE	AUXILIARY-EQUIPMENT OPERATOR, DATA PROCESSING	2	3	213.685-010
CRE	BACK PADDER	2	2	780.684-010
CRE	BACK TENDER, INSULATION BOARD	2	2	532.685-010
CRE	BAG REPAIRER	2	2	794.684-010
CRE	BALANCE RECESSER	2	3	604.685-010
CRE	BALL ASSEMBLER	2	3	732.684-026
CRE	BAND-AND-CUFF CUTTER	2	2	784.685-010
CRE	BARREL INSPECTOR, TIGHT	2	4	764.687-022
CRE	BARREL POLISHER, INSIDE	2	3	603.685-014
CRE	BARREL RIFLER	2	3	605.685-010
CRE	BASEBALL SEWER, HAND	2	3	732.684-034
CRE	BASKET MENDER	2	3	762.684-022
CRE	BATTERY ASSEMBLER, PLASTIC	2	2	727.684-014
CRE	BATTERY CHARGER	2	3	727.587-010
CRE	BEAD INSPECTOR	2	3	725.687-010
CRE	BEAD STRINGER	2	3	735.684-010
CRE	BEARING-RING ASSEMBLER	2	3	706.684-038
CRE	BEATER OPERATOR	2	3	555.685-010
CRE	BELLOWS ASSEMBLER	2	3	710.687-010
CRE	BELT MAKER	2	2	776.684-010
CRE	BENCH ASSEMBLER	2	2	706.684-042
CRE	BIRD-CAGE ASSEMBLER	2	4	709.684-026
CRE	BIT SHAVER	2	2	754.684-018
CRE	BLINDSTITCH-MACHINE OPERATOR	2	2	786.682-046
CRE	BLUEPRINT TRIMMER	2	2	920.687-038
CRE	BOARDING-MACHINE OPERATOR	2	3	589.685-010
CRE	BOBBIN INSPECTOR	2	2	769.687-014

Code	Title	GED	SVP	DOT No.
CRE	BONDER, AUTOMOBILE BRAKES	2	3	620.685-010
CRE	BONE-CHAR KILN TENDER	2	2	553.685-018
CRE	BOW MAKER	2	3	789.684-010
CRE	BOW-MAKER-MACHINE TENDER, AUTOMATIC	2	3	689.685-030
CRE	BOWLING-BALL WEIGHER AND PACKER	2	4	732.487-010
CRE	BRAKE ADJUSTER	2	2	620.684-018
CRE	BRIM-AND-CROWN PRESSER	2	2	583.685-022
CRE	BRINE MAKER 2	2	4	522.685-022
CRE	BRINE-MIXER OPERATOR, AUTOMATIC	2	2	520.685-034
CRE	BROOMMAKER	2	4	739.684-018
CRE	BUCKLE-STRAP-DRUM OPERATOR	2	2	554.485-010
CRE	BUNCH MAKER, MACHINE	2	2	529.685-038
CRE	BURNISHER	2	2	603.685-042
CRE	BURNISHER AND BUMPER	2	3	807.684-018
CRE	BURNISHER, BALANCE WHEEL ARM	2	3	715.684-038
CRE	BURRER	2	3	715.684-042
CRE	BURRER, MACHINE	2	2	603.685-046
CRE	BURSTING-MACHINE TENDER	2	2	217.685-010
CRE	BUTT MAKER	2	2	529.685-042
CRE	CADDIE	2	2	341.677-010
CRE	CAN INSPECTOR	2	3	920.687-050
CRE	CAP MAKER	2	4	784.684-018
CRE	CASE FINISHER	2	2	739.684-034
CRE	CASER	2	3	715.684-054
CRE	CASING-MATERIAL WEIGHER	2	2	520.687-026
CRE	CASTING INSPECTOR	2	3	514.687-010
CRE	CATHETER BUILDER	2	4	752.684-026
CRE	CELL REPAIRER	2	3	727.684-018
CRE	CELL TUBER, MACHINE	2	2	692.685-046
CRE	CELLULOID TRIMMER	2	2	732.684-046
CRE	CENTRIFUGE OPERATOR	2	3	521.685-046
CRE	CENTRIFUGE-SEPARATOR TENDER	2	4	541.585-010
CRE	CERAMIC CAPACITOR PROCESSOR	2	3	590.684-010
CRE	CHAINSTITCH SEWING MACHINE OPERATOR	2	2	786.682-054
CRE	CHAIR INSPECTOR AND LEVELER	2	3	763.687-014
CRE	CHILLER OPERATOR	2	3	551.685-042
CRE	CHIP UNLOADER	2	3	921.663-018
CRE	CHOKE REAMER	2	3	606.685-022
CRE	CIGAR PACKER	2	3	790.687-014
CRE	CIGARETTE-FILTER-MAKING-MACHINE OPERATOR	2	3	529.685-062
CRE	CIGARETTE-LIGHTER REPAIRER	2	3	709.684-034
CRE	CLARIFIER	2	3	521.685-058
CRE	CLEANER, HOUSEKEEPING	2	2	323.687-014
CRE	CLEANER, HOSPITAL	2	2	323.687-010
CRE	CLIP COATER	2	2	713.687-010
CRE	CLIP-AND-HANGER ATTACHER	2	4	739.684-038
CRE	COATER OPERATOR, INSULATION BOARD	2	2	539.685-010
CRE	COATER, BRAKE LININGS	2	2	574.685-010
CRE	COFFEE ROASTER, CONTINUOUS PROCESS	2	3	523.685-026
CRE	COIN-MACHINE COLLECTOR	2	2	292.687-010
CRE	COLD-ROLL INSPECTOR	2	4	751.584-010
CRE	COLOR MATCHER	2	4	788.687-034
CRE	COMPOSITION-WEATHERBOARD APPLIER	2	4	863.684-010

CLASSIFIED INDEX

Code	Title	GED	SVP	DOT No.
CRE	CONVEX-GRINDER OPERATOR	2	2	673.685-042
CRE	CORE EXTRUDER	2	2	557.685-010
CRE	COUNTER FORMER	2	2	690.685-098
CRE	COVERING-MACHINE TENDER	2	2	783.685-010
CRE	COVERSTITCH-MACHINE OPERATOR	2	2	786.682-078
CRE	CROWN POUNCER, HAND	2	3	784.687-018
CRE	CRUSHER	2	2	780.684-042
CRE	CULLER	2	3	764.687-054
CRE	CUTTER	2	2	976.685-010
CRE	CUTTER, MACHINE 2	2	2	699.685-014
CRE	DATER ASSEMBLER	2	2	733.687-030
CRE	DEBURRER	2	2	603.685-050
CRE	DECORATOR	2	3	784.684-022
CRE	DEFLECTOR OPERATOR	2	2	529.687-058
CRE	DEICER-ELEMENT WINDER, HAND	2	4	739.684-058
CRE	DESIGN INSERTER	2	3	692.685-070
CRE	DESKIDDING-MACHINE OPERATOR	2	2	690.685-126
CRE	DIAL MARKER	2	2	729.684-018
CRE	DIAL-SCREW ASSEMBLER	2	2	715.684-082
CRE	DISK-AND-TAPE-MACHINE TENDER	2	2	783.685-018
CRE	DOLL REPAIRER	2	3	731.684-014
CRE	DRAWSTRING KNOTTER	2	2	689.685-058
CRE	DRIER OPERATOR 2	2	2	553.685-046
CRE	DRILLER, BRAKE LINING	2	2	676.685-010
CRE	DRILLER, HAND	2	2	754.684-026
CRE	DRILLING-MACHINE OPERATOR, AUTOMATIC	2	3	606.685-030
CRE	DRUM-DRIER OPERATOR	2	3	553.665-030
CRE	DRY CLEANER	2	2	589.685-038
CRE	DUST-COLLECTOR OPERATOR	2	3	551.685-050
CRE	DYED-YARN OPERATOR	2	2	582.685-058
CRE	DYER	2	2	599.685-034
CRE	EDGE STAINER 1	2	3	589.685-046
CRE	EGG PROCESSOR	2	2	559.687-034
CRE	ELECTRIC-CONTAINER TESTER	2	3	727.687-050
CRE	ELECTRIC-MOTOR ASSEMBLER	2	3	721.684-022
CRE	ELECTRIC-SEALING-MACHINE OPERATOR	2	2	690.685-154
CRE	ELEVATOR OPERATOR	2	2	388.663-010
CRE	EMBOSSER	2	3	713.684-022
CRE	EMBOSSING-PRESS OPERATOR	2	2	652.685-030
CRE	EMBROIDERY-MACHINE OPERATOR	2	2	786.685-018
CRE	END FINDER, FORMING DEPARTMENT	2	2	681.687-010
CRE	END POLISHER	2	4	715.685-026
CRE	ENDBAND CUTTER, HAND	2	2	784.687-026
CRE	ENDING-MACHINE OPERATOR	2	3	641.685-042
CRE	ENGRAVER, AUTOMATIC	2	2	609.685-014
CRE	ETCHER, HAND	2	3	704.687-014
CRE	EVAPORATOR OPERATOR	2	2	532.685-018
CRE	EXPLOSIVE OPERATOR 1	2	3	737.687-042
CRE	EXTRACTOR OPERATOR	2	3	521.685-118
CRE	EXTRACTOR OPERATOR, SOLVENT PROCESS	2	2	551.685-062
CRE	EXTRACTOR-AND-WRINGER OPERATOR	2	2	551.685-066
CRE	EXTRUDER TENDER	2	3	557.685-014
CRE	EYE-DROPPER ASSEMBLER	2	2	739.687-086

Code	Title	GED	SVP	DOT No.
CRE	EYELET-MACHINE OPERATOR	2	2	699.685-018
CRE	EYELET-PUNCH OPERATOR	2	2	699.685-022
CRE	FABRICATOR, FOAM RUBBER	2	2	780.684-062
CRE	FACING-MACHINE OPERATOR	2	3	604.685-014
CRE	FEATHER-DUSTER WINDER	2	3	734.684-014
CRE	FINAL INSPECTOR	2	2	727.687-054
CRE	FINER	2	3	715.684-098
CRE	FINISHER	2	2	731.687-014
CRE	FINISHER	2	4	732.584-014
CRE	FIRER	2	3	590.685-034
CRE	FIRER HELPER	2	2	553.665-034
CRE	FISHING-REEL ASSEMBLER	2	2	732.684-062
CRE	FISHING-ROD ASSEMBLER	2	2	732.684-066
CRE	FISHING-ROD MARKER	2	3	732.684-070
CRE	FLANGER	2	3	712.684-018
CRE	FLANGER	2	2	784.684-026
CRE	FLAT POLISHER	2	4	603.685-054
CRE	FLAT SURFACER, JEWEL	2	3	770.685-010
CRE	FLATWORK TIER	2	2	361.587-010
CRE	FLOORWORKER- DISTRIBUTOR	2	2	784.687-030
CRE	FLYER REPAIRER	2	3	628.687-010
CRE	FOLDER	2	2	686.685-030
CRE	FOLDING-MACHINE OPERATOR	2	2	690.685-178
CRE	FOOD ASSEMBLER, KITCHEN	2	3	319.484-010
CRE	FOOT-MITER OPERATOR	2	2	739.684-066
CRE	FORM COVERER	2	3	739.684-070
CRE	FOUNTAIN SERVER	2	2	319.474-010
CRE	FRAME CARVER, SPINDLE	2	3	713.684-030
CRE	FRAMER	2	3	739.684-078
CRE	FRONT-SIGHT ATTACHER	2	2	736.684-030
CRE	FUR CLEANER, MACHINE	2	3	369.685-014
CRE	FUR TRIMMER	2	3	783.687-014
CRE	FUR-CUTTING-MACHINE OPERATOR	2	2	585.685-046
CRE	FUR-GLAZING-AND-POLISHING-MACHINE OPERATOR	2	3	369.685-022
CRE	GAGE-AND-WEIGH-MACHINE OPERATOR	2	3	737.685-010
CRE	GAGER	2	2	712.687-018
CRE	GARMENT INSPECTOR	2	3	789.687-070
CRE	GAS-METER MECHANIC 2	2	3	710.684-026
CRE	GAS-TRANSFER OPERATOR	2	2	914.585-010
CRE	GASKET INSPECTOR	2	2	739.687-102
CRE	GIG TENDER	2	2	585.685-054
CRE	GINNER	2	3	429.685-010
CRE	GLAZIER	2	2	712.684-026
CRE	GLAZING-MACHINE OPERATOR	2	2	573.685-018
CRE	GLUE SPREADER, VENEER	2	3	569.685-042
CRE	GLUER, WET SUIT	2	2	795.687-018
CRE	GOLF-BALL TRIMMER	2	2	732.587-010
CRE	GRAIN PICKER	2	2	529.687-110
CRE	GRINDER OPERATOR	2	2	521.685-166
CRE	GRINDER 2	2	3	715.685-030
CRE	GRINDER, HAND	2	2	716.685-018
CRE	GRINDER, LAP	2	3	603.685-066
CRE	GROOVING-MACHINE OPERATOR	2	2	733.685-018

Code	Title	GED	SVP	DOT No.
CRE	GUIDE-BASE WINDER, MACHINE	2	2	732.685-022
CRE	HAIR WORKER	2	5	739.684-086
CRE	HAIRSPRING CUTTER 1	2	2	715.687-038
CRE	HAND SEWER, SHOES	2	2	788.684-054
CRE	HARNESS RIGGER	2	2	789.687-082
CRE	HAT BRAIDER	2	3	784.684-038
CRE	HAT FINISHER	2	4	589.685-062
CRE	HEADING MATCHER AND ASSEMBLER	2	3	764.687-062
CRE	HEADING REPAIRER	2	3	764.687-066
CRE	HEADLINER INSTALLER	2	2	806.684-058
CRE	HEEL GOUGER	2	3	690.685-214
CRE	HEEL SCORER	2	2	690.685-222
CRE	HEEL-NAILING-MACHINE OPERATOR	2	2	690.685-226
CRE	HEMMER, BLINDSTITCH	2	2	786.682-126
CRE	HEMMER, CHAINSTITCH	2	2	786.682-130
CRE	HEMMER, LOCKSTITCH	2	2	786.682-134
CRE	HEMMER, OVERLOCK	2	2	786.682-138
CRE	HOGSHEAD MAT INSPECTOR	2	3	764.687-086
CRE	HOLIDAY-DETECTOR OPERATOR	2	2	862.687-014
CRE	HOLLOW-HANDLE-KNIFE ASSEMBLER	2	2	700.684-042
CRE	HOOKING-MACHINE OPERATOR	2	3	605.685-018
CRE	HOP STRAINER	2	2	521.685-178
CRE	HYDRAULIC-PRESS OPERATOR	2	2	583.685-058
CRE	INSPECTOR	2	3	709.587-010
CRE	INSPECTOR, WIRE PRODUCTS	2	3	709.687-026
CRE	INSPECTOR, SURGICAL INSTRUMENTS	2	2	712.687-026
CRE	INSPECTOR, HAIRSPRING 2	2	3	715.684-122
CRE	INSPECTOR, BALANCE-BRIDGE	2	3	715.687-058
CRE	INSPECTOR, CASING	2	3	715.687-062
CRE	INSPECTOR, CONTAINER FINISHING	2	2	727.687-066
CRE	INSPECTOR, FINAL ASSEMBLY	2	3	733.687-050
CRE	INSPECTOR, SALVAGE	2	2	737.684-026
CRE	INSPECTOR, PUBLICATIONS	2	2	653.687-014
CRE	JACQUARD-TWINE-POLISHER OPERATOR	2	3	583.685-062
CRE	JET WIPER	2	2	557.684-014
CRE	JEWEL STRINGER	2	2	770.687-026
CRE	JEWELRY COATER	2	2	590.685-046
CRE	JUMPBASTING-MACHINE OPERATOR	2	2	786.682-146
CRE	KICK-PRESS OPERATOR	2	2	692.685-102
CRE	KNITTING-MACHINE OPERATOR	2	4	685.685-010
CRE	LABEL PINKER	2	2	585.685-062
CRE	LACER	2	2	774.687-014
CRE	LACER 2	2	2	690.685-254
CRE	LAMINATOR	2	3	899.684-018
CRE	LAMINATOR 2	2	2	783.685-022
CRE	LAST CHALKER	2	2	788.687-078
CRE	LAST MARKER	2	2	739.684-102
CRE	LAST-REPAIRER HELPER	2	2	739.684-114
CRE	LAYBOY TENDER	2	2	649.685-066
CRE	LAYER	2	2	673.686-026
CRE	LEACHER	2	3	551.685-090
CRE	LEAD FORMER	2	2	691.685-018
CRE	LEAD-CASTER HELPER	2	2	502.687-018
CRE	LEAF STAMPER	2	3	979.682-018

Code	Title	GED	SVP	DOT No.
CRE	PANEL INSTALLER	2	2	869.684-038
CRE	PANEL MAKER	2	3	780.684-086
CRE	PAPER COATER	2	3	534.685-022
CRE	PAPER-CONE GRADER	2	2	649.687-014
CRE	PAPER-CORE-MACHINE OPERATOR	2	2	640.685-042
CRE	PAPER-NOVELTY MAKER	2	2	794.684-022
CRE	PARADICHLOROBENZENE TENDER	2	2	556.685-054
CRE	PASTEURIZER	2	2	523.685-110
CRE	PATCHER	2	2	585.687-022
CRE	PATCHER	2	3	739.687-146
CRE	PATTERN ASSEMBLER	2	3	685.685-014
CRE	PATTERN HAND	2	3	652.687-030
CRE	PEGGER, DOBBY LOOMS	2	2	689.687-054
CRE	PELLET-MILL OPERATOR	2	2	520.685-178
CRE	PERFORATOR	2	3	781.684-042
CRE	PHOTOLETTERING-MACHINE OPERATOR	2	4	652.585-010
CRE	PICK-UP OPERATOR	2	2	689.685-098
CRE	PICKED-EDGE SEWING-MACHINE OPERATOR	2	2	786.682-206
CRE	PINKING-MACHINE OPERATOR	2	3	686.685-042
CRE	PINKING-MACHINE OPERATOR	2	2	692.685-130
CRE	PIPED-POCKET-MACHINE OPERATOR	2	2	786.685-022
CRE	PLANING-MACHINE OPERATOR	2	3	605.685-034
CRE	PLATE SLITTER-AND-INSPECTOR	2	2	727.685-010
CRE	PLEATER, HAND	2	3	583.684-010
CRE	PLUG CUTTER	2	2	690.685-306
CRE	POCKET-MACHINE OPERATOR	2	3	616.685-050
CRE	POCKETED-SPRING ASSEMBLER	2	3	780.684-090
CRE	POLISHER, BALANCE SCREWHEAD	2	3	715.685-046
CRE	POLISHER, IMPLANT	2	2	713.687-034
CRE	POLY-PACKER AND HEAT-SEALER	2	2	920.686-038
CRE	PRECISE WINDER	2	2	681.685-066
CRE	PRESS OPERATOR	2	3	686.685-050
CRE	PRETZEL-TWISTING-MACHINE OPERATOR	2	2	520.685-190
CRE	PRINTING-MACHINE OPERATOR, FOLDING RULES	2	2	652.685-074
CRE	PRODUCTION-MACHINE TENDER, GLASS CUTTING-OR-GRINDING	2	2	679.685-014
CRE	PROFILING-MACHINE OPERATOR	2	2	605.685-038
CRE	PULLER AND LASTER, MACHINE	2	3	788.684-086
CRE	PULP-PRESS TENDER	2	3	521.685-258
CRE	PUMPER HELPER	2	3	549.684-010
CRE	PUZZLE ASSEMBLER	2	2	731.687-030
CRE	QUILT STUFFER, MACHINE	2	2	689.685-102
CRE	REBRANDER	2	2	559.685-150
CRE	RECOVERY-OPERATOR HELPER	2	3	519.485-014
CRE	REMNANT SORTER	2	2	789.687-146
CRE	REPAIRER, AUTO CLOCKS	2	3	715.584-014
CRE	RIBBON INKER	2	2	692.685-142
CRE	RIBBON WINDER	2	3	733.685-022
CRE	RIBBON-HANKING-MACHINE OPERATOR	2	2	640.385-010
CRE	RIM-TURNING FINISHER	2	3	604.685-030
CRE	RIVET-HOLE PUNCHER	2	2	686.685-054
CRE	RIVETER, HAND	2	2	789.687-154
CRE	ROLL INSPECTOR	2	3	554.587-010

Code	Title	GED	SVP	DOT No.
CRE	ROLLER CHECKER	2	3	682.684-010
CRE	ROLLER-BEARING INSPECTOR	2	3	706.687-034
CRE	ROOTER OPERATOR	2	3	731.685-010
CRE	ROUNDING-MACHINE OPERATOR	2	2	585.685-086
CRE	ROUTER	2	2	222.587-038
CRE	RUBBER-GOODS ASSEMBLER	2	2	752.684-038
CRE	RUBBER-MOLD MAKER	2	3	559.684-018
CRE	RUBBER-THREAD SPOOLER	2	2	681.685-090
CRE	SACK REPAIRER	2	2	782.687-046
CRE	SAMPLER	2	2	529.687-178
CRE	SANDER	2	2	690.685-346
CRE	SANDER, PORTABLE MACHINE	2	2	761.684-034
CRE	SANDFILL OPERATOR	2	3	939.485-010
CRE	SANDING-MACHINE BUFFER	2	2	662.685-022
CRE	SANITARY-NAPKIN-MACHINE TENDER	2	2	692.685-150
CRE	SCRIBING-MACHINE OPERATOR	2	2	605.685-042
CRE	SEAL-EXTRUSION OPERATOR	2	2	692.685-154
CRE	SEAM PRESSER	2	3	583.685-098
CRE	SEAM-RUBBING-MACHINE OPERATOR	2	2	690.685-350
CRE	SEASONING MIXER	2	2	520.687-054
CRE	SEASONING MIXER	2	3	550.685-106
CRE	SELECTOR	2	3	579.687-030
CRE	SET-STAFF FITTER	2	2	715.684-178
CRE	SEWER, HAND	2	3	782.684-058
CRE	SEWING-MACHINE OPERATOR, SEMI- AUTOMATIC	2	2	786.685-030
CRE	SEWING-MACHINE OPERATOR	2	4	787.682-062
CRE	SEWING-MACHINE OPERATOR, SPECIAL EQUIPMENT	2	2	689.685-118
CRE	SHADE MATCHER	2	3	582.687-022
CRE	SHADOWGRAPH-SCALE OPERATOR	2	2	737.687-126
CRE	SHANK INSPECTOR	2	2	788.687-110
CRE	SHAPER AND PRESSER	2	2	583.685-102
CRE	SHEET-METAL-PATTERN CUTTER	2	3	730.684-074
CRE	SHEETROCK APPLICATOR	2	3	869.684-050
CRE	SHOTGUN-SHELL-REPRINTING-UNIT OPERATOR	2	2	659.685-018
CRE	SHOTGUN-SHELL-LOADING-MACHINE OPERATOR	2	3	694.665-010
CRE	SILK-SCREEN ETCHER	2	3	704.684-014
CRE	SIZING-MACHINE OPERATOR	2	3	554.685-026
CRE	SKIVER, MACHINE	2	3	690.685-378
CRE	SLATE MIXER	2	2	570.685-094
CRE	SLEEVE MAKER, LOCKSTITCH	2	2	786.682-226
CRE	SLICKER	2	3	784.684-062
CRE	SLIDE-FASTENER REPAIRER	2	2	734.684-022
CRE	SLIDE-FASTENER-CHAIN ASSEMBLER	2	2	734.687-074
CRE	SLIP LASTER	2	2	788.684-106
CRE	SMOOTHER	2	2	733.685-026
CRE	SOAP-DRIER OPERATOR	2	2	553.685-098
CRE	SOLDERER	2	2	715.685-058
CRE	SOLE LEVELER, MACHINE	2	2	690.685-382
CRE	SPARK TESTER	2	2	727.687-078
CRE	SPARK TESTER	2	4	728.684-018

Code	Title	GED	SVP	DOT No.
CRE	SPICE MIXER	2	2	520.687-062
CRE	SPINNER, FRAME	2	3	682.685-010
CRE	SPINNING-BATH PATROLLER	2	4	557.685-030
CRE	SPLICER	2	2	759.684-058
CRE	SPLICER	2	2	976.684-026
CRE	SPONGE CLIPPER	2	2	447.687-026
CRE	SPOT CLEANER	2	3	582.684-014
CRE	SPREADING-MACHINE OPERATOR	2	3	559.685-170
CRE	SPRING INSPECTOR 2	2	2	709.687-038
CRE	SQUARING-MACHINE OPERATOR	2	2	605.685-046
CRE	STAB SETTER AND DRILLER	2	3	709.684-082
CRE	STAKER	2	3	715.684-182
CRE	STAKER, MACHINE	2	2	580.685-050
CRE	STEAMING-CABINET TENDER	2	2	582.685-150
CRE	STITCHER, HAND	2	4	977.684-022
CRE	STRAP-CUTTING-MACHINE OPERATOR	2	2	690.685-402
CRE	STRAW-HAT PRESSER, MACHINE	2	2	583.685-110
CRE	STRING-TOP SEALER	2	2	641.685-086
CRE	STRINGING-MACHINE TENDER	2	2	689.585-018
CRE	STRIPER, SPRAY GUN	2	2	741.687-022
CRE	STRIPPING-MACHINE OPERATOR	2	2	641.685-090
CRE	SUBASSEMBLER	2	2	729.684-054
CRE	SUBLIMER	2	3	542.685-014
CRE	SYNTHETIC-GEM-PRESS OPERATOR	2	2	575.685-078
CRE	TACKING-MACHINE OPERATOR	2	3	787.685-042
CRE	TAPE-FASTENER-MACHINE OPERATOR	2	2	649.685-122
CRE	TAPE-MAKING-MACHINE OPERATOR	2	3	689.685-138
CRE	TEMPLATE CUTTER	2	2	703.684-018
CRE	TESTER AND INSPECTOR, LAMPS	2	2	723.687-014
CRE	TESTER, WASTE DISPOSAL LEAKAGE	2	3	723.687-018
CRE	TICKET PULLER	2	2	221.687-014
CRE	TICKETER	2	2	229.587-018
CRE	TICKETER	2	2	652.685-098
CRE	TILE SETTER	2	2	861.684-018
CRE	TIRE SETTER	2	2	731.685-018
CRE	TOBACCO-PACKING-MACHINE OPERATOR	2	3	920.685-098
CRE	TOBACCO-SAMPLE PULLER	2	2	529.587-022
CRE	TOOTH CUTTER	2	3	605.685-050
CRE	TOP-HAT-BODY MAKER	2	3	784.684-074
CRE	TOWEL-CABINET REPAIRER	2	3	709.364-014
CRE	TOY ASSEMBLER	2	2	731.687-034
CRE	TRANSPLANTER, ORCHID	2	2	405.687-018
CRE	TRIMMER	2	2	784.684-078
CRE	TUBE ASSEMBLER, ELECTRON	2	2	725.384-010
CRE	TUBE SIZER-AND-CUTTER OPERATOR	2	3	640.685-086
CRE	TUBER-MACHINE CUTTER	2	2	690.685-446
CRE	TURNING-AND-BEADING-MACHINE OPERATOR	2	3	679.685-026
CRE	TWISTER	2	3	681.685-126
CRE	ULTRASONIC-SEAMING-MACHINE OPERATOR	2	2	786.682-258
CRE	ULTRASONIC-SEAMING-MACHINE OPERATOR, SEMI-AUTOMATIC	2	1	786.685-038
CRE	UNDERCOATER	2	3	843.684-014
CRE	UPPER-AND-BOTTOM LACER, HAND	2	3	788.684-122

Code	Title	GED	SVP	DOT No.
CRE	VACUUM PLASTIC-FORMING-MACHINE OPERATOR	2	2	556.685-082
CRE	VACUUM-BOTTLE ASSEMBLER	2	1	739.687-194
CRE	VENEER REPAIRER, MACHINE	2	2	669.685-098
CRE	VENEER TAPER	2	3	569.685-074
CRE	WAD LUBRICATOR	2	2	590.685-058
CRE	WADER-BOOT-TOP ASSEMBLER	2	2	795.684-026
CRE	WAISTBAND SETTER, LOCKSTITCH	2	2	786.682-266
CRE	WAITER/WAITRESS, BUFFET	2	3	311.674-018
CRE	WALLPAPER INSPECTOR AND SHIPPER	2	3	652.687-046
CRE	WASHER	2	3	713.684-042
CRE	WATCH-BAND ASSEMBLER	2	3	700.684-082
CRE	WATCHER, AUTOMAT	2	4	689.685-150
CRE	WATER-TEST RIDER	2	3	807.587-010
CRE	WAX MOLDER	2	2	549.685-038
CRE	WAX POURER	2	2	737.685-018
CRE	WAX-MACHINE OPERATOR	2	3	584.685-050
CRE	WEAVER	2	4	739.684-170
CRE	WEAVER	2	4	769.684-054
CRE	WEAVER, HAND	2	3	782.684-062
CRE	WEIGHER	2	2	732.687-086
CRE	WET MIXER	2	2	550.685-126
CRE	WET-END HELPER	2	2	534.685-034
CRE	WHEEL-PRESS CLERK	2	2	221.587-046
CRE	WHIZZER	2	2	581.685-070
CRE	WINDOW-SHADE CUTTER AND MOUNTER	2	3	692.685-250
CRE	WINTERIZER	2	2	521.685-374
CRE	WIRE INSERTER	2	2	784.687-082
CRE	WIRE-STRIPPING-AND-CUTTING-MACHINE OPERATOR, AUTOMATIC	2	2	691.485-010
CRE	WOOD INSPECTOR	2	2	663.687-010
CRE	WOOD-HEEL FINISHER	2	3	788.684-126
CRE	WOOL PULLER	2	3	589.687-050
CRE	WOOL-WASHING-MACHINE OPERATOR	2	2	582.685-166
CRE	YARN EXAMINER, SKEINS	2	3	689.687-082
CRE	YARN-MERCERIZER OPERATOR 1	2	2	584.685-054
CRE	YARN-TEXTURING-MACHINE OPERATOR 2	2	3	689.685-158
CRE	YARN-TEXTURING-MACHINE OPERATOR	2	3	589.685-102
CRE	YARN-TEXTURING-MACHINE OPERATOR 1	2	3	681.685-158
CRE	YEAST-CUTTING-AND-WRAPPING-MACHINE OPERATOR	2	2	529.665-022
CRE	ZIGZAG-MACHINE OPERATOR	2	2	786.682-278
CRE	ZIPPER TRIMMER, MACHINE	2	2	692.685-266
CRE	ZIPPER TRIMMER, HAND	2	2	734.687-094
CRE	ACETONE-BUTTON PASTER	1	2	734.687-010
CRE	ASSEMBLER	1	2	734.687-018
CRE	BOTTLING-LINE ATTENDANT	1	1	920.687-042
CRE	BUCKLE-WIRE INSERTER	1	1	734.687-034
CRE	BUTTON SPINDLER	1	2	740.687-010
CRE	BUTTONER	1	1	782.687-014
CRE	CEMENTER, MACHINE	1	2	692.685-050
CRE	CENTER-PUNCH OPERATOR	1	2	690.685-078
CRE	CHECK WEIGHER	1	2	737.687-026
CRE	CHEESE SPRAYER	1	2	524.685-014

Code	Title	GED	SVP	DOT No.
CRE	CRACKER SPRAYER	1	2	524.685-022
CRE	CRAYON SAWYER	1	2	677.685-022
CRE	DIAL BRUSHER	1	2	715.687-022
CRE	DROP-WIRE ALINER	1	2	689.685-062
CRE	FELT-HAT STEAMER	1	1	582.687-018
CRE	FITTER-PLACER	1	2	753.687-022
CRE	FUSING-MACHINE FEEDER	1	1	583.686-014
CRE	GLUING-MACHINE OPERATOR	1	2	692.685-098
CRE	HOT-STONE SETTER	1	2	734.687-058
CRE	LEVEL-GLASS-VIAL FILLER	1	2	692.685-114
CRE	MEASURING-MACHINE OPERATOR	1	2	589.685-070
CRE	NAILER	1	2	739.687-126
CRE	NUT GRINDER	1	2	521.685-234
CRE	NUT SORTER	1	2	521.687-086
CRE	PAPER-PATTERN FOLDER	1	1	794.687-034
CRE	PATTERN RULER	1	2	794.687-038
CRE	PLEAT TAPER	1	2	789.487-010
CRE	PROTECTOR-PLATE ATTACHER	1	2	692.685-138
CRE	PULLER, MACHINE	1	2	589.685-078
CRE	PUNCHBOARD ASSEMBLER 2	1	1	794.687-046
CRE	RAVELER	1	1	782.687-034
CRE	REEL-BLADE-BENDER FURNACE TENDER	1	2	504.685-030
CRE	SAMPLE FINISHER	1	2	789.687-162
CRE	SAMPLE SAWYER	1	2	677.685-034
CRE	SAUSAGE INSPECTOR	1	2	529.587-014
CRE	SCRAP SEPARATOR	1	2	529.587-018
CRE	SHOE SHINER	1	2	366.677-010
CRE	SKEIN-WINDING OPERATOR	1	1	559.687-054
CRE	SORTER 2	1	2	769.687-042
CRE	SPRAYER, HAND	1	2	584.687-014
CRE	STICKER	1	1	734.687-090
CRE	STONE SETTER	1	2	735.687-034
CRE	STRINGER	1	1	794.687-054
CRE	TABBER	1	1	794.687-058
CRE	TAPE STRINGER	1	1	782.687-054
CRE	TRIMMER, HAND	1	1	794.687-062
CRE	TUMBLER TENDER	1	2	520.685-222
CRE	VACUUM TESTER, CANS	1	2	920.687-194
CRE	VENEER-JOINTER HELPER	1	2	665.686-018
CRE	VINE PRUNER	1	1	403.687-022
CIS	POLYGRAPH EXAMINER	5	5	199.267-026
CIS	CHECK-PROCESSING CLERK 2	4	3	216.367-010
CIE	INSPECTOR, BUILDING	5	7	168.167-030
CSR	ACCOUNTING CLERK	4	4	216.482-010
CSR	ADVICE CLERK	4	5	216.382-014
CSR	BIBLIOGRAPHER	4	7	100.367-010
CSR	BOND CLERK	4	5	216.362-010
CSR	BRAILLE TYPIST	4	5	203.582-014
CSR	BROKERAGE CLERK 1	4	5	219.482-010
CSR	BUDGET CLERK	4	5	216.382-022
CSR	CLASSIFICATION-CONTROL CLERK	4	5	210.382-030

Code	Title	GED	SVP	DOT No.
CSR	CLASSIFIER	4	6	100.367-014
CSR	COLLECTION CLERK	4	5	216.362-014
CSR	COMPUTER-PERIPHERAL-EQUIPMENT OPERATOR	4	4	213.382-010
CSR	DATA TYPIST	4	4	203.582-022
CSR	FLIGHT-CREW-TIME CLERK	4	5	215.362-018
CSR	FOOD-AND-BEVERAGE CONTROLLER	4	5	216.362-022
CSR	INTEREST CLERK	4	5	216.382-038
CSR	INVOICE-CONTROL CLERK	4	4	214.362-026
CSR	MAIL CENSOR	4	5	243.367-010
CSR	ORTHOTICS TECHNICIAN	4	6	712.381-034
CSR	PAYROLL CLERK, DATA PROCESSING	4	4	215.382-010
CSR	POLICY-CHANGE CLERK	4	5	219.362-042
CSR	REAL-ESTATE CLERK	4	5	219.362-046
CSR	REINSURANCE CLERK	4	5	219.482-018
CSR	VOUCHER CLERK	4	4	219.362-066
CSR	ACCOUNTS-ADJUSTABLE CLERK	3	3	214.462-010
CSR	ASSIGNMENT CLERK	3	3	215.367-010
CSR	BALANCE CLERK	3	4	216.382-018
CSR	BISQUE GRADER	3	3	774.687-010
CSR	BROKERAGE CLERK 2	3	4	219.362-018
CSR	C.O.D. CLERK	3	3	214.382-018
CSR	CABINET ASSEMBLER	3	3	763.684-014
CSR	CABLE MAKER	3	3	728.684-010
CSR	CASHIER, TUBE ROOM	3	3	211.482-010
CSR	CHART CLERK	3	4	221.382-010
CSR	CHECKER, FILM TESTS	3	4	714.687-010
CSR	COMPLAINT CLERK	3	4	221.387-014
CSR	CREDIT-CARD CLERK	3	3	210.382-038
CSR	DEPOSIT-REFUND CLERK	3	4	214.482-014
CSR	DISPATCHER CLERK	3	4	215.362-014
CSR	DIVIDEND-DEPOSIT-VOUCHER CLERK	3	3	216.482-026
CSR	DOCUMENTATION-BILLING CLERK	3	4	214.362-014
CSR	EMBROIDERER, HAND	3	5	782.684-018
CSR	FEE CLERK	3	3	214.362-018
CSR	FILE CLERK 1	3	3	206.362-010
CSR	FILE CLERK 2	3	5	206.367-014
CSR	FILM-REPLACEMENT ORDERER	3	3	976.567-010
CSR	GARMENT-ALTERATION EXAMINER	3	4	789.687-078
CSR	HEEL SORTER	3	4	788.584-010
CSR	INSURANCE CHECKER	3	5	219.482-014
CSR	LAUNDRY CLERK	3	3	221.387-038
CSR	LIBRARIAN, MORGUE	3	4	206.387-018
CSR	MAIL CLERK	3	2	209.587-026
CSR	MEDICAL-VOUCHER CLERK	3	3	214.482-018
CSR	NIB INSPECTOR	3	3	733.687-058
CSR	ORDER DETAILER	3	4	221.387-046
CSR	PAINTER, PLATE	3	6	970.681-030
CSR	PAIRER	3	4	684.687-010
CSR	PRODUCTION ASSISTANT	3	4	221.387-050
CSR	PRODUCTION CLERK	3	4	221.382-018
CSR	QUALITY-CONTROL CLERK	3	3	229.587-014
CSR	RAILROAD-MAINTENANCE CLERK	3	4	221.362-026
CSR	RATER	3	4	214.482-022

Code	Title	GED	SVP	DOT No.
CSR	RECORD CLERK	3	3	206.387-022
CSR	REINSPECTOR	3	4	684.687-014
CSR	SALVAGER 1	3	4	737.687-114
CSR	SAMPLE WORKER	3	3	920.687-154
CSR	SCOREBOARD OPERATOR	3	2	349.665-010
CSR	SILK-SCREEN PRINTER, MACHINE	3	3	652.665-010
CSR	SLIDE PROCESSOR	3	3	574.684-018
CSR	STATEMENT CLERK	3	4	219.362-058
CSR	STRING-WINDING-MACHINE OPERATOR	3	5	692.682-062
CSR	STRIPING-MACHINE OPERATOR	3	3	652.682-026
CSR	THREAD INSPECTOR	3	3	681.687-018
CSR	TICKETING CLERK	3	4	248.382-010
CSR	TIP-LENGTH CHECKER	3	3	529.467-010
CSR	TIRE INSPECTOR	3	4	750.687-018
CSR	TRAIN CLERK	3	3	219.462-014
CSR	TRUST-SAVINGS-ACCOUNT CLERK	3	3	216.382-074
CSR	VERIFIER OPERATOR	3	4	203.582-070
CSR	WIRES-TRANSFER CLERK	3	4	203.562-010
CSR	WORK-ORDER-SORTING CLERK	3	5	221.367-082
CSR	ASSEMBLER	2	3	781.687-010
CSR	ASSEMBLER, SMALL PRODUCTS	2	2	739.687-030
CSR	BOOKING CLERK	2	3	216.587-010
CSR	BUCKLE INSPECTOR	2	2	734.687-026
CSR	CHECKROOM ATTENDANT	2	2	358.677-010
CSR	COLLATOR	2	2	653.687-010
CSR	DECORATING INSPECTOR	2	2	579.687-014
CSR	DECORATOR	2	3	524.684-014
CSR	DEFECT REPAIRER, GLASSWARE	2	3	772.684-010
CSR	FRAME REPAIRER	2	3	739.684-074
CSR	GOLF-CLUB ASSEMBLER	2	3	732.684-078
CSR	HAT-BODY SORTER	2	2	784.587-010
CSR	INSPECTOR	2	3	369.687-022
CSR	INSPECTOR-PACKER	2	2	784.687-042
CSR	INSPECTOR, BICYCLE	2	2	806.687-030
CSR	LABEL CODER	2	2	920.587-014
CSR	MARKER	2	2	209.587-034
CSR	MARKER, COMPANY	2	3	529.567-014
CSR	MEXICAN-FOOD-MACHINE TENDER	2	2	524.685-038
CSR	MICROFILM MOUNTER	2	2	208.685-022
CSR	PAINTER, SKI EDGE	2	2	749.687-022
CSR	PART MAKER	2	3	739.687-138
CSR	PLASTIC-CARD GRADER, CARDROOM	2	4	343.687-010
CSR	PRESSROOM WORKER, FAT	2	2	559.685-146
CSR	RIDING-SILKS CUSTODIAN	2	2	346.677-014
CSR	ROUTE-DELIVERY CLERK	2	3	222.587-034
CSR	SAMPLE CLERK	2	3	789.587-026
CSR	SEAL MIXER	2	2	540.687-010
CSR	SPOUT TENDER	2	3	921.685-058
CSR	SPRAYER, LEATHER	2	4	364.684-018
CSR	STAMPER	2	2	781.687-062
CSR	STENCILER	2	2	781.687-066
CSR	SWAGE TENDER	2	2	617.685-042
CSR	TILE GRINDER	2	2	679.685-022
CSR	TOUCH-UP PAINTER, HAND	2	2	740.684-026

Code	Title	GED	SVP	DOT No.
CSR	PRODUCE WEIGHER	1	1	299.587-010
CSI	ABSTRACTOR	5	6	119.267-010
CSI	FINANCIAL ANALYST	5	7	020.167-014
CSI	PROOFREADER	4	5	209.387-030
CSE	ACCOUNTANT, SYSTEMS	5	8	160.167-026
CSE	MEDICAL RECORD TECHNICIAN	5	6	079.367-014
CSE	SUPERVISOR, CARTOGRAPHY	5	8	018.131-010
CSE	TITLE EXAMINER	5	7	119.287-010
CSE	TITLE SUPERVISOR	5	8	119.167-018
CSE	UNDERWRITER	5	7	169.167-058
CSE	ACCOUNT ANALYST	4	5	214.382-010
CSE	ACCOUNT-INFORMATION CLERK	4	6	210.367-010
CSE	ADMINISTRATIVE CLERK	4	4	219.362-010
CSE	ATTENDANCE CLERK	4	6	219.362-014
CSE	BOOKKEEPER 2	4	4	210.382-018
CSE	BRAILLE PROOFREADER	4	5	209.367-014
CSE	BUILDING INSPECTOR (RCE)	4	7	168.267-010
CSE	BULK-PLANT OPERATOR	4	5	520.362-010
CSE	CADET, DECK	4	6	911.133-010
CSE	CASHIER 1	4	5	211.362-010
CSE	CATALOG LIBRARIAN	4	5	100.387-010
CSE	CHECK WRITER	4	3	219.382-010
CSE	CHIEF CLERK, MEASUREMENT DEPARTMENT	4	7	221.132-010
CSE	CITY PLANNING AIDE	4	6	199.364-010
CSE	CLAIMS CLERK 1	4	4	241.362-010
CSE	CONTRACT CLERK, AUTOMOBILE	4	5	219.362-026
CSE	COPY HOLDER	4	4	209.667-010
CSE	COUNTER CLERK	4	5	249.362-010
CSE	COUPON CLERK	4	5	219.462-010
CSE	COURT CLERK	4	6	243.362-010
CSE	CREDIT CLERK	4	4	205.367-022
CSE	DATA-CODER OPERATOR	4	4	203.582-026
CSE	DATA-EXAMINATION CLERK	4	3	209.387-022
CSE	DIALYSIS TECHNICIAN (ISC)	4	6	078.362-014
CSE	EDITOR, TELEGRAPH	4	7	132.267-010
CSE	ENGINEERING-DOCUMENT-CONTROL CLERK	4	6	206.367-010
CSE	EXCHANGE CLERK	4	4	216.362-018
CSE	EXPEDITER	4	4	222.367-018
CSE	FOREIGN-EXCHANGE CODE CLERK	4	6	209.367-030
CSE	GAS-DISTRIBUTION-AND-EMERGENCY CLERK	4	6	249.367-042
CSE	GRADING CLERK	4	3	219.467-010
CSE	INDUSTRIAL-ORDER CLERK	4	4	221.367-022
CSE	INSPECTOR, CHIEF	4	6	729.131-010
CSE	INSURANCE CLERK	4	5	214.362-022
CSE	INSURANCE CLERK 1	4	5	219.362-034
CSE	INSURANCE CLERK 1	4	4	219.387-014
CSE	LEGAL SECRETARY	4	6	201.362-010
CSE	MEMBERSHIP SECRETARY	4	3	201.362-018
CSE	NEW-ACCOUNTS CLERK	4	5	205.362-026
CSE	PAYMASTER OF PURSES	4	6	211.367-010
CSE	PERSONNEL CLERK	4	4	209.362-026

Code	Title	GED	SVP	DOT No.
CSE	PERSONNEL SCHEDULER	4	4	215.367-014
CSE	POLICYHOLDER-INFORMATION CLERK	4	6	249.262-010
CSE	PROBATE CLERK	4	5	216.362-030
CSE	PROMPTER	4	7	152.367-010
CSE	PROOF-MACHINE-OPERATOR SUPERVISOR	4	6	217.132-010
CSE	RATE ANALYST, FREIGHT	4	6	214.267-010
CSE	RATE CLERK, PASSENGER	4	4	214.362-030
CSE	RELAY-SHOP SUPERVISOR	4	7	729.131-014
CSE	RESERVES CLERK	4	5	216.362-034
CSE	SCHOOL SECRETARY	4	6	201.362-022
CSE	SCRIPT SUPERVISOR	4	6	201.362-026
CSE	SECRETARY	4	6	201.362-030
CSE	SECURITIES CLERK	4	5	219.362-054
CSE	SECURITIES CLERK	4	6	210.382-062
CSE	SPACE SCHEDULER	4	4	238.367-022
CSE	STENOTYPE OPERATOR	4	5	202.362-022
CSE	SUPERVISOR, TELEGRAPHIC-TYPEWRITER OPERATORS	4	7	203.132-010
CSE	SUPERVISOR, PERSONNEL CLERKS	4	6	209.132-010
CSE	SUPERVISOR, TRANSCRIBING OPERATORS	4	6	203.132-014
CSE	SUPERVISOR, MONEY-ROOM	4	6	211.137-018
CSE	SUPERVISOR, BILLPOSTING	4	6	841.137-010
CSE	SUPERVISOR, ACCOUNTING CLERKS	4	7	216.132-010
CSE	SUPERVISOR, UNDERWRITING CLERKS	4	7	219.132-022
CSE	SUPERVISOR, TRUST EVALUATION	4	6	219.132-018
CSE	SUPERVISOR, POLICY-CHANGE CLERKS	4	7	219.132-010
CSE	TAPE LIBRARIAN	4	4	206.387-030
CSE	TARIFF INSPECTOR	4	5	214.362-034
CSE	TELEVISION-SCHEDULE COORDINATOR	4	4	199.387-010
CSE	TELLER	4	5	211.362-018
CSE	TERMINAL OPERATOR	4	4	203.582-054
CSE	TICKET AGENT	4	5	238.367-026
CSE	TOURIST-INFORMATION ASSISTANT	4	6	237.367-050
CSE	TRAFFIC CLERK	4	4	221.367-078
CSE	TRAFFIC-RATE CLERK	4	5	214.362-038
CSE	TRUST-VAULT CLERK	4	6	216.367-014
CSE	WIRE-PHOTO OPERATOR, NEWS	4	5	239.382-010
CSE	ADVERTISING-DISPATCH CLERK	3	4	247.387-014
CSE	ADVERTISING CLERK	3	4	247.387-010
CSE	ADVERTISING-SPACE CLERK	3	5	247.387-018
CSE	APPOINTMENT CLERK	3	3	237.367-010
CSE	BACK-SHOE WORKER	3	4	221.387-010
CSE	BILLING TYPIST	3	4	214.382-014
CSE	BILLING-CONTROL CLERK	3	5	214.387-010
CSE	BOARD ATTENDANT	3	2	249.587-010
CSE	BORDEREAU CLERK	3	4	203.382-010
CSE	BOUFFANT-CURTAIN-MACHINE TENDER	3	4	689.685-026
CSE	BRAILLE TRANSCRIBER, HAND	3	4	209.584-010
CSE	BRAILLE-AND-TALKING BOOKS CLERK	3	3	222.587-014
CSE	BRAND RECORDER	3	4	206.587-010
CSE	CALCULATING-MACHINE OPERATOR	3	3	216.482-022
CSE	CALL-OUT OPERATOR	3	2	237.367-014
CSE	CANCELLATION CLERK	3	5	203.382-014
CSE	CAR CHECKER	3	2	222.387-014

Code	Title	GED	SVP	DOT No.
CSE	CARBONATION TESTER	3	2	522.587-010
CSE	CASHIER 2	3	2	211.462-010
CSE	CASHIER-WRAPPER	3	3	211.462-018
CSE	CASHIER, GAMBLING	3	4	211.462-022
CSE	CD-REACTOR OPERATOR	3	4	558.385-010
CSE	CENTRAL-OFFICE OPERATOR	3	3	235.462-010
CSE	CHARGE-ACCOUNT CLERK	3	2	205.367-014
CSE	CHARGER 1	3	3	740.684-010
CSE	CHECK CASHIER	3	3	211.462-026
CSE	CHECK-PROCESSING CLERK 1	3	3	216.387-010
CSE	CHECKER	3	5	559.165-010
CSE	CIVIL-SERVICE CLERK	3	3	205.362-010
CSE	CLASSIFIED-AD CLERK 2	3	5	247.387-022
CSE	CLERK-TYPIST	3	4	203.362-010
CSE	CLERK, GENERAL	3	2	209.562-010
CSE	CODING CLERK	3	3	209.387-010
CSE	COMMAND AND CONTROL SPECIALIST	3	5	235.662-010
CSE	COMPILER	3	4	209.387-014
CSE	CONTACT CLERK	3	4	209.387-018
CSE	CONTINUITY CLERK	3	5	209.382-010
CSE	CONTROL CLERK, AUDITING	3	3	209.362-014
CSE	CORRESPONDENCE-REVIEW CLERK	3	5	209.367-018
CSE	CREDIT CLERK, BLOOD BANK	3	3	245.367-022
CSE	CREDIT-CARD-CONTROL CLERK	3	3	249.367-026
CSE	CREEL CLERK	3	2	205.367-026
CSE	DECORATOR	3	5	740.684-014
CSE	DISPATCHER, RADIO	3	4	379.362-010
CSE	DRIVERS'-CASH CLERK	3	3	211.462-030
CSE	ELECTION CLERK	3	2	205.367-030
CSE	ENAMELER	3	4	740.684-018
CSE	FLOOR-SPACE ALLOCATOR	3	3	222.367-030
CSE	GAMBLING DEALER	3	3	343.467-018
CSE	GAS-VOLUME COMPUTER	3	3	216.585-010
CSE	GIN CLERK	3	3	221.467-010
CSE	HOSIERY MENDER	3	4	782.684-030
CSE	IDENTIFICATION CLERK	3	3	205.362-022
CSE	IN-FILE OPERATOR	3	4	203.362-014
CSE	INFORMATION CLERK-CASHIER	3	5	249.467-010
CSE	KEYPUNCH OPERATOR	3	3	203.582-030
CSE	KOSHER INSPECTOR	3	2	529.687-126
CSE	LABORATORY ASSISTANT, BLOOD AND PLASMA	3	6	078.687-010
CSE	LAYAWAY CLERK	3	3	299.467-010
CSE	LIBRARY ASSISTANT	3	4	249.367-046
CSE	LICENSE CLERK	3	3	205.367-034
CSE	LINE-UP WORKER	3	3	221.367-026
CSE	MANAGER, TRAFFIC 2	3	6	237.367-030
CSE	MAP CLERK	3	3	209.587-030
CSE	MATERIAL ASSEMBLER	3	3	784.687-050
CSE	METER READER	3	4	209.567-010
CSE	MILK SAMPLER	3	4	410.357-010
CSE	MORTGAGE-LOAN-COMPUTATION CLERK	3	3	210.382-050
CSE	ORDER CLERK, FOOD AND BEVERAGE	3	2	209.567-014
CSE	OUTPATIENT-ADMITTING CLERK	3	4	205.362-030

Code	Title	GED	SVP	DOT No.
CSE	PAPER-CONTROL CLERK	3	5	219.367-022
CSE	PARIMUTUEL-TICKET CASHIER	3	2	211.467-018
CSE	PARIMUTUEL-TICKET SELLER	3	2	211.467-022
CSE	PEDIGREE TRACER	3	3	249.387-018
CSE	PERFORATOR TYPIST	3	4	203.582-038
CSE	PETROLEUM INSPECTOR	3	5	222.367-046
CSE	POLICE AIDE	3	3	243.362-014
CSE	POSTING CLERK	3	3	216.587-014
CSE	PRODUCTION PROOFREADER	3	4	247.667-010
CSE	READER	3	4	249.387-022
CSE	RECEPTIONIST	3	5	237.367-038
CSE	RECEPTIONIST, AIRLINE LOUNGE	3	3	352.677-014
CSE	RECONSIGNMENT CLERK	3	4	209.367-042
CSE	RECORDER	3	2	221.587-026
CSE	REFERRAL-AND-INFORMATION AIDE	3	3	237.367-042
CSE	REGISTERED-MAIL CLERK	3	3	209.587-038
CSE	REGISTRATION CLERK	3	5	249.365-010
CSE	REGISTRATION CLERK	3	3	205.367-042
CSE	REHABILITATION CLERK	3	4	205.367-046
CSE	REPAIR-ORDER CLERK	3	3	221.382-022
CSE	RETURN-TO-FACTORY CLERK	3	3	209.587-042
CSE	REVIEWER	3	4	209.687-018
CSE	RIDE OPERATOR	3	3	342.663-010
CSE	RURAL-MAIL CARRIER	3	2	230.363-010
CSE	SAMPLE-DISPLAY PREPARER	3	3	222.687-026
CSE	SHORTHAND REPORTER	3	6	202.362-010
CSE	SPOTTER, PHOTOGRAPHIC	3	5	970.381-034
CSE	STENOGRAPHER	3	5	202.362-014
CSE	STENOGRAPHER, PRINT SHOP	3	5	202.362-018
CSE	SUGGESTION CLERK	3	4	209.387-034
CSE	SURVEY WORKER	3	3	205.367-054
CSE	TAKE-DOWN SORTER	3	3	976.665-010
CSE	TALLIER	3	2	221.587-030
CSE	TELEGRAPHER AGENT	3	5	236.562-014
CSE	TELEGRAPHIC-TYPEWRITER OPERATOR	3	4	203.582-050
CSE	TELEPHONE CLERK, TELEGRAPH OFFICE	3	3	239.362-010
CSE	TELEPHONE OPERATOR	3	3	235.662-022
CSE	TELEPHONE-ANSWERING-SERVICE OPERATOR	3	3	235.662-026
CSE	TELLER	3	3	211.462-034
CSE	TEST TECHNICIAN	3	4	249.367-078
CSE	THROW-OUT CLERK	3	4	241.367-030
CSE	TICKET MARKER	3	3	216.567-010
CSE	TIMEKEEPER	3	3	215.367-022
CSE	TOOTH CLERK	3	4	222.687-038
CSE	TOWER-CRANE OPERATOR	3	5	921.663-054
CSE	TRANSCRIBING-MACHINE OPERATOR	3	4	203.582-058
CSE	TRUST-MAIL CLERK	3	4	209.562-014
CSE	TYPIST	3	3	203.582-066
CSE	UNDERWRITING CLERK	3	4	219.367-038
CSE	WEIGHT TESTER	3	2	539.485-010
CSE	WEIGHT-YARDAGE CHECKER	3	3	589.487-010
CSE	YARD CLERK	3	3	209.367-054
CSE	ASSEMBLER, HOSPITAL SUPPLIES	2	2	712.687-010

Code	Title	GED	SVP	DOT No.
CSE	CALLER	2	2	215.563-010
CSE	CHECKER	2	2	221.587-010
CSE	COOLING-ROOM ATTENDANT	2	2	335.677-010
CSE	FINISHER	2	2	789.687-050
CSE	MARKER	2	2	781.687-042
CSE	PRINTER, MACHINE	2	3	652.685-070
CSE	RUG BRAIDER, HAND	2	2	782.687-042
CSE	SECOND	2	2	346.677-018
CSE	SHOE DYER	2	3	364.684-014
CSE	SHOW GIRL	2	2	159.647-022
CSE	SORTER	2	3	706.587-014
CSE	TELEGRAPH-SERVICE RATER	2	2	214.587-010
CSE	THREADING-MACHINE TENDER	2	3	683.685-030
CSE	TOOTH INSPECTOR	2	2	712.687-038
CSE	TUFTING-MACHINE OPERATOR, SINGLE-NEEDLE	2	3	687.685-022
CER	PROCUREMENT ENGINEER	5	7	162.157-034
CER	CRYPTOGRAPHIC-MACHINE OPERATOR	4	5	203.582-018
CER	MATE, SHIP	4	7	197.133-022
CER	SUPERVISOR	4	7	716.130-010
CER	TELEGRAPHER	4	4	236.562-010
CER	TERMINAL-SYSTEM OPERATOR	4	5	203.362-018
CER	ACID-PLANT HELPER	3	4	558.565-010
CER	AUTOMOBILE-SELF-SERVE-SERVICE-STATION ATTENDANT	3	3	915.477-010
CER	BROADCAST CHECKER	3	4	249.387-010
CER	CELLOPHANE-BATH MIXER	3	3	550.585-014
CER	CREDIT-CARD CLERK	3	3	209.587-014
CER	DETAILER, SCHOOL PHOTOGRAPHS	3	4	976.564-010
CER	DIRECTORY-ASSISTANCE OPERATOR	3	3	235.662-018
CER	ELECTRIC-METER INSTALLER 2	3	4	821.684-010
CER	INSPECTOR, BALANCE TRUING	3	3	715.687-050
CER	LOCOMOTIVE LUBRICATING-SYSTEMS CLERK	3	5	221.367-030
CER	NODULIZER	3	3	579.685-034
CER	OVERHEAD CLEANER MAINTAINER	3	3	628.684-022
CER	PAINTER, ANIMATED CARTOONS	3	4	970.681-026
CER	PURIFICATION-OPERATOR HELPER	3	4	551.465-010
CER	QUALITY-CONTROL INSPECTOR	3	3	725.687-026
CER	ROUGH-RICE GRADER	3	5	529.367-026
CER	SECOND OPERATOR, MILL TENDER	3	3	555.685-054
CER	SKI-TOW OPERATOR	3	3	341.665-010
CER	STATEMENT-REQUEST CLERK	3	4	209.382-018
CER	STOCK PATCHER	3	3	761.684-042
CER	STOCKING INSPECTOR	3	3	684.684-010
CER	TICKET WORKER	3	2	221.482-018
CER	ASSEMBLER, LEATHER GOODS 2	2	2	783.687-010
CER	BARREL FILLER	2	2	529.485-010
CER	BATCH-TANK CONTROLLER	2	3	521.685-022
CER	BROOMCORN GRADER	2	3	739.687-042
CER	BRUSH FILLER, HAND	2	3	739.687-046
CER	CAR COOPER	2	2	910.687-014
CER	CENTRAL-SUPPLY WORKER	2	3	381.687-010

Code	Title	GED	SVP	DOT No.
CER	CENTRIFUGE OPERATOR, PLASMA PROCESSING	2	2	599.685-018
CER	COLLET GLUER	2	2	715.685-010
CER	COLORER, CITRUS FRUIT	2	2	529.685-070
CER	COOLER TENDER	2	2	523.685-038
CER	CROSSING TENDER	2	3	371.667-010
CER	CUTTER-AND-PASTER, PRESS CLIPPINGS	2	2	249.587-014
CER	EGG CANDLER	2	2	529.687-074
CER	ESCORT-VEHICLE DRIVER	2	2	919.663-022
CER	FOLDER-TIER	2	2	759.684-034
CER	GLASS INSPECTOR	2	3	579.687-022
CER	GRADER, DRESSED POULTRY	2	3	529.687-102
CER	GRAIN MIXER	2	2	520.485-014
CER	HOSPITAL ENTRANCE ATTENDANT	2	2	355.677-014
CER	ION EXCHANGE OPERATOR	2	2	521.685-190
CER	LEAF SORTER	2	2	529.687-134
CER	LINE-OUT WORKER 1	2	2	920.687-110
CER	MIXER OPERATOR	2	3	520.685-146
CER	MOUNTER, HAND	2	2	976.684-018
CER	PAINTER	2	2	735.687-018
CER	PAPER SORTER AND COUNTER	2	2	649.687-010
CER	PASSENGER SERVICE REPRESENTATIVE 2	2	2	910.677-010
CER	PEGGER	2	2	788.687-102
CER	PENCIL INSPECTOR	2	2	733.687-062
CER	PROCESSOR, GRAIN	2	2	521.685-254
CER	PULL-OUT OPERATOR	2	3	739.687-162
CER	RAW SHELLFISH PREPARER	2	2	311.674-014
CER	RESTROOM ATTENDANT	2	2	358.677-018
CER	ROLL EXAMINER	2	2	640.687-010
CER	SAMPLE CLERK, HANDKERCHIEF	2	2	920.587-022
CER	SAMPLE COLLECTOR	2	2	550.587-014
CER	STEWARD/ STEWARDESS, BATH	2	3	350.677-018
CER	TAB-MACHINE OPERATOR	2	2	754.685-010
CER	TABLET TESTER	2	3	559.667-010
CER	TUBE OPERATOR	2	2	239.687-014
CER	TWITCHELL OPERATOR	2	3	558.585-042
CER	WEIGHER, PRODUCTION	2	3	929.587-014
CER	WHEAT CLEANER	2	3	529.685-262
CER	WRAPPER SELECTOR	2	3	529.687-218
CER	FARMWORKER, DIVERSIFIED CROPS 2	1	2	407.687-010
CER	LABORER, GENERAL	1	2	589.687-026
CER	MILL OPERATOR	1	2	521.685-226
CER	RACKER	1	2	659.687-010
CER	SANDWICH-BOARD CARRIER	1	1	299.687-014
CEI	PROGRAMER, CHIEF, BUSINESS	5	7	020.167-018
CEI	CUSTOMS INSPECTOR	4	6	168.267-022
CEI	FINGERPRINT CLERK 2	4	4	206.387-014
CEI	PARIMUTUEL-TICKET CHECKER	3	2	219.587-010
CES	ACCOUNTANT, COST	5	8	160.167-018
CES	FIRE-PREVENTION RESEARCH ENGINEER	5	7	012.167-022
CES	INSPECTOR, ELECTRICAL	5	7	168.167-034
CES	MEDICAL TECHNOLOGIST, TEACHING			

Code	Title	GED	SVP	DOT No.
	SUPERVISOR (ISE)	5	7	078.121-010
CES	AIRLINE-RADIO OPERATOR, CHIEF	4	8	193.162-022
CES	CHART CALCULATOR	4	5	214.487-010
CES	COPY CUTTER	4	8	221.167-010
CES	EMPLOYMENT CLERK	4	5	205.362-014
CES	FOREIGN BANKNOTE TELLER-TRADER	4	5	211.362-014
CES	INFORMATION CLERK	4	2	237.367-018
CES	LETTER-OF-CREDIT CLERK	4	5	219.387-018
CES	MAGNETIC-TAPE-COMPOSER OPERATOR	4	5	203.382-018
CES	MANAGER, GUN CLUB	4	6	187.167-118
CES	MANAGER, MUTUEL DEPARTMENT	4	5	187.167-134
CES	MEDICAL SECRETARY	4	7	201.362-014
CES	PHOTOCOMPOSING-PERFORATOR-MACHINE OPERATOR	4	6	203.582-042
CES	PLACER	4	5	239.267-010
CES	PROCUREMENT CLERK	4	4	249.367-066
CES	PRODUCTION SCHEDULER, PAPERBOARD PRODUCTS	4	6	221.162-010
CES	QUALITY-CONTROL COORDINATOR	4	6	168.167-066
CES	RESERVATIONS AGENT	4	4	238.367-018
CES	SCRIPT READER	4	6	131.267-022
CES	SOCIAL SECRETARY	4	6	201.162-010
CES	SUPERVISOR, CENTRAL SUPPLY	4	6	079.164-010
CES	SUPERVISOR, STENO POOL	4	6	202.132-010
CES	SUPERVISOR, PRODUCTION CLERKS	4	7	221.137-014
CES	SUPERVISOR, ADJUSTABLE-STEEL-JOIST-SETTING	4	7	869.134-014
CES	SUPERVISOR, WORD PROCESSING	4	6	203.137-010
CES	TELLER, COLLECTION AND EXCHANGE	4	5	211.362-022
CES	TELLER, NOTE	4	5	211.362-026
CES	ANIMAL-SHELTER CLERK	3	3	249.367-010
CES	BLACK-MILL OPERATOR	3	4	553.665-014
CES	BONDACTOR-MACHINE OPERATOR	3	3	899.684-010
CES	BRAKER, PASSENGER TRAIN	3	4	910.364-010
CES	BUS ATTENDANT	3	2	352.577-010
CES	CALENDAR-CONTROL CLERK, BLOOD BANK	3	3	245.367-018
CES	CASHIER-CHECKER	3	3	211.462-014
CES	CLASSIFIED-AD CLERK 1	3	5	247.367-010
CES	COLOR TESTER	3	3	511.667-014
CES	COUPON-REDEMPTION CLERK	3	2	290.477-010
CES	CREDIT AUTHORIZER	3	3	249.367-022
CES	CREDIT-REFERENCE CLERK	3	4	209.362-018
CES	CUSTOMER-SERVICE REPRESENTATIVE	3	5	239.367-010
CES	DIET CLERK	3	3	245.587-010
CES	DISBURSEMENT CLERK	3	4	209.367-022
CES	DISPATCHER, MAINTENANCE SERVICE	3	3	239.367-014
CES	DISPATCHER, SHIP PILOT	3	4	248.367-026
CES	DISPATCHER, OIL WELL SERVICES	3	5	939.362-010
CES	DOG BATHER	3	2	418.677-010
CES	FERMENTER, WINE	3	4	522.685-062
CES	FINGERPRINT CLERK 1	3	2	209.367-026
CES	FOOD TABULATOR, CAFETERIA	3	3	211.582-010
CES	FORECLOSURE CLERK, MOTION-PICTURE LOANS	3	4	249.367-038

Code	Title	GED	SVP	DOT No.
CES	GATE TENDER	3	3	372.667-030
CES	GRAIN ELEVATOR CLERK	3	4	222.567-010
CES	HAIR-SAMPLE MATCHER	3	5	739.387-014
CES	HISTORY-CARD CLERK	3	4	209.587-022
CES	INSURANCE CLERK 2	3	4	205.567-010
CES	INSURANCE CLERK 2	3	4	219.367-014
CES	LOST-CHARGE-CARD CLERK	3	3	209.367-034
CES	ORDER CLERK	3	4	249.367-054
CES	PAGE	3	2	353.367-022
CES	PLANIMETER OPERATOR	3	3	219.387-022
CES	PLANT OPERATOR, CHANNEL PROCESS	3	2	542.685-010
CES	REDYE HAND	3	3	789.687-142
CES	RELAY-RECORD CLERK	3	5	221.367-054
CES	RESERVATION CLERK	3	5	238.362-014
CES	RESERVATION CLERK	3	3	238.367-014
CES	ROUTING CLERK	3	3	249.367-070
CES	SHIPPING-ORDER CLERK	3	4	219.367-030
CES	SKATE-SHOP ATTENDANT	3	3	341.464-010
CES	TAX CLERK 1	3	3	219.487-010
CES	TAXICAB STARTER	3	3	913.367-010
CES	TELEPHONE-QUOTATION CLERK	3	2	237.367-046
CES	TEMPERATURE-CONTROL INSPECTOR	3	4	559.467-010
CES	TICKET SELLER	3	2	211.467-030
CES	TOLL COLLECTOR	3	2	211.462-038
CES	UNIT OPERATOR	3	3	542.685-018
CES	WAITER/WAITRESS, DINING CAR	3	3	311.477-022
CES	WAITER/WAITRESS, FORMAL	3	3	311.477-026
CES	WAITER/WAITRESS	3	3	350.677-030
CES	ABRASIVE-BAND WINDER	2	2	692.685-010
CES	ADDRESSER	2	2	209.587-010
CES	AUCTION ASSISTANT	2	2	294.667-010
CES	AUCTION CLERK	2	3	294.567-010
CES	CARDROOM ATTENDANT 2	2	2	343.577-010
CES	COLLATOR, HAND	2	3	977.687-010
CES	COLOR MIXER	2	3	589.464-010
CES	COUNTER ATTENDANT, LUNCHROOM OR COFFEE SHOP	2	2	311.477-014
CES	DELIVERER, OUTSIDE	2	2	230.667-010
CES	DRIER HELPER	2	2	553.687-010
CES	DRIVE-IN THEATER ATTENDANT	2	2	349.673-010
CES	FLOOR ATTENDANT	2	2	343.467-014
CES	HOSPITAL-TELEVISION-RENTAL CLERK	2	2	295.467-018
CES	IMPREGNATION OPERATOR	2	3	539.685-014
CES	MESSENGER, COPY	2	2	239.677-010
CES	MICA SIZER	2	3	779.687-030
CES	PAINT-SPRAY INSPECTOR	2	2	741.687-010
CES	PARKING ENFORCEMENT OFFICER	2	2	375.587-010
CES	PASSENGER ATTENDANT	2	2	350.677-014
CES	RACKER	2	2	340.477-010
CES	REGENERATOR OPERATOR	2	4	573.685-034
CES	RIDE ATTENDANT	2	2	342.677-010
CES	SIZING-MACHINE TENDER	2	2	690.685-366
CES	SORTER	2	3	209.687-022
CES	SUTURE WINDER, HAND	2	2	712.687-034

Part III. From Occupations to Holland Codes

The Alphabetical Index lists occupations in alphabetical order to make it easy to find the Holland code for any occupation. The entries in this index under "Code" are three-letter Holland codes. The entries under "Group" indicate the six-digit code number in the *Guide for Occupational Exploration* (GOE; U.S. Department of Labor, 1979). In the GOE the user can find out more about the kind of work involved, the skills or abilities needed to do the work, how to prepare for the work, and other things he or she might want to consider. The entries under "Page" show the page number in the Classified Index in this volume where users can find closely related occupations, DOT codes, GED levels, and SVP rating or training time estimates.

Title	Code	Group	Page
BAND SALVAGER	REC	06.04.24	107
BAND TUMBLER	REC	06.04.07	107
BAND-AND-CUFF CUTTER	CRE	06.04.05	218
BAND-MACHINE OPERATOR	REC	06.04.07	92
BAND-REAMER-MACHINE OPERATOR	RCS	06.04.02	119
BAND-SAW OPERATOR	REI	06.04.03	47
BAND-SAW OPERATOR	REI	06.04.15	47
BAND-SAW OPERATOR	RCS	06.02.05	114
BAND-SAW OPERATOR	RCE	06.04.03	152
BAND-SAWING-MACHINE OPERATOR	RCE	06.04.09	132
BAND-SCROLL-SAW OPERATOR	RCE	06.02.03	125
BAND-TOP MAKER	RCE	06.04.22	132
BANDER	RCE	06.04.23	132
BANDER	RCE	06.04.25	152
BANDER-AND-CELLOPHANER HELPER, MACHINE	RCE	06.04.38	132
BANDER-AND-CELLOPHANER, MACHINE	RCE	06.04.38	132
BANDER, HAND	RCS	06.04.38	120
BANDER, HAND	RCE	06.04.38	152
BANDING-MACHINE OPERATOR	RES	06.04.20	74
BANDING-MACHINE OPERATOR	REC	06.04.20	92
BANDING-MACHINE OPERATOR	CRS	06.02.08	208
BANDOLEER PACKER	RCE	06.04.38	152
BANDOLEER STRAIGHTENER-STAMPER	RCE	06.04.37	152
BANK BOSS	SER	05.11.04	171
BANK BOSS	ERS	05.12.12	180
BANK-NOTE DESIGNER	AER	01.06.01	165
BANKING PIN ADJUSTER	REC	06.01.04	87
BAR AND FILLER ASSEMBLER	RCS	06.04.22	120
BAR ATTENDANT	ERC	09.04.01	185
BAR EXAMINER	AES	11.04.02	166
BARBED-WIRE-MACHINE OPERATOR	RCS	06.02.02	114
BARBER	ESR	09.02.02	195
BARBER APPRENTICE	ESR	09.02.02	195
BARGE CAPTAIN	REI	05.12.03	34
BARK-PRESS OPERATOR	RCS	06.04.14	120
BARKER	ESA	01.07.02	202
BARKER OPERATOR	RES	06.04.03	74
BARLEY STEEPER	REC	06.04.15	92
BARN BOSS	ESR	03.02.04	189
BARREL ASSEMBLER	RCS	06.02.20	114
BARREL ASSEMBLER	RCS	06.01.04	114
BARREL BRANDER	RCE	06.04.37	132
BARREL CHARRER	RCE	06.04.18	132
BARREL DRAINER	RES	06.04.40	84
BARREL FILLER	RES	06.04.36	84
BARREL FILLER	RCE	06.04.37	132
BARREL FILLER	CER	06.04.15	235
BARREL FINISHER	RCS	06.04.24	120
BARREL FINISHER	RCE	06.02.02	132
BARREL INSPECTOR, TIGHT	CRE	06.03.02	218
BARREL LINER	RCS	06.04.33	120
BARREL LOADER AND CLEANER	RCE	06.04.34	132
BARREL MARKER	RCE	06.04.25	132
BARREL POLISHER, INSIDE	CRE	06.04.02	218

Title	Code	Group	Page
BELT PICKER	REC	05.12.07	107
BELT REPAIRER	RCE	05.12.15	132
BELT SANDER, STONE	RIE	06.04.08	19
BELT-BUILDER HELPER	REI	06.04.29	47
BELT-MAKER HELPER	CES	06.04.38	239
BELT-PRESS OPERATOR 1	RIE	06.02.13	14
BELT-PRESS OPERATOR 2	RCE	06.04.13	132
BELTING-AND-WEBBING INSPECTOR	REC	06.03.01	93
BEN-DAY ARTIST	RES	01.06.03	63
BENCH ASSEMBLER	CRE	06.04.23	218
BENCH CARPENTER	RSC	06.04.25	33
BENCH GRINDER	REI	06.04.24	47
BENCH HAND	RSC	06.01.04	31
BENCH HAND	REI	06.02.24	38
BENCH HAND	RES	06.02.28	63
BENCH HAND	RCE	06.04.22	132
BENCH HAND	RCE	06.04.23	152
BENCH WORKER	REC	06.04.24	93
BENCH WORKER	RCE	06.02.02	132
BENCH WORKER, HOLLOW HANDLE	RCE	06.04.23	132
BENCH-MOLDER APPRENTICE	RSE	06.02.24	22
BENCH-SHEAR OPERATOR	RCS	06.02.25	114
BENDER, HAND	REC	06.04.25	93
BENDER, MACHINE	REC	06.04.04	93
BENDER, MACHINE	RCE	06.04.03	132
BENDING-MACHINE OPERATOR 1	RCS	06.02.02	114
BENDING-MACHINE OPERATOR 2	REC	06.04.02	93
BENZENE-WASHER OPERATOR	RIE	06.02.11	14
BEVEL POLISHER	CRS	06.02.02	211
BEVELER	RIE	06.04.08	19
BEVELER	REI	06.02.30	38
BEVELER	RES	06.02.30	63
BEVELER	RCS	06.04.08	120
BEVELER	RCE	06.02.24	132
BEVELING-AND-EDGING-MACHINE OPERATOR	RIE	06.02.08	14
BEVELING-AND-EDGING-MACHINE-OPERATOR HELPER	RES	06.04.08	84
BEVELING-MACHINE OPERATOR	REC	06.04.05	107
BIAS-CUTTING-MACHINE OPERATOR	REC	06.02.05	87
BIAS-MACHINE OPERATOR	RCE	06.02.09	125
BIAS-MACHINE-OPERATOR HELPER	REC	06.04.07	107
BIBLIOGRAPHER	CSR	11.02.04	228
BICYCLE REPAIRER	RSC	05.10.02	31
BICYCLE-RENTAL CLERK	ERC	09.04.02	185
BILLET ASSEMBLER	RCS	06.02.22	114
BILLING TYPIST	CSE	07.02.04	232
BILLING-CONTROL CLERK	CSE	07.02.04	232
BILLING-MACHINE OPERATOR	CRS	07.06.02	208
BILLPOSTER	REC	05.12.12	93
BILLPOSTER	CRS	05.12.14	211
BIN CLEANER	REC	06.04.39	107
BIN FILLER	RCE	06.04.38	152
BINDER	RCE	06.02.05	125
BINDER AND BOX BUILDER	CRS	06.04.34	212

Title	Code	Group	Page
BINDER CUTTER, HAND	RCE	06.04.28	152
BINDER LAYER	RCE	06.04.15	132
BINDER SELECTOR	REI	06.03.02	47
BINDER TECHNICIAN	REI	06.04.11	38
BINDER-AND-WRAPPER PACKER	RES	06.04.38	74
BINDER, CHAINSTITCH	RCE	06.02.05	132
BINDER, COVERSTITCH	RCE	06.02.05	132
BINDER, LOCKSTITCH	RCE	06.02.05	132
BINDERY WORKER	RES	06.04.04	74
BINDERY WORKER	REC	06.04.04	93
BINDING CUTTER, SYNTHETIC CLOTH	RSE	06.02.05	25
BINDING FOLDER, MACHINE	RCS	06.04.27	114
BINDING PRINTER	CRS	06.04.05	212
BIOCHEMIST	IRS	02.02.03	157
BIOGRAPHER	ESC	01.01.02	203
BIOLOGICAL AIDE	RSI	02.04.02	21
BIOLOGICAL PHOTOGRAPHER	RIS	02.04.02	1
BIOLOGIST	IRE	02.02.03	158
BIOLOGY SPECIMEN TECHNICIAN	RCS	02.04.02	113
BIOMEDICAL ENGINEER	IRE	02.02.01	158
BIOMEDICAL EQUIPMENT TECHNICIAN	RIE	05.05.11	4
BIOMEDICAL EQUIPMENT TECHNICIAN	RIE	02.04.02	5
BIOPHYSICIST	IRE	02.02.03	158
BIRD-CAGE ASSEMBLER	CRE	06.04.23	218
BIRTH ATTENDANT	SER	10.03.02	172
BISQUE CLEANER	RCE	06.04.30	132
BISQUE GRADER	CSR	06.03.02	229
BIT BENDER	CRS	06.04.02	212
BIT SHARPENER	RCE	06.02.02	132
BIT SHAVER	CRE	06.04.34	218
BIT-SHARPENER OPERATOR	CRS	05.12.02	212
BITE-BLOCK MAKER	RES	06.02.23	63
BLACK-ASH-BURNER OPERATOR	RES	06.02.14	63
BLACK-MILL OPERATOR	CES	06.04.19	237
BLACKSMITH	RIE	05.05.06	5
BLACKSMITH APPRENTICE	RIE	05.05.06	5
BLACKSMITH HELPER	RES	05.12.10	74
BLADE BALANCER	RCE	06.03.02	152
BLADE GROOVER	RCE	06.04.24	132
BLANCHING-MACHINE OPERATOR	RES	06.04.15	74
BLANKET WASHER	RES	06.04.27	74
BLANKET-CUTTING-MACHINE OPERATOR	REC	06.04.05	93
BLANKET-WINDER HELPER	RES	06.04.04	74
BLANKET-WINDER OPERATOR	RSE	06.02.04	25
BLAST-FURNACE KEEPER	RSE	06.04.10	25
BLAST-FURNACE-KEEPER HELPER	RES	06.04.10	74
BLASTER	RIE	05.10.06	5
BLASTER	RSE	05.10.06	22
BLASTER HELPER	RCS	05.12.02	120
BLASTING-CAP ASSEMBLER	RCE	06.04.23	132
BLEACH PACKER	REC	06.04.11	107
BLEACH-BOILER FILLER	REC	06.04.14	93
BLEACH-LIQUOR MAKER	RES	06.02.14	63
BLEACH-RANGE OPERATOR	REC	06.04.16	93

ALPHABETICAL INDEX

Title	Code	Group	Page
BRIAR CUTTER	RCE	06.04.03	133
BRICK TESTER	REI	06.02.30	47
BRICK-AND-TILE-MAKING-MACHINE OPERATOR	RSE	06.02.17	26
BRICKLAYER	RSE	05.05.01	22
BRICKLAYER	REI	05.05.01	39
BRICKLAYER APPRENTICE	RIE	05.05.01	5
BRICKLAYER HELPER, FIREBRICK AND REFRACTORY TILE	RES	05.12.09	75
BRICKLAYER SUPERVISOR	ERS	05.05.01	180
BRICKLAYER, FIREBRICK AND REFRACTORY TILE	REI	05.05.01	34
BRIDGE INSPECTOR	RSI	05.07.01	20
BRIDGE OPERATOR, SLIP	RCS	05.11.04	114
BRIDGE-OR-GANTRY-CRANE OPERATOR	RCS	05.11.04	114
BRIGHT CUTTER	RCE	06.02.24	125
BRILLIANDEER-LOPPER	REI	05.05.14	39
BRIM CURLER	REC	06.04.05	93
BRIM IRONER, HAND	CRS	06.04.27	212
BRIM PRESSER 1	RCE	06.04.05	133
BRIM RAISER	REC	06.04.27	93
BRIM STITCHER 1	CRS	06.04.05	212
BRIM-AND-CROWN PRESSER	CRE	06.04.05	219
BRIM-POUNCING-MACHINE OPERATOR	RCE	06.04.16	133
BRIM-STRETCHING-MACHINE OPERATOR	RCE	06.04.05	133
BRIMER	REC	06.04.33	107
BRINE MAKER	RIE	06.04.11	14
BRINE MAKER	REC	06.04.11	93
BRINE MAKER 1	REC	06.04.15	93
BRINE MAKER 2	CRE	06.04.15	219
BRINE-MIXER OPERATOR, AUTOMATIC	CRE	06.04.15	219
BRINE-TANK TENDER	REI	06.04.15	47
BRINE-TANK-SEPARATOR OPERATOR	RCE	06.04.15	152
BRINE-WELL OPERATOR	RSE	06.04.11	26
BRINER	REI	06.04.28	51
BRIQUETTE-MACHINE OPERATOR	REC	06.02.17	88
BRIQUETTE-MACHINE-OPERATOR HELPER	RES	06.04.12	75
BRIQUETTER OPERATOR	RES	06.04.11	64
BRIQUETTING-MACHINE OPERATOR	RCE	06.04.10	133
BROACHING-MACHINE OPERATOR, PRODUCTION	RIE	06.02.02	14
BROACHING-MACHINE SET-UP OPERATOR	RIE	06.02.02	14
BROADCAST CHECKER	CER	11.10.02	235
BROKER-AND-MARKET OPERATOR, GRAIN	EAS	11.06.04	187
BROKER'S FLOOR REPRESENTATIVE	ERS	11.06.04	180
BROKERAGE CLERK 1	CSR	07.02.02	228
BROKERAGE CLERK 2	CSR	07.02.02	229
BROOM BUNDLER	REC	06.04.38	93
BROOM STITCHER	RCE	06.02.09	125
BROOMCORN GRADER	CER	06.03.02	235
BROOMCORN SEEDER	REC	06.04.09	107
BROOMMAKER	CRE	06.04.34	219
BROTH MIXER	REI	06.04.15	39
BROWN-STOCK WASHER	REC	06.04.14	93
BROWNING PROCESSOR	REC	06.04.10	93
BRUSH FILLER, HAND	CER	06.04.23	235

Title	Code	Group	Page
CLEANER	REC	06.04.39	107
CLEANER AND POLISHER	RCE	06.04.39	153
CLEANER AND PREPARER	REC	06.04.33	107
CLEANER 2	REI	05.12.18	47
CLEANER 3	REC	05.12.18	94
CLEANER-TOUCH-UP WORKER	REC	06.03.02	94
CLEANER, COMMERCIAL OR INSTITUTIONAL	REC	05.12.18	107
CLEANER, FURNITURE	RCE	06.04.39	153
CLEANER, HOSPITAL	CRE	05.12.18	219
CLEANER, HOUSEKEEPING	CRE	05.12.18	219
CLEANER, INDUSTRIAL	RSE	05.12.18	30
CLEANER, LABORATORY EQUIPMENT	RES	05.12.18	76
CLEANER, SIGNS	RCE	05.12.18	135
CLEANER, WALL	REC	05.12.18	107
CLEANER, WINDOW	RES	05.12.18	85
CLEARANCE CUTTER	REC	06.02.02	94
CLEARING SUPERVISOR	RES	05.11.01	53
CLEARING-HOUSE CLERK	RCI	07.02.01	112
CLEAT FEEDER	REC	06.04.40	107
CLERGY MEMBER	ASE	10.01.01	165
CLERICAL-METHODS ANALYST	SEC	05.01.06	175
CLERK-OF-SCALES	REI	12.01.02	39
CLERK-TYPIST	CSE	07.06.02	233
CLERK, GENERAL	CSE	07.07.03	233
CLERK, ROUTE	RCE	07.05.04	125
CLERK, TELEGRAPH SERVICE	SEC	07.02.02	176
CLICKING-MACHINE OPERATOR	RCS	06.02.05	115
CLINCHING-MACHINE OPERATOR	REC	06.04.20	94
CLIP COATER	CRE	06.04.33	219
CLIP-AND-HANGER ATTACHER	CRE	06.04.34	219
CLIP-BOLTER AND WRAPPER	REC	06.04.22	94
CLIP-LOADING-MACHINE ADJUSTER	RSC	06.02.20	32
CLIP-LOADING-MACHINE FEEDER	RCE	06.04.20	153
CLIPPER	RES	06.04.29	76
CLIPPER	REC	06.03.02	107
CLIPPER	RCE	06.04.09	135
CLIPPER AND TURNER	RES	06.04.24	85
CLIPPER, AUTOMATIC	RCE	06.04.03	135
CLIPPER, MACHINE	RCE	06.04.06	153
CLOCK ASSEMBLER	RCE	06.04.23	135
CLOCKER	ESC	12.01.02	205
CLOTH DESIGNER	AER	01.02.03	165
CLOTH DOFFER	RES	06.04.06	76
CLOTH DRIER	RCE	06.04.05	135
CLOTH EXAMINER, HAND	RES	06.03.02	76
CLOTH EXAMINER, HAND	RCE	06.03.02	135
CLOTH EXAMINER, MACHINE	REI	06.03.02	39
CLOTH FEEDER	RES	06.04.16	85
CLOTH FINISHER	ERS	05.09.02	181
CLOTH FOLDER, HAND	REC	06.04.27	94
CLOTH FRAMER	RSE	06.04.38	30
CLOTH GRADER	RES	06.03.01	64
CLOTH INSPECTOR	REC	06.03.02	95
CLOTH MEASURER, MACHINE	RCE	06.03.02	135

ALPHABETICAL INDEX

Title	Code	Group	Page
DIAL BRUSHER	CRE	06.04.33	228
DIAL MAKER	RES	06.01.04	65
DIAL MAKER	REC	06.02.31	88
DIAL MARKER	CRE	01.06.03	220
DIAL REFINISHER	RCS	06.04.33	121
DIAL-SCREW ASSEMBLER	CRE	06.04.23	220
DIALER	CRS	06.02.23	209
DIALYSIS TECHNICIAN	CSE	10.02.02	231
DIAMOND BLENDER	RCE	06.04.19	136
DIAMOND CLEAVER	REC	05.05.14	88
DIAMOND DRILLER	CRS	06.01.04	209
DIAMOND EXPERT	RSE	05.05.14	22
DIAMOND MOUNTER	RCE	06.02.32	126
DIAMOND SELECTOR	REI	05.05.14	34
DIAMOND SIZER AND SORTER	REC	06.03.02	88
DIAMOND-DIE POLISHER	RCE	06.01.04	126
DIAMOND-POWDER TECHNICIAN	RCS	06.04.08	121
DIANETIC COUNSELOR	SEI	10.01.02	173
DICE MAKER	RCE	06.02.24	126
DICER OPERATOR	REC	06.04.02	96
DICTATING-TRANSCRIBING-MACHINE SERVICER	RES	05.05.09	53
DIE BARBER	REI	05.05.06	40
DIE CLEANER	REI	06.04.39	48
DIE CUTTER	CRS	06.02.09	209
DIE DESIGNER	RIE	05.03.02	6
DIE FINISHER	RIS	05.05.07	1
DIE MAKER	RIE	05.05.07	6
DIE MAKER	RIE	05.05.06	6
DIE MAKER	RIE	01.06.01	6
DIE MAKER, BENCH, STAMPING	RIE	05.05.07	6
DIE MAKER, STAMPING	RIE	05.05.07	6
DIE MAKER, TRIM	RIE	05.05.07	6
DIE MAKER, WIRE DRAWING	RIE	05.05.07	6
DIE MOUNTER	RES	06.02.31	65
DIE POLISHER	RES	05.05.07	65
DIE PRESSER	RCE	06.02.08	126
DIE SETTER	RIE	06.01.02	6
DIE SINKER	RIE	05.05.07	6
DIE TRIPPER	RES	06.04.17	77
DIE-CASTING-MACHINE OPERATOR 1	RIE	06.02.10	15
DIE-CASTING-MACHINE OPERATOR 2	RCE	06.04.10	136
DIE-CASTING-MACHINE SETTER	RIE	06.01.02	6
DIE-CUTTING-MACHINE OPERATOR, AUTOMATIC	RSE	06.02.05	26
DIE-DESIGNER APPRENTICE	RIE	05.03.02	6
DIE-DRAWING CHECKER	IRE	05.03.02	160
DIE-MAKER APPRENTICE	RIE	05.05.07	6
DIE-MAKER APPRENTICE	RIE	05.05.06	6
DIE-TRY-OUT WORKER, STAMPING	RIE	05.05.09	6
DIELECTRIC-PRESS OPERATOR	CRS	06.04.05	212
DIESEL MECHANIC	REI	05.05.09	34
DIESEL-ENGINE ERECTOR	REI	05.05.09	34
DIESEL-ENGINE TESTER	RSI	06.01.05	20
DIESEL-MECHANIC APPRENTICE	REI	05.05.09	34
DIESEL-MECHANIC HELPER	RCE	05.12.15	136

Title	Code	Group	Page
EDITOR, CITY	AES	11.08.01	166
EDITOR, DEPARTMENT	AES	11.08.01	166
EDITOR, DICTIONARY	SIA	11.08.01	169
EDITOR, FILM	AES	01.01.01	166
EDITOR, GREETING CARD	AES	01.01.01	166
EDITOR, INDEX	SIC	11.08.01	170
EDITOR, MANAGING, NEWSPAPER	SEA	11.05.01	174
EDITOR, MAP	RIE	05.03.02	6
EDITOR, NEWS	AEC	11.08.01	167
EDITOR, NEWSPAPER	AES	11.08.01	166
EDITOR, PUBLICATIONS	AES	01.01.01	166
EDITOR, SCHOOL PHOTOGRAPH	SER	01.06.01	173
EDITOR, TECHNICAL AND SCIENTIFIC PUBLICATIONS	ASE	11.08.01	165
EDITOR, TELEGRAPH	CSE	11.08.01	231
EDITORIAL ASSISTANT	SCI	11.08.01	178
EDITORIAL WRITER	AES	01.01.02	166
EDUCATION SUPERVISOR, CORRECTIONAL INSTITUTION	SEA	11.07.03	174
EDUCATIONAL SPECIALIST	EIS	11.07.03	186
EDUCATIONAL THERAPIST	SEC	10.02.03	175
EFFERVESCENT-SALTS COMPOUNDER	RES	06.04.11	66
EGG BREAKER	REC	06.04.28	108
EGG CANDLER	CER	06.03.01	236
EGG PROCESSOR	CRE	06.04.34	220
EGG WASHER, MACHINE	RCE	06.04.39	153
EGG-BREAKING-MACHINE OPERATOR	REC	06.04.15	108
ELASTIC ATTACHER, CHAINSTITCH	RCE	06.02.05	137
ELASTIC ATTACHER, COVERSTITCH	RCE	06.02.05	137
ELASTIC ATTACHER, OVERLOCK	RCE	06.02.05	137
ELASTIC ATTACHER, ZIGZAG	RCE	06.02.05	137
ELASTIC-TAPE INSERTER	RES	06.04.27	77
ELECTION ASSISTANT	ESA	11.05.03	198
ELECTION CLERK	CSE	07.04.03	233
ELECTRIC MOTOR REPAIRING SUPERVISOR	ESR	05.05.10	190
ELECTRIC POWERLINE EXAMINER	RCE	05.07.01	126
ELECTRIC-CABLE DIAGRAMER	RIE	05.03.02	6
ELECTRIC-CELL TENDER	RES	06.02.11	66
ELECTRIC-CONTAINER TESTER	CRE	06.03.02	220
ELECTRIC-DISTRIBUTION CHECKER	RES	05.05.05	54
ELECTRIC-FORK OPERATOR	RES	03.04.01	85
ELECTRIC-GOLF-CART REPAIRER	REI	05.10.03	40
ELECTRIC-METER INSTALLER 1	RES	05.05.05	54
ELECTRIC-METER INSTALLER 2	CER	05.10.03	235
ELECTRIC-METER REPAIRER	RIE	05.05.10	6
ELECTRIC-METER TESTER	RIE	05.05.10	6
ELECTRIC-METER-REPAIRER APPRENTICE	RIE	05.05.10	6
ELECTRIC-MOTOR ANALYST	RSE	05.07.02	22
ELECTRIC-MOTOR ASSEMBLER	CRE	06.04.23	220
ELECTRIC-MOTOR ASSEMBLER AND TESTER	REI	06.02.23	34
ELECTRIC-MOTOR FITTER	RES	05.05.05	54
ELECTRIC-MOTOR REPAIRER	RIE	05.05.10	6
ELECTRIC-MOTOR WINDER	RES	06.02.23	66
ELECTRIC-MOTOR-AND-GENERATOR ASSEMBLER	RSE	06.01.04	22

Title	Code	Group	Page
ELEVATOR REPAIRER	RIS	05.05.05	1
ELEVATOR STARTER	ERS	09.05.09	184
ELEVATOR-CONSTRUCTOR HELPER	RCE	05.12.12	126
ELEVATOR-CONSTRUCTOR SUPERVISOR	RES	05.05.09	54
ELEVATOR-REPAIRER APPRENTICE	RIS	05.05.05	1
ELEVATOR-REPAIRER HELPER	RCE	05.12.15	126
ELIGIBILITY WORKER	SCE	07.01.01	178
ELIGIBILITY-AND-OCCUPANCY INTERVIEWER	SEC	07.01.01	176
EMBALMER	RIS	02.04.02	1
EMBALMER APPRENTICE	RIS	02.04.02	1
EMBLEM DRAWER-IN	RCE	06.01.02	126
EMBOSSER	RIE	05.10.05	7
EMBOSSER	RIC	06.02.05	20
EMBOSSER	REC	06.04.05	97
EMBOSSER	RCE	06.04.02	137
EMBOSSER	CRE	06.04.37	220
EMBOSSER OPERATOR	REI	06.02.09	40
EMBOSSING TOOLSETTER	RES	06.01.02	54
EMBOSSING-MACHINE OPERATOR	RCS	06.04.02	116
EMBOSSING-MACHINE OPERATOR	RCS	06.02.03	116
EMBOSSING-MACHINE OPERATOR	RCE	06.04.02	137
EMBOSSING-MACHINE OPERATOR	RCE	06.04.02	137
EMBOSSING-MACHINE OPERATOR 1	CRS	06.02.02	209
EMBOSSING-MACHINE OPERATOR 2	CRS	06.02.02	209
EMBOSSING-MACHINE TENDER	RES	06.04.04	77
EMBOSSING-MACHINE-OPERATOR HELPER	RCE	06.04.02	137
EMBOSSING-PRESS OPERATOR	RES	06.02.04	66
EMBOSSING-PRESS OPERATOR	CRE	06.04.09	220
EMBOSSING-PRESS OPERATOR, MOLDED GOODS	REI	06.02.09	40
EMBOSSING-PRESS-OPERATOR APPRENTICE	RES	06.02.04	66
EMBOSSOGRAPH OPERATOR	CRS	06.02.09	209
EMBROIDERER, HAND	CSR	06.02.27	229
EMBROIDERY PATTERNMAKER	IRE	01.06.03	161
EMBROIDERY SUPERVISOR	RES	06.02.01	54
EMBROIDERY-MACHINE OPERATOR	REI	06.02.05	40
EMBROIDERY-MACHINE OPERATOR	CRE	06.04.05	220
EMERGENCY MEDICAL SERVICES COORDINATOR	SER	11.07.02	171
EMERGENCY MEDICAL TECHNICIAN	ESI	10.03.02	197
EMPLOYMENT CLERK	CES	07.04.01	237
EMPLOYMENT INTERVIEWER	SEC	11.03.04	175
EMPLOYMENT-AND-CLAIMS AIDE	ESC	07.04.01	205
ENAMELER	RES	06.04.33	66
ENAMELER	CSE	01.06.03	233
ENCAPSULATOR	RCS	06.04.34	116
ENCAPSULATOR	RCE	06.04.24	137
END FINDER, FORMING DEPARTMENT	CRE	06.03.02	220
END FINDER, ROVING DEPARTMENT	RCE	06.04.27	137
END FINDER, TWISTING DEPARTMENT	RCE	06.04.27	137
END FRAZER	RCE	06.04.03	137
END POLISHER	CRE	06.02.02	220
END STAPLER	REI	06.04.20	48
END-TOUCHING-MACHINE OPERATOR	RCE	06.04.09	153
ENDBAND CUTTER, HAND	CRE	06.04.27	220
ENDING-MACHINE OPERATOR	CRE	06.04.04	220

Title	Code	Group	Page
GINNER	CRE	05.12.07	221
GIRDLER	RCS	05.05.14	116
GLASS BENDER	REI	01.06.02	35
GLASS BLOWER	RCS	06.01.04	116
GLASS BLOWER, LABORATORY APPARATUS	RAE	05.05.11	20
GLASS CALIBRATOR	RCE	06.02.31	127
GLASS CHECKER	RCE	06.03.02	139
GLASS CUT-OFF TENDER	RCS	06.04.08	121
GLASS CUTTER	RCS	06.02.30	116
GLASS CUTTER, HAND	REI	06.01.04	41
GLASS CUTTER, OVAL OR CIRCULAR	RCS	06.04.30	121
GLASS DECORATOR	REI	01.06.01	35
GLASS DRILLER	CRS	06.04.30	213
GLASS FINISHER	RSC	06.04.30	32
GLASS GRINDER	RSC	06.02.30	32
GLASS GRINDER	CRS	06.04.30	213
GLASS GRINDER, LABORATORY APPARATUS	REI	06.02.08	41
GLASS INSPECTOR	CER	06.03.02	236
GLASS INSTALLER	RCS	06.04.30	121
GLASS INSTALLER	RCE	05.10.01	127
GLASS POLISHER	RCE	06.04.30	139
GLASS SANDER, BELT	REC	06.04.30	98
GLASS TINTER	REC	06.04.33	98
GLASS-BLOWING-LATHE OPERATOR	RCE	06.02.08	127
GLASS-BULB SILVERER	RCE	06.04.33	154
GLASS-BULB-MACHINE ADJUSTER	RSI	06.01.02	21
GLASS-BULB-MACHINE FORMER, TUBULAR STOCK	RSE	06.02.13	27
GLASS-CLEANING-MACHINE TENDER	RCE	06.04.08	139
GLASS-CUT-OFF SUPERVISOR	RSE	06.02.01	23
GLASS-CUTTER HELPER	RSC	06.04.30	33
GLASS-CUTTING-MACHINE OPERATOR, AUTOMATIC	CRS	06.02.08	209
GLASS-FURNACE TENDER	RCE	06.04.13	139
GLASS-LATHE OPERATOR	RCS	06.02.08	116
GLASS-LINED TANK REPAIRER	REC	05.10.01	89
GLASS-RIBBON-MACHINE OPERATOR	RSE	06.02.13	23
GLASS-RIBBON-MACHINE-OPERATOR ASSISTANT	RES	06.02.13	67
GLASS-ROLLING-MACHINE OPERATOR	REI	06.02.13	41
GLASS-UNLOADING-EQUIPMENT TENDER	REC	06.04.08	98
GLASS-VIAL-BENDING-CONVEYOR FEEDER	RCE	06.04.13	139
GLASS-WOOL-BLANKET-MACHINE FEEDER	RCE	06.04.09	139
GLASS-WORKER, PRESSED OR BLOWN	CRS	06.02.30	213
GLAZE HANDLER	RES	06.04.17	78
GLAZE MAKER	RSE	06.02.09	27
GLAZE SUPERVISOR	REI	06.02.01	35
GLAZE SUPERVISOR	RES	06.02.01	55
GLAZIER	RSE	05.10.01	27
GLAZIER	CRE	06.04.30	221
GLAZIER APPRENTICE	RSE	05.10.01	27
GLAZIER SUPERVISOR	RCE	05.10.01	124
GLAZIER, METAL FURNITURE	RCE	06.02.22	127
GLAZIER, STAINED GLASS	RIS	01.06.02	2
GLAZING OPERATOR, BLACK POWDER	RSE	06.04.19	27
GLAZING-MACHINE OPERATOR	CRE	06.04.13	221

Title	Code	Group	Page
GLOBE MOUNTER	RSE	06.04.26	30
GLOVE CLEANER, HAND	REC	06.04.35	98
GLOVE FORMER	REC	06.04.27	109
GLOVE PAIRER	REC	06.03.02	98
GLOVE PRINTER	RCE	06.04.37	139
GLOVE SEWER	CRS	06.02.05	209
GLOVE TURNER	REC	06.04.27	109
GLOVE TURNER AND FORMER, AUTOMATIC	REC	06.04.05	109
GLOVE-PARTS INSPECTOR	SRE	06.03.02	169
GLUCOSE-AND-SIRUP WEIGHER	RCE	06.04.28	154
GLUE MAKER, BONE	REI	06.02.18	41
GLUE MIXER	RCE	06.04.19	127
GLUE SPREADER, VENEER	CRE	06.04.03	221
GLUE-MACHINE OPERATOR	RCE	06.04.09	139
GLUE-MILL OPERATOR	RES	06.04.19	78
GLUE-SIZE-MACHINE OPERATOR	RCE	06.04.21	139
GLUE-SPREADING-MACHINE OPERATOR	REC	06.04.05	98
GLUED WOOD TESTER	RES	06.03.01	55
GLUER	RES	06.04.22	78
GLUER	RCE	06.04.34	154
GLUER AND SLICER, HAND	RES	06.04.26	78
GLUER-AND-WEDGER	RCE	06.04.25	139
GLUER, WET SUIT	CRE	06.04.29	221
GLUING-MACHINE OFFBEARER	RES	06.04.03	78
GLUING-MACHINE OPERATOR	REC	06.04.03	98
GLUING-MACHINE OPERATOR	CRE	06.04.21	228
GLUING-MACHINE OPERATOR, AUTOMATIC	RCE	06.02.20	127
GLUING-MACHINE OPERATOR, ELECTRONIC	RCE	06.04.03	139
GLUTEN-SETTLING TENDER	REC	06.04.15	109
GOAT HERDER	REC	03.04.01	98
GOLD BURNISHER	REC	06.04.24	98
GOLD CUTTER	CRE	06.02.24	216
GOLD RECLAIMER	RCS	06.04.02	121
GOLD-NIB GRINDER	CRS	06.04.02	213
GOLDBEATER	RSE	06.01.04	27
GOLF-BALL TRIMMER	CRE	06.04.34	221
GOLF-BALL-COVER TREATER	RCS	06.04.11	121
GOLF-CLUB ASSEMBLER	CSR	06.04.23	230
GOLF-CLUB FACER	RES	06.02.25	67
GOLF-CLUB HEAD FORMER	RES	06.02.24	67
GOLF-CLUB REPAIRER	RES	05.10.01	67
GOLF-CLUB WEIGHER	RCS	06.03.02	121
GOLF-CLUB WEIGHTER	CRS	06.04.34	213
GOLF-COURSE RANGER	ESC	12.01.02	205
GOLF-RANGE ATTENDANT	RCS	05.12.18	121
GOLF-SHOE-SPIKE ASSEMBLER	RCE	06.04.27	139
GOODS LAYER	RES	05.09.02	78
GOODWILL AMBASSADOR	ESC	11.09.01	205
GOVERNOR ASSEMBLER, HYDRAULIC	RIE	06.01.04	7
GRADE CHECKER	REA	05.03.01	52
GRADER	RIE	06.03.02	16
GRADER	ESC	06.03.02	206
GRADER TENDER	RCE	03.04.01	139
GRADER, DRESSED POULTRY	CER	06.03.02	236

Title	Code	Group	Page
HELPER, ELECTRICAL	RSE	05.12.16	30
HELPER, LIQUEFACTION-AND-REGASIFICATION	RCS	05.10.02	116
HELPER, MANUFACTURING	REC	06.04.34	98
HELPER, METAL BONDING	RES	06.04.40	78
HELPER, METAL HANGING	RCE	06.04.22	154
HEMMER	RCE	06.02.05	127
HEMMER, AUTOMATIC	CRE	06.04.05	216
HEMMER, BLINDSTITCH	CRE	06.02.05	222
HEMMER, CHAINSTITCH	CRE	06.02.05	222
HEMMER, LOCKSTITCH	CRE	06.02.05	222
HEMMER, OVERLOCK	CRE	06.02.05	222
HEMMING-AND-TACKING-MACHINE OPERATOR	RCE	06.04.05	140
HEMSTITCHING-MACHINE OPERATOR	RCE	06.02.05	140
HIDE HANDLER	REI	06.04.27	49
HIDE INSPECTOR	RSE	06.03.02	27
HIDE INSPECTOR	REC	06.03.02	98
HIDE PULLER	REI	06.04.15	49
HIDE SPLITTER	REI	06.02.05	41
HIDE TRIMMER	RES	06.04.39	78
HIGH RIGGER	RES	05.10.01	68
HIGH-DENSITY FINISHING OPERATOR	RIE	06.02.18	16
HIGH-ENERGY-FORMING WORKER	RIE	06.01.03	8
HIGHWAY-ADMINISTRATIVE ENGINEER	IEC	11.05.03	164
HIGHWAY-MAINTENANCE SUPERVISOR	SER	05.11.01	171
HIGHWAY-MAINTENANCE WORKER	CRS	05.12.12	209
HISTOPATHOLOGIST	IRS	02.02.01	157
HISTORIAN	ESC	11.03.03	203
HISTORIAN, DRAMATIC ARTS	ESC	11.03.03	203
HISTORY-CARD CLERK	CES	07.05.03	238
HOBBING-PRESS OPERATOR	CRS	06.02.02	209
HOG TENDER	REC	06.04.03	98
HOGSHEAD COOPER 1	RES	06.04.22	78
HOGSHEAD COOPER 2	RES	06.04.22	78
HOGSHEAD COOPER 3	RES	06.04.22	78
HOGSHEAD HOOPER	REC	06.04.22	109
HOGSHEAD INSPECTOR	RSE	06.03.01	27
HOGSHEAD MAT ASSEMBLER	REC	06.04.22	98
HOGSHEAD MAT INSPECTOR	CRE	06.03.02	222
HOGSHEAD OPENER	RES	06.04.28	79
HOIST OPERATOR	RCS	05.11.02	116
HOIST OPERATOR	RCS	05.11.02	116
HOISTING ENGINEER	RCS	05.11.04	116
HOLIDAY-DETECTOR OPERATOR	CRE	05.07.01	222
HOLLOW-HANDLE-KNIFE ASSEMBLER	CRE	06.04.23	222
HOME ATTENDANT	SER	10.03.03	173
HOME ECONOMIST	SEA	11.02.03	174
HOME-SERVICE DIRECTOR	ESA	11.02.03	198
HOMEMAKER	SER	11.02.03	171
HONEY EXTRACTOR	REC	06.04.15	109
HONEY GRADER-AND-BLENDER	RIS	06.01.04	2
HONEY PROCESSOR	REC	06.04.15	98
HONEYCOMB DECAPPER	RES	06.04.28	79
HONEYCOMB-BLANKET MAKER	RES	06.02.09	68
HONING-MACHINE OPERATOR, PRODUCTION	RIE	06.02.02	16

Title	Code	Group	Page
INSURANCE CLERK 2	CES	07.05.03	238
INTELLIGENCE CLERK	RES	07.05.03	68
INTELLIGENCE RESEARCH SPECIALIST	AEI	11.03.02	165
INTELLIGENCE SPECIALIST	AES	11.03.02	167
INTELLIGENCE SPECIALIST	ERS	04.01.02	181
INTEREST CLERK	CSR	07.02.02	229
INTERIOR DESIGNER	AES	01.02.03	167
INTERLACER	RCE	06.04.27	140
INTERLINE CLERK	CRS	07.02.04	208
INTERN	IRS	02.03.01	157
INTERNAL CARVER	RIE	06.01.04	8
INTERNAL-COMBUSTION-ENGINE INSPECTOR	RIE	06.01.05	8
INTERNAL-COMBUSTION-ENGINE SUBASSEMBLER	RCE	06.02.22	127
INTERNIST	IRS	02.03.01	157
INTERPRETER	ESA	11.08.04	198
INTERPRETER, DEAF	SCE	01.03.02	179
INVENTORY CLERK	RCI	05.09.01	113
INVESTIGATOR	SIE	11.10.01	170
INVESTIGATOR	ESR	04.01.02	195
INVESTIGATOR	ESC	11.06.03	204
INVESTIGATOR, CASH SHORTAGE	SCE	11.10.01	179
INVESTIGATOR, FRAUD	SEC	11.10.01	176
INVESTIGATOR, NARCOTICS	SRE	04.01.02	168
INVESTIGATOR, PRIVATE	ESI	04.01.02	197
INVESTIGATOR, UTILITY-BILL COMPLAINTS	ESR	07.05.02	190
INVESTIGATOR, VICE	SER	04.01.02	171
INVOICE-CONTROL CLERK	CSR	07.02.04	229
ION EXCHANGE OPERATOR	CER	06.04.15	236
ION-EXCHANGE OPERATOR	RSC	06.04.11	32
ION-EXCHANGE OPERATOR	RES	06.02.18	68
ION-EXCHANGE OPERATOR	RCE	06.04.10	127
IRISH-MOSS BLEACHER	REC	03.04.03	99
IRISH-MOSS GATHERER	REC	03.04.03	109
IRISH-MOSS OPERATOR	RSE	06.02.11	27
IRON-LAUNDER OPERATOR	CRS	06.04.10	210
IRON-PLASTIC BULLET MAKER	RIE	06.02.10	16
IRONER	RCE	06.04.02	140
IRONER	RCE	05.12.18	154
IRONER, SOCK	REC	06.04.35	109
IRONWORKER-MACHINE OPERATOR	RSC	06.02.02	32
IRRADIATED-FUEL HANDLER	RSC	05.11.04	32
IRRIGATION ENGINEER	IRE	05.01.03	160
IRRIGATION SYSTEM INSTALLER	REI	05.11.01	42
IRRIGATOR, GRAVITY FLOW	REI	03.04.05	49
IRRIGATOR, HEAD	RES	03.04.05	68
IRRIGATOR, SPRINKLING SYSTEM	REC	03.04.05	99
IRRIGATOR, VALVE PIPE	REC	03.04.05	99
JACK SETTER	RCS	05.12.02	117
JACKET PREPARER	CRS	07.05.03	210
JACKHAMMER OPERATOR	RCS	05.12.02	121
JACQUARD-LOOM WEAVER	REC	06.02.06	90
JACQUARD-LOOM WEAVER	RCS	06.02.06	117
JACQUARD-PLATE MAKER	RES	06.02.23	68
JACQUARD-TWINE-POLISHER OPERATOR	CRE	06.04.16	222

Title	Code	Group	Page
JOGGER	RSE	06.04.26	30
JOINER	RES	05.05.02	55
JOINER	RCE	06.04.30	140
JOINER APPRENTICE	RES	05.05.02	55
JOINER HELPER	RCS	05.10.01	117
JOINT CUTTER, MACHINE	RCE	06.04.05	140
JOINT-CLEANING-AND-GROOVING-MACHINE OPERATOR	RIE	05.11.01	16
JOINTER OPERATOR	RIS	05.05.08	3
JUDGE	ESA	11.04.01	197
JUGGLER	SEC	12.02.01	177
JUMPBASTING-MACHINE OPERATOR	CRE	06.02.05	222
JUNCTION MAKER	RCE	06.02.30	140
KAPOK-AND-COTTON-MACHINE OPERATOR	REI	06.04.16	49
KEG VARNISHER	REC	06.04.33	109
KELP CUTTER	REI	03.04.03	49
KENNEL MANAGER, DOG TRACK	SRE	12.01.02	169
KERFER-MACHINE OPERATOR	RCE	06.04.03	140
KETTLE OPERATOR	REI	06.02.13	42
KETTLE OPERATOR	REI	06.02.11	42
KETTLE OPERATOR	RES	06.02.15	68
KETTLE OPERATOR	REC	06.04.10	90
KETTLE TENDER	REI	06.04.15	49
KETTLE TENDER	REI	06.04.15	49
KETTLE TENDER	RCE	05.12.10	154
KETTLE TENDER 1	RSC	06.04.10	32
KETTLE TENDER 2	REC	06.04.10	90
KETTLE TENDER, PLATINUM AND PALLADIUM	RES	06.04.10	68
KETTLE WORKER	REI	06.02.18	42
KEY CUTTER	RCE	05.12.13	140
KEYBOARD-ACTION ASSEMBLER	RES	06.02.23	68
KEYING-MACHINE OPERATOR	RCE	06.04.37	140
KEYPUNCH OPERATOR	CSE	07.06.02	233
KEYSEATING-MACHINE SET-UP OPERATOR	REI	06.02.02	42
KICK PRESS SETTER	RCS	06.01.02	117
KICK-PRESS OPERATOR	CRE	06.04.20	222
KICK-PRESS OPERATOR 1	RCE	06.02.20	127
KILN BURNER	RSC	06.04.17	32
KILN CLEANER	RCE	06.04.39	140
KILN DRAWER	REC	06.04.17	99
KILN DRAWER	ERI	05.12.03	180
KILN LOADER	REC	06.04.40	109
KILN OPERATOR	REC	06.02.18	90
KILN OPERATOR	RCS	06.02.10	117
KILN OPERATOR	RCS	06.04.10	121
KILN OPERATOR, MALT HOUSE	RSE	06.02.15	27
KILN PLACER	REC	06.04.17	99
KILN WORKER	RCE	06.04.17	154
KILN-BURNER HELPER	RES	06.04.17	79
KILN-DOOR BUILDER	RCE	05.10.01	140
KILN-FURNITURE CASTER	REC	06.04.17	99
KILN-OPERATOR HELPER	REC	06.04.11	99
KILN-OPERATOR HELPER	RCS	06.04.10	122
KILN-TRANSFER OPERATOR	REI	05.11.04	49

Title	Code	Group	Page
LINING SCRUBBER	REC	06.04.35	109
LINING SETTER, LOCKSTITCH	RCE	06.02.05	141
LINING-MACHINE OPERATOR	RCE	06.04.21	141
LINK-AND-LINK-KNITTING-MACHINE OPERATOR	REI	06.01.03	42
LINKER	RES	06.04.28	80
LINKER	CRE	06.04.23	223
LINKING-MACHINE OPERATOR	REC	06.04.15	100
LINOTYPE OPERATOR	RIE	07.06.02	9
LINSEED-OIL REFINER	RSE	06.02.11	28
LINSEED-OIL-PRESS TENDER	RES	06.04.19	80
LINTER TENDER	RCE	06.04.19	141
LINTER-SAW SHARPENER	REI	06.02.02	42
LIP CUTTER AND SCORER	RCE	06.04.05	141
LIP-OF-SHANK CUTTER	CRE	06.04.05	223
LIQUEFACTION-AND-REGASIFICATION-PLANT OPERATOR	RSC	05.06.04	31
LIQUEFACTION-PLANT OPERATOR	REC	06.02.12	90
LIQUID-FERTILIZER SERVICER	CRI	05.08.03	208
LIQUID-SUGAR FORTIFIER	REC	06.04.15	100
LIQUID-SUGAR MELTER	REI	06.02.15	42
LIQUOR BLENDER	REI	06.02.15	35
LIQUOR INSPECTOR	RCE	06.03.02	141
LIQUOR-BRIDGE OPERATOR	REI	06.04.15	49
LIQUOR-BRIDGE-OPERATOR HELPER	RSE	06.04.15	30
LIQUOR-GRINDING-MILL OPERATOR	REC	06.04.15	100
LITERARY AGENT	ESA	11.12.03	198
LITHO-MAKE-READY ASSISTANT	ERS	01.06.01	184
LITHOGRAPH-PRESS OPERATOR, TINWARE	REI	06.02.02	42
LITHOGRAPHED-PLATE INSPECTOR	RES	06.03.02	86
LITHOGRAPHIC PLATE MAKER	REI	01.06.01	35
LITHOGRAPHIC-PLATE-MAKER APPRENTICE	REI	01.06.01	35
LITHOGRAPHIC-PROOFER APPRENTICE	REI	05.05.13	42
LIVESTOCK RANCHER	RSI	03.01.01	21
LIVESTOCK-YARD ATTENDANT	REI	03.04.01	42
LOAD CHECKER	REI	05.09.01	42
LOAD DISPATCHER	ERS	05.06.01	181
LOAD TESTER	RCS	06.03.02	122
LOAD-OUT SUPERVISOR	REI	05.12.04	42
LOAD-TEST MECHANIC	RES	06.03.01	68
LOADER	RES	05.12.04	80
LOADER HELPER	CRE	05.12.06	223
LOADER 1	CRS	06.04.40	210
LOADER-UNLOADER, SCREEN-PRINTING MACHINE	RES	06.04.05	80
LOADER, MAGAZINE GRINDER	RES	06.04.14	80
LOADER, MALT HOUSE	ERI	05.12.04	180
LOADING INSPECTOR	RCE	05.07.01	128
LOADING-MACHINE ADJUSTER	RCS	06.01.02	117
LOADING-MACHINE OPERATOR	RIE	05.11.02	16
LOADING-MACHINE OPERATOR	CRE	06.04.20	223
LOADING-MACHINE TOOL-SETTER	RCS	06.01.02	113
LOADING-MACHINE-OPERATOR HELPER	REC	05.12.02	100
LOADING-RACK SUPERVISOR	ESC	05.12.03	204
LOADING-SHOVEL OILER	RES	05.12.08	80
LOADING-UNIT OPERATOR	CRE	06.04.09	223

Title	Code	Group	Page
LOADING-UNIT TOOL-SETTER	REC	06.01.02	90
LOAN CLOSER	ESR	07.01.04	190
LOAN COUNSELOR	ESA	07.01.01	198
LOAN INTERVIEWER	ESC	07.04.01	204
LOAN OFFICER	SEI	11.06.03	173
LOBBYIST	ESA	11.09.03	198
LOCATION MANAGER	EAR	11.12.02	186
LOCATION-AND-MEASUREMENT TECHNICIAN	RIE	06.01.04	9
LOCK ASSEMBLER	RES	06.02.22	69
LOCK ASSEMBLER	RCS	06.04.23	122
LOCK INSTALLER	REC	06.04.24	100
LOCK MAINTENANCE SUPERVISOR	RES	05.10.04	55
LOCK OPERATOR	RSC	05.11.04	32
LOCK TENDER 2	REI	05.11.01	43
LOCK TENDER, CHIEF OPERATOR	RES	05.05.09	55
LOCK-CORNER-MACHINE OPERATOR	RIE	06.02.03	16
LOCKER-PLANT ATTENDANT	RSE	05.09.01	28
LOCKER-ROOM ATTENDANT	RES	09.05.07	80
LOCKET MAKER	RES	06.01.04	69
LOCKSMITH	REC	05.05.09	87
LOCKSMITH APPRENTICE	REC	05.05.09	87
LOCKSTITCH-MACHINE OPERATOR	CRE	06.02.05	223
LOCKSTITCH-SEWING-MACHINE OPERATOR, COMPLETE GARMENT	REC	06.02.05	90
LOCOMOTIVE ENGINEER	RES	05.08.02	55
LOCOMOTIVE INSPECTOR	RES	05.07.01	55
LOCOMOTIVE LUBRICATING-SYSTEMS CLERK	CER	07.05.01	235
LOCOMOTIVE OPERATOR HELPER	REA	05.12.20	52
LOCOMOTIVE-CRANE OPERATOR	RSI	05.11.04	21
LOFT WORKER	RES	05.05.08	55
LOFT WORKER APPRENTICE	RES	05.05.08	55
LOFT WORKER, HEAD	RES	05.05.06	55
LOG COOKER	REC	06.04.18	100
LOG GRADER	REI	05.07.06	43
LOG INSPECTOR	RCS	03.04.02	122
LOG LOADER	RCE	05.11.04	128
LOG LOADER HELPER	RCE	05.12.04	154
LOG MARKER	RIE	05.07.06	16
LOG MARKER	REI	03.04.02	49
LOG ROLLER	RCS	06.04.40	122
LOG SCALER	REI	05.07.06	43
LOG SORTER	REI	03.04.02	43
LOG WASHER	RCE	06.04.39	154
LOG-CHIPPER OPERATOR	RCS	06.02.03	117
LOG-CUT-OFF SAWYER, AUTOMATIC	REI	06.02.03	43
LOG-HAUL CHAIN FEEDER	RCE	05.12.04	141
LOG-TRUCK DRIVER	RIS	05.08.01	3
LOGGER, ALL-ROUND	RES	03.04.02	80
LOGGING-EQUIPMENT MECHANIC	REI	05.05.09	35
LOGGING-OPERATIONS INSPECTOR	RES	03.01.04	52
LOGGING-TRACTOR OPERATOR	RCS	03.04.02	117
LOGISTICS ENGINEER	ESC	05.01.06	203
LONG-CHAIN BEAMER	RCE	06.04.06	141
LONG-GOODS HELPER, MACHINE	RES	06.04.15	80

Title	Code	Group	Page
LONG-WALL-MINING-MACHINE TENDER	RCE	05.11.02	128
LOOM CHANGEOVER OPERATOR	RES	06.04.05	80
LOOM CHANGER	REI	06.01.02	35
LOOM FIXER	RSE	06.01.02	23
LOOM SETTER, WIRE WEAVING	RES	06.01.02	55
LOOM STARTER	RSE	06.01.02	23
LOOM-FIXER SUPERVISOR	RES	06.01.01	55
LOOM-WINDER TENDER	RES	06.04.06	80
LOOPER	RCE	06.02.06	128
LOOPER	CRE	06.04.24	223
LOOSE-END FINDER, BOBBIN	REC	06.04.27	109
LOST-AND-FOUND CLERK	ESC	07.07.03	205
LOST-CHARGE-CARD CLERK	CES	07.05.03	238
LOUNGE-CAR ATTENDANT	ECS	08.03.01	207
LOWERATOR OPERATOR	REC	06.03.02	109
LOZENGE MAKER	RIE	06.02.15	16
LOZENGE-DOUGH MIXER	RES	06.04.15	80
LUBRICATING-MACHINE TENDER	REC	06.04.21	100
LUBRICATION SERVICER	RES	05.12.08	80
LUBRICATION-EQUIPMENT SERVICER	RES	05.10.02	69
LUBRICATOR-GRANULATOR	CRE	06.04.10	223
LUGGAGE MAKER	REC	06.02.27	90
LUGGAGE REPAIRER	RSE	05.10.01	28
LUMBER ESTIMATOR	CRS	05.09.02	210
LUMBER HANDLER	RSE	05.12.03	30
LUMBER SCALER	RCE	05.09.01	128
LUMBER SORTER	RES	06.03.02	86
LUMBER STRAIGHTENER	RES	06.04.40	80
LUMITE INJECTOR	RCE	06.04.05	141
LUMP INSPECTOR	CRS	06.03.02	213
LUMP-MACHINE OPERATOR	RCE	06.04.15	141
LUNCH-TRUCK DRIVER	ERS	09.04.01	185
LUSTER APPLICATOR	RSE	01.06.03	28
LYE TREATER	RIE	06.04.11	16
LYE-PEEL OPERATOR	RCE	06.04.15	154
LYRICIST	ASE	01.01.02	165
MACHINE ASSEMBLER	RES	06.02.22	69
MACHINE BUILDER	RIE	05.05.09	9
MACHINE CLEANER	REC	06.04.39	100
MACHINE FEEDER	REC	06.04.31	100
MACHINE FEEDER	REC	06.04.09	109
MACHINE FEEDER	RCE	06.04.09	154
MACHINE FEEDER, RAW STOCK	RES	06.04.16	86
MACHINE FIXER	REI	06.01.04	35
MACHINE FIXER	RES	06.01.02	55
MACHINE HELPER	RSE	06.04.24	30
MACHINE HELPER	RES	06.04.05	80
MACHINE HELPER	RES	05.12.11	80
MACHINE MOLDER	RIE	06.04.32	16
MACHINE OPERATOR 1	RIE	06.01.03	9
MACHINE OPERATOR 2	RCE	06.04.02	141
MACHINE OPERATOR, CENTRIFUGAL-CONTROL SWITCHES	REI	06.02.02	43
MACHINE OPERATOR, CERAMICS	CRS	06.04.08	213

Title	Code	Group	Page
MANUGRAPHER	REC	01.06.03	90
MAP CLERK	CSE	07.05.03	233
MAP-AND-CHART MOUNTER	REC	06.02.26	90
MAPLE-SIRUP MAKER	RES	06.02.15	69
MARBLE SETTER	RIE	05.05.01	9
MARBLE-MACHINE TENDER	RCE	06.04.13	141
MARGIN CLERK 1	CRS	07.02.02	210
MARGIN CLERK 2	RCS	07.02.02	113
MARINE ENGINEER	IRE	05.01.03	159
MARINE OILER	REI	05.12.08	43
MARINE RAILWAY OPERATOR	RSE	05.11.04	28
MARINE SURVEYOR	REC	05.03.06	87
MARK-UP DESIGNER	RCS	06.02.31	117
MARKER	REC	05.09.01	100
MARKER	RCE	06.02.02	128
MARKER	CSR	05.09.03	230
MARKER	CSE	06.04.27	235
MARKER 1	RCE	06.02.31	128
MARKER 2	RCE	06.04.37	141
MARKER, COMPANY	CSR	05.09.03	230
MARKER, HAND	REC	06.04.27	100
MARKER, MACHINE	RCE	06.04.05	142
MARKET-RESEARCH ANALYST 1	SCE	11.06.03	178
MARKING STITCHER	RCE	06.04.27	142
MARKING-MACHINE OPERATOR	REC	06.04.37	100
MARKING-MACHINE OPERATOR	CRE	06.04.05	223
MARKING-MACHINE TENDER	CRE	06.04.05	223
MARKSMANSHIP INSTRUCTOR	ESR	11.02.01	195
MARSHALL	RES	12.01.02	69
MASH GRINDER	REC	06.04.15	100
MASH-FILTER OPERATOR	REC	06.04.15	110
MASH-FILTER-CLOTH CHANGER	RES	06.04.15	86
MASH-TUB-COOKER OPERATOR	RCS	06.02.15	113
MASHER	REC	06.02.15	90
MASKER	REC	06.04.34	100
MASKER	RCE	06.04.33	154
MASKING-MACHINE FEEDER	REC	06.04.02	100
MASKING-MACHINE OPERATOR	RCE	06.04.38	128
MASSEUR/MASSEUSE	RES	09.05.01	69
MASTER, PASSENGER BARGE	REI	05.04.02	36
MASTER, RIVERBOAT	ESR	05.04.02	191
MASTER, SHIP	IES	05.04.02	164
MASTER, YACHT	RSC	05.04.02	31
MAT CUTTER	CRE	06.04.34	223
MAT INSPECTOR	REI	06.03.02	43
MAT PACKER	RCE	06.04.38	142
MAT PUNCHER	REC	06.04.07	100
MAT REPAIRER	RCE	06.04.29	142
MAT SEWER	REC	06.04.27	100
MAT TESTER	REI	06.03.01	43
MAT-MACHINE OPERATOR	RES	06.02.09	69
MAT-MAKING MACHINE TENDER	RCE	06.04.09	142
MATCH-UP WORKER	CRE	06.04.27	223
MATCHBOOK ASSEMBLER	RES	06.04.04	80

Title	Code	Group	Page
MILK-POWDER GRINDER	RES	06.04.15	86
MILK-RECEIVER, TANK TRUCK	REC	05.09.01	90
MILKER, MACHINE	RCE	03.04.01	142
MILKING-SYSTEM INSTALLER	RIE	05.05.09	9
MILL ATTENDANT	RIE	05.12.07	16
MILL ATTENDANT	RCE	06.04.11	142
MILL FEEDER	REC	06.04.15	110
MILL HAND, PLATE MILL	RES	06.04.10	80
MILL HELPER	RIE	06.04.24	19
MILL OPERATOR	REI	06.02.17	43
MILL OPERATOR	RCE	06.04.10	142
MILL OPERATOR	CER	06.04.15	236
MILL OPERATOR, ROLLS	REI	06.02.02	43
MILL PLATFORM SUPERVISOR	REI	06.02.15	36
MILL RECORDER, COMPUTERIZED MILL	CRE	05.03.03	217
MILL SUPERVISOR	ERC	06.02.01	185
MILL SUPERVISOR	EAS	06.04.01	187
MILL-AND-COAL-TRANSPORT OPERATOR	REC	06.04.08	100
MILL-LABOR SUPERVISOR	RES	06.04.01	56
MILL-OPERATOR HELPER	REC	06.04.19	110
MILL-ROLL REWINDER	RCE	06.04.02	142
MILLED-RUBBER TENDER	REI	06.04.13	49
MILLER	REI	06.02.11	43
MILLER	REI	06.04.08	49
MILLER	RES	06.04.17	80
MILLER	REC	06.04.11	100
MILLER	REC	06.04.15	110
MILLER HELPER, DISTILLERY	REI	06.04.15	49
MILLER SUPERVISOR	SER	06.02.01	171
MILLER, DISTILLERY	REI	06.02.15	43
MILLER, HEAD, ASSISTANT, WET PROCESS	REC	06.04.30	100
MILLER, HEAD, WET PROCESS	REI	05.05.01	43
MILLER, WET PROCESS	RSE	06.02.15	28
MILLER, WOOD FLOUR	REI	06.02.03	43
MILLINER	AES	01.06.02	167
MILLING SUPERVISOR	ESR	06.04.01	191
MILLING-MACHINE OPERATOR, NUMERICAL CONTROL	RES	06.01.03	69
MILLING-MACHINE OPERATOR, PRODUCTION	RCE	06.04.02	142
MILLING-MACHINE SET-UP OPERATOR 1	RIE	06.01.03	9
MILLING-MACHINE SET-UP OPERATOR 2	RIE	06.02.02	9
MILLWRIGHT	RES	05.05.06	56
MILLWRIGHT APPRENTICE	RES	05.05.06	56
MILLWRIGHT HELPER	REC	05.12.12	100
MILLWRIGHT SUPERVISOR	REC	05.05.06	87
MIME	AEI	01.03.02	166
MINCEMEAT MAKER	RCE	06.04.15	128
MINE INSPECTOR	EAC	11.10.03	187
MINE SUPERINTENDENT	ESR	05.02.05	188
MINE-CAR REPAIRER	RIE	05.05.06	9
MINER	RIE	05.11.01	9
MINER 1	RIE	05.11.02	9
MINER, PLACER	REC	05.12.02	90
MINERALOGIST	ISR	02.01.01	162

Title	Code	Group	Page
MODEL BUILDER	REI	05.05.06	43
MODEL MAKER	RIS	05.05.07	2
MODEL MAKER	RIS	01.06.02	2
MODEL MAKER	RIE	05.05.07	10
MODEL MAKER	RAE	01.06.02	20
MODEL MAKER	RSE	01.06.02	23
MODEL MAKER	REI	01.06.02	36
MODEL MAKER 1	ARI	01.06.02	164
MODEL MAKER, FIBERGLASS	RIS	01.06.02	2
MODEL MAKER, FIREARMS	RES	05.05.07	56
MODEL MAKER, FLUORESCENT LIGHTING	RIS	05.05.06	2
MODEL MAKER, SCALE	RIE	05.05.11	10
MODEL MAKER, WOOD	REI	05.05.08	36
MODEL-AND-MOLD MAKER	RIE	01.06.02	10
MODEL-AND-MOLD MAKER, PLASTER	REI	01.06.02	36
MODEL-MAKER APPRENTICE	REI	01.06.02	36
MODEL, ARTISTS'	AES	01.08.01	167
MODEL, PHOTOGRAPHERS'	AES	01.08.01	167
MODELER	ARI	01.06.02	164
MOHEL	SCE	10.01.01	179
MOISTURE TESTER	CRE	06.03.02	223
MOISTURE-CONDITIONER OPERATOR	RCE	06.04.14	142
MOISTURE-MACHINE TENDER	CRE	06.04.15	223
MOISTURE-METER OPERATOR	CRE	06.03.02	223
MOLASSES AND CARAMEL OPERATOR	REI	06.02.15	43
MOLASSES PREPARER	REI	06.04.15	43
MOLD CLEANER	RES	06.04.39	80
MOLD CLEANER	REC	06.04.39	110
MOLD CLOSER	RES	06.04.32	80
MOLD DRESSER	RCE	06.04.24	142
MOLD FILLER AND DRAINER	RCE	06.04.32	142
MOLD FILLER, PLASTIC DOLLS	RES	06.04.32	80
MOLD FINISHER	RES	06.02.24	69
MOLD LAMINATOR	REI	06.02.32	43
MOLD MAKER	RES	06.02.30	69
MOLD MAKER	RCS	06.04.32	122
MOLD MAKER	RCE	06.02.30	128
MOLD MAKER 1	RES	01.06.02	56
MOLD MAKER 2	RES	06.01.04	69
MOLD MAKER, DIE-CASTING AND PLASTIC MOLDING	RIE	05.05.07	10
MOLD MAKER, TERRA COTTA	RCE	06.04.32	142
MOLD OPERATOR	CRS	06.02.32	210
MOLD PARTER	RES	06.04.40	80
MOLD POLISHER	RCS	06.04.39	122
MOLD PREPARER	RCS	06.04.39	122
MOLD PRESSER	RES	06.04.28	80
MOLD SETTER	RIE	06.01.02	17
MOLD SETTER	REI	06.04.32	43
MOLD SHEET CLEANER	ERC	06.04.39	186
MOLD STAMPER	RES	06.02.31	69
MOLD STAMPER AND REPAIRER	RSE	05.10.01	28
MOLD STRIPPER	REC	06.04.24	110
MOLD WORKER	CRS	06.04.32	214

Title	Code	Group	Page
NEEDLEMAKER	RIE	06.01.03	10
NEGOTIATOR, LETTER OF CREDIT	ESI	11.06.03	197
NEMATOLOGIST	IRS	02.02.01	157
NEON-SIGN SERVICER	RSE	05.05.10	23
NEON-TUBE PUMPER	RSE	05.05.10	28
NET MAKER	CRE	06.04.27	223
NET REPAIRER	RES	05.10.01	69
NET WASHER	RCE	06.04.39	155
NETTING INSPECTOR	RCE	06.03.02	143
NEUROLOGIST	IRS	02.03.01	157
NEUTRALIZER	REI	06.04.15	43
NEUTRALIZER	REC	06.04.19	101
NEW-ACCOUNTS CLERK	CSE	07.04.01	231
NEW-CAR GET-READY MECHANIC	RIS	05.10.02	3
NEW-CAR INSPECTOR	RIE	06.03.01	17
NEWS ASSISTANT	SEC	07.05.03	176
NEWSCASTER	ESR	11.08.03	188
NEWSPAPER CARRIER	ESC	09.04.02	206
NEWSPAPER-DELIVERY DRIVER	RSE	05.08.03	28
NEWSWRITER	ESR	11.08.02	188
NIB FINISHER	CRS	06.04.24	214
NIB INSPECTOR	CSR	06.03.02	229
NIBBLER OPERATOR	RCS	06.04.02	122
NICKEL-PLANT OPERATOR	RES	06.02.10	69
NICKER	RCE	06.04.05	143
NICKING-MACHINE OPERATOR	RES	06.02.02	69
NIGHT AUDITOR	CRS	07.02.02	208
NIGHT-PATROL INSPECTOR	RCI	05.08.03	113
NITRATING-ACID MIXER	RCE	06.04.11	128
NITRATOR OPERATOR	RSE	06.02.11	28
NITROCELLULOSE OPERATOR	RES	06.04.34	69
NITROGLYCERIN DISTRIBUTOR	RES	06.04.40	80
NITROGLYCERIN NEUTRALIZER	RSC	06.04.11	32
NITROGLYCERIN SUPERVISOR	RES	06.01.01	56
NITROGLYCERIN-SEPARATOR OPERATOR	SCR	06.02.18	178
NODULIZER	CER	06.04.19	235
NOODLE MAKER	RES	06.04.15	80
NOODLE-CATALYST MAKER	REC	06.04.11	101
NOODLE-PRESS OPERATOR	REI	06.02.15	43
NOTCH GRINDER	RCE	06.04.08	143
NOVELTY MAKER 1	REI	06.02.15	43
NOVELTY MAKER 2	REI	06.02.15	43
NOVELTY WORKER	REC	06.04.28	101
NOZZLE TENDER	RCE	06.04.10	143
NOZZLE-AND-SLEEVE WORKER	RCE	06.04.24	143
NUCLEAR ENGINEER	IRE	05.01.03	159
NUCLEAR MEDICAL TECHNOLOGIST	RIS	10.02.02	1
NUMBERER AND WIRER	RCE	06.04.06	143
NUMERICAL-CONTROL-MACHINE OPERATOR	REI	06.02.02	43
NURSE AIDE	SER	10.03.02	173
NURSE ANESTHETIST	ISE	10.02.01	163
NURSE PRACTITIONER	IRS	10.02.01	158
NURSE-MIDWIFE	SIR	10.02.01	169
NURSE, CONSULTANT	SEC	10.02.01	175

Title	Code	Group	Page
OFFSET-PRESS OPERATOR 1	RIE	05.05.13	10
OFFSET-PRESS OPERATOR 2	REC	06.04.09	101
OFFSET-PRESS-OPERATOR APPRENTICE	RIE	05.05.13	10
OIL BOILER	RIE	06.02.18	17
OIL DIPPER	REC	06.04.25	101
OIL PUMPER	RES	05.06.03	69
OIL-BURNER-SERVICER-AND-INSTALLER	RES	05.05.03	69
OIL-BURNER-SERVICER-AND-INSTALLER HELPER	RSE	05.12.12	31
OIL-FIELD EQUIPMENT MECHANIC	RIE	05.05.09	10
OIL-FIELD EQUIPMENT MECHANIC SUPERVISOR	RES	05.05.09	56
OIL-PIPE INSPECTOR	REC	05.07.01	87
OIL-PIPE-INSPECTOR HELPER	RSC	05.07.01	32
OIL-RECOVERY-UNIT OPERATOR	RIE	06.02.12	17
OIL-SEAL ASSEMBLER	CRS	06.04.23	214
OIL-SPOT WASHER	RCS	06.04.39	122
OIL-WELL-SERVICE OPERATOR	RIS	05.11.03	2
OIL-WELL-SERVICE-OPERATOR HELPER	RCS	05.12.07	117
OIL-WELL-SERVICES SUPERVISOR	RSE	05.11.03	23
OILER	RCS	05.12.08	122
OILER	RCE	06.04.33	143
OILING-MACHINE OPERATOR	REI	06.04.14	49
OILSEED-MEAT PRESSER	RES	06.04.19	86
OLIVE BRINE TESTER	CRS	06.03.02	214
OLIVING-MACHINE OPERATOR	RCE	06.01.04	128
OPAQUER	RES	06.02.32	69
OPEN-DEVELOPER OPERATOR	RCE	06.04.16	128
OPENER	REC	06.04.07	110
OPENER TENDER	RES	06.04.06	80
OPENER 1	RCE	06.04.27	143
OPENER 2	REC	06.04.16	110
OPENER-VERIFIER-PACKER, CUSTOMS	RIE	05.09.03	17
OPERATING ENGINEER	RIS	05.11.01	2
OPERATING-ENGINEER APPRENTICE	RIS	05.11.01	2
OPERATING-TABLE ASSEMBLER	RIE	06.01.04	10
OPERATIONS AND INTELLIGENCE ASSISTANT	ESC	04.02.02	205
OPERATIONS MANAGER	ESI	11.11.03	197
OPERATIONS MANAGER	ESA	11.05.02	198
OPERATIONS OFFICER	ESC	11.06.01	203
OPERATIONS-RESEARCH ANALYST	IRE	11.01.01	159
OPERATOR, AUTOMATED PROCESS	REI	06.02.18	43
OPERATOR, CATALYST CONCENTRATION	RIE	06.02.13	17
OPERATOR, CAVITY PUMP	RCS	06.02.18	117
OPERATOR, PREFINISH	RSC	06.02.21	32
OPHTHALMOLOGIST	ISR	02.03.01	162
OPTICAL ENGINEER	RIC	05.01.07	19
OPTICAL-ELEMENT COATER	RES	06.02.21	69
OPTICAL-GLASS ETCHER	RCE	06.02.30	128
OPTICAL-GLASS SILVERER	RES	06.04.33	69
OPTICAL-INSTRUMENT ASSEMBLER	RIE	06.01.04	10
OPTICIAN	REI	05.05.11	36
OPTICIAN	RES	05.05.11	56
OPTICIAN APPRENTICE	REI	05.05.11	36
OPTICIAN APPRENTICE, DISPENSING	RCE	05.05.11	124
OPTICIAN, DISPENSING 1	RCE	05.05.11	124

Title	Code	Group	Page
OUTPATIENT-ADMITTING CLERK	CSE	07.04.01	233
OUTSIDE CUTTER, HAND	CRS	06.02.24	210
OUTSIDE PRODUCTION INSPECTOR	RIE	05.07.01	10
OUTSIDE PROPERTY AGENT	ESA	08.01.03	200
OUTSIDE-PLANT ENGINEER	IRE	05.01.03	160
OUTSOLE CUTTER, AUTOMATIC	RCS	06.02.09	117
OUTSOLE FLEXER	RCE	06.04.05	155
OUTSOLE SCHEDULER	CRS	05.09.03	214
OVEN DAUBER	RCS	06.04.30	122
OVEN OPERATOR	RES	06.04.15	80
OVEN OPERATOR	REC	06.04.14	101
OVEN OPERATOR, AUTOMATIC	RES	06.02.15	70
OVEN TENDER	RES	06.04.15	70
OVEN TENDER	RES	06.04.21	70
OVEN TENDER	RCE	06.04.14	143
OVEN TENDER	RCE	06.04.19	143
OVEN TENDER	RCE	06.04.13	143
OVEN-EQUIPMENT REPAIRER	RES	05.10.01	70
OVEN-HEATER HELPER	RCE	06.04.12	143
OVERCOILER	CRS	06.04.23	214
OVEREDGE SEWER	CRS	06.02.05	210
OVERHAULER	RIE	05.05.09	10
OVERHAULER HELPER	RCS	05.12.15	117
OVERHEAD CLEANER MAINTAINER	CER	05.10.01	235
OVERLAY PLASTICIAN	RES	06.02.24	81
OVERLOCK SEWING MACHINE OPERATOR	CRE	06.02.05	223
OVERLOCK-MACHINE OPERATOR, COMPLETE GARMENT	REC	06.02.05	90
OXIDIZED-FINISH PLATER	RCS	06.04.10	122
OXIDIZER	RCE	06.04.24	143
OXYGEN-FURNACE OPERATOR	RIE	06.02.10	17
OXYGEN-PLANT OPERATOR	REI	06.02.11	43
OYSTER FLOATER	REC	03.04.03	110
PACK-ROOM OPERATOR	RIE	06.04.30	17
PACKAGE CRIMPER	RCS	06.04.16	124
PACKAGE DESIGNER	AEI	01.02.03	166
PACKAGE SEALER, MACHINE	RCE	06.04.38	143
PACKAGE-DYEING-MACHINE OPERATOR	REI	06.02.16	43
PACKAGER, HAND	RES	06.04.38	81
PACKAGER, HEAD	RCE	06.04.03	143
PACKAGER, MACHINE	REC	06.04.38	101
PACKAGING ENGINEER	SCI	05.03.09	178
PACKAGING SUPERVISOR	REI	06.04.01	36
PACKAGING TECHNICIAN	RES	06.01.04	56
PACKER	RCS	06.04.38	122
PACKER	RCS	06.04.38	122
PACKER OPERATOR, AUTOMATIC	CRE	06.04.15	223
PACKER-FUSER	REC	06.04.38	110
PACKER, AGRICULTURAL PRODUCE	RES	03.04.01	81
PACKER, DENTURE	RES	05.05.11	70
PACKER, INSULATION	RES	06.04.09	81
PACKING-FLOOR WORKER	RES	06.04.40	81
PACKING-HOUSE SUPERVISOR	ESR	06.02.01	191
PACKING-LINE WORKER	RCE	06.04.38	143

Title	Code	Group	Page
ROLL-UP-GUIDER OPERATOR	RCS	06.04.09	123
ROLLER	RES	06.04.27	82
ROLLER	RCE	06.02.02	129
ROLLER CHECKER	CRE	06.03.02	225
ROLLER CLEANER	REC	06.04.39	111
ROLLER COVERER	RCE	06.02.09	129
ROLLER ENGRAVER, HAND	RES	01.06.01	71
ROLLER MAKER	RSI	06.02.32	21
ROLLER OPERATOR	REC	06.04.05	102
ROLLER OPERATOR	RCE	06.04.21	145
ROLLER REPAIRER	RIE	01.06.01	11
ROLLER VARNISHER	RES	06.02.21	71
ROLLER 1	REI	06.04.28	44
ROLLER-BEARING INSPECTOR	CRE	06.03.02	225
ROLLER-LEVELER OPERATOR	REC	06.04.02	102
ROLLER-MACHINE OPERATOR	RIE	06.02.02	18
ROLLER-MACHINE OPERATOR	REI	06.04.16	50
ROLLER-MILL OPERATOR	RCS	06.02.11	118
ROLLER-PRINT TENDER	RIE	05.10.05	18
ROLLER-SKATE ASSEMBLER	RCE	06.04.23	145
ROLLER-SKATE REPAIRER	CRS	05.12.15	214
ROLLER-STITCHER	CRS	06.04.29	214
ROLLER, GOLD LEAF	RCE	06.04.34	145
ROLLER, HAND	RCE	06.04.28	145
ROLLER, PRIMARY MILL	RIE	06.02.10	11
ROLLING ATTENDANT	RCE	06.01.03	125
ROLLING-DOWN-MACHINE OPERATOR	REC	06.04.05	102
ROLLING-MACHINE OPERATOR	RES	06.04.15	82
ROLLING-MACHINE OPERATOR	REC	06.04.16	102
ROLLING-MACHINE OPERATOR	REC	06.04.04	102
ROLLING-MACHINE TENDER	RCE	06.04.05	155
ROLLING-MILL OPERATOR	RSE	06.01.03	29
ROLLING-MILL-OPERATOR HELPER	REC	06.04.10	102
ROOF ASSEMBLER 1	RSC	06.04.22	32
ROOF BOLTER	RCE	05.11.02	129
ROOF FITTER	REI	06.02.22	44
ROOF-CEMENT-AND-PAINT MAKER	RIE	06.02.18	18
ROOF-CEMENT-AND-PAINT-MAKER HELPER	RES	06.04.11	86
ROOF-TRUSS-MACHINE TENDER	REC	06.04.20	102
ROOFER	REC	05.10.01	91
ROOFER APPLICATOR	CRS	05.12.14	210
ROOFER APPRENTICE	REC	05.10.01	91
ROOFING SUPERVISOR	RES	05.10.01	57
ROOFING-MACHINE OPERATOR	REI	06.02.18	44
ROOM-SERVICE CLERK	ECS	09.05.03	207
ROOTER OPERATOR	CRE	06.04.09	225
ROPE CLEANER	RCE	06.04.27	155
ROPE MAKER, MACHINE	REC	06.04.06	102
ROPE-LAYING-MACHINE OPERATOR	RCE	06.04.06	145
ROPE-MACHINE SETTER	RES	06.01.02	71
ROPE-MAKER, ROPEWALK	REI	06.02.09	44
ROPE-SILICA-MACHINE OPERATOR	RCS	06.04.16	123
ROSIN-BARREL FILLER	RCE	06.04.36	155
ROTARY CUTTER	RCE	06.04.05	145

Title	Code	Group	Page
ROTARY DERRICK OPERATOR	REC	05.11.03	91
ROTARY DRILLER	REI	05.11.03	45
ROTARY-CUTTER FEEDER	RCE	06.04.04	145
ROTARY-CUTTER OPERATOR	REI	06.04.05	51
ROTARY-DRIER FEEDER	RCE	06.04.11	145
ROTARY-DRILLER HELPER	RCE	05.12.02	145
ROTARY-FURNACE TENDER	REC	06.04.11	102
ROTARY-HEAD-MILLING-MACHINE SET-UP OPERATOR	RIE	06.02.02	12
ROTARY-KILN OPERATOR	REI	06.02.17	45
ROTARY-KILN OPERATOR	RCS	06.04.10	118
ROTARY-RIG ENGINE OPERATOR	RES	05.06.02	57
ROTARY-SCREEN-PRINTING-MACHINE OPERATOR	RIE	06.02.06	18
ROTARY-SHEAR OPERATOR	RIS	06.02.02	3
ROTOGRAVURE-PRESS OPERATOR	REI	05.05.13	45
ROTOR ASSEMBLER	CRS	06.04.23	214
ROTOR CASTING-MACHINE OPERATOR	RSE	06.02.10	29
ROUGE MIXER	REC	06.04.19	111
ROUGE SIFTER AND MILLER	RCE	06.04.09	155
ROUGH OPENER, JEWEL HOLE	RCS	06.02.30	123
ROUGH-AND-TRUEING-MACHINE OPERATOR	RCE	06.04.09	145
ROUGH-RICE GRADER	CER	06.03.01	235
ROUGH-RICE TENDER	REC	06.04.15	102
ROUGH-ROUNDER, MACHINE	RCE	06.04.05	145
ROUGHER	RES	06.02.02	71
ROUGHER OPERATOR	RCS	06.02.02	118
ROUND-CORNER-CUTTER OPERATOR	RCS	06.04.04	123
ROUND-UP-RING HAND	RES	06.04.22	82
ROUNDER	RCE	06.04.05	145
ROUNDER, HAND	CRS	06.04.27	214
ROUNDING-AND-BACKING-MACHINE OPERATOR	CRE	06.02.09	217
ROUNDING-MACHINE OPERATOR	CRE	06.04.05	225
ROUNDING-MACHINE TENDER	RES	06.04.03	82
ROUSTABOUT	RCS	05.10.01	118
ROUTE AIDE	RCE	07.07.02	145
ROUTE SUPERVISOR	SER	07.05.04	172
ROUTE-DELIVERY CLERK	CSR	07.05.04	230
ROUTER	REC	06.02.02	91
ROUTER	CRE	07.07.02	225
ROUTER OPERATOR	RIE	06.02.02	18
ROUTER OPERATOR	RIE	06.02.03	18
ROUTER OPERATOR	RIE	06.02.08	18
ROUTER OPERATOR, PORTABLE	RSC	06.02.24	32
ROUTER OPERATOR, RADIAL	RES	06.02.02	71
ROUTER SET-UP OPERATOR, NUMERICAL CONTROL	RIE	06.01.03	12
ROUTING CLERK	RCE	07.07.02	146
ROUTING CLERK	ESC	07.05.04	204
ROUTING CLERK	CES	07.05.04	238
ROUTING-EQUIPMENT TENDER	RCE	06.04.40	146
ROVING INSPECTOR	RES	06.03.01	71
ROVING SIZER	RSE	06.03.01	29
ROVING WINDER, FIBERGLASS	RCS	06.04.06	123
ROVING-WEIGHT GAGER	REC	06.03.02	102

Title	Code	Group	Page
SUPERVISOR	RES	06.01.01	57
SUPERVISOR	RES	06.02.01	58
SUPERVISOR	RES	06.02.01	58
SUPERVISOR	RES	06.01.01	58
SUPERVISOR	RES	06.02.01	58
SUPERVISOR	RES	06.01.01	58
SUPERVISOR	RES	06.02.01	58
SUPERVISOR	RES	06.02.01	58
SUPERVISOR	RES	06.01.04	58
SUPERVISOR	RES	06.02.01	58
SUPERVISOR	RES	01.06.02	58
SUPERVISOR	RES	06.02.01	58
SUPERVISOR	RES	06.02.01	58
SUPERVISOR	RES	06.02.01	58
SUPERVISOR	RES	06.02.01	58
SUPERVISOR	RES	06.02.01	58
SUPERVISOR	RES	06.02.01	58
SUPERVISOR	RES	06.01.01	58
SUPERVISOR	RES	06.02.01	72
SUPERVISOR	RCS	06.02.01	113
SUPERVISOR	SRE	06.01.01	168
SUPERVISOR	SER	11.05.03	172
SUPERVISOR	SEA	06.04.01	174
SUPERVISOR	ERS	06.04.01	182
SUPERVISOR	ERS	06.02.01	182
SUPERVISOR	ERS	06.02.01	182
SUPERVISOR	ERS	06.02.01	182
SUPERVISOR	ERS	06.02.01	182
SUPERVISOR	ERS	06.02.01	185
SUPERVISOR	EAS	06.04.01	187
SUPERVISOR	ESR	06.02.01	193
SUPERVISOR	ESR	06.02.01	193
SUPERVISOR	ESR	06.02.01	193
SUPERVISOR	ESR	06.02.01	193
SUPERVISOR	ESA	06.02.01	202
SUPERVISOR	ESC	06.01.01	204
SUPERVISOR	CER	06.01.01	235
SUPERVISOR OF COMMUNICATIONS	ESC	05.02.04	204
SUPERVISOR OF SALES	ESR	11.09.01	193
SUPERVISOR OF WAY	ESC	05.02.02	203
SUPERVISOR 1	RES	06.02.01	72
SUPERVISOR 1	SEC	06.02.01	177
SUPERVISOR 1	ERS	06.02.01	182
SUPERVISOR 2	RES	06.01.01	58
SUPERVISOR 2	ERS	06.02.01	182
SUPERVISOR 2	ESR	06.02.01	193
SUPERVISOR, ABATTOIR	RES	06.02.01	58
SUPERVISOR, ACCOUNTING CLERKS	CSE	07.02.02	232
SUPERVISOR, ACCOUNTS RECEIVABLE	SEC	07.02.02	177
SUPERVISOR, ACOUSTICAL TILE CARPENTERS	ERS	05.10.01	184
SUPERVISOR, ADJUSTABLE-STEEL-JOIST-SETTING	CES	05.05.06	237
SUPERVISOR, ADVERTISING-DISPATCH CLERKS	ESR	07.05.01	195

Title	Code	Group	Page
SUPERVISOR, MOLD YARD	RES	06.04.01	58
SUPERVISOR, MOLD-MAKING PLASTICS SHEETS	ERS	06.04.01	185
SUPERVISOR, MONEY-ROOM	CSE	07.02.02	232
SUPERVISOR, MOTION-PICTURE EQUIPMENT	ESR	05.05.11	194
SUPERVISOR, MOTORCYCLE REPAIR SHOP	ERS	05.05.09	183
SUPERVISOR, NATURAL-GAS PLANT	RES	05.06.04	59
SUPERVISOR, NATURAL-GAS-FIELD PROCESSING	RSE	06.01.01	24
SUPERVISOR, NET MAKING	REI	06.02.01	37
SUPERVISOR, NUT PROCESSING	RES	06.02.01	58
SUPERVISOR, NUTRITIONAL YEAST	RES	06.02.01	59
SUPERVISOR, OFFSET-PLATE PREPARATION	ESR	01.06.01	194
SUPERVISOR, OPEN-HEARTH STOCKYARD	RES	05.12.03	61
SUPERVISOR, OPTICAL INSTRUMENT ASSEMBLY	SEC	06.02.01	177
SUPERVISOR, ORDER TAKERS	ESC	07.04.02	205
SUPERVISOR, ORDNANCE TRUCK INSTALLATION	SER	05.10.01	172
SUPERVISOR, ORNAMENTAL IRONWORKING	RSE	05.05.06	24
SUPERVISOR, OVENS	ERA	06.04.01	180
SUPERVISOR, PACKING	RES	06.02.01	61
SUPERVISOR, PACKING	RES	06.04.01	61
SUPERVISOR, PACKING ROOM	ESA	06.02.01	202
SUPERVISOR, PAINT	ESR	06.01.01	194
SUPERVISOR, PAINT DEPARTMENT	ESA	06.02.01	202
SUPERVISOR, PAINT ROLLER COVERS	RES	06.02.01	60
SUPERVISOR, PAINTING	ERS	05.10.07	183
SUPERVISOR, PAINTING DEPARTMENT	ERS	06.02.01	183
SUPERVISOR, PAINTING, SHIPYARD	ESA	05.10.07	202
SUPERVISOR, PAPER COATING	SRE	06.02.01	168
SUPERVISOR, PAPER MACHINE	RES	06.02.01	59
SUPERVISOR, PAPER PRODUCTS	REI	06.02.01	37
SUPERVISOR, PAPER TESTING	SEC	06.02.01	177
SUPERVISOR, PARACHUTE MANUFACTURING	RIE	06.02.01	12
SUPERVISOR, PARK WORKERS	RES	03.02.03	58
SUPERVISOR, PARKING LOT	SER	09.04.02	173
SUPERVISOR, PARTICLE BOARD	ERI	06.02.01	180
SUPERVISOR, PASTE MIXING	RES	06.04.01	59
SUPERVISOR, PASTE PLANT	RSE	06.02.01	24
SUPERVISOR, PATTERN MARKING	RSE	05.03.02	24
SUPERVISOR, PERSONNEL CLERKS	CSE	07.05.03	232
SUPERVISOR, PHOSPHATIC FERTILIZER	ESR	06.01.01	195
SUPERVISOR, PHOSPHORIC ACID	SRC	06.04.11	169
SUPERVISOR, PHOSPHORUS PROCESSING	ERS	06.02.01	183
SUPERVISOR, PHOTOENGRAVING	RSC	01.06.01	31
SUPERVISOR, PICKING	ESR	06.04.39	194
SUPERVISOR, PICKING CREW	RES	03.04.01	58
SUPERVISOR, PIG-MACHINE	RES	06.02.01	58
SUPERVISOR, PIGMENT MAKING	ERS	06.02.01	183
SUPERVISOR, PILE DRIVING	RES	05.11.01	61
SUPERVISOR, PIPE FINISHING	RSE	06.01.01	24
SUPERVISOR, PIPE JOINTS	RES	06.02.02	61
SUPERVISOR, PIPE MANUFACTURE	RES	06.04.01	60
SUPERVISOR, PIPE-LINE MAINTENANCE	RSE	05.12.12	24
SUPERVISOR, PIPE-LINES	RCS	05.11.01	113
SUPERVISOR, PIT-AND-AUXILIARIES	RES	06.04.10	72
SUPERVISOR, PLASTERING	ERS	05.05.04	184

Title	Code	Group	Page
TEACHER, MUSIC	AES	01.04.01	167
TEACHER, PRESCHOOL	SEC	10.02.03	177
TEACHER, SECONDARY SCHOOL	SEC	11.02.01	176
TEAMSTER	RCS	03.04.05	123
TECHNICAL COORDINATOR	ESR	07.05.03	195
TECHNICAL DIRECTOR, CHEMICAL PLANT	IER	05.01.08	163
TECHNICAL ILLUSTRATOR	IRE	05.03.02	161
TECHNICAL OPERATOR	RIE	05.03.04	12
TECHNICAL TESTING ENGINEER	RIE	05.10.03	13
TECHNICIAN, PLANT AND MAINTENANCE	RIE	05.05.05	13
TECHNICIAN, SUBMARINE CABLE EQUIPMENT	REI	05.05.05	37
TELECINE OPERATOR	RCE	05.10.05	125
TELEGRAPH-PLANT MAINTAINER	RSE	05.05.05	25
TELEGRAPH-SERVICE RATER	CSE	07.07.03	235
TELEGRAPHER	CER	07.04.05	235
TELEGRAPHER AGENT	CSE	07.04.05	234
TELEGRAPHIC-TYPEWRITER OPERATOR	CSE	07.06.02	234
TELEPHONE CLERK, TELEGRAPH OFFICE	CSE	07.04.05	234
TELEPHONE OPERATOR	CSE	07.04.06	234
TELEPHONE OPERATOR, CHIEF	SEC	07.04.06	177
TELEPHONE SOLICITOR	ESC	08.02.08	206
TELEPHONE-ANSWERING-SERVICE OPERATOR	CSE	07.04.06	234
TELEPHONE-DIRECTORY DELIVERER	RSC	07.07.02	33
TELEPHONE-DIRECTORY-DISTRIBUTOR DRIVER	RCE	05.08.03	149
TELEPHONE-QUOTATION CLERK	CES	07.04.04	238
TELEVISION INSTALLER	RCS	05.10.03	119
TELEVISION-AND-RADIO REPAIRER	REI	05.10.03	37
TELEVISION-CABLE INSTALLER	RIE	05.10.03	13
TELEVISION-SCHEDULE COORDINATOR	CSE	07.05.01	232
TELLER	CSE	07.03.01	232
TELLER	CSE	07.03.01	234
TELLER, COLLECTION AND EXCHANGE	CES	07.02.02	237
TELLER, HEAD	SER	07.03.01	172
TELLER, NOTE	CES	07.03.01	237
TEMPERATURE INSPECTOR	CRS	06.03.02	215
TEMPERATURE REGULATOR, PYROMETER	RES	06.03.02	83
TEMPERATURE-CONTROL INSPECTOR	CES	06.03.01	238
TEMPERER	RIS	06.02.10	3
TEMPLATE CUTTER	CRE	06.04.24	226
TEMPLATE MAKER	RIE	05.05.07	13
TEMPLATE MAKER, EXTRUSION DIE	RIE	05.05.07	13
TEMPLATE MAKER, TRACK	RSC	05.10.01	33
TEMPLATE REPRODUCTION TECHNICIAN	RIE	06.02.31	13
TENNIS-BALL COVERER, HAND	RCE	06.04.27	149
TENNIS-BALL-COVER CEMENTER	REC	06.04.34	112
TENONER OPERATOR	RIS	05.05.08	3
TENONER OPERATOR	RCE	06.02.09	130
TENSIONING-MACHINE OPERATOR	RCE	06.04.02	149
TENTER-FRAME OPERATOR	RCE	06.04.16	149
TERMINAL OPERATOR	CSE	07.06.01	232
TERMINAL SUPERINTENDENT	ESC	11.11.03	205
TERMINAL-MAKEUP OPERATOR	CRS	07.06.01	211
TERMINAL-SYSTEM OPERATOR	CER	07.06.01	235
TERRAZZO WORKER	REI	05.05.01	37

Title	Code	Group	Page
TRIPE COOKER	REC	06.04.15	105
TRIPLE-AIR-VALVE TESTER	RSE	05.07.02	29
TROLLEY CLEANER	REC	06.04.39	112
TROLLEY OPERATOR	RCE	06.04.40	156
TROMBONE-SLIDE ASSEMBLER	RCS	06.01.04	119
TROMMEL TENDER	REC	06.04.10	105
TROPHY ASSEMBLER	RCS	06.02.24	119
TROUBLE LOCATOR, TEST DESK	RCS	05.06.01	114
TROUBLE SHOOTER 1	RES	05.10.03	73
TROUBLE SHOOTER 2	RSE	05.05.05	25
TRUCK DRIVER, HEAVY	RSE	05.08.01	29
TRUCK DRIVER, LIGHT	RIE	05.08.01	19
TRUCK SUPERVISOR	ERS	05.12.04	184
TRUCK-BODY BUILDER	RIE	05.05.06	13
TRUCK-BODY-BUILDER APPRENTICE	RIE	05.05.06	13
TRUCK-CRANE OPERATOR	REC	05.11.04	91
TRUCK-DRIVER HELPER	RES	05.12.03	84
TRUCKLOAD CHECKER	REC	05.09.03	92
TRUER	RCE	06.03.02	150
TRUER, PINION AND WHEEL	REC	06.01.04	105
TRUSS ASSEMBLER	RSC	05.10.01	33
TRUST OFFICER	ESR	11.06.05	189
TRUST-MAIL CLERK	CSE	07.05.04	234
TRUST-SAVINGS-ACCOUNT CLERK	CSR	07.02.02	230
TRUST-SECURITIES CLERK	CRS	07.02.02	211
TRUST-VAULT CLERK	CSE	07.02.02	232
TUBBER	REC	06.04.02	105
TUBE ASSEMBLER, CATHODE RAY	REC	06.02.23	105
TUBE ASSEMBLER, ELECTRON	CRE	06.01.04	226
TUBE BALANCER	RCS	06.04.29	123
TUBE BENDER, BRASS-WIND INSTRUMENTS	RES	06.02.02	73
TUBE BENDER, HAND 1	RES	06.02.24	73
TUBE BENDER, HAND 2	RCE	06.04.24	150
TUBE BUILDER, AIRPLANE	CRS	06.02.29	215
TUBE CLEANER	REC	05.12.18	105
TUBE CLEANER	RCE	06.04.27	156
TUBE COATER	REC	06.04.21	105
TUBE COVERER	REC	06.04.27	112
TUBE DRAWER	REI	06.04.02	51
TUBE HANDLER	REC	06.04.27	112
TUBE MOLDER, FIBERGLASS	RCE	06.04.09	150
TUBE OPERATOR	CER	07.07.02	236
TUBE REBUILDER	RIS	05.05.10	3
TUBE REPAIRER	RCS	06.04.29	123
TUBE SIZER-AND-CUTTER OPERATOR	CRE	06.04.04	226
TUBE SORTER	REC	06.03.02	105
TUBE SPLICER	RCE	06.04.07	150
TUBE WINDER, HAND	RCE	06.04.09	150
TUBE-AND-MANIFOLD BUILDER	RCE	06.02.29	150
TUBE-BUILDING-MACHINE OPERATOR	REC	06.04.05	105
TUBE-CLEANING OPERATOR	RCE	06.04.02	150
TUBE-MACHINE OPERATOR	RSE	06.02.04	29
TUBE-MACHINE-OPERATOR HELPER	REC	06.04.04	105
TUBER-MACHINE CUTTER	CRE	06.04.07	226

Title	Code	Group	Page
WARP SPOOLER	RCE	06.04.06	151
WARP-DYEING-VAT TENDER	REC	06.04.16	106
WARP-KNITTING-MACHINE OPERATOR	RCS	06.02.06	119
WARP-TENSION TESTER	REC	06.03.02	106
WARP-TYING-MACHINE TENDER	RCE	06.04.06	130
WARP-YARN SORTER	CRS	06.03.02	215
WARPER	RCS	06.04.06	124
WASH HELPER	REI	06.04.19	46
WASH OPERATOR	RCE	06.02.18	130
WASH-HOUSE WORKER	REI	06.04.39	51
WASH-MILL OPERATOR	REC	06.04.19	106
WASH-OIL-PUMP OPERATOR	RCE	06.02.17	130
WASH-OIL-PUMP OPERATOR HELPER	RCE	06.04.12	151
WASH-TANK TENDER	RCE	06.04.11	151
WASHER	RES	06.04.39	87
WASHER	REC	06.04.39	106
WASHER	REC	06.04.16	106
WASHER	REC	06.04.39	106
WASHER	REC	06.04.39	106
WASHER	CRE	06.04.39	227
WASHER ENGINEER	CRS	06.04.14	215
WASHER-AND-CRUSHER TENDER	RES	05.12.07	84
WASHER-ENGINEER HELPER	RCS	06.04.14	124
WASHER, AGRICULTURAL PRODUCE	REC	06.04.39	112
WASHER, CARCASS	REC	06.04.39	112
WASHER, HAND	REC	06.04.35	106
WASHER, MACHINE	REI	06.04.35	46
WASHER, MACHINE	REC	06.04.39	106
WASHING-AND-SCREENING PLANT SUPERVISOR	REI	06.02.01	38
WASHING-MACHINE LOADER-AND-PULLER	REI	06.04.35	51
WASHING-MACHINE OPERATOR	REI	06.04.39	51
WASHROOM CLEANER	REC	06.04.39	112
WASHROOM OPERATOR	REC	06.04.15	106
WASTE CHOPPER	REC	06.04.16	106
WASTE SALVAGER	CRS	06.02.27	211
WASTE-DISPOSAL ATTENDANT	RSE	05.12.03	29
WASTE-MACHINE OFFBEARER	RCS	06.04.16	124
WASTE-MACHINE TENDER	RCE	06.04.06	157
WASTE-PAPER-HAMMERMILL OPERATOR	RCE	06.04.14	157
WASTE-TREATMENT OPERATOR	RCS	06.02.11	114
WASTEWATER-TREATMENT-PLANT ATTENDANT	RIE	05.12.07	19
WASTEWATER-TREATMENT-PLANT OPERATOR	REI	05.06.04	38
WATCH ASSEMBLER	RIE	06.01.04	13
WATCH MANUFACTURING SUPERVISOR	RCS	06.01.01	114
WATCH REPAIRER	REI	05.05.11	38
WATCH REPAIRER APPRENTICE	REI	05.05.11	38
WATCH-AND-CLOCK-REPAIR CLERK	ERS	05.09.02	185
WATCH-BAND ASSEMBLER	CRE	06.04.23	227
WATCH-CRYSTAL EDGE GRINDER	RCE	06.04.30	151
WATCH-CRYSTAL MOLDER	RCE	06.02.32	131
WATCHER, AUTOMAT	CRE	06.04.05	227
WATCHER, PANTOGRAPH	RCE	06.04.05	151
WATER CONTROL SUPERVISOR	ESA	05.02.01	199
WATER REGULATOR AND VALVE REPAIRER	REI	05.10.02	46

Title	Code	Group	Page

Part IV. Theoretical and Technical Origins

The *Dictionary of Holland Occupational Codes* was developed to make some important but unwieldy sources of occupational information more accessible to clients, counselors, and researchers. Specifically, the voluminous information disseminated by the U.S. Department of Labor through its *Dictionary of Occupational Titles* (DOT; 1977) and supplements will be of more value if the information is linked directly to a theory of careers that serves as an underpinning of vocational assistance in schools, colleges, and industry. The largest single group of purchasers of the DOT is vocational and career counselors (Miller, Treiman, Cain & Roos, 1980), most of whom use interest inventories or other forms of vocational assistance based on the Holland (1973a) occupational classification and theory of careers.

To make this extensive information more accessible and easy to interpret, an empirically based translation of the DOT classification into the Holland classification was required. The following pages provide some background on Holland's theory and classification, describe the technical procedures used to produce the translation, and assess the quality of the product. Also described are some spin-offs from the research: more evidence of the construct validity of the occupational classification; more evidence on the distinctions among occupational groups; and more evidence about the distributions of one-, two-, and three-letter occupational codes. Finally, some suggestions for future research and experimental uses of the classification are made.

THEORY AND CLASSIFICATION

The present *Dictionary*, like the SDS and its associated tools, is the product of a theory of personality types and environmental models (Holland, 1973a). Its usefulness therefore depends on the usefulness of the underlying theory. Holland's theory is probably now the most widely used organizing principle for vocational interest assessments in the world. Holland's (1979) manual noted that there were more than 300 articles, books, chapters, and reviews examining the theory in experimental tests of its predictions, its value in organizing personal and occupational information, and its practical use. Although the research is impossible to summarize here, we evaluate the theory as follows.

The virtues of the theory are easily summarized: (1) The typology is easily grasped. (2) It has many characteristics of a useful theory—clear definitions, internally consistent structure, broad scope, and formalizations for dealing with personal development and change. (3) It has a broad base of research support based on studies of children, adolescents, college students, and adults, both men and women, up to 70 years old. (4) The theory is easily applied to practical problems: the development of vocational-assessment devices, the classification and interpretation of personal and environmental data, and the conduct of vocational counseling.

Further suggested studies of the Holland typology include: (1) The hypotheses about vocational environments are only partially tested and require more exploration. (2) The hypotheses about person–environment interactions (congruence) have received some support (Helms & Williams, 1973; Wiggins, 1976; Wiener & Vaitenas, 1977; Mount & Muchinsky, 1978), but they require more testing through experimental research. (3) The formulations about personal development and change (Holland, 1973a; Holland & G. D. Gottfredson, 1976) have received some support (Edwards, Nafziger, & Holland, 1974; Grandy & Stahmann, 1974a, 1974b; Holland, 1973a, pp. 53–54; Kelso, 1976), and they accord with the persuasive social learning perspective spelled out by Krumboltz (1978), but they also need more comprehensive examination. (4) The classification of occupations and of persons may differ depending on the devices or samples used to assess the types. (5) The evidence about some propositions involving consistency and satisfaction is weak, although it is generally positive (Nafziger, Holland, & G. D. Gottfredson, 1975; G. D. Gottfredson, 1977; Rounds, Shubsachs, Dawis, & Lofquist, 1978). (6) Important personal and environmental contingencies lie outside the scope of the typology. For example, the distribution of influence or status within a social environment, social class, special advantage or disadvantage, intelligence, special aptitudes, and demographic and economic conditions are all important influences on careers that are incorporated in the theory only indirectly. Such conditions must be taken into account in counseling and in research applications.

One of the investigations suggested above is addressed by the research to develop the present *Dictionary*. Alternative identifications (Sokal, 1974) of the occupational classification sometimes differ depending on the method used to derive them (for example, inventories such as the SDS, VPI, or SCII, or the job analysis data from the *Position Analysis Questionnaire* [PAQ; McCormick, 1979] or other sources) and on the samples of persons or jobs. The present translation uses a single source of job analysis data to assign Holland codes for all occupations by a common method. The results of interest inventory information about an occupation's incumbents are used only indirectly in the resulting classification. Accordingly, this *Dictionary* has fewer scientific flaws than the earlier classifications that relied on information from divergent sources.

DEVELOPMENT

This section summarizes how the classification was developed, what data were employed, and how the results support the validity of the classification.

Data

Occupational Analysis. The occupational data developed by the U.S. Department of Labor (1972, 1974, 1977) to produce the fourth edition of the DOT was the main source of occupational information used. In producing the DOT, the Department of Labor aimed to analyze all occupations in the U.S. economy. The economy was categorized by industries, and industries were assigned to occupational analysis field centers around the country. These field centers approached business establishments and other organizations with requests that they be allowed to inventory and analyze the jobs in those firms. If granted permission, the centers proceeded with their job analyses. Miller et al. (1980) have described the methods used to select organizations for examination and some limitations of the sampling. Generally, it appears that established production and other highly structured occupations are covered more extensively than less-structured and newly emerging occupations; and large organizations are overrepresented.

Occupations were rated by occupational analysts on three worker functions; educational development required in reasoning, mathematics, and language; specific vocational preparation; 11 aptitudes; 10 temperaments; 5 interests; 6 physical demands; and 7 environmental conditions. Table 3 (based on Miller et al., 1980, Tables 7-8 and 7-11) summarizes the ratings made. These ratings are more fully described by U.S. Department of Labor (1972) and by Miller et al. (1980), who also present information about their factor structure and reliability. In a partial simulation of the procedures used to rate Data, People, Things, GED, SVP, one physical demand, and one working condition, Cain and Green (1980) estimated lower-bound reliability coefficients ranging from .25 to .84. These results indicate that the ratings have useful but not high levels of reliability.

Evidence about the construct validity of the DOT ratings is limited. Definitions of some of the variables to be rated are cursory, and few validity studies have been conducted (Miller et al., 1980, Chap. 7). Nevertheless, these ratings have been shown to be strongly related to patterns in occupational mobility in much the same way as are the *Position Analysis Questionnaire* (PAQ; McCormick, 1979) dimension scores (G. D. Gottfredson, in press). An inspection of the ratings implies that they appear reasonable and that they are the most comprehensive source of systematic occupational information available. Equally important, there is no reason to suspect that "women's work" is undervalued relative to "men's work" in the fourth edition of the DOT (Miller et al., pp. 188–191).

Construction Sample. Occupations were selected from the *Occupations Finder* (Holland, 1978a) to represent occupations in each of the six major groups (R, I, A, S, E, and C) approximately equally. We selected occupational titles for which the evidence supporting the code assigned in the *Occupations Finder* appeared strongest. In all, 189 titles were chosen in this way: 37 Realistic, 35 Investigative, 27 Artistic, 31 Social, 28 Enterprising, and 31 Conventional occupations. This sample is called the construction sample.

Table 3
Occupational Ratings Made in Producing the DOT

Characteristic	Range	Mean	SD
Worker Functions [a]			
Data	0 to 6	4.11	2.09
People	0 to 8	6.83	1.85
Things	0 to 7	4.32	2.31
Education and Training			
General educational development	1 to 6	3.00	1.09
Specific vocational preparation	1 to 9	4.46	2.06
Aptitudes [a]			
Intelligence	1 to 4	3.19	0.72
Verbal aptitude	1 to 5	3.43	0.78
Numerical aptitude	1 to 5	3.63	0.78
Spatial perception	1 to 5	3.47	0.71
Form perception	1 to 5	3.36	0.67
Clerical perception	1 to 5	3.89	0.79
Motor coordination	1 to 5	3.46	0.56
Finger dexterity	1 to 5	3.56	0.61
Manual dexterity	1 to 5	3.21	0.53
Eye-hand-foot coordination	1 to 5	4.67	0.60
Color discrimination	1 to 5	4.52	0.70
Temperaments			
Direction, control, and planning	0 or 1	0.18	0.38
Feelings, ideas, or facts	0 or 1	0.01	0.10
Influencing people	0 or 1	0.04	0.20
Sensory or judgmental criteria	0 or 1	0.17	0.38
Measurable or verifiable criteria	0 or 1	0.39	0.49
Dealing with people	0 or 1	0.23	0.42
Repetitive or continuous processes	0 or 1	0.46	0.50
Performing under stress	0 or 1	0.02	0.16
Set limits, tolerances, or standards	0 or 1	0.60	0.49
Variety and change	0 or 1	0.20	0.40
Interests [b]			
Communication of data versus activities with things	-1 to 1	-0.57	0.66
Scientific and technical activities versus business contact	-1 to 1	-0.12	0.45
Abstract and creative versus routine, concrete activities	-1 to 1	-0.47	0.53
Activities involving processes, machines, or techniques versus social welfare	-1 to 1	0.62	0.55
Activities resulting in tangible, productive satisfaction versus prestige, esteem	-1 to 1	-0.05	0.47

(continued)

[a]
Low numbers indicate a high rating.

[b]
Interests are bipolar: "1" means first interest in pair present. "0" means neither present, "-1" means second interest in pair present.

Table 3 Cont.
Occupational Ratings Made in Producing the DOT

Characteristic	Range	Mean	SD
Physical Demands			
Lifting, carrying, pulling, pushing	1 to 5	2.39	0.91
Climbing, balancing	0 or 1	0.08	0.27
Stooping, kneeling, crouching, crawling	0 or 1	0.20	0.40
Reaching, handling, fingering, feeling	0 or 1	0.89	0.31
Talking, hearing	0 or 1	0.29	0.45
Seeing	0 or 1	0.57	0.49
Working Conditions			
Outside working conditions	1 to 3	1.22	0.56
Extreme cold	0 or 1	0.01	0.08
Extreme heat	0 or 1	0.05	0.21
Wet, humid	0 or 1	0.07	0.25
Noise, vibration	0 or 1	0.29	0.45
Hazardous conditions	0 or 1	0.15	0.35
Fumes, odors, dust, gases, poor ventilation	0 or 1	0.12	0.33

Source: Miller et al. (1980)

Method

Multiple discriminant analysis was used to develop classificatory functions based on occupational analysis data to classify the 189 titles chosen from the *Occupations Finder* into occupational categories. In a subsequent step, the classificatory functions developed in the construction sample were used to estimate the probability that each of the 12,099 occupations defined in the DOT belonged to each Holland category. Specifically, Fisher's linear discriminant functions (Norusis, 1979) were adjusted for estimated prior probabilities of category membership by adding the natural log of the prior probability to the constants in the functions estimated by SPSS (which do not include adjustments for prior probabilities [Nie, Hull, Jenkins, Steinbrenner & Brent, 1975]). Estimates of prior probabilities were made judgmentally by directly classifying a random sample of 296 occupations from the DOT. These estimates closely accord with estimates made by using the L. S. Gottfredson and Brown (1978) translation for census codes for the same sample of DOT titles (see Table 8). Each occupation in the DOT was assigned a three-letter Holland code by using the category with the largest classificatory function score (equivalent to the most probable category) to determine the first letter, the function with the second highest score to determine the second letter, and the function with the third highest score to determine the third letter.

Validation

The following subsections review the analyses that were performed to assess the scientific soundness of the classification and to clarify the relation of the classification to the U.S. Department of Labor's *Guide for Occupational Exploration* (GOE) categories and the DOT ratings.

The John Henry Technique. To assess the efficiency of the classification, and as a quality control check, two authors independently classified a randomly selected validation sample of 289 occupations from the DOT (excluding occupations included in the construction sample). We agreed on the classification of 87.5% of these occupations (kappa = .63), and we resolved nonagreements through discussion. The pooled judgment about the classification of validation sample occupations was compared with the classification of these occupations using the new empirical procedure to assess the degree of agreement.

The results of the empirical classification of occupations in the construction sample are shown in Table 4. In general, 87.8% of occupations in the construction sample were correctly classified (kappa = .85). Validation sample results are shown in Table 5. The empirically derived code matched the code based on our pooled judgment 77.4% of the time (kappa = .47). Most disagreements between the empirical and the pooled-judgment codes are for occupations with an empirical code in the Conventional category that were judged to belong to the Realistic category.

Table 4
Concurrent Validity of Classification:
Construction Sample

Imputed Code	Code Listed in Occupations Finder					
	R	I	A	S	E	C
Realistic (R)	36	1	1	0	0	2
Investigative (I)	1	34	1	0	0	0
Artistic (A)	0	0	20	1	1	0
Social (S)	0	0	0	24	2	0
Enterprising (E)	0	0	5	5	25	2
Conventional (C)	0	0	0	1	0	27

Note: Underscoring shows the frequency of occupations for which the imputed code matches the code listed in the Occupations Finder (hits). Hit rate is 87.8%, kappa=0.85.

Table 5

Validity of Imputed Codes in a Cross-
Validation Sample: The Lower Bound

Classification	Imputed Classification					
Based on Judgment	R	I	A	S	E	C
Realistic (R)	185	0	0	5	8	39
Investigative (I)	0	6	0	0	1	0
Artistic (A)	1	0	1	0	0	0
Social (S)	0	0	0	6	3	0
Enterprising (E)	4	0	1	1	22	1
Conventional (C)	1	0	0	1	1	2

Note: Classification based on judgment is based on independent classifications by Holland and Gottfredson, with discrepant classifications resolved by discussion. Underscored entries are hits (77.4%), kappa=0.47.

Holland and GOE Interest Categories. The GOE is organized according to "interest areas" based for the most part on 11 factors derived from a factor analysis of the items in the U.S. Employment Service Interest Inventory (Droege & Hawk, 1976; U.S. Department of Labor, 1979). Of the 12 categories in the GOE, 11 correspond to these 11 interest dimensions; the twelfth was added to accommodate a small number of occupations in physical performing that did not seem to fit into the first 11 categories. The assignment of DOT titles to GOE categories by Employment Service Occupational analysts therefore forms one method of examining the validity of the present classification. According to the U.S. Department of Labor (1979), the GOE categories should map into the Holland categories as shown in Table 6.

A comparison of the Holland category assigned by the empirical formula, and the occupational analysts' judgments about the GOE interest group for the same occupations, is shown in Table 7.

Overall, 76.8% of the occupations are classified into the category predicted by the U.S. Department of Labor (1979, p. 325). At the same time, the simple rules suggested in the GOE for translating "interest groups" into Holland occupational categories did not always work well. For example, more GOE "artistic" occupations are classified in the present system as Realistic than as Artistic. In addition, substantial numbers of "protective" occupations are classified as Enterprising and Social. Most "accommodating" occupations are classified as Enterprising, and a large proportion of "physical performing" occupations are classified as Enterprising.

Table 6
GOE and Holland Interest Categories

GOE Interest Group	Holland Category
01 Artistic	Artistic
02 Scientific	Investigative
03 Plants and Animals	Realistic
04 Protective	
05 Mechanical	
06 Industrial	
07 Business Detail	Conventional
08 Selling	Enterprising
09 Accommodating[a]	Social
10 Humanitarian	
11 Leading-Influencing[b]	
12 Physical Performing	

a
Also includes a few occupations included in
Holland's Realistic category.
b
Also includes occupations included in Holland's
Enterprising and Conventional categories.
Note: From Guide for Occupational Exploration,
U.S. Department of Labor, 1979, 325.

Table 7
Holland Category for Occupations Classified in
Each GOE Interest Group

| GOE Interest Group | Holland Category (%) | | | | | | N |
	R	I	A	S	E	C	
01 Artistic	45.3	1.3	32.8	8.4	7.4	4.8	311
02 Scientific	25.4	69.4	0.0	1.9	1.4	1.9	209
03 Plants and Animals	77.7	0.4	0.0	5.3	13.3	3.4	264
04 Protective	25.0	0.0	0.0	25.0	47.3	2.7	112
05 Mechanical	75.7	6.2	0.3	2.7	9.1	6.0	2,547
06 Industrial	80.9	0.1	0.0	1.1	3.1	14.8	6,936
07 Business Detail	6.3	0.2	0.2	11.4	22.9	59.1	589
08 Selling	2.4	0.0	2.4	1.4	92.4	1.4	210
09 Accommodating	15.4	0.5	0.0	7.4	54.3	22.3	188
10 Humanitarian	6.3	8.0	1.8	68.8	14.3	0.9	112
11 Leading-Influencing	2.6	6.7	4.8	28.2	54.0	3.6	581
12 Physical Performing	22.5	0.0	7.5	25.0	42.5	2.5	40

Note: Underscoring shows predicted categories. Overall, 76.8%
of the occupations (N=12,099) fall in the predicted cells.

These deviations from predictions notwithstanding, the high degree of correspondence we found lends considerable support both to the GOE classification and to the present classification. Less than perfect correspondence is to be expected because of the judgmental nature of the classification in the GOE, the relatively new interest measures underlying that guide, the limitations of the occupational analysis data used to empirically assign Holland codes in this project, and the sampling and measurement error in the codes of the *Occupations Finder*.

Sore Thumbing. As a final step, John Holland scrutinized the 12,099 empirically derived codes to locate grossly misclassified occupations. This procedure identified 35 occupations for which the empirically derived code did not appear in agreement with common knowledge or interest data. In most other cases, the codes generated by the empirical procedure appeared sensible or were reversals in ordering of codes that appeared in the *Occupations Finder*. The 35 anomalous occupational titles are listed in the Classified Index with an alternative code in parentheses.

Distribution of Occupational Codes. The distribution of one-letter codes assigned by the empirical formula is shown in Table 8. Of the 12,099 occupations in the DOT, 66.7% are classified as Realistic—somewhat fewer than estimated by direct judgment or by the census code translation of the random

Table 8
Distribution of Occupational Titles in the DOT
According to Three Estimates

Occupational Category	Method of Estimation		
	Judgment (N=296) (Per Cent)	Census Conversion (N=295) (Per Cent)	Imputation (N=12,099) (Per Cent)
Realistic	75.7	77.8	66.7
Investigative	6.4	4.7	3.0
Artistic	1.7	1.0	1.2
Social	6.1	6.4	4.6
Enterprising	6.8	6.8	11.1
Conventional	3.4	3.7	13.4

Note: For the Judgment method a random sample of occupations was classified by a judge using the Occupations Finder and a working knowledge of the classification as guides. In the Census Conversion method the first census code listed by the Occupational Analysis Branch of the U.S. Department of Labor was recoded to Holland codes using the L.S. Gottfredson and Brown (1978) table. One occupation could not be translated using this table. Imputation is based on the classification functions.

sample. In addition, 13.4% are classified as Conventional—somewhat more than estimated by direct judgment or by the census code translation of the random sample.

Table 9 summarizes the frequency of the results of the empirical classification in another way by showing the number of occupations with each of the six codes appearing somewhere in the three-letter code. As might be expected for occupations in the U.S. economy, most occupations have the letters R or E appearing in their codes, and occupations with A in the code are rare (fewer than 5% of titles in the DOT).

The entire distribution of three-letter codes is shown in Table 10. RE and RC codes are very common, accounting for 33.8% and 19.3% of the occupations, respectively. Some codes that involve inconsistent combinations according to the hexagonal model occur only rarely, or do not occur at all. For instance, the CA combination does not occur. The pattern of rare and frequent codes found in the *Dictionary* resembles the pattern found in other research based on census data (G. D. Gottfredson & Daiger, 1977) or interest measurement results (G. D. Gottfredson & Holland, 1975). As in earlier research, however, some inconsistent codes occur relatively frequently. Notably, the RS combination, which is very inconsistent according to the hexagonal model, accounts for 5.6% of the occupations. Because the distribution shown in Table 10 is based on the codes for what is purportedly a listing of *all* occupations in the U.S. civilian economy, it implies that the search for the "perfect match" between an interest profile and an occupational code is futile for persons with certain rare codes. This underscores the importance of examining all permutations of a person's code when using this *Dictionary* or the *Occupations Finder*, especially if the person has a rare or inconsistent code.

Table 9
Number of Occupations with Each
Code Appearing Somewhere in
the First Three Letters

Code	Number of Occupations
Realistic (R)	10,708
Investigative (I)	2,551
Artistic (A)	570
Social (S)	6,064
Enterprising (E)	10,405
Conventional (C)	5,999

Table 10
Frequencies of Three-Letter Holland Codes in the Dictionary

Code	F*	%age	Code	F*	%age	Code	F*	%age
RI		7.9	IS		0.3	AC		0.0
RIA	2	0.0	ISR	17	0.1	ACR	0	0.0
RIS	144	1.2	ISA	2	0.0	ACI	0	0.0
RIE	786	6.5	ISE	17	0.1	ACS	2	0.0
RIC	24	0.2	ISC	4	0.0	ACE	0	0.0
RA		0.1	IE		0.6	SR		0.7
RAI	1	0.0	IER	39	0.3	SRI	3	0.0
RAS	3	0.0	IEA	11	0.1	SRA	0	0.0
RAE	9	0.1	IES	13	0.1	SRE	58	0.5
RAC	0	0.0	IEC	5	0.0	SRC	16	0.1
RS		5.6	IC		0.0	SI		0.2
RSI	54	0.4	ICR	4	0.0	SIR	6	0.0
RSA	0	0.0	ICA	0	0.0	SIA	2	0.0
RSE	486	4.0	ICS	0	0.0	SIE	20	0.2
RSC	142	1.2	ICE	0	0.0	SIC	1	0.0
RE		33.8	AR		0.1	SA		0.0
REI	933	7.7	ARI	2	0.0	SAR	0	0.0
REA	31	0.3	ARS	0	0.0	SAI	0	0.0
RES	1,791	14.8	ARE	7	0.1	SAE	3	0.0
REC	1,332	11.0	ARC	0	0.0	SAC	0	0.0
RC		19.3	AI		0.0	SE		3.2
RCI	32	0.3	AIR	1	0.0	SER	147	1.2
RCA	0	0.0	AIS	0	0.0	SEI	30	0.2
RCS	591	4.9	AIE	2	0.0	SEA	52	0.4
RCE	1,709	14.1	AIC	0	0.0	SEC	150	1.2
IR		2.1	AS		0.2	SC		0.5
IRA	1	0.0	ASR	2	0.0	SCR	12	0.1
IRS	75	0.6	ASI	0	0.0	SCI	6	0.0
IRE	164	1.4	ASE	17	0.1	SCA	1	0.0
IRC	11	0.1	ASC	0	0.0	SCE	44	0.4
IA		0.0	AE		0.9	ER		2.7
IAR	0	0.0	AER	18	0.1	ERI	28	0.2
IAS	1	0.0	AEI	14	0.1	ERA	14	0.1
IAE	0	0.0	AES	79	0.7	ERS	258	2.1
IAC	0	0.0	AEC	5	0.0	ERC	32	0.3
								(continued)

*F=Frequency

Worker Functions, Aptitudes, and Interests. To provide additional insight into the meanings of the Holland categories, selected tables showing occupational analysis information were prepared. These tables describe the job content of typical jobs in each Holland category at GED levels 5 and 6 and levels 3 and 4. Mean worker function ratings are shown in Table 11.

Code	F*	%age	Code	F*	%age	Code	F*	%age
EI		0.3	EC		0.6	CA		0.0
EIR	16	0.1	ECR	15	0.1	CAR	0	0.0
EIA	3	0.0	ECI	3	0.0	CAI	0	0.0
EIS	10	0.1	ECA	0	0.0	CAS	0	0.0
EIC	2	0.0	ECS	52	0.4	CAE	0	0.0
EA		0.3	CR		9.0	CS		2.8
EAR	5	0.0	CRI	4	0.0	CSR	116	1.0
EAI	6	0.0	CRA	0	0.0	CSI	3	0.0
EAS	30	0.2	CRS	407	3.4	CSA	0	0.0
EAC	2	0.0	CRE	679	5.6	CSE	221	0.9
ES		7.2	CI		0.0	CE		1.6
ESR	403	3.3	CIR	0	0.0	CER	78	0.6
ESI	42	0.3	CIA	0	0.0	CEI	4	0.0
ESA	242	2.0	CIS	2	0.0	CEA	0	0.0
ESC	176	1.5	CIE	1	0.0	CES	111	0.9

*F=Frequency

(Recall that the DOT scores worker functions in the reverse direction. A high number means a low complexity of involvement in Data, People, or Things, and a low number means a high complexity of involvement.) These ratings generally accord with theoretical expectations. For example, for occupations at GED levels 5 and 6, Artistic and Investigative occupations are rated as having the most complex involvement with

Table 11
DOT Worker Function Ratings for Occupations by GED
Level and Holland Category*

Holland Category	Data		People		Things		N
	M	SD	M	SD	M	SD	
GED Level 5 and 6							
Realistic	1.16	0.88	6.03	1.26	3.04	2.58	94
Investigative	0.79	0.81	5.44	2.10	2.90	2.76	340
Artistic	0.32	0.58	5.11	1.81	4.67	2.91	102
Social	1.21	0.56	2.79	2.35	6.50	1.53	227
Enterprising	1.08	0.36	4.36	2.30	6.77	1.10	326
Conventional	1.22	0.65	5.67	1.28	5.72	2.47	18
GED Level 3 and 4							
Realistic	3.65	1.80	6.90	1.70	2.45	1.93	4,235
Investigative	3.25	1.42	7.04	1.30	3.08	2.38	24
Artistic	1.96	1.87	5.70	1.59	3.65	2.81	46
Social	2.07	1.49	4.59	2.00	4.75	2.58	315
Enterprising	1.88	1.25	4.54	1.52	5.81	2.20	942
Conventional	4.22	1.51	7.09	1.19	4.27	2.18	695

Note: The Department of Labor (1977) scores worker functions in the reverse direction. A low number indicates a high degree of involvement.
*p < .001

Data. At these GED levels Social occupations are rated as having the most complex involvement with People, and Realistic and Investigative occupations are rated as having the most complex involvement with Things. For occupations at GED levels 3 and 4, Artistic and Enterprising occupations are rated as having the most complex involvement with Data, although the involvement is less complex than that of occupations at the higher GED levels. Among occupations at GED levels 3 and 4, Enterprising and Social occupations are rated as having the most complex involvement with People, and Realistic and Investigative occupations are rated as having the most complex involvement with things. For Realistic occupations, the mean complexity of involvement with Things for GED level 3 and 4 is

Table 12
DOT Worker Aptitude Ratings for Occupations
at GED Levels 5 and 6 by Holland Category*

Holland Category (N)		R (94)	I (340)	A (102)	S (227)	E (326)	C (18)
Intelligence							
	M	4.08	4.54	4.30	4.13	4.12	4.00
	SD	0.43	0.51	0.48	0.44	0.36	0.00
Verbal							
	M	3.97	4.37	4.27	4.14	4.12	4.22
	SD	0.58	0.65	0.58	0.49	0.41	0.43
Numeric							
	M	3.87	4.20	2.99	3.17	3.63	3.67
	SD	0.64	0.63	0.70	0.62	0.62	0.77
Spatial							
	M	3.91	4.04	3.25	2.36	2.61	3.00
	SD	0.70	0.73	0.98	0.66	0.76	0.91
Form Percep.							
	M	3.50	3.78	3.26	2.50	2.61	2.78
	SD	0.67	0.72	0.92	0.66	0.68	0.73
Clerical							
	M	2.97	3.04	2.67	3.07	3.02	3.78
	SD	0.56	0.63	0.67	0.70	0.64	0.43
Motor Coord.							
	M	2.78	2.81	2.70	2.08	2.03	2.22
	SD	0.66	0.70	0.85	0.50	0.37	0.43
Finger Dexterity							
	M	2.79	3.10	2.82	2.10	2.02	2.17
	SD	0.70	0.89	1.10	0.52	0.37	0.38
Manual Dexterity							
	M	2.80	2.99	2.55	2.11	2.00	2.22
	SD	0.63	0.83	0.80	0.55	0.35	0.43
Eye-Hand-Foot coord.	M	1.66	1.56	1.22	1.19	1.13	1.39
	SD	0.96	0.66	0.66	0.55	0.39	0.70
Color Discrim.							
	M	1.97	2.26	2.30	1.45	1.34	1.44
	SD	0.80	0.88	1.48	0.80	0.63	0.62

*$p < .001$

slightly higher than the degree of complexity for GED level 5 and 6.

Mean worker aptitude ratings also generally correspond with expectations (see Table 12 for occupations at GED levels 5 and 6 and Table 13 for occupations at GED levels 3 and 4). For instance, the higher-level occupations (GED 5 and 6) are rated as requiring more general intelligence. Among GED level 5 and 6 occupations, Investigative occupations are rated highest, among GED level 3 and 4 occupations, Artistic occupations are rated highest.

Most of these aptitude ratings, however, relate to cognitive, perceptual, or motor skills. Accordingly, with some exceptions, clear-cut expectations are difficult to specify. One might expect

Table 13
DOT Worker Aptitude Ratings for Occupations
at GED Levels 3 and 4 by Holland Category*

Holland Category (N)		R (4,235)	I (24)	A (46)	S (315)	E (942)	C (695)
Intelligence	M	3.01	3.21	3.39	3.11	3.24	2.96
	SD	0.32	0.41	0.54	0.42	0.44	0.41
Verbal	M	2.54	3.00	3.11	3.03	3.19	2.66
	SD	0.54	0.59	0.60	0.52	0.46	0.61
Numeric	M	2.54	3.12	2.50	2.54	2.92	2.46
	SD	0.55	0.61	0.66	0.52	0.46	0.63
Spatial	M	2.88	3.04	3.15	2.37	2.49	2.17
	SD	0.63	0.86	0.89	0.63	0.63	0.56
Form Percep.	M	2.94	3.21	3.09	2.58	2.59	2.59
	SD	0.61	0.66	0.89	0.66	0.60	0.61
Clerical	M	2.15	2.62	2.11	2.80	2.79	2.88
	SD	0.55	0.71	0.74	0.66	0.56	0.90
Motor Coord.	M	2.74	2.92	2.83	2.38	2.31	2.65
	SD	0.50	0.58	0.64	0.60	0.51	0.61
Finger Dexterity	M	2.62	2.67	2.93	2.30	2.28	2.69
	SD	0.60	0.64	0.80	0.53	0.51	0.63
Manual Dexterity	M	2.99	3.08	2.91	2.48	2.36	2.60
	SD	0.44	0.41	0.69	0.58	0.55	0.53
Eye-Hand- Foot Coord.	M	1.40	1.79	1.59	1.33	1.30	1.21
	SD	0.66	0.93	1.11	0.70	0.62	0.49
Color Discrim	M	1.62	2.62	2.72	1.78	1.65	1.42
	SD	0.74	0.97	1.26	0.88	0.72	0.63

*$p < .001$

Artistic occupations generally to require more form perception and color discimination aptitude than other occupations (and it does receive the highest ratings in color discrimination). Conventional occupations would certainly be expected to require more clerical aptitude than other categories (and it does receive the highest rating on this aptitude). Finally, Investigative occupations would be expected to require more numeric aptitude than other occupations and, on average, they are rated highest. No ratings of interpersonal or social aptitudes are included in the job analysis data available.

Because the Holland occupational classification is rooted in the interest measurement tradition, the pattern of DOT interest ratings for occupations classified into each of the six categories is of special importance. The DOT interest ratings are made on bipolar scales that were influenced by Cottle's (1950) factor analysis of the Strong and other inventories. Although their bipolar nature and the casual method job analysts used to make these ratings are limitations for the present purposes, the results shown in Table 14 nevertheless are strongly in accord with theoretical expectations. For example, Realistic, Investigative, and Conventional occupations are rated, on average, at one end of the scale for "scientific and technical activities versus business contact," and Enterprising occupations are rated, on average, at the other end. Realistic and Conventional occupations are rated, on average, at one end of the scale for "activities involving processes, machines, or techniques versus social welfare," and Social occupations are rated at the other end. On average, Artistic occupations are rated at one end of the scale for "abstract and creative versus routine, concrete activities," and Conventional occupations are rated at the other end. In short, the pattern for hexagonally opposite occupational types (Holland, 1973a) is reproduced in the pattern of mean ratings for these scales.

Distinguishing Adjacent Occupational Categories. Some final analyses, using the construction sample, were performed to clarify the distinctions between adjacent types (R and I, I and A, S and E, E and C, and C and R) in the hexagonal model. Theoretically, the adjacent types are closely related, although they also have some distinguishing characteristics. Earlier accounts (Holland, 1966, 1973a) of the differences and similarities among the types were helpful, but more definitive information is needed.

Table 14

Mean Interest Ratings for Occupations by GED Level and Holland Category*

Holland Category	Communication of Data vs. Activities with Things		Scientific and Technical Activities vs. Business Contact		Abstract and Creative vs. Routine, Concrete Activities		Activities Involving Processes, Machines, or Techniques vs. Social Welfare		Activities Resulting in Tangible, Productive Satisfaction vs. Prestige, Esteem		N
	M	SD	M	SD	M	SD	M	SD	M	SD	
GED Levels 5 and 6											
R	-0.40	0.64	0.71	0.62	0.07	0.26	0.65	0.54	-0.03	0.43	94
I	-0.01	0.62	0.84	0.43	0.13	0.35	0.18	0.69	-0.18	0.44	340
A	0.74	0.50	-0.30	0.56	0.67	0.47	0.00	0.28	0.03	0.90	102
S	0.58	0.58	-0.20	0.76	0.50	0.25	-0.43	0.56	-0.46	0.54	227
E	0.52	0.54	-0.77	0.55	0.05	0.22	0.08	0.42	-0.77	0.42	326
C	0.33	0.84	0.78	0.55	-0.06	0.24	0.61	0.50	-0.28	0.46	18
GED Levels 3 and 4											
R	-0.75	0.45	-0.05	0.35	-0.31	0.48	0.91	0.29	0.08	0.56	4,235
I	-0.33	0.70	0.38	0.58	-0.17	0.48	0.58	0.58	0.12	0.34	24
A	0.48	0.65	-0.26	0.44	0.56	0.50	0.37	0.61	0.20	0.81	46
S	0.11	0.62	-0.44	0.58	-0.05	0.39	-0.04	0.64	-0.21	0.61	315
E	0.32	0.58	-0.82	0.40	-0.07	0.28	0.35	0.53	-0.54	0.52	942
C	-0.42	0.74	-0.22	0.45	-0.79	0.41	0.47	0.51	-0.01	0.24	695

*p < .001

Table 15
Variables Discriminating between Adjacent Occupational Types

Realistic versus Investigative (N=72)

Realistic rated higher than investigative in:
  Strength
  Stooping
  Hazards
  Activities involving processes, machines, or techniques versus
    social welfare
  Activities involving tangible productive satisfaction versus
    prestige, esteem
Investigative rated higher than realistic in:
  Intelligence
  Verbal aptitude
  Numerical aptitude
  General educational development
  Scientific and technical activities versus business contact

Investigative versus Artistic (N=62)

Investigative rated higher than artistic in:
  Intelligence
  Numerical aptitude
  Measurable or verifiable criteria
  Seeing
  Scientific and technical activities versus business contact
Artistic rated higher than investigative in:
  Feelings, ideas, or facts
  Influencing people
  Talking, hearing
  Communication of data versus activities with things
  Abstract and creative versus routine, concrete activities

Artistic versus Social (N=58)

Artistic rated higher than social in:
  Data
  Spatial perception
  Feelings, ideas, or facts
  Abstract and creative versus routine, concrete activities
  Activities involving processes, machines, or techniques versus
    social welfare
Social rated higher than Artistic in:
  People
  Clerical aptitude
  Dealing with people
  Variety and change
  Talking, hearing

Social versus Enterprising (N=59)

Social rated higher than enterprising in:
  Scientific and technical activities versus business contact
Enterprising rated higher than social in:
  Numerical aptitude
  Activities involving processes, machines, or techniques versus
    social welfare

Table 15
Variables Discriminating between Adjacent Occupational Types

Enterprising versus Conventional (N=59)

Enterprising rated higher than conventional in:
  Data
  People
  Dealing with people
  Talking, hearing
  Abstract and creative versus routine, concrete activities
Conventional rated higher than enterprising in:
  Finger dexterity
  Repetitive or continuous processes
  Set limits, tolerances, or standards
  Seeing
  Scientific and technical activities versus business contact

Conventional versus Realistic (N=68)

Conventional rated higher than realistic in:
  Clerical aptitude
  Dealing with people
  Repetitive or continuous processes
  Communication of data versus activities with things
Realistic rated higher than conventional in:
  Specific Vocational Preparation (SVP)
  Spatial perception
  Measurable or verifiable criteria
  Strength
  Stooping

Note: This table shows significant differences ($p < 0.05$) for up to five variables. When more than five variables significantly discriminate, only the five largest differences are shown.

The job analysis ratings that most strongly distinguish between these adjacent types are shown in Table 15. The table lists the biggest differences found in an examination of R versus I occupations, I versus A occupations, and so on. It lists up to five occupational analysis variables on which one adjacent type was rated significantly ($p < .05$) higher than the other. In some cases fewer than five ratings were significantly higher for adjacent types, and fewer are shown. In other cases more than five ratings were significantly higher for one adjacent type than another, and only the five biggest differences are shown.

The differences shown in Table 15 are useful in understanding the distinctions between adjacent types. For instance, Investigative work generally requires greater intelligence, more verbal and numerical aptitude, and more education than does

Realistic work; but Realistic work requires more strength, stooping, exposure to hazards, and it involves more activity with processes or machines than does Investigative work. And Artistic work more often requires a temperament for working with feelings, ideas, or facts, and greater interest in abstract or creative activities than does Investigative work. These, and other distinctions shown in Table 15, generally accord with the earlier characterizations of the types (for example, Holland, 1973a).

DISCUSSION

The limitations of the present translation lie largely in the quality and comprehensiveness of the job analysis information accumulated during the production of the fourth edition of the DOT. The occupational analysis methods used in producing the DOT are no longer the state-of-the-art technology they once were. These methods have remained for the most part unchanged over the years, failing to take into account more recent methods of analyzing jobs (McCormick, 1979). In addition, for most occupations only one or two job analysis schedules were available, and in some cases schedules produced for an earlier edition were used (Miller et al., 1980).

Despite these limitations, the translation is based on the most comprehensive source of job analysis data available, and the present results appear meaningful and generally in accord with expectations and other occupational information. In addition, other research using these DOT occupational analysis data (Cain & Green, 1980; G. D. Gottfredson, in press; L. S. Gottfredson, 1978; Miller et al., 1980, Chap. 7; Mortimer, 1974; Spaeth, 1979; Spenner, 1977) and numerous practical applications of the occupational information (Chronicle Guidance, n.d.; Dawis & Lofquist, 1974, 1975; Time Share Corporation, 1976) support the usefulness of the DOT information.

Accordingly, the following outcomes are of special interest.

1. The empirical classification resulted in many more occupations being designated Conventional than did the judgmental process or the census code approximation—also ultimately based on judgment (L. S. Gottfredson & Brown, 1978). We speculate that this outcome is due to a persistent misperception of judges—including ourselves—about the

nature of Realistic and Conventional work. Despite evidence from the SCII (Campbell, 1977) that some occupations heretofore classified as Realistic might appropriately be classified as Conventional, persistent notions that machine operation means R may have led to judgmental errors in classification in the past. The current *Dictionary* classifies many occupations previously supposed to resemble Realistic work as Conventional. The balance of the evidence now supports the *Dictionary* classification.

2. More insight about the psychological meaning of Enterprising work, and therefore the theoretical category itself, was suggested by our review of the numerous occupations heretofore not available in an extensive listing by major category and subcategory. Briefly, Enterprising work, in addition to its obvious involvement in persuasive and manipulative activities, appears also to involve power via the control of information, independent decision making and judgment, responsibility for crucial information with little or no supervision, and mental or physical risk taking. These qualities appear to hold in different combinations and to different degrees for many, perhaps most, Enterprising occupations.

3. The distinctions among occupational types are less marked among lower-level occupations. This blurring of categorical distinctions is demonstrated by the low-level RC and CR occupations, which appear to closely resemble each other.

4. Some kinds of occupational content are much more common than others. Realistic and Enterprising work is common (Table 9), whereas Artistic work is rare—fewer than 5% of occupations contain an A anywhere in the three-letter code.

5. The present classification, which is based *entirely* on occupational analysis data, for the most part accords closely with (a) the classification based primarily on vocational interest data according to the *Occupations Finder*, and (b) the judgmental classification of occupations. Accordingly, the construct validity of this *Dictionary* as an independent classification of occupations to implement the person-job matching model according to Holland's typology is strongly supported.

SUGGESTIONS FOR PRACTICE AND RESEARCH

The ready accessibility of Holland codes for all 12,099 occupations in the *Dictionary* makes possible a number of new applications of the typology for practice and research. We encourage, therefore, explorations of the following applications of the *Dictionary*.

Broadening the Occupational Search

Clients can now more easily examine a larger number of occupations suggested by their assessment results. The availability of long lists of occupations associated with many three-letter codes may, however, cause some clients to focus on a single three-letter code. Clients should be urged to avoid such a narrow search and to explore other permutations of their codes.

The availability of longer lists of occupations and the availability of occupations with three-letter codes not present in earlier lists may stimulate research on the process of occupational exploration. Do clients with longer lists search fewer categories? If so, what are the consequences of this? Are clients who obtain rare codes on interest assessments more satisfied with a *Dictionary* that includes entries for more rare codes than does the *Occupations Finder*? To what extent are the occupational definitions contained in the DOT actually used? What structures would promote their use? Would a shorter *Dictionary* have any advantages over the present voluminous listing?

Applications with Disadvantaged Clients

Most users of the Holland classification have worked with relatively advantaged persons—college students, adults seeking career redirection, and people able to pay to attend career seminars. Despite the availability of an SDS for the blind (Barker, 1978), Form E of the SDS (Holland, 1973b) for the poor reader, and the extremely low cost of the VPI, the use of the typology with disadvantaged clients has fallen short of its potential. The availability of the present compendium makes possible a number of experimental applications. (1) Does the present classification provide meaningful and satisfying occupational exploration for low ability users of the SDS Form E or the VPI? (2) Can the *Dictionary* be used in conjunction with other job search methods to provide vocational assistance to young people or adults experiencing difficulty finding employment? Can it, for example, be integrated with methods such as the Job Club (Azrin & Besalel, 1980) or the Milwaukee Youth Employment Center (Yamasaki, 1982) to supplement the *Yellow Pages* as a source of job leads? Does limiting the job search for persons with poor work histories or low levels of education to consistent occupations (that is, RC and CR at modest GED levels) result in greater employment stability (compare G. D. Gottfredson and Lipstein, 1975)?

Research on Labor Market Behavior

The comprehensive classification of occupations makes possible many psychological, sociological, and economic investigations of labor markets and career development using the Holland typology. Research that examines the theoretical predictions about the divergent talents required in different types of work can now be pursued more easily. Similarly, psychological and economic investigations of the operation of labor markets can be more easily performed. Do internal labor markets more often involve jobs with consistent codes, higher levels of SVP, or a combination of these? To what degrees are firms segregated by sex and race according to Holland category? What categories or subcategories of occupations are primarily involved in secondary labor markets, listed by the U.S. Employment Service job banks, or projected for growth or decline in work force requirement forecasts?

Research on Occupational Classification

The classification of occupations is a complex and error-prone process. No single approach to the development of a classification is likely to be flawless. Accordingly, research on the construct validity of the present occupational analysis–based classification is required. What VPI or SDS profiles characterize samples of workers classified according to occupational analysis data? More evidence about the interest profiles characteristic of large samples of computer operators, tractor mechanics, assemblers, midwives, steelworkers, hair stylists, and various military specialties is required. Explicit comparisons of large sample interest profiles for carefully delimited occupations with the codes presented in this *Dictionary* are required for additional quality control checks on the classification.

Validity Generalization for Personnel Selection Tests

Does the present classification provide a basis for the development of selection or placement batteries that have a high a priori probability of predictive validity according to a "synthetic validity" or validity generalization model (Guion, 1976)? Because the present classification is based on comprehensive occupational analysis data, it should hold promise as a method to systematize the accumulation of validity evidence with broad applicability in business and industry.

Part V. User Self-Test

1. What are the purposes of this dictionary?

   a. To make it easy for clients to see the full range of occupational options associated with a particular interest inventory profile (code).

   b. To make it easier to organize occupational information.

   c. To make it easier to perform research in which the coding of occupations is necessary (career data, personnel classification systems, aspirations, and so on).

   d. All of the above.

2. List 10 occupations that would be classified in each of the following groups:

   a. Realistic

   b. Investigative

   c. Artistic

   d. Social

   e. Enterprising

   f. Conventional

3. How were codes assigned to occupations in this *Dictionary*?

   a. "Sore thumbing"—the authors got together on a mountaintop and reviewed the DOT.

   b. The Viernstein technique was used.

   c. SDS profiles for all 12,099 occupations were obtained.

   d. A computer program based on 44 variables for each of the 12,099 occupations was keyed to selected occupations from the *Occupations Finder* to create a three-letter code.

4. What does "GED" stand for?

5. What does "SVP" stand for?

6. The 9-digit codes are from the _____.

7. The 6-digit codes are from the _____.

8. This classification is imperfect and not precise because:

   a. The occupational data on which it is based are not perfectly valid.

   b. Occupational titles are sloppy summaries, not precise definitions.

   c. Holland's theory of classification is itself incomplete and imperfect.

   d. Some occupations belong in two or three occupational groups to about the same degree.

   e. All of the above.

(The key to the Self-Test appears on page 500.)

References

Azrin, N. H., and Besalel, V. A. *Job club counselor's manual: A behavioral approach to vocational counseling.* Baltimore: University Park Press, 1980.

Barker, S. B. An evaluation of the development of the Self-Directed Search for use by visually disabled individuals. Doctoral dissertation, College of Education, Florida State University, 1978.

Cain, P. S., and Green, B. F., Jr. The rating of DOT worker functions and worker traits. In A. R. Miller, D. J. Treiman, P. S. Cain, and P. A. Roos (Eds.), *Work, jobs, and occupations: A critical review of the Dictionary of Occupational Titles.* Washington, D.C.: National Academy Press, 1980.

Campbell, D. P. *Manual for the Strong-Campbell Interest Inventory T325 (Merged form).* Stanford, Calif.: Stanford University Press, 1977.

Chronicle Guidance Publications. *Chronicle Occupational Library.* Moravia, N.Y.: Author, n.d.

Cottle, W. C. A factorial study of the Multiphasic, Strong, Kuder, and Bell inventories using a population of adult males. *Psychometrika,* 1950, *15,* 25–47.

Dawis, R. V., and Lofquist, L. H. *The Minnesota occupational classification system (MOCS).* Minneapolis: University of Minnesota, Department of Psychology, 1974.

Dawis, R. V., and Lofquist, L. H. Toward a psychological taxonomy of work. *Journal of Vocational Behavior,* 1975, 7, 165–171.

Droege, R. C., and Hawk, J. Development of a U.S. Employment Service interest inventory. *Journal of Employment Counseling,* 1976, *14,* 65–71.

Edwards, K. J., Nafziger, D. H., and Holland, J. L. Differentiation of occupational perceptions among different age groups. *Journal of Vocational Behavior,* 1974, *4,* 311–318.

Gottfredson, G. D. An assessment of a mobility-based occupational classification for placement and counseling. *Journal of Vocational Behavior,* in press.

Gottfredson, G. D. Career stability and redirection in adulthood. *Journal of Applied Psychology,* 1977, *62,* 436–445.

Gottfredson, G. D., and Daiger, D. C. Using a classification of occupations to describe age, sex, and time differences in employment patterns. *Journal of Vocational Behavior,* 1977, *10,* 121–138.

Gottfredson, G. D., and Holland, J. L. Some normative self-report data on activities, competencies, occupational preferences, and ability ratings for high school and college students, and employed men and women. *JSAS Catalog of Selected Documents in Psychology*, 1975, *5*, 192. (Ms. No. 859)

Gottfredson, G. D., and Lipstein, D. J. Using personal characteristics to predict parolee and probationer employment stability. *Journal of Applied Psychology*, 1975, *60*, 644–648.

Gottfredson, L. S. The construct validity of Holland's occupational classification in terms of prestige, census, Department of Labor, and other classification systems (Report No. 260). Baltimore: Johns Hopkins University, Center for Social Organization of Schools, 1978.

Gottfredson, L. S., and Brown, V. C. Holland codes for the 1960 and 1970 censuses: Detailed occupational titles. *JSAS Catalog of Selected Documents in Psychology*, 1978, *8*, 22. (Ms. No. 1660)

Grandy, T. G., and Stahmann, R. F. Family influence on college students' vocational choice: Predicting Holland's personality types. *Journal of College Student Personnel*, 1974, *15*, 404–409. (a)

Grandy, T. G., and Stahmann, R. F. Types produce types: An examination of personality development using Holland's theory. *Journal of Vocational Behavior*, 1974, *5*, 231–239. (b)

Guion, R. M. Recruiting, selection, and job placement. In M. D. Dunnette (Ed.), *Handbook of industrial and organizational psychology*. Chicago: Rand McNally, 1976.

Helms, S. T., and Williams, G. D. *An experimental study of the reactions of high school students to simulated jobs* (Report No. 161). Baltimore: Johns Hopkins University, Center for Social Organization of Schools, 1973. (ERIC No. ED 087 882)

Holland, J. L. A psychological classification scheme for vocations and major fields. *Journal of Counseling Psychology*, 1966, *13*, 278–288.

Holland, J. L. *Making vocational choices: A theory of careers*. Englewood Cliffs, N.J.: Prentice-Hall, 1973. (a)

Holland, J. L. *Self-Directed Search (Form E)*. Palo Alto, Calif.: Consulting Psychologists Press, 1973. (b)

Holland, J. L. *Occupations Finder*. Palo Alto, Calif.: Consulting Psychologists Press, 1978. (a)

Holland, J. L. *Vocational Preference Inventory Manual*. Palo Alto, Calif.: Consulting Psychologists Press, 1978. (b)

Holland, J. L. *Professional manual for the Self-Directed Search*. Palo Alto, Calif.: Consulting Psychologists Press, 1979.

Holland, J. L., and Gottfredson, G. D. Using a typology of persons and environments to explain careers: Some extensions and clarifications. *Counseling Psychologist*, 1976, *6*, 20–29.

Holland, J. L., and Holland, J. E. Vocational indecision: More evidence and speculation. *Journal of Counseling Psychology*, 1977, *24*, 404–414.

Kelso, G. I. *Explorations of the developmental antecedents of Holland's occupational types*. Unpublished doctoral dissertation, Johns Hopkins University, 1976.

Krumboltz, J. D. A social learning theory of career selection. In J. M. Whiteley and A. Resnikoff (Eds.), *Career counseling*. Monterey, Calif.: Brooks/Cole, 1978.

McCormick, E. J. *Job analysis: Methods and applications*. New York: AMACOM, 1979.

Miller, A. R., Treiman, D. J., Cain, P. S., and Roos, P. A. (Eds.). *Work, jobs, and occupations: A critical review of the Dictionary of Occupational Titles*. Washington, D.C.: National Academy Press, 1980.

Mortimer, J. T. Patterns of intergenerational occupational movements: A smallest-space analysis. *American Journal of Sociology*, 1974, *79*, 1278–1299.

Mount, M. K., and Muchinsky, P. M. Person-environment congruence and employee job satisfaction: A test of Holland's theory. *Journal of Vocational Behavior*, 1978, *13*, 84–100.

Nafziger, D. H., Holland, J. L., and Gottfredson, G. D. Student-college congruency as a predictor of satisfaction. *Journal of Counseling Psychology*, 1975, *22*, 132–139.

Nie, N. H., Hull, C. H., Jenkins, J. G., Steinbrenner, K., and Bent, D. H. *Statistical package for the social sciences*. New York: McGraw-Hill, 1975.

Norusis, M. J. *SPSS statistical algorithms (Release 8.0)*. Chicago: SPSS, Inc., 1979.

O'Dowd, D. D., and Beardslee, D. C. *Development and consistency of student images of occupations* (Cooperative Research Project No. 5-0858). Rochester, Mich.: Oakland University, 1967.

Rounds, J. B., Jr., Shubsachs, A. P. W., Dawis, R. V., and Lofquist, L. H. A test of Holland's environment formulations. *Journal of Applied Psychology*, 1978, *63*, 609–616. (A more complete version was disseminated as Work Adjustment Project Research Report No. 54, Department of Psychology, University of Minnesota, August 1977).

Sokal, R. R. Classification: Purposes, principles, progress, prospects. *Science*, 1974, *185*, 1115–1123.

Spaeth, J. L. Vertical differentiation among occupations. *American Sociological Review*, 1979, *44*, 746–762.

Spenner, K. I. *From generation to generation: The transmission of occupation*. Unpublished doctoral dissertation, University of Wisconsin, Madison, 1977.

Time Share Corporation. *The guidance information system: GIS guide*. West Hartford, Conn.: Houghton Mifflin, 1976.

U.S. Department of Labor. *Handbook for analyzing jobs*. Washington, D.C.: U.S. Government Printing Office, 1972.

U.S. Department of Labor. *Definition writer's manual*. Washington, D.C.: U.S. Government Printing Office, 1974.

U.S. Department of Labor. *Dictionary of occupational titles* (Fourth edition). Washington, D.C.: U.S. Government Printing Office, 1977.

U.S. Department of Labor. *Guide for occupational exploration*. Washington, D.C.: U.S. Government Printing Office, 1979.

Viernstein, M. C. The extension of Holland's occupational classification to all occupations in the Dictionary of Occupational Titles. *Journal of Vocational Behavior*, 1972, *2*, 107–121.

Wiener, Y., and Vaitenas, R. Personality correlates of voluntary midcareer change in enterprising occupations. *Journal of Applied Psychology*, 1977, *62*, 706–712.

Wiggins, J. D. The relation of job satisfaction to vocational preferences among teachers of the educable mentally retarded. *Journal of Vocational Behavior*, 1976, *8*, 13–18.

Yamasaki, C. The Milwaukee Youth Employment Center. In Gottfredson, G. D. (Ed.), *School Action Effectiveness Study: First interim report*. Baltimore: Johns Hopkins University, Center for Social Organization of Schools. 1982.

Self-Test Key

1. (d)
2. Use Classified Index (Part II) to check your responses
3. (d)
4. General Educational Development
5. Specific Vocational Preparation
6. *Dictionary of Occupational Titles*
7. *Guide for Occupational Exploration*
8. (e)